Annual Survey of Eastern Europe and the Former Soviet Union 1997

EWI

The EastWest Institute (EWI) works to defuse tensions and conflicts which threaten geopolitical stability while promoting democracy, free enterprise and prosperity in Central and Eastern Europe, Russia, and other states of Eurasia.

The EWI is an independent, international, not-for-profit institution established in 1981. It works through centers in New York, Moscow, Prague, Kyiv, Budapest, Brussels, and Košice. The EWI, formerly known as the Institute for EastWest Studies, operates with an international staff of some 90 professionals from 14 countries and maintains a large global network of relationships with leaders in the business, governmental, non-governmental and intellectual communities. This network is based on shared values and is dedicated to providing assistance to regional leadership to address critical issues at both the local and global levels.

The EWI seeks to cooperate with individuals and institutions sharing our values and mission. We invite you to visit our web site in English or Russian at http://www.iews.org/.

John Edwin Mroz
Founder and President

EASTWEST INSTITUTE
New York Prague Moscow Kyiv Budapest Brussels Košice

ANNUAL SURVEY
of Eastern Europe and the Former Soviet Union 1997

The Challenge of Integration

Edited by Peter Rutland

With Introductions by
Gale Stokes and Peter Rutland

EASTWEST INSTITUTE
New York Prague Moscow Kyiv Budapest Brussels Košice

M.E. Sharpe
Armonk, New York
London, England

EastWest Institute.
Annual Survey of Eastern Europe and the former Soviet Union:
1997—The Challenge of Integration / by the EastWest Institute
p. c.m.
Includes bibliographical references (p.) and index.
ISBN 0-7656-0359-4 (alk. paper)
1. Europe, Eastern—Politics and government—1989 .
2. Former Soviet republics—Politics and government.
3. Europe, Eastern—Economic conditions—1989– .
4. Former Soviet republics—Economic conditions.
5. Post-communism—Europe, Eastern.
6. Post-communism—Former Soviet republics.
I. Title
CIP

Printed in the United States of America

The paper used in this publication meets the minimum requirements of
American National Standard for Information Sciences—
Permanence of Paper for Printed Library Materials,
ANSI Z 39.48-1984.

ISSN: 1521-1452

∞

BM (c) 10 9 8 7 6 5 4 3 2 1

Contents

PREFACE

The Open Media Research Institute in Prague published an annual survey of developments in the former Soviet Union and Eastern Europe for the years 1995 and 1996. After the closure of OMRI in 1997, the EastWest Institute decided to take over sponsorship of the annual survey for 1997 and future years. The institute will use the survey to promote research into new areas, such as regional policy, community development, and trans-national cooperation, and will draw upon their own network of specialists across the region. It should be noted however that the individual chapters reflect the views and analysis of their authors and not those of the institute itself.

Given that these countries no longer share a common socialist political orientation, it is legitimate to ask why they should be treated as a common subject of study for a survey of annual developments. The first and most practical reason is that scholars, journalists, business executives, and policy-makers may find it useful to have a single, concise source which summarizes recent developments in these countries. Accurate and reliable information about the political life of some of these states, particularly the smaller ones, is not easy to come by.

With the passage of time since the collapse of communism, the 27 countries of the region have less and less in common. However, they do still face many similar challenges, and there are distinct patterns emerging amongst various blocs of countries. So it still makes intellectual sense to treat them together for reference purposes, at least as a conglomerate of regional blocs.

* * *

Coordinating the work of the dozens of authors of this volume, scattered across the countries of the region, was not an easy task. I would like to thank the authors for the care they took in writing their contributions, and their patience in seeing this project to completion.

Several institutions provided facilities and support for the production of this volume at various stages in the course of the year. Jan Urban, the publisher at the Institute for Journalism in Transition in Prague, kindly agreed to allow the survey to reprint some articles that had previously appeared in *Transitions.* Bill Geimer, president of the Jamestown Foundation, similarly authorized the re-publication of some pieces from *Prism.* (The publications of these two institutes can be found on the Web at www.ijt.org and www.jamestown.org.) All of the country surveys were specifically written for this volume.

At Wesleyan University, Fran Warren, Andrei Muchnik, and Dana Rappaport provided editorial and research assistance, and Wesleyan's office of research programs provided some financial support. Finishing touches on the manuscript were completed while the editor was in residence at the Slavic Research Center in Hokkaido University, Sapporo, on a fellowship from the Japanese government. I would like to thank the center's director, Professor Koichi Inoue, and the staff and colleagues who helped make my stay productive and enjoyable.

The main thanks must go to the EastWest Institute, for taking on this Sisyphus-scale project and turning it into a reality. Vasil Hudak and the staff at the Institute's Prague offices provided a most congenial work environment at various points in the year. John Mroz, Stephen Heintz, and Dag Hartelius gave the project their support and encouragement. Ambassador Heyward Isham, Natan Shklyar, and Bob Orttung rendered vital help in turning the idea into reality. And without Patricia Kolb at M.E. Sharpe the annual survey would never have happened in the first place.

It was with great sadness that we learned that Andrei Fadin, a Moscow-based journalist who was a regular contributor to *Transitions* magazine, died in a car accident on 19 November 1997. His article on Russia's media empires is included in this volume.

Peter Rutland

Annual Survey of Eastern Europe and the Former Soviet Union 1997

NORWEGIAN SEA
ARCTIC OCEAN
NORWAY
SWEDEN
FINLAND
RUSSIA
Tallinn
ESTONIA
Moscow
Riga
LATVIA
LITHUANIA
Vilnius
Minsk
BELARUS
Kazan
POLAND
Warsaw
CZECH REPUBLIC
Prague
Kyiv
SLOVAKIA
UKRAINE
Bratislava
AUSTRIA
Budapest
HUNGARY
MOLDOVA
Chisinau
Ljubljana
Zagreb
ROMANIA
SLOVENIA
Belgrade
Bucharest
CROATIA
Sarajevo
SERBIA
BOSNIA-HERZEGOVINA
BULGARIA
BLACK SEA
GEORGIA
Sofia
MONTENEGRO
Tirana
Skopje
Tbilisi
ARMENIA
ITALY
ALBANIA
MACEDONIA
Yerevan
TURKEY
GREECE
SYRIA
CYPRUS
MEDITERRANEAN SEA
IRAQ

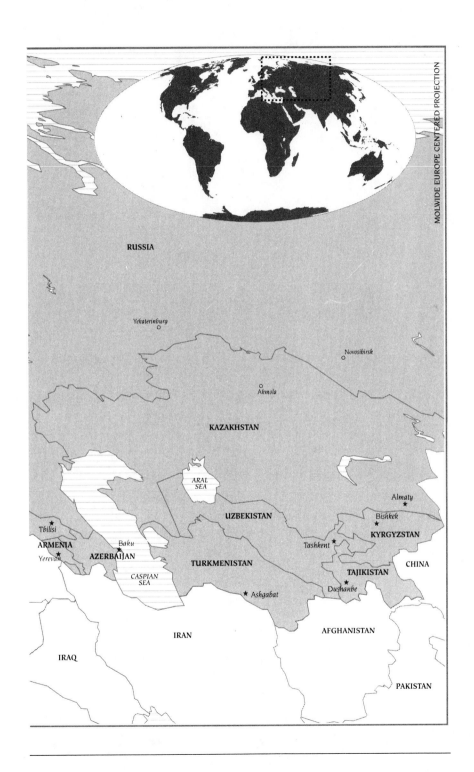

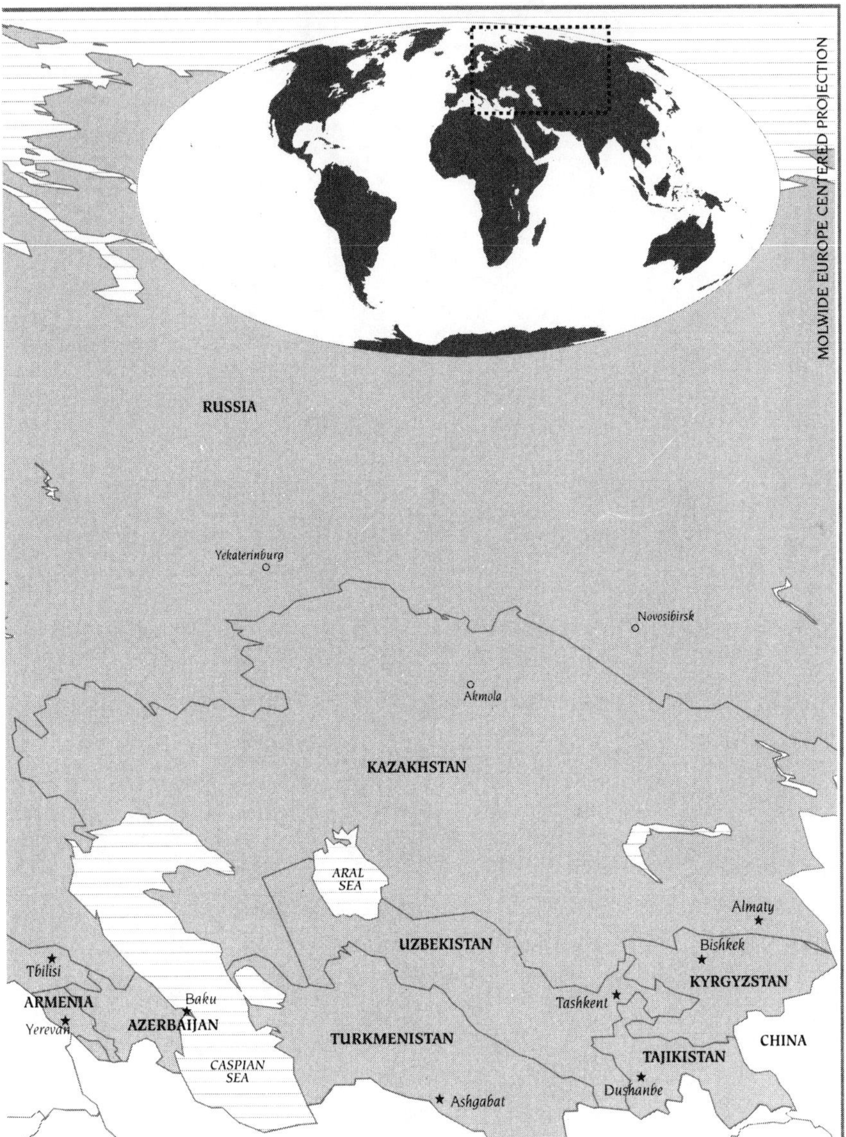
MOLWIDE EUROPE CENTERED PROJECTION
RUSSIA
Yekaterinburg
Novosibirsk
Akmola
KAZAKHSTAN
ARAL SEA
Almaty
Bishkek
UZBEKISTAN
KYRGYZSTAN
Tbilisi
ARMENIA
Yerevan
Baku
AZERBAIJAN
CASPIAN SEA
TURKMENISTAN
Tashkent
CHINA
TAJIKISTAN
Dushanbe
Ashgabat
AFGHANISTAN
IRAN
IRAQ
PAKISTAN

INTRODUCTION

I

IS EASTERN EUROPE "NORMAL" YET?

by GALE STOKES

In the first year that followed the collapse of communism in Eastern and East-Central Europe, one of the most commonly heard aspirations of ordinary people in the region was for their country to become "normal." The exact meaning of this term was quite unclear, of course, but one easily conjured up images: not standing in line for consumer goods, voting in contested elections, traveling abroad for vacations, or confronting a wide range of cultural and political views in the media. Some things that people probably did not have in mind included working harder, or, at the other extreme, being laid off, having reduced pensions, or paying for medical care. The reports gathered in this collection do not address these mundane issues, but they do suggest that many countries in Eastern Europe have begun to conduct their public affairs in ways that Europeans from the West can recognize. Except for some Southeast European countries, the free fall of production brought on by the collapse of the centrally planned economies has stopped and regrowth has begun, most countries hold bona fide elections, and the media are varied and vigorous.

Surely the most important milestones of 1997 were the invitations that the North Atlantic Treaty Organization and the European Union (EU) extended to several Central European countries in July. NATO expansion had been a matter of vigorous public discussion for several years. Originally founded as a purely military alliance to defend against a Warsaw Pact invasion of the West, NATO had to reassess its mission after the collapse of its main adversary.

The eventual adopting of a peacekeeping role in Bosnia was one of the painfully arrived at changes. In the new conditions, some favored expansion of NATO into Eastern Europe as a security measure against a possibly resurgent Russia, but the argument that won the day favored expansion as a democratizing agent more than as a purely military initiative. Advocates of this position argued that security in Europe today is not primarily military, but rather is based on a broadly overlapping system of democratic mechanisms of interaction. If East European states were to adopt NATO norms of civilian control, open budgets passed by democratically elected legislatures, and operational transparency, the argument went, democracy would be strengthened. Others argued that expansion would threaten Russia, which still had its pride and its nuclear weapons, undermine stability in Ukraine, and strengthen undemocratic forces in both countries. By the beginning of 1997, it had become clear that the expansion arguments, strongly supported by the United States, had won the day. In May, the alliance mollified Russia by creating the Russia-NATO Permanent Joint Council and satisfied Ukraine with a "Distinctive Partnership" agreement. With the decks cleared, in July it invited Poland, Hungary, and the Czech Republic to begin discussions that would lead to NATO accession by April 1999. Vigorous last-minute campaigns by Romania and Slovenia proved unsuccessful, although discussions regarding a second round could start in 1999.

Shortly before the NATO decision, the European Union announced that six countries had met its criteria for possible membership: Estonia, Poland, Hungary, the Czech Republic, Slovenia, and Cyprus. These criteria had been set out at the Copenhagen Summit in 1993: (1) democracy in political life; (2) protection of human rights; (3) guarantees of minority rights; (4) a functioning market economy; (5) ability to cope with a single market; (6) acceptance of the principles of monetary union. With the approval of the Luxembourg summit in December, negotiations got under way.

Despite the significance of these major developments, they were only the most important of an entire family of arrangements that in the last eight years have transformed the international situation in Eastern Europe. Since World War II West Europeans constructed a vast alphabet soup of interlocking and overlapping international agencies that as a whole constitute the European security system. WEU, OECD, OSCE, IMF, NATO, and UN are only some of the more easily recognizable acronyms in this mix. Relations among Eastern and East-Central European countries during most of their relatively short history as national states earlier this century were marked either by border disputes, protective tariffs, and nationalist accusations, or by forced bilateral relations with a hegemonic power. In the past few years, a new understanding of the sources of East European stability has emerged, based on the postwar West European example. Bi- and multi-lateral agreements among neighbors are now the order of the day. Some of the most important arrangements include the Central European Free Trade Association (CEFTA), which took in Slovenia in 1996 and Romania in 1997; the Black Sea Economic Cooperation organization (BSEC), which includes 11 states from Romania to Azerbaijan; the Southern Europe Cooperation Initiative (SECI), which consists of border-regulation negotiations among Balkan countries and is sponsored by the U.S. State Department; the Central European Initiative; the Weimar Triangle (Germany, France, and Poland); the German friendship treaties with Poland and the Czech Republic and the similar agreement between Hungary and Romania; and a multitude of bilateral agreements of all kinds. Not every issue has been ironed out. The Hungarian minority in Slovakia remains a problem, as does the Gabcikovo/Nagymaros dam dispute between Hungary and Slovakia. And not all of the international initiatives will prove viable over the long run. But on balance an entirely new level of commitment to regional cooperation now characterizes Eastern Europe.

This positive development reflects the completely different situation Eastern and East-Central European countries face in the post-1989 era compared to the one they faced in 1918 or 1948. This time the pressures are all on the side of pluralist, multilateral democracy. Anti-Semitic outbursts are immediately deplored in the European press and by Western governments; the desire to share in NATO and the EU push governments toward viable democratic and market mechanisms; and extreme nationalist or revolutionary parties (outside the former Yugoslavia at least) find themselves peripheralized rather than encouraged by external forces. In Poland, the study of Jewish life as an important part of Polish history picks up steam; in the Czech Republic agreement is reached with Germany on a treaty of friendship; in Romania, the Party of Romanian National Unity rejects its leader Gheorghe Funar.

The ongoing processes of NATO and EU enhancement suggest that two kinds of countries have emerged in post-1989 Eastern Europe: those the Western states recognize as most like them, and the rest. In actuality, however, there are at least three categories: those offered membership in NATO and the EU, those that could be offered membership if they change or develop significantly, and those unlikely to be offered membership for some while.

In the first category, the relative strengths of the three so-called Visegrad countries (Poland, Hungary, and the Czech Republic), favored by foreign investors since the very collapse of communism, have fluctuated over the years. Hungary, ahead at first because of reforms already instituted prior to 1989 and because of its moderate privatization policies, slumped by the mid-1990s and is now recovering after introducing an austerity policy in 1995. Poland, which was the only country to undergo radical "shock therapy," albeit an incomplete one, now boasts the strongest economy in Eastern Europe and is the only one to have surpassed its 1989 gross domestic product. The Czech Republic, at first the darling of neo-conservatives, has fallen on harder times. Vaclav Klaus turns out to have talked a tougher game than he played. Advocating markets, he relied on an informal social compact reached among labor, business, and government which kept unemployment low and slowed the pace of industrial restructuring. The voucher system, while successful as a device for mobilizing popular support for privatization, left too much power in the hands of banks, which continued to advance soft loans to near-insolvent large enterprises while their managers "tunneled" profitable assets out of the company. By the end of 1997, Klaus had fallen from power, and the Czech economy was in disarray.

Also increasingly included in the first category of developed states is the relatively prosperous Slovenia, which has had one major success along with a number of minor ones. Slovenia's main foreign policy for the past few years has been to assert successfully that it is not a Balkan country. It has approached the European Union and other entities directly, but it has also succeeded in redefining itself as a Central European state by achieving a free trade agreement with the Czech Republic and membership in CEFTA. In 1997, it began looking again at its potential markets to the south, but only under the proviso that it remain primarily northward oriented.

The second category of states, those with some hope of entering the charmed circle, include Slovakia, Croatia, Romania, Bulgaria, and the Baltic countries. As 1997 began, Bulgaria was perhaps the most problematic of these. After several years of serious mismanagement and growing economic crisis (the inflation rate was almost 250 percent per month in February 1997), it finally took drastic measures. After a bitter political struggle, the two main political formations, the socialists and the Union of Democratic Forces, finally managed to create an interim government; to establish, with the help of the IMF, a currency board; and to complete an election that brought the UDF to power. Inflation dropped almost immediately and confidence began to return, but it remained to be seen whether the new government could vitalize the Bulgarian economy.

Croatia's main problem was not economic. Its economy has privatized to a considerable extent (albeit largely into the hands of politically well-connected cronies), GDP is back on the upswing, and inflation is more or less under control. But President Franjo Tudjman shows little or no inclination for pluralism. Croatian voters returned him to the presidency in 1997, but Tudjman has consistently failed to recognize the election of opposition figures to local offices, particularly that of mayor of Zagreb, and government pressure on media that criticize Tudjman is unremitting.

The Slovak story is similar to the Croat in two major respects: its economy has done well in recent years (although it seems headed for a fall in 1998), and its political leadership does not understand or desire pluralism. The erratic Vladimir Meciar has demonstrated time and again an unwillingness to countenance real democratic procedures. In 1997 his personal battles with President Michal Kovac emasculated the power of the presidency and put even more power in his hands. Despite clear diplomatic messages from the European Union and the United States, it seems highly unlikely that Meciar will restructure the Slovak economy or its politics in a way that will make his country acceptable to NATO or the European Union.

For some time, it appeared that the same story might hold true for Romania under the leadership of Ion Iliescu. But in 1996, Iliescu lost an election and, without great ado, stepped down. At the beginning of 1997, therefore, the hopeful story in the second group seemed to be Romania. The long-delayed friendship treaty with Hungary had been signed in September 1996. Emil Constantinescu and Victor Ciorbea, the new president and prime minister who took office in November 1996, rather quickly transformed Romania from almost a pariah state into one with favorable atmospherics. The new team purged the government of many quasi-communists, spoke boldly of massive privatization, and tried valiantly to create a groundswell for NATO membership. By the end of the year, however, momentum had stalled for three reasons. First, miners and unions vigorously protested reforms that closed factories, forcing the government to go back on its budgetary restraints; second, the ruling coalition spent most of the year squabbling over a variety of accusations and secondary issues that prevented the implementation of a vigorous policy; and third, the nationalist opposition was unrelenting in its often irresponsible criticism of the government.

By the end of the year, these difficulties returned Romania to doubtful status as a European partner.

Six years after regaining their independence, the Baltic countries have shown that they have the capacity to put the legacy of Soviet rule behind them and move forward to join the community of Western nations. They have functioning democracies, with governments coming and going as a result of elections and coalition maneuverings. Despite a wave of bank crashes in 1994–95, and a serious problem with corruption, they have moved quickly forward with economic stabilization and market reform. Economic growth restarted in 1993, although living standards are still very low and the competitiveness in the European market of many of their core industries, including agriculture, is in doubt. The Estonians were delighted to be included in the first wave of candidates for EU entry, although the Latvians and Lithuanians complained bitterly that their preparedness was no less than that of Estonia.

The Balts also were disappointed that they were not invited to join the first track for NATO membership, although the declaration adopted at NATO's Madrid conference in July did describe them as "aspiring members." However, several serious obstacles remain to be overcome before the Baltic countries can be integrated with Western institutions. The chief hurdle has been the reluctance of Estonia and Latvia to adopt citizenship laws giving full political rights to the non-titular ethnic groups residing there, mainly Russians. These make up around 35 percent and 45 percent, respectively, of their population. Russian obstructionism also could delay the pace of their progress. Russia has delayed signing treaties confirming its borders with Estonia and with Latvia, although the treaty with Lithuania was signed in October 1997.

Finally, the third category, the also-rans: Moldova, Albania, Macedonia, Yugoslavia (Serbia and Montenegro), and Bosnia-Hercegovina. Despite the horrendous cataclysm of the Yugoslav wars, it was actually Albania that suffered the most in 1997. Its president, Sali Berisha, entered office with great promise and significant support from the West. In 1996, he undermined his legitimacy with a completely rigged election, and by 1997 he had created a personal regime and imprisoned his most important rival. In a collapsed economy surviving on smuggling and banditry, many people invested their scant funds in a vast array of pyramid schemes. When these inevitably began to collapse early in 1997, Albania descended into chaos. Eventually a European force headed by Italians had to intervene to prevent criminal gangs and the government police from destroying the country. A not entirely fraudulent election removed Berisha and brought his socialist rival, Fatos Nano, to power. Given the anarchic conditions, not to mention the rock bottom economic situation, Albania's prospects remained poor.

Moldova and Macedonia, although troubled by different specific issues, both faced the most heartrending situations in the region. Both are landlocked and surrounded by potentially threatening neighbors, Romania and Ukraine in the case of Moldova, and Greece and Serbia in the case of Macedonia. Both have intractable ethnic minorities, although Moldova has done a better job of granting the Gagauz measures of autonomy than Macedonia has done with its Albanian minority. Moldova has to deal with a recalcitrant breakaway state, the Transdnistrian Republic, a problem that at least Macedonia does not face yet, but both have not privatized to any great extent, both suffer from the infiltration of gangs into the economy, and both remain poverty stricken. The Macedonian economy is not declining, at least, but Moldova seems poised to abandon any pretense of economic reform.

In Serbia, hope for an important change was strong early in 1997. Tens of thousands of demonstrators tramped the streets of Belgrade daily to protest the unwillingness of the Milosevic government to permit opposition members to take their seats as the duly elected mayors of a number of Serb cities. As so often in the past, however, Milosevic proved able to master the situation. He waited, then made apparent concessions by allowing the new mayors to take office, and then arranged things in such a way that the mayors had very little power. Later in the year, to evade the constitutional requirement that he could not succeed himself as president of Serbia, he engineered his election as president of the Federal Republic of Yugoslavia. Outside observers watched aghast when in the subsequent election for president of Serbia Vojislav Seselj, a violent extremist almost surely guilty of massacres and devoted to the most narrowly defined Serb mission, came within a hair of winning. Tiny Montenegro provided further drama to the Serbian situation when Milo Djukanovic unseated Momir Bulatovic as president in a vicious electoral struggle. Bulatovic, a supporter of Milosevic, did everything in his power to stay in office, but in the end Djukanovic, who has been critical of Milosevic, was able to prevail.

Overarching all of the problems facing the former Yugoslav states and Albania, of course, were two fundamental issues: resolution of the Wars of Yugoslav Succession, and the Kosovo issue. The Dayton Agreement of 1995 brought an end to the wars, but not to the tensions, hatred, obstruction, and misery that the wars had produced. In theory, Bosnia was to become a multi-national state and refugees were to return to their homes. In fact, very few refugees have returned, the government elected late in 1996 has proven unable to bridge the enormous psychological gap between the former belligerents, and economic development has stalled. Most believe that had the international community not replaced its international force with a stabilization force (SFOR) a vicious three-sided war would have broken out again.

In the Serbian portion of Bosnia, Republika Srpska (RS), 1997 saw a bitter struggle between the forces of Radovan Karadzic, the actual if not nominal head of the kleptocracy that runs RS, and Biljana Plavsic, Karadzic's former ally who established her headquarters in Banja Luka and led a successful electoral challenge to Karadzic. Western countries, seeing in Plavsic a way of breaking the deadlock surrounding the Dayton Accords (even though she is a determined Serb nationalist), supported her, even to the extent of seizing Karadzic's TV transmitter, which had been broadcasting anti-Dayton propaganda. At the end of 1997 many issues remained not only unsolved, but seemingly insoluble: the fate of Brcko and Prevlaka; the virtual Croat seizure of Hercegovina; Croat intransigence in Mostar; the inability of the war crimes tribunal in The Hague to arrest and try those it had indicted; and the hostility on all fronts to refugees trying to return to their homes. Small, incremental steps were being made, but only a semi-permanent international force seems likely to keep the Bosnian situation inching forward.

But Bosnia, bad as it is, is not the worst potential problem in the Balkans. That problem is the political fate of the Albanians living outside the borders of Albania. Given that one of the main trends of European history in the past century and a half has been to re-map state borders onto ethnic borders, there seems every reason to think that at some point such a redrawing will take place regarding the Albanians. In fact, it would be possible to draw a line on a map that would include in one entity the overwhelming majority of Albanians living in the Balkans and exclude almost all other ethnic groups, but at the expense of several other countries. The focus in 1997 was Kosovo, the Albanian region of Serbia. Patient, non-violent leaders such as Ibrahim Rugova had created a shadow Albanian state within Kosovo, as Albanians withdrew from participation in formal public affairs, which are conducted by Serbs. In 1997, however, a new element entered the picture, the Kosovo Liberation Army, which began assassinating Serbs and even Albanians it perceived as cooperating too much with the Serbs. A violent Albanian revolution stands little chance of success at the moment, because the Serbs overwhelmingly outgun the Albanians. But the appearance of such a movement almost certainly portends trouble in the future, especially given the almost pathological intransigence of the Serbs regarding Kosovo.

What is the bottom line, then? Has Eastern Europe become "normal?" As the above thumbnail review suggests, the question turns out to be illegitimate. One cannot talk about "Eastern Europe" as an entity. The differences between Poland and Albania are almost as great as those between Singapore and Somalia. If we look at all the experiences, however, several common factors stand out. The first and foremost is the importance of leadership. Despite the literally thousands of analyses of "transition" that have filled social science journals in the past decade, which stress the importance of trans-national, structural explanation, the personal turns out to be vital. Nothing of fundamental importance differentiates the Czech Republic and Slovakia, for example, but diametrically opposed styles of leadership have brought the two countries to quite different positions. Paradoxically, one of the most useful characteristics of good leadership has been a willingness to leave office. Iliescu in Romania might not be the best example of a progressive leader, but he provided a salutary example of democratic civility when he stepped down after electoral defeat. By contrast, the socialists in Bulgaria had to be blasted out of office by the almost complete collapse of the Bulgarian economy. Even here, however, the Bulgarian socialist leaders made recovery possible by agreeing not to attempt a new government, even though they had not lost an election. Surely Serbia has no hope of restoring its economy or its position in Europe under Milosevic, and even Croatia's Tudjman keeps shooting himself in the foot with his narrow, nationalist style. Poland, on the other hand, has had exemplary leadership, despite bitter political struggles and occasional deadlock. The fact that its current government includes Leszek Balcerowicz, finance minister from the first Solidarity government, Hanna Suchocka, a former conservative prime minister, and Jerzy Buzek, a Protestant, as its prime minister suggests the ability of the Polish elites to find ways to continue fruitful developmental policies.

Corruption is another leitmotiv, but one that needs to be put into perspective. Every year Transparency International ranks fifty-two countries in an index of corruption perception. Denmark is considered the least corrupt place to do business, and Nigeria the most corrupt. The Visegrad countries stand near the middle of these rankings, not the best, but not the worst. Privatization has provided many opportunities for co-opting of public assets into private hands, while actual criminal activities (smuggling, "protection" rackets, and the usual combination of drugs and prostitution) have prospered as governments seek to establish their control over societies. Nevertheless, increasing integration into international markets is exerting a steady pressure to improve business practices.

Finally, ethnic conflicts are endemic. Here too, however, some perspective is needed. The hatreds engendered by the Wars of Yugoslav Succession will not abate soon, even if leadership changes for the better, and the Albanian problem will almost certainly evoke violence sooner or later. One wonders also if Moldova will in the long run be able to resist incorporation into Romania, although that is not on the immediate agenda. In Central Europe, however, the situation is relatively calm. The disputes regarding Hungarian minorities in Transylvania are being dealt with by Romania and Hungary in a cooperative spirit. Although the same spirit is not evident in Slovakia, the dispute there is not likely to become violent. The key to maintaining this relative calm is the expansion of the international community of buffering mechanisms throughout Central and Southeastern Europe as conditions permit. Whether this will create a "normal" life for everyone or not, the project is sufficiently challenging to keep Europeans occupied into the foreseeable future.

MARKING TIME IN THE FORMER SOVIET STATES

by PETER RUTLAND

In theory, the former Soviet republics that gained independence in 1991 are in "transition" to a market economy and liberal democracy. In reality, they have so far managed to construct a less-than-perfect market economy and a very shallow and unsatisfying democracy. Worse still, there were few signs of positive trends toward a brighter future.

On the contrary, stagnation was the dominant feature of political and economic life in the member-countries of the Commonwealth of Independent States (CIS) in 1997. Life did not get any better; the best one can say is that it did not get any worse. The peoples of the region showed tremendous patience in the face of adversity, and a resolute faith that the future will bring better times. The trajectory of the Baltic states of Estonia, Latvia, and Lithuania, which are not members of the CIS, has been quite different. (So much so that they are analyzed alongside the other Eastern and Central European countries, and not in this article.)

Amidst the general gloom, there were some positive developments. An uneasy peace settled upon the war-torn countries of Chechnya and Tajikistan. And cease-fires held in other conflict zones, notably Nagorno-Karabakh and Abkhazia. But peace, in all these cases, meant simply the absence of fighting, and not any real progress toward resolution of the underlying sources of conflict. In Tajikistan the government and opposition agreed to share power because of the threat posed by the northward march of the Taliban in Afghanistan. In Chechnya, Russian forces withdrew in line with the peace accords of August 1996. A formal peace treaty was signed in May 1997, but this left the status of Chechnya in limbo, neither recognized as an independent country nor functioning as part of the Russian Federation.

PROSPERITY? NOT YET

The other positive sign was the revival of economic growth in the Transcaucasus, Kazakhstan, and Kyrgyzstan. However, the double-digit growth recorded in those countries did not translate through into improved living standards for the population. Rather, it was a result of the fact that after several years of sharp economic decline, growth was bound to start sooner or later. And because those economies had shrunk to less than a quarter of their 1991 level, growth when it came—starting from such a low base—was bound to be spectacular. But this was more an artifact of arithmetic than a sign of economic health.

In general, there was little sign that the shattered Soviet command economy had been replaced by a functioning market system. True, the dragon of hyperinflation had been slain. Inflation was running at an annual rate of only about 10 percent in most of the countries, rising to 25 percent in Kyrgyzstan and somewhat higher in Uzbekistan. Inflation hit 80 percent in Tajikistan and at least 65 percent in Belarus. At the insistence of international financial institutions, most of the countries were running tight monetary policies and had established convertible currencies. Uzbekistan was an exception, in that it had reintroduced currency controls in 1996. Belarus was in a league of its own, since President Alyaksandr Lukashenka seemed bent on recreating a Soviet-style economy. Several of the countries ran up large foreign debts—most notably, the unpaid deliveries of energy from Russia to Belarus and Ukraine. Armenia's blockaded economy would have expired without the hundreds of millions of dollars of foreign aid and remittances from the Armenian diaspora. Turkmenistan experienced an economic meltdown in 1997, with GDP falling perhaps by one third. The reason was Russia's refusal to allow Turkmenistan to export its natural gas to paying customers in the West. (Its earlier deliveries to Ukraine and Georgia had gone largely unpaid).

Great hopes continued to swell in the southern tier of countries, where the oil riches of the Caspian basin were expected to turn the region into a second Kuwait. However, for the time being the riches are hypothetical rather than actual. 1997 did see a trickle of Caspian oil make its way out—some by rail into Iran, some through the pipeline across Chechnya to Novorossiisk, which was re-opened in November. But large-volume exports remain 3–5 years further off. The immediate task is to rehabilitate the existing Baku-Supsa pipeline and then build new pipelines for the major export volumes. One line is already under construction—the Caspian Pipeline Consortium's line across southern Russia that will carry oil from Kazakhstan's Tengiz field.

An intense debate was underway over what route to choose for the second major export pipeline. The heady mix of politics and oil was seen as a replay of the "Great Game" which had been played in the nineteenth century by Britain and Russia for control over inner Asia. But this time around, the United States emerged as a major player in the Caspian region, which was surprising given the lack of previous U.S. contacts in the area. The United States was pushing hard for the export pipeline to cross Georgia and then head south through Turkey to reach the Mediterranean at Ceyhan. This would bind Azerbaijan, Georgia, Turkey, and even perhaps Armenia into a mutually beneficial, U.S.-led alliance. It would have the added advantages of reducing the region's current dependency on Moscow, and preventing Iran from becoming a major export route for the energy riches of Central Asia.

However, there were still many ducks to be lined up before this U.S. scheme would come to fruition. In the meantime, as of late 1997 only one oil rig was actually operating in the Caspian, and oil output in Kazakhstan and Azerbaijan was well below the level attained in 1991, when the Soviet economy was still functioning. There was only slow progress toward resolution of the dispute over the legal status of the Caspian Sea. Russia, having been given a share in some of the oil projects in the Azeri zone, did start to shift its position in favor of dividing the sea into national sectors (the option favored by all the other littoral states save Iran). The political deadlock over the disputed Azerbaijani enclave of Nagorno-Karabakh remained unresolved, which is a barrier to full-scale development of the region. Azerbaijan's President Heydar Aliev received a red-carpet reception during his first-ever visit to the United States in August. Western pressure produced some concessionary statements from Armenian President Levon Ter-Petrossian in September, but this provoked a strong counter-reaction in Yerevan, not to mention Karabakh.

Behind all the great-power maneuvering, there was a growing fear among opposition forces in the region that the oil wealth, when it comes, will benefit a thin layer of the ruling elite (not to forget the Western investors) and will pass by the vast majority of the region's inhabitants.

The simple facts of geography—as amended by 75 years of central planning—weigh very heavily upon the countries of the former Soviet Union, especially Central Asia. Even if Moldova, or Kyrgyzstan, are astute pupils of IMF policies, their economies are stranded hundreds or thousands of miles from Western markets. Export-led growth, based on manufacturing plants assembling imported parts and materials, is simply not an option for most of these countries because of their geographic isolation. The Baltic countries are highly favored in this regard—this being yet another reason why they are pulling rapidly away from the rest of the ex-Soviet pack of countries.

There was general talk of Central Asia and the Caucasus serving as a land bridge between Europe and Asia, creating the "new Silk Road" to China, and so forth. However, the old Silk Road fell into disuse for a reason—sailing ships were a lot cheaper and faster than camels. Distances in the region are vast, and the climate and geography harsh. Many thousands of kilometers of new railway and pipelines will have to be laid before land transport across the region can compete with tanker freight across the open seas. It will be well into the next millennium before these dreams turn into reality.

As a result of the hand which history and geography have dealt them, most of the countries of the former Soviet Union have been thrown back onto a role as an exporter of primary products. Some of the countries, such as Ukraine, Belarus, and Armenia, have virtually nothing to sell in this regard. They desperately need radical economic reform to start moving forward—but political deadlock in Ukraine, and idiosyncratic leadership in Belarus, stopped economic reform dead in its tracks.

Russia itself is well-endowed by nature: its oil, gas, and minerals generate exports worth $80 billion a year. Unfortunately, the flawed economic reforms that were implemented in Russia meant that this resource wealth was not channeled into the development of new fields or ancilliary industries. Rather, it has been siphoned off into pockets of the "New Russian" elite, and has financed the creation of a new political class in which media manipulation has taken the place of communist ideology as the glue holding the system together.

FRIENDS AND NEIGHBORS

As a forum for the conduct of international relations, the Commonwealth of Independent States reached its nadir in 1997. At the abortive Chisinau summit in October, leader after leader stood up to denounce the uselessness of the organization. Countries seemed to compete to show how little they needed the CIS. And yet, the leaders keep coming back to the CIS summits. And efforts to create smaller, more effective associations (such as the customs union of Russia, Belarus, Kazakhstan, and Armenia) have not fared any better, but have been riven by internal bickering. The best one can say for the CIS is that it provides a forum within which the leaders can talk, even if it is only to complain.

One should be thankful that—apart from the conflict over Karabakh—none of the post-Soviet countries have gone to war with each other. There were plenty of potential reasons for such conflicts—contested territories, ethnic groups living outside their titular homeland, refugee flows, economic privation, and trade disputes. But common sense, and a certain mutual political understanding that came from the shared heritage of the Soviet past, persuaded the region's leaders to avoid conflict. It also helped that their national armies were weak to non-existent (with the exception of Russia's).

As in post-colonial Africa, all the countries accepted the idea that the borders separating their countries at the time of the Soviet breakup should become the new international borders, except for Armenia, which disputes Azerbaijan's claim to Nagorno-Karabakh. However, the process of physically demarcating and recognizing the precise border has been proceeding rather slowly. Recognition of the existing borders has undoubtedly minimized the likelihood of major conflict. However, it has left many anomalous situations where compact ethnic minorities live in territories ruled by leaders of a different ethnicity. In a minority of cases, the ethnic minority took up arms in pursuit of self-determination. This has led to the appearance of a rash of anomalous, rump states: Chechnya, Nagorno-Karabakh, Abkhazia, Transdniestrian Republic, and South Ossetia. These entities have some of the attributes of statehood, but are not recognized by the international community and are unlikely to make it into the world community of nation-states anytime soon.

In some cases, most notably the 22 million Russians living in Ukraine, Kazakhstan, and the Baltic states, the politically subordinate ethnic groups left stranded by the Soviet collapse have accepted the new rules of the game, and show no sign of rushing to the barricades. Even so, smoldering conflicts remain in these areas over language policy as it affects access to education, the media, and jobs. It requires careful and sensitive leadership (helped by close monitoring from the international community) to keep these disputes in check. In general, one has seen less trouble on this score than one would have expected back in 1992. It is not clear why this is the case. Perhaps Chechnya and Bosnia served as sobering examples of where confrontation leads. Perhaps also it is a product of the complex and differentiated nature of ethnic identity (especially Russian identity) in the former Soviet Union.

A major step forward in 1997 was the signing of a friendship treaty between Russia and Ukraine, which among other things signaled Russian recognition of Ukraine's title to the Crimean peninsula (which had been detached from the Russian Federation only in 1954). The treaty came after compromise was reached over the future of the Black Sea Fleet, giving Russia basing rights in Sevastopol for 20 years.

Sevastopol became a rallying cry for Russian nationalists, a symbol of their incredible shrinking empire. The Russian political elite drew the line at further territorial losses—hence the suicidal desire to hang onto Chechnya. But they were divided and unsure over where to go from here. They generally favor cooperation with the West. The West is peaceful and prosperous, as Russia wants to be. The Soviet experiment, an abortive search for another way, had proved disastrously bad for Russia. There was no point in picking a fight with the West—hence Russia's calm acceptance of NATO enlargement, when it finally came in July 1997.

But Moscow cannot shake off some superpower fantasies when it comes to the "near abroad"—the term Russians use for the former Soviet Union. Psychologically, many Russians still regard these countries not merely as a sphere of influence, but as part and parcel of their own political identity. And Russia still has sufficient military muscle to play the role of school bully. Looked at from the West, Russia's armed forces are a pathetic shadow of their former selves. However, viewed in a regional context, it is important to remember that Russia is still the dominant military power in the post-Soviet space. Its border guards patrol the "external" frontier of most CIS countries (all except Ukraine, Azerbaijan, and Uzbekistan). Its troops play a "peacekeeping" role in the conflicts in Tajikistan, Abkhazia, and South Ossetia. It maintains military bases in most of the CIS countries. And it still has the military hardware—communications infrastructure, transport aircraft, and air strike forces—to dwarf the military capacity of its new neighbors. Russia could not win the Chechen war, but it could devastate Chechnya. It has sufficient stocks of weapons to feed them into the hands of determined groups willing to use them, such as the Karabakh Armenians and the Abkhazians. The question arises, does this "bully" role serve Russia's best interests? Most of Russia's economic elite would answer that question in the negative. But such is the fragmented nature of the Russian political system that no clear and coherent policy has evolved. Security policy was left in the hands of the military services, in some cases even devolving down to the level of field commanders. Russia's political leaders surely realize that Russian security is best served through cooperation rather than conflict with Russia's neighbors.

RULERS AND RULED

If economics is the dismal science, then politics is not much better. The events of 1997 provide few grounds for optimism about the political trajectory of the newly independent states. In his discussion of Eastern and East-Central Europe, Gale Stokes underlines the importance of leadership (see preceding chapter). It makes a big difference if you are ruled by an Aleksander Kwasniewski or a Vladimir Meciar; a Franjo Tudjman or a Vaclav Havel.

The same holds true for the former Soviet countries. But they have been much less successful in the leadership lottery than their Central European colleagues. Most of the CIS countries are ruled by authoritarian presidents: some benign, some less so. Parliaments are generally fractious and reactionary bodies, which to the extent they had any power at all tended to wield their influence to block needed change.

In 1997 four of the five Central Asian countries were ruled by the very same men who had commanded the Communist Party at the time of the Soviet collapse. The exception was Kyrgyzstan (the smallest country in the region), which is ruled by the ex-physicist Askar Akaev. Organized political opposition in those countries was weak to non-existent, although street protests by desperate workers became increasingly common. It was left to a few brave journalists to point out that the emperor left something to be desired in the hosiery department.

The three Caucasus republics also have strong presidents, with a pliant parliament in Baku and more assertive legislatures in Yerevan and Tbilisi. Eduard Shevardnadze and Heydar Aliev were Soviet-era leaders who returned to power after their countries experienced a (disastrous) interregnum of several years under the rule of democratic-nationalist presidents. In Armenia, Levon Ter-

Petrossian rose to power as head of the democratic-nationalist movement and managed, unlike his neighboring presidents, to win re-election (in 1996, in elections of dubious equity). Even during Soviet times, the Caucasus republics were known to have vibrant societies and a clear sense of national identity. These qualities have seen them through difficult times, and Stephen Jones (see pages 333–34) detects the resurgence of civil society in Georgia. However, the strong sense of ethnic identity has also been fuel to many of the regions' conflicts (overlapping with other causes, from banditry to opportunistic leaders).

Further north, one has the enigmatic figure of Boris Yeltsin. To some he is the father of Russian democracy, to others he is the butcher of Chechnya. Events in 1997 did nothing to solve the riddle of Yeltsin's true historical rôle. Rather, one saw more of the political dancing that has become his calling card—the firing of ministers, the promotion of ministers, even an attempted launch of a second "liberal revolution" in economic policy in the spring. Yeltsin's health seemed to be much improved over 1996: there was no doubt that he was still the decisive figure in Russian political life. However, he continued to make embarrassing gaffes at international gatherings, and it was reported that he could only work for a few hours per day. The banking elite that had joined together to secure Yeltsin's re-election in June 1996 fell to bickering among themselves in 1997, arguing over the division of the spoils as some of Russia's last remaining state industries were put up for sale. Their political weapon of choice was *kompromat:* the leaking of scandalous material about corruption through the press and TV outlets that the business magnates controlled. (The low point of the year was a videotape of the justice minister cavorting in a bathhouse.) While the financial elite bickered, there was a steady leakage of power from the federal center to the regions. In July, Yeltsin tried and failed to remove the obstreperous governor of Primorskii Krai, when the other regional leaders who make up the upper house of parliament, the Federation Council, came to his rescue.

The political landscape was equally bleak in Belarus and Ukraine. The autocratic behavior of President Alyasksandr Lukashenka, who had long since alienated the Western powers, proved too much even for Russia in 1997. Having dismissed parliament in 1996, Lukashenka turned his attention to mopping up the last remnants of a free press. The arrest of a team of Russian TV journalists in July proved too much for Moscow, but Lukashenka refused to back down in the face of pressure from President Yeltsin. (At one point, Lukashenka was refused permission to fly into Russia.) He calculated, correctly, that Moscow sees Belarus as an important piece of strategic real estate, a chip that may perhaps be cashed in when NATO enlargement creeps up to the Baltic.

In Ukraine, the political standoff between president and parliament continued. President Leonid Kuchma maintained the usual practice of appointing a new prime minister each year, by firing Pavel Lazarenko on suspicion of corruption in July. There were dimensions of deadlock not seen in Russia: the parliament itself was deeply riven between nationalist, pro-market, and communist forces. At least in September, at its thirteenth attempt, the parliament passed a new election law which reduced the previous high turnout requirement and adopted a

Russian-style electoral system, with half of the parliamentary seats allotted by party list and half in individual races. This set the scene for more effective party competition in the elections scheduled for spring of 1998. The main political achievement of the year was the signing of friendship treaties with Russia and Romania.

CONCLUDING THOUGHTS

What, then, had been gained in the CIS after six years of democratization? Political power is more nakedly exercised, stripped of the illusionary screen of ideology. Ordinary citizens have few opportunities to exercise meaningful influence over their political leaders. The presidents are subject to popular election—but have proved very good at getting themselves re-elected. Elections to legislatures are more competitive, but also less meaningful, in the absence of well-organized parties to present clear choices to voters. The parliaments are generally feeble bodies, unable to exert much control over the selection of the government.

Corruption has become more entrenched—and certainly more rewarding—than in Soviet times. The international monitoring agency, Transparency International, ranks Russia as one of the half-dozen most corrupt countries on earth in which to do business. The other CIS member states are not far behind.

None of these societies have made much progress in developing rule of law, separation of powers, or civil society. Most of them do have a much freer press than in communist times. It is harder to judge whether there has been progress in respect for individual civil rights. In Russia, for example, constitutionally guaranteed rights such as the right to alternative military service, to own land, or to live where one chooses, are not implemented in law. And new forms of rights violation have arisen, from the collapse of state health and education services to the widespread arrears in payment of wages and social benefits.

Gale Stokes asks if East Europe is becoming "normal," and concludes that it is, for the most part. The same can also be said of the former Soviet Union—except that the standards of "normality" to which they are converging are not those of Western Europe, but those of much of the developing world.

REGIONAL ISSUES

II

NATO ***Enlargement***

European ***Union***

NATO Enlargement

FROM DREAM TO REALITY

by MICHAEL MIHALKA

The North Atlantic Treaty Organization (NATO) began its move East in 1997. In July of that year at the Madrid summit, NATO announced that it would accept as new members the Czech Republic, Hungary, and Poland. At the 16 December semi-annual meeting of the North Atlantic Council, the gathering of NATO's foreign ministers, those countries signed accession accords. In an attempt to assuage Russian fears that it would become increasingly isolated as NATO enlarged, the Russia-NATO Founding Act was signed in May. In the same month Ukraine's pivotal security position in Europe was recognized with the Distinctive Partnership agreement (later signed at Madrid).

NATO attempted to meet the concerns of those countries which did not qualify for the first wave of new members, in particular Slovenia and Romania, by creating the Euro-Atlantic Partnership Council (EAPC) and enhancing the Partnership for Peace (PfP) program. Meanwhile NATO agreed to stay in Bosnia indefinitely. One sign that NATO had increasingly become the center of the European security architecture was the changing attitude toward the organization in the formerly non-aligned and neutral states. By December 1996 even Switzerland had joined the PfP and support for NATO membership was growing in Austria, Sweden, and Finland.

In the Madrid communique NATO singled out several different groups of countries. First, NATO invited the Czech Republic, Hungary, and Poland to begin accession talks. In the same section, reaffirming that it will remain open for membership, NATO said it would review applications again in 1999 and took note of "the positive developments toward democracy and the rule of law in a number of southeastern European countries, especially Romania and Slovenia." In addition, the declaration recognized "the progress achieved toward greater stability and cooperation by the states in the Baltic region which are also aspiring members." Those words gently deferred the candidacy of Romania and Slovenia until 1999 while not dashing the hopes of the Baltic countries that they may eventually be invited to join. The wayward behavior of Slovakia's President Vladimir Meciar had removed that country from the list of potential early members.

THE ENLARGEMENT DEBATE

With the decision to enlarge the alliance having been taken by NATO leaders, the debate then shifted to the parliaments of the NATO members and those invited to join. All of the NATO member-country parliaments must approve the treaty changes to allow new members to join, which meant in the United States that two-thirds of the Senate, the U.S. upper house of the legislature, must agree to enlargement. Each new accession country must also agree, but this required only a majority vote of their respective parliaments. Both Hungary and Poland had wide cross-party support for enlargement. In the Czech Republic, all major parliamentary parties were also supportive, although if the Social Democrats win the election scheduled for June 1998, they may call for a referendum.

Support for NATO in Poland has always been high. Polls have usually shown support in favor of joining NATO consistently over 80 percent. Support in Hungary and the Czech Republic has been much lower. Both countries showed support from only a little over half of the population in 1995. Alarmed by these polls, the Hungarian government initiated a program to inform the public of the advantages of NATO enlargement. This proved effective. When Hungary held a referendum on accession to NATO on 16 November 1997, around 85 percent voted in favor and almost half of the eligible voters participated. By contrast the government in the Czech republic had done little to promote support for NATO accession. In November 1997, only 43 percent of Czech poll respondents favored Czech accession.

The elite debate regarding enlargement in the United States became somewhat difficult to categorize. One way to organize the debate in the United States is to think of a two-by-two table. Along one axis individuals would be differentiated as to whether they were "realist" or "liberal."[1] The other axis would distinguish between a regional and a Russian perspective. In general liberals who take a regional perspective support NATO enlargement. A prime example would be Anthony Lake, the former U.S. national security advisor who was the architect of the Clinton administration's NATO enlargement policy. Wilsonian internationalists, those who favor a leading U.S. role in creating effective international organizations, would also fall into this category. Russia-focused liberals such as Strobe Talbott have tended to oppose NATO enlargement: Talbott had to switch his position publicly in order to fall in line with the Clinton administration's policy. The father of Cold War studies, George Kennan, has called NATO enlargement the worst error the West could make.[2] By and large Russia experts oppose NATO enlargement because they think it will impede Russian progress toward a liberal democracy. Realists such as Zbigniew Brzezinski and Henry Kissinger who focus on Russia tend to favor NATO enlargement because they view this as an important opportunity to contain what they see as the long-term trend of Russian expansion. By the same token realists who take a regional view oppose NATO enlargement, because they do not see the strategic necessity. Michael Mandelbaum and John Mearsheimer are representative of this point of view.[3] In the final analysis, the elite debate in the United States came late and made little difference, while the public itself was never really engaged.

Although early on after the fall of communism the Central European countries pushed for NATO membership, they had to wait for a change in the U.S. administration to gain the necessary support with the alliance. Enlargement was really the brainchild of the Clinton administration which took over in January 1993. Even as late as the fall of 1993, the State Department was arguing against enlargement in language reminiscent of the Bush administration, which had opposed enlargement on the grounds that the obligations incurred by allowing the new members to join were not clearly compensated by their military capability. At the beginning of the Clinton administration, the State Department Russian experts around Strobe Talbott opposed enlargement because of its perceived negative consequences for Russia's transition to democracy, while the Defense Department opposed it because the United States would incur new obligations without any clear benefits for the country. However, Anthony Lake at the National Security Council and Madeleine Albright (who was born in Czechoslovakia) at the UN found a sympathetic ear in Bill Clinton and changed U.S. policy in favor of enlargement and engagement.[4] The disastrous results of the 1994 midterm elections for the Democrats (Clinton's party), which saw the Republicans win control of the House of Representatives for the first time in fifty years, also added to the appeal of enlargement for Clinton who would face reelection in 1996. Key electoral states have large concentrations of Americans with Central European ancestry, in particular Illinois, where Chicago is considered by some to be the second-largest Polish city in the world. Indeed, Clinton could appropriate yet another policy from the Republicans whose "Contract with America" in 1994 supported NATO enlargement.

Despite what seemed to be broad bipartisan support for enlargement in the Senate, as evidenced by successive non-binding resolutions in favor, the Clinton administration was particularly concerned about how the debate on enlargement would unfold in that body. One of the seemingly surprising features of the NATO enlargement process to date has been the almost total lack of public debate on the subject throughout NATO, especially since enlargement will entail as yet indeterminate costs but very real and clear obligations. Except in times of crisis, the American public rarely departs from its concerns about the economy to focus on foreign policy and thus has had little interest in the debate over NATO enlargement. The Senate and the American public are probably willing to defend Warsaw but have trouble distinguishing Slovenia from Slovakia and Budapest from Bucharest. The need to simplify the debate and enhance the likelihood of passage was one reason that the United States wanted to limit the first wave to Poland, the Czech Republic, and Hungary.

However, support even for these three countries was not a foregone conclusion within the rest of NATO. The alliance usually operates on consensus, but as the strongest military power in the alliance, the United States often tends to get its way. Nevertheless, the Europeans had become increasingly disenchanted with U.S. policy in Bosnia. The United States advocated forceful military action, the so-called "lift and strike" policy of lifting the arms embargo against the non-Serb parties to the Bosnian conflict and using air strikes against the Bosnian Serbs. Yet at the same time, the United States was unwilling to commit its own ground troops. The U.S. policy in Bosnia reached its nadir in the fall of 1994, when the U.S. Congress dictated that the U.S. naval forces no longer participate in the embargo against the former Yugoslav states. Some Europeans saw this shift in U.S. policy as the biggest threat to the unity of the alliance since the 1956 Suez crisis. However, by the summer of 1995, the United States was willing to provide troops, and midwifed the Dayton accord, which ended the Bosnian war in December 1995. This U.S. commitment to European security facilitated European support for enlargement.

Attitudes toward Russia also figured strongly in the rhetoric and logic of several West European countries. Germany has routinely strongly advocated enlargement. Clearly one of the more important reasons is that enlargement to the East, particularly by the inclusion of Poland, takes Germany off the front lines of any future East-West conflict. Equally as important, Germany receives a buffer zone to the East against a region perceived as politically unstable by many Germans. But Germany wanted to keep the first wave of NATO enlargement as small as possible in order not to antagonize Russia and ruin the deal over Poland. In addition, with enlargement (and re-unification), Germany also becomes firmly grounded in the West. Some people, especially in the United Kingdom, had feared a resurgent Germany would embark again on a drive to expand its influence on the continent, which led to the two major wars in Europe in the twentieth century. Indeed, many Russians support the continued presence of a non-enlarged NATO under U.S. leadership to ensure stability in Europe.

Britain, too, had raised concerns about the Russian response, but these arguments were largely tactical. The British initially argued that NATO was not a club with open membership for friendly parties, but a serious military alliance. Hence the Central Europeans needed to demonstrate that they could make a military contribution to the alliance that corresponded with the obligations that other countries incur under Article V of the 1949 Washington Treaty—which obliges them to go the aid of a NATO member if that country is attacked. Britain also feared that enlarging the alliance would also dilute it and diminish Britain's own influence.

After initially opposing NATO enlargement (and any other suggestion made by the Americans), France came to rather like the idea of a slightly diluted and broader alliance, as this would make Paris less isolated and also increase the European counterweight to the United States within the alliance. To balance the northern tilt of the leading enlargement candidates (Poland, the Czech Republic, and Hungary), France took up the cudgels for Romania, with whom it had traditionally close relations. The Danes promoted the Balts. After settling its rancorous bilateral dispute with Ljubljana over territory and property issues, Italy argued strongly for Slovenia.

As the Madrid summit approached, NATO divided into two camps: one favoring a smaller, the other a larger, group of candidates. None opposed the candidacy of Poland, the Czech Republic, and Hungary. France pushed strongly for Romania, which had helped its own position by its lobbying and considerable progress in reforming its military after the democrats came to power in the November 1996 elections. Slovenia found little opposition and some even argued, rather disingenuously, that including that country would provide a strategically important land bridge to Hungary, even though the single road connecting the two countries could not support much traffic.

Faced with the possibility that Romania and Slovenia might be included and the Baltic countries not, Denmark switched to restricting the first wave to only Poland, the Czech Republic, and Hungary. The Danes and other friends of the Balts reasoned that it would take a long time for the Alliance to integrate five members and thus Baltic membership would be put off indefinitely to the corresponding detriment of the security in the Baltic region. The Russian argument made little difference in the argument between five and three candidates. Some thought that taking in five would simply be too many for Moscow, others believed that would reassure the Russians that no further enlargement would take place for a very long time.

Carrying their argument into the Madrid discussions, the French fought extremely hard to at least give Romania a promise for the next round. Several members, including the British, opposed any special promises and wanted simply to retain the language that NATO remained open to new members. In this situation, Denmark and Norway, eventually supported by the United States (which has a strong domestic Baltic lobby of its own), came up with the drafting on the Baltic countries, which was then used to find a compromise solution. The favorable reference in the Madrid declaration to the Baltic states, "also aspiring members," was the least expected outcome of the summit. There was not much discussion about Slovenia; everyone agreed that this was the least controversial and most developed candidate. At the same time it would have been politically impossible to include Slovenia but not Romania.

The Madrid summit covered a number of other topics that will also command the attention of the alliance. One of the more important changes in the short run was the relatively unheralded enlargement of NATO's integrated military structure to include Spain and possibly France. NATO's structure will need to be further adapted to include the Czech Republic, Hungary, and Poland. With these countries, enlargement would actually involve five countries. Romania and Slovenia would have made seven. At the end of 1997, however, France decided to back off on its earlier interest of rejoining NATO's integrated military structure. This was, in part because it was unable to secure American acquiescence in appointing a European national to head NATO's southern command; but also because the new socialist government of Lionel Jospin was decidedly less enthusiastic about NATO than its predecessor.

INTEGRATING OR DESTABILIZING RUSSIA?

Russians criticize NATO enlargement for two main reasons: because Russia will lose influence as it becomes increasingly isolated, and because enlargement will strengthen the hand of anti-democratic forces in the country. If either one of these statements is demonstrably true, then a persuasive case can be made that European security writ large (as opposed to the security of individual countries) has been undermined by NATO enlargement. If so, enlargement should not proceed. However, at best the balance of evidence suggests that Russia is no worse off on either score.

Russia has become increasingly integrated into European security over the last eight years. The contrast with the Soviet period could not be more striking: at that time the only European organization to which the Soviet Union belonged was the predecessor of the Organization for Security and Cooperation in Europe (OSCE). In the first step toward integration, the Council of Europe granted membership to Russia even though many of its members and its own expert panel believed that Russia had not made enough progress to qualify. The European Union (EU) signed a partnership accord with Russia to promote trade even though many of its members had concerns about Russian actions in the Chechen war. The International Monetary Fund made several loans to Russia which some say allowed that country to finance that war. The Group of Seven major industrial countries (G7) agreed to allow Russia to participate in their councils even though Russia has a GDP less than that of Brazil (which is not a member).

Russia's relations with NATO, while rocky, have also seen greater cooperation. Russia joined the Partnership for Peace program. More importantly, Russia agreed to send troops to Bosnia, largely on NATO's terms. The relatively small size of the Russian contingent in Bosnia and the willingness of the Russians to subordinate their troops to American command reflected Russia's relatively weak power position in Europe. The commander of the Russian troops in Bosnia called the cooperation in Bosnia "the first real, tangible achievement in [Russia-NATO] relations since the end of World War II." Nevertheless Colonel General Leontii Shevtsov, who also served as the deputy to the Supreme Commander for IFOR and then SFOR for Russian forces, cited NATO enlargement as the "chief obstacle to broader cooperation."

The most obvious example of Russian-NATO cooperation was the Founding Act signed on 27 May 1997. Russian President Boris Yeltsin announced that the act prevented a new dividing line in Europe. He argued that "our vigorous political and diplomatic efforts" had "forced [NATO] to take into account Russia's legitimate interests." In his assessment of Russian foreign policy for 1997, Foreign Minister Yevgenii Primakov singled out the agreement along with other activities that showed Russia becoming increasingly integrated in the global community (joining the Group of Eight industrial countries and the Asia-Pacific Economic Community and the EU-Russia partnership accord). The Founding Act was designed to allow Russia and NATO to consult on a regular basis regarding European security. For its part, NATO agreed that it was not currently in its interest to deploy foreign troops and nuclear weapons on the soil of new members. Russia still said enlargement was a bad idea, and still vehemently opposed the membership of the Baltic states and Ukraine.

Russia believes that it has grounds for not trusting NATO, and this lack of trust figured in the desire to establish a formal consultative mechanism. Commenting on the value of the NATO-Russia Founding Act, Primakov contended that the United States, Germany, France, and Britain had reneged on their promise in 1990–1991 to Soviet President Mikhail Gorbachev and Foreign Minister Eduard Shevardnadze that NATO would not expand eastward. In addition, NATO statements that foreign troops and nuclear weapons could be deployed in some circumstances on the territory of new members seemed to threaten Russian security. Therefore, Primakov saw only two choices, either conclude an agreement with NATO to minimize the negative consequences of enlargement or return to a policy of confrontation. Russia chose the first course.

Primakov was satisfied with the first session of the Russia-NATO Permanent Joint Council on 26 September 1997. He said that he had initially feared that the council would turn into merely a "discussion club," but he was pleased to see that they accomplished some real work at the meeting. In particular he cited the establishment of a commission to address the nature of the principles and tasks concerning peacekeeping, including Bosnia. Primakov's statements showed yet again the important role that the joint peacekeeping in Bosnia was playing in furthering cooperation.

At the same time that Western countries were trying to ensure that Russia was not isolated, they were also making an effort to further democracy there. Support for Boris Yeltsin occurred largely because Western countries believed that he remained the best hope for democracy in Russia. Several Western countries, international organizations, and non-governmental organizations have programs to further democracy in Russia, although it is difficult to critically assess their effectiveness. In this light, the evidence that NATO enlargement would destabilize Russia by strengthening the hand of anti-democratic forces seems mixed and certainly unproven. For one, the theory of how countries can influence the domestic policies of other states remains underdeveloped. Without such a theory it is difficult to distinguish internal from external influences on the development of domestic politics in a given country and most theories of democratization do not single out external effects. Thus, those that argue that there is a connection between NATO enlargement and democratic transition in Russia do so without citing theory and a body of empirical evidence. Rather they are struck by the contrast between the pro-Western policies pursued by the then Russian Foreign Minister Andrei Kozyrev in 1992 and the more even-handed, some would say confrontational, approach taken by Primakov.

Almost all Russian and arms control experts oppose NATO enlargement as strategically unnecessary and threatening the basis for the arms control measures reached at the end of the Cold War.[5] The Strategic Arms Reduction Treaty II, originally signed in January 1993, was ratified by the U.S. Senate in 1996 but had yet to be approved by the Russian Duma, and NATO expansion made it less likely that the Russian parliament would approve the treaty anytime soon. In addition, many Western observers expressed concern about the implications of a deteriorating U.S.-Russian relationship for cooperation in helping to control the vast amount of nuclear materials and quantities of non-strategic nuclear weapons in Russia.

In conclusion, it appears there remain considerable differences of opinion on the net effect of NATO enlargement on Russia.

UKRAINE: STABILIZING THE WOBBLY PIVOT

NATO also signed a Charter on Distinctive Partnership with Ukraine, in Madrid on 9 July. Although this agreement received little press attention, it represented one of the important cornerstones for security in Europe after the Cold War. The agreement stated that "independent, democratic and stable" Ukraine is one of the best guarantees of security for Europe. Norman Davies, a scholar best known for his work on Poland, has noted that the importance of Muscovy's seventeenth-century takeover of Ukraine could not be "overestimated. It gave Muscovy the economic resources and geopolitical stance to become a great power. [. . .] The formula Muscovy + Ukraine = Russia does not feature in the Russians' own version of their history; but it is fundamental."[6] Some would dispute this statement, not least because Russians commonly trace the origins of their own state to the Kievan Rus. But it illustrates two important points. First, without Ukraine and its resources, Russia cannot again become a global power. Second, because of its historical links with Moscow, Ukraine will remain the focal point of Russian foreign policy. Thus, Ukraine is the pivot on which European security rests.[7]

Ukraine had few friends in its quest for a separate charter. However, the Ukrainian lobby was strong in the United States with good links to key senators. In addition, the United States was grateful Ukraine had decided to forego nuclear weapons. The Polish connection also proved useful. Poland supported Ukraine under the 3 + 2 formula: that is, three new members and two charter agreements. The Poles of course realize better than anyone that the best guarantee of their security is not NATO membership but an "independent, democratic and stable" Ukraine. The Charter for Distinctive Partnership between NATO and Ukraine calls for a regular meetings between Ukraine and the North Atlantic Council, to occur twice a year and otherwise as needed. Ukraine will also set up a military liaison mission at NATO headquarters.

On 27 May Ukraine had signed an agreement with Russia on dividing the Black Sea Fleet, granting Russia a 20–year lease on the port of Sevastopol. This colored the reaction to the NATO accord among the media and experts in Ukraine. Although many felt that the accord continued the tilt toward the West begun in the fall of 1996, they also thought that Ukraine remained caught between Russia and the West. Some commentators viewed the Black Sea accord as an indication that Ukraine had "de facto entered a military union" with Russia. Several felt that the changes in Ukrainian foreign policy and in particular the approaches to NATO were occurring too quickly and without preparing the way among the Ukrainian people.

What some saw as confusion and indecision in Ukrainian foreign policy, others see as a sophisticated balancing act intended to ensure Ukrainian independence. Following a visit by Russian Defense Minister Igor Sergeev in August 1997, the Ukrainian president Leonid Kuchma called his country "a state without a bloc." While saying on the one hand that Ukraine did not intend to "join

NATO structures," Kuchma also stated that Ukraine would no longer respect the 1992 Tashkent collective security treaty signed by several members of the Commonwealth of Independent States (CIS). Those comments seemed to contradict earlier statements by Ukrainian officials that Kyiv intended to join the Alliance. Kuchma seemed to be using his links to the West to slowly disengage from Russia. The Charter plays an important role in that policy.

THE COSTS OF ENLARGEMENT

Early on, one of the more contentious issues about NATO enlargement was the question regarding costs. In part this question resulted from studies which showed costs running to over $100 billion over 10–15 years.[8] The Western and Russian media often took these estimates uncritically at face value. In a letter that President Clinton sent to Congress in February 1997, the estimated costs were much lower.

One common and pervasive fallacy that appeared in the media was that new members must replace their current equipment with Western gear. In fact, new members need only make their current forces interoperable with NATO. This means English language courses, changing command and control and air defense procedures to make them compatible with NATO, and perhaps the purchase of communication equipment. The outspoken German Defense Minister Volker Ruehe called claims that the new members must buy Western equipment, "pure drivel." He added, "It is perverse to say that modern tanks and aircraft are necessary in the new member states. We are not talking about EU agriculture here. The purchase of tanks can wait."

Another fallacy was the belief that requirements drive defense budgets. In fact, politics drive defense budgets, not requirements. Many of the studies of the costs of NATO enlargement specify tasks that would need to be performed by the new members. Costs are then associated with those tasks. The higher estimates are based on a scenario of hedging against the threat of a large-scale, short-warning attack such as NATO faced during the Cold War. In this scenario, NATO would deploy large forward air and ground combat forces in the new member states. The costs in one such study run up to $110 billion. However, NATO has already decided that it is not necessary to plan for such a scenario in the near future.

In addition, NATO cannot require member countries to upgrade their militaries. NATO has certainly said what it expects aspirants to do to prepare for membership, but once these countries become members they can do as they please. Some NATO members, such as Iceland or Luxembourg, have no or only notional armed forces. Other NATO members, such as Norway, refuse to have foreign troops or nuclear weapons stationed on their territories. Still others, such as Spain, Greece, and France, have decided, on occasion, not to participate in the integrated military structure. During the Cold War, the United States routinely jawboned its alliance partners to spend more on defense; they rarely did.

Moreover, in the long run countries should spend less on defense if they participate in an alliance than if they had to assure their security on their own.

For example, Romania has stated that its defense costs may be 40 percent greater if it does not join NATO.

Policy-makers in Central and Eastern Europe are well aware of what they need and can do to prepare for NATO membership. Most of them think that the costs associated with NATO enlargement will be small and manageable, and that they needed to modernize their forces anyway whether or not they joined NATO. The assessment of costs by the Czech Republic, Poland, and Hungary, and especially by the heads of the parliamentary Defense Committees who must examine those costs, fall far short of those estimated in the initial American studies.

The former Czech Deputy Defense Minister, Peter Necas, in an interview given in April 1997 when he was chairman of the Defense and Security Committee in the Czech parliament, distinguished between the indirect and direct costs of NATO enlargement. The indirect costs, those involved in modernizing the army, had to be met anyway unless the army was simply to be used as a "castle guard in handsome uniforms for parades." The part of the direct costs to ensure interoperability with NATO was already being paid to enable Czech units to participate in exercises with NATO members and in the Stabilization Force (SFOR) in Bosnia. The other part of the direct costs, the contribution to NATO's budget, he estimated at about $10–12 million per year.

A Polish study group, which included members from Polish defense and foreign affairs ministries, estimated the essential costs for Poland to join NATO at about $1.5 billion. This cost included integrating the Polish command system with NATO, modernizing airfields, and ensuring the compatibility of the Polish telecommunications and air defense systems with those of NATO countries. The group assumed that Poland would need to contribute $35–40 million annually to the NATO joint budget. The Polish defense budget would increase by no more than 4 percent. In writing an introduction to this report, Janusz Onyszkiewicz, later appointed defense minister but at the time writing as the chairman of the defense committee in the Polish Sejm, said "the cost of NATO enlargement presents no major difficulty to either new or current members."

Prior to Madrid, Hungary did not publish an official estimate of the costs of enlargement. However, the chairman of the defense committee in the Hungarian Parliament, Imre Mecs, said in March 1997 that defense expenditure might increase by 15–20 percent but most of that was needed to modernize a military which had not been upgraded in 15 years. Joining NATO itself would not pose an economic burden for the Hungarian people.

Finally, it should be noted that the purpose of the May 1996 Congressional Budget Office study, which has the highest estimates of the costs of NATO enlargement, was to define the "worst-case" scenario, so that U.S. legislators would know the upper bound that they might have to contribute. Even that study concluded that it would cost only about $21 billion for training and exercises and upgrading air defense and command, control, and communications gear (for the Czech Republic, Hungary, Poland, and Slovakia). Of that sum, those countries would pay 70 percent, the United States $1.9 billion, and the European allies $3.7 billion. This cost did not differ significantly from the one provided in the

February 1997 State Department study of the costs of NATO enlargement which said that the United States would need to pay about $150–200 million a year, or less than one tenth of one percent of the annual U.S. defense budget. Finally, NATO itself conducted a study that concluded that the costs of enlargement need only be minimal.

THE NEXT STEPS

A number of questions remain about the readiness of the Czech Republic, Hungary, and Poland to join the alliance. An assessment of their military readiness was made only after the Madrid summit. Serious questions have been raised about the personnel structure in these countries (in the Soviet style, they still have officers performing many jobs that non-commissioned officers perform in NATO armies) and the lack of English-speaking personnel. Command, control, and communications also remain issues. On the other hand, their infrastructure is not as poor as some initially supposed.

To deal with the security concerns of its non-members, NATO set up the Euro-Atlantic Partnership Council (EAPC) to provide a forum for European security issues to replace the North Atlantic Cooperation Council, which included the 16 member nations and 27 partnership countries. NATO also decided in May 1997 "to substantively enhance the Partnership for Peace in a number of ways, including strengthening political consultation, increasing partner involvement in PfP decision-making, and rendering PfP as a whole more operational." Despite this decision, at the end of 1997 NATO had not yet changed its basic fact sheet on PfP and still used the NACC fact sheet for information on the EACP. The "enhanced" nature of both programs could probably have been handled without changing their names, which appears to have been more cosmetic than substantive.

Slovenia and Romania both lobbied hard for admission and several important countries supported their candidacy. Speaking at a meeting of the North Atlantic Assembly held in Bucharest in October 1997, NATO Secretary General Javier Solana said, "NATO's door stays open, Romania has been mentioned in the Madrid document and in 1999 we are going to re-examine the existing situation." The visit of U.S. President Bill Clinton to Romania immediately after the July NATO Madrid Summit was taken as a sign that Romania would join in 1999. Nevertheless, prior to that summit, the pro-government newspaper *Romania Libera* on 21 July warned that "[Romania's] missing the train to early membership in NATO would be a threat to the economic reforms and the anti-corruption drive in the country." Although disappointed, the Romanian military continued its program to make its forces ready for NATO, especially by emphasizing interoperability.

Russia was also active in trying to forestall further NATO enlargement. Primakov has suggested that Russia may offer security guarantees to those countries not involved in the first wave of NATO enlargement, in particular Bulgaria, Romania, and the Balts. He argued that just trying to seek security from the West, "orientation solely to the West without boosted relations with the Eastern neighbors is a one-sided policy which will not bring major success."

Although many see Romania and Slovenia as the major candidates for joining

NATO in the next wave, much longer odds are given to the Baltic countries. To reassure the Baltic countries, the United States concluded the Baltic Charter in January 1998. The Baltic countries had already rejected Russia's earlier offer of security guarantees.

Thus NATO accelerated the process of Euro-Atlantic integration in 1997. At year's end, none of the negative predictions of the impact of enlargement had come true, but opinion still remains fiercely divided. NATO enlargement did not lead to Russia's isolation or undermine Russia's democratic development. Rather than concern itself with NATO enlargement, Russia can now turn to its more pressing security concerns involving relations with its immediate neighbors. In this regard, it is noteworthy that the Russian National Security Strategy document published in December 1997 mentioned NATO only twice but the CIS at least 13 times.[9]

NOTES

I want to thank Dag Hartelius and Milada Vachudova at EWI, as well as my many colleagues at the George C. Marshall European Center for Security Studies for their comments.

[1]Michael Doyle, *Ways of War and Peace: Realism, Liberalism, and Socialism* (New York: Norton, 1997)

[2]George Kennan, "A Fateful Error," *The New York Times,* 5 February 1997.

[3]Michael Mandelbaum, *The Dawn of Peace in Europe* (New York: Twentieth Century Fund, 1996).

[4]James Goldgeier, "NATO Expansion: The Anatomy of a Decision," *The Washington Quarterly,* Winter 1998.

[5]Michael MccGwire, "NATO expansion: a policy error of historic importance," *Review of International Studies* (1998), 24, 23–42.

[6]Norman Davies, *Europe* (Oxford: Oxford University Press, 1996), p. 558.

[7]Donald McDonnell, "Charter with NATO will help Ukraine regain its rightful place in Europe," *NATO Review,* 45:4, Jul/Aug 1997, pp. 22–25; Ihor Kharchenko, "The new Ukraine-NATO partnership," *NATO Review,* 45:5, Sept/Oct 1997, pp. 27–29.

[8]Ronald D. Asmus, et al., "What Will NATO Enlargement Cost?" *Survival*, 38: 3, autumn 1996, pp. 5–26; Congressional Budget Office, "The Costs of Expanding the NATO Alliance," Congressional Budget Office, March 1996.

[9]*Rossiiskaya gazeta,* 27 December 1997, as appearing in FBIS *Daily Report,* FBIS-SOV-97–364.

A CHANCE TO STOP EXPORTING WARS AND VIOLENCE

by VACLAV HAVEL

(Vaclav Havel has been president of the Czech Republic since 1993. He was president of Czechoslovakia from 1990 to 1992.)

Central and Eastern Europe's move toward democracy in 1989 brought about the collapse of the principal threat that had jeopardized the whole democratic world until then: the threat represented by the Soviet empire and communism. Many people were under the impression that the danger of a European or global war could, therefore, be crossed off the list of potential future developments. While such a belief may have been understandable in the euphoria of the years 1989 and 1990, it can hardly be justified after the shocking experience of the war in the former Yugoslavia.

True, the nature of the dangers has changed. The free world is no longer threatened by a gigantic strategic adversary, as was the case in the Cold War era. Instead, we are confronted with innumerable new types of threats, in the form of national or local conflicts lacking clear distinctions from war, terrorism, and organized crime.

It has been said many times that after the West and democracy have won the Cold War, it is essential that they win the peace as well. Eight years after the fall of communism, I am deeply convinced that winning the peace will be much the more difficult task. Time and again, we have witnessed a strange inability of the democratic powers to draw a lesson from the history of this century. Time and again, they have shown themselves unable to understand that thinking in terms of particular interests is suicidal for all democratic nations regardless of their size or strength, failing to recognize that if democrats do not jointly forge a new security order while they can, a new order will be built by somebody else.

The threats looming over us in the present era can be averted only when we all awaken—with renewed vigor and a renewed ethos—to a sense of our responsibility for the world as a whole, and for its long-term future. We can no longer afford a lack of solidarity among democratic nations. Once and for all, we must discard the illusion that enemies of democracy will be stopped by a policy of appeasement. The experience of the 1938 Munich Agreement should be a sufficient warning. At that time, in the foolish belief that they would save themselves from the threat of war, the Western allies let a democratic Czechoslovakia fall prey to Nazi Germany, and they paid for it dearly themselves shortly thereafter.

AMERICA MUST ENGAGE

American isolationism is another concrete expression of that kind of particularism. It has had a long tradition in modern American history, recurring again and again and taking a different form each time. Never throughout that history, however, has isolationism saved America from any threat. On the contrary, its effect was that America's involvement always came too late. By the time the United States stepped in, the conflicts were fully ablaze and had begun to pose a vital threat to America itself. Consequently, the price Americans had to pay for their initial indifference or reluctance was a thousand times higher than any costs that may have been entailed in a political or military action taken right at the beginning of the conflict or, better still, even before that. Their shortsightedness eventually cost not only much higher material expenditures, but also great numbers of lost lives.

Despite that historical experience—and despite the fact that thousands of Americans now live in Prague, and that many people of Czech origin have settled in the United States—some Americans still consider involvement in Central and Eastern Europe an unnecessarily costly, unneeded, and untimely undertaking. Europe, however, is connected with America through thousand-fold links and bonds. Europe is the cradle of the present civilization, but also the birthplace of two world wars. Notwithstanding its cultural, ethnic, and economic diversity, the European continent has always been, and still remains, one body. For the first time in its history, this body now has a chance to build its internal order on the principle of cooperation and equality of the large and the small, the strong and the weak alike—to build on a sharing of common democratic values.

That means a chance to stop exporting wars and violence for good, and to become a model of peaceful cooperation. If Europe were to waste this chance, the result could be a new global catastrophe, possibly worse than the previous ones. This time, instead of the forces of freedom opposing a single totalitarian adversary, we might see a strange war of all against all, a war that would have no clear fronts and that could not be separated from terrorism, organized crime, and other forms of crime that have emerged in our contemporary civilization. Inevitably, such a war would have immediate repercussions throughout the world in many direct and indirect ways.

NEW THREATS, NEW SOLUTIONS

In most cases, foreseeing conflicts and averting them is more difficult than intervening in them, often even more difficult than winning them. The former, however, is a thousand times more advisable. At the NATO summit in Madrid, the Czech Republic was invited, together with Hungary and Poland, to accede to the North Atlantic Treaty. I see that decision as a breakthrough, an act that marked the end of a long hesitation in the search for a new security order after the fall of the Iron Curtain. In the face of the Balkan tragedy, we have perhaps become more keenly aware that all those who profess to share Euro-Atlantic values must join forces to protect them, that we must recognize that defense of our common values is in our common interest and act accordingly.

Life has proved NATO capable of dealing effectively with the new types of threats as well. The IFOR (Implementation Force) presence in Bosnia-Herzegovina bears witness to that. The countries to whom Madrid has offered membership in the alliance are by far not only consumers of security provisions, as is maintained by some uninformed critics of NATO enlargement. Those nations are fully conscious of their own share of responsibility for the preservation of peace and protection of Euro-Atlantic values. The Czech Republic sent a battalion to Bosnia-Herzegovina at its own expense; that unit is now part of the SFOR (Stabilization Force) contingent. Czech troops also took part in a number of other international missions, often alongside their partners from NATO. To give just one example, let us remember the Persian Gulf.

The Madrid decision represents a unique historic chance to finalize the security arrangements. It has respected the free will of the nations of Central Europe and their political representatives that wish to be integrated into organizations based on a shared commitment of their members to a shared set of values. While the European Union focuses on political and economic integration, NATO constitutes an irreplaceable instrument for the collective defense of those values. Nevertheless, from time to time we meet in the United States with an argument that is hard to understand, an argument that conflates the EU and NATO enlargement processes—an opinion we have never heard from any European government.

NATO has also provided room for a cooperation that has removed old disputes and hatreds and fostered confidence among its member states. Enlarging NATO thus means enlarging a sphere of peace and stability. It is my conviction that the alliance will gradually proceed to offer accession also to other European democracies that show interest in joining it and become eligible for membership. Who will be admitted, and when, depends on many different circumstances. What is more important is giving everyone assurance that their determination will not go unheeded. It must be made clear that the era when the large and powerful decided the fate of the smaller and less powerful, and divided the world between themselves into spheres of interest and influence, is now over. That, of course, does not preclude partnership with the democratic authorities of Russia, with whom NATO members will share many common tasks in the future.

If the great European unification process were not allowed to deepen its security dimension as well, and were made to halt at the gates of NATO, the only working European defense alliance at present, it would probably fail. The pernicious consequences of such failure—whatever form they would take, and no matter whether they would befall us three years or 15 years from now—could eventually cost us all much more than both world wars combined.

NOTE

Reprinted with kind permission from *Transitions* magazine, December 1997.

THE LEAST EXPENSIVE WAY TO GUARANTEE SECURITY

by ARPAD GONCZ

(Arpad Goncz has been president of Hungary since 1990.)

July saw a significant and historic step in the process of Hungary's Euro-Atlantic integration. NATO's decision in Madrid to invite Hungary into the alliance offers the historic opportunity for Hungary to become a full member of the community of the developed democracies over a relatively short period. The message of this decision was clear. The Euro-Atlantic community appreciates and sympathizes with the effort Hungary has been making to strengthen its political, economic, and social stability and to meet the criteria of accession. The Euro-Atlantic community also values Hungary's contribution to strengthening security in Central and Eastern Europe.

The Hungarian people received this message with great satisfaction and pride. Not only Hungary, but the other two selected countries unanimously support the transatlantic idea.

The rhetoric of NATO enlargement suggests that NATO is moving eastward at the instigation of the present 16 allies. Instead, what is happening is that the countries of Central and Eastern Europe are moving westward. Separated from West European and Euro-Atlantic institutions for 40 years, these countries now have the freedom and opportunity to join institutions such as NATO, the European Union, and the Western European Union. The dream of the late U.S. Secretary of State George C. Marshall may finally be coming true: the countries of Central and Eastern Europe will join a free, democratic, and united Europe.

I would say the reasons why we want to join the alliance are very much the same as those that make the current members want to stay in. In striving to join NATO, Hungary does not seek protection from a specific military threat. Hungary's determination to become a member in the alliance is motivated by shared values and the desire to belong to a favorable security environment, not by fear. In our opinion, NATO enlargement means the expansion of a region of security and stability. It is our goal to be part of this region, and to enjoy the benefits of its security guarantees. It is also clearly understood that by joining the alliance, Hungary will assume the obligation to contribute to an increased effectiveness of mutual defense as well as to the enhanced security and stability in our region and in Europe as a whole.

Hungary wishes full membership in NATO. That is, it desires to become an integral part of both the political and the military structure of the alliance. Euro-Atlantic integration does not just mean joining one organization; it is part of a deeper transformation: adherence to the shared values and community of the democratic countries, and the reinforcement of stability and prosperity. Enlargement increases the security not only of future member countries, but also of those neighboring countries that—whether in the short or long run—remain outside the alliance.

PREVENTIVE ALLIANCE

Opponents argue there is no military rationale for enlargement because there is no military threat to the applicants. The inclusion of new members in NATO is not aimed against any country or any specific threat. Rather, it is a process of integration into a community. NATO is, and will remain, a purely defensive alliance whose fundamental purpose is to preserve peace in the Euro-Atlantic area and to provide security to its members. Extension of the alliance is not an isolated event; it must be seen in a larger context. It is only one element—but an important one—of a broad European security architecture that transcends the idea of dividing lines in Europe and renders them obsolete.

NATO enlargement will not only provide an effective means to handle current and foreseeable risks to security, it will also be a pre-emptive response to future threats to security. Some people say that NATO enlargement means that in the case of a major conflict, American soldiers would die protecting Central European cities. I think those people are wrong. The very enlargement of the alliance guarantees that soldiers of NATO countries will not have to sacrifice their lives for a new member state. The history of NATO so far is a great success story: the alliance has succeeded in carrying out its mission as enshrined in the North Atlantic Treaty.

Under the bipolar world order, in the years of bitter enmity, not a single soldier of NATO died for a member state of the alliance. For more than four and a half decades, the alliance has proved to be the one and only organization that could and still can guarantee the security and stability of the entire continent. That is in the interest of the United States, as well as all European nations. As the inconceivable human tragedy in the states of the former Yugoslavia and in Bosnia-Herzegovina has shown, the European allies cannot handle crises alone in the continent without the active role of the United States.

I am convinced that NATO enlargement is the most effective and the least expensive way to guarantee security in Europe and to strengthen stability on the entire continent. Hungary is a small, almost indefensibly exposed country surrounded by seven other states, and its only wish is to avoid being a sentinel outpost on the periphery of Europe. We would like every neighbor to share the same level of security and safety. Therefore, I think, one cannot imagine a more willing and voluntary ally of NATO than Hungary would be.

On the other hand, the NATO alliance is tirelessly working on developing and strengthening cooperation with its onetime brother-in-arms and later antagonist, Russia. Today Russia is as important an economic and political partner for NATO and the European Union as Hungary is.

ONE FOR ALL

Back in the days of our revolution, in October 1956, we were dreaming of neutrality; these days, however, we know that neutrality can exist for a country between two opposing powers only in one case: if both of them acknowledge and are ready to guarantee its position.

Being neutral naturally means that a country has to be prepared to defend its borders—and capable of successfully defending its borders—against any kind of aggression by either power. Yet being armed to the teeth is the privilege of rich countries; it is far too expensive and unsuitable for Hungary. We must choose collective defense: all for one and one for all.

During the accession talks, Hungary intends to confirm that it fully agrees with the objectives, the strategic concept, and the security policy of NATO. Hungary is ready to assume all obligations stemming from the North Atlantic Treaty and from full membership. Hungary intends to participate in NATO's integrated military structure and in the defense planning process. It is ready to provide troops to collective defense and joint activities of the alliance. I hope that the accession talks will be successfully concluded in a relatively short time, and that the accession protocol will be approved and signed by the end of 1997. As it enlarges, NATO will have to be restructured and adapted, and we can contribute to that effort.

New members will have to contribute to alliance security and stability, and not be mere net consumers of security. While the risk of a large-scale military threat has declined over the years, risks to European security stemming from local crises and conflicts remain, risks that are multifaceted and multidirectional and thus hard to predict and assess. NATO must be capable of responding to such new risks and challenges as they develop if stability in Europe and the security of NATO members old and new are to be preserved. The enlargement process of NATO is neither intended to be nor can be a substitution for the expansion of the European Union. In fact, the two expansions can complement each other.

Through membership, Hungary would be able to export stability to those of its neighbors that do not wish to join the alliance or have not yet been invited. Our policy is to share with them the experiences we have already gathered and help them become members of the alliance. Over the past few years, we have managed to come to terms and sign basic treaties with all our neighbors except for the former Yugoslavia. So there should be no concerns that we might bring new problems to deal with into the alliance.

Concerns are repeatedly raised about Russia's reaction to NATO enlargement. Russian Foreign Minister Yevgenii Primakov has said: "This is the most catastrophic decision in the history of the alliance." Well, I wish all catastrophes were like this one. We have to ask the question: "Will enlargement create tension between NATO and Russia, or between the prospective new members and Russia?" I'm fully convinced that the partnership between NATO and Russia, which is embodied in the Founding Act on NATO-Russian relations, makes such an eventuality highly unlikely. The reform and development of democracy in Russia mostly depends on the country's internal affairs. Democracy cannot exist without democrats in the long run.

One of Hungary's greatest politicians, the late Istvan Bibo, wrote: "To be a democrat means not to fear." I think we should bear that in mind when we are talking about Russia. I also believe that the enlargement won't directly affect Russia's attitude concerning nuclear disarmament. Furthermore, President Boris Yeltsin announced in May that all the Russian strategic nuclear missiles had been de-targeted and are no longer aimed at any NATO country. Russia has already been invited to join the Group of Seven industrialized countries, and the Permanent Joint Council of Russia and NATO will be set up soon. Those measures should convince anyone who is alarmed at the possibility of Russia's exclusion from Euro-Atlantic integration. NATO also has signed a charter on a distinctive partnership with Ukraine that will contribute to the stability of Eastern Europe and the Crimea.

Hungary is maintaining a new kind of partnership with Poland and the Czech Republic, and the three of us are supporting each other in order to conclude the accession talks successfully. Our cooperation has been fruitful so far and we intend to keep it up. We have gone through the same history: wars, migration, suppressed revolutions, and lost opportunities. Now we must have the same future.

NOTE

Reprinted with kind permission from *Transitions* magazine, December 1997.

ISOLATIONISM IS AN ANACHRONISM

by ALEKSANDER KWASNIEWSKI

(Aleksander Kwasniewski has been president of Poland since 1995.)

Before our eyes, one of the fundamental divisions of the world is fading and disintegrating. Europe, once divided into East and West, is becoming a cultural unity, returning to its historic roots within a new Euro-Atlantic security environment.

After the democratic upsurges in the countries of the former Warsaw Pact helped bring about the fall of the USSR, the interests of Central and Eastern Europe and the interests of Western Europe and the United States began to converge. Western Europe, enjoying prosperity and security, re-evaluated the Yalta-era division of the continent and reoriented relations with the Central European countries, which shared the same values and were ready to assume responsibility for the safe development of Europe. Neither end of the continent wanted to see a "gray zone of security," in which the outbreak of conflict could threaten European stability.

The idea, born in the early 1990s, to expand NATO and to link what had been separate originated equally from a community of values and from the fear that conditions might arise to threaten peace. Before, the guarantee of peace was based on the Yalta system of balanced fear that thrived on adverse relations between the two global systems. The dismantling of the Warsaw Pact caused three parallel risks: that Russia would close itself off, wrestling with problems of deep transformation; that Western Europe would become isolated and self-centered; and that Central European states would be left with no security guarantees for their recovered sovereignty.

Fortunately, NATO almost immediately rejected the formula of continued adversity toward its former opponents. Instead it changed the strategic concept of the alliance and established institutional forms of cooperation, such as the North Atlantic Cooperation Council and the Partnership for Peace.

The new democracies approached their new opportunities in different ways, according to their needs. Poland chose the quickest possible integration with the West, while also pursuing friendly policies with Eastern Europe. In deciding to join NATO, we were aware of the expenses and willingly shouldered the costs, conscious that membership in the alliance would open the road to an institutional return to Europe. Having our security guaranteed by NATO makes us more trustworthy in our endeavor to obtain membership in the European Union.

THE UNITED STATES AS A EUROPEAN COUNTRY

The two world wars proved to the peoples of Europe and America that without a U.S. presence in Europe, European security is unlikely to be achieved. That U.S. presence has become a lasting factor in the international balance of armed forces and economic power. At a time of concurrent industrial and post-industrial civilizations, at a time of the global information village, isolationism is an anachronism.

The inward-looking policy the United States pursued in the 1920s and 1930s was a result of the sacrifice made by the thousands of American soldiers who fell on the battlefields of World War I. Americans questioned the point of that sacrifice. Yet had the United States remained in Europe at that time, might not the power of America's democracy and economy and the success of the New Deal have influenced European and international policy, perhaps even halting German fascism and taking the wind from the sails of Stalinism? We will never know.

It is surely obvious today that the absence of the United States in European policy in the years preceding both world wars was not the best way to defend America's vital interests. The very high price paid has convinced the American nation of the commonality of our security interests. We are a community, as expressed in the phrases "Euro-Atlantic security environment" or "Euro-Atlantic community."

Poland stands alongside those countries which perceive the future system of security in Europe as a system of Euro-Atlantic security based on the lasting political and military presence of the United States in Europe. Therefore, with Poland's history in mind, in particular the historical experiences connected with the causes and the courses of both world wars, we oppose attempts to marginalize the presence of the United States in uniting Europe. It is in that spirit that we shall pursue our policy within the region and outside it.

Europe needs America and America needs Europe. Having learned a lesson from the painful fall of democracy in Germany and Italy, America developed a model of democracy armed with values and protected by appropriate military potential. That model is based on the assumption that assistance is extended to all who are ready to defend its values. It is with that idea in mind that we are consolidating our own democracy and modernizing our defense potential.

Poland is situated in Europe. Through acceding to NATO, it wishes to define its role as ally by according special treatment to the United States' presence in the European system of collective security. Poland is ready to defend freedom, democracy, respect for individuals, and solidarity among all people and nations. The enhancement of well-being on the Vistula, Vltava, or Danube promotes well-being on the Potomac, Rhine, or Volga.

We want to be a full member of NATO. We are realistic and wish to adhere to our obligations, confirming in practice the values that we cherish, and to make our national contributions to common defense. At present, Poland allocates 2.7 percent of its gross domestic product for defense purposes. In Brussels, we declared our readiness to make suitable contributions to the common funds of the alliance: civil, military, and investment. In Maastricht, we informed the NATO defense ministers that we intend to increase our defense budget by 3 percentage points faster than our economic growth rate. We want to occupy a place in the civil and military structures of the alliance proportional to our contribution and our strategic position. We cherish a strong hope that the internal reform of the alliance will allow agreement on a new command structure enabling all the allies to fully participate.

JOINT EFFORTS

Because of our common objectives with the Czech Republic and Hungary and our friendly relations with other countries, particularly Germany and Ukraine, our foreign policy is establishing regional programs and structures. In that way, we will contribute to the creation of a stability zone that promotes economic and democratic development. Thus, we are implementing the general strategic idea of the alliance, which provides that, in the construction of international security, political factors must dominate over the military factor, whose driving force in turn depends on the economy.

The 1989 "spring of nations" created a new regional policy in Central and Eastern Europe based on cooperation among sovereign and democratic states. The magnitude of the transformations can be measured by the fact that without even one shot the number of Poland's neighbors grew from three to seven.

At that time, a reunited Germany was born, and immediately the Polish-German alliance played a stabilizing role in the absence of any larger regional stabilization. By contributing to stabilization on that part of the continent, Poland extended its helping hand to other nations. It entered the new era easily and, to the extent of its ability, paid back part of its historic debt to West European countries incurred in the struggle for Polish freedom and democracy. We attach great importance to political cooperation within NATO, for example, in the form of the Weimar triangle linking France, Germany, and Poland and stabilizing the central part of Europe. We are eager to help in the adaptation process of other countries that wish to join the alliance, such as Romania, Slovenia, and the Baltic states.

It is only in that way that we can obliterate the trenches of the Cold War. Like Western Europe, which had its Marshall Plan, the remaining part of the continent can create a new "Marshall Plan B," through joint cooperation.

Poland is shifting the critical point of the European security environment by its very decision to join the alliance. Poland's geographical situation—the curse of our history—offers NATO a strategic chance to stabilize all of Europe. Fitting Central Europe into the Euro-Atlantic security environment reduces almost to zero the threat of a regional conflict that could escalate to nuclear war.

TROUBLESOME QUESTIONS

In discussions of Poland's motives in seeking NATO membership, an implied question frequently emerged, even if it was never asked directly. Is Poland afraid of Russia? Or does it perhaps fear another country?

Of course, like any country, we fear aggression and situations in which, contrary to our efforts and intentions, we would have to fight and put national accomplishments, human happiness, and lives at stake. Everyone is afraid of that, even the mightiest. But do we specifically fear the Russian Federation? No, we are not afraid of our neighbor, provided it unswervingly pursues the road of democratic development and avoids chaos, the father of the worst of revolutions. Chaos in the post-Soviet space would be incomparably more dangerous than elsewhere in Europe. Bearing in mind the almost-peaceful dismantling of the Soviet Union (which commands high respect in view of the conflict in the former

Yugoslavia), we are confident in the wisdom of Russia's political elite and believe that they will do their utmost to prevent chaos.

Trustworthy Russian opinion polls prove that Russians do not consider the alliance a threat to their vital interests in Europe. Rather, Russian security experts perceive a threat in Islamic fanaticism and Chinese expansionism. Democratic Russia knows that not only is it not threatened by the free world, but the free world is ready to extend it assistance. However, it would be counterproductive to offer Russia a place in NATO. That would be a false attempt to buy Russia's approval to the expansion of the Euro-Atlantic security network in return for false guarantees. Besides technical and organizational questions, it would mean the reconstruction of the pre–World War I balance of power.

If, however, a hotbed of chaos were to emerge in the east of Europe, which cannot be excluded for the time being, appropriate military potential would have to be used. We trust that the Russian Federation and the other members of the Commonwealth of Independent States will pursue a road that will augment the security system in the Euro-Atlantic sphere. That hope is rooted in the mechanisms that have enabled Russia to become NATO's friendly partner in the architecture of the new security system. Far from destabilizing the region, NATO's expansion will have beneficial effects. First and foremost, it will make debates on the "gray zone of security" redundant. Those debates are dangerous because they could encourage anti-democratic forces to attempt to reconstruct the Warsaw Pact by undermining the legality of democratic institutions of the Russian state. A larger sphere of stabilization, prosperity, and peace will give Russian reformers more time to get through the difficult restructuring period.

And finally, since a troublesome question has been asked, let an easier question also be posed. Does Poland meet military and systemic requirements of NATO membership? My answer is unequivocal: Yes.

We have proved that we are ready and able to pay our financial contribution to NATO. And civil control over the armed forces is no longer a problem; the groundwork has been laid in the new constitution and in Polish laws. Neither do I entertain any doubts that we have a sufficient potential supply of English-speaking officers and troops, as well as civil servants, to ensure interoperability of our and NATO's defense systems.

ONE VOICE

Poland, the Czech Republic, and Hungary are linked by time-honored friendship and respect. We have in common the struggle against totalitarian power and our contributions to the creation of a free and undivided Europe. That is why we are working with such determination for a stable and friendly Central Europe. That common heritage, our strategic situation, and our contributions to democracy allow me to be an optimist about the ratification of the protocols of accession to NATO. I believe 4 April 1999 will be an important day in Poland's history and an important day in the history of the free world.

NOTE

Reprinted with kind permission from *Transitions* magazine, December 1997.

European Union

LEARNING ABOUT THE BOTTOM LINE

by DAVID ROCKS

Under a cold fluorescent glare, the 11 students shift wearily in their seats while a ventilation fan hums unrelentingly in the background. "If you've got a debt to someone, you should know whom you're supposed to pay . . .," the professor intones, his head buried in the book in front of him. One student, a 40-ish woman, scratches her nose and stifles a yawn. A balding man surreptitiously opens his briefcase and fidgets with a mobile phone inside. Another stares at the blank white board at the front of the class and picks at the blue upholstery of his chair.

Welcome to accounting qualification training, Czech style. Not very exciting, to be sure, but in a very real sense the future of the country depends on it. The class, sponsored in part by the European Union's PHARE assistance program, aims to bring Czech accounting into compliance with the EU's rigorous standards—a basic requirement for admission. "During the communist times, the accounting profession lost all of its meaning because the communists didn't care about economic results," says Jaroslav Louka, director of the Union of Accountants Institute, which offers the courses. "But then after 1989, there was a huge growth in the need for accountants as entrepreneurs and businesses started up."

Classes such as these are just a small part of the EU's multi-pronged effort to bring Central and Eastern Europe's capital markets and financial services sectors up to snuff as the region approaches EU membership. While the push is going on in all ten countries that are expected to eventually join, activity is doubly intense in the six—the Czech Republic, Estonia, Hungary, Poland, Slovenia, and Cyprus—that have been short-listed for early membership.

In areas ranging from banking supervision and market regulation to accounting rules and capital adequacy standards, which determine the amount of loans banks can have outstanding, EU officials are working with their counterparts in Central Europe to build the legal and commercial framework necessary to successfully integrate the prospective members into the single European market. In all, the candidate countries will need to comply with about 50 EU directives (2-to-15-page policy statements) concerning financial affairs.

The issues run from the mundanely arcane—for example, the development of a system of tax-free warehouses in Hungary—to the painfully obvious, such as improving transparency on the Czech Republic's notoriously under-regulated capital markets, or bringing the thousands of unregistered businesses in Poland out of the gray economy and onto the tax ledgers.

Like accounting class, it's hardly scintillating stuff. But these discussions make up the nuts and bolts of union membership, and without proper preparation the new members are just as likely to sink in the union's treacherous commercial waters as swim prosperously with their neighbors. "We don't want to become a member of the European Union because we think it's nice to be a member of the club, but because we see the process as an instrument for the modernization of the economy, for strengthening the economy, for putting in place consistent legal regulations," says Jaroslaw Pietras, undersecretary at Poland's Committee for European Integration. "In the long run, these will be absolutely helpful to our citizens and our welfare."

At the heart of the union's effort to bring the prospective members into compliance lies PHARE assistance. The program has budgeted 4.5 billion ecu ($5.5 billion) over the next two years in the ten candidate countries plus three countries of the former Yugoslavia for thousands of projects, from basic infrastructure development to training local officials in negotiating with the union itself. In the case of the Czech accounting classes, the fledgling Czech Union of Accountants prepared course materials, translated a series of accounting textbooks from English, and set up a system of exams and certification for accountants—something that didn't exist in the country.

PENCIL PUSHERS WANTED

Just six months into the program, about 1,700 individuals have signed up for the courses or the exams, and 90 have achieved one of three levels of certification. While those numbers reflect only a tiny fraction of the estimated 15,000 people working as accountants in the Czech Republic, officials are confident businesses will begin to demand that their accountants be certified, which should boost the numbers dramatically.

In the financial sector, the primary areas of concern for the union are the free movement of capital and the free movement of financial services, and PHARE has paid out more than 200 million ecu over the last six years to spur their development. Free movement of services and capital, of course, implies free competition as stronger financial institutions from abroad open branches in the region, something that makes local bankers in Prague, Warsaw, and Budapest quake in their wingtips. Consumers in the region would presumably benefit from the greater efficiency that would stem from increased competition. But local banks and financial institutions—in many respects still mired in the stone-age ways of communist banking, when all they had to do was allocate credits to enterprises deemed worthy by central planners—still need time to beef up their services, credit-risk analysis, and management skills before they can face the full force of competition.

In practical terms, the union is using two measures, one more and one less objective, to evaluate progress. On the objective side, for example, is compliance with the EU's directives. To comply, the candidate countries need to update various laws so they match EU legislation on, say, the regulation of capital markets, the supervision of banks, and controls on non-bank financial service providers such as brokerage firms and investment houses—already on the books in EU countries. "These laws don't have to be identical to EU law," says Roman Gardea, who oversees financial sector issues at the Prague delegation of the European Commission, the EU's executive arm. "But there has to be a strict minimum in compliance with legislation in EU countries, and it has to follow basic principles that are non-negotiable."

The laws might concern areas such as specific products subject to reduced value-added tax rates, the minimum and maximum amounts covered by government deposit guarantee schemes, or regulations governing the flow of capital in and out of the country. All of these tread on areas the countries often consider their sovereign turf. Tax rates are often tailored to suit specific local conditions, giving preference to products that authorities deem strategic, while free capital flows can wreak havoc on the efforts of central banks in transitional countries to maintain stable currencies. Authorities generally welcome an influx of capital from investors wanting to reap the benefits of soaring stock markets, but if those same investors turn skittish and leave the markets en masse the currency can tumble, as was the case in the Czech Republic in May 1997 and throughout Asia later in the year.

DETAILS, DETAILS

To date, European Commission officials estimate, the five fast-track countries from the former Soviet bloc have managed to implement more than half the laws they will need to bring their legal codes into line with the union's. But while many of the basic laws are in compliance, the details may still need some finessing to fulfill the union's requirements.

Officials say the leader in this process is clearly Poland, which went through "shock therapy" early in its reform process. This threw both Polish banks and the enterprises they were lending to into crisis but ultimately forced them to improve their operations long before banks in the rest of the region. Although the largest Polish banks remain in state hands, privatization should be completed this year. And Poland's capital market, although scrawny when the Warsaw Stock Exchange opened in 1991 in the monolithic former headquarters of the Communist Party with just a handful of tradable issues, has grown to 159 listed companies and funds and today is praised for its openness and transparency.

Hungary, Slovenia, and Estonia all have made substantial progress, with their legislation more or less in line with EU requirements, and banking supervision and capital market regulation proceeding on schedule. The Czech Republic, on the other hand, is only now beginning to realize the importance of implementing EU-mandated legislation. The country's capital markets continue to be the most loosely regulated in the region. The Prague Stock Exchange was at one time a big draw for foreign investment capital but in recent years lost attraction to foreigners after too many cases of "tunneling," in which companies and investment funds were stripped of cash and other assets via various criminal scams. "For the first four or five years, the real issues were not really tackled" in the Czech Republic, Gardea says. "Now the Czechs will have to move quickly. We are reaching the point where it must be done, otherwise it will be too late."

The practical implementation of the laws called for in the EU's directives is evaluated more subjectively. While the EU clearly wants to see better-regulated, more transparent markets in Prague to eliminate problems such as tunneling, and the legal framework establishing such a system is coming into place, it remains untested. Take the Czech law creating a commission to oversee the country's capital markets, which the Czech parliament—finally disgusted with the country's plunging reputation in the foreign investment community—passed earlier this year. Most observers cheered the measure, but the body has yet to begin its work in earnest, and EU officials want to see how it functions before giving it full approval.

Another thorny issue in both the Czech Republic and Poland is bank privatization. In Poland, the remaining state shares in commercial banks are scheduled to be sold this year, and the banks themselves are working to upgrade the level and range of services they offer. Problems persist in the rural banking sector, where nearly 1,400 small cooperative banks still operate. In the Czech Republic, three of the four largest banks remain to varying degrees in state hands, and two have seen falling profits in recent years as they struggle to get out from under portfolios that suffer from two to three times the amount of bad loans as Polish and Hungarian banks. Furthermore, the lack of clear ownership of the banks, as well as the tangled web of relations between the banks and Czech industrial firms, are blamed by many for the country's overall lack of restructuring in industry. Although the government of then-Prime Minister Vaclav Klaus finally came up with a plan to privatize the banks last autumn, the program has been put into question by the Social Democrats, who are favored to take over power after elections expected in June.

PRIVATIZE, PLEASE

The EU would clearly like to see applicant countries' banks privatized, and many economists say the banks would likely run aground in the single market if left in their current condition. But it would be disingenuous for the union to require privatization as a condition for membership because some EU countries have substantial state participation in the banking sector themselves. Instead of demanding privatization, the union is recommending that the Central Europeans ensure the competitiveness of their banks—and hinting strongly that privatization would be the best way to do that.

"Nobody can say that they have to privatize immediately," says Eva Thiel, a senior economist at the Organization for Economic Cooperation and Development in Paris. "You can tell them that [state ownership] creates uncertainty, and they could miss the boat in terms of efficiency. If there were interventions in credit allocation decisions, you could complain, but you can't really say per se that government should not own banks."

One area of particular concern for union officials is money laundering. Soon after the opening of the region in 1989 and 1990, casinos, currency exchanges, and bookie agencies sprouted along the region's gray highways and boulevards, while banks began to offer anonymous, numbered accounts and hard-currency savings schemes. These proved a strong attraction for dirty money from around the globe, especially from the criminal gangs flourishing in the former Soviet Union. "After the liberalization of the political situation there was practically nothing—no legislation, no law enforcement—and the countries were not prepared to tackle the problem, which of course has given some advantages to money launderers," says Paolo Clarotti, an EU advisor on Central and Eastern Europe.

Of the five short-listed countries in the region, Slovenia has made the most progress in controlling the problem, commission officials say. It has a legal framework based on international standards, as well as a disclosure office, which acts as an information clearing house and liaison between banks and other financial institutions. The Czech Republic and Hungary have also made substantial progress, while Poland and Estonia are expected to bring their regimes into relative compliance this year or next. In all of those countries, though, the officials in charge of the programs remain relatively inexperienced and will need some time before they are able to efficiently control money laundering. "Now at least they are aware that they have to tackle this problem properly if they want to be members of the European Union," Clarotti says.

THE GOING GETS ROUGH

While the push for compliance with EU legislation and regulations is accelerating, the countries on the short list are not newcomers to the pitfalls of negotiating with Brussels. As associate EU members since the early 1990s, they've had plenty of experience in dealing with the union. But that doesn't mean the integration process will run smoothly, and in fact there have already been many conflicts.

Hungary, for example, came under criticism from the union for taxing citrus fruit at the 25 percent rate of a luxury good rather than the 12 percent rate of other foods. Although Hungary's finance ministry said it needed the extra income from the fruit, the EU said the tax favored Hungarian-grown non-citrus fruit over imports. In the end, the Hungarians relented and reduced the rate.

The Czechs, when faced last year with a soaring trade deficit, introduced a scheme that required importers to deposit 20 percent of the value of their goods in a non-interest-bearing account for six months—a move that effectively made imports more expensive than domestic items. The EU cried foul there as well, and the deposit was soon revoked. The Czechs also have a quota system in place for apple imports that the EU opposes. "It's not difficult to adapt the legislation," says the EU's Thiel, "but the political resistance to some of this is very strong."

In spring 1998, the European Commission will release documents outlining what exactly the candidate countries need to do to bring themselves into compliance with EU regulations. Shortly thereafter, the countries will publish plans detailing a timetable for their accession, with deadlines for the various steps they need to take. And while EU officials privately acknowledge that there will likely be some room for negotiation, they say they want all of the countries to comply fully with EU requirements.

"All of the measures are important," says Luis Garcia, principal administrator in the banking division of the European Commission's directorate of financial affairs. "Without accounting, for example, we wouldn't know what the situation of a company is, and if they haven't transposed the directive on consolidated results, then the accounting won't work. We are going to proceed to the screening of the legislation article by article, and we hope that in two years' time all of the measures will be implemented."

By then the 11 students in the Prague accounting class—and the thousands of others in similar courses throughout the region—should have yawned their way through enough lectures to make sense of those measures and put them to work the way the politicians want them to.

NOTE

Reprinted with kind permission from *Transitions* magazine, April 1998.

Document: AGENDA 2000 AND THE SINGLE MARKET: A BRIDGE TO CENTRAL AND EASTERN EUROPE (October 1997)

There follow highlights from the European Commission's 10 Opinions on the state of preparedness of the applicant countries.

Table: Harmonization Program

(Number of White Paper measures that the country claims to have transposed into domestic legislation, out of a possible total of 899.)

Bulgaria	126
Czech Republic	417
Estonia	283
Hungary	579
Latvia	253
Lithuania	316
Poland	405
Romania	426
Slovakia	664
Slovenia	415

BULGARIA

The country is not able to cope with competitive pressure and market forces in the EU. There has been little progress over the last six years. The stability of democratic institutions must be reinforced by fuller respect for rule of law. Considerable effort is needed to fight corruption, improve the judiciary, and protect individual liberties.

The fundamental elements of Single Market (SM) legislation still need to be adopted in all areas. Complete restructuring of the financial sector is the top priority. The capacity of government as well as businesses to implement Single Market rules is lagging. Bulgaria is not yet ready to abolish internal SM borders or manage external EU borders.

CZECH REPUBLIC

Has a functioning market economy, but corporate governance and financial systems must be strengthened. Enterprise restructuring must be accelerated. Press freedom laws are weak. Citizenship laws discriminate against Roma (gypsies).

Core Single Market legislation on company and accounting law, technical rules and standards are in force and well implemented. There are problems with financial services, securities, intellectual property rights, and personal data protection. Public procurement is only partially transposed; however, legal remedies are working well. No problems in the medium term to fully participate in the Single Market, including abolition of borders.

ESTONIA

Estonia has a functioning market economy. It needs investment in environmental protection, and must strengthen its administrative capacity to enforce EU laws. Political institutions are effective, but the fight against corruption must be sustained. It must accelerate the naturalization of Russian-speaking non-citizens.

The core Single Market rules have been partly adopted, and there is a credible commitment by the government to do the rest and make the necessary amendments within two years. Problems persist with public procurement, intellectual and industrial property, and financial services. There are problem with implementation, and generally weak administration. There was no final statement on Estonia's readiness for abolition of borders.

HUNGARY

Hungary is able to cope with EU competitive pressure and market forces. The reform of pensions and social security needs to advance rapidly. Stable institutions guarantee rule of law, human rights, and respect for minorities, but Roma need better protection.

Most Single Market legislation including public procurement, intellectual property, company and accounting law, product liability, and financial services is in place. In some of these areas implementation measures are in place (public procurement). However, problems remain with implementing measures and establishment of an efficient administrative structure. No problems in the medium term to fully participate in the Single Market, including abolition of borders.

LATVIA

Latvia has made considerable progress in establishing a market economy, but lags in implementing new laws. Privatization is incomplete, and Latvia would face difficulties competing in the Single Market. The country must accelerate the integration of Russian-speaking non-citizens. Ethnic minorities' access to the professions and the democratic process is inadequate.

A degree of alignment with EU legislation has been achieved in the fields of industrial property rights, conformity assessments and standards, and in the area of free movement of services. Problems remain with public procurement, intellectual property, and data protection. Weakness of administration is a severe problem for implementation. There was no final statement on Latvia's ability to fully participate in the SM, including abolition of borders.

LITHUANIA

Financial discipline at Lithuanian enterprises is still missing. More progress is needed in price adjustment, bankruptcy proceedings, and large-scale privatization. Lithuania would have serious difficulties competing. The banking sector is weak, and agriculture must be modernized. There is a stable democratic system guaranteeing the rule of law, human rights, and minorities protection.

There is a degree of alignment with EU legislation in the fields of industrial property rights, conformity assessments and standards, and free movement of goods. Problems remain with public procurement, intellectual property, and financial services. Weakness of administration is a severe problem for implementation. There was no final statement on Lithuania's ability to fully participate in the Single Market, including abolition of borders.

POLAND

Growth and investment are strong in Poland. The financial services are underdeveloped, and more reform is needed in banking. Administrative reform is indispensable. Particular effort is needed in agriculture, environment, and transport. The fight against corruption must be intensified. There is some concern over press freedom and access for some categories to public service.

Large parts of the Single Market rules are already in place with some important gaps (implementation structures for technical regulations and standards), some not even foreseen in the country's future legislative programs. Problems remain with public procurement, data protection, and liberalization of capital movements. An efficient administrative structure is lagging. Foresees no problems in the medium term to fully participate in the Single Market, including abolition of borders.

ROMANIA

Romania has made considerable progress toward a market economy, but would face serious difficulties competing in the medium term. A big reform effort is needed in environment, transport, employment, social affairs, justice, and home affairs and agriculture. Gaps remain in respect for fundamental rights, and there is poor integration of Roma.

In general only a very sketchy transposition of Single Market legislation has taken place, with the positive exception of intellectual and industrial property. The complete restructuring of the financial sector is a priority. The capacity of government as well as businesses to implement Single Market rules is lagging. The country is not yet ready for the abolition of internal SM borders and the management of external EU borders.

SLOVAKIA

Slovakia does not fulfill the political conditions for entry, being characterized by unstable institutions and democratic shortcomings. The government too often disregards the rights of the opposition, and resorts to a worrying use of police and secret services. The rights of minorities must be improved. The country could cope with Single Market competition in the medium term, although enterprise restructuring has been slow.

Legislative alignment on company law, banking, securities, and free movement of capital has been achieved. Problems remain with standards and certification, intellectual and industrial property (in particular copyright), public procurement, and insurance. Implementing rules and efficient administrative structures are lagging. There was no final statement on Slovakia's ability to deal with the abolition of border controls.

SLOVENIA

Slovenia must reform its administration to apply EU internal market laws. Progress was slow in environment, employment and social affairs, energy, and enterprise restructuring. There is a lack of competition especially in the finance sector. Slovenia must strengthen the fight against corruption.

Core Single Market legislation, in particular accountancy, mutual recognition of professional qualifications and intellectual property is practically in place. There are problems with public procurement, insurance, freedom of capital movements, product conformity, and standardization. Concrete implementing measures and an effective administrative infrastructure are lacking. There was no final statement on Slovenia's capacity to cope with the abolition of border controls.

REGIONAL ECONOMIES

III

CENTRAL AND EASTERN EUROPE: GROWING ECONOMIC DIFFERENCES

by MICHAEL WYZAN *and* BEN SLAY

The year 1997 in the economic sphere in Central and Eastern Europe was dominated by relations with the European Union (EU). The year's biggest event was the European Commission's recommendation in July to invite only five of the ten candidate countries to begin accession negotiations, a recommendation adopted at the EU summit in Luxembourg in December.

In Central Europe, Slovakia was the only country not invited, likely isolating it further from the rest of the region and impelling it to strengthen its ties with Russia and Ukraine, especially if the current group remains in power in Bratislava. Slovenia was invited to negotiate, clearly demonstrating the distance between it and the rest of former Yugoslavia in the EU's eyes. Most controversial was the decision to invite Estonia but not the other two Baltic states to begin talks. Still, with relations with Russia remaining troubled (particularly in Latvia), that country and Lithuania are unlikely to turn eastward.

CENTRAL EUROPE: MOSTLY GOOD YEARS ON ROAD TO EU

The invitations extended to Poland, Hungary, and the Czech Republic to begin membership negotiations with the EU dominated the headlines in 1997. However, current account developments in these countries were undoubtedly more important in forming the countries' macroeconomic outlooks over the next few years. While Poland managed to keep its growing current account deficit from getting out of hand—and thereby record another year of rapid economic growth—the Czech Republic lost control over its external accounts, and fell victim to a currency crisis and economic stagnation. Slovakia's current-account deficit spun further out of control in 1997, possibly setting the stage for serious difficulties in 1998. Hungary, meanwhile, continued to recover from its own current-account crisis of 1994–95: strong export growth in 1997 paved the way for above-forecast growth of gross domestic product (GDP) and large reductions in external red ink. At year's end the task of reining in current account deficits is therefore a key economic-policy challenge for Poland and Slovakia in 1998; the Czech Republic was trying to restart economic growth; while Hungary looked to build upon the past year's economic successes.

Electoral (and constitutional) politics could be the greatest obstacles to meeting these challenges. Hungary, the Czech Republic, and Slovakia all faced parliamentary elections in 1998; while the constitutional crisis precipitated by Prime Minister Vladimir Meciar's play for the presidency suggested that politics will push economic issues ever further into the background in Slovakia. Only in

Poland, where the September 1997 parliamentary elections produced a government with a reasonably reformist economic policy, did political circumstances favor the adoption of the measures needed to deal with these external deficits.

Poland

To the surprise of many, the September 1997 parliamentary elections in Poland produced a relatively cohesive coalition government for whom tackling the nation's economic problems was a major priority. This turn of events was symbolized by the appointment of Leszek Balcerowicz, the author and instigator of Poland's economic transition during 1990–91, as the new government's deputy prime minister and minister of finance. The economy for which Balcerowicz assumed responsibility in 1997 was in infinitely better shape than the one he inherited in 1989. Inflation in 1997 fell to 13.0 percent (on a December to December basis, as are all inflation figures in this chapter). GDP growth continued at a torrid 6.5 percent pace; the unemployment rate dropped from 13.6 to 10.5 percent during the year; and the budget deficit claimed only 1.8 percent of GDP.[1]

On the other hand, Poland's current account deficit grew dramatically, from 1 percent of GDP in 1996 to around 4.0 percent in 1997. While last year's 8.0 percent growth in dollar exports exceeds the 6.8 percent growth recorded in 1996, these increases pale in comparison with the 32 and 18 percent growth in dollar imports recorded during 1996 and 1997, respectively. Although the zloty remained fairly stable, the National Bank did have to fight off speculative attacks on it in July and October. Over the longer term, Poland faces the need to reform its out-of-control pension system, which absorbed more than 15 percent of GDP in 1996.[2] Left unchecked, these trends could produce a currency crisis and a current-account meltdown.

Balcerowicz therefore faced the challenge of slowing the growth in domestic demand in 1998. Fortunately, the nearly $5 billion in direct foreign investment attracted in 1997 (bringing the cumulative total to $17.1 billion),[3] and the fact that increases in investment continued to outpace consumption and GDP growth, suggested that Poland still had room for a soft landing. Balcerowicz's tighter 1998 budget, projecting a fiscal deficit of only 1.5 percent of GDP, suggested that for once politics may not get in the way of Poland's economic prospects.

Hungary

Hungary during 1994–96 provided an object lesson in the dangers of ignoring fiscal and external deficits. Due to a budget deficit that had risen to 7.4 percent of GDP even before the country's large external debt-servicing payments were made, Hungary's current account deficit in 1994 exceeded 9 percent of GDP. The stabilization program (Bokros plan) of March 1995, which devalued the forint and imposed restrictions on imports, pushed yearly inflation rates close to 30 percent, and kept yearly GDP growth rates down to 1–1.5 percent during 1995–96.[4] External imbalances therefore prevented Hungary from sharing in the strong post-1994 recovery enjoyed by the other Central European economies.

As it turns out, 1997 was the year in which Hungary harvested the fruits planted in March 1995. Strong export growth—led by shipments from Hungarian subsidiaries of multinationals—pushed GDP growth up to 4 percent, and reduced the current-account deficit to about 2 percent of GDP. Inflation fell below 20 percent for the year, while unemployment dropped to 9.7 percent.[5] Hungary seemed likely to attract another $2.4 billion in direct foreign investment by the end of 1997, pushing its cumulative total to above $17 billion. Alone among the Central European countries, Hungary seemed poised to turn solid, export-led growth in 1997 into faster, yet still sustainable growth in 1998. It remains to be seen whether these trends will help the political fortunes of the parties forming Prime Minister Gyula Horn's coalition government, which faced parliamentary elections in May 1998.

Czech Republic

The year 1997 was not a good one for the Czech Republic's economy, nor for Vaclav Klaus. The Czech prime minister, who had argued that the Czech transition to a market economy was successfully completed, saw his economic miracle collapse, and was himself unceremoniously removed from office in December. The country's current-account deficit climbed to 8.0 percent of GDP in 1996, precipitating a currency crisis in May 1997, which culminated in the floating of the crown. Over the course of 1997, the Czech currency depreciated by some 24 percent against the dollar, but the current account deficit at the end of the year still stood at 6.7 percent of GDP.

As was the case in Hungary in 1995, these external problems slowed the Czech economy to a crawl. GDP, which grew by 5.9 percent in 1995 and 4.1 percent in 1996, recorded only a 1.2 percent increase last year. For the first time since 1993, retail price inflation in 1997 was in double figures (10.0 percent) and was likely to rise further in 1998. The unemployment rate, which stood at an other-worldly 2.7 percent in May 1996, had nearly doubled to 5.2 percent by December 1997, with higher (8 percent) rates reported in Northern Bohemia and Northern Moravia.[6] Both inflation and unemployment were likely to increase further in 1998.

These problems were exacerbated by the uncertainties of Czech politics. Intra-party feuding throughout 1997 prevented the resolution of important questions about privatization and financial regulation. While the June 1998 parliamentary elections could end this interregnum, they could also produce a government dominated by the Social Democrats, a party with much populist baggage and no experience in governing. The Czech Republic's economic prospects in 1998 are therefore difficult to evaluate.

Slovakia

Alone among the Central European economies, Slovakia seemed likely to undergo a bruising correction in 1998. The "Slovak economic miracle" of 1994–97, when GDP grew on average by 6.1 percent and consumer prices rose 7.7 percent annually, was unlikely to continue into 1998. The reason: Slovakia's current account, which went from a surplus equivalent to 3.7 percent of GDP in 1995 to annual deficits in excess of 11 percent of GDP during 1996–97. These external deficits in turn reflected a dramatic deterioration in Slovakia's fiscal stance: the government deficit increased from 1.7 percent of GDP in 1995 to 5.8 percent of GDP last year.

While large fiscal and current account deficits need not spell imminent disaster, the specifics of the Slovak case overwhelmingly suggest that such an event is waiting to happen. First, unlike the other Central European economies, Slovakia is largely closed to direct foreign investment. Per capita FDI in Slovakia at the end of 1997 was only $235 compared to $442 for Poland, $1,278 for the Czech Republic, and $1,671 for Hungary.[7] Only $200 million of Slovakia's $2.2 billion current-account deficit was financed by foreign direct investment (FDI) in 1997; the remainder was financed by short-term capital attracted by real interest rates as high as 13–15 percent (on government debt). Second, these high interest rates, and the growing fiscal imbalances underlying them, suggested that resources were being reallocated away from the investment and export activities needed to maintain economic growth.

Third, government officials in 1998 will be largely absorbed with the country's politics, especially the constitutional crisis precipitated by Meciar's play for the presidency and the parliamentary elections due in the fall of 1998. Slovakia is therefore unlikely to be as able as Poland to undertake the measures needed to slow domestic demand and reduce external imbalances. Fourth, the Meciar government's unwillingness to permit the Slovak crown to depreciate meant that the national currency appreciated about 7 percent in real terms against the currencies of Slovakia's two largest trading partners, the Czech Republic and Germany. Subsequent reductions in export competitiveness were likely to further exacerbate Slovakia's external imbalances.

Slovakia's constitutional crisis of 1998 could therefore be accompanied by an economic crisis, featuring a large devaluation of the crown, inflation surging to double-digit levels, and large slowdowns in GDP and consumption growth. The unfortunate political developments in the country may have made the international community less likely to rush to the country's aid. That is especially so if the United States leans on the International Monetary Fund (IMF) not to lend to the country (as it has done in the case of Croatia) and the EU decides not to provide assistance (unlike its generosity toward Bulgaria's new reformist government). Such decisions would increase the size of the domestic correction needed to restore external balance. Accordingly, 1998 could well see an accentuation of the differences between Slovakia and the other Central European economies.

THE NON-YUGOSLAV BALKANS: DREADFUL PERFORMANCE BUT BETTER GOVERNMENTS

All three Balkan countries outside former Yugoslavia experienced high drama during 1997. For Bulgaria and Albania, this meant near-total economic collapse, followed by the achievement of a fragile stability under new governments formed in April in Bulgaria and in July in Albania. Romania also saw its economic performance deteriorate, but oddly this occurred after a reformist (but internally divided) government was formed in November 1996.

Romania

In Romania, the former communists remained in power after 1989, through 1995 presiding over a slow improvement in macroeconomic performance, but losing an election to reformist forces in November 1996. In 1997, many measures of macroeconomic performance deteriorated sharply, even as the country embarked on a radical reform program. Meanwhile, disagreements within the ruling coalition increasingly paralyzed economic policy, relations with the IMF deteriorated, and organized labor became more restive.

During 1997 laws were passed that liberalized those prices still under control; created a unified, market-driven exchange rate, reduced import tariffs; and removed subsidies and phased out directed credits to agriculture. Fiscal and monetary policy were tightened, with wages and benefits partially indexed.[8] The share of enterprises that had been privatized rose from 45 percent at end-1996 to 60 percent eight months later. In February, the government began liquidating 62 large enterprises.[9] In August, miners began to accept severance pay equivalent to 12–20 average monthly wages in return for agreeing to become unemployed. However, the government, concerned that up to 150,000 miners might accept these offers, halted the closures in October.

Domestic macroeconomic performance was poor in 1997. GDP contracted by 6.6 percent, after rising by 4.1 percent the year before, while industrial production fell by 5.9 percent, compared to growth of over 9 percent in 1995 and 1996. The unemployment rate rose to 8.8 percent in December from 6.3 percent a year earlier.[10] The average monthly wage in November was $139, little changed from November 1996.[11]

The consumer price index (CPI) rose by 152 percent (versus 57 percent in 1996). Although the high inflation during the first quarter was the necessary concomitant of price liberalization, its acceleration in the autumn resulted from such policies as generous wage and pension indexation and looser monetary policy.[12] Still, the government managed to hold the budget deficit to 4.5 percent of GDP.

External developments were more favorable than domestic ones. The trade deficit narrowed from $1.7 billion in January–October 1996 to $1.2 billion in the same period of 1997, with the current account imbalance falling from $1.9 billion to $1.6 billion between these periods. The depreciation of the leu—from 4,035 to the dollar at end-1996 to 7,983 at end-1997—undoubtedly contributed to this improvement. Interest among foreign investors rose, with FDI at $806 million in January–September 1997, compared with $624 million in all of 1996.[13]

Relations with the IMF were troubled, with the latter concerned over a large budget deficit, high inflation, price controls on energy and food products, and slow privatization. The decision in August to close 17 enterprises and the lower inflation that was recorded that month convinced the IMF to release the second tranche of a standby loan in September (a month late). But continuing concerns over these and other issues resulted in the fund's postponing of a tranche release scheduled for November until well into 1998.

Bulgaria

The crisis in Bulgaria that began in May 1996 reached its apogee in February 1997. The consumer price index (CPI) rose by 243 percent that month, while the lev fell from 487 to the dollar at the end of 1996 to 2,046 on 28 February. The national bank's foreign reserves fell to $380 million in January, and the average monthly wage plummeted to $25 in February 1997.[14] The crisis and its aftermath saw many large enterprises and banks go bankrupt. After February, the economy began to stabilize, as policy-making improved under two new reformist governments. The key move was the introduction of a currency board on 1 July, which rendered impossible long-standing inflationary banking and fiscal practices.

In April, all price controls except those on eight staples were removed. Legislative highlights included the lifting in July of most restrictions on foreign currency transactions; elimination in July of discrimination against foreign insurance companies; legal amendments in October providing tax breaks for "priority investment projects"; and a move in October to strip debtors of the right to bank secrecy. A program was launched to privatize 30 large firms with the assistance of foreign consultants.[15] The liquidation of some 80 enterprises responsible for 25 percent of state enterprise losses was completed by July.[16]

While CPI inflation for the year was 579 percent, in July–December the average monthly rate had fallen to 2.5 percent. Average monthly wages reached $108 in December 1997. GDP fell by 7.4 percent over the year, although most of the decline occurred early on; industrial production was down by 11.5 percent in January–September. The budget deficit, at 3.6 percent of GDP, was smaller than expected, as was the end-year unemployment rate of 13.7 percent.

Confidence returned to the banks, with people converting their money back into leva and redepositing it. The international financial institutions resumed lending, with Bulgaria receiving during 1997 $320 million from a loan awarded in April by the IMF. Bulgaria also signed loan agreements with the World Bank ($100 million) and the EU ($250 million) last year. These factors contributed to a rise in the national bank's foreign reserves to $2.48 billion at the end of 1997. The economic collapse early in the year depressed imports and, despite a recovery late in the year, there was a trade surplus of $396 million; the current account was also in the black, to the tune of $456 million.[17]

The key issues facing Bulgaria at year's end were securing sources of finance for the investment needed for economic recovery and accelerating privatization. Banks, understandably cautious, have so far been interested only in buying government bonds. An encouraging sign is a rise in foreign investment to about $600 million,[18] with sales of such firms as Sodi Devnya and the Pirdorp Copper Combine, and progress made toward selling shares in the airline, telecommunications monopoly, and two oil refineries to foreign interests.[19] The government announced in July the sale of the United Bulgarian Bank to several investors. However, there remains disappointment over the slow pace and insider-dominated nature of privatization and the build-up of enterprise tax arrears.[20]

Albania

Albanian society descended into chaos in 1997 in the wake of the collapse of pyramid schemes that had collected $1.2 billion (about half of GDP) from domestic depositors. After growing by between 8.3 and 13.3 percent annually during 1993–96, GDP fell by 7 percent in 1997; industrial production fell by 5.6 percent.[21] Consumer price inflation rose to 42 percent, up from 17.4 percent in 1996. The budget deficit at 11.4 percent was little changed from 1996's 11.1 percent, which was already higher than in previous years, as financial discipline began to break down.

Monthly wages fell to $55 in the private sector and $50 in the state sector by year's end.[22] Although registered unemployment had declined from 24.8 percent at the end of 1994 to 12.1 percent two years later, it increased in 1997 as the economy collapsed.[23] The chaos in 1997 saw exports and imports nose-dive, the former from $244 million in 1996 to $159 million in 1997 and the latter from $922 million to $694 million over this period. The lek closed the year at 155 to the dollar, compared with 100 at the end of 1996.[24]

In August, the IMF set as conditions for renewed lending that the authorities close the remaining pyramid schemes, privatize or liquidate two of three state banks, reform the civil service, create an agricultural land market, improve the collection of customs duties, raise the value-added tax rate, and cut government spending. In early October, Albania reached agreement with the fund on $12 million in "emergency post-conflict assistance"; two weeks later in Brussels, a donors' conference approved a $600 million, three-year aid package. The IMF and World Bank also lent money to audit the pyramids, but refused to bankroll the return of depositors' money.

THE BALTIC STATES: ECONOMIES KEEP GROWING, AS DO EXTERNAL IMBALANCES

The year 1997 was another strong one for all three Baltic economies, with economic growth accelerating and inflation further declining. However, their current account deficits reached alarming proportions, calling into question their fixed exchange rate regimes. The EU's decision to invite only Estonia among them to begin accession talks ruffled feathers, but is unlikely to deflect Latvia or Lithuania from their reform paths.

Estonia

The Estonian GDP grew by about 9 percent in 1997, up from 4 percent in 1996, with a stock market slump in the autumn seemingly affecting the economy rather little.[25] Labor market developments were consistent with a booming economy: unemployment as a share of the labor force declined from 5.5 percent in December 1996 to 4.6 percent in December 1997, and the average monthly wage rose from $295 in the former month to $302 in the latter.[26] CPI inflation fell from 14.8 percent in 1996 to 12.5 percent in 1997.[27] The consolidated budget was in slight surplus.

The trade deficit last year was $1.4 billion, up from $1.1 billion in 1996. The current account imbalance in January–September was up by 59 percent over

January–September 1996,[28] likely pushing the annual figure to over 10 percent of GDP. But FDI inflows remained large at $800 million in the first three quarters of the year, compared with $298 million cumulatively through end-1996,[29] and the foreign reserves were increasing rapidly.[30]

Privatization was virtually complete, with assets worth $283 million sold through February 1997, and the remaining effort focused on utilities and infrastructure enterprises. The method used was based on sales to owners, including foreigners, willing and able to restructure enterprises and improve corporate governance.[31] The banking system was healthy and tightly regulated, with 93 percent of its assets in private hands (and 40 percent of them owned by non-residents); and was rapidly expanding into Latvia and Lithuania.[32]

Latvia

Latvia's macroeconomy continued to perform well. The year 1997 built on the previous year's strong recovery from 1995's downturn, which was caused by a banking crisis. During January–September, GDP grew by 5.6 percent, compared to 2.8 percent in all of 1996;[33] the growth of industrial production accelerated from 1.4 percent in 1996 to 6.1 percent in 1997.[34] Relatedly, labor market conditions were tightening, with the unemployment rate falling from 7.2 percent in December 1996 to 6.7 percent a year later,[35] while the average monthly wage in the public sector rose from $242 in December 1996 to $272 in December 1997.[36] CPI inflation fell to 7.0 percent from 13.1 percent in 1996, in both years the lowest in the Baltic states,[37] while the budget was in surplus—about 0.7 percent of GDP—for the first time since 1993.

Although Latvia had not introduced a currency board, unlike Estonia and Lithuania, the lats was pegged to the IMF's Special Drawing Right since 1994, so the foreign-sector balances needed to be watched, as disequilibrium could threaten the stability of the currency. The trade deficit rose from $877 million in 1996 to $1.1 billion last year,[38] while the current account imbalance was projected at about $460 million, similar to 1996's and a high 9 percent of GDP.[39] Cumulative FDI rose from $645 million at the end of 1996 to $850 million on 30 September 1997, helping to finance the current account deficit.[40]

Despite macroeconomic performance as respectable as Estonia's, observers criticized Latvia's approach to structural issues. They pointed to slow privatization; the prevalence of unrestructured state enterprises, especially in export-oriented sectors; and the weakness of the banking system.[41] A scandal involving the privatization of Latvenergo, the state electrical distributor, erupted in 1997, with allegations that the company transferred up to $14 million to a Liechtenstein company with links to Latvenergo's management.

Lithuania

Lithuania also experienced a good 1997, although its external imbalances were worrisome and its currency board (introduced in April 1994) periodically came under speculative attack. Moreover, FDI and other capital inflows to Lithuania have been weaker than in Estonia, making the sustainability of the Lithuanian board more doubtful. In any case, the intention is to replace the board by pegging to a basket of currencies, perhaps as early as 1999.

In January–November 1997, the trade deficit was $1.4 billion, up from $665 million in January–November 1996. The current account deficit was $500 million in the first half of 1996 (a high 10 percent of GDP), versus $642 in all of 1997.[42] But there were encouraging signs: the national bank's foreign reserves rose from $834 million at end-1996 to $1.06 billion at end-1997;[43] and the national bank announced that beginning in September no further IMF credits would be needed.[44]

The year 1997 was a solid one for the domestic economy. GDP grew by 6.4 in January–September 1997, compared with 4.2 percent in all of 1996,[45] while sales of industrial production were up by 6.1, versus 1.3 percent the year before.[46] Under a budget amended in October; the deficit was under the target of 1.9 percent of GDP, down from 2.5 percent in 1996.[47] Consumer prices rose by 8.4 percent in 1997, down from 13.1 percent in 1996.[48] Unlike in Estonia and Latvia, the unemployment rate rose during 1997, from 6.2 percent in December 1996 to 6.7 percent a year later.[49] The dollar wage increased, from $194 in December 1996 to $223 in November 1997.

Privatization had made less headway in Lithuania than in Estonia or Latvia, with strategic enterprises excluded from the process in December 1994 and little foreign participation. But there was progress in 1997 on privatizing a shipping company, the Baltic state's only oil refinery, and the country's largest hotel. Banking regulation improved in the wake of the 1995 banking crisis.

FORMER YUGOSLAVIA: NOTHING IN COMMON

Yugoslavia split into five countries with little in common economically. Slovenia was stable and prosperous, but saddled with interest groups resistant to reform. Political factors isolated Croatia, but its economy was healthy, albeit with worrying external imbalances. Macedonia had sound macroeconomic policy but was slow to resume growth. Federal Yugoslavia remained isolated and anti-reform, while Bosnia-Herzegovina's recovery was slowing as emergency reconstruction neared completion.

Slovenia

Slovenia's indicators in 1997 were respectable and similar to 1996's. GDP grew by between 2.9 and 3.3 percent, versus 3.1 percent in 1996. However, macroeconomic policy was hampered by the failure to pass the budget until December; the deficit was 1.2–1.4 percent of GDP, the largest since independence.[50] Retail price inflation was 9.4 percent, up from 8.8 percent in 1996.

Growth of industrial production, at 1.3 percent, was trending downward after hitting 6.4 percent in 1994. Weak industrial performance resulted from slow enterprise restructuring, with firms hostage to pressures against layoffs from workers' representatives on supervisory councils.[51] It also resulted from high interest rates that depressed investment. Moreover, banks demonstrated their own resistance to reform by suing the government over a tax aimed at forcing them to consolidate and increase lending to enterprises.[52] Wages in November were up by 8.0 percent on November 1996, half their growth rate in the twelve months prior to the latter month. Nonetheless, gross wages, at $890 in November, remained the highest among transition countries. The unemployment rate according to the official method was 14.5 percent in November, although a survey according to internationally accepted methods found 7.1 percent in May, both figures little changed over 1996.

External developments were favorable, with a trade deficit of $767 million, compared with $882 million in 1996; the current account was in surplus ($70 million). The national bank's foreign reserves reached a comfortable $3.3 billion in December. FDI inflows were $246 million during the first nine months, compared with $186 million during all of 1996.[53] The government took steps in 1997 to align legislation with EU standards; its priorities were taxation, pensions, the financial sector, government services, and price liberalization.[54] New legislation called for removing barriers to FDI, except in defense industries and health and pension insurance, and allowing foreigners to become the sole owners of firms.[55]

Croatia

Croatia saw GDP grow by 5.5 percent last year, up from 4.2 percent in 1996.[56] Industrial production rose by 6.8 percent, up greatly from 1996, due largely to strong growth in power generation; manufacturing grew by only 3 percent.[57] Tourism was recovering, with night-stays up by 42 percent in 1997.[58] The healthy economy resulted in a budget deficit of 1 percent of GDP, versus a projected 2.6 percent.[59] Retail price inflation was only 3.6 percent, although there was skepticism on data accuracy.[60] The gross wage of $588 in October 1997 exceeded those of all Visegrad countries except Slovenia, a misleading fact because prices are correspondingly higher.[61] The unemployment rate was high and rising, closing 1997 at 17.6 percent, versus 15.8 percent the year before,[62] and there were signs of growing social discontent.

External sector developments were worrisome in 1997, with a trade deficit of $4.79 billion, up from $3.28 billion in 1996, and a current account imbalance of $2.34 billion, up from $881 million in 1996 and a very high 12.1 percent of GDP.[63] The central bank's foreign exchange reserves rose only modestly, from $2.3 billion in 1996 to $2.5 billion in 1997. These developments led many observers to predict that the kuna would be devalued, something that had not happened by year's end.[64] In July, the IMF refused under U.S. pressure to release two $40 million loan tranches. When ten accused war criminals left for Holland in October, the IMF released the money. Croatia then decided that it did not need the loans, although the central bank governor soon announced a new agreement with the fund.[65]

The rehabilitation of the giant Privredna Banka was progressing. Voucher privatization, which mainly benefited refugees and veterans, began in 1997, and there was official support for privatizing utilities and banks. Nonetheless, many industrial concerns had restructured little and inter-enterprise arrears were substantial.[66]

Macedonia

Macedonia's recovery slowly gathered steam, with social product growing by 1.4 percent in 1997 (versus 0.7 percent in 1996), and industrial production by 3.5 percent (compared to 3.1 percent in 1996).[67] Retail price inflation was 4.6 percent, up from 1996's 0.3 percent. The denar monthly wage barely moved, so with a weaker denar, the dollar wage fell to $166 in December from a high of $228 in August 1996. Even so unemployment, estimated at 31.7 percent in September, was up from 30.4 percent at end-1996.[68]

The major economic event was July's 16 percent devaluation against the Deutsche mark. The external position improved during the year, with the trade deficit at $385 million and the current account deficit at $272 million.[69] Foreign investment remained negligible, but there were plans to sell shares in the telecommunications monopoly and the largest bank to foreign interests in 1998.

Serbia and Montenegro

In the Federal Republic of Yugoslavia retail price inflation was 20 percent in the twelve months prior to October 1997. Industrial production was up by 9 percent during this period, while GDP grew by about 6 percent in 1997.[70] But inflation was expected to rise, spurring a weakening of the dinar on the black market late in 1997.[71] The numbers of unemployed barely rose, but the rate has been estimated at fully 28.5 percent; the average wage was $156 in October. Through November, the trade deficit was $2.1 billion, a 19 percent increase over January–November 1996. Not a member of the IMF, the country had limited possibilities to finance external imbalances.

Bosnia

Bosnia's recovery was hampered by restrictions on the movement of people, goods, and capital. As emergency reconstruction neared completion in 1997, GDP growth slowed to 25–35 percent from 50 percent in 1996 (these figures obviously reflecting the low base from which recovery began).[72] Consumer prices in the Muslim-Croat federation rose by 12.2 percent October 1996–October 1997; the monthly wage was $145 there and $47 in Republika Srpska during the summer.[73] Laws were passed in June on the budget, central bank (which opened in August), customs, and foreign debt, and in October on privatization.[74] A July donors' conference raised $1.24 billion to aid the country's revival.[75]

NOTES

[1]Unless otherwise mentioned, all data for the Central European economies come from PlanEcon's *Review and Outlook for Eastern Europe,* December 1997.

[2]Ben Slay and Louisa Vinton, *Poland to 2005: The Challenge of Europe,* Economist Intelligence Unit, Vienna, 1997, p. 85.

[3]WEFA's *World Economic Outlook (vol. 1),* January 1998, p. 8.21.

[4]These figures come from WEFA's *Eurasian Economic Outlook,* November 1997, p. 8.4; from PlanEcon's *Hungarian Economic Monitor,* 8 August 1995, p. 27; and from the author's calculations.

[5]WEFA's *World Economic Outlook (vol. 1),* January 1998, p. 8.18; and PlanEcon's

Review and Outlook for Eastern Europe, December 1997, p. 107.

[6]The inflation and unemployment data come from PlanEcon's *Czech Economic Monitor,* 30 January 1998, pp. 19, 36, 38.

[7]According to PlanEcon and WEFA data.

[8]*1998 Romanian Economic Survey: Assessment and Recommendations,* Center for Cooperation with the Economies in Transition, Organisation for Economic Cooperation and Development, February 1998 (available on Web site http://www.oecd.org/sge/ccnm/romecon98/asses_rec.htm).

[9]*Transition Report 1997: Enterprise Performance and Growth,* European Bank for Reconstruction and Development, 1997, pp. 192–94.

[10]*Business Central Europe* Web site (http://www.bcemag.com/_bcedb/ act_fig.idc).

[11]Ibid.

[12]*Eurasia Economic Outlook,* WEFA Group, February 1998, pp. 11.4–11.5; *Transition Report 1997: Enterprise Performance and Growth,* European Bank for Reconstruction and Development, 1997, pp. 192–94.

[13]Gabor Hunya, "Romania: Recovery and Reforms in Delay," in Leon Podkaminer *et al., Transition Countries: 1997 External Deficits Lower Than Feared, Stability Again a Priority,* Vienna Institute for Comparative Economic Studies, No. 243, February 1998; 44–46; Robert Lyle, "Romania Polishes Global Image," *RFE/RL Newsline,* 26 September 1996.

[14]All data on Bulgaria, unless otherwise noted, are taken from the regular publications of the Bulgarian National Bank and the National Statistical Institute.

[15]Rumen Dobrinsky, "Bulgaria: Distorted Financial Markets Impede Recovery," in Podkaminer *et al.,* pp. 26–28.

[16]*Transition Report 1997,* pp. 158–61.

[17]*Weekly Bulletin: Bulgaria,* Expandia Finance, 23 March 1998.

[18]*Business Central Europe: The Annual, 1997/98,* p. 37.

[19]*Country Report, Bulgaria, 4th Quarter 1997,* Economist Intelligence Unit, pp. 26–28.

[20]*Transition Report 1997,* pp. 161–63.

[21]These and all other data on Albania presented here, except where indicated otherwise, were supplied by Marta Muço, Associate Professor, Economics Faculty, Tirana University.

[22]Fabian Schmidt, "Sleaze Spreads in Pauperized Albania," *Transitions,* vol. 5, no. 3, March 1998, pp. 50–53.

[23]*Transition Report 1997,* p. 214; *Country Report, Albania, 4th Quarter 1997,* Economist Intelligence Unit, pp. 20–21.

[24]OANDA Web site (http://www.oanda.com/cgi-bin/ncc).

[25]RFE/RL *Newsline,* 24 February 1998, citing the Bank of Estonia.

[26]*Statistical Datasheets,* Bank of Estonia, 2 March 1998, p. 36.

[27]Ibid., p. 27.

[28]*Statistical Datasheets,* p. 29.

[29]Ibid., pp. 24, 29; Ardo Hansson, "The Baltic States: Performance Much Improved," *Stockholm Report on East European Economies,* vol. 9, nos. 1–2, 4 July 1997, p. 8.

[30]*Eesti Pank Bulletin,* Bank of Estonia, no 1: 36, 1998 pp. 26–27.

[31]Hansson; *Transition Report 1997,* pp. 167–68.

[32]Ibid.

[33]*Survey of the State Budget,* Ministry of Finance, Republic of Latvia, January 1998; *Monthly Bulletin of Latvian Statistics,* Central Statistical Bureau of Latvia, no. 12, 1997 (January 1998), p. 23.

[34]*Monthly Bulletin of Latvian Statistics,* p. 16.

[35]Ibid., p. 9.

[36]Hansson; *Monthly Bulletin of Latvian Statistics,* pp. 52–53.

[37]*Monthly Bulletin of Latvian Statistics,* pp. 12–13.

[38]Ibid., p. 110; *Monetary Bulletin,* no. 1, 1998, Bank of Latvia; Hansson.

[39]*Country Report, Estonia, Latvia, Lithuania, 4th Quarter 1997,* Economist Intelligence Unit, p. 29.

[40]*Transition Report 1997,* p. 228; *Monthly Bulletin of Latvian Statistics,* pp. 36, 39.

[41]Hansson; *Country Report, Estonia, Latvia, Lithuania,* p. 24.

[42]Hansson; *Business Central Europe* Web site.

[43]*Monthly Bulletin,* Bank of Lithuania, no. 1, 1998, p. 13.

[44]*Country Report, Estonia, Latvia, Lithuania,* p. 40.

[45]*Economic and Social Development in Lithuania,* Department of Statistics of the Government of the Republic of Lithuania, no. 12, 1997.

[46]Ibid., pp. 61–62; Hansson.

[47]*Country Report, Estonia, Latvia, Lithuania,* p. 40.

[48]*Economic and Social Development in Lithuania,* pp. 8–9.

[49] Ibid., p. 11.

[50]Hermine Vidovic, "Slovenia: Remaining on Its Moderate Growth Trajectory," in Leon Podkaminer *et al.*, pp. 53–55.

[51]*Country Report, Slovenia, 4th Quarter 1997,* Economist Intelligence Unit, pp. 19–20.

[52]*Eurasia Economic Outlook,* WEFA Group, February 1998, pp. 13.4–13.11.

[53]Ibid.

[54]*Country Report, Slovenia,* pp. 13–14.

[55]*Eurasia Economic Outlook.*

[56]*Croatian Economic Forecast,* March 1998, Zagrebacka banka.

[57]Ibid., *Bulletin,* Croatian National Bank, February 1998, p. 9. All unattributed figures on Croatia are from the latter.

[58]*Croatian Economic Forecast,* December 1997, Zagrebacka banka.

[59]*Country Report, Bosnia and Hercegovina, Croatia, 4th Quarter 1997,* Economic Intelligence Unit, p. 27.

[60]*Country Report, Bosnia and Hercegovina, Croatia,* p. 31.

[61]The figure is from PlanEcon's Web site (http://www.planecon.com/wage.html).

[62]*Bulletin,* p. 14. There is an alternative unemployment series which shows an even higher rate, e.g., 22.8 percent in October 1997; see the PlanEcon Web site cited in footnote 61.

[63]*Croatian Economic Forecast,* March 1998.

[64]RFE/RL *Newsline,* 29 January 1998.

[65]Ibid., p. 28.

[66]*Business Central Europe,* pp. 37–38; *Transition Report 1997,* pp. 161–63.

[67]Vladimir Gligorov, "FYR Macedonia: Slow Transition Continues," in Podkaminer *et al.,* pp. 38–40.

[68]Ibid.

[69]The external-sector data were provided by Zoran Stavreski, Director, Research Department, National Bank of the Republic of Macedonia.

[70]*Indeks,* December 1997, Federal Statistical Office (Belgrade), p. 2; available on Web site http://www.szs.sv.gov.yu/indeks/decembar/. All unattributed figures on Federal Yugoslavia are from that source. The GDP figure is from *Business Central Europe,* p. 40.

[71]*Country Report, Yugoslavia (Serbia-Montenegro), Macedonia, 4th Quarter 1997,* p. 26. Officially, the dinar is fixed at 3.3 to the Deutsche mark.

[72]*Transition Report 1997,* p. 218; *Business Central Europe,* p. 36.

[73]*Country Report, Bosnia and Hercegovina, Croatia,* pp. 16–17.

[74]*Transition Report 1997,* p. 157.

[75]*Country Report, Bosnia and Hercegovina, Croatia,* p. 13.

THE CIS ECONOMIES: A YEAR OF GROWING PARADOXES

by BEN SLAY *and* MICHAEL WYZAN

The economies in the Commonwealth of Independent States (CIS) were full of paradoxes in 1997.[1] While most of the CIS economies pushed inflation down to (or below) Central European levels, and economic recovery trends strengthened throughout the region, recovery bypassed three of the countries with the lowest inflation rates—Ukraine, Russia, and Moldova. By contrast, if the official numbers are to be believed, Belarus's neo-Soviet economy reported strong growth in 1997. While Georgia and Kyrgyzstan also reported very high growth rates, they continued to be afflicted by serious shortages of such utilities as electricity, heat, and hot water. And although the bounty of Azerbaijan's energy riches began to be realized in 1997, Turkmenistan's immense natural gas reserves experienced such severe problems in getting to market that both gas production and overall industrial output plummeted. Individual CIS economies seemed increasingly to be moving in their own directions, and references to a "common CIS economy" were becoming increasingly pointless.

TRANSCAUCASUS: STRONG RECOVERIES CONTINUE

Some of 1997's best economic news was found in the Transcaucasus, the only CIS region in which all of the constituent states have since 1996 experienced economic growth and enjoyed good relations with the international financial institutions. The three countries nonetheless enjoyed very different years in 1997: Armenia displayed its weakest performance since 1993; Georgia continued to perform strongly, its main macroeconomic categories little changed from 1996; and Azerbaijan saw its best year since independence.

Armenia

Most economic indicators in Armenia deteriorated in 1997 and, although respectable, were worse than projected. GDP growth was 2.7 percent, compared to a projected 6 percent, and down from 5.3 percent in 1996.[2] Consumer price inflation was a disappointing 22 percent for the year, up from 5.7 percent in 1996. In contrast to most other macroeconomic indicators, the fiscal picture improved in 1997, but the budget deficit remained high at 6.8 percent of GDP. The trade deficit for the first eleven months was $608 million, compared to 1996's $556 million.[3]

Despite this deterioration, the IMF and World Bank continued to display confidence in Armenian policy-makers. In November, the World Bank announced that it would provide $200 million in 1997–98 to finance the budget deficit and infrastructure investment.[4] Although the IMF was less supportive, it ultimately released both annual tranches of the three-year, $50 million enhanced structural adjustment facility (ESAF) agreed to in February 1996. Better economic policy-making that followed the formation of Prime Minister Robert Kocharian's government in March 1997 may also have solidified external support for Armenia. In addition to passing new banking legislation and undertaking further liberalization initiatives, privatization acquired greater impetus based on market (as opposed to voucher) mechanisms. This change resulted in the sale of 90 percent of the Armentel telecom monopoly in December.

Azerbaijan

Azerbaijan's GDP grew by 5.8 percent in 1997, following 1.3 percent growth in 1996 (the first increase in GDP recorded since independence).[5] Consumer prices rose by only 0.3 percent for the entire year, well down on 1996's already low 6.7 percent. The state budget deficit was 3.2 percent of GDP during the first nine months of 1997, essentially unchanged from the 1996 level.[6]

Azerbaijani foreign trade was essentially in balance during the first ten months of 1997, and although imports of capital equipment for the oil sector could eventually turn this surplus into a deficit, capital inflows to that sector should keep foreign-exchange reserves healthy.[7] Indeed, the manat strengthened from 4,440 to $1 at the end of 1995 to about 3,900 at the end of 1997. In late December, the IMF awarded Azerbaijan $64 million in a one-year, combined ESAF and extended fund facility. The award followed on the heels of a similar action almost exactly a year earlier in the amount of $219 million.

Privatization also progressed during 1997: mass privatization using voucher auctions got under way in March; while more than 15,000 small firms (70–80 percent of the total) had been auctioned off for cash by the end of the year. Foreigners may participate in cash privatization by purchasing options.

Overall, Azerbaijan's macroeconomic prospects seemed bright. Oil deals worth a prospective $30 billion have already been signed, and the country's Caspian oil fields are expected to yield oil worth $100 billion over the next thirty years. Moreover, these figures do not take into account the revenues that Azerbaijan will gain from the transit of Central Asian oil and gas through its territory. However, Azerbaijan's leaders must avoid excessive optimism, as fundamental domestic and international uncertainties remain. Moreover, the record of other developing countries that experience sudden bursts of oil wealth and do not have long-standing democratic traditions is not encouraging.

Georgia

Georgia's economic performance in 1997 was probably the most impressive in the region. GDP grew by 11.3 percent (slightly above 1996's 11.0 percent), giving Georgia the fastest economic growth in the CIS for the second year in a row.[8] Consumer price inflation was 7.9 percent, while the budget deficit fell from 4.4 percent of GDP in 1996 to around 3.5 percent last year. The tax intake remained astonishingly low, however, with tax revenue a mere 8 percent of GDP.[9]

Due among other things to problems with the customs service, a significant proportion of Georgia's foreign trade went unregistered. The trade deficit in 1997 was about $600 million, more than twice the level of the year before.[10] Balance-of-payments problems abounded, including tensions with Russia over the transit of alcohol from third countries and a $400 million debt to Turkmenistan for natural gas, part of Georgia's total $1.485 billion foreign debt (as of 31 October 1997).[11] A second IMF loan granted in March from the $76 million ESAF agreed upon in February 1996 helped alleviate these tensions, but Georgia's difficult external position suggested that such support would be necessary for some time.

Some 266 Georgian medium-sized and large enterprises were sold in July in "zero cash auctions," in which shares were distributed in proportion to funds paid in by buyers. 1997 also saw the sale of several major enterprises—including a brewery, a bottling plant, and a champagne factory—to foreign investors.[12]

The generally good economic news did not change the fact that these three Transcaucasian countries remained desperately poor. The years of political upheaval and conflict after gaining independence in 1991 had taken their toll, and the collapse of their economies that occurred during that time will take many years to reverse. Despite the country's impending oil bounty, per capita GDP in Azerbaijan ranked below all other CIS countries except for Tajikistan. The average monthly wage in Azerbaijan was only $31 in August 1997; the equivalent figure in Armenia was $22. Georgian salaries (at all of $50 in the third quarter of 1997) were the highest in the Transcaucasus region.[13]

THE WESTERN CIS: STAGNATION AND "LUKANOMICS"

The performance of the Ukrainian, Belarusian, and Moldovan economies in 1997 was perhaps the most paradoxical, warning us against the adoption of simple explanations for economic outcomes. After years of following IMF prescriptions, Moldova fell victim to reform weariness and as of the end of 1997 the Fund was withholding financial support. Although Ukraine, like Moldova (and Russia), reduced inflation rates significantly in 1997, none of these countries were unable to definitively break out of recession. Meanwhile, *dirigiste* "Lukanomics" in Belarus produced what looked like a strong recovery, albeit one with high and rising inflation.

Ukraine

While retail price inflation fell from 40 percent in 1996 to 10.1 percent in 1997 and the hryvnya remained stable in 1997, economic recovery continued to elude Ukraine, as GDP declined by some 4.0 percent.[14] Plummeting trade with Russia, Ukraine's largest trading partner (the dollar value of Russo-Ukrainian trade fell by some 18 percent in 1997),[15] as well as the inability of Ukraine's government and populist parliament to work together, were probably the most important causes of the continuing decline. Political tensions prevented the passage of important tax legislation, kept the 1997 budget from being passed until mid-year, and slowed enterprise and bank privatization and restructuring to a snail's pace. Little progress was made last year in reducing the vast scope of the underground economy, which conservative government estimates place at 43 percent of GDP.[16]

All of this convinced the IMF to hold off on Ukraine's long-awaited $2.4–$2.7 billion Extended Funding Facility (EFF) in 1997, and although a $542 million standby credit was authorized in July, only $152 million had been released by December.[17] While Ukraine did raise $450 million through a Eurobond issue in August, the outbreak of the East Asian financial crisis in October made subsequent attempts to tap the international capital markets ineffective. Ukraine therefore faced a financial squeeze at the end of the year, with the National Bank's refinancing rate rising from 15 percent to 35 percent between November 15 and 26, and yields on Treasury notes rising from 22 to 40 percent.[18]

Ukraine's economy thus ended 1997 in a weak state, the victim of yet another year of indecisive economic policy. Political uncertainty associated with the parliamentary elections in March suggests that more of the same may be in store for 1998.

Moldova

On the one hand, the 1.3 percent increase in Moldovan GDP reported for 1997 by the Statistical Office was quite an improvement on 1996's 8.0 decline, and last year's 11.8 percent increase in consumer prices was below even the 15.1 percent figure reported for 1996.[19] On the other hand, Moldova's fiscal and external deficits spun out of control during 1996–97. The budget deficit rose from 4.9 percent of GDP in 1995 to nearly 10 percent of GDP in the third quarter of 1997; while the current-account deficit seemed likely to have climbed to an unsustainable 15 percent of GDP by the end of 1997, relative to 1995's still-large 6.8 percent.[20]

The IMF reacted to this fiscal collapse by freezing disbursements of the $185 million three-year EFF approved in 1996: only $52 million had been paid out as of February 1998.[21] The IMF also decided not to renew funding until after the March 1998 parliamentary elections, in the hope that the "reform weariness" that overtook Moldovan economic policy during 1996–97 will be reversed.

Belarus

In contrast to the mixed results of reform efforts in Ukraine and Moldova, Belarus seemed to score major successes in 1997 by back-pedaling on reform and closing the door on Western assistance and investment. The autocratic regime of President Alyaksandr Lukashenka, which effectively re-nationalized the Belarusian economy's "commanding heights" in 1996, recreated the (late) Soviet-era controls over prices and commerce last year. These levers, once in place, allowed the regime to issue production targets for key sectors, and then to "convince" managers to attain them. Special foreign-currency stores were another Soviet economic throwback to re-emerge in Belarus in 1997.

On paper, the results of "Lukanomics" were impressive. GDP increased by 10.0 percent, due to 17.6 percent growth in industrial production and 20 percent growth in investment spending.[22] Exports to other CIS countries—mostly Russia, with whom Belarus formed a free-trade area after the 1996 "union" treaty—increased by 35 percent. Abundant credit funneled through the politically subservient banking system kept enterprises awash with liquidity, so that most Belarusian workers got paid on time.

On the other hand, consumer prices rose 64 percent during 1997, one of the highest rates in the CIS last year.[23] These price increases occurred in spite of controls on many consumer-goods prices, suggesting that underlying trends were stronger than the official inflation rate would indicate. The increased energy imports needed to fuel Belarus's economic "miracle" had produced a $1 billion trade deficit (equal to some 15 percent of GDP) by the third quarter of the year.[24] Since Belarus received no commercial or official capital inflows from Western sources, prospects for financing this deficit in 1998 must be viewed as at best uncertain.[25] Data during the first half of 1997 indicated that inventories of industrial products were growing faster than industrial production, suggesting that factories were not producing goods that consumers wanted to buy.[26] Moreover, the absence of IMF supervision of Belarusian statistics lends credence to charges that the official numbers are tailored to fit the regime's "propaganda of success."[27] Skeptics wondered whether Lukashenka's economic strategy would run out of steam before his propagandists run out of hot air.

CENTRAL ASIA: A MIXED BAG

Kyrgyzstan posted double-digit growth in 1997 by closely following IMF prescriptions; and Kazakhstan, Uzbekistan, and Tajikistan also reported increases in GDP last year. Turkmenistan, by contrast, apparently underwent an economic collapse.

Kazakhstan

Although the strong recovery some had predicted for Kazakhstan in 1997 did not materialize, GDP did increase by some 2.0 percent last year, while consumer price inflation fell from 39 percent in 1996 to 17 percent.[28] The relatively weak GDP numbers are somewhat difficult to reconcile with the strong growth in investment (19 percent), retail sales (23 percent), and industrial production (4 percent). Foreign trade suffered a decline. Exports to other CIS countries declined by 18 percent last year, while imports from these countries fell by 22 percent. Russia alone still accounted for 79 percent of Kazakh trade.[29]

Like Azerbaijan's, Kazakhstan's future is tied to its energy sector, and to the pipelines needed to bring its energy to market. A $9.5 billion deal concluded with China in September to develop two large oil fields in the Uzen and Aktyube regions would, upon completion, more than double the cumulative $4.3 billion in foreign direct investment Kazakhstan had attracted by mid-1997.[30] The government also approved a plan to raise annual oil production from approximately 26 million metric tons last year to at least 140 million metric tons by 2010. But while large increases in foreign direct investment must play a large role in such scenarios, the replacement in October of Prime Minister Akezhan Kazhegeldin by Nurlan Balgimbaev may make this more difficult, as Balgimbayev seemed less committed to attracting foreign investment than his predecessor.

Kyrgyzstan

Kyrgyzstan was Central Asia's star performer in 1997. According to Statistical Office data, GDP grew by 10.4 percent, largely on the strength of a whopping 47 percent increase in industrial production, as well as 14 percent export growth. Sales to non-CIS countries increased by a stunning 141 percent last year, so that some 46 percent of Kyrgyzstan's exports were directed outside of the CIS (chiefly to China, Turkey, and Germany).[31] Consumer price inflation also continued to fall, from 31 percent in 1996 to 25 percent last year.

As with much official data produced by the Central Asian countries, there are some peculiarities in Kyrgyzstan's numbers. Perhaps the most striking is the 35 percent decline in capital investment reported for 1997, which is difficult to reconcile with the large increases in GDP and industrial production mentioned above. Still, IMF monitoring of Kyrgyzstan's official numbers suggests that their quality probably did not deteriorate last year, and that a powerful economic recovery is therefore underway.

Uzbekistan

Uzbekistan also reported solid GDP growth of 5.2 percent in 1997, reducing the cumulative decline in GDP during 1991–97 to 13 percent—the smallest among the Soviet successor states.[32] However, the availability and quality of Uzbekistan's official statistics deteriorated in 1997. This may have been due to the country's estrangement from the IMF for much of the year, following the December 1996 suspension of payments from a $185 million standby credit.

That suspension was precipitated by the government's introduction of foreign-exchange controls that month, a move that it justified by referring to foreign exchange shortages that had followed bad cotton and wheat harvests. (Agricultural output officially declined by 6.0 percent in 1996, and cotton exports generally supply around 60 percent of Uzbekistan's foreign-exchange earnings.[33]) However, the official data for 1997 show 4.0 percent growth in agricultural output, as well as 6.5 percent growth in industrial production, and a 13.0 percent increase in retail sales. Although producer price inflation last year was still high—54 percent—it nonetheless represented a reduction from 1996's 133 percent.[34]

Tajikistan

The year 1997 brought the first good news for Tajikistan's economy since the country collapsed into civil war after independence. The peace treaty signed in June 1997 paved the way for a nascent economic recovery, as official data report a 1.7 percent increase in GDP, and consumer-price inflation fell from 255 to 78 percent for the year.[35] Foreign trade flows as of mid-year were up by some 27 percent on 1996, with aluminum and cotton accounting for more than 40 percent of total exports. Still, the country remained desperately poor, with average per-capita monthly wages of only $50.[36]

Turkmenistan

Although the autocratic regime of President Saparmurad Niyazov did manage last year to release historical data for the 1993–95 period, the availability and quality of Ashgabat's official numbers are probably the worst in the CIS. As of February 1998, almost no data for 1997 had been made available to either CIS or UN reporting agencies. However, preliminary data released earlier in the year indicated that Turkmenistan experienced an economic collapse in 1997. Industrial production during the first seven months was down a whopping 35.2 percent over the same period in 1996; natural gas production was down 39 percent during the first five months of the year; while cotton processing was down a stunning 75 percent.[37]

Russia's decision in March to stop pumping Turkmenistan's natural gas through Gazprom's pipeline system was certainly a major cause of these problems, so the Niyazov regime stepped up its efforts to bypass the Russian pipeline grid in 1997. Turkmenistan opened a southern-route gas pipeline to Iran in December 1997, and future plans to construct other pipelines to or through Turkey, Iran, Afghanistan, and Pakistan also moved close to fruition last year. In the long term, however, the government's unwillingness to undertake serious reform, the U.S. sanctions against Iran, and the continuing turmoil in Afghanistan, could frustrate these hopes.

NOTES

[1]Unless otherwise specified, data in this article come from PlanEcon's *Review and Outlook for the Former Soviet Republics,* September 1997. This article does not consider the Russian economy, which has a separate chapter.

[2]Interfax, 3 February 1998.

[3]The information on the budget deficit and the trade balance were provided by Gagik Bakhshian, Deputy Director, Center for Economic Policy Research and Analysis, Yerevan.

[4]RFE/RL *Newsline,* 4 November 1997.

[5]Interfax, 3 February 1998.

[6]Economist Intelligence Unit, *Country Report, Azerbaijan, 4th quarter 1997,* p. 8.

[7]According to official projections, the petroleum sector will run a negative trade balance through 2001 (as imports for use by that sector will exceed oil exports), after which it will generate large and rising trade surpluses. See Christoph B. Rosenberg and Tapio O. Saavalainen, "How to Deal with Azerbaijan's Oil Boom? Policy Strategies in a Resource-Rich Transition Economy," IMF Working Paper WP/98/6, January 1998, p. 11.

[8]Interfax, 3 February 1998.

[9]Ibid., p. 16.

[10]Caucasian Institute for Peace, Democracy and Development, Annotated Daily Headlines of the Georgian Press, 28 January 1998.

[11]TACIS European Expertise Service, p. 38.

[12]Ibid., pp. 41–44.

[13]*Delovoy Mir,* 9 January 1998; TACIS European Expertise Service, p. 49.

[14]These figures come from statements made by Prime Minister Valerii Pustovoitenko and National Bank Governor Viktor Yushchenko, reported in the *Eastern Economist,* 12 and 19 January 1998. The CIS Statistical Committee in February reported a 3.2 percent decline in GDP for January–December 1997, relative to the same period in 1996. (Source: http://www.unicc.org/unece/stats/cisstat/ukr_q.htm.)

[15]Interfax-Ukraina, 20 February 1998.

[16]UNIAN, 3 January 1998.

[17]UNIAN, 8 December 1997.

[18]Interfax-Ukraina, 27 November 1997.

[19]Source:http://www.unicc.org/unece/stats/cisstat/mold_q.htm.

[20]These are author's calculations, based on data presented in PlanEcon's *Review and Outlook for the Former Soviet Republics,* September 1997, pp. 179, 181.

[21]Infotag, 11 February 1998.

[22]Source:http://www.unicc.org/unece/stats/cisstat/bel_q.htm.

[23]Ibid.

[24]Interfax-Belarus Business Report, 3 November 1997.

[25]Russia did provide an $86 million loan at mid-year (Interfax, 13 June 1997), but this credit would not have been able to finance much of a $1 billion trade deficit.

[26]Unsold products accounted for 51 percent of industrial production in June 1997. Source: PlanEcon's *Review and Outlook for the Former Soviet Republics,* September 1997, p. 86.

[27]This point was argued forcefully by Henadz Karpenka, chairman of Belarus's National Economic Council, who termed official rhetoric about rapid economic growth in Belarus "a regular lie" (*Zerkalo Nedeli,* 12 July 1997).

[28]Source:http://www.unicc.org/unece/stats/cisstat/kazakh.htm.

[29]*Delovoy Mir,* 23 October 1997.

[30]*World Economic Outlook,* vol. 2 (Developing and Eurasia), WEFA Group, January 1998, p. 9.11.

[31]Source: http://www.unicc.org/unece/stats/cisstat/kyrgyz.htm, and author's calculations.

[32]Source: http://www.unicc.org/unece/stats/cisstat/uzb.htm.

[33]Ibid.

[34]Ibid.

[35]Source:http://www.unicc.org/unece/stats/cisstat/tajik.htm.

[36]Source: Asia Plus agency, bulletin no. 32.

[37]Source: Interfax, 28 August, 17 June 1997.

CENTRAL EUROPE

IV

Czech Republic

Slovakia

Hungary

Poland

Czech Republic

Population:	10,331,206
Capital:	Prague (pop. 1,215,000)
Major cities:	Brno (pop. 391,000), Ostrava (pop. 331,000), Plzen (pop. 175,000)
Area:	78,864 sq. km.
Major ethnic groups:	Czech 94%, Slovak 3%, Romani 2.4%
Economy:	GDP growth: 1.2%
	Inflation rate: 10.0%
	Average monthly wage: $346
	Unemployment rate: 5.2%

THE END OF THE KLAUS ERA

by MILADA ANNA VACHUDOVA

The year 1997 in the Czech Republic was marked by an economic slowdown, widespread flooding, an exodus of Czech Roma to the West, and the dramatic fall of the government of Prime Minister Vaclav Klaus. Klaus had managed to convince the West (and the Czech public) that the Czech political and economic transition was all but complete. In 1997, it became evident that the privatization process was severely flawed, that important economic reforms still lay ahead, and that the Czech government had neglected critical tasks such as building a middle class, reforming the state administration, battling racism, and supporting a vigorous civil society. More positively, the Czech Republic was invited to begin negotiations on full membership by the European Union (EU) and NATO.

WESTWARD DIPLOMACY

EU membership has been the primary goal of Czech foreign policy since 1990, to be attained through economic reform, political stability, and strong ties with the West. While Klaus lobbied for rapid membership in the EU, he also identified with the so-called "Euroskeptics," questioning the ambitious integration projects envisioned by the Maastricht process. Meanwhile, support for EU membership among Czechs was consistently higher than was support for NATO membership: 61 percent in January 1998 (as compared to 58 percent in September 1997 and 42 percent in March 1996). Klaus had rejected cooperation with Poland and Hungary within the Visegrad group in 1993–94, seeing this as an obstacle to membership in the EU. From the perspective of 1997, when the Czechs found themselves near the bottom of the Visegrad heap, this was amusing at best. A Eurobarometer poll of citizens of the 15 EU member states conducted in 1997 found that 41 percent of respondents favored Czech entry into the EU, which placed the Czech Republic third after Hungary (47 percent) and Poland (44 percent).

The European Commission published a formal Opinion on the Czech Republic's Application for Membership in the European Union in July 1997. The overconfidence of Klaus's Czech Republic was alluded to in a single laconic sentence: "Confident of its progress toward meeting the obligations of EU membership, the Czech Republic has at times shown reluctance to acknowledge difficulties and seek a collaborative approach to resolving them." The Commission found that although the Czech government had made great strides, for example in fulfilling the White Book criteria regarding economic harmonization, it would have to implement very demanding reforms to prepare for EU membership. The Opinion sharply criticized the neglect of state administration reform. It also stressed that the Czech Republic must prepare for adherence to all internal EU market rules; further reform agriculture, commercial banks, and capital markets; improve the environment; and strengthen border controls.

The arms of the state administration in greatest need of reform were the judiciary and the civil service. The judicial system was incompetent and inefficient, and the EU regarded existing reform efforts as insufficient. Meanwhile, the absence of a civil service statute blocked the development of an efficient, independent civil service. The Commission report cited the lack of any coherent plan for public administration modernization as "the single greatest cause for concern" regarding the administrative capacity to apply the acquis communautaire (the body of laws which all new member states must adopt), and characterized existing reform measures as "thoroughly inadequate." It observed that "a wide-ranging reform process will need to be instigated and sustained [. . .] to establish a civil service of the overall quality, level of training, motivation, and flexibility" which is required. This was grave indeed since, among other things, it is the quality and the efforts of the state administration which will qualify the Czech Republic for EU membership.

Negotiations with the EU were due to commence in April 1998 with the so-called "screening process" which will include minute examination of each state's application of the acquis communautaire. The demands on Czech negotiators and ministry officials will be great, as they will be called upon to provide the Commission with immense amounts of well-ordered information. However, dynamic, English-speaking bureaucrats able to think in European dimensions are in short supply. This led some to wonder whether the Czech government can cope simultaneously with the demands of NATO and EU expansion.

The Czech-German Declaration was finally signed by Klaus and German Chancellor Helmut Kohl on 21 January 1997. The declaration was intended to bring about a reconciliation between Czechs and Germans, and draw to a close half a century of strained relations between the two countries. It failed to achieve this goal. In the final document Germany accepted responsibility for World War II (although the Holocaust was not mentioned), while the Czechs apologized for the forced expulsion of three million ethnic Germans from the Sudetenland at the war's end, an action based on the principle of collective guilt. However, the document bypassed several issues, such as the question of reparations for Czech victims of Nazism, Sudeten German support for Hitler, and allied countries' support for the expulsion of the Germans.

The declaration was ratified by the Czech Parliament on 14 February 1997 after a week of stormy debate, marked by the racist and anti-Semitic diatribes of Republican deputies. Party Chairman Miroslav Sladek observed at a January rally that "we can only regret that during the war we killed so few Germans." (For this remark, Sladek was charged with inciting racial hatred, but acquitted in January 1998.) While the coalition parties voted for the declaration, almost one half of the Social Democrats played to anti-German sentiment by voting against. Despite the efforts of President Vaclav Havel and others, reconciliation between Czechs and Germans remained elusive, as Czech society proved unable to accept that it, too, should apologize for past ethnic cleansing.

A GREEN LIGHT FROM NATO

On 8 July 1997 NATO invited the Czech Republic to begin negotiations on membership, along with Hungary and Poland. The Klaus government had actively sought admission to NATO, but exhibited its trademark overconfidence in the Czech Republic's qualifications for membership. Meanwhile, NATO membership enjoyed the support of only a slim majority of Czechs. In the Klaus-dominated period of Czech politics (1993–1997), the government did not exert itself to explain to the public the benefits and responsibilities of NATO membership, nor to underscore that NATO could prevent the security failures which had twice in this century spelled the end of Czechoslovak democracy.

The absence of a pro-NATO campaign by the government created political space for the extremists, the Communists and the extreme right-wing Republicans, who in 1997 painted NATO as the tool of (respectively) American and German imperialists. Opinion polls in 1996 and 1997 showed that as few as one third of Czechs supported NATO membership, while one-third were against and one-third expressed no opinion. By early 1998, those in favor had increased to 54 percent, while 24 percent were against and 22 percent did not know.

The three coalition parties and the Social Democratic Party (CSSD) promised American Secretary of State Madeleine Albright to do their all for Czech entry into NATO during her visit to Prague on 14 July 1997. However, only strong pressure from NATO members in late 1997 compelled the Klaus government to seek greater popular support for NATO membership. Western pressure included reprimands from Albright, who no doubt wondered why she was battling American critics of expansion so fiercely on behalf of the torpid Czechs. As arguments in favor of entry, Czech officials highlighted that the Czech Republic will receive more from the NATO budget than it will contribute, and that no nuclear weapons or foreign troops will be stationed on Czech soil.

Albright laid down three requirements for prospective members in 1997: the adoption of a new strategic concept, the improvement of military interoperability, and the acceptance of a "new responsibility" for European security. Albright asked each candidate to reassess the threats to its security. The Czech "National Strategy Concept," in the making for five years, remained unfinished in 1997. As for interoperability, it became clear in 1997 that the greatest hurdle for the Czech military would be knowledge of English, and that NATO grants for language training had been squandered. The Social Democrats joined the extremists in early 1998 to delay a law on the protection of sensitive information, a requirement for NATO membership. Until it is passed, Czech representatives at NATO—unlike their Polish and Hungarian counterparts—are excluded from negotiations pertaining to classified information.

Prospective members were also to be judged by their participation in joint projects, the level of their defense spending (to reach 2 percent of GDP), and the support of their public for membership. The Czechs were praised for the conduct of their troops serving in United Nations peacekeeping efforts in the former Yugoslavia and for their participation in NATO's Partnership for Peace (PfP). However, unlike most PfP members, the Czechs had not created a joint unit with another PfP state, despite an abiding interest on the part of the Poles. Defense spending rose in 1997 (to 1.7 percent of GDP), but the low level of public support for NATO membership troubled the West.

ECONOMIC MISADVENTURES

The Klaus government, elected in 1992, devoted itself to creating the image that market reform was "complete" in the Czech Republic. It managed for several years to preserve low inflation and very low unemployment, while balancing budgets and attracting foreign investment. In 1997, however, the Czech economic miracle was decidedly over. GDP growth fell to 1.2 percent due to weak export performance, a consequence of insufficient enterprise restructuring and the summer floods. The trade deficit swelled due to an over-valued crown and strong household consumption fueled by overly high wage growth. Lower exports combined with high consumer spending on imports resulted in a steady increase of trade and current account deficits from 1995 to 1997.

Weak tax revenue forced the government to adopt an austerity package in April, which cut expenditures by 23 billion crowns ($750 million) to counter a growing current account deficit. The problems of excessive household consumption and an overvalued exchange rate, however, remained unaddressed and resulted in downward pressure on the crown. The crown fell sharply on 27 May, tumbling from 27 to 35 to the U.S. dollar, when the central bank was finally forced to let the currency float. In June, the government approved another 17 billion crowns in budget cuts, and was unable to pay public sector employees on time due to budget problems.

To counter the rising trade deficit, the Czech government introduced an import deposit scheme in April for a large number of consumer products. The scheme required importers to deposit in a bank account an amount equal to 20 percent of the value of the goods they wished to import. This scheme violated the terms of the Czech Republic's association agreement with the EU, and the European Commission called for its withdrawal. Citing an improvement in the trade deficit (not EU pressure), the Czech government suspended the scheme in August 1997. By the end of 1997, the economy had recovered somewhat, in part due to dramatic growth in exports due to the more competitive exchange rate.

To shore up a sharp decline in popular support resulting from privatization scandals (see sidebar) and from the economic downturn, several key ministers including Finance Minister Ivan Kocarnik and the long-time Minister of Trade Vladimir Dlouhy were replaced in May. As the government began to totter, the coalition parties admitted that they had lacked the courage to implement difficult economic reforms, and that the privatization process had suffered from fundamental flaws. Meanwhile, disagreements on economic policy among (and within) the coalition parties escalated, particularly over price deregulation which was strongly opposed by Josef Lux, chairman of the Christian Democratic Union–Czechoslovak People's Party (KDU-CSL).

There was a general expectation that 1998 would bring higher unemployment, rising prices, and for many a real decline in their standard of living. Future reforms will be painful, as energy, transportation, and rent prices are due to be deregulated and some large "privatized" firms may be allowed to go bankrupt (see sidebar). Because Czech society was persuaded by Klaus that radical reform was complete, the ensuing economic hardships will be difficult for Czechs to understand.

A dramatic test of the government's ability to respond to social needs came with the heavy rains that engulfed large parts of Moravia and Eastern Bohemia in July. The floods left about one-third of the country under water for several days, killed 56 people and caused over $2 billion in damages. Some 58,000 people had to be evacuated from 536 flooded towns and villages. Over 8,000 soldiers were mobilized by the government to direct rescue efforts, help with emergency repair work, and guard against looting. Thousands of people were left homeless by the floods, which in some cases swept away the totality of their possessions. The government promised aid to families who lost their homes, and was generally praised for the way that it coped with the floods. Czechs responded to the tragedy with admirable solidarity, sending donations to various humanitarian agencies.

RACISM AND THE ROMA

The Roma represent the only significant ethnic minority in the Czech Republic (up to 300,000 persons), and suffer widespread discrimination, occasional violence, and a deteriorating socio-economic position in Czech society. Racism and xenophobia were represented in parliament by the extreme right-wing Republican Party of Miroslav Sladek. While Sladek's party and skinheads were its most visible and brutal face, racism was widespread among ordinary citizens and also among "moderate" politicians, especially at the local level. In surveys up to 90 percent of Czech respondents said that they would not want to have a Roma as a neighbor. In 1997 racist violence increased in the Czech Republic, and thousands of Roma left the country in search of political asylum in Canada and Western Europe.

In November 1997 skinheads murdered a Sudanese student in Prague. The killing occasioned a few demonstrations and a long-overdue public discussion on racism in Czech society. The officially reported incidence of violent, racially motivated attacks on Roma and dark-skinned foreigners was not high. From 1990 through 1997, 1,210 racially motivated attacks were recorded in the Czech lands by the Documentation Center for Human Rights. In a country where the police were generally thought indifferent or sympathetic to such attacks, it is likely that many more went unreported. The number of reported attacks per year rose steadily since 1990. Of the 1,210 attacks noted by the independent center, only one-third were officially classified as racially motivated; and of the 19 incidents in which people were killed, only two were classified as racially motivated. Only about 10 percent of attackers ended up in court, and more than 95 percent of those convicted received suspended sentences.

The government, the police, and the courts failed to make a stand against the rise of racially motivated crime. While police were accused by human rights organizations and Roma leaders of doing little to investigate even violent crimes against the Roma, judges usually refused to rule a crime to have been racially motivated even when it was plainly so. Only 146 people were convicted in the Czech lands for racially motivated crimes in 1997 (up from 5 in 1991). Light sentences sent the message that such attacks were not considered serious crimes.

Several hundred Roma families left for Canada after an August 1997 television documentary portrayed Canada as a wealthy country free of racism. Some local authorities reacted by encouraging Roma to leave the country and even offering them financial assistance on the condition that they abandon their tenancy rights. Between January and August 1997, Canada granted refugee status to 22 Roma from the Czech Republic on the grounds that their homeland was unable or unwilling to provide protection for them. Over 1,200 Roma had applied by late 1997. In October 1997, Canada reinstated visa requirements for Czech citizens.

Another wave of Roma left for the United Kingdom in October 1997. Roma representatives believed there to be some 800 Roma seeking political asylum in the United Kingdom or France by the close of 1997. At that time, about ten Czech Roma families had been granted asylum since 1990 in the United Kingdom. However, soon after the October 1997 exodus British authorities returned 563 Czech and Slovak Roma to their countries.

Even in the face of this international embarrassment, many Czech politicians maintained that the Roma were merely economic migrants. Still, in response to the exodus and the international pressure, the Klaus government in its waning days did emphasize its willingness to work to improve the situation of the Roma, and held talks with Roma leaders. In September it agreed to create a new commission for Romani affairs to advise the government. In November CSSD Chairman Milos Zeman called for making the skinhead movement illegal, which was criticized by human rights groups as a useless, populist move. Meanwhile, the parliament ratified the Council of Europe's Framework Convention for the Protection of National Minorities in December 1997. The Framework Convention will require the Czech government to report on the anti-discrimination measures taken by each state organ; there were no such measures taken in 1997.

The Citizenship Law of 1993 left most Czechoslovak Roma residing in the Czech Republic stateless, for various reasons. Some had a criminal record, or could not prove residence in the Czech lands for the two previous years. Others had not annulled Slovak citizenship, or simply failed to navigate the complex bureaucratic path to citizenship. Despite a constructive amendment to the law in 1996, international foundations and organizations were still assisting Czech Roma in overcoming the bureaucratic obstacles to citizenship in 1997. Several European human rights groups advised the EU to require candidate countries to improve their treatment of the Roma minority as a condition of membership. The Roma have already proven that they can migrate in large numbers, which will make their treatment a particularly sensitive issue for the EU when considering the Czech application. As the Czech Republic nears EU membership, humanitarian and self-interested advocacy of the Romani cause in Western Europe is bound to increase.

THE SHIFTING POLITICAL LANDSCAPE

The dissolution of Czechoslovakia aside, the first four years of government by Klaus were marked by political calm. After the June 1992 elections, Klaus's victorious Civic Democratic Party (ODS) formed a coalition with the Civic Democratic Alliance (ODA) and the Christian Democratic Union–Czechoslovak People's Party (KDU-CSL). This coalition controlled 105 out of 200 parliamentary seats, and held together until the elections of 1996. Klaus's three-party coalition fell short of a parliamentary majority in the June 1996 elections. In the 200-seat parliament, Klaus's coalition won 99 seats, while the Social Democratic Party (CSSD) won 61, the Communist Party (KSCM) 22, and the extreme right-wing Republican Party (SPR-RSC) 18. From this point on, Klaus headed a minority government that had to contend with a deteriorating economy and mounting political opposition until its fall in November 1997. The two extremist parties—the Republicans and the Communists—together garnered around 20 percent of the vote in 1992 and 1996. The fact that one fifth of Czech voters opt for extremist parties, that were unacceptable partners for all the other parties made it much harder to put together coalition governments with a majority in parliament.

Throughout 1997, popular support for Vaclav Klaus and his coalition government declined, and disagreements among the coalition parties increased. In June the coalition government only survived a confidence vote (101–99) thanks to support from the independent deputy Jozef Wagner. Meanwhile, conflicts within the ODA and the ODS further weakened the coalition. In October the most popular ODS politician, Josef Zieleniec, dramatically resigned as foreign minister, explaining that "very serious decisions" were made regarding the party's financing without the knowledge of the political leadership. This presaged a series of financial scandals which first doomed Klaus's government, then split the ODS, and seemed likely to obliterate the ODA. The independent deputy and former dissident Jaroslav Sedivy replaced Zieleniec as foreign minister, and shielded the Czech Republic's foreign policy from its domestic turmoil as best he could well into 1998.

ODS ministers Jan Ruml and Ivan Pilip called upon Klaus to resign as prime minister on 28 November (while he was away in Sarajevo). Klaus would have fallen in any case, as the KDU-CSL left the government later the same day. He resigned on 30 November. Klaus and other ODS leaders were accused of financing the ODS through illegal means and disposing of a secret bank account abroad. Several individuals who were listed as having given the ODS millions of crowns turned out to be fictitious: the real donors were allegedly the new owners of recently privatized firms and of investment funds. While the three coalition parties and the Social Democrats have all faced various party financing scandals, it became apparent that money flowed into the ODS and also the ODA party coffers in exchange for favors related to privatization and banking. These two parties were in charge of the finance ministry, the economic ministries, the state banks, and the institutions created to oversee privatization.

President Havel's political importance increased dramatically at the end of

1997 as he brokered the creation of a new government. On 10 December, Havel delivered a dramatic "state of the union" speech to the parliament and senate. Havel forcefully criticized the outgoing government for its "petty bourgeois provincialism," and for its suppression of Czech civil society. He lamented the government's inattention to rules and laws, particularly in privatization and the capital markets, which resulted in the most immoral becoming the most successful. He called for sweeping reforms in many spheres and a "merciless war" against Czech chauvinism. The speech represented a forceful and thorough attack on the ousted Klaus.

On 16 December Havel asked Czech National Bank Governor Josef Tosovsky to form a new interim government. By the end of December, Tosovsky had constructed a center-right government which included independents as well as members of the ODA, the KDU-CSL, and the anti-Klaus wing of the ODS. Klaus complained bitterly that he was excluded from the process of forming a new government. The CSSD promised to support the new government in exchange for elections in June 1998.

Klaus triumphed over Ruml's anti-Klaus faction to win re-election as chairman of the ODS in mid-December. Ruml, Pilip, and others then left the ODS to create a new party, the Freedom Union (US) in January 1998. It must convince the electorate that it is truly a new, uncorrupted force in Czech politics, despite harboring many former ODS and ODA members. Unlike the ODS, the Freedom Union presented itself as open to input from all corners of society and to influences from abroad. The Freedom Union (like Havel) rebuked the Klaus government for tolerating a market without rules, and for undermining law, morality, and the middle class. The party called for a revival of civil society and the creation of reliable state institutions.

CSSD Chairman Milos Zeman was widely expected to become prime minister after the June 1998 elections (probably in a coalition government with the KDU-CSL). Improving dramatically on its modest 7 percent showing in 1992, the CSSD had received 26 percent of the vote in 1996, and it received over 30 percent in some opinion polls in 1997. CSSD Vice Chairman Petra Buzkova was the most popular politician in the country in 1997. The CSSD called for a battle against corruption, reform of the health and education systems, and protection of living standards. It thus opposed the prompt deregulation of rent, transportation, and energy prices.

Anticipating the June 1998 elections, the CSSD also played to Czech parochial sentiments. Although they had renounced cooperation with the Republicans and the Communists, CSSD deputies voted with the extremists on certain issues, such as the Czech-German Declaration and entry into NATO. In early 1998, the Social Democrats voted to defer the parliament's ratification of NATO accession. They feared that if they voted for NATO membership in parliament before the June 1998 elections they would lose anti-NATO voters to the extremists. The party's program did call for NATO membership, subject to a national referendum. However, although only one half of the social democrat electorate supports Czech entry into NATO, Zeman made no attempt to persuade the other half.

KLAUS'S POLITICAL LEGACY

From June 1992 to June 1996, the Klaus government enjoyed a striking degree of political freedom, which it augmented by excluding and undermining alternative poles of opinion, such as non-governmental organizations, the media, and an independent civil service. This practice stunted Czech civil society and impeded the creation of a new class of Czech elites. The Klaus government delayed the creation of a legal framework for non-governmental organizations, and avoided dialogue or cooperation with civic groups. No law was passed providing for an independent civil service. No effort was made to foster public discussion and few public information campaigns were attempted. No freedom of information law was passed. An obsession with the economy led to disregard for reform in other spheres. As President Havel argued in his December 1997 address, the absence of civic involvement and the loss of faith in government cannot be measured by economists, but is a legacy of the Klaus governments. To Klaus's credit, however, the Czech Republic was kept on a resolutely pro-Western and pro-market trajectory.

If the CSSD wins the June 1998 elections, a Zeman government will perhaps tackle some of the problems neglected by Klaus, particularly the crumbling health-care and education systems. Its European orientation, however, is bound to be less pronounced. Pressure from European institutions and particularly from West European social democratic parties (with which Zeman likes to identify) will be integral in transforming Zeman from a populist to a statesman. As the European Commission studied Czech political and economic reform more closely in 1997, it equipped itself to steer the next Czech government toward addressing the deficiencies of the Czech reform process under Klaus.

GLOSSARY

CSSD	Social Democratic Party
KDU-CSL	Christian Democratic Union–Czechoslovak People's Party
KSCM	Communist Party of Czech Lands and Moravia
ODA	Civic Democratic Alliance
ODS	Civic Democratic Party
SPR-RSC	Republican Party
US	Freedom Union

Sidebar: WAS IT PRIVATIZATION?

by MILADA ANNA VACHUDOVA

The privatization program launched in 1992, the crown jewel of Vaclav Klaus's reforms, began to seem less impressive in 1997. Serious problems became evident in the Czech economy, many of them related to the privatization process. Voucher privatization had failed to restructure and to privatize enterprises, while government policy had stifled the creation of new enterprises and set the stage for corruption in the distribution of the firms inherited from communism.

That the Klaus government allowed only Czech actors to take part in privatization severely hampered necessary enterprise restructuring. The exclusion of foreign investors from the voucher privatization meant that most "privatized" enterprises generally received no influx of capital or know-how, and thus lacked the tools to increase their competitiveness. Meanwhile, the financial structure of the Czech Republic became an opaque maze of interconnected banks, investment funds, and newly privatized firms. Many Czechs sold their vouchers to so-called investment funds, allowing such funds to gain control of perhaps 70 percent of privatized firms. Most of these funds were in turn controlled by one of four major banks, which in their turn were still partly owned by the state in 1997. The "privatized" firms were greatly indebted to the banks, and the banks were often called upon by the government to decide which enterprises would receive state financing. State-owned banks were therefore simultaneously the owners, the creditors, and sometimes the auditors of "privatized" firms. In 1997, the Czech Republic was criticized by the International Monetary Fund, World Bank, and the Organization for Economic Cooperation and Development for the slow pace of bank privatization. The Social Democratic Party (CSSD), however, declared that it will put off bank privatization for two years if it heads the next government.

Privatization not only failed to restructure and to privatize, it created an investment climate distinctly unfavorable to new, legitimately private firms. To forestall the shocks of economic restructuring, communist-era managers were offered advantageous loans and loan-forgiveness. State-owned banks, after "privatization" the indirect owners of old communist enterprises, were happy to oblige, as they could always turn to the state for more cash. The liquid capital available to new firms was thus limited. Moreover, new firms were subject to burdensome taxes. All of this slowed the rise of a new middle class.

In addition, voucher privatization led to massive corruption. Three deficiencies in the privatization process produced the conditions for "tunneling," defined as financial operations by which the managers of investment funds, banks, and enterprises transfer their firm's most choice assets to other businesses which are owned by the managers themselves (or by their relatives and associates). While these "managers" enriched themselves, the legal owners—for example the shareholders in an investment fund—were effectively robbed. One of the greatest instances of tunneling was from the CS Investment Fund, whose shareholders lost $40 million to the managers' bank accounts abroad in early March 1997. (Observers charged that the Ministry of Finance could have intercepted the stolen money had it acted promptly on a warning from the mediating bank.)

The first such deficiency sprang from Klaus's desire to jump-start the Czech economy by privatizing as much and as rapidly as possible. This priority led to a disregard for the details of who got rich by what means. Some advisors close to

Klaus advocated "switching off the light": allowing the initial property allocations to sort themselves out without state oversight. Secondly, gaping holes in the legal code governing the capital market and the banking sector created the opportunity for managers to legally steal from owners. As of 1997 there was still no law to effectively protect shareholders or members of cooperatives from tunneling. Thirdly, even when confronted with persistent tunneling, the Klaus government failed to use what instruments it had to staunch the flow of assets into foreign bank accounts. When attempted, state oversight in banking and the capital markets was hampered by a shortage of able and experienced staff. Instead of building a society of shareholders, privatization thus alienated the average citizen from a political system increasingly seen as corrupt.

TRUTH, FREEDOM, AND THE PURSUIT OF PROFITS

by JAN CULIK

With holdings in 10 commercial broadcasting ventures or production companies in a region that stretches from Germany to Ukraine, Central European Media Enterprises (CME) is building a broadcast empire in Central and Eastern Europe. *The Financial Times* estimates that if CME obtains broadcast licenses in Poland and Ukraine, the company's combined stations will reach 100 million viewers by the year 2000. CME will have access to advertising markets worth nearly $3 billion.

In launching commercial television stations, CME often evokes the ideals of free enterprise, pluralism, and independent journalism. Ronald Lauder, a CME founder and an heir to the Estee Lauder cosmetics fortune, has argued that he created a commercial television empire to help champion independent thought and democracy. "I felt that in order to have a democracy, you had to have free media," he said in a 1996 *New York Times* interview.

Yet part of the key to CME's success may lie in exploiting post-communist governments' inexperience in media regulation. As CME stated in its October 1996 U.S. Security and Exchange Commission (SEC) prospectus summary, "In many countries the regulatory systems as they apply to private (and especially foreign) investors in broadcasting stations are relatively new and untested."

In commenting on CME's management of its media holdings in the Czech Republic, Vladimir Zelezny, chief executive of Nova TV, CME's highly profitable Czech television station, said in 1995: "Unfortunately, we are in a situation when we—the media—sometimes have to use methods which, well, they are legal, but perhaps they are not quite correct."

CME was dealt a surprise blow in late June when the Hungarian government awarded two broadcast franchises to a consortium, rejecting CME's bid. That left CME without a presence in the top unclaimed market in Central and Eastern Europe. Later in the year a $750 million lawsuit was filed against CME and

Lauder for allegedly undermining another Western company's contract to provide programming and sell advertising for Ukrainian state television's UT-2 (which reaches 93 percent of Ukrainian viewers). The suit charges CME with bribery and cooperation with groups alleged to have "criminal connections" and "corrupt methods." A CME spokesperson has said the suit filed by Perekhid Media Enterprises "is legally and factually meritless and [CME] will vigorously contest it."

Whatever techniques CME used in Ukraine, its strategies in the Czech Republic have been highly effective. In 1996, its third year of operations, Nova earned $44 million in station operating income on revenues of $108 million, according to *Forbes* magazine. In 1996, CME reported to the SEC that the company had received a 107 percent return on its original investment. CME owns a 93.2 percent stake in Nova as well as an 83.7 percent interest in the nationwide Radio Alfa.

In Nova, CME has created a highly commercial enterprise that is almost fully owned by a foreign company and which broadcasts in a practically unregulated environment. In much of Western Europe and in the United States, where television broadcasting is regarded as a specialized business because it can influence public attitudes and the political and cultural climate, such a situation would be illegal at worst, questionable at best. In the Czech Republic, Jan Kasal, the head of the parliamentary media commission, has said that television broadcasting is a business like any other. The most important thing, he said, is that Nova TV pays taxes.

As critic Jaroslav Veis, writing in *Literarni noviny* in February, pointed out:

> "When, four years ago [. . .] the Council for Radio and Television Broadcasting chose the CET 21 group [for the nationwide broadcasting license], there were several reasons. The CET 21 project promised to fulfill a number of informational, cultural, educational and other aims. [. . .] I cannot say [. . .] that some people did not suspect [. . .] the end result of the process [of creating a commercial television station] in a country with imperfect laws. [. . .] It was highly likely that [. . .] the station would turn into a money-making machine and that all the pledges of high-quality programming would be forgotten."

SEX AND SITCOMS

CME operates Nova, currently its only profitable station, on behalf of the Czech and Slovak company CET 21, which holds the broadcast license. CME now has financial control over Nova, and, were it not for public outcry and media and political scrutiny, CME would also have complete control over Nova's broadcasting license, a license originally awarded to CET 21 and which, by law, is nontransferable.

Taking advantage of the inexperience of the Czech parliament and the Council for Radio and Television Broadcasting, CME has evaded the spirit of parliamentary regulation and created a largely unregulated environment for Nova. Standards of objectivity and quality in programming as originally required in the broadcast license agreement now seem forgotten; there are no teletext subtitles for the deaf, no children's educational programs, no music apart from pop-music videos.

That situation helps to further destabilize Czech cultural identity, which was already undermined by the communist regime. Politicians are reluctant to publicly criticize Nova. "Nova's political influence ensures the company will probably prevail," *The Wall Street Journal* wrote on 30 April. "They can make or break us," a senior parliament member told the reporter.

Nova's impact on the Czech media scene could be beneficial if intelligently regulated by parliament. Milan Smid, a specialist in Czech television broadcasting at Charles University, says Nova has brought plurality to the Czech television scene. "In most of the other post-communist countries, public service television still enjoys a monopoly and is subservient to the government. I know that when it comes to the crunch, Nova will also support those who are in power. [. . .] Maybe Nova has released Czech public service television from intense political pressure by the government, to which public service television stations are directly exposed in many other post-communist countries."

CME-produced programs have adapted Western television formats to local tastes. CME's October 1996 SEC prospectus describes the company's programming strategy as: "A mix of locally and internationally produced movies, series, talk shows, variety shows, sports, and news. [. . .] Broadcasting a significant amount of locally produced programming and developing a distinctive independent news program give[s] a strong local identity, [. . .] appeal[s] to local tastes, and [is] desired by the local regulatory authorities." Yet CME also relies heavily on popular American entertainment. Nova does not hesitate to use sex, violence, nudity, and voyeurism to assure itself of an audience—a situation comparable to the excesses of Italian commercial stations and some European satellite broadcasters. The Hungarian government, in rejecting CME's bid for broadcast franchises, cited Nova's entertainment programming.

Yet that formula has been hugely successful: estimates of the number of Czechs who watch Nova range from 54 percent to 70 percent, depending on the audience monitoring method. While Nova is at times more daring than Czech public service television, especially in tabloid-style news coverage, its news and current-affairs coverage is not universally admired. In a 1996 survey, 39 percent of respondents regarded Nova's news programs as objective compared with 46 percent who deemed Czech state television's news programming objective. In January and again in May, the Council for Radio and Television Broadcasting warned Nova that its license was in jeopardy because of biased news broadcasts and derogatory comments toward the council and Czech (public service) television made by Nova chief executive Zelezny on the program "Ask the Director."

FROM DIPLOMACY TO BUSINESS DEALS

The chairman of CME is the fifty-two-year-old Lauder, who left Estee Lauder in 1983 after 17 years with the firm. In 1986 and 1987, he served as U.S. ambassador to Austria and, in 1989, made an unsuccessful bid for New York City mayor. As ambassador, according to Frederick Kempe writing in *The Wall Street Journal* in 1991: "Mr. Lauder was criticized by the Austrian press and his own staff for traveling with a team of personal bodyguards paid for by his mother, who was worried about terrorists. When he departed, newspapers attacked him for leaving Austria with national art treasures that he had bought. [. . .] In Prague, government official Richard Wagner boiled as Mr. Lauder talked about the urgent need to shape up the historic Wenceslas Square with a development plan of his own conception. 'If you want to do business here, don't ever come back with that man,' Mr. Wagner told two of Mr. Lauder's partners."

Early in 1990, Lauder recruited Robie Mark Palmer, a career diplomat and then-U.S. ambassador to Hungary, as chief executive officer for the Central European Development Corporation (CEDC). Lauder more than tripled Palmer's salary, to $350,000 annually, and gave him a generous stake in the business.

As ambassador to Hungary from 1986 to 1990, Palmer promoted contacts between East and West and untrammeled, American-style entrepreneurship. Palmer was on close terms with Hungarian Communist Party head Karoly Grosz, Prime Minister Miklos Nemeth, and politburo members Imre Poszgay and Rezso Nyers. On taking up the ambassadorial post, Palmer quickly aligned himself with Hungarian dissidents. As a publicity stunt, he held separate "hamburger summits" in the Budapest branch of McDonald's restaurant with Karoly Grosz and the Soviet ambassador to Hungary. As early as July 1989, Palmer suggested the idea of launching independent newspapers and broadcast stations in Hungary, with American backing.

Palmer made headlines when he announced his CEDC appointment. He said he would not leave Hungary until after the March 1990 general elections and that he would not resign from the U.S. State Department until July. The State Department, however, considered it "unseemly of Mr. Palmer to stay on any longer than it took to pack his bags."

CEDC began business by purchasing half a Hungarian bank, a Hungarian vineyard, and some other businesses. In 1992, CEDC invested $400 million (which later grew to $1 billion) in a business center at Checkpoint Charlie, near the former Berlin Wall. But complex legal negotiations delayed the start of construction until 1994. Investments in broadcasting were more successful, especially after CME was incorporated in 1990 as the media arm of CEDC.

LEGAL LOOPHOLES

In 1993, CME joined forces with a group of Slovak and Czech intellectuals who had formed CET 21. CET 21 won the broadcasting license for the first Czech nationwide commercial television station. That station became Nova TV.

According to the 1995 CME annual report, the company invested $9.265 million dollars to launch Nova TV—although Palmer told *The New York Times* in 1994 that CME contributed $47 million. The $9.265 million represented 66 percent of the original investment in the station. When Nova began broadcasting in February 1994, its programs were much more down-market than the programs described in the proposal submitted to the licensing committee. One of the original owners of CET 21, Fedor Gal, now calls that proposal "nonviable." As the parliamentary media commission revised legislation after pressure from various lobby groups, most of the 31 broadcasting conditions stipulated when the license was granted were removed. Commission member Martin Priban, writing *in Mlada fronta Dnes* in 1997, explained that "all the quality conditions were abolished so that every broadcaster could have the same conditions."

By 1996, with Nova's financial success assured, CME began taking steps to ensure it had firm control over the jewel in the crown of its broadcasting empire. The original plan was for CET 21 to remain as license holder but for CME to have veto power over all CET 21's decisions. If CET 21 continued to control the broadcasting license, it could eventually return the license to the Council for Radio and Television Broadcasting. And without controlling the license, CME could never sell Nova. In July 1996, CME crafted a loan agreement to pay Zelezny $5.2 million so he could buy a 43.31 percent stake in CET 21 from four of the original five CET 21 members. Zelezny's holdings in CET 21 rose to a majority 60 percent. In the loan agreement, he pledged to exercise his voting rights only as directed by CME.

But CME could not fully carry out that plan in public. Details of the loan agreement, made public in late 1996 and early 1997, provoked public outcry. In March 1997, the original loan agreement was amended. Zelezny now has a controlling interest in CET 21 but has seemingly been released from his duty to ensure that CME can veto all CET 21 decisions. Yet according to the 1996 CME annual report: "CET 21 has agreed to provide Nova TV with exclusive access to the use of the broadcast license. CME [may now] appoint five of the seven members of Nova TV's Committee of Representatives, which directs the affairs of Nova TV." The Council on Radio and Television Broadcasting launched an investigation into charges that the scheme invalidated Nova's broadcast license but ended the investigation in June, apparently approving the existing arrangement. One of the former owners of CET 21, Peter Krsak, is suing CME because he says the way CME gained control over the shares of the other four former owners is illegal. The sale made them millionaires.

In December 1996, the Czech government lost all formal control over changes in the ownership of Nova after parliament changed the media legislation and the broadcasting council annulled Condition 17 of Nova's broadcast license, the last of the original 31 conditions, which required proposed changes in license ownership to be approved by the council. Thus, the Bermuda-registered CME now controls the Czech Republic's most influential and profitable commercial television station.

As a result of the abolishment of Condition 17, the value of CME's shares on the American NASDAQ had risen to $37 by January 1997 from an August 1996 level of $22. Shares dropped sharply in April and May, however, possibly in connection with political and economic difficulties in the Czech Republic, and by July had leveled off at $26 following the news of CME's failed bid for the Hungarian television market.

IN THE (CLOSED) PUBLIC EYE

Until recently, the Czech government did not seem interested in monitoring Nova's adherence to the country's media law. But in late June, the parliamentary media commission launched an investigation into whether Nova's use of the CET 21 broadcast license is legal. The public still seems unconcerned about Nova's escalating influence. Vladimir Mlynar, editor in chief of *Respekt,* a current affairs weekly, said in a public debate that Nova can broadcast whatever it likes because, after all, it is a private station.

Also in March, David Stogel, a CME director, wrote to the East European Media List, an e-mail discussion list with more than 600 members, and offered to provide information about his company. In a letter posted to the list, Stogel was asked about several topics, including whether CME infringed on the Czech media law by obtaining control of the Nova license; whether CME's business strategy in Central and Eastern Europe is based on exploiting those countries' weak media regulatory systems; whether it would be permissible for a foreign company to own more than 90 percent of a nationwide terrestrial television broadcaster in the United States or Great Britain; and whether CME regards the statements by Zelezny on "Ask the Director" as conforming to the requirement that Nova TV should "provide objective and balanced information, which is necessary for [the viewer to form his/her own] free opinions," as stated for instance in the October 1996 CME prospectus. Stogel never responded to those questions.

CME has repeatedly tried to raise capital in the United States to extend its television empire. In enticing investors, it has held up Nova's stunning financial success. Yet the operating conditions Nova enjoys are exceptional and it is doubtful whether they can soon be replicated in other post-communist countries. Nevertheless, Romania and Ukraine seem the most likely countries for the next CME success. Why? They are the countries where media legislation is weakest.

NOTE

Reprinted with kind permission from *Transitions* magazine, July 1997.

Slovakia

Population:	5,324,632 (1993)
Capital:	Bratislava (pop. 448,785)
Major cities:	Kosice (pop. 238,886); Presov (pop. 90,963), Nitra (pop. 86,679)
Area:	49,036 sq. km.
Major ethnic groups:	Slovak 86%; Hungarian 10.7%; Romani 1.6%; Czech, Moravian, and Silesian 1.1%; Ruthenian, Ukrainian 0.6%
Economy:	GDP growth: 6.0%
	Inflation rate: 6.2%
	Average monthly wage: $321
	Unemployment rate: 12.5%

FALLING BEHIND

by SHARON FISHER

Continued political struggles and foreign policy failure were the main features of 1997 in Slovakia. It will be remembered as the year the country officially fell out with the group of fast-track states for integration with NATO and the European Union (EU), mainly because of Slovakia's perceived "democratic deficit." Although political conflict had been raging in Slovakia ever since the fall 1994 election victory of Prime Minister Vladimir Meciar's Movement for a Democratic Slovakia (HZDS), it grew even fiercer in 1997 as the government's respect for the rule of law further deteriorated. While the ruling parties continued to show their intolerance for opposition, attacks were made on the foundations of the state, including the presidency, the Constitutional Court, and even the National Bank of Slovakia (NBS).

The most memorable political event in 1997 was the 23–24 May referendum. The ballot was supposed to ask four questions: if the people favored Slovakia's entry into NATO, if they wanted nuclear weapons deployed on Slovak territory, if they favored having military bases in Slovakia, and if they wanted direct presidential elections. The first three questions were put forward by the HZDS and approved by the parliament in February, while the last question was proposed by the center-right opposition parties, which collected 521,580 valid signatures in a petition drive in order to launch a referendum. President Michal Kovac decided to call the two referenda on the same day.

In launching the NATO referendum, the ruling parties were apparently looking for an excuse, since they knew that Slovakia's chances of obtaining a membership invitation at the July Madrid summit on NATO enlargement were extremely slim. By including the controversial second and third questions, the cabinet was clearly hoping that the people would vote "no" to all three. In fact, although NATO and EU integration were listed in the government's program as its top foreign policy objectives, the HZDS's junior coalition partners—the Slovak National Party (SNS) and the Association of Workers of Slovakia (ZRS)—openly encouraged their supporters to vote "no" to each of the three referendum questions relating to NATO.

The main reason why the opposition demanded a referendum on direct presidential elections was its fear that when President Kovac's term expired in March 1998, the country would be without a president; since any given candidate would find it difficult to muster the three-fifths parliamentary majority needed to replace him. In that case, the Meciar government would take over some presidential duties, thereby further strengthening its control over society and leaving the country in an unclear constitutional position, particularly since the president's signature is required for passing laws. Meciar was clearly surprised by the opposition's proposal, which marked the opposition parties' first real attempt to "take matters into their own hands" to prevent the ruling coalition from doing what it wanted. Apparently increasingly nervous about the chances for the opposition's success, the government asked the Constitutional Court to decide whether it was possible to change the constitution through a referendum. The court finally addressed the issue just days before the referendum was to take place, ruling that a referendum on direct presidential elections was legal and that a constitutional change could be the subject of a referendum. However, the court declared that even if citizens voted in favor of direct presidential elections, the question of how the law would be changed remained uncertain. The constitution states that deputies are expected to vote "according to their conscience."

The government argued that the court's decision meant that the question on direct presidential elections would not be legally binding and should therefore not be included on the ballots, and Interior Minister Gustav Krajci ordered that ballots be printed with only the three questions on NATO. More than 90 percent of eligible voters boycotted the referendum, making it invalid. In a press conference on 26 May, President Kovac noted that the referendum would have "very important internal and external consequences for Slovakia," and he warned that the country risked "international isolation." That same day, Pavol Hamzik resigned as foreign minister, noting that he wanted his resignation to signal that Slovakia's "vital international interests" were being subordinated to domestic battles for power. Zdenka Kramplova, a virtually unknown woman with a degree in agriculture, became Slovakia's sixth foreign minister since independence after several others refused the job. Her appointment as foreign minister was surprising even to the HZDS's coalition partners. Although Prosecutor Michal Barila on 19 September proposed that Krajci be charged in the referendum affair, ten days later the charges were dropped because of "insufficient evidence."

Another case in which the government ignored the Constitutional Court was that of parliamentary deputy Frantisek Gaulieder. Gaulieder, a founding HZDS member, was stripped of his deputy mandate in December 1996 after he publicly criticized the government and quit the HZDS parliamentary caucus. The parliament removed Gaulieder's mandate on the basis of a letter in which he allegedly offered to give up his seat, even though Gaulieder claimed he had never signed the letter and wanted to retain his mandate. The Constitutional Court on 24 July ruled that the parliament had violated Gaulieder's constitutional rights when it revoked his mandate; however, it said that the mandate could not be restored automatically but only through a parliamentary vote. The ruling parties apparently feared that if they reinstated Gaulieder's seat, more coalition deputies would follow him in deserting their parties, and a number of top HZDS representatives—including Meciar, parliament chairman Ivan Gasparovic, and legal expert Jan Cuper—launched verbal attacks against the Constitutional Court. On 30 September, the parliament voted against reinstating Gaulieder's seat.

Several cases of politically related violence remained unresolved in 1997, demonstrating the weakness of the police and further undermining the rule of law. The most important of these were the August 1995 kidnapping of President

Kovac's son and the April 1996 death in a car explosion of ex-policeman Robert Remias, who had links to the Kovac Jr. case. The Slovak Information Service (SIS) was widely accused of taking part in these two cases, as well as others. In April, Kovac called on the parliament to dismiss Prosecutor General Michal Valo, whom Kovac held primarily responsible for numerous unresolved crimes. On 12 December, President Kovac used his presidential right and pardoned all persons accused in an international fraud case involving the Technopol firm, including his own son. Highly politicized, the case had been dragging on for years in Slovakia. It was clear that Kovac would not be elected to a second term as president, and he wanted to enable his son to travel to Germany to receive a fair trial.

By late 1997, Meciar's behavior was becoming increasingly erratic. In early October, the opposition parties suggested that they wanted Meciar's mental health professionally examined after he accused the Christian Democratic Movement (KDH) of considering having him murdered. In early November, Meciar began an extended stay at the Piestany spa for unspecified health problems, but the visit apparently did not help him. Speaking on Slovak TV on 10 December, he said that he was reevaluating his political future and was not even sure whether he would remain in his position until the next elections. One source noted that during that appearance, Meciar still looked tired and seemed to be on sedatives. On 5 December, Meciar's spokeswoman Magda Pospisilova and government spokeswoman Ludmila Bulakova left their positions, reportedly in connection with the role of Meciar's new aide, Blazena Martinkova. Martinkova, the wife of the former director of the Slovak-Russian Devin banka, appeared at Meciar's side during a number of official appointments throughout the year.

In 1997, the ruling coalition quarreled over bank and TV privatization, as well as the 1998 state budget. Although the ZRS said it would oppose the privatization of Slovakia's four largest financial institutions, even if it caused the government's collapse, several deputies from the party eventually voted in March to allow for the privatization of two of these firms—Vseobecna uverova banka (VUB) and Investicna a rozvojova banka (IRB). The government hoped to sell Slovakia's banks to domestic industrial firms, a move which foreign and domestic experts said could have a disastrous effect on Slovakia's economy. Meanwhile, the conflict over TV privatization raged in June, when the ZRS and SNS joined the opposition in the parliament to prevent HZDS plans for the privatization of Slovak Television's second channel. The HZDS wanted to have a private channel of its own to compete with TV Markiza, which began broadcasting in September 1996 and was largely seen as pro-opposition. The final major conflict within the ruling coalition emerged in mid-November, when the SNS opposed the 1998 state budget, saying that funding for defense and education was insufficient. After considerable wrangling, funding for both ministries was raised when the parliament discussed the bill, and the budget was approved on 12 December. Meanwhile, Meciar unexpectedly announced on 16 December that he was proposing Miroslav Maxon, head of the parliamentary finance and budget committee, to replace Sergej Kozlik as finance minister. Kozlik would remain deputy prime minister.

OPPOSITION'S PROSPECTS IMPROVE

In 1997, the opposition presented an increasingly united front against the ruling coalition. Although three center-right opposition parties—the KDH, the Democratic Union (DU), and the Democratic Party (DS)—had formed the "blue coalition" in late 1996, this was not a pre-election coalition but simply an effort to coordinate the parties' policies. In June, however, these three parties were joined by the Social Democratic Party (SDSS) and the Greens (SZS) in forming a formal pre-election coalition. Public support for this group, called the Slovak Democratic Coalition (SDK), immediately surpassed that for the HZDS. This gave the opposition hope that the SDK, not the HZDS, would be asked to form a government after the next parliamentary elections, scheduled for 25–26 September 1998. The SDK on 30 August released a 15-point memorandum in the historic town of Martin, declaring its basic priorities after the next elections (see sidebar). The coalition also resolved to punish crimes committed by the Meciar government. In September, KDH economic specialist Mikulas Dzurinda was chosen as SDK spokesman, and in December, the SDK signed an agreement with the Hungarian Coalition, forming the basis for cooperation after the next elections. Meanwhile, the post-communist Party of the Democratic Left chose to stay out of the SDK and present itself as an "independent opposition party," a decision that boosted the party's popularity rating.

Regardless of the opposition's tactics, the parties' attempts to block the ruling coalition normally failed, usually because the opposition deputies were simply overruled in the parliament. In 1997, the opposition attempted several times unsuccessfully to dismiss government ministers, including Krajci and Culture Minister Ivan Hudec. Another problem centered on the fact that after the 1994 elections, the opposition was not given adequate representation on various key parliamentary bodies, including those overseeing the SIS, the National Property Fund (FNM), and Slovak TV and Radio. In February, all parties were finally given proportional representation on the parliamentary mandate and immunity committee. However, the center-right opposition parties had to wait until November to gain representation on the committees overseeing SIS and military intelligence, and even then the KDH's candidate for the SIS committee was again rejected. Also in November, the parliament finally elected a fourth deputy parliament chairman. Although the post was supposed to go to the opposition, the parliament chose the "independent" deputy Rudolf Filkus, who had quit the opposition DU earlier in the year and had since voted with the ruling parties.

In any case, these "democratization" steps came only after repeated warnings from the EU on the need for proportional representation. On 18 June, the EU-Slovak parliamentary committee set three conditions for Slovakia to be included in the first round of enlargement talks: improving government-opposition relations, altering the composition of parliamentary committees to achieve a fair coalition-opposition ratio, and passing a minority language law. Although the government promised on 17 September to meet EU demands by the end of November, the question of the minority language law was especially controversial. The legislation had been promised by Meciar and other government representatives following the parliament's passage in November 1995 of the Slovak state language law, which banned the use of languages other than Slovak in official contexts and declared that financial penalties would be issued to violators of the law's provisions. The question of the minority language law was especially crucial after 1 January 1997, the first date that violators of the law could be charged fines. The Constitutional Court ruled on 9 September that the state language law's provision requiring all citizens to use Slovak when addressing state bodies contradicted the constitution. On 4 November, the cabinet approved a memorandum stressing that current legislation on the use of minority languages was sufficient and deeming that a separate law on minority languages was unnecessary. Despite the difficult political situation in Slovakia, the largest anti-government demonstration was the commemoration of the eighth anniversary of the "Velvet Revolution" on 17 November, which only attracted about 15–20,000 people.

ECONOMIC GROWTH CONTINUES

Although many analysts were predicting a considerable economic slow-down in 1997, preliminary figures estimated annual GDP growth at 5.9 percent, while inflation was only 6.4 percent at year's end. The state budget deficit was more of a problem, reaching 37 billion crowns by the end of the year, more than 4 percent of anticipated GDP. By late August, government interventions in the economy were intensifying in an effort to deal with certain problem areas. The cabinet put special emphasis on controlling wage growth, passing a law on wage regulation in early September. Another area of concern was the trade deficit, which was soaring out of control in the early months of the year following the cabinet's move under international pressure to lift the import surcharge on 1 January. The Finance Ministry announced on 16 July that the government had decided to reintroduce a temporary 7 percent import surcharge on consumer goods and food. Growth in the trade deficit began to slow in late 1997, with the deficit reaching 50 billion crowns for the year, or approximately 7.7 percent of GDP. This was considerably less than the previous year's trade deficit, and the 17 percent growth in exports was also encouraging. Following the Czech economic crisis that sent the Czech crown plummeting downwards, officials from the Slovak government and the NBS insisted that there would be no devaluation of the Slovak crown. By the end of the year, the exchange rate was 34.8 Slovak crowns to $1 and the Slovak crown had closed the previous gap and was almost equal in value to the Czech crown.

Meanwhile, the government continued in its efforts to build a business class that would be subordinate to the ruling parties. In April, former economy minister Jan Ducky of the HZDS became head of Slovensky plynarensky priemysel (SPP), a hugely profitable state-owned energy firm; shortly afterwards, the company signed a controversial joint venture agreement with Russia's Gazprom. The HZDS also had close relations with the east Slovak steel giant VSZ. The party started a membership drive at VSZ in January, reportedly focused on staff in "higher positions." Not long after Transport, Postal Services, and Telecommunications Minister Alexander Rezes left his cabinet post in March—allegedly for health reasons—he was elected president of VSZ's five-member board of directors. An owner of shares in VSZ, Rezes said in February that after leaving his post he would publicly, economically and politically stay with Meciar, adding that Slovakia needed "ten Meciars." Against the wishes of the NBS, VSZ and its partner firms had purchased an estimated 43 percent of the shares in IRB long before the decision to privatize the bank was approved by the parliament. With VSZ actively buying up steel firms abroad and investing in media, sport teams, and other enterprises, it appeared that the firm wanted to use the IRB for its own needs. In December, the NBS placed the IRB under forced administration after a large deficit was discovered and after the IRB had stopped fulfilling its obligations on the inter-bank market. Although the NBS had always had considerable independence and had been praised internationally for keeping inflation and currency fluctuations under control, in September the government approved a draft law that would limit the bank's autonomy. The legislation was withdrawn from the parliament's agenda in December, but it was expected to be resubmitted in 1998.

EUROPE TURNS AWAY FROM SLOVAKIA

Slovakia's biggest foreign policy failure in 1997 was its lack of success in gaining entry into NATO and EU talks, which was especially disappointing since the transformation of Slovakia's military and economy was comparable, or in some cases even superior to that of countries that were chosen as candidates. At the start of the year, many Slovak government representatives gave the impression that they still believed Slovakia had a chance of entering NATO and the EU in the first round, despite a series of statements to the contrary by Western officials. Even so, Meciar began to prepare his supporters for the government's failure, telling a HZDS rally on 21 March that Slovakia might not be admitted to NATO in the first round, not because of domestic political problems, but due to "global agreements" between superpowers.

In an apparent attempt to improve communication, some West European countries altered their approaches to Slovakia in 1997 by no longer avoiding formal contacts with Meciar. In his first official visit to a West European country since 1994, Vladimir Meciar visited France in March. Although Meciar's much desired official visit to Germany to meet German Chancellor Helmut Kohl remained elusive, Germany did send both Bundestag Chairwoman Rita Suessmuth and Foreign Minister Klaus Kinkel to Bratislava. Still, these visits had little effect on the Slovak government's behavior.

Not only did 1997 bring Slovakia problems with NATO and the EU, it also brought a cooling of ties with two of its neighbors: the Czech Republic and Hungary. The issue of the common state border between Slovakia and the Czech Republic was finally settled on 25 July, with the swap of two villages and some other border land. However, other complications arose in early April during preparations for Meciar's first official bilateral meeting in several years with his Czech counterpart, Vaclav Klaus. The major issue of conflict involved completing the division of former Czechoslovakia's common property. Tensions heightened further when Czech President Vaclav Havel alleged in an interview with the French daily, *Le Figaro,* that Meciar suffered from paranoia, leading the HZDS to demand an apology. The controversy between Bratislava and Prague grew so serious that the Slovak government on 9 April recalled Ivan Mjartan, the country's ambassador to the Czech Republic, for 20 days. Meciar and Klaus finally met in Piestany on 10 October, where they agreed to swap bank shares as part of a plan to settle bilateral debts. The talks were set to continue in Prague in December, but bilateral meetings were again delayed due to changes in the Czech government. In early December, the Czech Republic demanded an apology after Meciar made vulgar jokes about Klaus and Havel during a HZDS rally. After new Czech Prime Minister Josef Tosovsky was appointed, Meciar said he did not consider him a partner for talks.

Meanwhile, relations between Slovakia and Hungary were also strained because of the latter's perception that Slovakia was not fulfilling the requirements set forth in the bilateral treaty that took effect in 1996. A particularly thorny issue concerned Slovakia's delay in approving the minority language law. Bilateral tensions heightened after a meeting between Meciar and his Hungarian counterpart, Gyula Horn, in Gyor on 15 August. Horn revealed on 5 September that one of the issues brought up by Meciar during the meeting was the possibility of a transfer of ethnic minority populations between the two countries. Horn stressed that he had refused to discuss the topic, since it evoked "tragic" historical memories. A meeting between Kramplova and her Hungarian counterpart Laszlo Kovacs, scheduled for 20 September, was canceled.

Slovakia's one success in the field of foreign policy was its partial victory over Hungary in the dispute over the Gabcikovo-Nagymaros dam complex. Emotions ran high in both countries over the issue, and Hungary apparently thought it would win because of its better international position and stronger foreign lobby. The International Court of Justice in The Hague ruled on 25 September that Hungary had violated international law by abandoning its 1977 agreement with Slovakia to build the Gabcikovo-Nagymaros dams and hydroelectric power stations on the Danube River. At the same time, however, the court said that the former Czechoslovakia was also wrong in unilaterally diverting Danube waters from Hungary into Slovakia. The court obligated the two countries to take all necessary measures to ensure the implementation of the 1977 accord. Meeting with Austrian Chancellor Viktor Klima on 15 December, Meciar and Horn said they would reach an agreement on Gabcikovo-Nagymaros by 25 March 1998, the deadline set by the court.

GLOSSARY

DS	Democratic Party
DU	Democratic Union
HZDS	Movement for a Democratic Slovakia
KDH	Christian Democratic Movement
SDK	Slovak Democratic Coalition

SDSS Social Democratic Party
SNS Slovak National Party
SZS Greens
ZRS Association of Workers of Slovakia

Sidebar: THE OPPOSITION PLANS FOR SLOVAKIA'S FUTURE

On 30 August 1997, the newly formed five-party Slovak Democratic Coalition (SDK) drew up a 15-point program in the historic town of Martin. The following are excerpts from the so-called Martin Declaration:

"Today, we stand at a crossroads. In 1989, after many decades, we obtained freedom and democracy. In 1993, we created an independent Slovakia. Today, we must decide about its character and face. There are only two possibilities: a democratic state or an undemocratic state. There is no third way. Therefore, we stand firmly and simply on the side of democracy. [. . .]

Our victory in the 1998 elections will be based on creating a Slovak government which is legal, lawful, and constitutional. [. . .] We therefore offer our Program for Slovakia. Its goals are:

1. To renew and build a democratic legal state.
2. To renew, promote, and safeguard parliamentary democracy.
3. To safeguard the independence of the judiciary and prosecutors.
4. To restore individual responsibility for criminal actions.
5. To safeguard freedom of speech, association, and assembly.
6. To create conditions for economic growth [and] higher standards of living.
7. To safeguard the state's social direction and renew the partnership with labor unions.
8. To guarantee the personal safety of citizens against petty and organized crime.
9. To control the intelligence agencies.
10. To safeguard the development of public media based of citizens' constitutional right to information.
11. To protect the environment.
12. To promote the development of the non-governmental sector, education, science and culture, based on the principle of self-government.
13. To safeguard the civil service, promote the development of local and regional self-governments, strengthening their financial positions.
14. To build good relations between Slovaks and ethnic minorities.
15. To secure Slovakia's position in European and Transatlantic structures, including the EU and NATO.

Hungary

Population:	10,277,000 (January 1994)
Capital:	Budapest (pop. 1,996,000)
Major cities:	Debrecen (pop. 218,000), Miskolc (pop. 190,000), Szeged (pop. 179,000)
Area:	93,030 sq. km.
Major ethnic groups:	Hungarian 90%, Romani 4%, German 2.6%, Slovak 1%
Economy:	GDP growth: 4.0%
....	Inflation rate: 18.4%
....	Average monthly wage: $367
....	Unemployment rate: 9.7%

A YEAR OF OPTIMISM

by ZSOFIA SZILAGYI

After two years of austerity measures, the third year under the governance of the Hungarian Socialist Party (MSzP) and its junior coalition partner, the Alliance of Free Democrats (SzDSz), was marked by significant growth in the economy. 1997 also witnessed success stories in the country's relations with NATO and the European Union (EU). In July, along with the Czech Republic and Poland, Hungary was invited to join the North Atlantic alliance as a full member and was given a special consultative status for the interim period. In its country reports on East-Central European associate countries, the European Union (EU) gave Hungary the best rating regarding its commitment to democracy, its economic competitiveness, and its advancement in adjusting its laws to EU standards. But the year also saw a significant change in the electorate's party preferences and loud public and political debates over NATO and the future of the hydroelectric dam on the Danube.

THE NATO DEBATE

Analysts and politicians agreed that Hungary's biggest foreign policy achievement in the post-communist era occurred when it received an invitation to join NATO at the alliance's Madrid summit in July. A glance back at 1997, however, shows a year filled with controversy and uncertainty on the bumpy road toward the security alliance. 1997 saw Western defense manufacturers swarm the country trying to sell the government NATO-compatible military equipment, and the passage of a risky national referendum on NATO membership, where concern over the costs of joining overshadowed all other expansion-related issues.

Over the course of the past two years, organizations both in Hungary and abroad had tried to estimate the costs of NATO entry. The varying figures reflected the fact that no one really knew what it would cost to bring the Czech Republic, Poland, and Hungary into the NATO security fold. In Hungary, what confused the issue further was the fact that Hungarian negotiators committed themselves to specific levels of increased defense spending in the fall, after the country received its invitation to join. According to Andras Simonyi, Hungary's NATO ambassador, no matter what the newest studies estimated, Hungary would still dish out what it had committed itself to earlier.

Speaking to a populace that had borne the weight of austerity measures for more than two years, the Hungarian government tried to play down the fact that the modest peace dividends following the end of the cold war would have to stop. With defense spending currently at 1.44 percent of GDP, Hungary committed itself to increasing defense expenditures until it tops out at about 2 percent of GDP in the year 2001, an amount close to the NATO average. When Hungary's economic growth is added to that figure, Hungary will actually be spending about $400 million a year more at that time than in 1997, an increase equal to ten times the annual gross salary of every teacher in the country. Government officials argued that the annual $400 million should not be counted as the cost of expansion, since the Hungarian defense forces would have to be modernized even if Hungary did not join NATO.

A RISKY REFERENDUM

The costs issue became central in the fall as citizens nationwide prepared to vote on the country's NATO membership in a national referendum on 16 November. The referendum, which passed with a 49 percent turnout and 85 percent voting in favor, brought deep relief to officials who had worried that a negative vote would put an abrupt end to years of planning and negotiations. Real opponents turned out to be few as nearly the entire media and political establishment supported NATO membership.

The victory, however, was tainted. While international newspapers covered the event, they also reported how the defense and foreign ministries had paid out over 112 million forints ($560,000) to a variety of television, radio, and print media organizations to publicize the importance of joining NATO. Opponents claimed that the money was not used to inform Hungarians, but to fund a highly biased propaganda campaign in which the government paid for pro-NATO characters on sitcoms and soap operas. Later the National Radio and Television Board ordered television show Familia Kft. to apologize on the air for never indicating to viewers that the Defense Ministry had paid the show 7 million forints ($35,000) to include a pro-NATO army colonel in the script that season.

In 1998, the legislatures of all 16 NATO countries must ratify documents on expanding the alliance to include Hungary, the Czech Republic, and Poland. The three countries are due to be admitted formally on NATO's 50th anniversary, 4 April 1999. As of 1997 Hungary was the only one of the candidate countries to hold a referendum on NATO membership. Holding a binding referendum, however, was not what the government originally intended to do. The government first adopted a plan to hold a referendum on entry to the alliance that would merely have been a test of public opinion, which was generally believed to favor NATO membership. Although all the parliamentary parties supported NATO membership, electioneering on both the government's and opposition's side turned the issue into a controversial debate, and a Constitutional Court ruling was requested several times.

In September the opposition Young Democrats proposed holding a fully binding referendum on NATO membership, and the cabinet decided to call one itself, in an effort to reap the political benefits of a successful referendum. But the public vote plan became bogged down in a political scandal because of the government's decision to link it with yet another vote, on the controversial land reform bill, on which the opposition had initiated another referendum and collected nearly 300,000 signatures. Opposition parties exploited public disquiet with the possible entry of foreign capital into the country's farm sector and pushed for a total ban on planned foreign ownership. The opposition's efforts to put their own questions on the referendum were turned down by the ruling coalition parties, which hold more than two-thirds of the seats in parliament. The

Constitutional Court finally ruled that in the opposition-supported land referendum, the original questions should be asked, and not the government's, which led the parliament to postpone the issue until next year.

Meanwhile, the public debate over NATO mainly centered around questions of financing membership-related costs, with several non-governmental organizations (NGOs) and extra-parliamentary parties on the radical left and right arguing that it would put too much of a burden on taxpayers.

GROWTH IN THE ECONOMY

Two years after the launch of an austerity program, known as the "Bokros package" after former Finance Minister Lajos Bokros, the economy in 1997 started to show swift development. Annual inflation dropped to 18 percent from 24 percent in 1996, and annual GDP growth increased to 3 percent from 0.5 percent. According to many observers, this was the first year since 1989 that economic prognoses by independent economic research institutes and those of government officials actually matched.

Despite the fall economic crisis in South-East Asia, which resulted in several black days on the Budapest Stock Exchange as well, the exchange closed its best year in trading since its establishment and it strengthened its position as the post-communist region's strongest exchange. Hungary also continued to attract the largest amount of direct foreign investment in East-Central Europe. Even so, growth figures stayed behind those of the fastest-growing economies in the region. That may have been due partly to the government's inability to tackle the shadow economy, which accounts for an estimated 30 percent of GDP. Privatization of state assets was largely finished by the end of 1997, and the country's privatization officials began debating the future management of state assets that are slated for long-term state ownership.

With a 4–5 percent GDP growth expected in 1998 and a current account deficit under control, Hungary is in a neck-and-neck competition with Poland for the top position in the region. Real wages in Hungary rose by a little under 5 percent in 1997, the first such increase in three years. Financial problems in traditional state-sponsored sectors, such as health care and education, however, resulted in considerable public discontent and led to trade-union protests. The crisis-ridden agricultural sector also had a rough year. In the spring, farmers blocked roads across the country, protesting government plans to raise their taxes and social security payments.

SHIFTING PARTY SUPPORT

In April, Ivan Pett stepped down as chairman and caucus leader of the junior coalition party, the Alliance of Free Democrats (SzDSz). With his resignation, which came in the wake of growing public distrust in governing parties after a privatization scandal in 1996, Pett wanted to give his party a chance to rebuild its image for the 1998 general elections. By the end of 1997, the Socialists (MSzP) had regained most of the supporters they had lost in 1996. But meanwhile the popularity of the moderate, center-right Young Democrats and the populist, right-wing Smallholders' Party reached that of the leading Socialists. That occurred partly as a result of general discontent with the economic austerity program launched in 1995, and partly because of high-level corruption charges in 1996.

The remaining opposition parties saw further fragmentation. 1996 had seen the break-up of the Hungarian Democratic Forum, which had won the first democratic elections back in 1990. In July the Christian Democrats became the second opposition party to split in two. In the fall, parties descending from the Democratic Forum and the Christian Democrats forged electoral alliances with the current major opposition parties. The Young Democrats joined hands with the rump Democratic Forum and the moderate group of the Christian Democrats, while the Smallholders struck an alliance with the Christian Democrats' radical splinter group, thus dividing the political scene into three major blocks of power. In the meantime, extra-parliamentary parties on the extreme left and extreme right also became significantly stronger. Both of those parties' platforms include fierce protests against Hungary's bid to join NATO.

In June, Hungarian Prime Minister Gyula Horn signed a concordat with the Vatican. Under this agreement, the Hungarian government will give $230 million in restitution to the Catholic, Lutheran, Jewish, Baptist, and Serbian Orthodox churches and synagogues. According to the pact, the state will return property seized from the Catholic Church under communism, or alternatively pay compensation. The agreement also stipulated that church-run schools are eligible for the same subsidies as public schools. Although coalition parties agreed on the necessity of the Concordat, they disagreed on some of the specifics. Together with other non-Catholic churches, the Alliance of Free Democrats objected to the fact that the government prepared the Concordat without prior consultation with the non-Catholic establishments, violating the equality of churches. The Jewish and Protestant establishments, for instance, rejected the Concordat's stipulations for return of property nationalized by the Communist regime. In these institutions, contrary to the Catholic Church, it was local communities and not the central religious body that owned the property.

HAGUE RULING FAVORS SLOVAKIA

In September, the International Court of Justice in The Hague ruled in favor of Slovakia in the Gabcikovo-Nagymaros dam dispute, which Hungary had taken to the Court in 1993. Originally negotiated in 1977 between Hungary and Czechoslovakia, work on the dam continued through the 1980s, until Hungarian environmentalists pressured the government to halt construction work in 1989. In 1992, Hungary unilaterally withdrew from the project, but the Slovaks proceeded with a temporary solution, the so-called C variant, and built a smaller-scale version of the dam, diverting the Danube and according to the Hungarian government violating the border between the two countries.

In a verdict which pleased neither side, the Court ruled that the 1977 treaty is still valid and that both Hungary and Slovakia were liable in the dispute. The Hungarians were upset that the Court disregarded their environmental concerns and based its ruling on international legal obligations. The Court said that Hungary broke international law when it pulled out of construction work in 1989 and when it unilaterally withdrew from the 1977 bilateral agreement. However, it also found that Slovakia did not have the right to divert the waters of the Danube to its own territory and that the C variant violated international law. The two governments were given six months to find a settlement acceptable to both sides. Soon after, negotiations began between the Slovak and the Hungarian delegation, but there was a public outcry in Hungary following a government proposal to build one or two new dams on the Danube.

The plan's opponents said the Hungarian delegation is overstepping the Hague ruling's requirements if it starts building dams on the Hungarian side. The opponents—opposition parties and environmentalists—also accused the government delegation of clouding the real costs of further construction work, and proposing to build without a comprehensive environmental impact study.

Relations between Hungary and Slovakia remained tense as the premiers quarreled over the establishment of a joint subcommittee to discuss the protection of minority rights and Slovakia's failure to draft a bill on the protection of minority languages. Slovak President Vladimir Meciar accused the Hungarian government of initiating a smear campaign against the Slovak government, by recording and publicizing the minutes of the meeting without Meciar's approval. Meciar also broached the idea of a population transfer of the two countries' respective minority populations, which drew international opprobrium.

MEDIA DEVELOPMENTS

In 1997, the most momentous event for Hungary's media was the long-awaited appearance of private investors. After the year-late sale of two national commercial television licenses in June, the National Radio and Television Board also sold off two nationwide commercial radio concessions in November. The emergence of private media started reshaping the market right after the October launch of the two new national television stations, bringing a wider choice to viewers and advertisers and tons of cheap imported programming.

The forty-year monopoly of state-fed public service Hungarian Television (MTV) evaporated with the launch of the new commercial stations. In spite of MTV's desperate attempts to augment its budget revenues by broadcasting more advertising than allowed and running sponsored programs despite the media law's ban, its viewership share had plummeted from around 75 percent to 29 percent by mid-December. Of the new commercial channels, it was TV2—owned by the Hungarian-Swedish MTM-SBS consortium—which managed to secure a 25 percent viewership share by mid-December. The station also landed a $28 million loan financed by the European Bank for Reconstruction and Development and two Hungarian banks. RTL Klub—majority owned by the Luxembourg-based media giant CLT-Ufa—launched its full broadcasting in late October, three weeks after TV2, and trailed behind its rival in terms of viewer figures. The real loser in the long run, however, was Central European Media Enterprises, which after success stories elsewhere in the region, lost its bid for a national channel. Currently its much-touted cable broadcast TV3 is only available in Budapest and has modest viewer ratings.

Poland

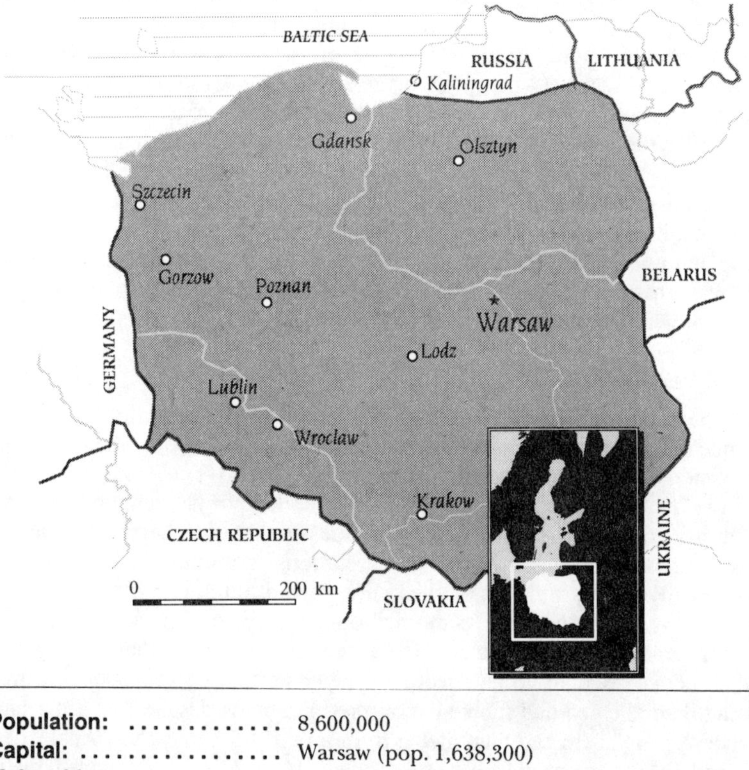

Population:	8,600,000
Capital:	Warsaw (pop. 1,638,300)
Major cities:	Lodz (pop. 825,600), Krakow (pop. 745,400), Wroclaw (pop. 642,700)
Area:	312,685 sq. km.
Major ethnic groups:	Polish 97.6%, German 1.3%, Ukrainian 0.6%, Belarusian 0.5%
Economy:	GDP growth: 6.5%
....	Inflation rate: 13.0%
....	Average monthly wage: $407
....	Unemployment rate: 10.5%

NEW CONSTITUTION, NEW PARLIAMENT, NEW GOVERNMENT

by JAKUB KARPINSKI

In May 1997, Poles accepted their long-awaited constitution in a referendum, and later in the year elected a new parliament and new government. The year also saw the adoption of a new penal code, one that abolished the death penalty. Pope John Paul II once again visited his native country in June. In July, widespread flooding mobilized social energy and created an additional opportunity for the opposition to attack the government for its supposedly delayed reaction to the calamity. The first half of the year was marked by heated arguments over the new draft constitution. In the second half, the Solidarity-led coalition won the parliamentary elections and, together with the centrist-liberal Freedom Union (UW), formed the new government.

THE NEW CONSTITUTION

Poles voted twice in 1997, first in the constitutional referendum on 25 May, and second in the parliamentary elections on 21 September. The referendum brought the long-awaited—and initially much contested—constitution, which had been developed by the four major parties in the 1993–1997 parliament. The co-ruling Democratic Left Alliance (SLD) and the Polish Peasant Party (PSL) were helped in the constitutional consensus by the centrist-liberal UW and left-wing Labor Union (UP). There was no constitution as a unified text in Poland until 1997, rather a patchwork of constitutional laws which were coordinated by the "small constitution" adopted on 17 October 1992. The new constitution was initially approved by the National Assembly (the Sejm and Senate in joint session) on 22 March (461 deputies and senators voted for, 31 against, and 5 abstained). On 2 April, the National Assembly accepted three quarters of the 41 amendments proposed by President Aleksander Kwasniewski. The assembly approved the president's prerogative to nominate the presidents of the Supreme Court, Constitutional Tribunal, and Supreme Administrative Court, as well as to nominate the chief of General Staff and commanders in chief of the land forces, air force, and navy. But the assembly rejected proposed limitations on the parliamentarians' immunity. On the same day, the assembly approved the whole text of the constitution in the final vote, so the constitution is known as the act of 2 April. (451 deputies and senators voted for, 40 against, and 6 abstained.) In the referendum on 25 May, with turnout of 43 percent, the constitution was approved by 53 percent and opposed by 46 percent.

The new constitution clarifies regulations that were ambiguous, limits presidential powers, and gives the citizens a judicial procedure for complaining if their constitutional rights are infringed. The opposition strongly criticized the new constitution, attacking not so much its concrete legal measures, but rather its ideological meaning and implied Weltanschauung, although compromise formulations were found to satisfy those who wanted an explicit reference to God in the constitutional preamble. The vague yet vivid polemics around the constitution contrasted with the rather calm and matter-of-fact tone of the subsequent electoral campaign. The polemics around the constitution notably diminished after the September elections.

THE FLOODS

The July floods in southwestern Poland diverted people's minds from divisive political issues. The widespread spontaneous help given to flood victims demonstrated the need and practical usefulness of citizens' solidarity. The opposition criticized the government, arguing that its reactions were not fast enough, prompting Labor Minister Tadeusz Zielinski to repeat in parliament an Italian saying: "Bad weather?—The government is responsible." Opinion polls showed that the public's evaluation of the government's performance during the floods was more positive than negative. The activities of ordinary people, the military, the fire services, the charity organizations, the church, the police, and the media were, however, more often appreciated than the performance of the government and provincial authorities. The 1997 electoral results of the SLD, the senior partner in the 1993–1997 government coalitions, were not worse in the flood area than elsewhere, despite several predictions to the contrary.

THE 1993–1997 LEFT-DOMINATED PARLIAMENT ENDS ITS TERM

The elections on 21 September 1997 led to a complete change in the composition of the parliament and hence the Polish political scene in general. The former elections in 1993, which took place under the 1993 electoral law that favored stronger parties, brought about a parliament dominated by two parties which both had communist origins and rather left-wing inclinations. The SLD won 20.4 percent of the votes and gained 171 seats in the 460-seat lower chamber of parliament, the Sejm, while the PSL gained 15.4 percent of votes and 132 deputies. Those two parties kept a very comfortable majority in the 1993–1997 parliament, approaching the two thirds that was needed to change constitutional laws. The consecutive SLD-PSL governments, under prime ministers Waldemar Pawlak (PSL), Jozef Oleksy (SLD), and Wlodzimierz Cimoszewicz (SLD), in general continued the reforms that were initiated by the governments in 1989–1993. That continuing program included financial stability, privatization, and a pro-Western foreign policy favoring Poland's entrance to NATO and the European Union (EU).

The 100-seat Polish Senate is elected together with the Sejm for four years, but electoral rules for the two chambers differ. The elections take place with party lists (and a 5 percent threshold for awarding seats), while the Senate seats are fought by individual candidates, with two seats in each district (except for Warsaw and Katowice, which elect three senators each). The 1993–1997 Senate, like the Sejm, was dominated by the SLD-PSL coalition. The SLD had 37 senators, while 36 senators represented the PSL. Senate Speaker Adam Struzik was from the PSL. Other Senate seats were divided between Solidarity, with 9 senators, the Democratic Union (UD, later transformed into UW) 4, and UP 2. The Non-Party Bloc for Support of Reforms (BBWR), which backed former President Lech Walesa, had 2 senators; six other political groupings had one senator each, and four senators were independent. The 1993–1997 Sejm was marked by significant absences. Solidarity received 4.9 percent of votes, thus missing the threshold by 0.1 percent. The right-wing coalition "Fatherland" did not enter the Sejm either—although it won 6.4 percent of votes, the threshold for coalitions of parties was set at 8 percent.

The proponents of the 1993 electoral law wanted a parliament with a strong majority that, unlike in the fragmented Sejm of 1991–93, would be able to select a stable government. The law-makers received what they wanted: a clear SLD-PSL majority dominated the parliament in 1993–1997. That left-wing majority was established thanks to the fact that numerous right-of-center parties were unable to agree and unite before the election.

The parliament that was replaced in 1997 was the only one since 1989 that had served its full term. The first parliament that was elected in June 1989, after roundtable talks between the communists and opposition in half-free elections, had some Solidarity representation but dissolved itself after two years. The next parliament, elected in 1991, was dissolved in 1993 by the then-President Lech Walesa who was criticized for that move by those who, following public opinion polls, correctly predicted that the elections would bring the post-communist coalition to power.

In the 1993–1997 parliament, the SLD-PSL coalition adopted a magnanimous policy of allowing other parties to have deputy speaker posts in both chambers and to chair parliamentary commissions. The SLD's Jozef Oleksy was the Sejm speaker in 1993–1995. When he became prime minister in 1995, he was replaced as speaker by the PSL's Jozef Zych. After the 1997 elections, the SLD demanded a proportional share in parliamentary posts as a gesture of reciprocity from the former opposition. But the coalition that was formed in 1997 argued that the staffing of parliamentary posts should reflect the electorate's preference by granting more freedom and resources to the new majority, that is that the AWS-UW majority should take nearly all posts. SLD deputy Marek Borowski was elected Sejm deputy speaker, but there is no SLD representative among the Senate deputy speakers.

In its personnel policy, however, the ruling SLD-PSL coalition had not always been generous toward the opposition. Not long before the parliamentary elections in 1997, the coalition assured its political influence in the media by nominating the public television supervising board. It also nominated judges to the Constitutional Tribunal, which became more important under the new constitution, because now in some cases the tribunal takes ultimate decisions that are not subjected to the Sejm's approval.

The left-wing coalition generally continued the reforms that had been initiated by its predecessors linked to Solidarity. The opposition in 1993–1997 complained that the reforms were proceeding too slowly, but the dark predictions from 1993 did not materialize. That point was repeatedly emphasized by the SLD in its electoral campaign in 1997: GNP, real wages, and pensions grew in 1993–1997, as did foreign investment, while the inflation rate and unemployment went down.

SOLIDARITY AS A UNIFYING FORCE

Paradoxically, Solidarity, a labor union, is often considered in Poland to be right-wing—mostly because of its anti-communism, but also because of its support for the Catholic Church. In other countries the left-right differentiation is usually understood in terms of economic policies rather than religious or cultural values. The "right" in the economic sense prefers less state intervention in the economy, lower taxes, and more privatization; while the "left" advocates the welfare state, and thus stands for higher taxes and more state intervention. The Polish custom of considering a labor union to be right-wing stems partly from an assumption that whoever confronts a leftist organization is on the right. Anti-communism is widely considered right-wing, although that identification is arguably mistaken. An undoubtedly left-wing, influential, and numerous Polish Socialist Party (PPS), existing in Poland until 1948, was strongly anti-communist in the inter-war period and in the underground during German occupation. The PPS leaders were persecuted for their anti-communism by the communist authorities after World War II.

Solidarity Electoral Action (AWS) was created in June 1996 in response to Solidarity's catastrophic performance in the 1993 elections. Marian Krzaklewski, Solidarity president since 1991, managed to unite three dozen political groupings under the union's banner and leadership. Those groups are mostly considered to be right-of-center and some are right-wing in terms of the economic policies that they advocate. The Solidarity labor union showed its understanding that labor prosperity depends on business performance. After the AWS electoral victory, both the Polish lobby group Business Center Club and the AWS stressed that the two sides had a good mutual understanding.

THE 1997 ELECTION RESULTS

After the 1997 elections, two coalitions dominated in the Polish parliament. The AWS was a clear winner, but neither the AWS nor the SLD could form a government alone. The electoral law brought similar results as in 1993, giving the winners additional bonuses. The newcomer in the parliament, the AWS received 34 percent of votes and 201 deputies, the SLD had 27 percent of votes and 164 deputies, the UW 13 percent of votes and 60 deputies, the PSL 7.3 percent of votes and 27 deputies, and the Movement for Poland's Reconstruction (ROP) 5.5 percent of votes and 6 deputies. Only those five parties entered the Sejm. Additionally, two deputies represent the German minority, owing to the electoral law that waives the 5 percent threshold for national minorities. With 51 senators, the AWS has the majority in the Senate, the SLD has 28 senators, UW 8, ROP 5, and PSL 3. Five senators are independent.

Right-wing parties of an anti-communist or conservative persuasion, practically absent in the 1993–1997 Sejm, came back in the union-led coalition. The SLD improved its performance: it received 6.7 percent of votes more than in 1993, although it received less seats, because less votes were lost, cast for the parties absent in the Sejm. The UW had a little fewer votes than its constituting parts, the UD and the Liberal Democratic Congress (KLD), had together in 1993.

THE LOSERS IN THE 1997 ELECTIONS

The PSL went through some struggles in the leadership over policies: deputy prime minister and agriculture minister Roman Jagielinski resigned in March. The party made efforts to represent the interests of its constituency, the millions of Polish peasants, but the PSL leadership were split over whether to favor the more modern and wealthy farmers or the more numerous poorer peasants. Over the last four years, the PSL took many advantages from its presence in the government by acquiring state-distributed posts and other resources. But from time to time the PSL tried to display its distance from the government and threatened to leave its coalition with the SLD. Those tactics of participation combined with half-opposition culminated in the no-confidence vote in the Sejm against the government of Wlodzimierz Cimoszewicz on 28 August. The vote was taken in response to a PSL initiative, but in the end the PSL did not support its own motion and the proposal failed. The voters showed that they did not appreciate the PSL's tactics of partial responsibility. The PSL lost 103 seats in the Sejm and 33 seats in the Senate, as the result of losing its electorate mostly to the SLD, but also to the AWS.

The UP attempted to build a left-wing alternative to the SLD. The UP avoided speaking in favor of the communist past, trying to suggest that the SLD has been catering to the needs of former communist party members. The UP did not enter the Sejm in 1997. As the public opinion polls show, its electorate was divided between the SLD, AWS, and UW. The UP leaders complained after the elections that results of opinion polls were published just before the elections (an infringement of the electoral law). Such publications might have convinced some voters not to vote for the UP because the polls predicted that the UP would not pass the threshold (as in fact happened).

The ROP, led by former Prime Minister Jan Olszewski, had a similar program and profile of supporters to the AWS, but decided to run separately. It lost voters mostly to the AWS. The ROP, according to a poll conducted by the Public Opinion Research Center (OBOP), lost 19 percent of its supporters to the AWS between June and August 1997. The internal fights in the ROP culminated in the secession of a group led by former Internal Affairs Minister Antoni Macierewicz who, elected to the Sejm as an ROP candidate, is now an independent deputy.

THE NEW GOVERNMENT

Since April 1995, Leszek Balcerowicz, a deputy prime minister and finance minister who the led Polish economic transformation in 1989–1991, was acting as the UW leader, replacing former Prime Minister Tadeusz Mazowiecki. As finance minister, Balcerowicz proved to be a man of character who knew where he was going despite harsh criticisms from the opposition. In 1997, as the UW leader, he proved to be a tough negotiator with the AWS. The UW resembles the AWS by its heterogeneity: it includes liberal, social-democratic, and Christian-democratic currents. The leadership managed to keep these diverse currents united, although there were some defections from the UW to the AWS before the elections (a few deputies left the UW in January and formed the Polish People's Conservative Party, SLK, that was admitted to the AWS). The UW's opponents often suspected that party of planning a coalition with the SLD, following the Hungarian example where a coalition of socialists (former communists) with liberals (former dissidents) took power in 1995. During the electoral campaign, the UW leaders did not exclude a coalition with the SLD, an attitude that improved the UW's position in the negotiations with the AWS, but after the elections the UW decided to form a coalition with the AWS.

According to the Polish constitution, the president is free in his choice of the prime minister, who later has to win the Sejm's approval. After the September elections, President Aleksander Kwasniewski met with representatives of the five political parties that entered the Sejm. The talks saved the decorum of presidential prerogatives and stressed his freedom of choice, but taking into account political expediency, the president nominated a candidate whom the AWS-UW coalition chose on 15 October, 57-year-old academic Jerzy Buzek. Former Gdansk province governor Maciej Plazynski (AWS) was elected Sejm speaker on 20 October and law professor Alicja Grzeskowiak (AWS) became Senate speaker the next day. Forming the government took two weeks and the government was sworn in on 31 October. Janusz Tomaszewski, AWS chief negotiator with the UW, became deputy prime minister and minister of internal affairs and administration. Balcerowicz, his UW counterpart in negotiations, returned to the posts of deputy prime minister and finance minister that he held in 1989–1991. The foreign affairs portfolio went to Bronislaw Geremek (UW), who in 1991–1997 had chaired the Sejm foreign affairs commission. Defense went to Janusz Onyszkiewicz (UW), who returned to the post he held in 1992–1993 in the Hanna Suchocka (UW) coalition government. The new government won a confidence motion on 11 November, with 260 votes for and 173 against.

During the AWS-UW negotiations, AWS leader Marian Krzaklewski declined to be a candidate for the prime minister's post, saying that he preferred to chair the AWS parliamentary caucus. UW representatives pressed Krzaklewski to consider taking the position of prime minister, arguing that otherwise he would become a supervisory prime minister from the sidelines, as then-SLD leader Kwasniewski was called during Oleksy's premiership in 1995. Commentators hinted that Krzaklewski was preparing himself for the presidential election in 2000, and was copying the actions of Kwasniewski, who, as the SLD leader in 1993, had declined the prime minister's post after the SLD won the 1993 parliamentary elections.

The first steps of the Buzek government showed that the prime minister and the government intended to continue the reforms initiated in 1989. Polish political life had already become familiar with union activists who became leaders of transformation to capitalism, however painful such a transformation was for union members and union electoral supporters. Formerly pro-Soviet and pro-Russian SLD politicians changed into ardent advocates of Poland's EU and NATO membership. Socialists or social democrats from the SLD conducted quite pro-capitalist and liberal policies that included mass privatization. Authority brings responsibility, electoral intransigence and posturing are often later forgotten.

In its electoral platform the AWS stressed that it wanted to watch closely the social context of economic reforms. In particular, the AWS wanted to link privatization with the reform of the pension system, so that the resources from privatization could be directed to the pension funds that were desperately in need of capital. The AWS also stressed the need for restitution of property to former owners, a policy that had been postponed by the previous parliaments and governments. The AWS's Solidarity core was registered as a new political party on 13 November. Meanwhile, many of the groupings that constitute the AWS have still separate legal identitities, fueling internal tensions and controversies within the AWS parliamentary caucus (although those controversies did not yet disrupt the overall work of the coalition).

At the year's end President Aleksander Kwasniewski flexed his political muscles. He vetoed the pension bill and a bill on the removal of sex education from schools. The AWS-UW coalition does not have the qualified Sejm majority of three fifths that is needed to overturn a presidential veto, so the president showed that new legislation depends on his approval. Kwasniewski called for better coordination of the presidency with the government, which was to be assured by allowing his representatives to participate in cabinet meetings. Premier Buzek saw no need for such an attendance, ending a seven-year tradition that had derived from the previous constitutional laws that had granted the president special prerogatives in foreign affairs, defense, and state security.

Abortion remained a central concern of lawmakers in 1997. The abortion law had been liberalized in 1996, and on 28 May the Constitutional Tribunal called for those modifications to be reexamined by the parliament. The 1996 amendments allowed for abortion until the twelfth week of pregnancy if the woman could not afford to have a child or had other personal problems. The outgoing Sejm ruled out a referendum on abortion on 17 June, but the new Sejm on 17 December restored the 1993 law that had been amended in 1996. The restored law allows for abortions only if the pregnancy poses a threat to the woman's life or health, if it results from rape or incest, or if the fetus is irreparably damaged.

Poland started the year with a reform of the governmental structure. New ministries, including one for the economy (headed by Wieslaw Kaczmarek) and internal affairs and administration (headed by Leszek Miller) started to work on 1 January. The year ended with a plan for a major administrative reform that was proclaimed by Janusz Tomaszewski, the new minister of internal affairs and administration, on 15 December. The provinces were to be reduced in number from the current 49 to 15 or fewer, and a new intermediate administrative entity, the *powiat*, was to be introduced between the province (*wojewodztwo*) and commune (*gmina*). The proposed reform led to widespread protests in the cities that were scheduled to lose their position as provincial capitals.

FOREIGN POLICY

Poland's foreign policy did not change in 1997. The year saw visible success in its two main priorities: the country's admittance to the EU and NATO. At the Madrid summit in July, Poland was invited to join NATO together with the Czech Republic and Hungary. In December, EU leaders agreed in Luxembourg to move ahead with expanding the EU to embrace five new members, including Poland. The country's Western orientation enjoys nearly unanimous support from Polish political elites and the population at large. In a public opinion poll conducted by OBOP in January, 90 percent of respondents supported Poland's NATO entry, while 88 percent were for the country's EU membership. When U.S. President Bill Clinton visited Poland after the Madrid summit, he said "Poland is coming home." Defense cooperation with the West was close. Polish, German, and Danish defense ministers met in May and August; Polish, French, and German defense ministers met in February; and the three countries decided in December to form a joint military corps. Polish and German navy exercises were conducted in November.

Poland was active on the regional scene. Meetings of Central European leaders in Poland and on Poland's initiative were frequent. Polish leaders repeatedly stated that they favor a wider NATO enlargement. Prime Minister Cimoszewicz said it in Strasbourg in June, Foreign Minister Dariusz Rosati related that to Slovakia in May, his successor Bronislaw Geremek said it with respect to the Baltic states in November. The Polish and Ukrainian presidents met in Warsaw in January and signed a declaration of reconciliation in Kyiv on 21 May. During the Pope's visit to Poland, the presidents of the Czech Republic, Germany, Hungary, Lithuania, Poland, Slovakia, and Ukraine met in Gniezno on 3 June. A Polish-Lithuanian cooperation council was launched in September, and Bronislaw Geremek went to Lithuania in November in his first visit abroad as the new Polish foreign minister. Polish-Russian relations remained tense, mostly over Russia's opposition to NATO enlargement. Polish-Belarusian relations were shadowed by Belarus's record in human rights and the limitations of democracy there, as well as by the Russian presence in Belarus.

GLOSSARY

AWS	Solidarity Electoral Action
BBWR	Non-Party Bloc for Support for Reforms
PSL	Polish Peasant Party
ROP	Movement for Poland's Reconstruction
SLD	Democratic Left Alliance
UD	Democratic Union
UP	Labor Union
UW	Freedom Union

EASTERN EUROPE

V

Lithuania

Latvia

Estonia

Belarus

Ukraine

Lithuania

Population:	3,709,100
Capital:	Vilnius (pop. 575,700)
Major cities:	Kaunas (pop. 415,300), Klaipeda (pop. 202,800)
Area:	62,500 sq. km.
Major ethnic groups:	Lithuanian 81.3%, Russian 8.4%, Polish 7%, Belarusian 1.5%, Ukrainian 1%
Economy:	GDP growth: 6.4%
....	Inflation rate: 8.4%
....	Average monthly wage: $223
....	Unemployment rate: 6.7%

A YEAR OF PROGRESS

by PETER RUTLAND

Lithuania experienced a year of political stability, good relations with its neighbors, and continuing economic recovery, but was disappointed to learn that it would not be among the first five countries of Central Europe to be offered entry to the European Union—an honor that was bestowed on Estonia. Vilnius decided in response to redouble its efforts to prove that it was worthy of EU entry.

1997 was the last year in office of Algirdas Brazauskas, the former Lithuanian Communist Party First Secretary who had been a dominant figure in the country's political life since 1988. Elected head of the parliament in 1993, he declined to run for a second term when his five years in office expired. During the rule of President Brazauskas, power in Lithuania lay not with the president, but with the parliament (Seimas), which had been decisively captured by the conservative Homeland Union in November 1996 after four years of rule by Brazauskas's Lithuanian Democratic Labor Party (LDLP). However, Vytautas Landsbergis was unable to follow up the success of the conservatives by recapturing the presidency, a position he had held prior to 1993. It was centrist Valdas Adamkus, a Lithuanian émigré from the United States, who won the elections to replace Brazauskas in December 1997 and January 1998.

END OF AN ERA

In October President Algirdas Brazauskas announced that he would not put himself up for a second term. Although polls showed that the 65-year-old Brazauskas was still the most popular politician in the country (with a 76 percent approval rating), he said it was time for a new leader to take over. He was also concerned that having a former communist in office was bad for Lithuania's international image. Brazauskas was not able to secure the election of his chosen successor, the 44-year-old former procurator Arturas Paulauskas. Brazauskas' decision to withdraw was a blow to the left, which had already been weakened by rivalry between the LDLP and the Social Democrats. While the LDLP backed Paulauskas, the Social Democrats put forward their own candidate. Paulauskas won the backing of the centrist Liberal Party, but only after he had refused the support of the hard-line Socialists.

The right's electoral strategy was to portray Paulauskas as a neo-communist figure who lacked a concrete policy agenda. The leading liberal/conservative candidate was the Center Union nominee Valdas Adamkus, a 71–year-old environmental administrator who had lived in the United States since leaving Lithuania in 1944. Parliamentary chairman and Homeland Party leader Vytautas Landsbergis also entered the race. In October the Chief Election Commission blocked the Adamkus candidacy on the grounds that he did not meet the three-year residency requirement for presidential candidates. That decision was overturned by the Vilnius regional court, which noted that he had been granted a

Lithuanian passport and residence card in 1992. In the end seven candidates gathered the 20,000 signatures required to enter the race.

In the first round election on 21 December Paulauskas led with 44.7 percent, followed by Adamkus at 27.6 percent and Landsbergis with 15.7 percent. Turnout was a respectable 72 percent—well above the 53 percent that had voted in the 1996 parliamentary election. Landsbergis urged his followers to support Adamkus in the 4 January run-off. Adamkus won the second round by a margin of only 14,000 votes, gaining 50.29 percent to Paulauskas's 49.71 percent.

A certain stable pattern has emerged in the Lithuanian political system. The parties have coalesced into two broad blocs—the post-communist left and the anti-communist right, both fairly close to the center. The five leading parties are relatively weak in organizational terms: they are riven by rivalries within their leadership, and have weak regional organizations. Still, the party system is fairly stable in comparison with those in Estonia and Latvia. The LDLP was the strongest party in the early 1990s, but by 1996–97 its aging supporters were less politically active. At the end of 1997 polls indicated that public support was fairly evenly divided: 16 percent for the Center Union, 15 percent for Homeland Union, 10 percent for the LDLP, and 7 percent for the Social Democrats. Other parties garnered less than 5 percent support each.

The conservatives were in the ascendant, but were divided between those seeking to restore traditional values and those of a more liberal inclination favoring rapid entry to the European Union. The labels of left and right do not neatly correspond to concrete political platforms, but derive more from the parties' anti-communist and post-communist images. Behind the rhetoric, all the parties had quite a strong social welfare orientation, and were united in their desire to restore Lithuania's place as a sovereign nation in an integrated European community.

WAITING AT THE DOORS OF EUROPE

In July the European Commission released its finding that Lithuania was not ready to start accession talks with the EU. Estonia would be one of the five countries in the first round of applicants, while Latvia and Lithuania would have to wait. The commission recognized that Lithuania was qualified to join on political grounds, but argued that its economy was not yet ready to compete in an open European market. The commission's recommendation was accepted at the EU's Luxembourg Summit in December.

The decision to accept only one new member from the Baltic re-opened simmering rivalries among the three Baltic states. At their summit 12 June in Tallinn, the Baltic premiers failed to come up with a joint declaration in response to the Commission's report. Latvia and Estonia were reportedly in favor of a statement saying that even if only one Baltic country were admitted, the other two would still benefit from its membership. Latvia and Lithuania still tried to persuade Estonia to insist on the other two countries being invited to accession talks, to no avail. Some Lithuanians accused Estonia of having deliberately pursued a policy of differentiating itself from its southern neighbors, by creating an image of being the leading reformer in the region.

Prime Minister Gediminas Vagnorius complained in August that Lithuania was left out not because of objective criteria, "which Lithuania more or less meets, but because of organizational and political factors." Partly the rejection stemmed from EU fears that it was administratively and politically impossible to absorb more than five new members at once. Partly also it was a reflection of concern that the Baltic countries were still too poor and would require too much financial support. The GDP per capita of Lithuania amounted to 24 percent of the EU average in 1995, while that of Estonia was 22 percent and Latvia 18 percent. (Poland was only a little better, at 31 percent.) In response to pressure from Sweden and Denmark the EU felt obliged to allow one Baltic country to join—and Estonia was chosen.

The EU made the concession to Latvia and Lithuania of allowing "preparatory talks" to continue in 1998, leaving them with the hope that these can be upgraded to bilateral accession talks. Prime Minister Vagnorius said in December: "We will accomplish so much that the EU will simply feel it is awkward not to begin negotiations with Lithuania. We are determined and we have enough political will to do more than the European Commission will require, and we will do it much faster than the European Union expects." Lithuania definitely did not intend to wait for a possible second wave alongside Romania and Bulgaria. Rubbing salt into the wound of rejection was the EU commission's proposal to allocate the five "fast track" countries 77 percent of its funding for transitional countries, with only 23 percent going to the rest—Bulgaria, Romania, Latvia, Lithuania, and Slovakia.

Lithuania also failed to make the cut for NATO entry. At its Madrid summit in July NATO decided to limit enlargement in the first round to Poland, Hungary, and the Czech Republic. At least in this case the three Baltic countries were treated equally. The Madrid summit made the concession of recognizing Estonia, Latvia, and Lithuania as "aspiring members" of NATO. Many Baltic observers were suspicious that in return for Moscow accepting NATO enlargement, NATO implicitly agreed not to accept the Baltic states as members. Meeting in Tallinn on 27 May, the Baltic, Polish, and Ukrainian presidents nevertheless issued a joint statement expressing their approval of the Russia-NATO Founding Act.

By October intense negotiations were under way on a special U.S.-Baltic charter which it was hoped would partly compensate for the lack of NATO membership. Negotiations took longer than planned. Some suggested this was because of disagreements between the Baltic countries, but it may simply have been delayed by scheduling problems on the American side.

In July, Lithuanian troops participated at the Baltic Challenge 97 international exercise which was held in Paldiskis, Estonia, involving soldiers from six Baltic countries plus the United States. In October plans were laid for an eleven-country Baltic Challenge peacekeeping exercise to be held in Lithuania in July 1998, again including U.S. troops.

GOOD NEIGHBORS

In foreign affairs Lithuania continued the pattern of earlier years, developing good relations with Russia and Poland while falling prey to some bickering with

Latvia and Estonia. The main achievement of the year was the 24 October signing of a border treaty with Russia, something which Estonia and Latvia had not achieved. In general the Baltic states were rather cool toward the idea of cooperation with each other, but pursue this strategy because the Western powers want them to cooperate with each other.

At the semiannual session of the Baltic Council of Ministers in Tallinn in February agreements had been signed promoting air travel and advancing plans to form a Baltic customs union, following up the free trade agreement on farm goods that came into effect at the beginning of 1997. Later in the year, however, Estonia was accused of having lost interest in the creation of a Baltic customs union once it was given the green light for EU. At least on 18 September an agreement on the abolition of non-tariff barriers was initialed in Riga by Estonia, Latvia, and Lithuania. Lithuania rejected charges in the Estonian press that Lithuania had been ignoring Baltic unity in favor of closer relations with Poland. It was thought that by building close ties with Poland Lithuania was trying to improve its chances for early NATO entry.

Regional cooperation received a boost with a "good neighbors" meeting in Vilnius on 5–6 September of the presidents of ten countries in the region between the Baltic and the Black seas. The summit failed to produce any specific agreements, or even a common declaration, but the simple fact that it took place was considered important, and the leaders hope to turn it into an annual event. The gathering saw tough criticism of Belarusian president Alyaksandr Lukashenka and a call for good relations with Russia as well as the West. Russian Prime Minister Viktor Chernomyrdin was also in attendance and pledged speedy resolution of lingering border questions, although the Baltic states rejected his offer of Russian security guarantees as a substitute for NATO enlargement. Presidents Brazauskas of Lithuania, Guntis Ulmanis of Latvia, and Lennart Meri of Estonia met at the Lithuanian resort of Palanga on 10 November to discuss President Boris Yeltsin's security proposals. They reaffirmed their common position that "unilateral security guarantees do not correspond to the spirit of the new Europe."

The border agreement with Russia had taken four years, and 17 rounds of talks, to prepare. The western border with the Russian enclave was not yet fully demarcated, although in October Lithuania agreed to accept 20 percent of the territory of Lake Vistytis, which had been the main stumbling block in the talks. Another area of concern is land access from Russia proper across Belarus and Lithuania to the Kaliningrad enclave. Given that only 8 percent of Lithuania's residents are ethnic Russians, unlike in Estonia and Latvia, Vilnius had no problem passing a liberal citizenship law (back in 1989) and granting ethnic minorities full political rights. Visiting Vilnius on 13 June, Russian Foreign Minister Yevgenii Primakov said that he hoped Lithuania would gain entry to the EU and praised its "civilized, good, and balanced measures . . . with regard to ethnic minorities and the Russian community, Lithuania meets all EU accession requirements." However, November saw the publication of a report by the Council for Foreign and Defense Policy in Moscow which urged the use of economic leverage to extract better terms from the Baltic states and heightened emphasis on the rights of ethnic Russians, which caused grave concern in Baltic capitals. It also advocated a policy of differentiation toward the three Baltic states.

By the end of 1997 Lithuania had managed to complete the demarcation of its border with Poland, while the 650-kilometer border with Belarus and 540-kilometer border with Latvia were in the process of being marked. Still unresolved was the demarcation of the sea border with Latvia. In 1995, Latvia signed oil exploration agreements with U.S. and Swedish companies in an area claimed by both Latvia and Lithuania. Relations between Riga and Vilnius were also strained in September when the Latvian environmental ministry wrote a letter to banks who were considering funding the Butinge oil terminal in Lithuania, expressing concern about possible ecological hazards.

Relations with Belarus were complicated by the scandal over Minsk's arrest of Russian journalists who had crossed the Belarus-Lithuanian border. Despite this, Lithuania strove to maintain normal, working relations with its eastern neighbor. In June it was decided to deploy more Lithuanian soldiers on the border with Belarus to staunch the flow of illegal immigrants from Asia and the Middle East hoping to transit further west. About 1,000 such refugees were being held in Lithuanian detention centers. Control of migrants is a matter of considerable concern to the European Union. Lithuania was accepting repatriated illegal immigrants from Poland, but Belarus would not take back refugees who had crossed into Lithuania from its territory. In July a new law on the status of refugees came into effect in Lithuania, granting them the right to apply for asylum. Visa-free travel agreements were signed with Sweden and later Finland in the course of the year. Denmark and Norway had signed such agreements several years previously.

Relations with Poland continued to blossom, with frequent visits by politicians from the two countries, joint operation of border points, and the like. Over the course of 1997 special joint gatherings were established for the presidencies, governments, and parliaments of the two countries. On 4 November, the Lithuanian parliament ratified the creation of a joint Lithuanian-Polish peacekeeping battalion. However, there was still some sensitivity over language policy with respect to the Polish minority in Lithuania (7 percent of the total population). In January Polish organizations in Lithuania protested Education Minister Zigmas Zinkevicius's statements to journalists the previous month, in which he suggested that Polish-language schools should be closed down. Talks continued over the issue of how to transliterate the names of Lithuanian and Polish minorities in the respective countries.

POLITICS AS USUAL

In the course of the year the Social Democrats tried to mobilize against privatization, with nothing much to show for their efforts. They sought to block the government's plans for extending privatization to strategic industries such as oil, energy, nuclear power-engineering, telecom, ports, and airlines. The opposition complained that the sale of these monopolistic companies to foreign buyers would result in price-gouging of customers and possible harm to Lithuania's national interests. In May they began collecting signatures to call a referendum on the subject, but in the three-month period allowed by law they collected only 180,000 signatures—short of the 300,000 required for a referendum to be called. Energy and utility rates were hiked by about one-third as of 1 July, leading to more protests and a court appeal from leftist parliamentary deputies.

The government's priority was to prepare for privatization the telecom monopoly Lietuvos Telekomas (LT), which they thought could raise $1 billion. In August the Swiss bank UBS was commissioned to prepare the public tender for LT.

The post-communist crime wave continued to be a central concern of politicians, the public, and the international community. President Brazauskas called in March for a strengthening of the State Security Department to enable it to "fight Lithuania's domestic ills—corruption, contraband, and the squandering of state property." In June and July new laws were passed on organized crime and money laundering, and one requiring top state officials to submit official declarations of income and gifts.

In July, in a case which drew wide and unwelcome international publicity, two Lithuanian nationals were arrested in Miami and were accused of offering to sell arms such as anti-aircraft missiles, tactical nuclear weapons, and a submarine complete with crew, to U.S. federal agents posing as Colombian drug lords. The same month the Vilnius police chief resigned following the beating and robbery of the French cultural attache.

There was a steady flow of corruption scandals. The 29-year-old finance minister, Rolandas Matiliauskas, resigned in February (less than a month after his appointment) after he was indicted on charges of embezzlement and foreign currency violations, stemming from a low-interest loan he allegedly received from a bank. He was subsequently cleared of the charges. In August parliamentary deputy Andrius Butkevicius, the first minister of defense in independent Lithuania, had his immunity lifted and was indicted for having offered to intervene on behalf of a businessman accused of fraud. Police caught Butkevicius accepting a $15,000 bribe.

Lithuania generally got a clean bill of health on the human rights front in the U.S. State Department's annual report for 1997. It did cite concern over police brutality toward subjects in detention, and complained about a law allowing detention without trial for up to two months for suspects of organized crime activity. In June the parliament began to discuss the abolition of the death penalty, implementation of which had been suspended in 1996 as a condition of Lithuania's entry to the Council of Europe.

The press was generally free but there was some concern about political pressure over the content of print media. In turn the press itself stood accused of blatant political partisanship. The parliament adopted its long-awaited media law in July: a draft public information law had failed to pass in November 1995 after journalists protested that it was too restrictive. Under the new law the media will create a special ethics commission and ombudsman to review complaints against the press.

GHOSTS OF THE PAST

Political disputes blew up around attempts to deal, or not to deal, with the communist and fascist past. Controversy over the prosecution of Nazi-era war criminals flared up in the fall. Shortly after Lithuania gained its independence, parliament had passed a law rehabilitating all those who had resisted occupying forces (Nazi and Soviet). This blanket amnesty gave immunity to several dozen suspects that international Jewish organizations accused of participation in Nazi war crimes.

In September parliament discussed some legal amendments to speed up efforts to prosecute suspected war criminals. Some nationalist deputies rebutted charges made in the Israeli parliament about the alleged enthusiastic participation of some Lithuanians in the Nazi Holocaust. The Simon Wiesenthal Center called for a boycott of the commemorations marking the 200th anniversary of the Talmudic scholar Gaon Elijahu Kramer of Vilnius, which took place in September. On 23 December the parliament eventually amended the criminal code to allow the prosecution of those accused of genocide regardless of their state of health, by allowing their lawyers to represent them by proxy. This cleared the way for the trial of Alesandras Lileikas, 90, whose case had been repeatedly postponed on health grounds. Lileikas had been the head of the National Security Police subordinate to the Nazis. His former deputy Kazys Gimzauskas, 89, who lost his U.S. citizenship in 1996, was also indicted in November. Antanas Mineikis, who had been stripped of U.S. citizenship in 1992 for concealing his membership in a Nazi execution squad, had returned to Lithuania and had not been prosecuted. He died of old age in November.

On the communist side of the ledger, the trial continued of six persons accused of leading the January 1991 hard-line coup attempt in Lithuania, including communist leaders Mykolas Burokevicius and Juozas Jermalavicius. President Brazauskas appeared as a witness in the case in October.

In June President Brazauskas vetoed a property restitution law which would have returned land and property to some 80,000 families dispossessed in the 1940s. There were fears that the new owners could threaten the tenure of the existing occupants, some 10,000 families. The parliament on 1 July voted by 80 to 24 to override Brazauskas's veto, arguing that legal guarantees for sitting tenants were adequate. Since its election in December the conservative parliament had overridden four of the five vetoes which Brazauskas imposed.

In May parliamentary chairman Landsbergis had to fend off accusations that he gave orders to the interior ministry to put other political leaders under surveillance. In September the parliament set up a commission to investigate charges in a book by former KGB General Vyacheslav Shironin that in Soviet times Landsbergis had offered to cooperate with the KGB in return for permission to travel abroad. The investigation established that Landsbergis had been monitored for his dissident activities but had not collaborated with his persecutors.

ECONOMIC RECOVERY CONTINUES

1997 was a good year for the Lithuanian economy. GDP grew by about 6 percent (up from 3.5 percent in 1996); inflation was held to 8.4 percent; and the budget deficit came in at 1.9 percent of GDP. In October, due to better than expected economic performance, the government was able to increase budget spending by 270 million litas ($68 million) above plan. The only really worrying indicator was the external trade deficit, which rose to $1.4 billion in January–November. However, Lithuania's total debt burden is fairly low relative to GDP (19 percent) and to exports (35 percent in 1997). Per capita GDP is still low, however. In purchasing power parity terms it is estimated at about $2,500 a year. Average working wages in Lithuania in December were 985 litas ($246), pulling ahead of Estonia ($240) for the first time. They rose 32 percent in dollar terms during the year.

The Index of Economic Freedom for 1998 prepared by the Heritage Foundation and the *Wall Street Journal,* ranked Lithuania 74th out of 156 countries, well behind Estonia (ranked 17) and even Latvia (62) but quite close to Poland (69) and ahead of Slovakia (74), Slovenia (80), and Romania (94).

The country's banking system seemed to have rebuilt itself after the devastating crash of 1995. One sign of recovery was that on 9 June Lithuania received its first investment grade rating from an international agency. Previously, its bonds had been rated as speculative grade. Standard and Poor put Lithuania's long-term debts at BBB. In December Moody upgraded the country's long-term foreign currency bonds and notes to Ba1.

By the end of 1997 over 40 percent of state property, and most housing and small businesses, had been privatized, employing some 66 percent of the labor force. Most of the privatization had taken place in previous years. In 1997 the second wave of cash auctions for the remaining small enterprises went slowly. Only 317 firms were sold, raising 84 million litas ($21 million). All that was on offer were small blocks of shares in already-privatized companies, or defunct enterprises and pieces of derelict real estate. There were plans to privatize a dozen or so major firms in the energy and transport sectors, including Lithuanian Airlines, the Mazeikiu oil refinery, and Lietuvos Telekomas (see discussion above). The new $270 million Butinge offshore oil terminal, which was scheduled for completion in 1998, will also be privatized.

The IMF granted Lithuania a three-year, $180 million Extended Fund Facility in October 1994 which was drawn down on schedule and ended in October 1997. During negotiations for renewing the final six months of the EFF loan Prime Minister Vagnorius expressed reluctance to implement some of the IMF's conditions, in particular the pledge to cut average food import duties from 27 percent to 20 percent by March 1997 and to 10 percent a year later. But agreement was reached, and in July 1997 Lithuania became the first post-socialist country to agree to the public release of its "article 4" review by the IMF. The report praised Lithuania's commitment to reform but identified privatization, agriculture, and social security as in need of further action. Farmers still accounted for 22 percent of the labor force, and were seen as the group most vulnerable to EU competition.

The IMF was undecided over whether it was time for Lithuania to drop the rather rigid currency board system, adopted in 1994, which fixed the litas at 4 to the U.S. dollar. The new government elected in November 1996 had made abolition of the currency board part of its campaign program. A steady real appreciation of the litas against the U.S. dollar over 1996–97 and the consequent yawning foreign trade deficit were arguments in favor of a move toward a more flexible crawling peg regime. But no decision on this issue was taken in 1997. The stable litas was seen as an important symbol of Lithuania's economic reliability.

Foreign direct investment was $220 million in the whole of 1996 and $190 million in the first half of 1997 alone, cumulating to a total of $970 million by October 1997. This was ahead of Latvia's $840 million and close behind Estonia's $1.1 billion. The three Baltic countries see themselves as direct competitors for investment, since foreign manufacturers will typically build one plant for the whole region. The United States was the largest single source of foreign capital (25 percent), followed by Sweden and Germany (each accounting for 12 percent). Philip Morris was the largest single investor. In September they opened a new $38 million factory in Klaipeda. In November Inkaras of Kaunas started producing shoes under license for Adidas, with half of the output intended for export. By November foreign investment in Lithuania's fledgling stock market increased by 20 percent to $290 million, 60 percent of the total market.

Last but not least there is the question of Lithuania's nuclear legacy. The country derives 84 percent of its electricity from the nuclear plant at Ignalina, which has two Chernobyl-style RBMK reactors and is located just 40 miles from Vilnius. One of the reactors was shut down for several days after the cooling system failed on 21 September. In June police seized 70 kilograms of uranium that had been stolen from the Ignalian plant in 1992. Foreign Affairs Minister Algirdas Saudargas expressed concern that the country would soon be facing problems over the long-term storage of spent fuel and would need international assistance.

Sidebar: UNCERTAINTY AROUND THE BALTIC SEA

by GERARD F. BRILLANTES

In the past, all Baltic Sea nations' defense scenarios centered on the potential expansion of the Soviet empire. But now, in the short run, the singular threat from the east has diminished—if not altogether disappeared—and has largely been replaced by multiple low-intensity threats. While six years have passed since the breakup of the USSR, the nations that border the Baltic are still adapting their defenses to the new order. Some countries have grown larger, some smaller. And the three small Baltic republics are grappling with the defense responsibilities of independence.

For more than 40 years, the Cold War imposed an uneasy stability on the Baltic Sea region. Within a short span of eight years, the fall of the Soviet Union and the loss of Soviet hegemony swept away that anxious peace. In its place is a volatile mix of nascent national boundaries, awkward new democratic systems, unpolished military alliances, and above all, new national security interests.

Russia has had perhaps the most difficult task: it has less access to the Baltic coast than before because of the loss of the Baltic states of Estonia, Latvia, and Lithuania. The three Baltic republics had been a vital part of the Soviet Union's national defense. Tallinn was once the home of the Northern Group headquarters of the Baltic Red Banner Fleet. The Estonian cities of Parnu, Haapsalu, and Tapa formed an air defense network, and the Latvian port of Liepaja served as a naval harbor. And the loss of the three Baltic republics made Kaliningrad Oblast vulnerable, isolated from Russia.

Given the dire situation of the navy and the nation as a whole, Russia has recognized the need to consolidate its naval presence in the Baltic Sea through excessive and rapid militarization in Kaliningrad. The exclave is 25 percent over its arms limitations defined by the Conventional Forces in Europe treaty (CFE). Another trend is the continued building and maintenance of the Russian Baltic Fleet. The Soviet navy possessed the largest fleet in the area and, from the end of World War II to the breakup of the Soviet Union, had enjoyed the great geographic advantage of having a long stretch of coastline under its control. Today, the Russian navy possesses only two outlets to the Baltic Sea: one in St. Petersburg to the north and one in Kaliningrad to the south. Kaliningrad is the current home of the Baltic Fleet, which is based in the city of Baltiisk due to the vulnerability of St. Petersburg's outlet to the Gulf of Finland (the gulf is bordered by Estonia and Finland). Russia still boasts five major shipyards, which produce surface vessels and submarines for domestic and foreign purchase. Naval aviation is land-based, since aircraft carrier operations would be vulnerable as well as redundant or even a hindrance in the confined theater of the Baltic Sea.

The limited union of Russia and Belarus contains provisions for future national security cooperation. Should those specific provisions be realized, such an alliance would greatly enhance Russia's current strategic advantage, particularly in the southern region of the Baltic Sea. However, given the dire condition of the Russian economy, support from the centrally planned and stagnant economy of Belarus is doubtful in the long term. Russia's Baltic moves are most likely a consolidation of Russian naval power and a reorientation toward perceived Western military threats, such as the expansion of NATO eastward.

Russia is therefore fortifying its remaining Baltic strategic assets in case new East European NATO members, particularly Poland, should prove a real threat. Kaliningrad Oblast is the only Russian foothold in northern Europe; it is the military card Russia can play should fears of NATO aggression prove justified. Otherwise, even in light of its violations of the CFE quotas, Russia does not seem intent on expanding to other Baltic regions. It cannot afford the gain of new territory, not to mention the costs of modernizing weapons or command, control, communication, and intelligence systems.

REGIONAL MAINTENANCE

Unlike Russia, Sweden is not experiencing difficult economic times for its armed forces. Sweden has neither lost nor gained territory vital to national security in the last decade. It views once-feared eastern threats as a dying danger and has adjusted its Baltic naval presence accordingly.

During the Cold War, Sweden detected Soviet incursions and took steps to deter and counter threats to its neutrality and its borders. That experience is reflected in the country's long-standing commitment to extensive littoral operations. Sweden's geography has always demanded improvements in anti-submarine warfare operations. While the number of anti-submarine ships, coastal vessels, and submarines in the Swedish navy is noteworthy, the defense capabilities of Sweden's other armed forces remain equally impressive.

Despite acquiring a new "stealth ship" and more modern submarines, Sweden is continuing a path of neutrality rather than returning to the empire-building of centuries past. Because of the diminishment of the Soviet naval threat, Sweden has reduced its force from 12 submarines to nine. The latest submarines, the A-19 Gotlands, can stay submerged longer than other diesel-electric boats, such as the Russian Kilo-class submarines in the Baltic Sea. Two of Sweden's submarines were transferred to Finland, which would never have acquired the submarines during the Cold War, for fear of provoking Russia.

After World War II, Finland's national policy of neutrality was framed within the context of the 1948 Treaty of Friendship, Cooperation, and Mutual Assistance with the Soviet Union. The present Finnish defense policy still follows the preamble of that treaty: a "desire to remain outside the conflicting interests of the Great Powers." In other countries, that policy came to be known as "Finlandization," which implies a loss of control of foreign policy in favor of compliance with the wishes of a larger, more powerful neighbor.

With the threat of Soviet territorial expansion eliminated, Finland continues its neutrality with respect to other Baltic Sea nations. On the waves, Finland continues to seek more modern patrol craft to replace aging, Soviet-built vessels. Finland's armed forces, well-suited for littoral warfare, will now include Swedish-built diesel submarines. It also seeks to acquire F-18 Hornet aircraft, designed for joint warfare. The new acquisitions come in light of Russia's diminishment to regional power status and Finnish security demands for in-depth defense.

One nation that requires an even more comprehensive security policy is Germany, because of its reunification. Germany's territory has increased to give the country greater access to the Baltic. It bears a resemblance to a newly formed empire, where newly acquired territories force changes in defense strategy.

Type-124 destroyers, Brandenburg-class frigates, Type-212 air-independent, propulsion-equipped submarines, and Frankenthal-class minehunters are all planned additions to the German navy for early next century. Like Russian and Swedish ships, all those vessels possess capabilities suited to Baltic Sea operations. Germany is likely to use its current naval forces toward coastal defense, split between the Baltic Sea and North Sea. Unlike Russia, however, Germany has NATO exercise and force obligations to fulfill. Its naval and security establishments will see further changes particularly in the political and cultural ramifications of taking into account differences between East and West.

Overall, national security concerns will expand as newly enlarged boundaries must be guarded, a problem facing the three Baltic nations, and national defenses must be reoriented to cope with a new alliance, a problem facing Poland.

Unlike the other nations that have a border with the Baltic Sea, Denmark's most pressing security interests are defined in two missions: defense of its home waters and the waters of the Faeroe Islands and Greenland, and whatever mission is assigned to the Danish units operating within NATO or other multinational forces. Thus there is much greater emphasis on Danish naval defense toward the North Sea and its immediate seaways and away from the Baltic Sea. Therefore, Baltic Sea concerns have a much lower priority for Denmark than for the other nations. However, under the Partnership for Peace program, Denmark has adjusted its security concerns with its regional concerns and has concluded several other bilateral and trilateral agreements.

NEW NATIONS, NEW DEFENSES

Poland and the Baltic nations are still redefining their defense strategies in the wake of the Warsaw Pact's dissolution. Under the current economic difficulties, those four nations share the onerous burden of having to create a new national defense policy and inheriting antiquated weapon systems. Although national defense spending is rapidly increasing, it remains a distant second to national welfare and infrastructure building. As a consequence, the Baltic nations are currently using small patrol craft, European-donated vessels or, in Lithuania's case, newly purchased Russian light frigates to maintain and secure national boundaries. Much like the Baltic states, Poland could only acquire German-built Sassnitz-class ships. Modern naval equipment will be beyond the reach of those nations for at least the next decade.

Soon after the end of World War II, the polarization and the threat of escalation to a major war deterred most aligned countries from seeking armed solutions for explosive territorial, ethnic, or religious conflicts. Today, ethnic tension or natural disasters are sufficient to cause major regional unrest: witness Bosnia. In general, geopolitical changes have created new threats.

Lithuanian Defense Minister Andrius Butkevicius set the following "hierarchy of threats": instability in the former Soviet Union, followed by ethno-religious and territorial conflicts, followed by crime and industrial disasters. With the threat of high-intensity conflicts unlikely in the short run, nations face subtler threats, including disaster-relief operations, peace operations, international crime and drug trafficking, illegal migration, and terrorism. The escalation of such threats to regional conflicts is a threat to long-term security. In the three Baltic republics, the potential for conflicts is particularly worrisome given the untested and vague laws against such "capitalist" problems as illegal immigration and drug dealing.

Fortunately for those nations, low-intensity conflict resolution mostly demands sufficient political will and naval presence. As Polish, Estonian, Latvian, Lithuanian, and German vessels are mostly small and fast, they will not demand complicated and expensive command and intelligence networks to secure national borders against criminal activity or illegal immigrants.

In the case of Lithuania, the problem is also its position as a buffer between East and West. The militarization of Kaliningrad Oblast is a major obstacle in securing Lithuania's national boundaries and could potentially start a regional arms race. In the short term, high-intensity conflicts are unlikely because of the economic and social instability caused by the dissolution of the Soviet Union. Domestic interests have taken priority over international concerns.

The turn of the century holds more uncertain issues. Porous national boundaries, ethnic issues, authoritarian tendencies, and extreme nationalism provide a dangerous impetus toward high-intensity conflicts. Among them is the persistent issue of Russian minorities in the Baltic states. Current and past officials of the Russian Foreign Ministry have vigorously complained about the alleged mistreatment of Russian minorities. The Russian government feels it retains the right to take whatever steps are necessary to protect Russian minorities in the "near abroad." All three nations construe those protestations as interference in internal matters and a pretext for invasion. While that may seem unlikely the remainder of this century, history has taught the Baltic nations to be wary.

To reduce tensions in the Baltic Sea region, there is an impressive array of international regional, subregional, and bilateral agreements that have greatly reduced the tensions caused by political and economic instability and uncertainty. By their inherent exclusivity, unions and alliances arouse feeling of either neglect, as in the three Baltic nations, or menace, as in Russia. The July 1997 visit from the U.S. secretary of state and continual Russian worries regarding the potential NATO membership of the Baltic states and Poland emphasize the pitfalls of regional security and integration agreements in this region.

One such pitfall is when matters of national principles and interests clash with treaties. Russia's pursuit of the war in Chechnya in 1994 brought widespread condemnation from European nations. Under the Partnership for Peace, Denmark and Russia had already signed a bilateral agreement concerning joint cooperation at all military levels, exchange visits, and exercises ranging from sea rescue to peacekeeping. But Denmark ceased cooperation because Russia was mobilizing its troops for action in Chechnya. Denmark felt that Russian conduct contradicted Western and Danish principles.

Security rests primarily on the ability of all Baltic Sea nations to adapt to changing institutions, to counter authoritarian tendencies, and to foresee potential trouble caused by the deteriorating economic and social conditions such as inflation, currency devaluation, and loss of social safety nets. Poland, the Baltic states, and Russia are in the midst of defining new national security policies in light of the historic changes of the last half of the decade. Long cherished and revered (or hated) pillars of communist rule have disappeared in favor of capitalism, free markets, and democracy and the strengthening of national integrity.

NOTE

Reproduced with kind permission from *Transitions* magazine, November 1997.

Latvia

Population:	2,485,400
Capital:	Riga (pop. 820,577)
Major cities:	Daugavpils (pop. 117,835), Liepaja (pop. 97,917), Jelgava (pop. 70,943)
Area:	64,610 sq. km.
Major ethnic groups:	Latvian 54.8%, Russian 32.8%, Belarusian 4.0%, Ukrainian 3.0%, Polish 2.2%, Lithuanian 1.3%, Jews 0.5%
Economy:	GDP growth: 5.6%
	Inflation rate: 7.0%
	Average monthly wage: $272
	Unemployment rate: 6.7%

KEEPING A COURSE TOWARD THE WEST

by ARTIS PABRIKS

The year 1997 was seen by local as well as foreign observers as the most hopeful period Latvia has experienced since its independence was regained. The main reason for Latvians' optimism about their future was the country's economic advancement. According to Dimitris Demecas, IMF representative in Latvia, the developments of 1997 placed Latvia among the leading countries in Central and Eastern Europe as far as reforms and macroeconomic data are concerned.

Within the political realm one of the most important events of 1997 was Latvia's acceptance by the European Union as one of the future candidates for membership. Domestically, the resignation of Prime Minister Andris Skele, the possible new rising star of Latvian politics, was the main focus of public attention. Improvements in daily life still remained wishful thinking, although the year 1997 provided people with the belief that they were on the right track and that tomorrow things might get better.

DOMESTIC POLITICS DESERVE BETTER

The broad coalition government, containing no less than seven parties, and the fragmented parliament led to a climate of political instability which culminated in the summer with the resignation of Prime Minister Andris Skele on 28 July. Skele had served as prime minister since December 1995. He had threatened resignation earlier in the year, in January, when the coalition balked at approving his candidate for finance minister. His resignation was caused by his disagreements with the leadership of the three largest coalition partners, namely Latvia's Way, For Fatherland and Freedom, and the Democratic Party Saimnieks. Skele was accused of dictating to parliament, while the prime minister blamed several leading politicians for corruption and inefficiency. No less than five ministers resigned in the months before Skele's departure, four of them amidst corruption allegations, none of which actually made it to court. The fifth official, Interior Minister Dainis Turlais, quit after an accident at a firefighting display in Talsi on 28 June claimed the lives of eight children. In August, the 40-year-old Gundars Krasts, the economic minister and a member of the right-of-center For Fatherland and Freedom, was approved by parliament as the new prime minister.

On 9 March municipal elections were held. The established political dominance of three parties, namely the center-right party Latvia's Way, the populistic Democratic Party Saimnieks, and the nationalist party For Fatherland and Freedom, was challenged by a newly emerged power, the Social Democrats led by Juris Bojars, a former KGB officer and lawyer. The above-mentioned party came up with slogans to "nationalize the denationalized," to fight corruption, and to increase the social well-being of the poor. It was noted by a number of politicians and analysts that the Social Democratic Party is concerned with social democracy in name only. Basically, it represents the values of the former Soviet regime. In the capital of Riga the Social Democrats were the most popular party, but were unable to find any coalition partners. Eventually, Latvia's Way formed the local government without the participation of the Social Democrats.

The congress of Latvia's Way that took place in autumn declared a slight turn of the party's policy toward the left. In 1997, Latvia's Way had lost its particular political identity and was unable to produce a viable program of future activities. During the congress of the Democratic Party (Saimnieks) its leadership, seeking to redefine its vision of politics, declared its wish to follow a policy of "state nationalism." In practice it would mean the protection of local producers in competition with foreign entrepreneurs. Saimnieks' announcement annoyed Prime Minister Krasts, as well as foreign investors. Above all, the third leading party For Fatherland and Freedom focused its efforts on blocking any liberalization of the citizenship law. Thanks to this strategy it seemed to be the party with the most stable electorate, namely nationalists (about 12 percent of the voters).

The latter half of the year was dominated by maneuvering for the parliamentary elections due to take place in 1998. All three leading parties of the coalition, namely Latvia's Way, Democratic Party (Saimnieks), and For Fatherland and Freedom, were trying to halt the appearance of new political forces able to challenge the status quo. Obviously, the worries of the leading parties in the coalition were caused by the emergence of several new parties. The National Reform Party was started by three leading members of the former Latvian Movement for the National Independence (LNNK) who unlike the majority of their former party comrades did not accept the unification of the LNNK with For Fatherland and Freedom. A second new party was being prepared by Latvian businessmen in the younger generation.

A third was launched on 18 December by Andris Skele, the former prime minister, who was still the most popular politician in Latvia. Many argued that it was his policies that made it possible to call the year 1997 economically successful and politically optimistic. Skele earned the respect and trust of large segments of the population despite—or perhaps because of—his tough character, authoritarian appearance, hard-nosed economic policy, and combative approach toward the established political elite and major parties. He pledged that his new party will adopt a long-run perspective and tackle the structural problems which still impede Latvia's further development.

LATVIA AND THE EUROPEAN UNION

In summer, 1997, the European Union announced that six countries from the former socialist camp were ready to start talks about joining the EU. Estonia was included in this group but Latvia was not, which led the Latvian prime minister to embark on an odyssey through almost all the EU countries seeking support. Mainly thanks to Denmark and Sweden at the EU summit in December 1997 it was decided to invite Latvia as well as four other previously "unqualifying" countries of the former Soviet bloc for talks about their possible entry into a second round of membership talks in the European Union. However, it was declared that substantial talks would be started only with those who "fit most" the requirements of the European Union, which applies to the earlier announced six countries.

Ultimately, for Latvia it means a lot of work over the next decade in order to make its economy, laws, and financial system compatible with West European standards. On 4 September during a meeting in Bergen the prime ministers of the Baltic and Nordic countries agreed to create a Nordic and Baltic Country Research Group that would assist the Baltic countries to adapt to EU norms. Though many Latvian politicians think that all three Baltic countries should join the EU simultaneously, there is a common understanding that even if Estonia starts first all three countries will finally benefit from Estonia's success. Estonia's success can positively influence Latvia to speed up its development as well as making the Latvian political elite estimate their policy failures and successes more realistically. At this moment Latvia in its transition toward a market economy is still behind Estonia. The high standards of the EU countries force Latvian authorities and entrepreneurs to stick to the proper path of reform. However, some EU analysts claim that Latvian entry to the European Union is not likely for at least ten years.

According to the Euro-barometer survey in 1997, about 32 percent of Latvia's respondents do not have a clear opinion about the European Union. Also, it seems that many Latvians still do not consider membership in the European Union to be in their near future. Some doubts were expressed by nationalists about the future of the Latvian identity and language as well as the future viability of the farm sector after EU entry. However, recent developments showed that there are increasing attempts on behalf of the government to fight corruption and stick to the market-oriented reforms.

LATVIA AND NATO

In June 1997, the Madrid Summit showed that the Latvian path to membership in NATO would be even more thorny than the road to EU. However, Latvian participation in the peace-keeping forces in Bosnia as well as cooperation with Western powers through the Partnership for Peace makes Latvia feel closer to NATO. In September alone three military training sessions took place in Latvia. On 8–11 September representatives of four NATO countries and ten countries from the Partnership for Peace program took part in the international training session Cooperative Best Effort '97 at the Adazi Training Centre. 475 soldiers from Canada, Netherlands, Norway, the United States, and the three Baltic states as well as Finland, Hungary, Macedonia, Moldova, Poland, Sweden, and Ukraine participated in the training session. At the same time, Open Spirit '97 and Cooperative Baltic Eye '97, the largest ever search-and-rescue training event on the Baltic Sea took place. During 1997 there was continued cooperation with Western partners on such projects as Baltron, the establishment of a common

Baltic navy unit and Baltnet. The latter project was developed during 1997 on the initiative of the United States as well as with the help of Norway and Denmark and the possible involvement of Sweden and Finland. The Baltnet program is designed to establish a common Latvian, Lithuanian, and Estonian system of airspace control based in Lithuania. During 1997, Latvia's government also seemed to show more efforts to improve the security of its eastern borders.

On 14 October in Washington representatives of all three Baltic countries and the United States had talks regarding the U.S.-Baltic Charter. On 4 November the Latvian Foreign Ministry rejected Russia's offer to provide unilateral security guaranties to Latvia and the two other Baltic states. In the foreseeable future it is very unlikely that Latvia could agree on any Russian security guaranties which are not part of the larger collective security agreement involving the major Western powers and NATO.

ECONOMIC REFORMS PROGRESS

Good economic results were achieved during 1997, and Latvia attained not only stability but also significant development. In 1997 GDP increased by 6 percent (up from 2.8 percent in 1996) while the inflation fell to 7 percent (13 percent in 1996), which is one of the lowest inflation rates in the region. The work of the Bank of Latvia was estimated with a "B+" or "very good" in the annual report on the activities of central banks prepared by Global Finance. For the first time since regaining independence the country ended the year with a budget surplus (of about $63 million). Revenues collected were 589 million lats ($980 million) while expenditures were about 548 million lats ($916 million). According to statistics, almost every branch of the Latvian economy showed an increase compared to the data of 1996. More than 60 percent of GDP was earned by services, indicated that Latvia's economy is taking on characteristics similar to those of developed industrial nations. However, imports were increasing much faster than exports. Some industries, such as fishing, experienced a decrease of activity in 1997. The banking sector seems to have put its earlier troubles behind it. Assets increased by 40 percent, loans by 55 percent, and capital and reserves by 35 percent, while savings increased by 36 percent.

JUSTICE AND CORRUPTION

The year 1997 marked slight changes in the attitude of the society as well as of the government toward criminality and corruption. Survey data showed that 40 percent of Latvia's residents had some personal experience connected with corruption, and 20 percent admitted their willingness to bribe. On the other hand, fully 52 percent of the respondents said that they did not experience cases of corruption since 1991. Still, 48 percent of respondents thought that the police are corrupted, and 47 percent believed the same of the courts and parliament. Only 6 percent regard journalists as corrupted.

In 1997 the Latvian authorities took a more serious stand in fighting criminality and corruption. At the end of the year the head judge of Valmiera region was arrested after being accused of taking bribes. Dzintars Rasnacs, the minister of justice, and Guntars Krasts, the prime minister, criticized the court system in connection with its inability to properly handle the cases of Banka Baltija and Ivans Haritonovs. The latter was publicly known as the leader of a local Mafia branch. However, due to the weakness of the court system his guilt could not be proven, and Haritonovs was released by court decision in the summer of 1997. Janis Legzdins, the leading Latvian parliamentary deputy in the fight against corruption, argued that the government needed to make the fight against corruption a top political priority instead of leaving it up to a handful of individual campaigners. After the unsuccessful trial against Haritonovs, the authorities finally introduced a witness protection program that had never formerly existed in Latvia. Prime Minister Krasts admitted that Latvia should use the experience of Scandinavia and Germany in the battle against corruption, as well as coordination, cooperation and better flow of information between the Baltic Sea countries. The survey data suggest some grounds for arguing that Latvian society was starting to understand that a crucial difference between the former Soviet regime and a democratic regime is that in the former people were proud of ignoring the laws, while in a democratic country people should feel shame following the same practice.

In June, Latvia ratified the European Convention on Human Rights and on 2 October the Latvian parliament finally ratified the Geneva Convention on Refugees. The ratification of the Convention will facilitate the creation of a refugee center in Latvia and regulate dealing with illegal refugees. Among the Baltic states, Latvia was the last country to ratify the Convention.

Estonia

Population:	1,466,900
Capital:	Tallinn (pop. 434,763)
Major cities:	Tartu (pop. 104,907), Narva (pop. 77,770), Kohtla-Jarve (pop. 55,415)
Area:	45,000 sq. km.
Major ethnic groups:	Estonian 64.2%, Russian 28.7%, Ukrainian 2.7%, Belarusian 1.5%, Finnish 1%
Economy:	GDP growth: 9.0%
....	Inflation rate: 12.5%
....	Average monthly wage: $302
....	Unemployment rate: 4.6%

BACK TO EUROPE

by JOAN LOFGREN

In 1997 Estonia was still the success story of post-Soviet reforms, as leaders used the term "Baltic tiger" to refer to its fast-growing economy. The year marked the end of Estonia's political transition from Soviet rule, as it was accepted into the first round of European Union (EU) enlargement talks and thus confirmed in its return to the community of democratic European states. Russia's continuing insistence, however, on Estonia's exclusion from NATO membership reminded leaders that although Estonia had returned to Europe, Russia's influence over its security environment was here to stay.

ANOTHER CHANGE OF GOVERNMENT

Domestic political events in 1997 were dominated by a change of government early in the year. Prime Minister Tiit Vahi, after having formed a minority government in November 1996 and barely surviving a no-confidence vote, finally resigned in February. Opposition leaders called a no-confidence vote after Vahi admitted to privatizing two apartments (including one for his daughter) that the Tallinn city government had previously neglected to auction publicly. Over 200 apartments had been channeled to prominent persons in the community, some at a fraction of their market prices, while Vahi was chair of the city council (1993–95). He explained that he was leaving office in order to defend himself against the accusations, aiming to return to active politics eventually. In September, however, he resigned from his seat in parliament, intending to return to private business full-time.

Vahi's center-left Coalition Party and its ruling partner, the Farmers' Bloc, agreed on Mart Siimann, the Coalition faction leader in parliament, to replace him. Siimann, a novice politician and regarded by the opposition as scandal-free, was elected in mid-March. The new government he formed included five representatives of the Coalition Party, two ministers from the Rural Union (the core of the original coalition agreement from 1995), six non-partisans, and one Progressive.

Siimann vowed to continue the government's liberal economic policy, although a conflict arose later in the year over agricultural tariffs. In forming his minority government, Vahi had promised the agricultural parties that the government would consider introducing tariffs on certain subsidized food imports that Estonian farmers considered to compete unfairly with local goods. Vahi later retreated from this commitment, under pressure from Estonia's international trading partners. Siimann was more sympathetic to the proposal, and in October the parliament adopted a law which allows the government to impose tariffs on certain food imports for up to 6 months.

Vahi continued to dominate the Coalition Party after his resignation and remained prominent in national politics, even semi-officially representing Estonian interests on a trip to Moscow. He shifted a bit rightward toward the Reform Party, whose cabinet members had resigned in late 1996 over the tariff issue.

CITIZENSHIP, RIGHTS, AND INTEGRATION

Estonia made progress in 1997 in clarifying the legal status of Russian-speaking non-citizens and began more intensive debates on the meaning of long-term social integration. The number of citizenship applications in 1997 reflected a slowdown in the pace of naturalization since the first waves of interest after independence. By the end of 1997, 65 percent of the 1.45 million population in Estonia were citizens, or over 1 million. Of that number about 90,000 had acquired citizenship through naturalization since the start of the process in 1992. About 100,000 residents hold Russian citizenship. An estimated 80,000 non-ethnic Estonians already hold Estonian citizenship by birth.

Registering the roughly 330,000 non-citizens continued to be a challenge for Estonian state officials, due to technical problems, mismanagement, and inertia among the unregistered. An estimated 30,000 non-citizens (mainly Russian-speaking elderly persons) had not filed for residency and were thus technically considered illegal residents. For those working within the system, the year showed progress. By late 1997, most applicants for alien passports had received them and the government had acted to speed up the granting of permanent residence permits. For those whose applications were in process, the government continued to issue temporary travel documents and to accept officially invalid former Soviet internal passports for identification in emergency situations, such as registering births and deaths.

Problems continued, however, with processing residence permit applications for some 19,000 military pensioners, which was complicated by the lack of Russian passports in which to place the permits. Instead of deporting the estimated 35 percent of pensioners who missed the registration deadline, the government decided to deal with them on a case-by-case basis. Finland, Sweden, and the Netherlands have provided financial assistance to the Estonian Migration Fund, which assists former Soviet military and their families to emigrate from the country.

Russian-speaking non-citizens still complained of work and housing discrimination because of Estonian language requirements. Estonian's status as the state language continued to be enforced, although the targets for Estonian language use were scaled down. For example, the Estonian parliament amended a previous law on schools stating that Russian-language instruction in secondary schools should be phased out by the year 2000, which was widely regarded as impossible. The target date was changed to 2007.

Generally, Estonia's human rights practices were accepted as fulfilling international standards. In early 1997 Estonia's human rights record was recognized in the international community as it became the first new member state of the Council of Europe to no longer be specially monitored on human rights practices. The Council nevertheless urged Estonia to move forward with the abolition of the death penalty (which was in de facto moratorium), to improve prison conditions and the treatment of refugees, and to speed up the integration of Russian speakers in society. Through improved border security and other reforms, Estonia managed to reduce the flow of illegal immigrants in 1997, most of whom were en route to the Nordic countries. The parliament also adopted the Geneva Convention on Refugees in February after having concluded return agreements with several neighboring countries. Visa-free travel agreements that were concluded with Scandinavian countries in 1997 were linked to the passage of these refugee laws and conventions.

In education, the high school system was overhauled in conformity with European norms, with the introduction of standardized final exams and college entrance exams for the first time. A one-hour teachers' strike in May in led to assurances that a 23 percent salary increase would be included in the 1998 budget.

NATO EXPANSION

Major developments occurred in NATO enlargement in 1997, affecting Estonia's security prospects. At the Madrid Summit in July the Baltic states were disappointed in their efforts to be included in the first group of former Warsaw Pact countries to start membership negotiations (Czech Republic, Hungary, and Poland). Instead, promises were made to consider Baltic applications in the following round of NATO enlargement and to expand Baltic involvement in the Partnership for Peace (PfP) program. Besides wanting to keep the first round of NATO enlargement small, Western leaders sought to avoid antagonizing Russia, which has strongly objected to Baltic membership in NATO. They did not, however, rule out future membership, allowing for some optimism among Estonian policy makers. If the first round of enlargement goes well, Estonia could be considered for membership again as early as April 1999, when NATO celebrates its 50th anniversary.

The Madrid Summit had been preceded in May by the signing of the Russia-NATO Founding Act, intended to ease Moscow's concerns about the alliance's expansion eastward into former Soviet territory. In addition, a new Euro-Atlantic Partnership Council was formed in May to coordinate cooperation between NATO and the 27 mostly former Soviet-bloc nations. It will coordinate any future military operations involving both NATO and partner nations, such as the peacekeeping force in Bosnia.

Baltic leaders were concerned over President Bill Clinton's Helsinki meeting with President Boris Yeltsin in March, seeing it as a sign of deal-making over their heads. They were somewhat reassured by the U.S.-Baltic Charter, concluded (but not yet signed) by year's end. The Charter was seen as an attempt to go beyond the PfP program, stating U.S. intentions to help integrate the Baltics into European institutions, encourage good Baltic-Russian relations, and to promote U.S. political and economic interests in the region. Overall it was an attempt to assuage Baltic fears of being left in a gray zone between NATO and Russia.

Since regaining independence, Estonia has pursued its security interests in a variety of international fora, without abandoning the search for military security guarantees of the sort provided in the NATO charter. In 1997 Western leaders increasingly tried to downplay NATO's military guarantees in the post–Cold War era, stressing the new types of internal conflicts and trans-national crime threats that NATO itself is not necessarily equipped to address. Decades of Soviet occupation and the persistence of reactionary elites in Moscow have nonetheless made Estonian leaders tenacious on this point, insisting on a more traditional view of security threats. Another point in favor of NATO membership is symbolic: it would herald Estonia's return to the club of stable and democratic European nations—although that purpose can also be served by EU membership.

A major accident in September near the coastal town of Kurkse, in which 14 peacekeeping troops died, shook Estonia's reputation as a peacekeeping partner and led to strained state-military relations. A unit of 22 soldiers, a reconnaissance unit in the Estonian company of the Trilateral Baltic Peacekeeping Battalion, was attempting to wade several kilometers across a shallow strait from Pakri island to the mainland. Fourteen were swept under due to high winds and waves; a harbor guard managed to save the remaining eight. The accident provoked debate about civilian control of the military and the role of the president, who is formally head of national defense, versus the defense minister and the cabinet. It also raised questions about the organization of the Baltic Peacekeeping Battalion itself. Its Commander in Chief, Johannes Kert, as well as Defense Minister Andrus Oovel, tendered resignations that were not accepted.

An earlier tragedy which continued to have international repercussions was the sinking of the ferry *Estonia,* which went down in September 1994 en route from Tallinn to Stockholm with the loss of 852 lives. The disaster was the focus of a long and contentious investigation conducted by an international committee. The committee finally released its report in December, provoking further controversy and calls for new probes. The Committee's report pointed to a number of factors which together led to the tragedy: unusually stormy weather; weak locking devices on the ferry's bow door; the ferry's speed; poor warning signals; lax safety procedures; and misunderstood distress calls heard by a rescue center on the coast of Finland. Plans of the Swedish government to encase the wreck in cement have been stalled due to protests by the victims' families.

RELATIONS WITH RUSSIA

The year began on an optimistic note concerning Estonia's impending border agreement with Russia, after Estonian negotiators agreed in late 1996 to omit reference to the 1920 Tartu Peace Treaty, which had implied Estonian claims on territory currently inside Russia. Technical preparations for the treaty were also completed, but hopes of an immediate signing were dashed as Russian foreign policy officials continued to use alleged "human rights abuses" in Estonia to delay signing the treaty. At the end of 1997, Estonian leaders were still hopeful but no date for signing had been set. Statements by Russian officials pointed to technical and procedural issues rather than political ones as the reason for delays. Statements of goodwill by Yeltsin and Prime Minister Viktor Chernomyrdin in 1997, especially regarding the border agreement, suggested that overall Estonian-Russian relations were thawing. This may have been in response to Estonian efforts to speed up the naturalization of non-citizens and grant permanent residency. Alternatively, Moscow may have realized that because the unresolved border issue did not stop Estonia from being in the first round of negotiations for EU membership, its value as a bargaining tool had diminished.

Relations with Russia also involved the ongoing dispute within the Orthodox Church, which reached a partial resolution during the year. Orthodox congregations supporting the Estonian Apostolic Orthodox Church (EAOC), whose legal rights were preserved in exile during the Soviet era, had restored the church's relationship to the Patriarchate in Constantinople, in contrast to the congregations wanting to remain under the Moscow Patriarchate. (While the majority of EAOC parishes are Estonian speaking and the pro-Moscow parishes Russian speaking, the conflict does not follow strictly ethnic lines.) According to Estonia's laws on property reform, the EAOC had legal right to church properties dating back to 1940, including many buildings now used by Moscow-affiliated congregations. Through efforts led by both patriarchates, congregations in Estonia were free to choose their affiliation, effectively splitting the Orthodox Church. Congregations loyal to Moscow refused to register as anything but the sole Orthodox Church in Estonia, leaving their right to use church properties in limbo. By the end of 1997 no solution to this impasse was in sight. One exception, however, proved to be the Puhtitse (Kuramae) convent in Northeast Estonia, which had always been directly under Moscow. The convent was registered by the Estonian state in October, improving relations between Estonia and the Russian patriarchate.

MAJOR ECONOMIC DEVELOPMENTS IN 1997

Estonia's GDP grew by 9 percent in 1997, more than twice the predicted rate. This justified the term "Baltic tiger," while at the same time causing concern for overheating. Declines in unemployment (from 5.5 percent to 4.6 percent) and inflation (from 14.8 percent to 12.5 percent) were seen as reassuring, however. Inflation from price liberalization is now over and pressures come from the high retail price of some imports, price rises in utilities and the pressure of consumer demand.

Estonia's rapid growth since regaining independence is due in part to growth in service industries. Manufacturing as a whole increased by about 15 percent in 1997, led by recovery in chemicals, plastics, glass, rubber, and metals. The food processing industry continued to decline, unable to compete internationally given the strong currency and absence of a favorable trade agreement with Russia. The agricultural sector's share of GDP continued to decline, with small farmers facing stiff competition in the domestic market from foreign producers.

The most difficult economic issue of 1997 was the trade deficit, which rose from $1.1 billion in 1996 to $1.4 billion in 1997, equal to 10 percent of GDP. While surpluses were noted in service industries such as tourism, and in the timber and furniture industry, they were offset by larger trade deficits in other areas. Food comprised about 15 percent of all Estonian exports and 17 percent of imports. Some analysts suggested abandoning the currency board system, which pegs the kroon to the German mark and requires parliamentary approval for any change in the exchange rate. Unpegging the kroon would allow devaluation to occur, making exports more attractive, but debates on monetary policy during the year resulted in no major changes in approach. Eventual devaluation will presumably occur when Estonia joins the European Monetary Union. The Bank of Estonia is limited in its ability to slow the economy by raising interest rates, since commercial banks do not use central financing. But it can increase the minimum reserve capital for commercial banks and did so in 1997.

Successive “crashes” or “corrections” occurred in the Tallinn Stock Exchange in October and November, with the market halving in value as a result. Considering the fact the market had been previously overvalued, analysts were not overly alarmed and the system withstood the fluctuations. Factors contributing to the crashes included a liquidity crisis in banking and speculative local investors.

Estonia’s major trading partners shifted somewhat in importance in 1997. Finland remained the most important partner. Sweden rose to second place and Estonia reached a positive trade balance with that country. Germany ranked third, with the trade deficit growing by 58 percent, in part due to vehicle imports. Russia fell to fourth place and increased the deficit because of double customs duties on Estonian exports. A major fisheries agreement was signed in February with Latvia, setting out conditions for fishing rights for both countries, including quotas, a major bone of contention since concluding the 1996 sea border agreement. Estonia moved away from its former zero-tariffs policy for agricultural goods, as the parliament voted to allow 6-month tariffs to be imposed.

Estonian business leaders and policy makers sought in 1997 to improve trade relations with Russia, and to promote their small country’s role as a gateway to Russian markets. In spite of double tariffs on Estonian exports, nearly half of Estonia’s agriculture exports went to Russia in the first half of 1997. The port of Tallinn continued to grow rapidly in 1997, handling an estimated 30 percent more passengers and freight than in the previous year. In addition, a “free zone” customs regime was set up for the Muuga port near Tallinn in October. Tourism in Estonia continued to expand in 1997, facilitated by visa-free travel agreements with Nordic neighbors, most notably Finland. By 1996 foreign visitors accounted for 18 percent of export income. $615 million was expected in tourism revenues for 1997.

Estonia continued to be the success story of the Baltics also in foreign investment, termed a “role model” by *Forbes* magazine in 1997. Earlier waves of foreign investment in distributing consumer goods shifted toward larger infrastructure projects. Foreign companies run about one third of the Estonian economy and account for over 50 percent of exports. Direct foreign investment in

Estonia had already reached $250 million by the end of September.

Estonia's credit ratings in 1997 were comparable to those of Hungary, Poland and the Czech Republic (Moody's Baa1). The Fraser Institute in British Columbia, Canada, rated Estonia 5.6 on a ten-point scale, ranking 52nd of 115 countries and the freest of all countries making the transition from Soviet rule or influence. The rating was based on the facility of opening foreign currency accounts, few restrictions on business activities, low income tax rates, free trade policies, and low government spending. Inflation was considered an ongoing challenge. The IMF considers the economic revival of Estonia to be due to the liberal and open economic environment, the currency board system, simple taxation, and successful privatization.

Challenges still remain, even if Estonia maintains the title of Baltic Tiger. For example, in 1997 the Estonian state lost an estimated $160 million in revenue, or 15 percent of GDP to the shadow economy, a holdover from the Soviet era when it was considered ethical to avoid cooperation with the state. An estimated 240,000 work in areas of the shadow economy in Estonia, often only temporarily. Privatization of enterprises was mainly complete in 1997 and began to be extended to large infrastructure and utilities projects. Land privatization was hindered, however, by registration difficulties, and businesses were slowed by the need to clear land ownership from restitution claims from former (pre–World War II) owners. A further concern to foreign investors is that the commercial code requires that 50 percent of company management boards must live in Estonia. In spite of these and other challenges, 1997 proved the resilience of Estonia's market reforms and its elite status as a post-Soviet success story.

The Estonian banking system maintained stability after several previous years of consolidation. The Estonian Union Bank and the North Estonian Bank merged in 1997 to create a bank almost as large as the Hansabank, until then the largest bank in the Baltic states. The government adopted the state budget for 1998, planning to run a 50 million kroon ($4 million) surplus. The surplus budget funds from 1997 and 1998 together with privatization proceeds will be used to create a 500 million kroon stabilization fund, still below the 1.3 billion kroon fund recommended by the IMF. The budget included for the first time 90 million kroon in subsidies to farmers.

The economic indicators listed above point to a market economy in consolidation and by all accounts Estonia is a "winner." Less obvious in such statistics are the "losers" in the transition, such as regions with particularly high unemployment, sectors with high unemployment such as agriculture, pensioners and families with small children. The United Nations Development Report for 1997 concluded that economic and regional inequality have increased in Estonia with the transition process. This is not in itself surprising, but the degree of inequality is striking: for example, one fifth of Estonia's households control almost half of the population's income. The development of a large and stable middle class will remain on Estonia's agenda into the next century.

Sidebar: ESTONIA IN EUROPEAN UNION: FIRST AMONG BALTIC EQUALS

by JOAN LOFGREN

While NATO membership continued in 1997 to be an important longer-term security goal, the Baltic leaders settled on the EU as the best (and only realistic) option for integration into Europe in the medium term. The conditions which countries must fulfill for EU membership are summarized broadly in the "Copenhagen Criteria," and include democratic institutions, rule of law, human rights, and protection of minorities; a functioning market economy; and the capacity to cope with competitive pressure and market forces within the Union. In the EU Commission's Opinion on Estonia's readiness for accession released in July, its success in economic reforms was decisive, with its economic policy since 1992 termed "remarkably consistent." Nonetheless, Estonia's per capita GDP is only 23 percent of the EU average, making it the poorest of the east European applicants to start negotiations in 1998.

The Opinion also pointed out areas where reforms had been less successful in Estonia, for example in justice and home affairs (pillar three) issues. Estonia shares problems with its Baltic neighbors in reforming police and customs administration, preparing for refugee reception, and dealing with large minority populations. In contrast, border guard reforms have been clearly more successful in Estonia than in its Baltic neighbors. In particular, the need for public sector reform was highlighted as Estonia prepares for membership, although the Commission considered current problems mainly transitional. The lack of a border agreement with Russia was considered to hinder Estonia from early negotiations, but Brussels officials seemed to understand that the delays were Russia's doing, especially after Estonia gave up the Tartu Peace Treaty reference in the agreement.

In its Amsterdam Council meeting in mid-1997, EU leaders confirmed Estonia's advanced position in the initial group of countries to start EU membership talks in 1998. Latvia and Lithuania subsequently launched campaigns in EU capitals, arguing that the differences between them and Estonia were either misunderstood, misinterpreted, or prompted by political motivations. In the event, they won some concessions at the Luxembourg meeting in December, as the Council changed its rhetoric to include "preparatory talks" with applicant countries not in the 1998 negotiations.

Why is EU membership so important for Estonia and its neighbors? While the EU is far from providing anything resembling security guarantees, joining the Union would provide the Baltic states with tangible security benefits, fostering political interdependence with other states. Estonia is a small state in need of alliances of some sort, and the European Union is the only conceivable place for such cooperation in the absence of likely prospects for NATO membership. In addition, while EU membership (or even associate status) implies less independence over certain policy areas, it also provides resources for state consolidation, thus enhancing sovereignty and, by extension, security. Most Estonian political elites have been convinced that there is no alternative to EU membership. In a 1997 study, 89 percent of the Estonian political elites surveyed were in favor of joining the EU and 65 percent considered it the only alternative for Estonia's future: 91 percent considered it a means for ensuring security. Yet by the end of 1997, Euro-skepticism was growing and a public debate about the EU had started. As many have pointed out, the EU itself must undergo considerable reforms before absorbing new members, but at its 1997 summits it was unable to reach consensus on fundamental changes in its institutions. The Union risks bankrupting itself if it accepts additional Eastern members without reforming its voting procedures, and its system of agricultural and regional funding. Even as Estonian leaders had cause to celebrate their success in getting into the "pre-member" group of EU applicants, they were also sobered by the long accession process that lies ahead toward a Union itself in need of reform.

Estonian leaders faced a diplomatic problem with their Baltic neighbors in the wake of the invitation to negotiations. Not surprisingly, Estonia deemed the EU's decision to invite only Estonia in the first round to be based on fair and objective criteria, while also generally supporting Latvian and Lithuanian attempts to enter negotiations as soon as possible. They tried to appease their disappointed neighbors by advancing the "spill-over" argument: that one Baltic country closer to accession will help the others, by making the EU more familiar with the problems and prospects of reforms in all three states. In contrast to other Nordic states, Finland supported Estonia's early start as a pragmatic guarantee that Baltic interests would be highlighted in EU fora. In 1997 the EU introduced an expanded pre-accession program and a more individualized approach to the accession process, using "road maps."

Practical steps in Baltic cooperation (such as the customs union) will likely be complicated by one country joining the EU ahead of the others, but it is not considered an immediate problem, since actual membership would not be possible for at least 5–7 years. By the November meeting of the Baltic Assembly, the initial indignation of Latvian and Lithuanian leaders was less in evidence, as they sought to make the best of the situation and use Estonia's success to their advantage.

Belarus

Population:	10,279,000
Capital:	Minsk (pop. 1,693,000)
Major cities:	Homel (pop. 383,000), Vitsebsk (pop. 297,000), Mahileu (pop. 290,000)
Area:	207,600 sq. km.
Major ethnic groups:	Belarusian 77.9%, Russian 13.2%, Polish 4.1%, Ukrainian 2.9%, other 1.9%
Economy:	GDP growth: 10.0%
....	Inflation rate: 64.0%
....	Average monthly wage: not available
....	Unemployment rate: 2.8%

FROM BAD TO WORSE

by USTINA MARKUS

The most notable aspect of the year for Belarus was its continuing international isolation. While the volume of criticism from the West had steadily increased since President Alyaksandr Lukashenka's election in June 1994, in 1997 even the country's main ally, Russia, aired its displeasure with the Belarusian president over his policies toward the press and human rights.

OPPOSITION AND AUTHORITARIANISM

A series of anti-government demonstrations were held during 1997, but none reached the scale of the 1996 demonstrations, which had numbered tens of thousands. The 1997 protests resulted in the arrests of the usual suspects, which prompted criticism of the regime at home and abroad over its treatment of peaceful demonstrators. March was a particularly busy month for protests. One was held on 2 March, the anniversary of the founding of the city of Minsk. Some 5,000 participated and 16 were arrested. Another was held on 11 March, resulting in around 100 arrests. On 23 March, the 79th anniversary of the establishment of the Republic of Belarus, a demonstration of 4,000 protesting Lukashenka's rule ended with clashes between demonstrators and security forces, and the arrest of some 100 protesters. Among the arrested were Yuriy Khadyka (who had been arrested and released after a hunger strike in 1996), Henadz Karpenka (a former presidential candidate and deputy speaker of the 1996 parliament), and Yuriy Zakharenka (former interior minister). All of the leading opposition figures arrested were becoming regular guests of the Interior Ministry following anti-government rallies.

Another anti-Lukashenka rally took place on 2 April, the anniversary of the signing of the Russian-Belarusian Treaty on the Formation of a Community in 1996, at which 107 people were arrested. On 23 November, the anniversary of the 1996 constitutional referendum, another rally was held. New rules passed in 1997 raised the fines for participating in unsanctioned rallies to 20–50 times the minimum wage. (In contrast, the fines for using firearms in populated settlements were only 5–10 times the minimum wage.) Along with the stricter penalties, the Committee of State Security (KGB) was given broader powers of search and infiltration, and they were explicitly given the right to use weapons and force. Under the new law, KGB informers were also given the right to use fake identity documents and receive remuneration.

Arrests and detentions without due process became more pronounced. One of the more notorious was the case of former Chairwoman of the National Bank of Belarus (NBB), Tamara Vinnikova. She was arrested at the beginning of the year and kept in detention over nine months on a variety of charges relating to irregularities during her tenure as head of the Belarusbank, a post she held before heading the NBB. In November, Vinnikova was released on remand owing to her deteriorating health. Another former Lukashenka appointee who found himself out of favor and charged with corruption was his old-time colleague from the pre-presidential Anti-Corruption Committee, Yuriy Malamau. Malamau was accused of being involved in some underhanded dealings in the sale of property. Minister of Agriculture and Food Supplies Vasyl Leonau was also arrested in November. He was detained on suspicion of embezzlement and corruption, charges similar to those lodged against Lukashenka's other erstwhile allies.

While former allies were finding themselves out of favor with the president, this was nothing new for the opposition. Among the legally dubious arrests that year was that of Uladzimir Kudzinau. Kudzinau was a member of the 1995 parliament who was arrested in February for allegedly attempting to bribe a police official. At that time he still had immunity from arrest as a legislator. In June a new law lifted immunity for deputies who did not cooperate with the president. In August, a court sentenced Kudzinau to seven years' imprisonment along with the confiscation of his property. Technically, such a sentence could only have been handed down to a repeat offender, but the police official said Kudzinau had offered him a bribe twice, making it a repeated offense.

The president made an attempt at reconciliation with the last democratically elected parliament, the 13th, which Lukashenka had disbanded in the aftermath of the November 1996 constitutional referendum. That parliament had continued to meet and refused to recognize the decision to disband it, since it had been elected for a four-year term at the end of 1995, while the new legislature had never been elected, but appointed by the president. With the exception of Russia, no other country recognized the new post-referendum legislature as the legal parliament. In June, talks were held between representatives of the president and the 1995 elected parliament, with the participation of representatives from the European Union and the Council of Europe. Talks stalled after the old parliament refused to accept the new post-referendum constitution as the basis for a compromise formula.

A new development in Belarus in 1997 was the appearance of terrorism. In April, a group calling itself the Belarusian Liberation Army (BLA) claimed responsibility for shooting at the Russian embassy in Minsk and two explosions at gas facilities. Since the group had never been heard of before, there were doubts as to whether it even existed. There was a prevalent belief that the authorities were blaming a conjured-up BLA for genuine accidents. In September, the BLA resurfaced and claimed responsibility for an explosion at a Minsk court, and in November there was yet another incident involving the placement of mercury and the BLA.

While the existence of the BLA remained dubious, terrorism connected with business matters made an appearance. In October the head of the Mahileu Committee for State Control and a close personal friend of Lukashenka, Yauhen Mikalutsky, was assassinated by a remote-control bomb. He was the second state official to be killed in a mob-style execution since independence.

(The first was the head of the Hrodna Executive Committee in 1992.) In response, a decree was issued raising the upper limit of prison terms to 25 years, and allowing authorities to hold anyone suspected of criminal activities for 30 days without pressing charges.

Another development was the creation of a pro-presidential youth organization, the Patriotic Union of Youth, in May. The organization was formed with Lukashenka's blessing and government money, and was granted an array of privileges. It was meant to be a successor to the communist-era Komsomol. Lukashenka said he would give the organization a role in job placements after university and in the distribution of student housing. He also made it plain that it would be a stepping-stone for careers in government ministries and agencies. He urged members of the movement to expose university professors who were stirring up students against the regime. The leader of the Patriotic Union of Youth, Usevalad Yancheusky, was a personal friend of President Lukashenka's son. Among the perks afforded to the organization by Lukashenka was control of radio station 101.2, which had been closed in 1996 and had been the only independent radio station in Belarus broadcasting in Belarusian. (Radio Liberty broadcasts in Belarusian from outside the country). The group also requested control over the travel of all youth abroad by requiring they receive approval from the Patriotic Union of Youth for trips along with other visa documentation. It was assumed that the new youth organization was created to counter support for the nationalist Belarusian Popular Front, which had a substantial following among students.

TIGHTENED GRIP ON THE MEDIA

Several new restrictions on the media were introduced over the year. In March, a decree by the Council of Ministers prohibited the transmission of any materials deemed damaging to the national interests of Belarus. A censor was to be on duty at the satellite communications center monitoring all transmissions. This same decree banned the import of printed materials, audio-visual products, and other forms of information that could harm the republic's interests or the morale of its citizens. A week later, on 26 March, foreign news agencies found their access to satellite communications was barred, and only journalists with accreditation from the Foreign Ministry were allowed into the communications center.

The head of the Presidential Security Council Viktar Sheiman threatened to impose severe sanctions against the media for its biased reporting on events in Belarus. On 25 March, the authorities made good on their threat when a correspondent from the Russian channel NTV, Aleksandr Stupnikov, was informed that his accreditation had been annulled and told to leave the country.

Under the new head of the State Committee for Print, hard-liner Uladzimir Zamyatalin, a new law on the media was drafted giving his committee almost unlimited power over the media. Whereas publications with a circulation of over 500 previously had to register with the State Committee for Print, under the new law even a publication producing a single copy would have to register. This law extended to school papers. Registration procedures were also tightened, and sanctions were introduced against publications for verbally assaulting the president. The law went on to ban the import and export of any materials which could be damaging to Belarusian political, economic, and security interests, without defining what those interests were. The list of agencies and officials with the power to suspend a publication was also expanded. Under the old law only a court of law could order a suspension after due process initiated by the registration authority or the Procurator General.

The law made the normally pliant lower house uneasy and there were problems mustering even the minimum quorum of 70 to have it pass. When it came before that chamber on 16 October, only 65 deputies were present during the debate, and several even tried to walk out of the session. Speaker Anatol Malafeyau had to order the deputies back to their seats so there would be a quorum during the vote. International criticism of the law was harsh, and when it came before the parliament's upper house two weeks later, the senate unexpectedly voted to amend some of the more controversial aspects of the legislation.

Independent papers continued to be harassed by the authorities. The oldest, *Svaboda,* was repeatedly served court summonses and fined. By the end of the year it had closed and reorganized itself as a new publication under the name of *Naviny. Belorusskii rynok* also was ordered to pay a series of fines for various transgressions. *Femida* closed by the end of the year. A Hrodna-based opposition paper, *Pahoniya,* was forcibly evicted from its premises by police and fined 224 million Belarusian rubles ($9,000) for alleged financial irregularities. Even the English-language *Minsk Economic News,* which had previously been left unscathed, was threatened with eviction from its premises.

The media incident which gained the most publicity was the 27 July arrest of journalist Paval Sheremet, a Belarusian citizen working for Russian Public Television (ORT). Sheremet and his crew were doing a story on the lack of controls on the Belarusian-Lithuanian border, and demonstrated this by filming themselves crossing it without being stopped by border troops. He and three colleagues were arrested for "systematic and deliberate distortion of information on Belarus." The arrests prompted a storm of protests in Russia. President Boris Yeltsin even threatened to review the Treaty on the Formation of a Community over the issue, but Lukashenka did not back down. Eventually on 7 October, after more than two months in detention, Sheremet was released from jail on the condition that he not leave his residence in Minsk. His case was scheduled to come to trial in December, but was postponed until the following year. An opinion poll conducted in Belarus by the independent NOVAK agency found 22 percent of respondents approved depriving the journalist of his accreditation, while 33 percent disapproved of the action.

RELATIONS WITH RUSSIA

Over the course of 1997 it became increasingly apparent that any union with Russia was unlikely owing to the conflicting interests of the two sides. This was highlighted during the anniversary of the Treaty on the Formation of a Community. The event was supposed to be marked by the signing of a new document strengthening ties between Russia and Belarus. Just days before the anniversary celebrations, Moscow refused to sign the Belarusian draft of the new agreement, and proposed a different version, which provided no binding commitments as to unification, and merely affirmed the original treaty's declaration of intent to form a union. Yeltsin assured the Russian people that they would not have to pay for any merger with Belarus, and noted that the different levels of development in the two countries would delay further progress toward economic union. Indeed, the year passed with no sign of monetary, political, or any other type of union. Lukashenka placed the blame for the lack of progress squarely on the shoulders of the Russian leadership.

Still, Lukashenka found some support for union among Russian conservatives. Lukashenka gave a speech to the third Congress of USSR Nations in February in front of Russia's most notorious hard-liners, among them former Communist Party Secretary Yegor Ligachev, leftist leader Viktor Anpilov, former Prime Minister of the USSR Nikolai Ryzhkov, and ex-generals Valentin Varennikov and Albert Makashov. The other group in Russia that reportedly favored integration with Belarus were the energy companies which had been able to gain concessions and operate in Belarus under the rubric of integration.

Russian opponents of integration were generally liberal democrats who were critical of Lukashenka's rule. The IMF also influenced the lukewarm attitude in Russia toward integration, since it warned Moscow that a condition for aid from the fund would be the discontinuation of Russian subsidies to Belarus.

The arrest of Sheremet exemplified the problem Lukashenka was having with his portrayal in the Russian media. Although the president had control over his own country's official media, the Russian media were not subject to his censors, and Belarusian airwaves throughout the country could pick up the frequently critical reports from Russia. On 15 August, shortly after Sheremet's internment, another group of ORT journalists was detained on the Belarusian-Lithuanian border. This time the situation with Russia became even more strained because most of the apprehended journalists were Russian citizens. After a week in jail the journalists were handed over to Russian Duma speaker Gennadii Seleznev, known to be sympathetic to Lukashenka. Seleznev called the incident a provocation by enemies of the Russian-Belarusian union, and did not condemn Minsk for arresting the Russians.

Meanwhile, Sheremet was still in custody. In September Russian Foreign Minister Yevgenii Primakov flew to Minsk in an attempt to persuade Lukashenka to release Sheremet, but he returned to Moscow empty-handed. Lukashenka demanded an apology from ORT and steps to correct Russian media "bias" against his regime. On 6 September Lukashenka was in Moscow for talks with Yeltsin on the subject. The Belarusian president was not inclined to compromise, despite Belarus's economic dependency on Russia. Lukashenka admitted that Minsk owed $120 million for Russian fuel deliveries for 1997, but claimed Moscow owed Belarus $1 billion for other, unspecified services.

By October Yeltsin's patience with Lukashenka was running out. He issued an order forbidding the governors of Russia's oblasts from meeting with the

Belarusian president. At that time Lukashenka was planning to meet the governors of Lipetsk and Yaroslavl in the Volga region. When Lukashenka continued to stall over releasing Sheremet, the Russian authorities denied his plane access to Russian airspace so he could not fly to the Volga for the scheduled meetings. Shortly thereafter, Sheremet was released but remained under house arrest.

INTERNATIONAL ISOLATION

While relations with Russia deteriorated, Belarus became even more distanced from the international community at large. On 16 March, the head of the Soros Foundation in Belarus, Peter Byrne, was deported, and the Belarusian authorities charged the foundation with $3 million in unpaid taxes. The Soros Foundation was the largest philanthropic organization operating in the country, providing the bulk of foreign grants.

Later in March the First Secretary of the U.S. Embassy in Minsk, Serge Alexandrov, was deported for his alleged participation in anti-government demonstrations. The United States retaliated by expelling the First Secretary of the Belarusian Embassy in Washington, and refusing entry to the newly appointed Belarusian Ambassador Valeriy Tsyapkala.

These incidents were followed by Minsk stepping up its activities against the international charitable organization Children of Chernobyl. The German parliament wrote to Lukashenka urging him to curb the Security Council's investigations into the fund. At the same time, the European Union program Technical Assistance to the CIS (TACIS) was notified that it would have to pay taxes on all aid provided to Belarus. TACIS informed the government that it would suspend all of its projects in the country if it were forced to pay taxes.

At the end of March the Inter-Parliamentary Assembly of the Council of Europe voted to suspend Belarusian membership in the organization on the grounds that the new parliament had not been formed on the basis of democratic principles. In addition, the Conference of Constitutional Courts of Europe refused to accept the Constitutional Court of Belarus as a full member because it did not meet the criteria for membership.

Minsk's posturing in response to NATO enlargement further alienated the country internationally. In August, Lukashenka's assistant Syarhei Pasakhau said Belarus could return nuclear weapons to its territory because of NATO expansion. It was unlikely that Moscow would agree to return nuclear weapons to Belarus. Russia had removed all nuclear weapons from the country ahead of schedule in 1996, and had been highly critical of Belarus for suspending the reductions on two occasions. Nonetheless, the comment was taken seriously by Belarus's neighbors.

In September, a European security conference took place in Vilnius attended by the presidents of ten states, including Belarus. Lukashenka looked upon it as an opportunity to demonstrate that Belarus was not subject to international isolation. Yet five of the attendant presidents, including all those from neighboring states, used the opportunity to reprimand Belarus for its poor human rights record.

That same month the Soros Foundation finally closed its Belarusian offices after haggling with the government for several months over conditions for the foundation's continued operations. As a sign of its displeasure over Minsk's policies toward the foundation, the United States suspended $40 million in aid to Belarus. European aid was also suspended. In October, the Council of Europe held a meeting in Strasbourg. Belarus was the only country left off of the invitation list, underlining its growing international isolation. At the end of the month the United Nations Human Rights Commission issued a report expressing concern over human rights abuses in Belarus.

ECONOMIC STAGNATION

Officially, the economy registered a number of positive developments over the year. At the end of May Lukashenka announced that investments in the country had grown 19 percent in the first four months of the year and GDP was up 10 percent—a turnaround that would have made Belarus the fastest-growing economy in the region. He also claimed that loss-making companies had declined from 30 percent in 1996 to 18 percent in 1997. In September, Lukashenka reported that GDP was up 10.5 percent from January to September over the same period in 1996; manufacturing was up 16 percent; and agriculture up five percent. Inflation, however, was higher than forecast. Official figures reported annual inflation of 65 percent, but some estimates reached double that figure. Lukashenka blamed the inflation on lax government control over prices.

Despite the optimistic statistics, there were signs that the economy was not actually in such great shape. The combination of goods shortages, price controls, and high inflation meant that it was very difficult to come up with reliable figures for the real level of GDP. One sign that all was not well was Belarus's inability to meet its energy payments to Russia. By the third quarter of the year Minsk owed $120 million to Gazprom. Economic minister Uladzimir Shimau admitted Belarus could pay for only 10 percent of the supplies in cash, while Gazprom was demanding 30 percent cash payment. The oil situation in the country was equally serious, and the shortages prompted the government to prohibit refineries from exporting refined oil products. Because Belarusian customers were unable to pay for their oil supplies in cash, work at the refineries ground to a virtual halt. Wage arrears were another indication that not all was well. In the first ten months of the year arrears totaled 900 billion Belarusian rubles ($324 million), or 14 percent of the total wages payable.

Privatization continued at its former snail's pace. Only 15 percent of municipal properties had been privatized. The gap between the value of privatization vouchers issued and the value of shares that could be bought for them continued to grow. In April, it was reported that only 25 percent of the vouchers issued could be exchanged for shares because so little property was being put up for auction.

The agricultural sector continued to be heavily subsidized. The Minsk region covered only 15 percent of the cost of its agricultural supplies, the rest being covered by the government. Collective farms continued receiving privileges from the state, such as the roll-over of outstanding loans and the writing-off of unpaid taxes. Not surprisingly, the strongest support for the president comes from the rural sector.

Officially recorded unemployment fell from 183,480 (3.2 percent of the workforce) in January to 157,429 (2.82 percent of the workforce) by July, but the reasons for this do not appear to have been the creation of more jobs. In March, Lukashenka issued a decree capping unemployment at 130,000, and tightening the criteria for being classified as unemployed. In another return to Soviet-era policies, the prospect of compulsory job assignments became more real as the government turned to this solution to cope with unemployment.

Another point Lukashenka failed to mention in his optimistic description of the economy was the country's poverty level. In the first four months of the year the Ministry of Statistics found that almost 4 million people (39 percent of the population) had incomes lower than the officially stated subsistence level. Other social indicators of economic problems were seen in health statistics. The infant mortality rate averaged 213 per 1,000 births in 1996. Ten years earlier it had been only 85.

International financial institutions became even less forthcoming with aid. In 1996 the government had expected to receive $110 million in aid, most of which was earmarked to cover the two percent budget deficit. Instead, it received only $45 million. Both Russia and the IMF discontinued financial support because Belarusian businesses failed to pay the state back for imports financed by external sources. In the summer the World Bank shut down its offices in Minsk, stating it found it unnecessary to maintain offices in a country that was not actively cooperating with the bank.

IMF representative Richard Haas suggested that the surge in official growth statistics had been produced by a massive injection of rubles into the economy, mostly into the construction sector. The resulting growth also triggered the high inflation rate. Haas described the country's economic policies as unsound owing to the continuing lack of financial liberalization, slow progress of privatization, continuing price controls, and generally poor business environment. However, he did commend Minsk for its fiscal policies, saying Belarus was the only CIS country that did not lose considerable revenue through tax evasion. Unfortunately, this was achieved through a high degree of state control over the economy, with the government sector accounting for over 75 percent of GDP. In a move that would increase state control over the economy, a new decree issued by Lukashenka made it mandatory for the first time for all residents to file income declarations.

The country ran a trade deficit in 1997. The main trading partner remained Russia, accounting for 55 percent of its total trade in the first quarter of the year. Ukraine followed with 11 percent of the trade, and Germany accounted for 6.5 percent. Although Lukashenka complained that the customs union with Russia had not resulted in the hoped-for revival of mutual trade, according to some estimates Russo-Belarusian trade rose by more than one third during 1997. Russia continued penetrating the Belarusian economy through investment and acquisitions. In August, two Russian banks, Oneksimbank and MFK, purchased 49 percent of the shares of the Belarusian Minsk Komplex Bank. It was also rumored that the Russian oil companies Yukos and LUKoil would obtain substantial shares in the Belarusian refinery Naftan. Western investment, however, remained low. In 1997 the amount of direct foreign investment did not exceed $20 million. Although there were negotiations over large deals that year, little came of these. Negotiations with the Korean company Daewoo over joint ventures in the country's automotive industry foundered. Initially, Minsk proposed that Daewoo invest as much as $1.3 billion in exchange for shares in Belarusian factories. Daewoo offered only $30 million and $10 million for two factories in exchange for half of their shares. Some of the conditions demanded by the Belarusian side, however, even threatened this deal. The government wanted Daewoo to assume responsibility for the factory's social structure and to keep the same number of personnel. Minsk also balked at Daewoo's request that it be exempt from social security payments and the Chernobyl tax.

The Ford joint venture producing Transit vans and Escort cars outside of Minsk began its assembly line production in July. Ford had invested slightly over $20 million in the deal and negotiated various tax exemptions. As this had been the largest investment deal so far concluded with a Western company, it was expected that Lukashenka would treat the deal with kid gloves to reassure other prospective investors. Instead, in October, Lukashenka revoked the company's tax privileges. On a brighter note in regards to foreign investment, McDonald's opened its fifth restaurant in Minsk in late November.

While Belarusian authorities had never been particularly friendly toward private businesses, over 1997 the laws pertaining to private enterprise were essentially penal and the detention of several businessmen for alleged irregularities made it even more difficult for entrepreneurs to operate in the country. In August, Lukashenka signed a decree allowing the Committee for State Control to impose fines on any legal entity or business, including foreign businesses. The law can be compared to that on the media, which widened the number of agencies that could control and impose fines on publications. In September, the Council of Ministers enacted a resolution setting new fees for the issue of operating licenses to foreign companies. There was little popular opposition to the government's enactment of such penal laws in regards to taxation and regulations on businesses because the Belarusian public by and large has a negative view of all private entrepreneurs. A February/March NOVAK opinion poll found only 14 percent of respondents believed businessmen were making money primarily through honest means, while 69 percent believed most businessmen were dishonest.

The most notorious example of the persecution of businesspeople was the previously mentioned arrest of the former Chairwoman of the NBB, Tamara Vinnikova. The hounding of businessmen reached new heights with the arrest of

Vasyl Staravoitau, director of the joint-stock company, Rassvet, a former collective farm. Unlike many private farms, Rassvet had steadily been making profits. Staravoitau refused to sell milk to the state reserve at the officially set price, and even had the temerity to demand payment of more than 5 billion Belarusian rubles ($180,000) for earlier supplies. Staravoitau's arrest was followed by a media campaign accusing him of profiteering and theft of state assets, none of which appeared to be true. Another salient case was the sentencing of the mayor of Salihorsk to eight years in prison, with slightly lighter sentences for five other officials in his administration. The officials were accused of extorting money from the city's business community for various municipal projects and pocketing the money themselves.

Thus over the year there was a succession of cases of businessmen either being arrested or harassed with accusations of some improprieties. The *Minsk Economic News* wrote that much of the persecution was related to the particular businessman's political behavior. A good portion of the 13th parliament members were involved in business and those who had not supported Lukashenka during the 1996 constitutional referendum were finding obstacles to their continued commercial activities. As a result, there was a noticeable exodus of the country's business elite, with many migrating to Russia to continue their activities. However, businesspeople who had supported the president during the 1996 political crisis appeared to be prospering.

Along with the persecution of individual businessmen, a new tax code came out at the end of the year that made it much costlier to run a business. Enterprises were expected to pay 75–80 percent of their taxes in advance, regardless of whether or not they would be able to sell their products that fiscal year. Private companies were already in an almost permanent state of audit. Another clause that was ominous for its potential abuse was the article allowing for the criminal prosecution of businessmen who made erroneous decisions leading to financial losses.

LUKASHENKA'S PROSPECTS

Despite the economic stagnation, authoritarianism, and international isolation, Lukashenka remained the most popular politician in the country, with no serious popular rivals. In an opinion poll conducted by the NOVAK agency, 57 percent of those surveyed said they trusted the president, while 39 percent said they did not, and eight percent were uncertain. The poll found two institutions that came out ahead of the executive in the people's esteem. The Church was trusted by 68 percent of respondents and the army by 63 percent. Amongst the least trusted institutions was one frequently relied on by Lukashenka to enforce his decrees—the police. Only 32 percent of those surveyed said they trusted the militia, while a full 61 percent said they did not.

There were still no serious alternative candidates to Lukashenka on the political horizon. According to polls, opposition leaders Syamyon Sharetsky, Stanislau Bahdankevich, Zyanon Paznyak, and Henadz Karpenka all could count on only about one percent of the vote if they were to run for the presidency. Even worse for the nationalists, Paznyak's negative rating (those who would not vote for him under any circumstances) reached 18 percent.

As the reprimands of the EU and United States seem to have had little impact on Lukashenka, the growing international isolation is also unlikely to curb his authoritarian tendencies. To date, the most effective instrument in influencing the Belarusian president's behavior has been Moscow's refusal to allow him to fly to Russia for official visits. The implication is that opponents of Lukashenka's regime, most of whom oppose integration with Russia, should look to Moscow to tame their president.

Ukraine

Population:	50,853,000
Capital:	Kyiv (pop. 2.5 million)
Major cities:	Kharkiv (pop. 1.5 million), Odesa (pop. 1.1 million), Dnipropetrovsk (pop. 1.1 million)
Area:	603,700 sq. km.
Major ethnic groups:	Ukrainian 72.7%, Russian 22.1%, Jewish 0.9%, Belarusian 0.9%, Moldovan 0.6%, Bulgarian 0.5%, Polish 0.4%
Economy:	GDP growth: –4.0%
....	Inflation rate: 10.1%
....	Average monthly wage: $94
....	Unemployment rate: 2.9%

UKRAINE PLODS ON

by USTINA MARKUS

Ukraine resolved some long-standing issues in 1997, most notably the signing of the Treaty on Friendship and Cooperation with Russia. In other areas, however, the country made little progress. Political deadlock between president and parliament continued to be characteristic of the political system, while the problem of corruption rose to such a level of visibility as to threaten the flow of foreign aid.

POLITICAL BICKERING

The conflict between President Leonid Kuchma and the parliament, which had been raging from the time he was elected president in June 1994, continued unabated in 1997. Among the highlights of that antagonism during the year was the dispute over the 1997 budget, which was not passed by parliament until the summer. Deputies also threatened impeachment proceedings against Kuchma over the law on local government. Although Kuchma signed a new law on parliamentary elections, he made it clear in public that he did not approve of some of the provisions which parliament had written into the law.

Along with Kuchma's ongoing battle with the legislature, the president replaced the unpopular prime minister, Pavlo Lazarenko, who was widely considered to be incorrigibly corrupt. The replacement, Valerii Pustovoitenko, barely held that post until the end of the year before he was ousted, likewise for corruption. The issue of corruption led the former Minister of Justice Serhii Holovaty to add his voice to criticism of Kuchma's regime for not seriously pursuing the anti-corruption campaign that Holovaty had launched in April 1997. At the same time, Lazarenko formed his own party in opposition to Kuchma. All in all, the political picture in Ukraine remained one of conflict between right and left, president and parliament, business elites and legislators. The scene did nothing to attract foreign investment, or encourage political and economic analysts to offer optimistic forecasts about progress in reforming Ukraine's economy.

At the start of the year the government came under attack for the continued lack of progress in reforming the economy and its failure to improve living standards. Kuchma proceeded to fire the minister of agriculture, the deputy transport minister, and the chairman of the organizing committee for corruption and crime. Two weeks later in February, in an attempt to demonstrate that he was trying to initiate some economic reform, Prime Minister Lazarenko reshuffled the cabinet. He fired the finance minister, economic minister, statistics minister, and the minister for engineering, the military-industrial complex, and conversion. The following day Yurii Yekhanurov was named minister for the economy and Ihor Mitiukov was appointed finance minister. Despite the reshuffles, pro-market reformers continued to complain that little was being done to reform the tax system or to implement appropriate legislation to promote fair competition and free enterprise. In April, a leading advocate of market-economic reform, Deputy Prime Minister for the Economy Viktor Pynzenyk, tendered his resignation, expressing his frustration with the barriers to economic reform. He was particularly put out by parliament's refusal to accept his tax reform package. This had been one of the main conditions set by international financial institutions for the disbursement of loans to Ukraine.

The February reshuffle did not deflect criticism from Lazarenko for long. In March, Kuchma severely criticized the prime minister, whom he had just appointed the year before, for submitting an unrealistic budget to parliament. Lazarenko's fall from grace continued to be the subject of rumor. On 1 July, the prime minister tendered his resignation citing health reasons. No one believed that Lazarenko, who continued to be politically active, had stepped down because of his health. The real reasons suggested for his resignation had more to do with pressure from the shroud of accusations against him for corruption and profiteering in office.

In the wake of his resignation, Lazarenko soon emerged as a vocal critic of Kuchma, denouncing the president's regime as undemocratic during a visit to Washington, D.C., in October. He also formed the Hromada Party. The party was composed largely of businesspeople from Eastern Ukraine, particularly those with interests in energy enterprises, and those who advocated the privatization of land. In November, the party announced it was creating a shadow government with Yuliya Tymoshenko, president of the United Energy Systems, serving as the shadow prime minister. By the end of the year, Lazarenko made it plain he would be contesting the presidency in the 1999 elections.

Following Lazarenko's resignation, Vasyl Durdinets was temporarily appointed acting prime minister. In July, he was replaced by Valerii Pustovoitenko, who was appointed prime minister. Parliament did not overwhelmingly confirm him. While 226 voted in his favor, 91 voted against, and 26 abstained. Within months Pustovoitenko became embroiled in a scandal surrounding the misappropriation of some $40 million during the renovation of the Palace of Culture in Kyiv, and in the questionable awarding of contracts for that renovation. Kyiv Mayor Oleksander Omelchenko and Minister of Culture Dmytro Ostapenko were also implicated in the scandal. In January 1998 the parliament called upon Kuchma to dismiss Pustovoitenko in light of the fraud allegations.

Another noteworthy appointment and dismissal that year was that of Justice Minister Serhii Holovaty. The minister's integrity was generally accepted, and Kuchma appointed him head of the anti-corruption campaign launched that year. The campaign was dubbed "Clean Hands," and was hailed as a whole-hearted initiative to deal with the problem of corruption. Despite the publicity surrounding the campaign when it was launched in April, it produced no substantive results. In August, Holovaty was dismissed by the new prime minister, Pustovoitenko, and replaced as justice minister by the former minister of families and youth, Suzanna Stanik. After his dismissal, Holovaty denounced the president and government, saying the Clean Hands anti-corruption program was thwarted at the highest levels, specifically accusing the acting premier, Vasyl Durdinets, of attempting to silence him and derail his efforts. He noted that not a single one of his recommendations regarding deadlines for performance reviews of government officials and guidelines had been implemented. Holovaty went on to accuse members of the cabinet of misappropriating World Bank and IMF money, and hinted that he too may run for the presidency in 1999.

Alongside the criticisms levied against Kuchma by individual politicians, the president continued to find himself at odds with parliament over legislation. There were even threats of impeachment against the president over the bill on local government self-administration. Kuchma vetoed the bill three times, using the excuse that the bill itself, or some part of its drafting process, had been unconstitutional. On 4 September parliament began the official impeachment process, with a 7–3 vote by the Committee on Legal and Judicial Reform to bring the issue to the legislature. The committee charged that Kuchma was neglecting his constitutional duties because of his three-time veto of the law on local self-rule. As neither the constitution nor legislation actually detailed the impeachment procedure, the recommendation was temporarily shelved by acting speaker Viktor Musiyaka, who felt the procedure should be codified before the process began. Under the constitution, the impeachment process is drawn out into several stages. First, a simple majority of deputies must put forward a motion to initiate impeachment proceedings. Afterwards, a parliamentary investigative committee must determine whether there are sufficient grounds for impeachment. If it finds the move is warranted, two-thirds of the total number of deputies must approve the decision to accuse the president of a crime. The committee's findings are then sent to the Constitutional Court and Supreme Court for review. If the court agrees with the findings, parliament may remove the president by a vote of 75 percent of the total number of deputies.

Kuchma was not the only one threatened with removal from office. There was an unsuccessful attempt to remove parliamentary speaker Oleksander Moroz in May. On 12 May the parliamentary committee chairs approved a resolution calling for his removal, and the next day a petition signed by 220 deputies and supported by the president was put forward to this effect. On that day, however, there was a shortage of leftist deputies at the session. It was suspected that the leader of the Ukrainian communists, Petro Symonenko, and the agrarian leader Moroz had collaborated and effectively organized a boycott so there would be no quorum. Fighting broke out twice that day in the parliament over the matter. In the end, it was decided to compromise and debate the no-confidence vote proposal. After the debate, the vote to remove the speaker came in at 186 for his removal, and 183 against. That was 40 votes short of the simple majority needed in the 450-seat legislature to remove Moroz. It was also the third time Moroz had faced a no-confidence vote, and the closest the vote had come to removing him. He had been consistently opposed by the nationalist and pro-reform groups, while his support base remained the agrarian party and the communists, which together formed the largest bloc in parliament.

Another highly controversial piece of legislation passed in 1997 was the new law on parliamentary elections, which was signed by Kuchma in October. It had been drafted after it became apparent that the previous legislation was seriously flawed. Essentially, the old law was a copy of Soviet-era legislation, which called for voter turnout of over 50 percent in order for an election to be valid, run-off elections if no candidate won over 50 percent of the ballots cast, and by-elections if the run-offs failed. In practice, this resulted in the holding of many costly repeat elections. Elections in a number of districts were repeatedly declared invalid because they did not meet the minimum turnout requirement, and those seats remained unfilled. The old law on elections was also perceived to be flawed because it allotted all seats to individual, first-past-the-post races and did not reserve any seats for party tickets. This created a parliament with weak parties and a large independent bloc of deputies. The new law was meant to redress these shortcomings.

In September, after thirteen reviews in six months, parliament approved a new election bill which replaced the 50 percent minimum turnout requirement with 25 percent, and also did away with the requirement that a candidate win over 50 percent of the votes cast. This meant that the continuous by-elections to fill vacant seats would no longer take place. In addition, under the new law, half of the legislators would be elected through a simple majority vote in individual races, while the other half would be drawn from party lists. This is the same dual system that was introduced for the Russian Duma by the 1993 constitution. Kuchma returned the bill to parliament on 13 October with a list of 15 recommendations that he demanded be implemented to avoid a presidential veto. Parliament accepted almost all of Kuchma's points, but refused to reinstitute the 50 percent minimum voter requirement. Despite his threat to veto the legislation, Kuchma signed the bill, while still expressing reservations about the law in that form.

The next parliamentary elections were scheduled for March 1998, and in preparation the Central Electoral Commission had to be appointed in 1997. The commission had to realign the 450 electoral districts, approve candidate lists and voter petitions, determine the budget for elections, print official ballots, and oversee the process. As with other matters, parliament and the president found themselves at odds over its composition. On two occasions, the legislature rejected all but six of Kuchma's nominees for the commission. Not until 12 November did parliament finally approve 11 members to the Central Electoral Commission, enabling it to begin its work in organizing the upcoming elections. This was still short of the full complement of 15, but it was enough to start work.

The situation in Crimea remained unchanged. Russian nationalist politicians continued to claim that at least Sevastopol was a Russian city, and the peninsula's aging, Russian majority population continued to support pro-Russian policies. In January, Moscow Mayor Yurii Luzhkov visited Crimea illegally after Ukrainian authorities denied him permission to visit the area. He reiterated his view that Sevastopol was a Russian city, prompting the usual protests from Kyiv. In October, the Crimean parliament voted to make Russian the official language on the peninsula as allowed for by the Crimean constitution, and to change the clocks over to Russian time. That constitution, however, had not been approved by Kyiv. That same month, Kuchma came out against the Crimean legislators' moves, and issued a decree which declared the change to Moscow time as contrary to Ukraine's constitution. In November, Kuchma warned the Crimean parliament against giving the Russian language a higher status than Ukrainian or Tatar.

Two assassinations of journalists emphasized the seriousness of the corruption problem in the country. In March, the body of Petro Shevchenko, who worked for the newspaper *Kyivskie vidomosti,* was found hanging in a warehouse outside of Kyiv. Shevchenko had written a series of articles criticizing the Luhansk branch of the Security Service of Ukraine (SBU). Although police initially claimed it was a suicide, the paper was adamant that it was an assassination because of his reports. In August, Borys Derevyanko was gunned down in Odesa. He was the editor-in-chief of *Vechernyaya Odesa,* and had made critical statements in the paper about corruption amongst the city's leading officials. Derevyanko had been beaten twice since 1995 over such stories.

A U.S. State Department report on human rights issued at the end of the year touched on the country's media, and found that government officials sometimes attempted to control the press and limit freedom of speech by suing editors for libel, initiating tax audits, and by keeping radio and television under government control.

The same report raised other concerns over continued government controls over freedom of association through complicated registration requirements. This applied particularly to non-native religious organizations and regional political parties. The report went on to say that many problems remained in Ukraine's attempts at democratization. These included continued delays with trials, beatings in the unreformed legal and prison systems, bullying in the armed forces, and political interference in the judicial process. The report also found that much of the legislation needed to safeguard human rights under the new 1996 constitution had yet to be passed.

FOREIGN RELATIONS

The one area in which Ukraine scored a number of successes over the year was in foreign relations. It signed treaties on friendship and cooperation that recognized the inviolability of its borders with Russia and Romania. The treaties had remained unresolved since 1992 despite lengthy negotiations. Most of the credit for the final signing of the treaties was not due to any particularly skillful diplomats in any of the countries, but to the prospect of imminent NATO expansion, which prompted Ukraine and its neighbors to conclude the treaties.

The most important of the friendship treaties with neighbors was the one with Russia. Negotiations had reached a standstill under the presidency of Leonid Kravchuk, and the treaty had been shelved. Following Kuchma's election as president, talks restarted, but foundered over the issue of the Black Sea Fleet. Thus, the fleet's division and basing rights had to be agreed on before the Treaty of Friendship and Cooperation could be signed.

On 28 May, the long-standing Black Sea Fleet dispute appeared to be resolved, when Russian Prime Minister Viktor Chernomyrdin and his Ukrainian counterpart Lazarenko initialed an agreement on the fleet's basing, paving the way for Yeltsin's visit to Ukraine to sign the Treaty on Friendship and Cooperation. The most controversial aspect of the treaty in Ukraine was the lease offered to Russia for its base in Crimea. Under the accord, Russia has a twenty-year lease on two of four bays in the port of Sevastopol, with an option for a five-year renewal, subject to Ukrainian approval. As of 12 June, Russian ships were to occupy Sevastopol Bay and Quarantine Bay, while Ukraine's navy was to be maintained in Striletsky Bay. Southern Bay was to be demilitarized.

The Russian navy was also given rights to use the test range in Feodosia, the Hvardiiskyi Aerodrome, the Yalta Stadium, a communications base, and a rocket fuel depot. Russia agreed to a limit of 25,000 personnel at the bases, with no more than 132 vehicles, up to 24 artillery pieces with a caliber exceeding 100 mm, and a limit of 22 aircraft. It was also stated that Russia would not deploy any nuclear weapons on the leased lands. Russia agreed to pay Ukraine $525 million for those ships in the fleet which had been allotted to Ukraine after the break-up of the Soviet Union, but which Kyiv agreed to hand over to Russia. While the exact amount that Russia was to pay Kyiv for leasing the Crimean bases was not divulged, it was reported that most of the payment would be made through writing off Ukraine's energy debts to Russia. There was speculation that Ukraine was to receive around $100 million per year for the lease. In addition, Russia and Ukraine signed another agreement in which Russia agreed that it owed Ukraine around $200 million for nuclear materials exported to Russia in 1992 when all tactical nuclear weapons were removed from Ukraine.

Not surprisingly, the agreement was controversial, and elicited criticism from those opposed to any Russian military presence on Ukrainian soil. Nationalist leader Vyacheslav Chornovil blasted the accord for allowing Russia to lease bays in Sevastopol for its part of the fleet for 20 years. He called for demilitarizing the Black Sea, with all countries bordering on it signing a charter to that effect. In reality though, the treaty did little more than affirm reality, since the Russian share of the fleet was already based there and nothing short of force could have removed it.

On 30 May, Yeltsin arrived in Kyiv for his first-ever official state visit to Ukraine, more than five years after the country established its independence. The following day, he signed the treaty of Friendship and Cooperation with his counterpart Leonid Kuchma. The treaty is valid for ten years, but will be automatically extended if neither side asks for a cancellation. It encompasses a broad range of issues, including military, political, cultural, educational, scientific, and economic exchanges between the two countries. Most of the treaty's contents had already been worked out by the end of 1994. The Black Sea Fleet issue was the main unresolved stumbling block delaying the final drafting. For Ukraine, the most important aspects of the treaty were the recognition of the inviolability of its territorial borders by Russia, and the fact that by signing the treaty between two sovereign, independent states, Moscow was accepting Ukraine's independent status.

Another long-standing friendship treaty which was signed in the run-up to the Madrid NATO summit was the treaty with Romania. The agreement almost failed to materialize. The points of controversy between Kyiv and Bucharest had been resolved in principle in late February. Less than two weeks later, the Romanian Ambassador to Ukraine, Ion Bestreanu, said his government wished to review the terms of the treaty. As with Russia, there was only one real stumbling block that had been delaying the treaty. In this case, it was ownership of Serpent's Island on the Black Sea, and the border along the Bukovyna region. Both of these territories had been a part of Romania prior to World War Two, and had then been absorbed into Soviet Ukraine. Kyiv now insisted on wording regarding Ukraine's territorial inviolability that would preclude any possible territorial claims on these lands by Romania in the future.

The "Treaty on Principles of Good-Neighborliness and Cooperation" formally recognized Serpent's Island as a part of Ukraine, but left out the issue of mineral rights in the area. It is believed there are substantial oil and gas reserves in the sea around the island. Both sides agreed to work out the mineral rights over the next two years, and bring it before an international tribunal for arbitration. As for the issue of Bukovyna, Romania had demanded wording that in some way denounced the 1939 Molotov-Ribbentrop Pact that gave the Soviet Union a part of northern Bukovyna. Ukraine preferred to avoid directly denouncing the pact, fearing that this could justify future claims to these territories. Instead, Kyiv agreed to denounce the acts of totalitarian regimes and dictatorships in general, including the Soviet-Nazi Pact. It also promised not to place offensive weapons near Romania's border. In return, Romania agreed to recognize the inviolability of existing borders.

Along with Ukraine's other neighbors, Poland signed an agreement just before the Madrid summit meant to address any animosities or historical conflicts between the two countries. Warsaw had recognized the inviolability of Ukraine's borders already in 1992, and relations between the two countries were good, despite a history of conflict in the past. Nonetheless, Polish President Aleksander Kwasniewski spent three days in Ukraine in May and signed a Declaration on Concord and Unity with Kuchma. Other agreements relating to cooperation between the coal industries and finance ministries of the two countries were signed as well, along with a series of agreements on technical, cultural, and educational cooperation.

As for relations with the West, the main event of the year was NATO's decision to expand into East-Central Europe. Ukraine was initially apprehensive about NATO expansion, fearing that such a move would put Ukraine in the uncomfortable position of a buffer zone between NATO and Russia. There were also concerns that it could lead Moscow to grow more aggressive in trying to co-opt Ukraine into a security pact with Russia and the CIS. Politicians in Kyiv adopted a policy of neutrality, which was meant to reassure Russia that Ukraine would not push for NATO membership anytime in the near future. At the same time, Kyiv strove to demonstrate to the West that Ukraine was not a part of any common security system with Russia. This was done mainly through actively cooperating with NATO in its Partnership for Peace Program. In 1997, Ukraine continued this type of cooperation. In April, Ukrainian Defense Minister Oleksander Kuzmuk visited the United States for talks with his U.S. counterpart William Cohen. He visited a number of U.S. bases, and returned with military medical cooperation agreements and an agreement promising $47 million more for disarmament. The funds were earmarked for use in destroying the remaining strategic delivery vehicles and silos.

In order to protect itself from any possible pressure from Russia in the event of NATO expansion, and so as not to be completely left out of an expanded Western alliance, Kyiv pushed for a separate agreement with NATO. Such an agreement would hopefully provide some sort of security guarantees to Ukraine, and at least allow for consultations and cooperation. After all, NATO had just signed a special agreement with Russia, in an effort to assuage the latter's concerns over enlargement. Ukraine was moderately successful in this endeavor. On 8 July, at a summit in Madrid, NATO invited Poland, the Czech Republic, and Hungary to join the organization. The following day a "Charter on a Distinctive Partnership between NATO and Ukraine" was signed by Kyiv and the sixteen NATO countries. The document reaffirmed the obligations and commitments undertaken by NATO members through previous accords such as the UN Charter, the Helsinki Final Act, and the charter of the Organization for Security and Cooperation in Europe (OSCE). None of these offered concrete security guarantees, merely stating that no country should pursue its security interests at the expense of any other state in the OSCE area. Two days later, U.S. Defense Secretary William Cohen visited the Transcarpathian Military District in Ukraine, symbolically reaffirming the special relationship with the country. There was some opposition to Ukraine's charter with NATO from Ukraine's conservatives. The head of Ukraine's Communist Party, Petro Symonenko, said it contradicted Ukraine's sovereignty declaration, which proclaimed Ukraine was a neutral and non-aligned state.

Other highlights in foreign affairs in 1997 included the unanimous election of Foreign Minister Hennadii Udovenko as president of the 52nd session of the UN General Assembly in September. The incumbent holds the post for one year, during which he oversees the work of six permanent assembly committees. The same month, Ukraine signed a series of arms control agreements along with Kazakhstan and Belarus, aimed at removing obstacles for Russian ratification of START II.

While Kyiv's relations with its neighbors and NATO were generally successful, Ukraine did come under criticism from the United States for corruption in the country. The United States earmarked $225 million in aid to Ukraine out of a total of $770 million for the former Soviet republics. Owing to the growing criticism of potential foreign investors over corruption and obstacles placed in the way of foreign projects, however, half of that sum was to be withheld until Ukraine showed more willingness to tackle the corruption issue and guarantee fair treatment for foreign investors. The issue was debated in Congress, and Ukraine came under fire from a number of witnesses who reported on the difficulties of investing in the country.

Overall, however, the West, particularly the United States, remained supportive of Ukraine. In May, during a visit to the United States, Kuchma was awarded the 1997 Democracy Award by the International Foundation for Election Systems. Kuchma met with U.S. Vice President Al Gore during that visit for the first full session of the U.S.-Ukrainian Bilateral Commission. Gore and Kuchma signed several documents relating to economic and security cooperation. Yet even during these upbeat visits, the Ukrainian delegation found itself under criticism for failing to tackle the corruption that was stymying U.S. investment in Ukraine.

THE ECONOMY

The conflict over economic policy between legislators, government, and the president was highlighted by the drawn-out debates over the national budget. Only in late July, seven months after parliament was presented with the draft, did the legislature finally approve the 1997 budget. The impetus for the delayed approval was the threat that the IMF would not dispense further aid if it were not approved. The IMF had established a series of preconditions for the release of funds to Ukraine. These included: approval of a budget with a deficit of less than six percent of GDP, a reformed tax system, and keeping inflation under 25 percent for the year. The legislature failed to pass the tougher tax collection package the IMF demanded, and instead passed more investment-unfriendly corporate tax legislation. Kuchma criticized the legislature for its delay in passing the budget and its recalcitrance over tax reform. In a speech marking the first anniversary of Ukraine's Constitution on 27 July, Kuchma claimed that one sixth of all people charged with corruption were deputies, and said parliamentary immunity should be lifted in cases involving corruption. This type of threat had been made before by the president, but given that he himself has had a history of promoting individuals of dubious moral character (such as Lazarenko), it seems likely that the threats were made with a view to swaying public opinion rather than with the intent of having any real impact.

Despite the budgetary fiasco, the IMF approved a $542 million stand-by loan to Ukraine in August, and agreed to release $49 million immediately. The remainder was to be disbursed in several installments over the next year, as long as Kyiv adhered to its promised economic reforms. Just a month earlier, the IMF had put a $2.5–3 billion long-term restructuring loan on hold because Ukraine was not proceeding with reforms fast enough. The IMF stated Ukraine's budget was not consistent with what had been agreed on as a condition for the release of funds, after parliament made last-minute changes.

The problems surrounding the passage of the 1997 budget prompted parliament to avoid a repeat of the circus for the following year. The 1998 state budget was approved on 30 December. The vote in favor of the budget was a surprising 240 to 45, assuring that there would be no repeat of the previous year's budget fiasco which had made it necessary to institute emergency budgets based on expenditures from the previous year for more than half of the year. In contrast to the 1997 budget debates, parliament and the government cooperated with each other in passing the 1998 budget. When disagreements over issues came up (such as the government's insistence that a bill to revamp the corporate tax structure be passed), it was agreed to omit it and work it out later. The 1998 budget authorized outlays of 21.1 billion hryvnya against revenues of 24.5 billion hryvnya. The planned deficit ceiling of 3.3 percent of GDP was satisfactory to the IMF. (Whether it would be realized in practice was another story.) Most of the deficit would be met by borrowing from international financial institutions, and internal borrowing. For the first time, the budget also included a list of items that were to be maintained as expenditure priorities. This included payment of wages to government workers, purchases of adequate food supplies, medicine purchases, and servicing the interest on the national debt.

The provision in the new budget making wage payments to government workers a priority expenditure was meant to address the serious problem of wage arrears. Wage and pension arrears had been a problem for the government since Kravchuk's presidency. In March 1997, some 85,000 demonstrated in cities throughout the country to protest the nonpayment of pensions and back wages. At that time the government owed workers some 2.7 billion hryvnya ($1.5 billion).

Although Ukraine managed to pass the 1998 budget by the end of year, in other areas there was little progress. On 3 December the World Bank announced that it ranked Ukraine as one of the ten most corrupt countries in the world. The corruption made foreign investors uneasy about sinking money into the country, and Kuchma's highly publicized but abortive Clean Hands campaign had not served to convince the international community that Kyiv was serious about tackling the problem. As Kuchma had made winning foreign investment one of his priorities when he was elected president, the low level of investment clearly indicated that despite his many international jaunts, he had not succeeded. Since 1991, only $1.6 billion had been invested in the country. In 1996, the largest investment deal ever put together in Ukraine, Motorola's contract to put together a $500 million dollar phone system, fell through when Motorola decided the ever-changing business legislation, excessive corporate tax rates, and general corruption made the deal untenable.

Following the World Bank's denunciation of Ukraine's ineffective drive against corruption, the procurator general's office brought charges of corruption against the highest ranking individuals yet. These included the head of the consular department of the Foreign Ministry, Vasyl Koval. The same day, the procurator's office asked parliament to lift the immunity of Lazarenko's crony, deputy Yuliya Tymoshenko, so it could bring an indictment against her. The procurator's office also announced in late December that it was investigating Lazarenko himself on charges of concealing foreign currency earnings. And in January 1998, as already noted, Pustovoitenko was removed from office for corruption.

One of the most telling signs of the user-unfriendly investment environment in the country was the late date of the opening of any McDonald's restaurants. Two finally opened in Kyiv in late May. This was two years after the first two had opened in Minsk, and by the end of 1997, Belarus could boast five McDonald's, while Moscow had already had the restaurant for over five years.

Some progress was made in the area of privatization. By the end of the year, Ukraine's collective farms had all been disassembled. The transfer of the lands into private hands had begun in August 1995. Over eight million hectares of land had been privatized, with plots averaging five hectares. In addition, 6,500 medium to large-scale enterprises had been privatized by the end of the year. Since problems with the privatization system had become apparent, it was announced that the process would be reformed. Toward the end of the year the acting chairman of the State Property Fund, Volodymyr Lanovy said the government would no longer issue stock certificates to Ukrainian citizens and legal entities in the privatization of enterprises. Instead, in 1998 all medium- and large-scale enterprises would be privatized on the basis of cash tenders. The certificate system had been criticized for allowing illegal deals to take place. During the second phase of privatization slated for 1998, foreigners would be allowed to bid so that the government could get the highest sum possible for the enterprises. Among the grievances aired in the first phase of privatization was that many assets had been undersold to cronies in pre-arranged deals.

The greatest success in regards to the economy was in the stabilization of the national currency. The hryvnya's exchange rate to the dollar remained steady until the fall, when the Asian financial crisis caused its value to fall.

The process of closing the Chernobyl nuclear power plant continued, amid calls for more aid from the international community toward the effort. Ukraine continued to criticize the Group of Seven leading industrial countries (G-7) for their slow pace in providing promised funds for the closure of the plant. In the spring, the European Bank for Reconstruction and Development refused to release funds for the completion of two nuclear power stations which were to compensate for the energy which would be lost by the decommissioning of Chernobyl. The bank argued the cost estimates for completing the new plants were too high. On 22 June, G-7 leaders meeting in Denver, Colorado, promised an additional $300 million toward Chernobyl's closure. Despite the generous gesture, that same month Udovenko complained at a press briefing in the UN that the G-7 were providing neither the financial aid promised, nor technical assistance. The G-7 had promised a total of $3 billion in loans and credits to decommission the power plant. Little of the aid had been dispersed however. In November, a conference in New York raised an additional $36 million from the international community for rebuilding the sarcophagus encasing the number-four reactor, which had been the site of the world's worst nuclear accident in April 1986.

At the plant itself, none of the reactors had been functioning since June, owing to maintenance problems, and it was not expected that the one working reactor would restart until sometime in 1998. Apart from the problems of funding for the plant's closure and maintenance, there was serious consideration for expanding the exclusion zone around the damaged reactor. It was reported that radiation had spread to regions beyond the 30-kilometer exclusion zone and there were recommendations to expand it by one third.

On a final note, Ukraine's population continued to drop. In July, the Ministry of Statistics reported it stood at 50.9 million—a drop of 1.15 million since independence. Life expectancy for males fell by 3.5 years during that time to 61.2 years, and for females it went down to 72.7 years. Almost a quarter of all deaths were in the working-age group, with the most common causes of death among the able-bodied population being traumas, accidents, malignancies, and circulatory, digestive or respiratory disorders.

Profile: YULIYA TYMOSHENKO: UKRAINE'S FIRST WOMAN PRIME MINISTER?

by OLEG VARFOLOMEYEV

Ukraine, a country until recently governed exclusively by men, in 1997 acquired a female premier, albeit only a "shadow" one. Yuliya Tymoshenko, one of the leaders of the Hromada party headed by former prime minister Pavlo Lazarenko, announced in November 1997 that she would form Hromada's shadow cabinet. Hromada was staunchly opposed to President Leonid Kuchma, and Tymoshenko had repeatedly called for Kuchma's impeachment or, failing that, early elections. Hromada had its sights set on winning the elections for the Ukrainian parliament, the Verkhovna Rada, scheduled for March 1998. Hromada refused to enter into electoral coalitions with any other of the 29 parties and blocs registered to participate in the elections.

All this may seem rather presumptuous for a party which had kept a low profile since it was registered in 1993. In fact, Hromada had a good chance if not of winning the 1998 elections outright, then at least of securing a substantial number of seats in the legislature. The party's stock went up sharply in August 1997, when Tymoshenko unexpectedly announced that she was joining it. With Tymoshenko came big money.

Yuliya Tymoshenko, 37, is a native of Dnipropetrovsk, hometown of Soviet president Leonid Brezhnev and of Ukrainian President Leonid Kuchma. Tymoshenko heads Ukraine's largest private company, United Energy Systems (YES, in its Ukrainian acronym). YES's turnover in 1996 equaled $10 billion, and its profits $4 billion. Much of that was linked to the sale of Russian natural gas in Ukraine. Ukraine is the world's third leading consumer of natural gas. It imports 80 percent of the gas it uses, and most of that comes from Russia. Dealing with gas imports is the most profitable business in this country. Until the summer of 1997, YES was estimated directly or indirectly to have controlled almost a half of the domestic wholesale gas market and, in consequence, around one-fifth of the Ukrainian economy. Up until last summer, too, the company was able to rely on the political patronage of Lazarenko.

YES's history dates back to 1989 when Yulia Tymoshenko, an economics graduate from Dnipropetrovsk State University, set up a family cooperative in Dnipropetrovsk. The business was started with only $5,000, and initially offered such services as sewing and hairdressing. In 1991, Tymoshenko switched focus and set up the Ukrainian Petrol Company. This sold gasoline to farmers in Dnipropetrovsk Oblast. At that time, Ukraine was in an energy crisis, and farmers were experiencing severe shortages of gas.

It was probably at about this time that Tymoshenko and Lazarenko, then head of the agricultural department of the Dnipropetrovsk Oblast administration, forged their business and political ties. Lazarenko does not deny that he helped Tymoshenko get her business off the ground. And neither of them denies that they have known each other for a long time, though both deny that YES finances Hromada's electoral campaign.

In 1995, Tymoshenko reorganized Ukrainian Petrol into United Energy Systems of Ukraine. In the fall of that year, Lazarenko was appointed deputy prime minister for energy in Yevhen Marchuk's cabinet. In that capacity, Lazarenko was given the difficult task of negotiating gas supplies with Russia and Turkmenistan. Lazarenko divided the Ukrainian gas market along territorial lines. The upshot was that YES secured the lion's share of the market and a dominant position in Dnipropetrovsk and Donetsk oblasts, where most of Ukraine's steel mills, machine-building plants, and chemical factories are concentrated. In 1996, for the first time since independence, Ukraine reported no debts to Russia's Gazprom. Tymoshenko claims this was thanks to her company's involvement and to the territorial division of the market introduced by Lazarenko.

Meanwhile, YES was actively expanding into other sectors of the economy. By early 1997 it controlled several banks, had stakes in dozens of enterprises in metallurgy and machine-building, was part-owner of Ukraine's third largest airline and its second largest airport in Dnipropetrovsk, participated in the development of Turkish and Bolivian gas pipelines, and controlled several local and national newspapers.

YES's problems began soon after Lazarenko succeeded Marchuk as premier in May 1997. A group of deputies of the Verkhovna Rada set up a commission to look into allegations that Lazarenko's reform of the gas market had been biased in favor of YES. In September 1996, they threatened to begin proceedings to dismiss Lazarenko. When Hryhory Vorsinov, the procurator general at the time, investigated these allegations, he found that no laws had been violated. At that time, however, rumors began to circulate about policy differences between Kuchma and Lazarenko. The media predicted that Lazarenko would soon lose his job. Tymoshenko had already taken precautions against hard times. To defend her business and her clout, she went into politics herself. In December 1996, she was elected to parliament from a constituency in Kirovograd Oblast. To comply with the law, she resigned as president of YES. Formally, her father-in-law, Hennady Tymoshenko, now heads the company. In reality, Yuliya Tymoshenko remains in change.

Meanwhile, Tymoshenko's activities and business connections with

Lazarenko had begun to attract international media attention. On 9 April 1997, the *New York Times* reported that Lazarenko owned a share in YES which, the paper claimed, earned the prime minister $200 million a year. The government rejected the report as "bare-faced libel" but, at the beginning of June, a group of Verkhovna Rada deputies accused YES of misappropriating $3 billion in humanitarian and technical aid. YES denied the accusations.

In July 1997, Lazarenko was forced to resign. This was a blow to Tymoshenko and her company. One sign of the company's loss of influence came when the Ukrainian government suspended a non-commercial competition for a 26-percent stake in Khartsyzsk Piping Plant in Donetsk Oblast, which YES had won. Khartsyzsk Piping, which manufactures large-diameter pipes for transporting Gazprom's gas from Russia to Europe, was to have been a major source of profits and would have played a key role in YES's efforts to force its rivals out of the gas market. Under Ukraine's new premier, Valerii Pustovoitenko, YES was edged out of the wholesale gas market and lost valuable tax privileges.

Pustovoitenko's administration dispatched an army of auditors and inspectors to Dnipropetrovsk, Lazarenko's and Tymoshenko's stronghold. This hamstrung YES's activities. Observers said the new government was using the same tactics against Lazarenko that he had used against his own political opponents in the past. The government accused YES of monopolizing the gas market and "barterizing" the economy. At the end of September 1997, the State Anti-Monopoly Committee brought several charges of dumping against YES before the procurator general's office. In late November, the Procurator General asked parliament to lift Tymoshenko's parliamentary immunity and to allow criminal charges to be filed against her.

Tymoshenko was accused of attempting to smuggle $26,000 from Ukraine to Moscow in 1995. When Lazarenko came to her defense, the procurator general launched criminal proceedings against Lazarenko himself, accusing him of embezzling 5 million hryvnyas ($2.7 million) from state coffers to restore his dacha outside Kyiv. Like Tymoshenko, however, Lazarenko enjoyed parliamentary immunity, and by the end of 1997 there was no sign that parliament was likely to lift it.

Tymoshenko and Lazarenko used the media they controlled to counter-attack and wage a smear campaign against the government in general and President Kuchma in particular. Tymoshenko has called for early presidential elections, to be held not in 1999, as scheduled, but in the fall of 1998. The Ukrainian press called this "the war of compromising information" (*krompromat*).

Lazarenko and Tymoshenko had a lot at stake. A loss in the 1998 parliamentary elections could lead to their losing everything, including their personal freedom. Tymoshenko may yet emerge from the shadows to become Ukraine's first woman prime minister.

NOTE

Reprinted with kind permission from the Jamestown Foundation's *Prism,* vol. IV, no. 3 (6 February 1998). Jamestown publications can be found on their web site at www.jamestown.org.

SOUTHEASTERN EUROPE

VI

Slovenia

Croatia

Bosnia-Herzegovina

Federal Republic of Yugoslavia

Macedonia

Albania

Bulgaria

Romania

Moldova

Slovenia

Population:	1,990,000 (1995)
Capital:	Ljubljana (population 270,000)
Major cities:	Maribor (pop. 103,512), Celje (pop. 39,942), Kranj (pop. 36,808)
Area:	20,251 sq. km.
Major ethnic groups:	Slovenian 90%, small numbers of ethnic Serbs, Croats, Albanians, Hungarians, and Italians
Economy:	GDP growth: 3.2%
	Inflation rate: 9.4%
	Average monthly wage: $890
	Unemployment rate: 14.8%

AN ISLAND OF STABILITY

by STAN MARKOTICH

Tracking developments in Slovenia in 1997 was a prospect as exciting as observing a chess game. What this in fact demonstrates is just how far removed from the former Yugoslavia and the Balkans in general the tiny alpine country has become in its roughly seven years of independence. The year's main issues were familiar. The political agenda was dominated by politicians working toward integrating the country into Western institutions—namely, NATO and the European Union (EU).

A NEW GOVERNMENT

The year opened with at least some element of suspense that was ultimately resolved by resort to the country's now preferred method of conflict resolution: compromise. Back in November 1996 parliamentary elections were held for the 90-seat legislature, and at least on the surface Slovenia's political landscape had changed considerably. The Liberal Democrats (LDS), led by Prime Minister Janez Drnovsek, emerged again as the single largest party, claiming 25 seats. However, a coalition of conservative parties (Janez Jansa's Social Democrats, the People's Party, and the Christian Democrats) grouped together as the conservative Slovenian Spring coalition and took a total of 45 seats.

The Slovenian Spring dedicated itself to forming a government on its own, and at least during the campaign identified the LDS as the political player that had to be kept from power. At least early on, their rhetoric suggested forging a working compromise with the LDS would be almost impossible. As 1997 unfolded, some drama took place as the parties jockeyed for power, but it was quickly evident that a brokered resolution was in the offing and that any rock-solid cohesion the Spring had, existed largely if not entirely in rhetoric. On 8 January STA reported that the parliamentary deadlock in naming a new premier was on the verge of ending. For its part, the LDS needed the support of only a simple majority and had secured the backing for Drnovsek's candidacy from the remaining minor parties holding the balance of 20 seats. It was, according to news reports, one of the Christian Democratic deputies, Ciril Pucko, who swung his support behind Drnovsek, justifying the move as a necessity "because we have economic and social problems that have to be solved not today, but yesterday." Hinting that petty politicking was destructive, Pucko proffered his support to the LDS and announced his intention to sit as an independent.

On 9 January Drnovsek was reelected prime minister and almost immediately began an attempt to broaden the base for a new cabinet. On 10 January STA reported that he would turn to the People's Party in search of coalition allies. On 19 January, however, the Spring flatly rejected Drnovsek's overtures, insisting that his proposal still left his own LDS with far too much influence and representation in government. On 24 January Radio Slovenija reported that Drnovsek had succeeded in forging a new administration with all members save the Spring, giving the new government a single-seat majority. Drnovsek, however, did not name ministers of agriculture and justice, in a move widely seen as his open door for Spring members to join the ranks.

On 6 February, however, the legislature split down the middle, failing to give Drnovsek the simple majority needed to legitimate his cabinet. It was back to the drawing board, and on 17 February local media reported that a coalition including the People's Party had been forged behind closed doors. A parliamentary rejection of that new cabinet line-up, Radio Slovenija accounts hinted, would spice up national politics by forcing new balloting. Such coverage, however, was short-lived and quickly offset by the Slovenian appetite for yet another compromise. On 27 February the legislature approved a government with the support of 49 legislators and consisting of the LDS, Marjan Podobnik's People's Party and the minor Pensioners' Democratic Party. Drnovsek had succeeded in both dividing the right and taking control of government.

EUROPE, YES!—BALKANS, NO!

And once the new government was formed, Slovenia turned to pursuits that it had worked for over the past several years. The centerpiece of Slovenian politics has been the twinning of EU and NATO membership, and in 1997 officials continued to be aggressive about making their aspirations known to the international community. The linking or twinning of membership in the two international bodies was underscored by officials throughout the first half of the year. In July, Anton Bebler, Slovenia's ambassador to the UN, succinctly yet unofficially defined the Slovenian aims, stressing that NATO and EU memberships were priorities. "The European Union has used some of those same criteria for membership. [. . .] It stands to reason that a top NATO candidate is required to show a satisfactory degree of social, economic, and political compatibility with the European Union. . . . The EU conditions are nevertheless more elaborate . . . [and] new NATO members will have several years to bring their compatibility to that required for full EU membership," he noted.

And relations with Italy, in the past marred by disputes which threatened to invoke an Italian veto of Slovenian membership in the EU, seemed to have hit their stride in 1997. Back on 11 March Italian Prime Minister Romano Prodi paid a one-day visit to Ljubljana and held meetings with Drnovsek and Slovenian President Milan Kucan. There he announced Rome's intention to back Slovenia's inclusion in the first round of NATO expansion and its membership in the EU. Prodi even went one step further and pledged that tensions, stemming from issues of foreign ownership in Slovenia and Slovenian treatment of Italian minorities in the years immediately following World War II, would be a thing of the past. "In the next months, a mixed Italian-Slovenian group will be established that will work on bilateral questions so that all shadows of the past will disappear," he said.

By late summer, however, Slovenian authorities had to quiet expectations and suffered what came as a setback to some of the political leadership. In early July the government learned that Slovenia had in fact not been named for the first wave of NATO expansion. Drnovsek, speaking from Madrid, acknowledged that Slovenia was favored for a second round, and thus stated he was "highly optimistic about the year 1999." Just a day later, the premier expressed his satisfaction upon hearing news that the European Commission was giving its support to Slovenian inclusion in the EU.

The ramifications of the NATO decision, however, did have an almost immediate impact on government. On 31 July Zoran Thaler, an LDS member and the foreign minister most identified as the architect of Slovenian regional and foreign policy since 1995, tendered his resignation. According to Thaler, his critics in government were sabotaging his attempts to integrate Slovenia into NATO and the EU, while his opponents counter-attacked, arguing Thaler's blundering had left the country out of NATO's first wave of expansion.

By year's end, however, the government showed few signs of wavering from its aim of integration in the international bodies. Its main strategy was to emphasize how far the country has gone in terms of domestic reforms, and how its strategic role as a land bridge between NATO members Italy and Hungary is indispensable to the integrity of Western security. What remains an open question is whether or not Slovenia may be held at bay, owing to fears that its inclusion in NATO and the EU may drag those organizations into uncomfortably close relations with regimes such as those headed or manipulated by Yugoslav President Slobodan Milosevic. For its part, Ljubljana was careful in late 1997 to signal to the international community that its own intent was to wash its hands of sustained dealings with Balkan problems. In early November it flatly rejected an invitation to attend a Balkan summit held on Crete, with Slovenian officials saying that participation was inappropriate given that Slovenia was not a Balkan state.

PLUS CA CHANGE. . .

Much of what took place in Slovenia during the year was in fact reflective of a holding pattern. By the end of the year, very little had changed on the economic front. Privatization did not take off, and the unemployment rate hovered at 14 percent, roughly where it had held for at least three years. Annual economic growth registered about 4 percent.

On 23 November elections were held for the presidency, and the result surprised no one. According to local reports, Milan Kucan, who had successfully forged the public image of a benevolent fatherly figure, fond of being featured in photos seen gardening, won handily over his opponent, Podobnik. The conservative political challenger suffered from the disintegration of the conservative alliance when he opted to support Drnovsek in government, leaving the Slovenian Spring coalition unable to reconstitute itself in agreement on a viable common presidential candidate.

And no year in Slovenian politics would be complete without at least a few minor scandals. Back on 10 January an investigation opened following allegations that the LDS had engaged in "vote buying" in an effort to reelect Drnovsek. The premier dubbed the accusations groundless, and, as with many tawdry scandals of recent years, the incident slid out of the headlines in short order.

Document: SLOVENE ATTITUDES TOWARD THE EUROPEAN UNION

Periodically, radical right-wing politicians have a minor resurgence on the Slovenian political scene. Their constituency tends to be the disenfranchised rural community, and nationalists concerned about the prospects of foreign, namely Italian, meddling in internal Slovenian politics. In July, the Institute of Macroeconomic Analysis and Development argued that most Slovenes were committed to the policies undertaken by the government, but left open the possibility that the years ahead may accommodate at least one or two more ultra-nationalist renaissances. What follows is a translation from the July 1997 monthly report, published in Ekonomsko ogledalo.

"The development of democracy and the protection of human rights are, in addition to economic development, important criteria for evaluating eligibility of accession to the EU. According to [our] poll respondents, Slovenia has made considerable progress in developing democracy, with the share of respondents who regard the development of democracy as satisfactory rising from 36 percent in 1995 to 42 percent in 1996. [. . .] Results concerning the protection of human rights, however, are not so good, with respondents who believe human rights are well protected declining from 41 percent in 1995 to 38 percent in 1996. [. . .] Only 18 percent of the respondents think that farmers will benefit from [EU] affiliation, a number that was even lower in 1995 (12 percent)."

Croatia

Population:	4,800,000 (1991 census)
Capital:	Zagreb (pop. 994,000)
Major cities:	Split (pop. 207,000), Rijeka (pop. 206,000), Osijek (pop. 165,000)
Area:	56,538 sq. km.
Major ethnic groups:	90% Croatian, 3–4% Serbian
Economy:	GDP growth: 5.5%
....	Inflation rate: 3.6%
....	Average monthly wage: $588
....	Unemployment rate: 17.6%

ANOTHER YEAR OF BLEAK CONTINUITY

by NEBOJSA BJELAKOVIC *and* SAVA TATIC

Croatia entered 1997 awash with speculations on its future fueled by reports and rumors of the faltering health of the two strongest figures in its political establishment, President Franjo Tudjman and his hard-line nationalist right-hand man, Defense Minister Gojko Susak. But as the year progressed, even those sinister hopes for change withered away. Tudjman not only lived to see a number of 75th-birthday specials in May—including a theater performance presenting his work and thoughts as the apogee of Croatian history and gold coins and postage stamps bearing his likeness—but he also won another five-year presidential mandate a month later. Moreover, toward the end of the year, he seemed to have shaken off his mysterious ailment, unlike the increasingly frail Susak, who was losing his battle with lung cancer.

The observers' fascination with the possibility of divine intervention in Croatian politics was not baseless—there was little else that seemed capable of changing the way the country had been ruled since 1990. In short, the seventh year of Tudjman's rule and the second year without war operations brought little new to Croatia. All the major patterns of the past few years remained in place, testifying to the maturing of Tudjman's brand of authoritarianism. The Croatian Democratic Union (HDZ) continued to enjoy an unrestricted hold on power as the fissiparous opposition parties remained divided and prone to striking back-room deals with the ruling elite. All significant attempts to create a coalition of opposition parties kept ending in failure. Moreover, the ruling party's tight control of state—especially electronic—media and its tailor-made electoral system ensured that the political playing fields remained sufficiently tilted in favor of the government. Croatia's independent media continued to be harassed, as did its Serbian minority. For his part, Tudjman slipped further into authoritarian behavior, increasingly reveling in his self-styled role of the "father of the nation." The commendable macroeconomic stability of the past few years was maintained, but the population largely failed to see the benefits as the main spoils from the country's privatization program continued to be split among HDZ cronies.

HDZ'S ELECTORAL JUGGERNAUT

The most significant formal challenges for Tudjman and the HDZ were the two elections held in spring and early summer. In the April local elections, the opposition parties mounted a good showing in major urban centers as well as in the Istria and Dalmatia regions, but it was not enough to overcome HDZ's nation-wide dominance. Tudjman's party did well in small towns and villages, but its most important success was in the elections for the Zagreb city council. The HDZ barely fell short of a majority, but its tried-and-true arsenal of pressures and bribes managed to produce a coalition that finally wrested the capital city out of the opposition's control.

The elections, which were carried out according to a single-round proportional system (with a 5 percent threshold), also strengthened the HDZ's parliamentary position, because each of the 21 counties (*zupanije*) was electing three deputies to the parliament's upper house, the House of Counties. The ruling party increased its number of seats in that chamber from 37 to 41, while its main opponent, the Croatian Social-Liberal Party (HSLS), experienced a significant electoral setback by going down from 16 to seven seats. The Croatian Peasant Party (HSS), performed slightly better, securing nine seats—a boost of four mandates in relation to the previous elections. The party of reformed communists, the Social Democratic Party (SDP), also increased its presence in the upper house from one to four seats. All in all, together with the constitutionally stipulated presidential appointees, the HDZ came to enjoy a comfortable majority of 46 votes in the 68-seat chamber—enough to secure the rubber-stamping of laws passed by the lower house.

As in the past, the opposition's strategy was one of the primary keys to the HDZ's electoral success. By effectively running independently from each other in the April elections and counting on eventual post-election coalitions in local councils, the opposition parties allowed the HDZ to scoop up more than 60 percent of upper-house seats with only 43 percent of the popular vote. Even at the local level, opposition parties spent more time quarreling among themselves than building workable coalitions. As a result, power slipped away from them in many city councils even where the HDZ was in a minority. Tudjman's party was successful in luring or pressuring opposition representatives—particularly those from the HSS—to split ranks in councils with slim opposition majorities. The HDZ's aim was to at least block the creation of a viable opposition majority if not form an outright coalition with individual opposition parties (as it did in Zagreb with the HSS). It was precisely due to the inability of the three strongest opposition parties (SDP, HSLS, and HSS) to agree on a power-sharing arrangement that local elections had to be repeated in numerous municipalities in December.

The June presidential election followed a similar scenario. The opposition made life easier for the incumbent by failing to come up with a single presidential candidate, even though such an approach could have forced Tudjman into a second round. Tudjman ended up winning comfortably, garnering 61 percent of the vote. The Social Democrat Zdravko Tomac came in second with 21 percent of vote, while the Liberals' candidate, Vlado Gotovac, had to content himself with 18 percent.

Though observers were justifiably quick to attribute the opposition's electoral failures to its disunity, it should not be forgotten that all electoral battles in today's Croatia are fought under HDZ rules. In the June election, for example, state media did their job for the "right candidate" with their proverbial efficiency: an OSCE media-monitoring report maintained that Tudjman received 300 times more coverage in the official media than his challengers. The electoral commission itself was closely controlled by the ruling party. Moreover, the opposition had no means to control the vote among the Croatian diaspora in the West or of the 300,000 Croats in Bosnia and Herzegovina. The voter lists in Croatia proper remained vulnerable to doctoring due to the huge demographic changes of the years of independence. International observer Paul Simon, the head of the OSCE monitoring team, said the poll was "fundamentally flawed" and "free but not fair," adding that the electoral campaign "did not meet the minimum standards for democracies."

PARTY-STATE SYMBIOSIS

The electoral manipulations are illustrative of a larger trend that continued in 1997—the increasing symbiosis between the ruling party and the state, which reached almost the same degree as in neighboring Serbia. Put simply, anything that matters in Croatia has the HDZ's hand in it, from quickly assembled financial and industrial empires to the country's secret service, headed by Tudjman's son Miroslav (until May 1998). Such a state of affairs in essence redirected the accountability of the state institutions away from the people to the ruling party, with all the predictable consequences.

Throughout 1997, the ruling party's perception of its role as the guardian of Croatian statehood evolved toward further intolerance of political opponents, with its undisputed boss leading the way. Proportionate with rumors about his faltering health, Tudjman's speeches increasingly resembled communist-era rhetoric about the enemy from within and from without, only that this time around that enemy was working against Croatian sovereignty and not the interests of the self-managing working people. The gist of Tudjman's message was that the protection of Croatian statehood must be the paramount goal for all Croats. In order to set more visible parameters in that respect, he came out with a list of Croatia's enemies at the end of 1996. The list included the handful of remaining independent media; prominent journalists and human rights activists; opposition leaders; and the majority of non-governmental organizations and "their foreign sponsors." As Tudjman himself put it addressing the congress of the HDZ youth organization: "Those who have drawn no lessons from history are either genetically programmed against the free and independent Croatia . . . or are paid yes-men of foreign centers [of power]."

Throughout 1997, individuals mentioned as "public enemies" were constantly attacked and humiliated in state-controlled media or physically intimidated. The most drastic examples of physical abuse against government opponents involved the two opposition presidential candidates. The Social Democrat Tomac had his van stoned by "unknown perpetrators" while campaigning, and Tudjman's second challenger, Vlado Gotovac, was assaulted and beaten by a uniformed officer of the Croatian army special forces at an election rally on 5 June in Rijeka.

ROUGH RIDE FOR INDEPENDENT MEDIA

The Croatian media scene was yet another area of bleak continuity. The state-controlled media continued to be in the exclusive service of the ruling party, while the handful of independent media faced various legal, financial, and political pressures.

In essence, the HDZ stuck to its strategy of controlling the primary information outlets, while keeping the few independent voices at bay. The key to the government's effective monopoly in electronic media continued to be the very restrictive frequency-allocation and licensing policy, whereby "politically incorrect" applicants faced constant delays in the processing of their requests for starting up a radio or television station. Unsurprisingly, a December study by PULS, a Croatian public opinion research agency, found that state television still figured as the main source of news for 75 percent of respondents.

While Croatia had a very liberal law on information, the government used the Law on Protection of Secrecy of Information and the criminal law as the main grounds for pressuring independent media. For example, legal provisions added in 1997 made "insult" a crime (even if the alleged libel turns out to be true) and criminalized critical reporting and commentary about the top five state officials. As a result, the number of lawsuits filed against those who published "inconvenient stories" spiraled. According to a working paper prepared for the Open Society Institute, by the end of 1997 the Split-based independent weekly *Feral Tribune* was faced with over 50 libel suits and $3 million in potential fines. *Globus,* a Zagreb weekly, was confronted with more than 100 cases and $5.3 million in fines; *Nacional,* another weekly from Zagreb, was subject to 32 suits and faced $2.4 million in potential damages; and Croatia's only major independent daily, Rijeka's *Novi list,* faced 51 suits and $1.6 million in fines. Moreover, on the sole occasion that *Feral Tribune*'s editors were cleared of charges (much to everyone's surprise), President Tudjman sacked the chief justice of the Supreme Court, Krunislav Olujic.

Nonetheless, the independent media, partly thanks to substantial international aid, proved to be resilient. In 1997, the independent media scene featured several independent local radio stations, most notably the influential Radio 101 from Zagreb; a handful of minor local television stations; one major daily (*Novi list*); and three weeklies (*Feral Tribune, Nacional,* and the Zagreb-based *Tjednik*).

A DEAL WITH ETHNIC SERBS?

Croatia continued to improve its cooperation in minority issues with Hungary and Italy, but it failed to follow the same approach toward other ex-Yugoslav states. For example, Muslims and Slovenes were erased from the list of minorities during the December revision of the constitution, despite the fact that they represent, after the Serbs, the two biggest minority groups within Croatia.

The Serb ethnic minority suffered constant harassment in the Knin region and western Slavonia. The rare returnees, who had fled Croatia in the wake of Croatian Army offensives that took those regions out of rebel Serb control in 1995, were frequent targets of physical intimidation. Besides those incidents, there were plenty of indications that the Croatian leadership was loath to give up the country's newly found ethnic purity. Despite the strong pressure by European and U.S. diplomats on the refugee-return issue, the cumbersome citizenship requirements for displaced persons remained in place, effectively making a larger-scale return of Serbian refugees highly improbable. Moreover, the government's newly specialized agency for trading real estate between Serbian and Croatian refugees was bound to contribute to a further population exchange.

On the brighter side, there were signs that a sort of a political modus vivendi between official Zagreb and Serbian political parties in Croatia could be reached. Milorad Pupovac's Zagreb-based Independent Serbian Party merged with the Democratic Serbian Party of Vojislav Stanimirovic from Vukovar, creating the Independent Democratic Serbian Party (SDSS). The new party proved a much more pragmatic and conciliatory partner for the HDZ than the more nationalistic Serbian People's Party of Milan Djukic, which, ironically, many had regarded as Tudjman's puppet ethnic-Serb party during the war in Croatia. The new party brought together the "urban" and "rural" Serbs, a feat that had eluded all previous ethnic Serb leaders in post-communist Croatia. The SDSS was crucial in supporting the latest changes in the constitution through the parliamentary vote, signaling that the remaining ethnic Serbs do not have any intention of undermining territorial sovereignty and democratic processes in Croatia.

ECONOMIC PAST STILL LOOKS BETTER

The second consecutive year of peace in Croatia saw good economic results, at least on paper. The general economic stability of the past few years, expressed in stable currency and a very low inflation rate (3.6 percent in 1997), was maintained, while economic growth accelerated. The GDP grew by 5.5 percent, while industrial production expanded by 6.8 percent.

The average Croat, however, could take little consolation in the good figures. The strong currency (which many experts consider overvalued) rendered Croatia a very expensive place to live, at a time when real salaries still lag far behind their pre-war levels (in 1996, they were at 56 percent of their 1990 level). The official unemployment rate hovered between 17 percent and 20 percent. This led to growing social tensions, with many trade unions, most notably those of transportation workers and teachers, staging strikes. According to some estimates, at least one-fifth of the population was living below the poverty line.

Privatization was well under way, but the whole process was marred with episodes smacking of clientelism. According to government critics, this entrenched cronyism has led to a situation where a bloc of 500 families allegedly controls half of all economic activity. Moreover, the state's role in the economy is still significant. The state budget ran at more than 40 percent of GDP, with defense expenditures being its biggest item: Croatia spent about 13 percent of its GDP on army and police.

In 1997, Croatia ran up a large trade deficit ($4.8 billion, up by more than $1.5 billion from the previous year). The foreign debt came to $4.7 billion, which is a higher burden in per capita terms than the one the former Yugoslavia had in 1990. Croatia's biggest hope for a quick economic recovery remained tourism, with a reported improvement in earnings of more than $2 billion in 1997. The recorded figure of 30 million overnight stays is still far behind the level back in 1987, which saw 68 million tourist overnights. Clearly, Croatia still has a long way to go in aligning its economic performance with the expectations of its citizens and desires of foreign investors.

SEEDS OF CHANGE

Despite the prevalence of trends of continuity, several new factors were integrated into the Croatian political equation during 1997: the political rise of the Social Democrats; the easing of tensions in the neighborhood; a tougher Western stance toward Croatian domestic and regional policies; and the re-incorporation of eastern Slavonia and consequent re-emergence of the Serbian minority issue.

After its good showing in the April elections, the even better result of its presidential candidate Tomac in the June election represented a big comeback for the SDP, which had been growing accustomed to electoral catastrophes. The SDP proved capable of pulling its ranks together and re-presenting itself not only as a nationwide voice of protest against HDZ rule, but also as a party with a clear and distinctive message, targeting social issues and advocating anti-corruption measures. In December, SDP won—alone or in coalition—in almost all the electoral districts where local elections had to be repeated. Although the victories were achieved in traditional anti-HDZ counties in Dalmatia and the Rijeka region, they boosted reformed communists' hopes for the general elections scheduled for 1999.

Another event that played into the Social Democrats' hands was the split-up of the formerly largest opposition party, the HSLS. The Liberals split over the issue of cooperation with the HDZ. Vlado Gotovac, HSLS's presidential candidate, opposed any deals with Tudjman, unlike the party's equally prominent leader, Drazen Budisa. The realignment could lead to the emergence of a political arena divided among a rightist bloc headed by HDZ, a leftist bloc headed by SDP, and Gotovac's Liberal Party—together with the Istrian Democratic Alliance and the Croatian National Party—occupying a very narrow center.

The easing of tensions in the region played an important role in Croatian foreign and domestic policy. On the domestic front, it gradually decreased the presence of the nationalistic political discourse and deprived the ruling party of its favorite practice of using the foreign threat to discipline and to homogenize the domestic political space. Nonetheless, the HDZ moved to amend the constitution in order to ban any future regional association with other ex-Yugoslav or Balkan countries. Croatia's relations with the Federal Republic of Yugoslavia, however, improved in minor ways. Regular bus lines were established and it became easier for citizens of both countries to obtain visas as new consulates were reciprocally established in Belgrade and Zagreb. The issue of dual citizenship—regarded as key to easing the ethnic Serbs' predicament—has remained unresolved. The Croatian side claimed it had no problem with the concept, while the Yugoslav side seemed reluctant to proceed in that direction.

The real dividends of peace for Croatia did not come in the form of a smaller military budget but in the lesser degree of Zagreb's political support for elements undermining peace in the region. Despite its strong reluctance to reach an agreement with Sarajevo on the free use of the Adriatic port of Ploce and its refusal to implement partnership relationships with the Bosnian (Muslim-Croat) Federation, Zagreb withdrew its support from the most radical elements among Herzegovinian Croats.

The gradually toughening Western stance toward Croatia was instrumental in limiting the damaging relationship between official Zagreb and its Herzegovinian brethren. Croatia's fall from the West's grace was primarily triggered by its noncompliance with the Dayton peace agreement. The United States in particular became very impatient with Zagreb's unwillingness to cooperate with the International War Crimes Tribunal in the Hague, as well as with the constant harassment of Serb returnees in Croatia. The May 1997 visit of U.S. Secretary of State Madeleine Albright to Croatia put Zagreb officials in a most embarrassing situation, since they did not know how to respond to her finger-pointing at recently burned ethnic Serb homes in Kostajnica region. As a consequence, Western economic assistance became conditional upon compliance with the requests from the Hague.

Croatia eventually budged in October, sending a group of 10 Bosnian Croat indictees to The Hague, including Dario Kordic, one of the key figures in the Bosnian Croat para-state Herceg-Bosna. In an earlier operation, two Herzegovinian warlords, Mladen "Tuta" Naletilic and Vinko "Stela" Martinovic, were arrested on Croatian soil and put in a Zagreb jail. As much as this move was aimed to please the Hague, it was also aimed at neutralizing dangerous witnesses, whose possible testimonies in the Hague could damage many high officials in Zagreb. The ability of a Zagreb court to deal efficiently with war crimes, however, can be seriously questioned. The official position that Croats could not have committed war crimes since they were waging a defensive war had not changed, despite fresh evidence to the contrary (see "Dealing with the Ugly Side of the 'Patriotic War'" which follows this article).

Croatia's compliance with Western demands was initially awarded with the release of the blocked loans, but later in the fall, Croatia's stubbornness in the face of demands for better treatment of its Serbian minority pushed Washington to propose that Croatia be expelled from the Council of Europe. The West's carrot-and-stick policy gave some hope for the successful incorporation of eastern Slavonia, the last Serb-held area, scheduled for 1998. The incorporation would lead to the re-emergence of the Serbian minority issue in Croatia, since the total number of ethnic Serbs living on Croatian territory would jump by 100,000. Throughout 1997, the creation of a joint police force and mixed municipality councils in eastern Slavonia occurred without major hitches. Hard-liners on the Serbian side either left for Yugoslavia or were overpowered by the nonnationalists. However, the reconciliatory politics of the current Croatian Serb political leadership may not be enough. Given the experience with HDZ policies vis-à-vis the Serbs in western Slavonia and the Knin region, an active guardian role on the part of the West will be necessary to provide arbitration and compliance with democratic procedures and minority-rights standards.

GLOSSARY

HDZ	Croatian Democratic Union
HSLS	Croatian Social-Liberal Party
HSS	Croatian Peasant Party
SDP	Social Democratic Party
SDSS	Independent Democratic Serbian Party

Testimony: DEALING WITH THE UGLY SIDE OF THE "PATRIOTIC WAR"

The government and its media for years conditioned the public to believe that the Croatian side could have done no wrong in the 1991–1992 war. Even the chief justice of Croatia's Supreme Court, Milan Vukovic, once said that Croats could not have committed war crimes since they were waging a defensive war. Reports in independent media that alleged otherwise were customarily slammed as the work of traitors and foreign agents operating with flimsy evidence.

Things changed when a phone rang at the Split-based weekly Feral Tribune *in late August. Feeling forgotten and betrayed, a disillusioned "hero" of Croatia's "Patriotic War" decided to go public with an account of the war exploits of his paramilitary unit (known as "Autumn Rains"), which had operated under the command of the Croatian Interior Ministry. Counter-accusations, denials, and personal insults against the teller of this tale almost immediately flooded the media. Both the public and the authorities were in a state of shock, although, as* Feral Tribune's *then-Editor in Chief Viktor Ivancic later noted, "the most shocking thing was that everybody was so shocked" by the whole affair.*

The authorities had known about the case since 1992, when Zagreb police arrested 16 members of "Autumn Rains" on murder charges, obtaining chilling testimonies from the perpetrators themselves during the course of investigation. But as the group's boss, Tomislav Mercep, was still on good terms with the ruling party, they were soon released on procedural grounds with no charges. Feral Tribune got hold of the testimonies and published them in 1994, but that effort only got them a 1996 court order to pay 130,000 kuna ($24,000) in damages to Mercep for "emotional suffering."

This time around, however, the HDZ correctly assumed that another cover-up was not possible. Miro Bajramovic and three of his comrades found themselves behind bars, where they awaited trial at the end of 1997. Most important, however, the testimony published by Feral Tribune *on 1 September (excerpted below), and similar confessions that followed, opened the doors to a public re-examination of the role of the Croatian side in the "Patriotic War." All this notwithstanding, the eminence grise of* Feral*'s story, Tomislav Mercep, escaped unscathed—up to the point of being able to prepare a political comeback.*

My name is Miro Bajramovic and I am directly responsible for the death of 86 people. I go to bed with this thought and I wake up with it—if I sleep at all. I killed 72 people with my own hands, nine of whom were women. We made no distinction, we asked no questions: for us they were Chetniks and enemies. The hardest thing is to set the first house ablaze and kill the first man. Afterward, everything becomes routine. I know the names and surnames of every single person I killed. [. . .]

I met Tomislav Mercep in 1991 in the village of Dalj [eastern Slavonia]. We fought together from that time on. We've been through a lot together. Our unit was called Autumn Rains, or officially: the Interior Ministry's First Zagreb Special Unit. Croatian defenders [soldiers] and Croats in general know very well who Autumn Rains were.

Before going to Pakracka Poljana [a village some 60 kilometers southeast from Zagreb] sometime in September 1991, we were in Gospic [northern Dalmatian hinterland]. [. . .] Being a Serb in Gospic was almost as good as being dead [at the time]. Our group executed between 90 and 100 people in less than a month there. [. . .] The order for Gospic was: "ethnically cleanse." So we killed the directors of the post office and the hospital, restaurant owners, and other assorted Serbs. The killing was done by shooting at point-blank range, since we did not have much time. I repeat, orders from above were to reduce the percentage of Serbs in Gospic. We went to [the Dalmatian town of] Slano four times and executed 13 people there, all of whom were Serbs. Their stronghold was in the village of Vukovici, between Dubrovnik and Slano. Out of the 13, I killed eight. [. . .]

We arrived in Pakracka Poljana on 6 October 1991, after returning from Gospic. In the beginning, our headquarters were at the fire station, and that's where the prison was as well. [. . .] We had orders to hold the territory around Pakrac, and later, [Josip] Boljkovac [then interior minister] and Mercep went out there and agreed that the base be established in Pakracka Poljana. [. . .]

We kept prisoners in the basement of the elementary school, and whenever we had more of them, we'd put them in the classrooms as well. Nights were the worst for them, since it was then that we "operatively processed" them, which meant finding out the best way to inflict the greatest possible pain so that they would tell the most. Do you know what's the best way? You burn the prisoner with a gas flame, and then pour vinegar over his wounds, and you concentrate on his genitals and eyes. Then there is that little field inductor-phone, you hook up a Serb onto that. It's direct current, it can't kill, but it's very unpleasant. Then you ask the hooked-up Serb where he is from, and he says [for example] "from Dvor na Uni," and then you "call" Dvor na Uni by rotating the handle on the phone. [. . .] We'd open wounds on them and then pour salt or vinegar on them. We usually made sure that they didn't stop bleeding. They also had to learn [the Croatian national anthem] right away. They were forced to do so by the prison commander, Mijo Jolic, who now owns restaurants throughout Croatia, just like [Munib] Suljic. And why don't I own anything?

When I think of all that torturing, I sometimes wonder how they managed to come up with all those methods. For example, the most painful one was to stick little nails under [prisoners'] fingernails. When you connect them to the three-phase current, nothing remains of a man. Ashes! I would never have thought of that. I also interrogated prisoners, but I never maltreated them, nor did I do it for pleasure. And there were those who enjoyed doing it, like Munib Suljic for example. But we only cared about the results he got, we did not care about his means. After all, we knew that they would all be killed, so it didn't matter if it hurt them more today or tomorrow. [. . .] In the beginning, we pretended to be a "democratic" police force. We'd give sheets of paper to Serbs to write all they knew, and we wanted as many names and places as possible.

Tomislav Mercep was the commander of the Pakracka Poljana [base], and I was his deputy. Mercep knew everything. He didn't participate directly in the executions, but he read all that we wrote him in our reports, though most of the information was communicated orally. He knew about each execution, because he was the commander and was a very charismatic person for us. He told us several times: "Tonight you have to clean all these shits." That meant that all prisoners had to be executed. If you didn't carry out everything that was ordered, then they said you were a traitor. And we killed Serbs and Croats alike in Pakracka Poljana. Local Croats also feared us. The villagers could hear screams and moans coming out of the prison all night long, people couldn't sleep, but they didn't dare say a word to us. They all knew that if they asked anything at all, they could also wind up in the prison. [. . .]

As far as I know, more than 50 Serbs were brought to Pakracka Poljana from Zagreb, and it was the closest circle of Mercep's associates [. . .] who brought them there. We worked in two groups, one brought them to [the collection center at] the Zagreb fairground, and the other one took them further. [. . .]

Great avarice reigned at the time. [. . .] Mercep told us to take away everything from the Serbs but that we had to hand over the money we found in their houses to headquarters, for buying weapons. But . . . Mercep [and a few others] split the money into equal shares among themselves. . . . [One day a] shoot-out [erupted], because [it turned out that] the money hadn't been split into equal parts. Posavec was removed from the unit, but the money was not taken away from him, and we aren't talking here about a 1,000 or 100,000 German marks but much, much more.

I can't say that mass executions were carried out in Pakracka Poljana; people were mostly killed in groups of seven to ten. That is, everything depended on how many people were in the prison. Sometimes, we went out and executed people in their homes and then blew up the houses. No bodies. [. . .] In those days, I absolutely had no feeling that Serbs are people like us, that they are someone's fathers, brothers, children. . . . No, we didn't kill children, except when Suljic killed Aleksandra Zec. I saved 19 kids in Vocin with my own hands. Had I killed children, I wouldn't be able to look my little daughter straight in the eye.

My estimate is that, altogether some 280 men were executed at Pakracka Poljana, along with ten or so women. [. . .] Except for [an] old woman, all women were first raped and then killed. Such is the truth. [. . .]

Ivan Vekic [interior minister of Croatia at the time of atrocities] . . . is lying, he knew everything. I can tell him how many orders our unit got from him. He would say "I want you to do this and this and that and that." We never returned without fulfilling our tasks, and those were mostly executions. [. . .] I repeat, Ivan Vekic knew everything. I was in jail from 2 January to 30 April 1992. What really made me sad was that Croatia was [internationally] recognized on 15 January and I was in the Remetinac jail. We were freed after [the hard-line HDZ nationalist Vladimir] Seks became attorney general, but we were released in two groups. [. . .]

Mercep, who organized our defense, exerted a great influence there, then there was Ivan Vekic, who is now talking gibberish in public. At that time, he was on our side. [. . .]

I kept silent about this for a long time, waiting for somebody in this country to remember that I also exist. My kids need to eat in the same way as Mercep's, who owns two houses in Zagreb, two apartments and a house on [the Adriatic island of] Brac, and he came without a dime to his name from Vukovar. Then there are Stipe Spajic, Mandjeralo. . . . How did they get all that they've got now? Let them tell me the way so that I also can get some property. If you have to dig canals, I'll dig, I'm not ashamed. After all this, I'm expecting [President] Tudjman to call me himself and ask me what got into me [to make this confession], and I'll tell him: "I just did it for my kids." I just want a job and housing for my family.

I'm a great believer. I wear a ring-rosary from Medjugorje [a major Catholic pilgrimage site in Herzegovina] on my finger. God forgives everything up to a limit. I believe that I've been punished enough so far for all that I've done. [. . .]

I'm not feeling relieved after I've told you all this. I'm scared of my own unit. These guys are hardened professionals who don't miss often. And I know that [the International War Crimes Tribunal in] the Hague is in the cards for me."

Translated by Sava Tatic

Bosnia-Herzegovina

Population:	3,200,000 Bosnian federation: 2,300,000 Republika Srpska: 900,000
Capital:	Sarajevo (pop. 350,000)
Major cities:	Banja Luka (240,000), Tuzla (pop. 240,000 including refugees), Zenica (pop. 160,000), Mostar (pop. 100,000)
Area:	51,233 sq. km.
Major ethnic groups:	Muslim 43.7%, Serbian 31.4%, Croatian 17.3%, other 7.6% (1991 census)
Economy:	(excluding Republika Srpska)
....	GDP growth: 25%–35%
....	Inflation rate: 12.2%
....	Average monthly wage: $145
....	Unemployment rate: 30%–40%

A YEAR OF WESTERN DETERMINATION IN BOSNIA

by DARIA SITO-SUCIC

At a moment when most political analysts, let alone common people, seriously started to question the U.S.-sponsored Dayton peace agreement that ended the three-year-long Bosnian war in 1995, the British troops with the NATO-led peace force took everyone by surprise. On 1 July 1997 they moved in to arrest two indicted war criminals in the Serb-controlled western town of Prijedor. One of the indictees was killed during the subsequent shoot-out, and the other was transferred to International Criminal Tribunal for Former Yugoslavia in The Hague.

This action opened the door for others to follow. In October, ten Bosnian Croats who were suspected of committing war crimes against Muslims during the 1993–94 Muslim-Croat war surrendered to the war crimes tribunal. NATO took yet another step in December and arrested two Bosnian Croat war crimes suspects. As was the case with their two Serb predecessors, they were accused in "sealed indictments," which had not been made public but were delivered directly to the NATO Stabilization Force (SFOR).

Some complained all of the arrested were just "small fish," while the "sharks" such as the former Bosnian Serb president Radovan Karadzic and his top army general Ratko Mladic were still at large. However, not all of those who found themselves in The Hague were "small fish." The fact that Dario Kordic, the notorious Bosnian Croat nationalist who allegedly organized most of the Croat atrocities toward the Muslims during the Muslim-Croat war, was before the tribunal, could still assure many Bosnians that justice was slow but reachable after all. In addition, the arrests coincided with the upheaval on the Bosnian Serb political scene, which no longer made them look like a coincidence.

BOSNIAN SERB POLITICAL CLIMATE CHANGED

A sudden turn on the Bosnian Serb political stage started during the summer when the Bosnian Serb President Biljana Plavsic ended her obedience to the ruling ultra-nationalist Serb Democratic Party (SDS), which was still controlled by Karadzic. Until that time, Plavsic had been only a puppet president, handpicked by Karadzic himself in the summer of 1996 when the Western powers forced him to leave his post as the self-proclaimed "first and only" Bosnian Serb president. Plavsic was invisible for one year, excluded from all major political decisions by her party fellows. She was only expected to sign the decisions already prepared by Karadzic's narrow circle in his mountain stronghold of Pale, near Sarajevo. She was not expected to act, especially not independently.

However, Plavsic surprised everyone when she sacked Interior Minister

Dragan Kijac in June, accusing him of corruption. Unexpectedly, the Bosnian Serb president had started a process that gathered an unstoppable momentum. Nobody was sure of her motives or intentions, but she distanced herself from her former party colleagues and found new partners whom she trusted. Plavsic became a Serbian Robin Hood, starting a crusade against the crime and corruption that were embodied in the SDS hard-liners. She also resigned her membership in the party, and formed a new one, the Serb National Alliance (SNS).

The West strongly supported Plavsic and her circle of pragmatic and allegedly moderate technocrats based in northwestern Banja Luka, the only big town in the Bosnian Serb entity. Nobody believed she had stopped being a Serb nationalist, but the international community needed someone among the Bosnian Serbs who was ready to cooperate. Plavsic proved to be a willing partner. She confronted Karadzic's Mafia elite, and effectively divided the territory of the Serb republic into two politically opposed parts.

SFOR supported her in several ways. Its troops guarded the replacement of the hard-line police force with those loyal to Plavsic in western parts of the Serb republic. In October, SFOR seized the television transmitters held by the Pale-based Serb hard-liners, and put the airwaves into the hands of Plavsic's supporters. In this way, the international community prevented Serb television from continuing to spread ethnic hatred through its inflammatory and nationalist language, and took away yet another powerful weapon from the formerly untouchable ideologists.

Soon enough, the SDS leadership, though they were unwilling, had to agree to hold early parliamentary elections in the Serb republic. They were aware that it was the only way to prevent the definitive split of the territory into two parts: the eastern region controlled by them and the western region which was Plavsic-controlled. The Organization for Security and Cooperation in Europe (OSCE) supervised the elections, trying to assure they were free, fair, and democratic.

THE YEAR OF ELECTIONS

The international community put quite a lot of effort and funds into organizing Bosnia's September municipal elections. They believed there was still a chance to change the gloomy political landscape in the country which was being run by nationalist groups from the Serbian, Croatian, and Muslim communities. They saw the municipal elections as providing an opportunity to move forward.

The municipal elections, originally scheduled for September 1996 along with the country's general elections, were delayed for one year "until the conditions for free and fair elections were created." Although it was highly questionable if these conditions existed in September 1997 (a major voter registration fraud was later discovered in the disputed Brcko area), the elections nevertheless passed without major incidents, although they demonstrated once again that it was difficult to beat nationalist parties in the Balkans.

The OSCE reported that the turnout in the entire country was close to 70 percent. The OSCE spent close to $50 million organizing the elections and supervising the voter registration procedure. Some 3,000 SFOR troops were deployed to provide security for the refugees who arrived to vote in their former place of residence, from which they had been expelled during the course of war.

Despite all these efforts, the Serb, Croat, and Muslim nationalist parties that represented Bosnia's three major nationalities unquestionably won the elections. Progress could still be seen since the opposition parties had secured more seats in the municipal councils than expected, and had won the elections in the northern Tuzla region, famous for its non-nationalist history.

An even bigger change was the fact that the deputies from the Muslim-Croat federation were elected to the municipal councils inside the Serb entity: only months earlier this would have been unthinkable. However, the installation of the councillors to their posts was to be a different matter.

The OSCE was generally satisfied with the way the elections had proceeded, but they were not happy about the pace at which the election results were implemented. The deadline for the installation of the new local authorities was initially set at 31 December, but this was later extended to 28 February 1998. At the end of 1997, the elected Muslim municipal councillors in Srebrenica, Foca, and other towns in the eastern parts of the Serb republic were as far from taking up their seats as ever.

In addition, the international community participated in the organization of the Bosnian Serb parliamentary elections which were held ahead of schedule on 22–23 November. This time the hard-line Serb nationalists, who scored well in the country's September local elections, failed to secure a parliamentary majority, though they remained the strongest faction in the parliament. The elections showed again that the territory of the Bosnian Serb entity was divided. The Serb Democratic Party and the Serb Republic Radical Party, representing the ultra-nationalist faction, won a majority of votes in the eastern parts, and Plavsic's party and a number of smaller independent parties prevailed in the western parts of the Serb republic. However, the SDS and radicals were three seats short of a majority in the 83-seat national assembly, so Plavsic was able to name a caretaker government until the next elections, which were scheduled for September 1998. According to the Dayton peace agreement, Bosnia's general elections in 1996 were to be followed by new elections in two years.

WEST FORCED TO INTERVENE

After U.S. President Bill Clinton announced that American troops in the NATO-led peace force would remain in Bosnia after their mandate was initially due to expire in June 1998, it was clear to everyone that NATO was going to stay in Bosnia with the mandate repeatedly renewed and with no time limitation. Since some progress had only just begun, more time was needed for it to be maintained and further developed in order to prevent a possible return to war.

The international community had also realized it had to step up the implementation of the civilian provisions of the Dayton peace agreement, even if it meant certain decisions had to be imposed upon Bosnia's rival political parties. Waiting for the ethnic representatives in the country's central government to agree upon any single issue proved to be a hopeless enterprise, because Bosnians demonstrated they were masters of delay regardless of their ethnicity. "They could only agree they were unable to agree," was a favorite phrase used by journalists when talking about the country's collective presidency and cabinet.

Bosnia's international Peace Implementation Council (PIC) met twice in 1997—first in May in Sintra, Portugal, and again in December in Bonn. The PIC consists of representatives of the countries taking part in promoting the peace process in the former Yugoslavia: suppliers of military personnel; donors; international institutions such as the EU; the United States and Russia; as well as the main parties, the Bosnian Muslims, Serbs and Croats.) The meeting of international representatives in Sintra resulted in a conditional decision on economic aid for Bosnian parties depending on their participation in the implementation of the peace accords. The first international peace coordinator for Bosnia, Carl Bildt, was replaced by the Spanish diplomat Carlos Westendorp. The decision to make economic aid conditional on the readiness of the parties to implement the peace accords primarily affected the Serb entity, whose government stubbornly opposed any kind of political and economic changes. But it was also applied in those municipalities in the Muslim-Croat federation where the return of refugees had been prevented or the peace agreement violated in any significant way.

Although the Sintra meeting had produced a declaration which set deadlines for the implementation of the civilian aspects of the peace agreement, none of them were respected. Two years after the Dayton peace agreement was signed, Bosnia still did not have a common passport, single currency, flag, coat of arms, citizenship law, or common car plates. The privatization laws regulating the ownership of enterprises, banks, and apartments still had to be adopted.

Hence, the West was forced to change its attitude and language significantly at its December ministerial meeting in Bonn. The international High Representative, Carlos Westendorp, was given much wider authority by the Bonn document, and was entitled to impose his decisions upon the country's impotent and obstructive leadership. Westendorp used this right for the first time on 16 December, and imposed a temporary law on citizenship after Bosnia's central government failed to adopt it by the agreed deadline. In this way, the Western powers started in effect to openly treat Bosnia as a protectorate under their charge, not capable of self-rule, in light of the repeated failure of the local politicians to cooperate and fulfill their promises given in Dayton.

ECONOMIC AID MADE CONDITIONAL

By the end of 1996, one year after the war had ended, Bosnia's Muslim-Croat federation saw a rapid economic growth that was estimated at nearly 50 percent, though it started to grow from a very low level. Such a growth in a country thoroughly devastated by war was possible thanks to more than $1 billion in reconstruction aid donated to Bosnia in 1996 by the international community. Growth in GDP in 1997 was estimated at some 35 percent, as suggested earlier by the World Bank experts. Still, at the beginning of the year, Bosnia had been included among the 63 least developed countries in the world, whose annual per capita income did not exceed $725.

Meanwhile, growth in the Serb entity in 1996 was estimated at some 20 percent, while no reliable figures for 1997 were available. The reconstruction program for Bosnia, drafted by the World Bank and other multilateral and bilateral donors, was estimated at some $5.1 billion in external financing over three to four years. At the first two international donor conferences $1.8 billion was pledged for Bosnia's postwar reconstruction. The third donor meeting was scheduled for the end of 1996, but was postponed several times due to the failure of the country's politicians to adopt a set of basic economic laws, a so-called Quick Start Package.

This Quick Start Package of laws governing state institutions, which included a budget, a law on central bank, customs, and responsibility for foreign debt, was adopted in June. But the donor conference, which was held in July and raised some $1.2 billion, came too late for major reconstruction undertakings because much of the building season had passed. Originally, the aim of the meeting had been to release $1.4 billion of aid, but, according to the World Bank, as the meeting had been postponed several times, several contributions were immobilized by the budget procedures of the donor countries.

The 23–24 July donor conference denied aid to the Bosnian Serbs until they started to cooperate fully with all aspects of the Dayton peace agreement.

The handover of indicted war criminals was stressed as one of the key provisions of the treaty. But the Serb Prime Minister Gojko Klickovic said nobody could force the Serb republic to yield to international demands for "a handful of dollars," nor force it to reintegrate into Bosnia and Herzegovina. In this way, the Bosnian Serb leadership was responsible for not getting the international aid in 1997, as in 1996. As a result the Serb republic received only two percent of the total aid for Bosnia's reconstruction. But its leadership continued to block the building of the new state institutions.

Although the international governor of Bosnia's central bank, Serge Robert of France, was appointed in October 1996, a law on the country's central bank was passed only in June 1997. The bank became operational in August, issuing a common currency (for monetary transactions only at this stage), and centralizing foreign exchange reserves. The bank operated as a single organization, with branches in both of Bosnia's entities being responsible for day-to-day activity, and operated under strict currency board rules (meaning that monetary emissions were tied to the level of hard currency reserves). An interim currency, the "convertible mark," was fully convertible and pegged at parity with the German mark. The introduction of a common currency for the whole of the country was vital to stop the chaos in the money market in Bosnia, where three currencies were flowing: the so-called Bosnian dinar in the Muslim-controlled areas of the Muslim-Croat federation, the Croatian kuna in the Croat-controlled parts of the federation, and the Yugoslav dinar in the Serb republic. The convertible mark (KM) had two different designs which had not been agreed upon by the end of 1997.

A week after the Dayton accords were signed, Bosnia had become a full member of the International Monetary Fund. But the IMF refused to grant Bosnia a $100 million stand-by arrangement due to the government's failure to adopt economic reforms and a common currency with an agreed design. Bosnia assumed 13.2 percent of the assets and liabilities of the former Yugoslavia, including a debt of $640 million to the World Bank. In December Bosnia reached an agreement with the London Club of commercial creditors, reducing the country's original debt of $1.04 billion to $404 million under favorable terms. Its relation with the Paris Club of government creditors remained unresolved. Although the international community demonstrated plenty of goodwill when dealing with Bosnia, the major condition for continuing financial aid to the country was a complete overhaul of its economic structure. Growth could be sustained only through privatization and other economic reforms, the foreign experts maintained.

Legislation regulating the privatization of state-run enterprises, the sale of state-owned apartments, and the settlement of war-related claims of Bosnian citizens was adopted in October by the federation parliament, and was praised by the West as a crucial step forward. But international experts criticized the Serb republic for adopting a flawed privatization package that allegedly could lead to fraud and manipulation.

BOSNIA—A PLACE TO VISIT

In 1997 Bosnia was probably the country that was most visited by all kinds of celebrities—political and religious leaders, royals and pop-stars. The trend was started by Pope John Paul II, who paid a two-day visit to Bosnia on 12 April to promote religious reconciliation and tolerance. His visit was very successful and was aimed at helping to improve the poor relations between Catholic Bosnian Croats and Bosnian Muslims in the federation. (Only a couple of months earlier, nationalist Croats in the western part of the divided southern town of Mostar attacked a group of Muslims who were attempting to visit a cemetery on their religious holiday. Two were killed and several persons were wounded.)

Princess Diana arrived in Bosnia in the beginning of August on her land-mine crusade, just three weeks before she died. The Irish rock band U2 held an impressive open-air concert in Sarajevo in September, bringing together fans from both Bosnian entities. Succeeding where everyone else had failed, they managed to gather and keep 50,000 people of different nationalities in one place without a single incident. The year was crowned by the visits of U.S. President Bill Clinton and German Chancellor Helmut Kohl before Christmas. Bosnians felt they were at the center of the world.

However, regardless of the very good relations Bosnia managed to establish and maintain with the major world powers, it failed to establish proper relations with its closest neighbors. Although its relations with Yugoslavia to the east and Croatia to the west were set as priorities for Bosnia's international relations, by the end of 1997 diplomatic relations with Yugoslavia had not yet been established, while the controversial agreement on parallel relations between the Muslim-Croat federation and Croatia had not yet been reached.

One major problem which still faced Bosnia, and which will continue in the long run, are the territorial claims of the neighboring countries. Despite all international efforts and the presence of a 35,000-strong NATO force, there is a real threat of secession by Bosnia's Croat- and Serb-controlled territories and their joining the parent states of Croatia and Serbia. This possibility is brought home by the continued practice of international peace mediators, who go to Belgrade and Zagreb when they need some urgent interventions with regard to the Bosnian Serbs and Croats.

Document: CONCLUSIONS OF THE BONN PEACE CONFERENCE

Summary of the most important conclusions made at the Bonn Peace Implementation Conference (Bonn, 9–10 December 1997):

The Council will continue its assistance to Bosnia and Herzegovina in 1998, reiterating the Sintra commitment to stay the course, but it concluded that an even more persistent approach on the part of the international community is required. The actions of the authorities in Bosnia and Herzegovina too often fall short of their words. The recent report by the World Bank and the European Commission's Customs and Fiscal Assistance Office (EC CAFAO) provide new sobering evidence of this attitude.

Continued procrastination may even endanger the progress achieved so far.

The Council made it clear to the authorities in Bosnia and Herzegovina that assistance by the international community remains conditional upon compliance with the Peace Agreement and subsequent obligations.

The Council reaffirmed that it will tolerate neither any tendencies to dominate the political institutions of Bosnia and Herzegovina, nor any attempts to undermine the sovereignty and territorial integrity of Bosnia and Herzegovina. The Council recalled that the Peace Agreement has primacy over previous Agreements between the Parties.

The High Representative was charged at Sintra to pursue deadlines adopted by the Steering Board, and to recommend and take measures in cases of noncompliance. This course has proved to be right. The Council welcomed the High Representative's intention to use his authority fully to facilitate the resolution of difficulties.

The Council insisted that all persons indicted for war crimes must be handed over to the International Criminal Tribunal for Former Yugoslavia (ICTY) for justice to be dispensed impartially, under the terms of the Peace Agreement and UN Security Council resolutions. It drew particular attention to the failure of the authorities of Republika Srpska and the Federal Republic of Yugoslavia to carry out this obligation.

The Council was convinced that until all persons indicted for war crimes were brought before the International Criminal Tribunal for Former Yugoslavia, the prerequisites for reconciliation and the rule of law in Bosnia and Herzegovina will remain seriously impaired. In this regard, the Council recalled the Sintra Declaration where the continuing influence of Radovan Karadzic on the political life of Republika Srpska was deemed unacceptable.

The Council reminded the Republic of Croatia and the Federal Republic of Yugoslavia of their obligations under the Peace Agreement and expected that these would be voluntarily and immediately discharged in their entirety. There would have been more progress in implementing the Peace Agreement if this commitment had been observed. In particular, this refers to special relations with the Entities, the ongoing discrimination between Entities' citizens with regard to visa regulations and, more generally, free movement.

The Council thanked SFOR for providing the secure environment necessary for the civilian implementation of the Peace Agreement and for the increased assistance rendered in this field. The Council recognized and supported the emerging consensus on the need for a military presence to continue beyond June 1998, considering it indispensable for the maintenance of a stable security environment and, in particular, for helping to create secure conditions for the conduct by the High Representative, as well as by the UN, OSCE, and other international organizations, of tasks associated with the Peace Agreement.

The Council stressed that the presence of IFOR and SFOR has been the greatest single contributor to sub-regional security since the signing of the Peace Agreement and will continue to be so in the short to medium term. It welcomed NATO's plans to consider options for a multinational follow-up force to SFOR beyond June 1998. The Council stated that any follow-up force should provide appropriate support to civil implementation while being readily available and effective enough to respond quickly to events on the ground in and across Bosnia and Herzegovina.

The Council thanked OSCE for the effective conduct of the municipal and Republika Srpska Assembly elections. It recognized that OSCE supervision remained essential to ensure free and fair elections in Bosnia and Herzegovina in 1998. It therefore invited OSCE to extend the mandate of its mission in Bosnia and Herzegovina accordingly.

NO FLYING COLORS FOR DAYTON—YET

by CHRISTOPHER BENNETT

In Bosnia-Herzegovina, street names generally offer a good pointer to the ethnicity of a town's ruling caste. Having cleansed an area of undesirable ethnic groups, nationalist leaders set about eradicating all traces of the former inhabitants' culture, including a purge of names of public places. One street that bucks the nationalist-exclusivist trend is Ulica Potporucnika Smajica in the center of the northeastern Bosnian town of Bijeljina, now in the Republika Srpska, the place where the Bosnian war originally broke out in March 1992.

Despite the Muslim association (Smajic is an unmistakably Muslim surname) the Second Lieutenant Smajic Street is itself a new epithet, the legacy of a sad tale reflecting many of the complexities both of Bosnia's war and of its peace. At the beginning of hostilities in Croatia in 1991, Second Lieutenant Smajic was a young officer in the Yugoslav People's Army. His regiment was dispatched to eastern Slavonia and he died in the assault on Vukovar, becoming one of the first casualties of the Croatian war. Out of respect, Bijeljina's municipal authorities named after him the street on which Smajic had grown up and where his parents had built a large house. Six months later, his mother was expelled from her home, one of the first victims of ethnic cleansing in the Bosnian war. She took refuge with Serbian friends, kept a low profile, and remained in Bijeljina throughout the war.

When hostilities finally ended, Mrs. Smajic hoped she might get her house back. After all, one of the clearest promises of the peace plan was the right of all refugees to return to their homes. At the very least, Mrs. Smajic hoped she might be allowed to live out her days in a single room in her family home, sharing the house with the current occupants, who had themselves been displaced during the war. To no avail. The local courts were not interested in the plight of an elderly Muslim woman. After 18 months of peace, Mrs. Smajic ran out of patience and emigrated to Syria.

A SLUGGISH START

Mrs. Smajic's experience was sadly typical of the 18 months following the signing of the General Framework Agreement for Peace (commonly referred to as Dayton) at Wright-Patterson Air Force Base in Dayton, Ohio, on 21 November 1995. The hope and expectation that accompanied the end of the war rapidly gave way to frustration and disappointment as the promises of peace proved illusory. After overseeing the cease-fire, the transfer of authority in some areas of Bosnia, and the creation of a zone of separation, the 60,000-strong NATO-led

Implementation Force (IFOR) largely focused on patrolling the boundary line between the two entities created by Dayton and avoiding casualties. Meanwhile, implementation of the civilian aspects of the peace treaty stalled even before it had begun.

Dayton's early difficulties were in part the result of the contradictions between partition and integration that were inherent in the peace plan and reflected the tortured negotiations that preceded agreement. The peace plan recognized Bosnia-Herzegovina as one state but divided it into two separate entities: the Republika Srpska and the (Muslim-Croat) Federation of Bosnia and Herzegovina, each with its own constitution, police force, and military. At the same time, it attempted to impose a structure that could, over time, draw the entities into a single, truly integrated state. Provisions to that effect included common institutions, such as a countrywide presidency, parliament, and central government, as well as a central bank and common currency. Other fundamental guarantees of basic human rights, such as freedom of movement and the right of refugees to return home, were also enshrined in the peace plan.

The leisurely start to Dayton's implementation also reflected U.S. domestic politics. In an election year, Bill Clinton did not want Bosnia to cost him the presidency and thus charted an ultra-cautious course aimed, above all, at avoiding body bags. That policy changed, however, after Clinton's successful re-election, when he appointed Madeleine Albright as secretary of state. Meanwhile, the change of government in Great Britain in May 1997 provided a willing partner for a more robust approach to Dayton implementation, which transformed the fortunes of the peace process during the second half of 1997.

A NEW RESOLVE

The key breakthrough was the Prijedor snatch operation. On 10 July 1997, elite British troops from the Special Air Services serving in the now renamed Stabilization Force (SFOR) staged manhunts for two key indicted war criminals, Milan Kovacevic and Simo Drljaca. They captured the former and killed the latter in a shoot-out, thus ending the cycle of impunity that had characterized the wars in the former Yugoslavia. Despite threats from the Republika Srpska authorities and the fears of those who had always been opposed to snatch operations, there were no reprisals of any significance.

Neither Kovacevic's nor Drljaca's indictment had been made public; instead, the International Criminal Tribunal for Former Yugoslavia in The Hague delivered the indictments and arrest warrants direct to SFOR. The instrument of sealed indictments was part of a new strategy toward war-crimes suspects that had already yielded results before the Prijedor snatch operations. At the end of June, Slavko Dokmanovic, a Croatian Serb wartime mayor of Vukovar, was lured to eastern Slavonia, where he was arrested by United Nations forces.

Though speculation about forthcoming arrests remained rife, SFOR did not step up its efforts to hunt down more indictees. Instead, the international community, in particular the United States, exerted maximum diplomatic pressure on Croatia and Yugoslavia to surrender further war-crimes suspects. In the case of Croatia, that tactic yielded results on 6 October, when ten Bosnian Croats, including one of the wartime leaders, Dario Kordic, gave themselves up voluntarily. As a result, the Hague tribunal's mid-November tally was as follows: of 78 named indictees, 20 (14 Croats, three Muslims, and three Serbs) were in custody, one (Serb) who had been in custody had died and one (Serb) was killed resisting arrest; two indictees (one Croat and one Serb) had already been tried and sentenced; and five (three Muslims and two Croats) were being tried in two separate trials.

As of mid-November 1997, all indicted Muslims and 14 out of 18 indicted Croats were in custody. In contrast, only three out of 57 Serbian indictees had been put behind bars. While four were believed dead, 50—including wartime leaders Radovan Karadzic and Ratko Mladic—remained free. In addition, both Yugoslavia and the Republika Srpska refused to cooperate with the Hague tribunal. As long as that remained the case and Karadzic, though officially out of the scene, kept exerting influence, the likelihood of large-scale returns of Croats and Muslims to the Republika Srpska remained minimal.

REFUGEES OLD AND NEW

According to the United Nations High Commissioner for Refugees (UNHCR), of the total of 2.3 million displaced persons at the end of hostilities, 381,000 had returned home by October 1997. Of that number, about 171,000 had been refugees abroad and 210,000 had been displaced within Bosnia. Most returned to areas where they belonged to the ethnic majority. At the same time, however, more than 80,000 people had been forced from their homes since Dayton came into force.

The Serbian exodus from Sarajevo suburbs, which were transferred to the federation under the peace plan in early 1996, remains probably the greatest stain on the peace process. Those Serbs, who left their homes amid large-scale arson and police intimidation while IFOR troops stood by, then moved into former Muslim homes in eastern Republika Srpska, including those in Brcko and Srebrenica. Moreover, with only some 25,000 Serbs left in the Bosnian capital—less than 8 percent of its population—Sarajevo was no longer the multicultural city it had once been.

The physical difficulties of reintegrating refugees into Bosnian society have been daunting, as some 60 percent of the country's housing stock was destroyed or damaged during the war. The deliberate and systematic destruction of houses in both Croat-controlled parts of the federation and the Republika Srpska made things even worse. Many early schemes—even in areas in which returnees belonged to the ethnic majority—foundered. That was in part because returnees, who often received economic inducements, were resented by those who had remained in Bosnia throughout the war.

The Open Cities project, launched by the UNHCR in March 1997, adopted a new approach. Instead of directing economic assistance exclusively toward returnees, aid was now distributed throughout the target municipality. In that way, the entire community benefits by welcoming back returnees. The UNHCR grants Open City status only to municipalities that demonstrate a genuine commitment to reaccept all former residents. By mid-November, only four towns—Konjic,

Busovaca, Vogosca, and Bihac—had qualified, all federation municipalities. During spring, summer, and autumn 1997, displaced Croats and Muslims began crossing former front lines to return to their homes in central Bosnia. Some 30 more municipalities were seeking Open City status, including a handful in the Republika Srpska.

THE UNLIKELY SERBIAN REBEL

In addition to ending Bosnia's cycle of impunity, SFOR's Prijedor snatch operation opened up the Republika Srpska's political arena. Drljaca had been the rallying point for hard-line supporters of Karadzic. His removal paved the way for Biljana Plavsic, the Banja Luka–based president of the Republika Srpska, to challenge the entity's Pale-based authorities.

Though herself a committed Serbian nationalist, Plavsic fell out with the rest of the Bosnian Serb wartime leadership over the extent of corruption in the Republika Srpska. Charging Karadzic and his associates with the economic rape of the Serbian statelet, Plavsic dissolved parliament and went on a media offensive in which she revealed details of her erstwhile friends' profiteering.

In the absence of international support, Plavsic's challenge may have faded. But shielded by British SFOR troops, which intervened to help police loyal to Plavsic take over Banja Luka and to prevent Karadzic from using force to crush the revolt, she built herself a power base in the west of the Republika Srpska. Plavsic's territorial advance was eventually halted on 28 August when Karadzic loyalists clashed with U.S. troops in the strategic town of Brcko.

Although the international community had been keen to see Plavsic make gains because of her more pragmatic approach toward Dayton, SFOR backed down in the face of the angry mob in that particular episode. That said, Pale's victory soon proved Pyrrhic. After Bosnian Serb television incited Serbs against SFOR, calling the peacekeepers SS-FOR and broadcasting images of the Nazi army, SFOR decided to move against the media. Following a series of warnings and repeated violations, SFOR seized four transmitters in eastern Republika Srpska on 1 October. Plavsic already controlled one transmitter in the west.

Having seized Pale's television transmitters, the Office of the High Representative (OHR)—the agency coordinating Dayton's civilian aspects, which had recently been granted the right to suspend media that contravened the peace process—demanded the restructuring of Bosnian Serb television, including the removal of Momcilo Krajisnik, Karadzic's ally and the Serbian member of the Bosnian presidency, from the station's governing board. Until those conditions were fulfilled, Pale's transmitters would exclusively broadcast Banja Luka's version of Bosnian Serb television.

FEW UPSETS FOR NATIONALISTS

Thanks to meticulous preparation and a complete voter registration effort that put a lid on fraud, September's municipal elections were not marred by an impossibly high turnout as were the national elections a year earlier. Nevertheless, they had little to do with democracy. Since displaced persons could choose to vote either in their current municipality or where they had been living at the time of the 1991 census, the nationalist parties worked hard to pack key municipalities with voters from the "correct" ethnic group. Moreover, they could and did work out the results of the elections in advance based on the complete electoral registers, determining their level of support by examining the distinguishable names of Muslim, Serbian, and Croatian voters. Armed with that information, the ruling Serbian and Croatian nationalist parties, the Serbian Democratic Party and Croatian Democratic Union, threatened a boycott unless the Organization for Security and Cooperation in Europe, which supervised the elections, granted them key concessions.

While the three nationalist ruling parties won a clear majority of council seats in the aggregate, a handful of municipalities threw up interesting results. In Tuzla, non-nationalists retained a majority of council seats. Elsewhere, candidates representing displaced persons and their right to return to their prewar municipalities won more than 50 percent of council seats in six municipalities: five in the federation (Bosanski Petrovac, Drvar, Grahovo, and Glamoc, which have Serbian majorities; and Zepce, with a Muslim majority) and one (Srebrenica, with a Muslim majority) in the Republika Srpska.

Final certification was to be conferred on a municipality-by-municipality basis once new council administrations have been installed and various other criteria, including representation of minority political parties and coalitions in executive posts, are fulfilled. The OSCE's elections-related mandate was to expire on 31 December, and if municipalities did not fulfill those criteria, the results would not receive final certification.

The most bitterly contested municipality was Brcko. The fate of the strategic town on the Sava River that links the eastern and western halves of Republika Srpska could not be resolved at Dayton and was instead left for international arbitration. Predictably, the Republika Srpska authorities attempted to abuse voter registration and pack Brcko with Serbs, thus engineering an absolute Serbian majority. Indeed, the scale of the fraud was so great that the voter-registration process had to be canceled and redone. Following the elections, which nonetheless produced a Serbian majority, Robert Farrand, a U.S. ambassador appointed as supervisor for Dayton implementation in Brcko, issued directives concerning the functioning of a multiethnic administration, judiciary, and police. Those directives met with significant opposition from the Bosnian Serb leadership, which slammed them as unconstitutional.

A LOPSIDED RECOVERY

The World Bank managed to put together a framework for reconstruction, and international donors have responded generously to Bosnia's needs. A total of \$1.8 billion was pledged in 1996 and a further \$1.24 billion was promised at the 1997 Donors' Conference. Moreover, donors more than fulfilled their pledges by committing a total of \$1.9 billion in 1996. Of the \$1.1 billion actually disbursed that year, the bulk went to Muslim-controlled regions of the federation and only 3 percent went to the Republika Srpska, since that entity had refused to attend the Donors' Conference. In the future, however, roughly 70 percent of aid will be earmarked for the federation and 30 percent for the Republika Srpska. (Such allocation was based on various criteria, including the level of physical destruction and the size of the population.)

Exact economic data are difficult to obtain. Nevertheless, it is clear that the economy, employment, and wages grew rapidly throughout 1996 but that the growth rates slowed in the first half of 1997. In the federation, the economy grew by almost 68 percent in 1996 and was expected to grow by another 40 percent in 1997. Average monthly wages had risen to 266 German marks ($145) in July 1997, from about 44 German marks ($31) in 1995.

Unemployment is estimated at between 60 percent and 75 percent of the work force. In the Republika Srpska, where data are even scarcer, the economy grew by some 20 percent in 1996. Average monthly wages rose from 21 German marks ($15) in 1995 to 88 marks ($50) in June 1997.

At the end of June, Bosnia agreed in principle with the London Club of commercial creditors on an effective 87.5 percent reduction of the state's $1 billion-plus debt inherited from the former Yugoslavia. If ratified, the agreement should make Bosnia's debt repayments manageable.

Reconstruction in Bosnia is especially complicated since the country is simultaneously recovering from a war and restructuring after half a century of socialist self-management. In many respects, the latter is actually the greater problem. Political control over the economy and a lack of transparency in accounting threaten to undermine the international community's efforts. Ominously, the International Monetary Fund refused to grant a $100 million standby arrangement to Bosnia, which reflects the international body's dissatisfaction with Sarajevo's economic policy.

A major problem in both entities was the diversion of tax revenue into private pockets. The European Union's customs and excise technical assistance team highlighted the scale of the problem regarding customs duties, and its mandate may be extended to cover all tax collection. Ironically, unless political issues are resolved first, the influx of international aid may actually enhance the strength and influence of the nationalist parties and work against reintegration, since those funds are generally channeled via the authorities.

On 20 June, after much delay, the Bosnian parliament passed key legislation known as the Quick Start Package, featuring laws on the creation of a central bank and a unified customs policy. But the laws were greatly watered down to enable consensus and persuade the Republika Srpska to sign. The central bank will issue a new currency, the convertible mark, once its design has been approved by the board of governors and the presidency. The entities are obliged to "undertake all efforts" to promote the use of the new currency, but no deadline or penalties in case of noncompliance were set.

THE JURY IS OUT

The ongoing bickering over the design of Bosnia's money was typical of the presidency. Although the rationale for holding the 1996 elections was that common national institutions were required to help weld the country back together, those institutions have largely failed to function. In practice, the 1996 elections conferred a pseudo-democratic mandate on many of the instigators of the 1992 war, which they then used to undermine the peace process.

The Peace Implementation Council—a body that brings together countries and international organizations involved in the peace process—attempted to resolve that problem by setting implementation deadlines at its Sintra meeting. Those included an integrated telephone system (15 July), a Civil Aviation Authority (end of July), citizenship laws and the appointment of ambassadors (1 August 1997), a new flag (1 September), and common vehicle license plates (1 January 1998). Despite the deadlines, the progress toward implementation remained slow. To break the political impasse, the OHR was looking to the next meeting of the Peace Implementation Council to strengthen its mandate with the power of binding arbitration.

Thus, two years after Dayton ended the war in Bosnia, the jury is still out both on the peace plan and the future contours of the Bosnian state. The peace has genuinely benefited all of Bosnia's peoples, though possibly not as much as hoped at Dayton. The pity is that the international community took so long to find the resolve to begin enforcing implementation of the peace plan and a year and a half was effectively wasted. SFOR is scheduled to remain in the country until the end of June 1998. The peace is not yet so firmly rooted that international forces can depart without the country slipping back into war. As a result, the details of a reduced follow-on force are currently being debated in world capitals. Meanwhile, the pressure is on in Bosnia to push implementation forward while 35,000 peacekeepers remain in the country. Whether the likes of Mrs. Smajic will be able to return home will probably not be clear for another couple of years.

NOTE

Reprinted with kind permission from *Transitions* magazine, December 1997.

Federal Republic of Yugoslavia

Population:	11,100,000
Capital:	Belgrade (pop. 1,087,915)
Major cities:	Nis (pop. 247,898); Novi Sad (pop. 170,029); Pristina, Kosovo (pop. 108,020); Podgorica, Montenegro (pop. 96,074)
Area:	102,350 sq. km.
Major ethnic groups:	Serbian 63%, Albanian 14%, Montenegrin 6%, Hungarian 4%, other 13%
Economy:	GDP growth: 6.0%
....	Inflation rate: 20.0%
....	Average monthly wage: $156
....	Unemployment rate: 28.5%

SLOW TO CHANGE

by STAN MARKOTICH

So many elections were held in the Federal Republic of Yugoslavia in 1997 that perhaps some observers may be excused for speculating that, if not democracy, at least some element of opposition to Slobodan Milosevic had finally made inroads.

Among others, it was Milosevic himself who had to submit to election. His second term as president of Serbia was due to expire by year's end, and rather than attempt to subvert the republic's constitution to extend his hold on power for a third term, he instead opted to consolidate his dictatorship by shifting to the federal presidency. So on 15 July the parliament voted Milosevic into that office.

Milosevic's Socialist Party of Serbia (SPS) did not hold a majority in the federal legislature, and so it was only by cutting a deal with its Montenegrin allies—the Party of Democratic Socialists (PDS)—that Milosevic obtained the requisite votes. But this deal proved costly for the Montenegrin ruling party, and it appears that institution began the road to irrevocable disintegration. Supporters of former Montenegrin Premier, Milo Djukanovic, agreed not to block Milosevic's move to federal politics, but only on the condition that the Yugoslav presidency remain a ceremonial office devoid of real political power. Meanwhile, backers of former Montenegrin President Momir Bulatovic opted to unconditionally back Milosevic.

A PLETHORA OF BALLOTS

In addition to Milosevic's own rise to the federal presidency, 1997 saw elections to fill his vacancy at the Serbian republic's level, and was a year that featured a hotly contested race for the Montenegrin presidency, ending in what some quickly dubbed a victory for forces standing in opposition to the Milosevic dictatorship. It was also a year for legislative elections in Serbia, and one that witnessed a dramatic resurgence for the ultra-nationalist Serbian Radical Party (SRS), headed by the accused war criminal Vojislav Seselj. (See accompanying article, "Demagogue in Waiting," by Slobodan Reljic.)

Immeasurably aiding Milosevic's political fortunes was the disintegration of the so-called democratic opposition, banding under the Zajedno (Together) banner, and led by its two most outstanding spokesmen, Vuk Draskovic, head of the Serbian Renewal Movement (SPO), and Zoran Djindjic, head of the Democratic Party (DS). As 1997 began to unfold, the Zajedno coalition appeared to be a rock-solid alliance, and one poised to deal a fundamental democratic death blow to the dictatorship. It was back on 17 November 1996 that the coalition secured a majority of votes in at least 12 municipalities in run-off balloting for Serbian republic-wide local elections. The SPS failure to recognize opposition victories ultimately led to a series of mass protests which, according to some estimates, prompted hundreds of thousands of people to flood Belgrade streets in support of Zajedno, to call for a validation of the returns, and to insist on Milosevic's resignation. Under mounting pressure, the regime seemingly gave in, but in stages.

On 14 January *Nasa Borba* reported that local electoral authorities, for at least a second time, conceded that Zajedno had won balloting in Belgrade, Nis, and another 12 municipalities. The regime, however, maintained a low profile, and refused to acknowledge this. Mass street demonstrations went on, and the state-controlled police forces continued to harass, intimidate and brutalize peaceful protesters. On 28 January, the opposition seemed to suffer an insurmountable setback after a municipal court in Belgrade ruled that the local elections commission was incorrect in deciding that the capital had gone to the opposition.

Nevertheless, undaunted demonstrators continued to flood streets, and only a few days later, on 30 January, federal President Zoran Lilic, speaking in Montenegro, seemed to offer Zajedno an olive branch. It was then that he said opposition victories should be recognized, but stressed the regime would not meet all demands, maintaining that calls for Milosevic's ouster would under no circumstances be tolerated. Again days later, the regime opted for an about-face, turning to brute force. Independent media reported on 2 February that a wave of police violence swept throughout Serbia. According to eyewitnesses, police resorted to the use of tear gas, water cannons, and an assortment of weapons, thereby transforming Belgrade into what more than one observer dubbed "a battleground with innocent civilians under siege." Vesna Pesic, leader of Zajedno's Serbian Civic Alliance, became the victim of police brutality. According to Radio Index accounts, she was beaten, but spared worse injuries thanks to the intervention of fellow protesters. For his part, Draskovic was allegedly shot at by plain-clothes officers.

Only days later, on 5 February, the government of Serbia submitted to parliament draft legislation calling for the recognition of opposition victories. That the government had real compromise and concessions in mind was in doubt even then. Mirjana Markovic, leader of the Yugoslav United Left (JUL) and the wife of Milosevic, chose the same day to issue a public declaration calling for an immediate halt to mass protests, and suggesting that a severe crackdown might ensue should the public fail to heed the message. Nevertheless, prospects seemingly brightened for opposition fortunes, with the regime apparently acquiescing to Djindjic's being named the first non-communist mayor of Belgrade on 21 February. And upon taking office, Djindjic underscored the significance of the event by having the red star removed from atop the municipal building.

WAS IT ALL THAT ATTENTION?

What undoubtedly aided Zajedno in its quest to have its victories recognized was the focus of the international community. From late November 1996 to at least the end of February 1997 events in Serbia were on front pages around the world and the subject of much discussion in influential political circles. At a Brussels meeting on 11 January representatives of the International Contact Group (the powers involved in bringing peace to Bosnia) focused talks on events in Serbia, and concluded that democratization, including measures prompting the growth of a free media, ought to be promoted. For his part, U.S. Assistant Secretary of State John Kornblum said Washington was contemplating a wide range of measures to pressure Belgrade, including maintaining economic sanctions and applying intensifying pressure against Milosevic.

And again, international condemnation was swift when Milosevic cracked down on peaceful protesters in the first few days of February. Washington's charge d'affaires Richard Miles met with Belgrade's foreign minister, Milan Milutinovic, in order to "condemn" the violence and "to call upon the Serbian government officially to refrain from using police force in the streets of Belgrade."

It remains an open question to what degree disunity within the Zajedno camp played a role in Milosevic's ultimate ability to roll back the opposition victory. Friction indeed surfaced almost immediately after Djindjic was poised to take power. Almost as soon as Serbian media reported that he was to take up the mayoralty post, Danica Draskovic, wife of the SPO leader, announced her intention to become head of the greater Belgrade district government, an office seen as a rival power base to the mayor's. And for his part, Vuk Draskovic seemed to indicate that his nomination for Zajedno candidate in upcoming elections for the Serbian presidency was a foregone conclusion, and that all that was left for Djindjic to do was to rubber-stamp the nomination. Already on 18 February *Nasa Borba* reported that Draskovic had gone on record as saying that he would press for the restoration of the Karadjordjevic dynasty if he were elected the republic's president.

ONE'S OWN WORST ENEMY?

By spring, an open split seemed to have emerged within the Zajedno coalition. For his part, Draskovic continued touting himself as the leader of an opposition coalition slated to contest republican presidential elections. His agenda, in addition to pledges of a monarchical restoration, came to include calls for resettling Serbian refugees in Croatia, and a declaration that the predominantly ethnic Albanian Kosovo should be recognized as an integral part of Serbia—a move to include incorporating the region as a part of "Old Serbia." While elements of the platform may not have been anathema to other members of Zajedno, it seems that at least a personality clash between Draskovic and Djindjic precluded cooperation. Throughout May, the two leaders waged a war of words in the press, with Draskovic alleging that Djindjic was bent on destroying Zajedno, while Djindjic did not endorse Draskovic's presidential bid. By the end of the month, Draskovic accused Djindjic of holding secret meetings with Milosevic and ostensibly attempting to cut a deal with Milosevic to keep the so-called democratic opposition out of office. For his part, Djindjic began to argue that participation in elections would be futile, given that the regime would undermine the democratic process.

All the accusations and counter-claims notwithstanding, it does seem that opposition divisions played into Milosevic's hands. From summer, the ruling

SPS was in fact in a position where it could both wipe out past Zajedno gains and ensure its inability to mount a unified campaign for the presidency. The first actions undertaken included muzzling the independent media. While exact figures vary, there is a consensus that beginning in June at least fifty local TV and radio stations were shut down during the summer months, with the regime following a time-honored practice, citing licensing irregularities as the basis for closing shop. In reality, it was little more than an insurance policy aimed at ensuring that no opposition party could readily get its message out.

Finally, the regime acted directly against the opposition, and at a time when its division was most severe and the attention of the international community apparently was focused elsewhere. By early October, and coinciding with election season, Djindjic was ousted from office, with the event recorded in the international press as almost a political footnote if not an obituary. A short paragraph appearing in the *Economist* the week of 4 October is not untypical of the coverage, stressing only that "Serbian police attacked thousands of people protesting against the removal as mayor . . . of Zoran Djindjic."

ELECTIONS . . . IN SERBIA FIRST

By late September, from the post of federal president, Milosevic was in a position to begin reaping the electoral dividends that the disarray within the opposition camp would pay. The DS boycott and Milosevic's own willingness to manipulate political outcomes guaranteed favorable returns. The first balloting began on 20 September, and resulted in the SPS's taking the lion's share of legislative seats in the 250-member assembly. After vote counting, the Socialists emerged with 40 percent of the seats, while the resurgent SRS claimed a third. The SPO took just under 20 percent of the seats. The remainder was apportioned among a host of minor parties.

What came unexpectedly to some commentators was the outcome of the balloting for the presidency. SPS candidate Lilic garnered 36 percent of the vote, while Seselj, in what has been described as the surprise, took 29 percent. Draskovic won only 22 percent of the vote. With no single candidate securing a majority, the stage was set for runoffs, which took place in early October. It was then that Seselj seemed to be gaining ground, and emerged with the greatest number of votes in a round that was canceled, owing to electoral commission claims that fewer than the requisite 50 percent of the electorate had bothered to turn out. With this twist, a new round of elections was to take place, beginning with the registration of candidates.

According to some observers, Milosevic had counted on Lilic to become president so as to be able to control republican politics through his loyal proxy and former federal executive. In reality, however, Milosevic's main objective may have been to profit from the resurgence of the radical right under the leadership of the accused war criminal Seselj. With the SRS holding large influence in the legislature and with Seselj seemingly attractive to voters, Milosevic's SPS was positioned to portray itself as a moderating political force in 1998, and may yet seek a tactical compromise with other opposition parties against the SRS.

At any rate, elections slated for 7 December featured a new SPS candidate, Milan Milutinovic, squaring off against Seselj. Even here, a runoff was required, and following voting on 21 December Milutinovic was declared winner in a process described by international monitors as "rife [with] irregularities."

. . . AND THEN MONTENEGRO

Montenegro seemed to hold out promise for opponents of the Milosevic regime, and at year's end it appeared that those objecting to the policies of the Yugoslav dictator were at the helm in the republic. As mentioned above, the Montenegrin ruling Democratic Party of Socialists (DPS) had agreed to back Milosevic's shift to the federal presidency. However, it was with that gesture that the dynamics within that party began to lead to a rift between those loyal to Premier Milo Djukanovic, an outspoken Milosevic critic, and those backing President Momir Bulatovic, a Milosevic loyalist and protege.

It seems that 2 September was the key date. Then some 17 DPS legislators openly stated their support would go to Bulatovic in upcoming 5 October presidential elections. This move stood in contrast to the wishes of what might have been the greater number of DPS deputies; namely, the backing of Djukanovic's candidacy. At the time, a Montenegrin statute stipulated that only one member from each party could contest the presidency, a situation that was remedied on 12 September when the Yugoslav Constitutional Court nullified the law. It was this ruling that set the stage for the electoral showdown.

Djukanovic campaigned in part on the platform that his administration would block any changes to the federal constitution that might make the office of federal executive anything more than ceremonial. But on election day, the results were close, with both candidates just missing 50 percent of the vote, but with Bulatovic slightly ahead. On 19 October, following runoffs, Bulatovic prepared to concede defeat. In a sudden about-face, and likely on orders from Milosevic, Bulatovic refused to relinquish his post, instead going public with trumped-up charges that Djukanovic rigged the election by resorting to tactics such as bussing Albanians across the border to stuff the ballot box. Furthermore, Bulatovic attempted to whip up mass demonstrations against the newly elected president, ostensibly in an effort to demonstrate public discontent with the allegedly fraudulent voting process.

THE MONTENEGRIN GREAT WHITE HOPE?

At year's end, Djukanovic retained the presidency, and his tenure in office seemed to hold out the promise that opponents of the Milosevic dictatorship would somewhat consolidate a grip on political offices in the Federal Republic of Yugoslavia. What remained unclear was Djukanovic's staying power. Will 1998 see him suffering a fate not unlike Djindjic's? Or, is he really immune to compromise with a Milosevic? If not, then Milosevic may continue to exert influence in Montenegro while using the Bulatovic loss at the polls as an excuse to elevate the former president to an influential post in federal politics.

For his part, Milosevic showed no signs in 1997 of retiring into a ceremonial presidency. On the contrary, he continued to exert control over Serbia's police, and by the end of the year had promoted his head of Serbian State Security, Jovica Stanisic, to the post of federal security advisor. If anything, these trends suggested that Milosevic was bent on centralizing his dictatorial power in the federal office.

Moreover, he seemed content to concern himself with the processes that would effect the transfer of power, rather than on fundamental questions and issues that might lift his regime, once and for all, from the status of an international pariah. On the question of the "outer wall" of sanctions, for example, Milosevic eschewed fundamental democratic and economic reforms, opting instead to appease civil servants by generating money to pay their salaries by selling a 49-percent share of the state phone company to Italy's STET and Greece's OTE at a bargain price.

GLOSSARY

DS	Democratic Party
JUL	Yugoslav United Left
PDS	Party of Democratic Socialists
SPO	Serbian Renewal Movement
SPS	Socialist Party of Serbia
SRS	Serbian Radical Party

Profile: VOJISLAV SESELJ: DEMAGOGUE IN WAITING

by SLOBODAN RELJIC

Impoverished, disillusioned, and apathetic Serbia was ripe for leaders with quick fixes up their sleeves, and the ultranationalist Vojislav Seselj patiently awaited his turn. "Our present is ever worse, our past ever better, and there is no future." That was how public opinion analyst Srecko Mihailovic of the Institute of Social Sciences in Belgrade described the state of affairs in Serbia. According to the institute's surveys, after an initial burst of trust in parliamentary democracy, nearly half the population slid into a mood where "we had best give all the power to a single leader." People perceived anxiety, fear, despair, helplessness, indifference, and passivity as the most common moods among their friends and colleagues. But 6 percent did see individuals around them "ready for action," and among those most ready was Vojislav Seselj.

In September 1997, Seselj, the leader of the ultranationalist Serbian Radical Party, came a whisker away from becoming Serbia's president. He defeated the

Socialist candidate Zoran Lilic in the second round of the Serbian presidential race, but Serbia's kingmaker (and Yugoslav President) Slobodan Milosevic and his cohorts hung tightly onto a law stipulating that more than 50 percent of registered voters must go to the polls for the election to be valid. In the rerun, the Socialist activists did their electoral homework better so the "right" candidate tallied more votes, and the turnout was "just right."

In normal times, it would be extremely difficult to understand Seselj's appeal. He is ungainly, obviously overweight, and his boyish face is always covered by a pair of glasses that went out of fashion at least a decade ago. From his native, rugged, and sparsely inhabited Herzegovina he brought the habit of shouting as a regular way of communicating. At different stages in his political career, this quintessential populist has been a monarchist, a Chetnik, a greater Serbia advocate, a staunch anti-communist, but also Milosevic's opposition darling. He engages in public antics and back-stabbing of former political mentors. Yet he heads a party that, at least in name, claims the tradition of the most successful Serbian parliamentary party before World War II and the most prominent Serbian politician of this century, Nikola Pasic.

He is a thug who has been known to slug people he doesn't like and the political force behind paramilitary forces accused of committing war atrocities in Croatia and Bosnia. Different phases of his "political activity" have featured physical assaults on students, fellow parliamentarians, teachers, cab drivers, and an ethnic-Croatian family and their lawyer. When explaining his actions, he has no scruples: "I left my job at the National Assembly, and the mob attacked me. When I am attacked by an inarticulate mob, boiling with rage and hatred, I don't stop to think if these are students or cobblers. . . . For me it's a mob threatening my life, and I must defend myself." Even privately, Seselj doesn't display traits traditionally appreciated by the Serbian voter. He doesn't smoke or drink, nor does he look like a ladies' man or, for that matter, like a family man.

So what is his secret? Why are there a million and a half adult citizens who, if the last election results are to be trusted, believed Seselj was the right man for Serbia?

THE LUMPEN HERO

The "Red Vojvoda," as cynics have dubbed him with reference to the unlikely melding of a communist and a Chetnik, has always been close to the government, and that definitely matters in Serbia. One of the most prominent opposition figures, the Serbian Renewal Movement leader Vuk Draskovic, was once told by a peasant from central Serbia in front of television cameras: "Once you come to power, we'll vote for you as well." The faltering and eventual virtual disintegration of the opposition coalition Zajedno, which won control of Serbia's major urban centers in 1997 following three months of demonstrations, further bolstered this traditional "trust in those in power." Thus "the Seselj solution" was awaited equally by impatient Socialist voters, who would not see this shift of political allegiances as particularly unprincipled, and by disillusioned democrats, to whom everything political had come to look the same.

Who are Seselj's activists? In part, they consist of the lumpen proletariat. But as *Vreme* reporter Milan Milosevic put it, the bulk of them are "elderly workers in 10-year-old jackets and three-and-a-half-year-old shoes, middle-aged women, a youngster here and there. Only a handful of flashy biznismeni in red jackets. . . . [Seselj's supporters] give an impression of people who have never really been wealthy but have known better times; they are people who now have almost nothing and are unsure whether they shouldn't expect a turn for the worse. These are the people who will readily tell you that a glitch must have occurred somewhere within the state apparatus and it has to be fixed by a specialist, like when a gasket is replaced. Or that somebody should be hanged as an example."

Such people are also magically attracted by Seselj's conspicuous abstention from the unscrupulous pillaging of state assets and common citizens that has marked the 1990s in Serbia. And this seems to be the only point where he has been really consistent. "He is a man who introduces order," says Predrag Djordjevic, an unemployed metal worker. "I sincerely believe there is no more corruption in the [Belgrade] municipality of Zemun," of which Seselj is mayor and where his Serbian Radical Party is in charge. "He is a man who puts the people first, not his own pocket," says Dragica Djordjevic, a homemaker of modest means, adding that "he would certainly never sell off the postal service or the railroad or anything."

FROM DISSIDENT TO BIGOT

Seselj first gained notoriety as a victim of communist repression in Tito's Yugoslavia. In 1984, at the age of 30, he was sentenced to eight years in prison. The promising, undisciplined young communist was a victim of a show trial. Such trials occurred in Yugoslavia from time to time, particularly in its central republic of Bosnia-Herzegovina. Witnesses were produced, claiming that Seselj had bad-mouthed Tito, the state, and the party during a train ride. The goal of such trials was to intimidate people and preclude a possible articulation of an organized critical questioning of "our road to socialism."

Mainly due to international pressure, Seselj's sentence was commuted to one-fourth of the original term. After a year and ten months in jail, Seselj joined the relatively small group of Yugoslav dissidents, which was not too heavily persecuted by communist-state standards. Besides the major names, such as Milovan Djilas and writers Dobrica Cosic and Matija Beckovic, it included the so-called Praxis philosophers (in the late 1960s, they had published the *Praxis* journal and organized the internationally renowned Korcula summer school of critical Marxist thought) who held tenures at the universities of Belgrade and Zagreb, as well as certain poets and theorists from Ljubljana. Nationalism was not at the core of this small and heterogeneous group. They were nationalists only insofar as the regime billed them as such during its periodic media campaigns against them.

After Seselj's release from jail, when few people dared communicate with him, Dobrica Cosic provided both moral and material support. But when in 1993 Slobodan Milosevic decided to get rid of Cosic (whom many credit with paving the way for Milosevic's ascent to power), Seselj had no qualms about taking on the role of executioner.

Seselj has always been a controversial figure, but despite much public focus on him, his inner workings remain unclear. Back in 1989, with the tacit blessing of Serbia's communist leadership, Seselj, Draskovic, and Mirko Jovic, a village cafe owner, shocked the Yugoslav public by proclaiming themselves the leaders of the Serbian Chetnik Movement (named after World War II royalist guerrillas, notorious for their atrocities against non-Serbs and communist sympathizers). The "movement" consisted of a dozen bearded men cruising Yugoslavia, slinging threats at non-Serbs. Seselj was a militant anti-communist and monarchist at the time. He was promoted to the rank of vojvoda (the highest Chetnik rank) by Momcilo Djujic, the notorious World War II vojvoda now living in the United States. But shortly thereafter, Seselj distanced himself from the Chetnik idea and went on to ridicule Crown Prince Aleksandar Karadjordjevic, the heir to the Yugoslav throne who lives in London, for his lack of knowledge of Serbo-Croatian and ignorance about the current situation in Serbia. Seselj went to Madrid and invited one Aleksei Dolgorukii Nemanjic Romanov to the Serbian throne. Among other titles, this dubious character claimed to be the long-lost heir of the medieval Serbian Nemanja dynasty and the Romanovs. The Seselj-engineered mockery proved effective, and popular support for the restoration of monarchy in Serbia shrank to its current 10 percent.

MAKING A MONSTER

Seselj owes his real start in national politics to Slobodan Milosevic. Nebojsa Covic, the former mayor of Belgrade and a rising star among the ruling Socialists before his fall from Milosevic's grace in April 1997, explained how the ruling party engaged in political engineering in 1992, "creating not only the [Serbian Radical] Party but its leader as well." When the writer and Socialist parliamentarian Miodrag Bulatovic died, a new deputy had to be elected from the Belgrade working-class municipality of Rakovica. "The Socialists had [deliberately] put up a weak, bad candidate, precisely because they needed somebody who would constantly destabilize and sabotage the opposition ranks," says Covic. "That person, who ended up winning the by-election in Rakovica, was Vojislav Seselj." He took up the task immediately. As a reward, he got the infrastructure for his party: offices, equipment, and "numerous opportunities for making advantageous business deals that he subsequently used to finance his party." Vojislav Seselj obviously did what he was told. By repeatedly staging incidents in the National Assembly, he discredited parliamentary life. In Covic's view, the consequences were permanent, because "the relations [among political parties in Serbia] today look more like a brawl among enemies than like a [civilized] contest among various options."

With exposure in the state media, Seselj's political rise was meteoric. In December 1992, finding fans mainly among disgruntled Socialists, Seselj's party collected 1 million votes in the parliamentary elections, a result second only to the ruling Socialists' 1.3 million. On the eve of the next year's elections, the

Radicals were so popular among the Socialist ranks and the military that it could no longer be tolerated. Milosevic's media started a ruthless campaign. Suddenly, Seselj was "contributing to the isolation of Serbia from the world" with his chauvinism, fomenting "hatred toward non-Serbs"; his paramilitary units in the Republika Srpska and the Republic of Serbian Krajina (Croatia) had committed "crimes against civilians, be they Croatian, Muslim, or Serbian;" and finally, Seselj was "the embodiment of violence and primitivism that must be stopped because it leads Serbia into dictatorship and fascism." After such "conditioning" of the public, the Radicals' support shrank by almost half, while the Socialists were reinforced by 200,000 new votes.

But as the mainstream opposition forces, such as Zoran Djindjic's Democrats and Draskovic's Serbian Renewal Movement, regrouped and became more of a threat to Milosevic, Seselj gradually moved out of the state media's "doghouse." He soon began delivering his roll call of national traitors and foreign agents on national television, with the opposition leaders topping the bill. And though the favorable treatment in the state media didn't ever match the days when he was Milosevic's "favorite opposition figure," Seselj had another big surge in September 1997, when he defeated the Socialist candidate Lilic.

BREAKING THE MONSTER

Seselj is a great communicator, and he is known as a dangerous adversary in public debates. He thinks quickly and logically, uses simple words and attacks mercilessly when he discovers his opponent's weak spot. He is capable of taking over the moderating of a television program from an unskilled host. He insults his interlocutors without restraint, and his insults are always designed as half-truths, forcing the opponent into self-justification. For instance, using the fact that General Veljko Kadijevic had spent some time at West Point, Seselj automatically drew the far-reaching conclusion that Kadijevic—the last federal defense minister and commander in chief of the Yugoslav People's Army—was following orders from the Pentagon during the early years of the Yugoslav wars. Republika Srpska President Biljana Plavsic, who has no children of her own, is a barren climacteric woman playing with the lives of our children. Peace groups from Belgrade that maintain links with Croatian pacifists are the Ustasha (Croatian fascist) lobby.

But in the run-up to the presidential election rerun in December, Seselj was at a loss for words in a public face-off with Draskovic, who had meanwhile broken ranks with his former opposition allies over participation in the election and was amid a rapprochement with Milosevic. Draskovic, incidentally the godfather of Seselj's eldest son, raised a painful question for the Radical leader: is he Serbian at all? With his communist background and materialist logic—all of it subsequently painted over by a thick layer of nationalism and poseur rightism—the usually unstoppable Seselj started gasping for air in front of television cameras when Draskovic showered him with comments such as: there was a time when you didn't know how to cross yourself, we taught you at the Ljubostinja monastery; you have no certificate of baptism; in the phone directory of Serbia there is not a single Seselj, while the Croatian cities of Zagreb, Split, and Rijeka are full of people named Seselj, all of them Croatian; in the 1980s you declared yourself a Yugoslav, not Serb; and after coming to Belgrade you became a member of the Croatian Sociological Society. To an outside observer it might seem irrational to fear such allegations, but that was not the case with Seselj the nationalist, who has been a proponent of a greater Serbia and with his paramilitary units part of a terror that targeted Croats and Muslims.

In 1993, when it suited the interests of the Milosevic regime, the authority of the National Assembly of Serbia and the Historical Institute of the Serbian Academy of Sciences and Arts was used to issue Seselj an unusual certificate—that he is indeed a Serb. At the parliament's request, the institute came out with a paper that established "historical and ethnographic facts about the genus of the Serbian Orthodox Seseljs."

When the anti-Seselj campaign was rekindled at the end of 1997, official Zagreb also joined in, rather discreetly, but not insignificantly. The Croatian ambassador in Belgrade, Zvonimir Markovic, otherwise a temperate and cautious man, said this: "I know the Seselj case very well. His father worked on a church estate in Herzegovina and fell in love with the priest's daughter. In order to marry her he converted to Orthodox faith." At a reception at the Czech Embassy on 27 November, Zarko Jokanovic, a Milosevic ally, asked Markovic to produce the certificate of Croatian citizenship of the Seselj family on the spot. Markovic declined, but the Split-based pro-regime newspaper *Slobodna Dalmacija* conducted its own probe a week later, sending a reporter to Orahov Do, a village in Herzegovina where the Seseljs used to live. The Belgrade press reprinted the resulting article under the headline: "No Dilemma—Seselj is a Croat." In fact, there was a dilemma, but who reads such articles closely? Electoral engineering took care of the rest, and Socialist Milan Milutinovic became Serbia's new president.

THE SPITE FACTOR

Despite the latest setback, Seselj's position remained strong. His Radicals were the second-largest party in Serbia's parliament, boycotted by the ex-Zajedno parties minus Draskovic's party, and public opinion polls indicated that he still enjoyed significant popularity.

The pressure of the international community on the Serbs played an important role in Seselj's enduring appeal. Severely affected both materially and emotionally by the war and the concurrent international sanctions against Serbia, as well as their bleak aftermath, the Serbs are every now and then tempted to behave like naughty schoolchildren and do the opposite of what they are told. "We won't let some [German Foreign Minister Klaus] Kinkel blackmail us as to who is going to be our president," says a worker who has not received his salary for years. A disappointed soldier explains: "What is it that we are getting from the world anyway? The West is taking our clothes off us every day. We are only left with our dirty laundry. . . . Seselj wants us to wash our laundry and to launch a fresh, real economic program." The fact that Seselj himself does not know of any such program obviously does not matter here.

When people are desperate, they tend to project their suppressed desires and frustrations into extreme solutions. In this frame of mind, there are no insoluble problems. All that is needed is a strongman. A young man from the Belgrade periphery, almost growling with anger, says: "I want to work and make money, I want to buy a car, to eat meat, to wear a new suit, to buy a half-meter robot [toy] for my son and a new coat for my wife. But how? I don't receive my pay, I have no land to cultivate, and there is nobody to help me. That's why I'll keep on voting for Seselj."

For the time being, it is certain that the number of such resolute people in Serbia is not sufficient to lift Seselj to power. The master Milosevic has been able to keep a lid on the bitterness and accumulated rage. But will he succeed the next time? The story of Dr. Frankenstein, whose creation breaks free and kills its creator, may prove to be more than a metaphor.

Translated by Milan Jelic

NOTE

Reprinted with kind permission from *Transitions* magazine, March 1998.

Sidebar: A STRIKING BALANCE IN MONTENEGRO

by JEREMY DRUKER

The founders of *Vijesti,* Montenegro's first independent daily newspaper, picked a potentially disastrous time for the inaugural issue of a paper determined to build a reputation for independence: 1 September, in the midst of a heated presidential campaign that highlighted the bitter split in the republic's ruling Democratic Party of Socialists. The political tensions of that moment guaranteed a readership but also left the paper's staff open to charges that they launched their publication to influence the October election. But as the candidates slung mud and the Serbian state media stooped to venomous propaganda, *Vijesti* persisted in offering carefully balanced coverage.

In issues leading up to the first-round 5 October election, approximately equal space was devoted to the two main presidential candidates, Prime Minister Milo Djukanovic and President Momir Bulatovic. "We are totally neutral," said Mihajlo Jovovic, a member of the foreign news department. "We do have our own attitudes and our own views, and we know whose views are close to ours. But we are independent in our editorial policy and not supported by any political party."

Montenegrins long accustomed to seeing only the drab, state-owned daily

Pobjeda and Belgrade newspapers on their local newsstands grabbed every one of *Vijesti*'s 10,000 copies on the first two days it appeared. Circulation by early 1998 had increased to 12,000, a respectable number for an economically depressed area of 600,000 where newspaper reading did not have a strong tradition. *Vijesti*'s blue masthead, which proclaimed the paper an "independent daily," was sandwiched between two advertisements, one of which touts the country's only mobile phone company, which purchased the ad for an entire year.

Inside, the Podgorica-based paper's 16 pages are full of international and domestic politics and information. Local news comes from a team of 20 correspondents scattered throughout the republic. The tabloid design, complete with frequent front-page photos of attractive young women, offered a new look when compared with *Pobjeda,* which resembled a 1960s relic.

Pobjeda also had a circulation of around 10,000, but that is likely a reflection of the previous lack of alternatives to the Belgrade press. The paper owed part of its readership to its traditional role of publishing official news and, even more important, obituary announcements—a custom playfully referred to in *Vijesti*'s marketing campaign: "*Vijesti* [News]. But from this world."

Zoran Radmanivic, an editor at *Pobjeda,* said, "[*Vijesti*] hasn't affected us at all. We already have our readership." Yet disputes within the ruling party have caused some changes at *Pobjeda.* Rather than slavishly mouthing the views of the Socialists, the newspaper has started running articles on the opposition and commentaries on previously taboo issues.

Vijesti readers, at least during the election period, found hardly any opinion pieces in their paper. Such sensitivity to charges of political meddling can be traced to *Vijesti*'s journalistic lineage; the newspaper was conceived at the newsmagazine *Monitor,* also based in Podgorica. The company that published *Monitor* put up one-third of the capital for *Vijesti,* private businessmen another third, and journalists from the new daily the final third. *Vijesti*'s publisher, Zeljko Ivanovic, and editor in chief, Ljubisa Mitrovic, are both veterans of *Monitor.*

If *Monitor*'s record of independent reporting is any gauge of what is in store for *Vijesti,* the prospects look good. Founded in 1990, *Monitor* quickly gained a reputation for independence and successfully avoided the warmongering rhetoric that consumed much of the Serbian and Montenegrin media during the Balkan wars.

With or without the weight of *Monitor*'s legacy, *Vijesti*'s discretion during the presidential campaign is admirable considering the two very different attitudes toward the independent media that Djukanovic and Bulatovic would be expected to take after winning the presidential race.

According to *Vijesti*'s Mitrovic, the recent opening up of the state media is part of Djukanovic's attempts to impress the West. "In order to solve the disastrous economic situation, Montenegro needs foreign investment. To get that, Djukanovic needs to show there is more democracy and all the things that go with it," he said. "For him, there is no turning back to the old methods of communism."

Bulatovic, for his part, backs a strong federal government and accuses Djukanovic of harboring separatist ambitions. He has portrayed himself as a defender of press freedom; he once told the French newspaper *Le Figaro:* "I am a principled advocate of free and independent media. I feel embarrassed in Yugoslavia regarding this issue. I have the impression that [people think] I am guilty, but really I am a reluctant accomplice." Reluctant or not, Bulatovic has long been seen as taking his orders from Belgrade, not known for its light-handed touch with independent media.

During its first two months, at least, *Vijesti* has had a comfortable relationship with the authorities. Minister of Information Bozidar Jaredic praised the new daily: "It looks very professional. They've been objective and haven't picked sides—unlike the press from Belgrade."

The authorities' tolerance for *Vijesti* may wear off soon, because the new daily plans on changing its tactics when the presidential race is decided. "We are going to criticize the government 100 percent," Mitrovic vowed. "The day after the elections, whoever wins will be under our magnifying glass."

NOTE

Reprinted with kind permission from *Transitions* magazine, November 1997.

THE KOSOVAR VOLCANO

by JANUSZ BUGAJSKI

Kosovar Albanians' pacifist approach to their dispute with Serbia has not worked. By late 1997 many were thinking about a change in tactics. Kosovo remained a center of crisis in the southern Balkans that perennially threatened to spark a regional conflagration. A viable solution to the conflict between Serbs and Albanians has evaded both the protagonists and the international community for nearly a decade. Instead, an inherently unstable stalemate existed between two diametrically opposed parties: the government in Belgrade, which was adamant that the territorial integrity of Serbia be maintained, and the Kosovar Albanians' internationally unrecognized government in Pristina, which was unwilling to back down on its demand of complete independence.

The Kosovar crisis in 1997 entered a new, unpredictable phase as a consequence of three destabilizing factors. First, growing sectors of the Kosovar Albanian population were becoming disenchanted with the peaceful approach of their leaders and could turn to radicalism as social and economic conditions deteriorate. Second, the Serbian authorities continued to pacify the territory through the use of forceful methods that threatened to provoke wide-scale violence. Third, Kosovar Albanians were increasingly losing faith in the international community as a force that was able or willing to promote their interests.

The omission of Kosovo from the ongoing Dayton peace process and the persistent opposition to Kosovo's independence among Western governments disillusioned many people who were banking on international intervention. Even

Kosovar leaders feared that their people had been sacrificed and abandoned by the West in the misplaced hope of democratizing Serbia and unseating Yugoslav President Slobodan Milosevic. That situation presented a major challenge to the West and a new sense of urgency lest the long-forecast eruption of the Kosovar volcano occur.

PACIFISM OR PASSIVITY?

The position of Kosovar shadow-state President Ibrahim Rugova and other Albanian leaders has been clear since the formal declaration of Kosovo's independence in September 1991. Neither the strategies nor the objectives of the governing Democratic League of Kosovo (LDK) underwent significant change. With state sovereignty as the ultimate goal, the key strategy has involved the creation of a separate political and social structure, including a system of media channels, economic activities, educational institutions, justice organs, health-care facilities, and cultural activities. Some activists described Kosovo as one big non-governmental organization in which the Serbian state controlled only the instruments of repression. Kosovo remained a territory of de facto apartheid, as Serbs and Albanians rarely intermingled.

The Kosovar Albanian leaders' strategy was based on the principles of nonviolence and passive resistance, despite frequent incidents of unwarranted brutality by Serbian police and acts of provocation by paramilitary forces implicitly sanctioned by Belgrade. The Albanians even avoided public demonstrations in order not to provide the pretext for a crackdown that could thwart all independent activities.

Rugova and his colleagues also calculated that the "internationalization" of the conflict was essential to give Kosovo high priority on the U.S. and European foreign-policy agendas. Pristina courted numerous international institutions and foreign governments to establish a presence in the province that would not only deter Serbian repression but also raise Kosovo's status as a distinct international subject.

Rugova's strategies appeared to be paying some dividends in the early days of the standoff. Bloodshed was minimized, the Albanians won praise and support from various governments for their steadfast and peaceful approach, and the authorities in Pristina seemed poised to gain international recognition. But as the stalemate continued, the benefits of pacifism and creating a parallel sociopolitical structure seemed to dwindle. Increasingly, Albanians began to question both the wisdom and the direction of the LDK's policies. Independence was at a standstill and high initial expectations were turning to frustration and resentment.

Not surprisingly, more radical options emerged in Kosovo, represented primarily by the writer Redzep Cosja and the former political prisoner Adem Demaci, as well as by a clandestine organization advocating armed resistance to Serbian policy. Cosja opposed Rugova's Gandhian methods, which he believed to have stifled the drive for independence. Although he did not represent any political force in Kosovo, Cosja advocated more active opposition through mass rallies and demonstrations. His stance reflected the belief that the Albanians may have missed the boat for independence when the Yugoslav tanker disintegrated in 1991. Instead of opting for passive declarations, he argued, Albanian leaders should have mobilized their people for active resistance even though there might have been casualties.

Demaci, leader of the opposition Parliamentary Party of Kosovo, was equally critical of the LDK. In 1997 he proposed more active measures against "Serbian occupation," including demonstrations, strikes, and other protests, with the aim of making Kosovo ungovernable while intensifying international attention. Paradoxically, Demaci's ultimate objective was more moderate than that of the LDK: he proposed confederation with Serbia once Kosovo attains independence. One wonders, however, why Kosovo would want to confederate with Serbia once statehood has been accomplished. In a confederation, Milosevic could capitalize on Albanian unrest to declare a state of emergency in Kosovo and conduct a sweeping crackdown.

The extent of Albanian frustration with the status quo was evident even within the LDK leadership. Prime Minister Bujar Bukoshi claimed that the government's moderate tactics had "come to a dead end" and called for stronger forms of civil disobedience. Student leaders also became more outspoken and petitioned the LDK to lead public demonstrations against the Milosevic government.

Meanwhile, Kosovar opposition leaders complained the LDK was using illegitimate means to maintain its political monopoly in Kosovo, exemplified by the repeated postponement of parliamentary and presidential elections that should have been held in late 1996. The LDK argued that convoking parliament or holding elections could provoke a police crackdown and the wholesale arrest of the Albanian leadership.

Dissatisfaction with the LDK was evident in another way: the emergence of a militant terrorist group. Organized anti-Serbian attacks began in the summer of 1995 and became more regular during 1997. The terrorists targeted Serbian policemen and officials as well as Albanian "collaborators." The clandestine Kosovo Liberation Army, the military arm of the National Movement for the Liberation of Kosovo, claimed responsibility for the deaths of 30 people. In May, the group issued a proclamation to the citizens of Kosovo to "reject the peace-making policy of Rugova and accept the liberation struggle against the invader."

Although Serbian police arrested, tried, and convicted several dozen people on charges of belonging to the army or its political wing, Albanian leaders claimed the arrests were merely part of a pattern of state-sponsored intimidation. Indeed, some believed the group was actually a creation of the Serbian secret service. There was evidence of rising sympathy for the terrorist group among young people. Many jobless youths were frustrated with pacifism and incessant police intimidation and sought alternative outlets for their anger. Even Prime Minister Bukoshi admitted that many Kosovars sympathize with the army.

Serbian officials claim the Kosovar terrorists receive training and weapons in neighboring Albania, although no evidence has been presented. Nonetheless, a substantial volume of weapons has undoubtedly crossed the border since Albania's arms stocks became open to the public during the rebellion against the government of Sali Berisha. No major Albanian party publicly affirmed its support for the Kosovo Liberation Army, but the more nationalist groupings, such as the Beli Kombetar, criticized Rugova and his peace policy and were outspoken about liberation struggles and the creation of a "greater Albania." However, such groups had little influence on the new socialist government in Tirana.

Kosovar Albanian leaders had long been dissatisfied with Tirana's cautious, hands-off policy toward Kosovo, and the crisis in Albania during the past year left the Kosovars feeling even more isolated. They had viewed Albania as a potentially stable ally whose rising international position would positively affect U.S. and European Union policy toward Kosovo.

REPRESSION FROM BELGRADE

Belgrade's repressive policies in Kosovo were low-key enough not to provoke any strong international reaction but sweeping enough to instill a sense of fear among the Kosovars. During 1996, at least 14 Albanians were killed by the police, and about a dozen more died in 1997. Hundreds were imprisoned or beaten by the security forces. Milosevic, who first used the issue of supposed threats to Serbdom in Kosovo when he was coming to power in Serbia in 1987, continued to promote the image of himself as the stern defender of Serbia's territorial integrity.

In June, Milosevic visited Pristina for a public rally in which he claimed Serbia would not "yield an inch of Kosovo and Metohija." In August, the Serbian government held its first session in Pristina since the elimination of the region's autonomy in 1990. Officials made promises about investment and economic development in order to secure the votes of Kosovar Serbs in the upcoming ballot. Because Albanians consistently boycotted Serbian elections, the small Serbian minority in Kosovo decided 42 of the Serbian parliament's 250 seats.

The Serbian opposition claimed that Milosevic hoped to engineer a crisis in Kosovo as a pretext for imposing martial law and eliminating dissent and independent activism throughout the country. Indeed, during the Belgrade demonstrations in late 1996 the state media tried to link the Zajedno opposition coalition with Albanian separatism. In fact, Serbian opposition leaders gave no support to Kosovar Albanian aspirations. At best, they avoided the Kosovar question for fear of being branded as national traitors. At worst, they sought to undermine Milosevic's support among nationalists by outdoing his anti-Albanian rhetoric. Vuk Draskovic, leader of the Serbian Renewal Movement and a candidate in the Serbian presidential election, declared during the campaign that Kosovo should be renamed Old Serbia.

Wary of any association with opposition parties whose position on Kosovo seemed no more accommodating than that of the Socialists, LDK leaders avoided any show of support for Serbian opposition parties or their leaders. As Kosovar Premier Bukoshi put it, the LDK only backed those forces in Serbia that had the political courage to support self-determination for the people of Kosovo. Nevertheless, he did not totally discount a dialogue with the Serbian opposition.

Parliamentary Party of Kosovo leader Demaci did express support for

Zajedno and even visited Belgrade during the mass demonstrations and granted interviews to the Serbian press. His presence was widely misinterpreted as a climb down from Kosovar demands for independence, heralding the initiation of a historic compromise with the Serbian opposition. The collapse of Zajedno and subsequent statements on Kosovo by its former leaders injected a dose of reality into that picture.

Western governments were avidly looking for signs of compromise in Belgrade and Pristina. In order to deflect Western criticism and improve the prospects for lifting economic sanctions, Milosevic made some gestures toward easing repression in Kosovo. In September 1995, he signed an agreement with Rugova to reintegrate Albanian pupils into the state school system that they had boycotted for six years. But two years later, the accord had still not been implemented.

One essential ingredient of Milosevic's strategy was to weaken and divide the Albanian movement by driving a wedge between the Kosovars and their leadership. Hence, he offered talks and illusory concessions in order to discredit any willing participants. Milosevic generally rejected international mediation of the conflict, and when U.S. institutions attempted to organize talks, Serbian officials boycotted them and any Serbian opposition figures attending were branded by the state media as traitors to the Serbian cause.

WASHINGTON'S CONTAINMENT

Washington at no time supported independence for Kosovo but focused on two strategies: containment of the conflict and the "restoration of human and political rights" (as if such rights had ever been a feature of either Tito's or Milosevic's Yugoslavia). Presidents George Bush and Bill Clinton both publicly affirmed that in case of armed conflict in Kosovo, the United States would unilaterally intervene to protect the Albanians. However, the precise threshold for intervention was not specified. That deliberate ambiguity was designed to keep both sides in check: the policy may have deterred massive Serbian repression and has not encouraged an Albanian revolt. Washington's overriding concern was that an armed conflict in Kosovo might spill into Albania and Macedonia. Hence the policy of containment involved measured pressures on Milosevic and consistent restraint on the Kosovars.

Milosevic for his part exploited other crises to mute the Kosovar question. During the Dayton process in Bosnia-Herzegovina, he cast himself as an indispensable peacemaker, calculating that such an image would provide him with greater leeway in Kosovo. The Albanians were dismayed when Kosovo did not appear on the Dayton agenda despite Pristina's incessant appeals. Their anger was aggravated during the visit to Kosovo by former U.S. Assistant Secretary of State John Kornblum, who reportedly told Rugova to abandon the idea of independence and take part in the Serbian elections. Albanian leaders complained that the question of Kosovo's self-determination should not be tied to Serbian democratization.

Despite Kosovar Albanian fears, Washington did not abandon Kosovo completely. Following Dayton, an "outer wall" of sanctions was maintained against Yugoslavia, which denied Belgrade access to international financial institutions. One of the conditions for lifting the sanctions was "substantial progress in Kosovo." Indeed, the United States was consistently more supportive than the European countries, which granted significant trading privileges to Belgrade in April despite appeals from Pristina.

Washington underscored its engagement in Kosovo by opening up a U.S. Information Office in Pristina in June 1996 and inviting Rugova to Washington in August to meet with Secretary of State Madeleine Albright. In a letter to Milosevic in February 1997, Albright urged Belgrade to "take positive steps to resolve the situation in Kosovo" and cautioned against the use of force. Indeed, Albright injected a new sense of urgency to defusing the Kosovar time bomb and maintaining pressure on Milosevic. The Clinton administration realized that an official and continuous U.S. presence in Kosovo was essential to demonstrate support for Rugova's peaceful strategy, even if Washington disagreed with his objectives.

Questions remained, however, whether Washington can maintain the balance between Belgrade and Pristina. The U.S. State Department was relying on Serbian democratization to help resolve its policy challenges in Kosovo. As prospects for an opposition takeover receded in 1997 and talks between Albanian and Serbian leaders remained stalemated, Washington seemed to be looking for fresh initiatives in Kosovo. For example, the notion of appointing a special envoy for Kosovo, with a mandate similar to that of Richard Holbrooke's in Bosnia-Herzegovina, was being taken seriously in policy circles.

FOUR OPTIONS

Given the prospect of continuous turmoil and instability in Kosovo, the Serbian government may eventually decide the status quo is either too costly or untenable. Then it would face at least four options: homogenization, division, disassociation, or federalization.

In the first option, Belgrade may decide to forcefully Serbianize the region in a Bosnian-type scenario of ethnic cleansing. That option would probably precipitate a bloodbath and an Albanian revolt, provoke American intervention, and destabilize the entire southern Balkans. It would also help seal Serbia's international isolation and further destroy the Yugoslav economy.

In the second option, Belgrade could territorially divide Kosovo and allow the region next to the Albanian border to secede—a proposal once discussed by Serbian writer and former Yugoslav President Dobrica Cosic. But such a scenario would also entail the large-scale "cleansings" of areas designated for Serbian habitation and thus follow the pattern outlined in the first option.

In the third scenario, Belgrade could simply disassociate itself from Kosovo and allow the region to gain de facto independence. Although such a move would probably earn Belgrade international praise and credit, the domestic impact could lead to a Serbian nationalist revolt and the attempted secession of an increasingly restless Montenegro.

The fourth option would probably be the most viable solution to the Kosovar challenge. The only possible compromise between the two diametrically opposed positions of Serbs and Albanians is federalization, in which Kosovo would obtain the status of a republic in a three-way federation alongside Serbia and Montenegro. Even LDK leaders privately concede that such a scenario may be the only way of defusing tensions in the absence of international support for outright independence.

Clearly, both sides would have to concede ground for federalization to work, but the institutional underpinnings of such an arrangement already exist. The constitution of the Federal Republic of Yugoslavia contains provisions for taking in other federal units, while the independence resolution of the Republic of Kosovo affirms that the state has the "right of constitutive participation in the alliance of states-sovereign republics [in Yugoslavia] based on full freedom and equality." A three-way federation would require prolonged negotiations. But the process would allow the international community to engage itself fully in the solution of a problem that bedevils the Balkans and constantly threatens to escalate into a regional conflict.

NOTE

Reprinted with kind permission from *Transitions* magazine, October 1997.

Macedonia

Population:	2,075,196 (1994 census)
Capital:	Skopje (pop. 450,000)
Major cities:	Bitola (pop. 80,000), Kumanovo (pop. 70,000), Prilep (pop. 70,000)
Area:	25,713 sq. km.
Major ethnic groups:	Macedonian 67%, Albanian 23%, Turkish 4%, Romani 2%, Serbian 2%, other 2%
Economy:	GDP growth: 1.4%
....	Inflation rate: 4.6%
....	Average monthly wage: $166
....	Unemployment rate: 31.7%

ETHNIC TENSIONS ON THE RISE

by STEFAN KRAUSE

In 1997, tensions between ethnic Macedonians and ethnic Albanians rose considerably, casting doubts on the country's future stability, despite progress made in the economy and in foreign relations.

Arguably the single most important development in Macedonia in 1997 was the further deterioration of relations between the country's sizable ethnic Albanian minority on the one side and the ethnic Macedonian majority and the government on the other. The Albanians, who according to official data account for some 23 percent of the country's population but claim that they make up 35–40 percent, had long demanded more freedom to regulate their own cultural and political affairs. Long-standing problems came to a head in 1997, resulting in violent clashes and harsh prison sentences against ethnic Albanian leaders.

STANDOFF BETWEEN MACEDONIANS AND ETHNIC ALBANIANS

Between January and March 1997, ethnic Albanian and ethnic Macedonian students protested for and against Albanian-language tuition at the Skopje University's pedagogical faculty. A parliamentary decision in early February allowing Albanian-language tuition sparked protests from nationalistic ethnic Macedonian students and from the opposition Macedonian Internal Revolutionary Organization–Party for Macedonian National Unity (VMRO-DPMNE). The students demanded the resignation of Education Minister Sofija Todorova and staged daily demonstrations in Skopje for some three weeks in February and March, while some even went on a hunger strike to prevent the law from taking effect. The VMRO-DPMNE for its part appealed to the Constitutional Court, claiming the Macedonian constitution allowed minority-language education only in primary and secondary schools, but not in institutions of higher education. The issue was settled when the Constitutional Court on 7 May decided not to start proceedings in this matter, de facto recognizing the law's constitutionality.

Macedonia's conflict with its Albanian community was also a focus of attention for the international community. In early March, the European Union (EU) expressed its concern over rising ethnic tension and its potential effect on Balkan stability. The EU noted that as a member of the OSCE (Organization for Security and Cooperation in Europe) and Council of Europe, Macedonia was obliged to guarantee minority rights and to strive for good relations with its neighbors. On 13 March, Prime Minister Branko Crvenkovski addressed a special parliamentary session on the issue of ethnic relations. He said Macedonia was in an "extraordinarily difficult situation" on the political, economic, social, and security fronts, admitting that many of those problems stemmed from the poor functioning of state institutions. He claimed that the constitution and the government's ethnic policies were based on "political coexistence, mutual tolerance, and respect" and said problems should be overcome using the existing institutional framework, with laws and procedures meeting "European norms."

Not long after Crvenkovski's speech, matters worsened. On 5 May, the Interior Ministry filed charges against the mayors of the predominantly Albanian towns of Gostivar and Tetovo, Rufi Osmani and Alajdin Demiri, and other local officials for ordering the Albanian flag to be flown from public buildings during recent public holidays. The Interior Ministry claimed that this contravened Macedonian laws on displaying foreign symbols.

Following the charges and the subsequent indictments, tensions between ethnic Macedonians and Albanians increased sharply, especially in western Macedonia, where about 70 percent of the population was Albanian. In Gostivar, police had to move in on 26 May to break up armed clashes between the various ethnic groups. The government reacted on 10 June by adopting a draft law enabling ethnic minorities to use their own national symbols at private, cultural, or sporting events. The draft also allowed minorities to display their flags on state holidays in areas where they constitute a majority, but only on municipal buildings and only alongside the Macedonian banner. It did not allow them to fly their flags from other public buildings on any occasion. Summing up ethnic Albanians' sentiments, Osmani rejected the draft law as a "degradation" of minority rights as set forth in the constitution and relevant laws.

Violence broke out after parliament passed the law on 8 July. In the single worst incident, three ethnic Albanians were killed and dozens wounded in clashes between Albanians and police in Gostivar on 9 July after police took down Albanian flags from Gostivar city hall and Albanians tried to re-hoist them. Some 300 Albanians were arrested during the clashes. Osmani was also detained and charged with inciting the riots and promoting ethnic hatred. Appeals for peace by President Kiro Gligorov did little to diffuse the tension. The situation remained tense over the following weeks as police continued taking down Albanian flags from public buildings in areas with an ethnic Albanian majority. Politicians from both camps blamed each other for the situation. Gligorov abandoned his relatively neutral and conciliatory position. In a statement which appeared in Belgrade's weekly *Ekonomska Politika*'s 25 August issue, the president said that all ethnic Albanian parties in Macedonia wanted to secede from Macedonia and worked toward that aim. On 4 November, Gligorov once again refused to legalize the self-proclaimed Albanian university in Tetovo, saying that Albanians who wanted higher education in their mother tongue should go to Tirana University.

On 17 September, Osmani was sentenced to 13 years and 8 months in jail for "fanning racial, national, and religious intolerance, [. . .] inciting rebellion, [. . .] and disregarding [decisions of] the Constitutional Court." Gostivar City Council President Refik Dauti received a three-year sentence on the last charge. The official reasoning was that Osmani had allowed Albanian and Turkish flags to fly from the town hall after the new law was passed. Osmani was temporarily released on 7 October because a 90-day detention deadline had expired before a final verdict was passed, but his case was still pending. On 14 October, Tetovo Mayor Alajdin Demiri and Tetovo City Council President Vehbi Bexheti were convicted on similar charges and each sentenced to 2 years and 6 months in prison.

Despite continued ethnic tensions, on 30 September, UN Human Rights Commission special envoy Elisabeth Rehn recommended that Macedonia be removed from her mandate because of its improved human rights record. She voiced concern, however, over the situation of the Albanian minority and about police abuses.

PYRAMIDS AND GOVERNMENT RESHUFFLES

Ethnic tensions were not the only problem plaguing Macedonia in 1997. In early March, the National Bank suspended operations of Macedonia's largest savings house, the Bitola-based TAT. The bank was accused of operating a pyramid scheme—that is, using the cash from new depositors to pay exorbitantly high (and unsustainable) interest rates to earlier depositors. TAT owner Sonja Nikolovska was arrested on 7 March and charged with forging documents, tax evasion, and abuse of office. National Bank Governor Tome Nenovski resigned over the scandal. Bitola Mayor Siljan Bicevski, his wife, and a deputy governor of the National Bank were detained for some time, while investigations were also launched against other officials. Many of the officials arrested apparently had a personal interest in TAT's fate. Bicevski and his wife reportedly deposited money from state companies they managed with TAT in order to avert the saving house's collapse, since this would have cost them their personal TAT deposits of over $1 million. In the end, some 30,000 clients lost between $28 million and $80 million (the exact figure is unknown because the results of the official investigation were classified). On 24 April, the government promised $12 million to partially reimburse victims of the pyramid scheme. Still, people staged demonstrations, demanding full compensation by the state. The trial against Nikolovska and her co-defendants began on 20 October but was then postponed, with no new date set by the end of the year.

The government was under pressure as a consequence of the TAT scandal, although Crvenkovski received a vote of confidence from the parliament on 25 March. Shortly afterwards, he reshuffled his cabinet. On 2 April, Construction Minister Jorgo Sundovski resigned, denying allegations of being involved in the TAT scandal. On 27 May a major government reshuffle took place. A majority of the old cabinet members either left the government or took over new portfolios. Among those sacked were Deputy Prime Minister Jane Miljovski and Foreign Minister Ljubomir Frckovski, both prominent reformers. Frckovski was replaced by Defense Minister Blagoj Handziski, who was himself succeeded by Lazar Kitanovski. Since more than one third of the ministers were replaced, the constitution stipulated that the new government had to be approved by the parliament, which the latter did on 30 May, by 78 to 23 votes.

The opposition intensified its protests against the government, staging mass rallies and demanding the cabinet's resignation and early elections. The government said talks on elections could only be held after the consequences of the TAT scandal had been dealt with, but ultimately, those talks never materialized.

SLOW PROGRESS IN FOREIGN RELATIONS

Despite continuing problems, Macadonia made some progress in foreign relations, and on the whole, emerged in a stronger position by the year's end. Influenced by developments at home, relations with Albania deteriorated, especially in the first half of the year. Skopje and Tirana, the capital of Albania, traded accusations and blamed each other for the events in western Macedonia. To make matters worse, several Albanians trying to cross into Macedonia were killed or injured by Macedonian security forces. Still, the second half of 1997 saw some rapprochement between the two countries. On 24 October, Kitanovski and his Albanian counterpart, Sabit Brokaj, signed an agreement to improve security on their common border, and on 4 December, Handziski and Albanian Foreign Minister Paskal Milo signed six bilateral agreements, again mostly concerning border security. Nevertheless, relations with Tirana remain a problem, especially since they were directly linked to Skopje's policy vis-à-vis its ethnic Albanian minority.

Relations with Greece remained stable, although no breakthrough on the disputed issue of Macedonia's name could be reached. Several rounds of UN-brokered bilateral talks failed to produce a viable compromise. Greece objected to the adoption of the name "Macedonia" by its northern neighbor, claiming that this implies a territorial claim on the region of northern Greece that goes by the same name. (Macedonia already altered its national flag in response to Greek complaints that it had appropriated an ancient Macedonian sunburst symbol.) But in January, Culture Minister Slobodan Unkovski became the first Macedonian government minister to visit Greece officially, and in June, Handziski participated in a Balkan foreign ministers' meeting in Thessaloniki. In March, Greek Foreign Minister Theodoros Pangalos had visited Skopje—the first such high-level visit by a Greek official to independent Macedonia. Gligorov participated in the Balkan summit in Crete in early November and returned saying that he and Greek Prime Minister Kostas Simitis had made good progress on improving relations. In May, Greece participated in a NATO-sponsored military exercise in Macedonia.

No agreement was reached in the quarrel with Bulgaria about the Macedonian language and its use in official documents, which Bulgaria refused to accept. The conflict has clouded bilateral relations ever since Macedonia declared its independence, leaving some 20 bilateral agreements unratified. Bulgaria recognized Macedonian statehood but refuses to accept that the Macedonians are a people distinct from the Bulgarians, with their own language. Despite signs that the new Bulgarian government might have been more willing to compromise on the issue, a meeting between Gligorov and Bulgarian President Petar Stoyanov on the sidelines of the Crete summit failed to break the impasse. Relations with Belgrade continued to be impaired by the failure of the bilateral border commission to delineate the common border. On 3 December, the Yugoslav commission members demanded that changes in Belgrade's favor be made in three strategically important places.

On the international front, Gligorov embarked on several high-profile official visits, most notably to the United States and China, while Italian President Oscar Luigi Scalfaro and NATO Secretary General Javier Solana were arguably the highest-ranking politicians who visited Macedonia in 1997.

The UN Security Council in late May voted to extend by six months the mandate of its peace-keeping force in Macedonia (UNPREDEP). The UN deployed the force in 1992 as a precautionary measure, to patrol the Macedonian borders with Albania and the Serbian province of Kosovo. It consisted of about 1,000 soldiers and 200 police observers, drawn from the Nordic countries and the United States. On 4 December, the UN extended the peacekeepers' mandate through August 1998, but said it will then end the mission. Macedonia tried to get elected to a non-permanent UN Security Council seat but lost out to Slovenia on 14 October.

Macedonia's relations with the EU and NATO remained largely unchanged throughout 1997. The country had not formally applied for membership in either organization and was therefore not directly affected by their decisions on which countries to invite for membership talks. On 18 February, the EU agreed to lend Macedonia $48 million, partly as the EU contribution to a donors' conference later the same month. The conference promised Macedonia a total of $65 million in loans for 1997, which was partly earmarked to cover a projected $85 million balance-of-payment deficit.

MINOR CHANGES IN THE ECONOMY

Economically, 1997 brought only minor changes over 1996. Economic growth continued but slowed down to just about 1 percent of GDP. The budget remained largely balanced. According to preliminary figures, the budget deficit was 0.1 percent of GDP. Inflation rose, but still remained low at 4.6 percent. However, the trade deficit remained high, $463 million according to preliminary estimates for all of 1997. The current account deficit for the first three quarters stood at $218 million. Unemployment also remained a cause of major concern. At the end of 1997, 253,410 persons were officially unemployed, some 8,000 more than the previous year. No official percentage figures are available, but estimates for the unemployment rate range from 25 percent upward. The average monthly wage fell to $159 in September. Following negotiations between the Macedonian government and the International Monetary Fund, on 9 July the National Bank depreciated the denar by 16.1 percent against the German mark, while freezing public sector wages for the rest of the year.

Albania

Population:	3,249,136
Capital:	Tirana (pop. 270,000–300,000)
Major cities:	Durres (pop.130,000), Elbasan (pop. 100,000), Shkoder (pop. 81,000–100,000)
Area:	28,750 sq. km.
Major ethnic groups:	Albanian 95%, Greek 3%, other 2%
Economy:	GDP growth: –7.0%
....	Inflation rate: 42.0%
....	Average monthly wage: $55
....	Unemployment rate: 20%–30%

FROM ANARCHY TO AN UNCERTAIN STABILITY

by FABIAN SCHMIDT

After five years of relative stability, anarchy broke out in Albania in February 1997. In the wake of the collapse of pyramid schemes in which hundreds of thousands had invested their savings it became obvious that economic and political progress was far from what the governing Democratic Party had claimed throughout the previous years.

Much of the prosperity that Albania had seen since 1992 did not derive from its own economic strength. Albania was living largely on imports, while domestic production was diminishing, despite large-scale privatization. Financial transfers from Albanians living abroad and the smuggling of oil and arms to the former Yugoslavia partly covered the trade deficit. The huge emigration, estimated at between 400,000 and 600,000 persons, helps to explain the low official unemployment rate.

Many of Albania's structural economic problems were disguised by the apparent speed of reform since 1991, such as the privatization of agricultural land. However, the small plots of land which the farmers received discouraged the use of machinery and fertilizers and led to inefficient production.

The lack of a proper private banking system was only slowly addressed with the opening of Greek and Malaysian private banks and a stock exchange in early 1996. The stock exchange never started to develop. Inexperienced savers preferred to invest in pyramid schemes, which offered astronomic interest rates, rather than serious banks. The companies running these pyramid schemes quickly became the symbol of Albania's apparent economic progress. It was no coincidence that these financial companies blossomed in 1994, a time when smuggling activities reached a peak during the Yugoslav crisis.

Italian investigators and intelligence sources suggested that these companies were able to rise so quickly only by laundering money from smuggling oil into Montenegro and drugs and refugees into Italy. Another important business was apparently the export of arms to Rwanda, Afghanistan, and Bosnia. These revenues were one of the reasons why the pyramid schemes were able to operate for as long as they did without collapsing for lack of income.

Once the Dayton accord was signed in December 1995 the lucrative market for illegal oil and arms dried up, and the pyramid schemes were in serious danger. In early 1996 they were still able to attract new domestic investors by advertising their earlier financial successes. In June 1996 the World Bank strongly urged the government to intervene against these companies, but parliament only stepped in six months later, as the schemes started to collapse. By then it was too late.

On the political front, President Sali Berisha's authoritarian policy became apparent already in 1994. Human rights groups documented ample cases of violations of human rights and judicial independence, reprisals against the free media, and numerous cases of violence against political opponents of the ruling Democratic Party.

The most blatant cases included the imprisonment of Socialist Party Chairman Fatos Nano, who was charged with assisting an Italian company in the misappropriation of humanitarian aid funds during his first term as prime minister in 1991. Even though an Italian court acquitted the Italian company of the charges, Nano remained in prison until March 1997.

Another indicator of increasing authoritarian tendencies in Berisha's government came with the holding of national parliamentary and local elections in 1996. Winning the vote, the Democratic Party (PD) managed to reach a peak in power consolidation, holding over two-thirds of the parliamentary seats. The opposition accused Sali Berisha and his PD of perpetrating election fraud, a view shared by international observers of the Organization for Security and Cooperation in Europe (OSCE). During those years the PD had managed to extend its control over the legislature, the executive, the judiciary, and the media.

OUTBREAK OF ANARCHY

The collapse of fraudulent pyramid investment schemes was the straw that broke the camel's back half a year after the elections. Thousands of cheated investors protested on the streets in December and January 1997 and demanded their money back from the government. These riots led to an uprising in southern Albania, which also spread north during March. People looted arms depots throughout Albania. The army and public order collapsed and the country appeared to be only a step away from a civil war. During these incidents public buildings were destroyed and banks looted, and according to official figures about 1,500 people were killed. Bullets fired randomly in the air apparently killed most of the victims.

At the same time criminal gangs used the opportunity to spread illicit activities ranging from robbery to smuggling of arms, drugs, and refugees. As occurred after the end of communism in 1991, tens of thousands fled by boat to Italy or otherwise to Greece. In the most dramatic incident over 80 people died after one refugee boat collided with an Italian coast guard vessel on 28 March. The trafficking of humans by boat, however, continued, and the local Mafia found a lucrative business in smuggling Kurds to Italy, since they did not need a visa to enter Albania as long as they were Turkish citizens.

The March 1997 crisis in Albania was caused not only by the collapse of pyramid investment schemes but more broadly reflected the failure to introduce functioning, independent, democratic and legal institutions. Another factor was the lack of democratic experience. In its history Albania had a democratic government only for several months in 1924, shorter than almost anywhere else in the Balkans. In no other country did communism isolate its citizens as much from the outer world as in Albania. Even though pyramid schemes appeared in many other countries besides Albania, nowhere else did their rise and fall have such devastating effects.

A NEW BEGINNING?

In March 1997 OSCE envoy Franz Vranitzky successfully mediated an agreement between President Sali Berisha and the opposition. Both sides agreed to the formation of a government of national reconciliation under Socialist Prime Minister Bashkim Fino, formerly the major of Gjirokaster, and announced early elections. The Albanians asked the international community to send a multi-national stabilization force to Albania. The West European Union (WEU) and North Atlantic Treaty Organization (NATO) declined to take full responsibility. Instead it was left to Italy to assemble the force after receiving the appropriate United Nations mandate. Various other European countries, including France, Greece, Turkey, Spain, Romania, Austria, and Denmark participated in the operation, landing without difficulties in Albania on 15 April.

Even though the process that led to the June 1997 parliamentary elections was by itself far from democratic and had pushed the country into a vicious circle of violence, the outcome was a free and fair ballot. Few observers expected this to be achieved, considering that the timeframe to organize the vote was extremely short. The parliamentary elections on 29 June and 6 July proceeded without the eruption of major violence, even though the Albanian government, assisted by the OSCE, had hardly two months to prepare. Despite widespread fears that they would be a failure, the elections turned out to be a success and by and large contributed to the stabilization of the country. The OSCE concluded that the ballot was "acceptable."

In August 1997 the new Socialist-led coalition government took office under Prime Minister Fatos Nano. The Socialists had gained over two thirds of the parliamentary seats. Berisha resigned and the parliament elected Rexhep Meidani in his place, a physicist who has subsequently played a moderate ceremonial role promoting national reconciliation, unlike his predecessor, who had used the presidency to wield political power.

Since then Albania witnessed another round of efforts to reform its administration and to strengthen its democratic institutions. The current government faces the same daunting problems as its many predecessors. The country is underdeveloped and faces a huge budget deficit, and the low salaries in the public sector make the administration vulnerable to corruption. The future of the government will depend on whether it finds an answer to the question of how to provide for economic prosperity and create jobs. Reviving the economy will be crucial for further democratic development. On one hand only a solid democracy will create the basis for long-term development, but on the other hand popular appreciation of democratic values and systems will grow only if the broad population remains involved in the democratic process and at the same time experiences its value by sharing the benefits of economic growth.

The new government presented a highly ambitious program. Foreign Minister Paskal Milo from the Social Democratic Party announced that his long-term aims are joining the European Union (EU) and NATO. Earlier, Prime Minister Fatos Nano had stressed that good relations with the United States and the EU were of primary importance to Albania. But Albania was far from reaching these ambitious goals.

Law and order remained a serious problem. The government was faced with the task of cracking down on the gangs that were still causing insecurity and waging gang wars, especially in remote parts of the country. Killings were running at about 70 people per month at the end of 1997. Interior Minister Neritan Ceka from the Democratic Alliance Party pledged to disarm the population, which is estimated still to hold over 600,000 arms, but this would not be easy. In order to achieve this, Ceka would have to continue with his police reform to improve their professional qualities. He was closely cooperating with Western countries in rebuilding law enforcement. There was a police training contingent from the WEU, supporting the police in training and providing equipment. Italy focused on reorganizing Albania's customs service, and kept 500 soldiers in the country after the multinational forces withdrew in late August. These soldiers helped rebuild the army, which fell apart shortly after the unrest started in February. Similar assistance was given by Greece, which helped rebuild a military hospital.

The pace of reform was not fast enough to satisfy increasing popular calls for harsher measures against crime, including capital punishment. Albania was obliged to observe the standards of the European Convention on Human Rights since its admission to the Council of Europe, and could not practice capital punishment. Local judges nonetheless continued to sentence people to death. None of the sentences were carried out, since every case needed presidential approval and none were approved. Some politicians have, however, demanded that the government negotiate special terms with the Council of Europe that would allow Albania to apply the death penalty.

That example shows that the respect for human rights and rule of law is still built on weak foundations. The roles state institutions have played in the past have not helped much in enforcing democratic principles. The police, courts, and state media were highly politicized institutions during the reign of the PD government. This led the new ministers to begin sacking a large number of high-ranking officials in the administration. The Socialists were, however, in danger of continuing with the Albanian tradition of appointing officials for their loyalty to the ruling political party, and may have missed an opportunity to break with that habit. Appointing officials with an awareness of professional esteem and loyalty to the democratic state rather than to a particular party was a necessary first step toward drying out the cultural basis on which corruption and abuse of political power grows.

The biggest dilemma faced by the new government was how to fire and hire employees without starting an orgy of political purges. There was an urgent need to fire many incompetent employees, downsize the administration, and hire fewer but better qualified people. But in doing this the government laid itself open to charges of starting political purges and bringing communist-era specialists back into duty.

At least some of these charges seemed justified. The network of regional branches of the Socialist Party served as a strong pressure group, demanding jobs in the administration for their supporters in the still strongly centralized state apparatus. The government often gave in, contributing to a perception of the government's role as a patron. As was the case with the previously governing Democratic Party, many Socialist Party members appeared to consider the state their own property, not that of the whole society.

There were clear indicators that the new government wanted radical changes in its personnel structure, contributing to the public perception that government employees would once again be primarily political appointees. Justice Minister Thimio Kondi and Defense Minister Sabit Brokaj both sacked a number of senior officials. Brokaj even indicated that some top-ranking officers might be put on trial for violating the constitution by sending troops against protesters or by leaving arms depots open to looters. The Democratic Party has already opened an office giving legal advice to those affected by the dismissals.

The question of where necessary administrative changes end and political purges begin is indeed difficult to answer. The government needed qualified personnel if it wanted to overcome the politicization of the administration. But even the people who may have had the qualities and professional integrity to change the political culture were wary of becoming the next generation of officials under pressure to behave loyally to the respective ruling political party. Even though many young and foreign-trained experts entered the administration, they faced problems and opposition deriving from the old mentality which still prevailed throughout the apparatus. Complicating the picture still further was the fact that the local government was by and large antagonistic toward the center, with most of the mayors coming from the opposition Democratic Party.

The judiciary also was largely antagonistic toward the government, while at the same time receiving little trust from the people. Its actions did little to inspire public confidence. The constitutional court in November 1997, for example, blocked a law allowing the government to administer pyramid schemes, on the grounds that the law violated private ownership rights. But previously, lower-ranking courts had also refused to accept cases from cheated investors against the pyramid companies. Under these circumstances the parliament was forced to amend the constitutional provisions on 19 November, allowing the auditing and administration of companies under extraordinary circumstances.

Another major conflict between the parliament and the constitutional court arose over the question of the rotation of its judges. According to the constitution the court has to rotate three judges by lot every three years. But after the court was created in May 1992, the first rotation did not take place by May 1995. Instead the court decided, meeting in June 1995, that it did not have to rotate, because three of its members had resigned the previous November. The three had resigned in protest over the constitutional court's refusal to allow a court case against Berisha's constitution referendum.

The rotation conflict broke out only in November 1997 when the Socialist-dominated parliament adopted a constitutional amendment with its two-thirds parliamentary majority, saying that the resignation of a judge did not constitute rotation and obliging the court to rotate by mid-December. The court refused to comply, and on 5 December declared the amendment invalid, implying that the constitution does not mean what it says. Constitutional Court judge Rustem Gjata later declared the vote a "constitutional coup d'etat."

The court controversy illustrates that probably the strongest hindrance to reforms is the undemocratic mentality that seems to have deep roots in both the common people and state officials, including the courts. Often civil servants consider themselves in a position of ownership rather than of public service, and act accordingly.

Many state employees lack a sense of duty and commitment. They have developed sophisticated methods for using their working hours for everything but what they are supposed to do. As a result there are delays and little gets done. Another problem is that government salaries have been low, compared to those of international organizations, NGOs, or some of the newspapers, keeping qualified people away from government jobs. The low salaries, usually between $70 and $120 per month, also made the administration liable to corruption.

At the same time few people were willing to organize themselves on a grassroots level, to start local initiatives and to defend their interests against either government or bigger businesses. Instead they tried to access officials through influential friends and patronage networks. Unfortunately, often enough these mechanisms worked faster and more efficiently than official channels.

Another heritage of a patronage-based social system was that people were reluctant to publicly join forces, having had bad experiences with collectivism under communism. The biggest hindrance for a reform of agriculture was the widespread ownership of small pieces of land and the peasants' unwillingness to form agricultural cooperatives. Thus agriculture, potentially the country's largest industry, was still on a primitive level without much hope for substantial change. The peasants lacked the necessary vision to become the basis of broad economic prosperity.

Beside private business, that lack of vision also persisted in government areas such as the state media. Politicians were enthusiastically promoting the idea of reforming the strongly controlled state radio and television, as well as the news agency ATA. A new broadcasting law was in preparation. But in the meantime the organization and structure of the institutions had not yet changed, nor the style of reporting. The ATA statute had stayed unchanged since communist times.

A positive development was that open conflicts between the parliament, the president, and the judiciary suggested that the separation of powers functions better than before. The bulk of work, however, was still ahead, including the drafting of a new constitution in mid-1998.

In order to avoid the mistakes of its predecessors the new government needed to develop a mentality of duty to the state rather than to the party in power. It is important therefore that the new constitution be based on a broad popular consensus and that it be openly discussed with a high level of public involvement prior to its adoption.

Bulgaria

Population:	8,487,317 (1992 census)
Capital:	Sofia (pop. 1,190,126)
Major cities:	Plovdiv (pop. 377,637), Varna (pop. 297,090), Burgas (pop. 188,367)
Area:	110,994 sq. km.
Major ethnic groups:	Bulgarian 85.7%, Turkish 9.4%, Romani 3.7%
Economy:	GDP growth: –7.4%
....	Inflation rate: 579.0%
....	Average monthly wage: $108
....	Unemployment rate: 13.7%

WINDS OF CHANGE SWEEP BULGARIA

by STEFAN KRAUSE

At the beginning of 1997, Bulgaria seemed on the verge of total collapse. But as the year progressed, the demise of the Socialist government and the takeover by the former opposition brought the beginning of long overdue reforms. Early 1997 found Bulgaria in a situation that almost amounted to a constitutional vacuum. Zhan Videnov had resigned as prime minister and Bulgarian Socialist Party (BSP) chairman in late December 1996, while President Zhelyu Zhelev was waiting to hand over power later in January to Petar Stoyanov, the opposition candidate who had convincingly won the presidential elections in October/ November 1996.

CIVIC PROTEST AND POLITICAL WRANGLING

Videnov resigned following widespread public and intra-party criticism. He was widely blamed for Bulgaria's sorry condition, especially for the economy's collapse. In November and December 1996 alone, the lev had dropped from 240 to around 500 against the U.S. dollar, bringing year-end inflation to 311 percent. Wages and pensions had fallen considerably, and by the end of the year, many people found themselves below the poverty line.

Against this dire economic background, political events gained momentum. As the BSP under its new leader Georgi Parvanov tried to regenerate itself and stay in power, popular protest against the party and calls for early parliamentary elections reached dimensions unseen since 1989–1990.

When the BSP Supreme Council met on 3 January to elect a new Executive Bureau, Parvanov proposed a list of 20 members. But the Supreme Council dealt a blow to his authority, reducing the number to 15 and voting against several prominent reformers on the list. The same day, over 40,000 people gathered in central Sofia at a rally organized by the United Democratic Forces (ODS), protesting against the BSP and demanding early elections. The ODS had been formed by the main opposition parties before the presidential elections and comprised the Union of Democratic Forces (SDS), the People's Union (NS), the mainly ethnic Turkish Movement for Rights and Freedoms (DPS), and the Bulgarian Social Democratic Party. Unimpressed by continuing protests in many towns, the BSP on 7 January nominated Interior Minister Nikolay Dobrev as prime minister.

On 10 January, protests reached a qualitatively new level. Protesters blocked the parliament building and some stormed it, trapping Socialist legislators inside and causing considerable damage. The government sent in riot police to break up the blockade. In the ensuing clashes, hundreds were injured, and 295 people had to be hospitalized. Those events further shattered the BSP's credibility and brought about the biggest demonstration thus far: on 12 January, between 50,000 and 200,000 people flooded downtown Sofia. Over the next weeks, protests continued every single day, while work stoppages and blockades of major traffic arteries brought public life to a virtual standstill.

Meanwhile, Zhelev on 10 January said the political situation made it impossible for him to give the BSP a mandate to form a new government. The next day, he called for early elections, while Stoyanov and Dobrev met and agreed that inter-party talks were necessary to solve the crisis. The BSP no longer ruled out early elections in late 1997 but insisted that Dobrev be made premier, while the opposition demanded elections overseen by a caretaker government by May.

On 22 January, Stoyanov and Vice President–elect Todor Kavaldzhiev took office. Stoyanov called for a new "social contract" and urged the Socialists and the opposition to resolve the political crisis, but the two sides were unable to reach a compromise. Finally, on 28 January, Stoyanov in accordance with the constitution gave Dobrev the mandate to form a new government, after unsuccessfully calling on the BSP to refuse that mandate and clear the way for early elections. Amid continuing protests, Dobrev on 3 February announced the lineup of his new government, saying he would present it to Stoyanov the following day.

But on 4 February, Stoyanov brokered a surprising compromise between the major parties to form a caretaker government and hold elections in April. Previously, Dobrev and Parvanov had gone to the president and asked him to choose between two documents—one containing the new government lineup, the other returning the BSP's mandate. Stoyanov instead called a session of the Consultative Council for National Security in which a compromise "in the name of civic peace" was reached. Dobrev and Parvanov had acted without informing their party, knowing their decision meant certain electoral defeat for the BSP, but realizing that if the BSP formed a new government, worse might happen. The Supreme Council on 8 February endorsed their move, knowing there was no alternative. Multi-party talks led by Stoyanov on 10 February led to an agreement to hold elections on 19 April and give the caretaker government extensive powers to deal with the economic crisis and corruption.

During this time, Bulgaria's economic collapse continued. The lev fell from around 500 to $1 in early January to an official record low of 2,937 to $1 on 14 February. On 6–7 February alone, the official exchange rate dropped from 1,638 to 2,608 to $1. By early March, the lev had partly recovered, trading for 1,667 to $1 on 6 March. Monthly inflation was 44 percent in January and 243 percent in February, but dropped sharply after that.

THE APRIL ELECTIONS

On 12 February, Sofia Mayor Stefan Sofiyanski, a leading SDS member, was sworn in as caretaker premier. The next day, the parliament approved his government and voted to dissolve itself. Stoyanov formally dissolved it on 19 February. Sofiyanski's government included many high-profile opposition politicians. Aleksandar Bozhkov was named deputy prime minister and industry minister, ambassador to Germany Stoyan Stalev took over as foreign minister, and Bogomil Bonev was appointed interior minister. Georgi Ananiev became defense minister, Svetoslav Gavriyski, the long-time deputy finance minister in various governments, was appointed finance minister, while Stoyanov's advisor Krasimir Angarski was put in charge of the economy. One of the country's leading trade unionists, the Confederation of Independent Trade Unions in Bulgaria's Deputy Chairman Ivan Neykov, became labor and social minister.

Sofiyanski's cabinet took many necessary but painful decisions, including several price hikes. Most utility prices tripled within days. The cabinet also started purging officials whom it accused of corruption, incompetence, or inefficiency (a move the BSP lambasted as politically motivated), while Bonev launched several high-profile campaigns against alleged criminals. The government started negotiations with the International Monetary Fund (IMF) and the World Bank on structural reform, financial assistance, and the introduction of a currency board. The IMF on 11 April approved a $657 million standby loan to support economic reforms.

An SDS conference on 15–16 February reelected Ivan Kostov as its chairman and decided to transform the SDS from a coalition of parties to a single party. On 22 February, a new party held its inaugural congress: the Euroleft, uniting the Civic Alliance for the Republic (GOR), BSP dissidents, and other reformist leftists. Euroleft elected GOR leader Aleksandar Tomov as its chairman. The SDS and NS after lengthy negotiations decided to contest the April elections together under the ODS banner. DPS Chairman Ahmed Dogan for his part left the ODS and took his party into a new coalition. The National Salvation Union (ONS) united the DPS, ecologists, monarchists, and several small liberal formations. Their ideological and programmatic diversity was overcome by the fact that none of them except for the DPS had any chance of clearing the four-percent threshold on their own, while polls showed that even the DPS could not be absolutely sure to make it alone.

The 19 April elections saw a clear ODS victory. The ODS got 52 percent of the vote, securing 137 out of 240 seats in the National Assembly. The BSP fell to 22 percent (58 seats), the ONS received 7.6 percent (19 seats), the Euroleft 5.6 percent (14 seats), and the Bulgarian Business Bloc of populist Georges Ganchev, 4.9 percent (12 seats). Turnout was just 58 percent, the lowest since the end of one-party rule. The Business Bloc faction was to fall apart in September after expulsions and defections reduced it to nine deputies, one less than the minimum number required for a parliamentary group.

The ODS's triumph was total. It doubled its share over the last elections while the BSP votes halved, and it won in all 31 constituencies, including the so-called "Red Districts" in northwestern Bulgaria. Even in the Vidin constituency, where they did best, the Socialists managed to get only about one third of the vote.

NEW GOVERNMENT INITIATES ECONOMIC REFORMS

On 24 April, the ODS nominated Kostov as prime minister, and Stoyanov invited him to form the new government. The new cabinet included several ODS heavyweights. Bozhkov, Bonev, Ananiev, and Neykov were among those who kept their posts. Evgeniy Bakardzhiev, who had successfully organized the three last SDS/ODS campaigns, became deputy premier and minister of regional development and public works. Nadezhda Mihaylova was named foreign minister, Muravey Radev took over finance, and Vasil Gotsev became justice minister. The new government was approved by the parliament on 21 May by 179 to 55 votes. Only the Socialists voted against it.

The parliament in its inaugural session on 7 May elected Yordan Sokolov of the SDS as its president. At its second meeting on 8 May, the parliament adopted a "Declaration of National Salvation," calling for the establishment of a currency board, the opening of communist secret police files on officials and judges, the full privatization of agricultural land, and membership in NATO and the European Union (EU). (See document on page 250.) Most of its sections were approved by all the parliamentary factions, although the BSP voted against NATO membership.

On 5 June, the parliament approved a law on the introduction of a currency board, an arrangement that automatically ties a country's monetary emissions to its level of hard currency reserves. Currency boards severely restrict the economic flexibility of national governments, but they were used with some success by Estonia and Slovenia to promote international confidence and limit inflation. The lev was pegged to the German mark at a rate of 1,000:1. The government nominated Gavriyski to replace Lyubomir Filipov as Bulgarian National Bank governor. The currency board was introduced on 1 July, the date agreed on with the IMF. Over the next months, the currency board proved to be quite efficient in bringing about economic and financial stabilization. By the end of the year the BNB's foreign-currency reserves had tripled, while inflation stabilized at a fairly low level.

Sofiyanski's government had already set the tone for future reforms. On 21 April, the caretaker government liberalized prices for all foodstuffs except for eight basic staples, and in July most restrictions on foreign currency dealings were lifted. Kostov voiced his determination to streamline the state administration and cut bureaucracy. Neykov announced that by the end of the year 160,000 jobs in the state sector would be scrapped. Bozhkov in March had said that privatization would be "total": on 28 May he announced that the government wanted to transfer 40 percent of state enterprises into private hands in 1997. That target was not met, and although privatization finally picked up, results were disappointing considering the high aims. Bozhkov attributed the slow pace of privatization to "resistance from the state administration." On 17 October, parliament passed a law halving profit taxes for 10 years for foreign investments of $5 million or more and for investments creating at least 100 new jobs. On 7 November, the parliament passed a law restituting all property confiscated by the communist regime to its former owners—including religious communities—or compensating them if their property no longer existed. Four days later, a law restituting forests was passed.

The new government also moved to safeguard economic reforms and crack down on economic and organized crime. The Interior Ministry on 20 May said it would closely monitor all voucher funds set up under the mass privatization scheme, noting that since the caretaker government took office in February, economic crimes amounting to $19 million had been uncovered. In May, Bonev said the National Security Service would investigate clandestine financial groups trying to undermine the new government's economic policies. Privatization Agency Director Asen Dyulgerov demanded heavy fines for regional governors and managers of state-owned companies who interfered with the privatization process, while the Interior Ministry on 24 June announced that Bulgaria will set up a gendarmerie to combat organized crime and guard strategic sites. On 16 July, the parliament amended the insurance law, in a move to stop organized crime from using "insurance companies" as a front for racketeering.

In early June, Kostov told the parliament that Bulgaria must tighten its laws, saying some former members of the state security services "play a vital role in crime." And on 8 July, he said organized crime threatened to destroy state authority and had already virtually replaced it in certain regions. In November, he proposed setting up a special financial police to fight corruption among politicians, police officers, and other state officials.

The start of economic reforms brought renewed backing from abroad. Bulgaria received badly needed loans from the IMF, the World Bank, the European Bank for Reconstruction and Development, and the European Union. And in September, the Central European Free Trade Association (CEFTA) decided to open membership talks with Bulgaria.

Despite the start of reforms, and mainly because of the crisis at the beginning of the year, economic figures for 1997 look disastrous. GDP fell by 7.4 percent, while the budget deficit amounted to 3.6 percent of GDP. Foreign debts equaled $10 billion. Average monthly wages went up slightly, reaching $95 in October. But unemployment also rose, reaching 13.7 percent. Year-end inflation stood at 579 percent, mostly stemming from the first months of the year.

DEALING WITH THE COMMUNIST PAST

Another major issue was the opening of the former communist secret police files. The government on 7 July approved a draft law requiring the opening of all files on members of parliament, ministers, senior state officials, and high-ranking judges. Citizens would have the right to read their own files. One year after the enactment of the law, all files would be transferred to the State Archives and be made available to the public.

On 18 July, the parliament started debating the draft law, which the BSP called unconstitutional and rejected on "national security grounds." On 30 July, the law was passed after the Socialist deputies walked out and the ONS abstained. On 8 August, deputies from the BSP, the ONS, and the BBB took the matter to the Constitutional Court. The court rejected their appeal on 22 September but ordered that the current president, vice-president, and judges of the Constitutional Court not be screened.

Bonev on 22 October disclosed the names of 23 persons who had been found to be former police informers. Among them were 14 parliamentarians from all factions. The most prominent one was undoubtedly DPS leader Ahmed Dogan. According to the files, Dogan cooperated with the secret police between 1974 and 1988; but he denied any wrongdoing and refused to resign. On 18 November, the first "ordinary" citizens were able to read their secret police files.

The government also moved on a new "lustration" law allowing for checks into the political background of civil servants in the communist era. Stoyanov on 23 July said it was too late to pass a law banning former communist officials from holding positions in the state administration. Still, in December the government approved a draft law banning former communist officials from holding such jobs for five years. The draft also stipulated that one year after the law takes effect, civil servants cannot be dismissed following a government change.

Finally, Stoyanov on 10 October signed the Council of Europe Convention for the Protection of National Minorities. But by the end of the year, it had yet to be ratified, as the BSP threatened to take the issue to the Constitutional Court, claiming it might encourage secessionist tendencies.

NEW PRIORITIES IN FOREIGN RELATIONS

1997 also brought major changes to Bulgaria's foreign-policy orientation. In a symbolic move, Stoyanov paid his first foreign visit to Brussels on 29 January, visiting the EU and NATO headquarters. This visit was followed on 17 February by the interim government's announcement that Bulgaria would seek full NATO membership, a position endorsed by Kostov's government. Ultimately, but not surprisingly, Bulgaria was not among the candidates for the first wave of NATO expansion nor on the fast-track list for EU membership talks.

With the accession of Stoyanov to the presidency and the arrival of the Sofiyanski and Kostov governments, Bulgaria's international standing improved considerably. All three, as well as Mihaylova, embarked on a number of high-level and high-profile visits abroad, while many leading foreign politicians visited Bulgaria. Clearly, the West wanted to show support for the former opposition and its bid to reform Bulgaria and bring it closer to European and Atlantic structures. Most of the damage done by Videnov's government to relations with the West and with international financial institutions had been repaired by the end of 1997.

Russia, predictably, was less happy about Sofia's new foreign policy, especially regarding NATO membership. In early October, tensions built up after Russian Foreign Minister Yevgenii Primakov refused to meet Mihaylova during the United Nations General Assembly session in New York. Mihaylova said that this was indicative of Moscow's "unwillingness or inability to use . . . civilized methods" in its foreign relations. Although Mihaylova a few days later said Sofia wanted to give its traditional relations with Russia "new impetus," relations remained tense because of allegations that Russian diplomats stationed in Sofia were engaging in spying, a claim Moscow categorically denied. The parliament on 24 October unanimously adopted a declaration saying relations with Russia should be based on "friendship, mutual benefit, and equal rights," but also in line with Bulgaria's "national interests." Yet, differences remained unresolved at the end of the year, and there were even new problems, this time over Russian gas deliveries to Bulgaria and the role of the joint Topenergy company.

There were also disputes with the United States, over Washington's demand in August that Bulgaria destroy its SS-23 medium-range conventional missiles. Kostov already on 26 July had said their destruction "does not correspond to Bulgaria's current interests and would lead to a serious imbalance of armaments" between Bulgaria and its neighbors, but Mihaylova on 22 August said Sofia was ready to discuss the issue. Washington also urged Sofia to take steps against the thriving pirate CD production in Bulgaria, and in November even threatened trade sanctions.

Bulgaria's relations with most of its neighbors improved in 1997. Relations with Romania and Greece were friendly, but the conflict with Skopje over the question of the existence of a distinct Macedonian nation and language remained unresolved and prevented further progress in bilateral relations. Most importantly, Stoyanov during an official state visit to Turkey removed one of the main obstacles for better relations with Ankara and the Muslim world by apologizing for Bulgaria's attempts to "Bulgarize" its ethnic Turkish minority in the 1980s, a campaign which involved compulsory name changes and other indignities, and caused many Bulgarian Turks to flee the country.

GLOSSARY

BBB	Bulgarian Business Bloc
BSP	Bulgarian Socialist Party
DPS	Movement for Rights and Freedoms
GOR	Civic Alliance for the Republic
NS	People's Union
ODS	United Democratic Forces
ONS	National Salvation Union
SDS	Union of Democratic Forces

Document: DECLARATION OF NATIONAL SALVATION

Declaration of National Salvation, adopted by the National Assembly on 8 May 1997.

We, the representatives of the people in the 38th National Assembly, declare our support for:

1. The agreements between Bulgaria and the international financial institutions, including the introduction of a currency board as a necessary step toward ensuring external support for our efforts to find a way out of the economic catastrophe.

2. A fair distribution of the social cost of the reform.
3. A speedy restitution of agricultural land and the creation of conditions for its effective use.
4. Decisive measures against crime and especially against organized crime and corruption at all levels of state administration regardless of its political color.
5. The opening of the secret files of politicians, senior magistrates and administrators in order to neutralize their dependency on the former security services.
6. The membership of Bulgaria in the European Union and all concrete steps taken in this direction.
7. The membership of Bulgaria in the North Atlantic Treaty Organization.

(*Source: The Insider,* The Documents, Special issue, January 1998, p. II.)

Romania

Population:	22,680,951 (November 1996)
Capital:	Bucharest (pop. 2,066,723)
Major cities:	Constanta (pop. 348,985), Iasi (pop. 337,643), Timisoara (pop. 325,359)
Area:	237,500 sq. km.
Major ethnic groups:	Romanian 89.4%, Hungarian 7.1%, Romani 1.8% (according to 1991 census—although Roma are generally estimated at 7% to 8% of the population)
Economy:	GDP growth: –6.6%
	Inflation rate: 152.0%
	Average monthly wage: $139
	Unemployment rate: 8.8%

A YEAR OF HOPE

by MATYAS SZABO

1997 was the first full year in which the newly elected Ciorbea cabinet exercised its power in Romania. The government, led by the former union leader and Bucharest's elected mayor, Victor Ciorbea, was installed after the 1996 November general elections. The three coalition members—the Democratic Convention of Romania (CDR), the Social Democratic Union (USD) and the Hungarian Democratic Federation of Romania (UDMR)—took power from former president Ion Iliescu's Party of Social Democracy in Romania (PDSR). November 1996 had the potential to be a historic turning point: truly democratic forces took power after seven years of rule by a political party and a president that were guided by neo-communist ideology. The year 1997, therefore, can be considered Romania's first democratic year since the December 1989 uprising.

It was not surprising that the results of a Gallup opinion poll, published on 2 January 1997, showed that Romania was the most optimistic former communist country. At that time 61 percent of Romanians believed that 1997 would be better than 1996.

"POLITICAL PURGES"

President Emil Constantinescu's 7 January vow to combat organized crime and the rampant corruption that had characterized the previous government added considerably to building the new leadership's image, but it was received with strong criticism from the country's nationalist-communist opposition. The ousting of the old guard at the Romanian National Television was the biggest shake-up at the institution since the fall of the communist regime, and it was described by the former ruling party (PDSR) as a "political purge" carried out by the new leadership.

The same label was attributed to the 10 January arrest of Miron Cosma, the leader of a miners' trade union in the Jiu Valley, who led thousands of miners in violent marches on Bucharest in 1990 and 1991. The replacement of the Romanian Army's Chief of the General Staff, Gen. Dumitru Cioflina, and head of logistics Gen. Florentin Popa, were in line with Romania's intention to adhere to "democratic principles," as noted by Ciorbea on 23 January. The move was seen by Adrian Nastase, PDSR deputy chairman, as unjust and having a "serious political motivation." It was also the last straw for the PDSR, which proposed on 25 January a "political and social pact" with Constantinescu, asking him to put an end to the governing coalition's "firings and hirings" among the heads of state institutions. The call fell on deaf ears, and together with Gen. Costica Voicu, head of the Romanian police force, some 20 generals and other high police officers were replaced by the end of February.

Charges of abuse of office did not bypass the banking sector either. Some leading coalition members said that the government would replace the managers of state-owned banks in order to "speed up the reform process," triggering opposition protests against politicizing the banking system. The resignation of Virgil Magureanu, chief of the Romanian Intelligence Service, and of Gen. Decebal Ilina, chief of the Military Intelligence Service, could also be connected to the "political purge" of the new government. The former resigned in April after numerous attacks from journalists and accusations of serving the interests of the KGB, while the latter's July resignation was connected to an earlier statement of Ciorbea, who said, "the country's secret services must undergo a process of de-Sovietization." The dismissal of high-ranking state officials continued with the dismissal on 25 August of Prosecutor-General Nicolae Cochinescu.

The last two months of 1997 brought a new wave of legal procedures launched against those suspected of involvement in efforts to put down the December 1989 uprising; Generals Victor Stanculescu and Mihai Chitac were charged with complicity in murder. Iliescu himself was the target of investigation for his role in the initial stage of the uprising. Together with other members of the provisional leadership, Iliescu ordered troops to open fire on crowds that attempted to assault the state television building.

ECONOMIC REFORMS, SOCIAL UNREST

Ciorbea's reforms were less successful than Constantinescu's efforts to combat crime and corruption. On 30 January Ciorbea told the country that the government's tough reform program, drafted jointly with representatives of the World Bank and the European Union (EU), was the last chance to avoid Romania's "Bulgarization." He accused the former government of giving false reports on economic performance and failing to take timely measures to fight economic deterioration. He pledged to carry out the necessary reforms "whatever the political price" would be, and predicted that the economy would register further decline in 1997.

As early as 5 February, the government announced that it had to delay promises made during the electoral campaign to cut income taxes. Minister of Labor Alexandru Athanasiu said the cabinet could not afford to do so because of an unexpected rise in unemployment due to the planned closing down or privatization of non-productive state enterprises. After several rounds of discussions with union leaders amid growing popular dissatisfaction over a wave of price hikes in January, the government proposed to index salaries, increasing them by more than 30 percent. The wage increase was estimated to compensate for some 75 percent of the price increases.

On 17 February, after consultations with international financial institutions and the major trade unions in Romania, Ciorbea presented the awaited "shock therapy" program of the government. He said 3,600 state companies would be privatized in 1997, those unprofitable would be closed or auctioned off. Within a negotiated social program, the International Monetary Fund (IMF) agreed to lend some $400 million to compensate those most affected by the measures, but

Ciorbea pledged that in the long run Romania would receive $1 billion from international lenders. The "shock therapy" included the immediate liberalization of all prices, and elimination of state subsidies for energy and staples.

The price hikes went into effect less than one day after the package was launched by the cabinet. Gasoline prices, which had already doubled in early January, rose again by 50 percent, the price of rail tickets by 80 percent, of telecommunications by 100 percent, and of electricity by 500 percent. Despite the government's efforts to moderate the effects of its radical reforms, and its 15 March announcement that in the 1997 budget over 10 percent of the GDP would go to social protection, the first large-scale protest against the cabinet's policies took place on 20 March. Energy workers in Bucharest and other Romanian cities demonstrated against the economic measures, calling for the resignation of the government and demanding new contracts and higher salaries.

The international reaction to the "shock therapy" was much more positive. EU finance ministers on 17 March authorized the second installment of a loan approved back in 1994. An installment of $81 million had been withheld because of the previous government's evasive reform implementation, but was now authorized in recognition of the new government's "courageous" reform drive. Poul Thomsen, chief IMF negotiator for Romania, also expressed satisfaction with the government's fiscal and monetary policies, and on 9 April signed a letter of intent with Romanian National Bank Governor Mugur Isarescu for a $400 million loan to support reforms. The loan was granted at the end of the month, and represented a "green light" for foreign investors, and proof of the government's "credible program," as Ciorbea proudly noted. Meanwhile, according to figures released by the Romanian National Agency for Development, foreign investment grew by 35 percent in the first quarter of 1997, compared with the same period of the previous year.

The month of April brought some major decisions concerning the privatization process as well. In less than ten days the cabinet made public the list of 10 state-owned companies facing imminent privatization. It also placed the State Property Fund under direct government control, while parliament approved the bill on the privatization of banks and passed the law on the 1997 budget. The government foresaw a trade deficit amounting to 4.5 percent of GDP, an annual inflation rate of 110 percent, and a 10-percent unemployment rate. With a $550 million World Bank loan approved on 3 June, the government authorized further reform legislation, in the form of an ordinance for the privatization of all state-owned companies within three months, and another providing considerable tax advantages for foreign investors.

The country's population was again hit by the hardships of economic reforms. Thousands of workers protested in the capital on 15 May, calling Ciorbea's cabinet a group of "liars" and "thieves," and demanding a reasonable welfare program. The labor protest quickly spread to other parts of the country, and in the following months Romania was hit by massive demonstrations of miners and of the National Syndicate Bloc, one of the largest trade unions in the country. Trade unions insisted that they should be involved in Ciorbea's negotiations with the IMF, and accused the government of failing to keep them informed about the discussions. Their leaders demanded the resignation of the whole government or an immediate reshuffle.

The second half of the year brought the first worrying signs of international discontent with the pace of reforms. Before a new round of talks with the IMF, in late July Ciorbea admitted that the privatization and restructuring was not as quick as expected, but he stressed that the government had succeeded in bringing about "macrostabilization." President Constantinescu, too, urged the government to speed up the reforms, otherwise he would propose a government reshuffle or possibly the dismissal of the whole cabinet. The government immediately restructured its budget on 6 August, and announced that although the budget continued to be one of "austerity," it would try to protect social welfare, health, and education. The IMF praised the revision, but added that more effort was necessary to liquidate loss-making industries and state farms. Following that criticism, Ciorbea announced on 7 August the "test of fire" for the government's reform program: the government would close down 17 enterprises, which would result in 30,000 people losing their jobs.

Poul Thomsen's proposal that the government offer compensation of a year's salary to those laid off came too late to avoid labor unrest. Some 5,000 workers at a petrol refinery broke the windows of the company's headquarters, while other workers in the same industry blocked the railways and stopped traffic between Bucharest and two major cities. After violent clashes with demonstrators, rail traffic was resumed on 8 August, while the representatives of the main trade unions reached an agreement with Ciorbea on wages for the period August–December. The cabinet kept its promise and on 21 August announced that wages would be raised by 15 percent in August and September and by an additional 14 percent on 1 October.

The conflict with the miners, however, continued in the following months. In late August, the leader of the largest miners' trade union said some 40,000 miners had agreed to the government plan whereby they would receive compensation for volunteering to be unemployed. The union expected some 150,000 of its 210,000 members to opt for the plan eventually, and return to the countryside in Romania's largest workforce migration in 30 years. Still, the miners staged a 24-hour strike on 8 October, demanding a 100-percent wage hike, and threatening a general strike if their demands were not met by 14 October. The conflict was settled on 8 October, when, after meeting with Ciorbea, miners said that a solution was found for all their grievances.

Other trade unions continued their protest against declining living standards. Several thousand members of the Alfa trade union confederation marched in Bucharest on 14 October, demanding immediate measures for social protection. Despite this, discussions between members of the coalition and between the cabinet, the IMF, and the World Bank continued. As of late September the World Bank was saying that it was still satisfied with the "general lines" pursued by the government. One month later, however, the IMF said it was not satisfied with the pace of reforms, particularly that of privatization. After the 4 November decision of Constantinescu and leaders of the ruling coalition to reshuffle the government, inflation soared in Romania, reaching an annual rate of 170 percent. Budget revisions and popular protests followed each other in rapid succession. On 20 November, more than 15,000 members of the Fratia trade union demonstrated in Bucharest and called on the cabinet to resign. Thus, the year ended with growing popular dissatisfaction over declining living standards, and foot-dragging negotiations with IMF on the continuation of the reform program.

POLITICAL COALITION CRISIS

The political situation in the country did little to help economic reforms. Efforts to privatize and restructure the economy were marred by political conflicts between coalition partners, and between the government and the opposition.

The first tension in the ruling coalition emerged on 13 January when Ticu Dumitrescu, head of the Former Political Detainees' Association which was affiliated with the coalition party Democratic Convention of Romania (CDR), suggested that Petre Roman, head of the coalition party Social Democratic Union (USD), shared responsibility with Iliescu for the miners' violent marches on Bucharest in 1990. Ion Diaconescu, chairman of the CDR's National Peasant Party Christian Democratic (PNTCD), the main force in the CDR, tried to prevent the conflict, saying it was natural that Roman, who was prime minister at the time, had to be on Iliescu's side.

The next couple of months were marked by relative peace between coalition partners. Only the split of the liberals spoiled the image: a dissenting wing of the National Liberal Party–Democratic Convention (PNL-CD), a CDR member, on 15 February suspended party chairman Nicolae Cerveni, for his efforts to unite with several liberal parties who were not members of the CDR. They also reproached Cerveni for having failed to gain ministerial posts for PNL-CD members. The two wings of the party finally split in mid-March, allowing Cerveni's supporters to merge with the Liberal Party '93 on 14 June. The bureau of the CDR on 1 August ruled that the new formation had to reapply for CDR membership because it was a "new political formation," but Cerveni refused to do so.

The most damaging conflict within the government coalition was that between the PD and the PNTCD. The first hints of that conflict surfaced in late June when Ciorbea was criticized by the press officer of the foreign ministry, a portfolio led by Adrian Severin of the PD. The Romanian daily *Ziua* quoted ministry spokeswoman Gilda Lazar as saying that Ciorbea was begging for NATO membership and financial assistance during his visit to Washington. The prime minister said it was inappropriate for a person who attacked the head of government to be employed by that administration. Parallel to that conflict, new tensions were growing within the coalition, when Valerian Stan, a member of the PNTCD, released a report that said PD chair Petre Roman, Foreign Minister Adrian Severin, and Transportation Minister Traian Basescu illegally acquired state apartments. Basescu rejected the accusations and said the PD would discuss whether it would be feasible to prolong the existing coalition partnership. PNTCD chairman Ion Diaconescu mentioned, too, the possibility of early elections and forming a new government without the PD. Under a compromise reached on 5 July, the PD agreed to remove the Foreign Ministry spokeswoman; in exchange, the government rebuffed Stan, by placing his department under the direct supervision of the cabinet.

The deal, however, did not calm spirits either in PD or PNTCD. Defense Minister Victor Babiuc, a member of the PD, said on 22 July that his party should prepare an alternative program that would make its "separate Social-Democratic options" more clear to the electorate. He said the dominance of the PNTCD in the present coalition was due to the influence of President Constantinescu.

Severin's 22 September claim that two or three directors of large-circulation dailies were foreign agents, and that two party leaders were also financed from abroad, led to the escalation of the PD-PNTCD conflict. Two intelligence agencies reported to Constantinescu that Severin's allegations were false, and Severin had to resign on 23 December. He was replaced by Andrei Plesu, a leading anti-communist dissident and the first post-communist minister of culture.

Only one week after Severin was replaced, a second PD minister, Traian Basescu, resigned on 29 December. The transport minister handed in his resignation after Ciorbea asked him to take back his critical statements or to step down. Basescu said in an interview that the "government did not have the strength to take important decisions" of the sort requested by foreign institutions.

Meanwhile, several attempts were made to overcome what Constantinescu called on 15 October "misunderstandings, confusion, and unnecessary tensions." The cabinet was reshuffled on 2 December. Three PNTCD ministers, heading the reform, education, and health portfolios, were replaced by ministers with no party affiliations. The PNTCD finance minister took over the industry and commerce portfolio, making room for yet another independent; and the newly established ministry of privatization was given to a former presidential councillor, a PNTCD member. To enhance Ciorbea's authority within the PNTCD and the coalition, he was elected the party's deputy chair on 5 December.

Another conflict that contributed significantly to the deepening of the coalition crisis was the dispute between the Hungarian Democratic Federation of Romania (UDMR) and the PNTCD. The UDMR entered the governmental coalition hoping that it would be able to influence decisions affecting the Hungarian minority. The government agreed, among other things, to amend a 1994 educational law that the UDMR saw as discriminatory. The 18 May amendments provided for instruction in the mother tongue at all levels of education and abolished the provision that national minorities must study subjects such as history and geography in Romanian. However, the amendments still had to be passed by the parliament. At the end of June the UDMR threatened to withdraw its support from the coalition unless the amendments were implemented by government ordinance in time for the new school year. Despite protests from the PNTCD, on 9 July the amendment was approved by government ordinance. Negotiations continued over drawing up a version of the law that was "mutually acceptable" to both the UDMR and PNTCD. In the senate, however, representatives of the PNTCD voted in favor of opposition amendments, forbidding separate universities for national minorities or separate minority sections in existing universities. The UDMR on 10 December announced that it had suspended its participation in the cabinet, but reversed itself after President Constantinescu promised that he would refuse to promulgate a law that infringed on the right of minorities to set up independent universities.

THE OPPOSITION GATHERS FORCE

The cabinet's work was hindered not only by internal conflicts but also by constant attacks and accusations that came from the side of the opposition. As expected, the rhetoric of the left-wing PDSR parties, and of the two extreme nationalist parties, the Greater Romania Party (PRM) and the Party of Romanian National Unity (PUNR), differed little when attacking the new government's and ruling coalition's economic, foreign, and minority policies.

As early as 4 January, the PDSR accused the cabinet of failing to keep its electoral promises, and at the beginning of March it announced that it would start monitoring the implementation of "Contract with Romania," the ruling coalition's electoral program. In June the opposition gathered the signatures of 140 deputies on a no-confidence motion but the motion was easily defeated by the ruling coalition. A second motion several days later condemning the government's new program also failed.

As workers' protests spread in the country during the second half of the year, the opposition used every opportunity to "politicize" their demands. At the beginning of October some 500 "revolutionaries" who took part in the December 1989 uprising started a demonstration in Bucharest, demanding that the government withdraw its earlier decision to limit their special benefits. Iliescu was present at the demonstration and denounced the cabinet's intention as a "political diversion." The "revolutionaries" went on a hunger strike, and one of them set himself ablaze. The PDSR walked out of the senate after Iliescu was accused by the ruling PNTCD of "destabilizing the country" by encouraging the strikers. One week later, at a 21 October press conference, Iliescu read aloud a "Letter to the Nation" calling upon the cabinet to "leave the political scene, making room for others who are more diligent and more loyal to the country's interests." On 30 October the government created a special commission to review the strikers' cases, and the demonstrators ended their 23-day protest.

In addition to attacking the government's economic performance, the opposition homed in on their foreign affairs and minority policies. After the UDMR joined the governmental coalition, the issue of inter-ethnic relations in Transylvania and the rights of the ethnic Hungarians became a constant field of tension. A leading role was played by Gheorghe Funar, chair of the Party of Romanian National Unity (PUNR), and after his March dismissal, mayor of Cluj. He tried to stop the reopening of the Hungarian consulate in Cluj; to cancel Hungarian President Arpad Goncz's visit to the town; and to remove the Hungarian flag from the Cluj consulate. He also hindered the implementation of the government ordinance that allowed the use of bilingual signs in localities where minorities made up at least 20 percent of the population. The unity of nationalist forces became more and more obvious in the second half of the year. On 21 September, the PUNR, the PRM, and the Socialist Unity Party organized a demonstration in Targu Mures against Hungarian ethnic minority influence on government policies. They called for an alliance of nationalist and leftist forces. In mid-November, the PUNR made an anti-Hungarian motion in the parliament, asking for a debate on the situation of Romanians in Harghita and Covasna, the two counties where Hungarians constitute a majority. The motion, which was supported by the PDSR, PRM, and the Alliance for Romania, also called for launching a "national program" to prevent the assimilation of the Romanians living there.

The cabinet's foreign policy, its intentions to improve Romania's relationship with its neighbors, and particularly its negotiations over the Romanian-Ukrainian basic treaty were also targets of the nationalist opposition's attacks. On 7 February PRM chair Corneliu Vadim Tudor demanded Constantinescu's impeachment for high treason for his statement that Romania had no territorial claims against Ukraine. After the treaty was initialed on 3 May, Tudor said the treaty "was the most serious act of national treason in Romania's modern history." The PUNR also opposed it because it did not include a denunciation of the 1939 Molotov-Ribbentrop pact and did not clarify the issue of Serpent's Island.

In contrast with the apparent unity of the opposition in criticizing all major steps taken by the Ciorbea cabinet, the PDSR and the PUNR went through serious internal crises. On 17 January, when Iliescu was elected PDSR chairman, he pledged to renew both the membership and the policies of the party, stressing the need to combat corruption within its ranks. In early May, however, the Sibiu branch of the PDSR accused Iliescu of failing to remove party members "with a dubious image," and urged Deputy Chairman Teodor Melescanu, the previous government's foreign minister, to replace Iliescu as party chair. Next month a new division appeared within PDSR when Iosif Boda, Iliescu's presidential campaign manager in 1996, demanded the resignation of Nastase. Other members joined the reformist wing, and demanded that the party dissociate itself from those involved in "notorious acts of corruption." The reformist group left the party at the end of the 20–21 June national conference, and announced the establishment of a new political formation, called the Alliance for Romania (APR). Melescanu, the acting chair, said the center-left, social-democratic APR was represented in the parliament by 13 deputies and two senators.

The PUNR had also entered a period of internal crisis in February, when it ousted its leader, Gheorghe Funar, blaming him for the party's poor performance in the November 1996 elections. Valeriu Tabara, a former agriculture minister, was elected interim president. The internal turmoil deepened: Funar refused to recognize the legality of his own dismissal. He was eventually expelled from the party in November for refusing to withdraw lawsuits against other party members. His supporters met in Cluj on 22 November and invalidated the decision to expel him, and suspended Tabara as chairman. On 29 November the two rival groups held separate gatherings: in Cluj Funar was reelected chairman, while Tabara's group in Bucharest decided to suspend all those members who attended the meeting in Cluj.

The only attempt to unite the opposition's forces was the 15 September agreement of PDSR, PRM, and the extra-parliamentary Socialist Labor Party (PSM) representatives, who said their main aim was to bring about a change in the ruling coalition. The alliance was called off by PRM chair Corneliu Vadim Tudor after Iliescu called on him and on PSM leader Adrian Paunescu to "temper" their extreme nationalist postures. Tudor said he rejected Iliescu's attempt to unite the opposition and to return as the head of state, and remarked that a "genuine national opposition" could only be formed around himself, Paunescu, and Funar.

FOREIGN POLICY

Last, but not least, 1997 also represented Romania's most intensive year after the fall of communism in boosting and improving its relations with foreign countries. As Severin announced on 28 January, outlining the new government's foreign policy priorities, in order to boost its chances of early admission into NATO, Romania put improved ties with its neighbors, particularly with Ukraine, at the top of its agenda.

In Bucharest on 9 January, U.S. Defense Under-Secretary for Policy Walter Slocombe said that Romania's chances of early admission to NATO had significantly increased following the democratic elections. Romania launched an unprecedented diplomatic "offensive" for NATO admission, both in the Western world and in the neighboring countries. Constantinescu's first official trip abroad since his election was to Poland, where he agreed with President Aleksander Kwasniewski that the two countries would cooperate in their efforts to join NATO. Severin suggested the same cooperation to his Hungarian counterpart Laszlo Kovacs: the two countries should join the alliance simultaneously, he wrote to Kovacs in mid-January. Hungary said the admission of one country into NATO ahead of the other would not destabilize the region, but Hungarian President Arpad Goncz promised in Bucharest that his country would do "everything it can" to push for Romania's inclusion in the first wave.

Since settling disputes with all neighbors was a condition for NATO integration, Romania appeared to be under pressure to finalize the basic treaty with Ukraine before the July NATO summit. In January the bilateral treaty negotiators agreed to resume talks in Kyiv after examining proposals submitted by each side. Severin said Bucharest would propose a "compromise package" to settle unresolved issues, but wanted the treaty to include the condemnation of the 1939 Molotov-Ribbentrop pact, and guarantees for the 400,000-strong Romanian minority living in Ukraine. The talks seemed to stall for a short while, after Ukrainian President Leonid Kuchma said in early February in Davos that Romania should not be allowed to join NATO before signing the bilateral treaty. Severin emphasized that Romania had no territorial claims on Ukraine, and said that Kuchma's attitude was "unsuitable" and amounted to "blackmail." Despite the opposition's strong attacks on the treaty, the friendship document was initialed on 3 May and signed by the two presidents on 2 June.

The Russian foreign ministry welcomed the signing of the treaty and said the document would in no way influence the still pending bilateral treaty between Russia and Romania. Russia wanted, however, to base the bilateral treaty on a text agreed upon with the previous Romanian government in April 1996. That text made no mention of the Molotov-Ribbentrop pact. The two sides agreed on 29 August to relaunch talks on the treaty. Though Romania renounced its insistence that the condemnation of the Ribbentrop-Molotov pact be included in the treaty, the problem of returning the Romanian treasury which had been sent to Russia for safekeeping during World War I became an issue that hindered the conclusion of the final text, which remained unsigned at year's end.

Another pending bilateral treaty on which talks were resumed after the November 1996 election was the one with neighboring Moldova. Severin and his Moldovan counterpart, Mihai Popov, agreed in Bucharest on 5 April to speed up the conclusion of the treaty. Moldova wanted to be certain that the treaty reflected "today's realities and the interests of both countries." As Romania was insisting on a document that mentioned the "special relationship" of the two countries based on their unity of culture, history and language, Moldovan Prime Minister Ion Ciubuc stressed on 17 May that the treaty must be "one of friendship and cooperation, and not one of fraternity."

A much stronger and more important element of Romania's foreign policy in 1997 was the diplomatic offensive that the country launched for admission to NATO in the first wave. Romanian high state officials' visits to Western capitals, including Brussels, Paris, Bonn, Madrid, and Washington, were all aimed at promoting the country's early admission. French President Jacques Chirac was the first one to say that his country would strongly plead Romania's case to its NATO allies. Italy, Spain, Greece, and Portugal also expressed their support for Romania's admission in the first wave, while the United States, Britain, Germany, Norway, and the Netherlands expressed in different ways that they had not yet decided which countries should be invited to join the enlarged NATO at the July Madrid summit.

U.S. President Bill Clinton announced on 12 June that only the Czech Republic, Hungary, and Poland should be included in the first round of NATO expansion. Ciorbea made a last trip to the United States, but the only encouraging words that he could get were those of Defense Secretary William Cohen, who said that the United States did not say "no" to Romania's bid, but only "not yet." Constantinescu told a NATO security forum in Prague on 23 June that the Romanian people would regard the United States as "cynical and incapable of analyzing global interests" if his country were left out.

The 8 July historic NATO summit in Madrid did not invite Romania to join the alliance. Two days later, the European Union Commission also rejected Romanian inclusion in its first enlargement wave. Clinton visited Romania and on 11 July addressed a huge crowd in Bucharest, urging them to "stay the course" in implementing economic reforms and democratization. Romania would be one of the strongest candidates to join NATO in the near future if they did so, he concluded.

Ciorbea sadly noted that "everything humanly possible" had been done to enable Romania to join NATO in the first wave, but that the gap left by the previous government between Romania and other contenders had been too large to bridge in seven months.

GLOSSARY

CDR	Democratic Convention of Romania
PDSR	Party of Social Democracy in Romania
PNL-CD	National Liberal Party-Democratic Convention
PNTCD	National Peasant Party Christian Democratic
PRM	Greater Romania Party
PSM	Socialist Labor Party
PUNR	Party of Romanian National Unity (PUNR)
UDMR	Union Hungarian Democratic Federation of Romania
USD	Social Democratic Union

Moldova

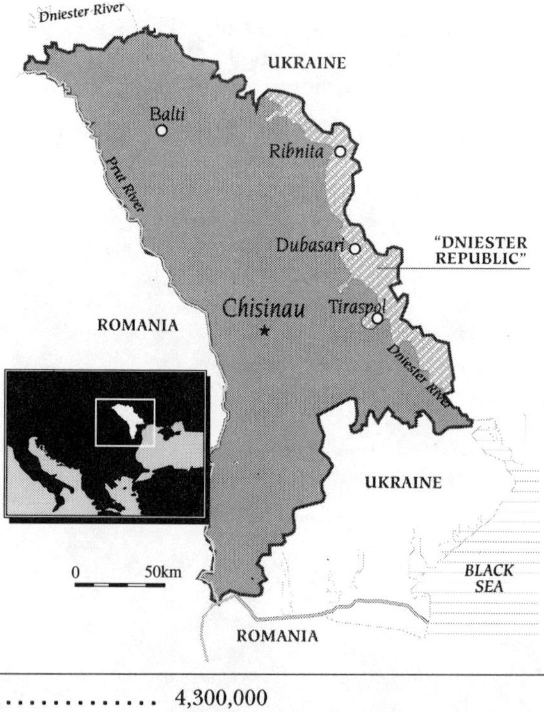

Population:	4,300,000
Capital:	Chisinau (pop. 754,000)
Major cities:	Tiraspol (capital of the self-proclaimed "Dniester Republic," pop. 185,000), Balti (pop. 158,000)
Area:	33,700 sq. km.
Major ethnic groups:	Moldovan 65%, Ukrainian 14%, Russian 13%, Gagauz 3.5%
Economy:	GDP growth: 1.3%
....	Inflation rate: 11.8%
....	Average monthly wage: $45
....	Unemployment rate: 1.7%

IN SEARCH OF STABILITY

by DAN IONESCU

The year 1997 started in the shadow of the November–December presidential election, which brought about a significant change in Moldova's leadership. President-elect Petru Lucinschi on 9 January handed in his resignation as parliament speaker. On 15 January, he was sworn in as the country's second president since Moldova declared its independence from the Soviet Union in August 1991. Lucinschi replaced Mircea Snegur, whom he defeated in a run-off on 1 December 1996. In his inaugural speech, the president repeated his electoral pledge to ensure the country's "stability, order, and prosperity," and proclaimed "normalization" of the situation in the breakaway Dniester region a top priority for his administration.

On 16 January, he nominated Ion Ciubuc, a trained economist and head of the State Auditing Office, to form a new cabinet, which was eventually approved by parliament—together with its governing program—on 24 January. Ciubuc claimed his cabinet was mainly one of technocrats, whose political views were irrelevant. He promised the government would restructure the economy, reduce budget expenditure, foster privatization in industry, launch privatization in agriculture, and break the state monopoly in the energy sector to help overcome an endemic crisis there. Lucinschi aired nevertheless dissatisfaction over the cabinet's lineup, suggesting that he was not able to keep his electoral pledge of including "young, promising professionals" in the executive, mainly because of a "stubborn parliamentary majority."

Despite his own background in parliament, the new president soon found himself trapped in a confrontation with the legislature reminiscent in many ways—albeit in a less overt and dramatic vein—of the one his predecessor had to face in 1995–96. Growing opposition from the Socialist Unity faction, the Communist Party (PCRM), and segments of the ruling Agrarian Democratic Party (PDAM) often made difficult the adoption of badly needed legislation to help reform the economy and society.

One of Lucinschi's main handicaps was that he had no clear political force behind him—a force able to defend his own views in parliament. Things changed on 8 February, when his supporters decided to set up the Movement for a Democratic and Prosperous Moldova (MPMDP), headed by Deputy Parliament Chairman Dumitru Diacov, who had previously quit the PDAM together with several other politicians. MPMDP declared itself a centrist organization with some affinities with both the moderate left and right, and vowed to overtly promote the president's political platform. Some ten months later (24 September), the pro-Lucinschi movement announced the creation of a political bloc to include several (minor) political and civic groupings.

In January, Diacov, who had been one of the organizers of Lucinschi's election campaign, failed in his effort to replace the latter as parliament's speaker. But he could garner enough support to delay for nearly two months the election to that post of the rival candidate, PDAM leader Dumitru Motpan, thus pushing the legislature to the verge of a serious crisis. After repeatedly failing to win the required 50 percent of the vote, Motpan was eventually elected on 5 March, to preside over a parliament dominated by conservative and leftist forces.

Some of those forces which had supported Lucinschi in the second round of the presidential election ostentatiously changed sides, declaring themselves against the new administration. On 22 March, the communist leader Vladimir Voronin asked his party to do its best to shorten the government's life. And in late April, he sharply criticized the new president, and suggested that the communists' electoral support for Lucinschi had been dictated by the "lesser evil" principle. Similarly, the Socialist Unity faction—the second-largest in parliament after the PDAM—announced on 26 March that it was moving into "constructive opposition" to the government. As early as late January, the faction, which largely represents the interests of the Russian-speaking population, had expressed "particular concern" over what it described as the cabinet's "mono-ethnic" (read: purely Moldovan) composition.

In a more diplomatic, though unequivocal tone, Motpan on 14 June told the PDAM fourth congress that his party was not prepared to "accept full responsibility" for the cabinet's policies, and denounced the latter's economic reform program as "rudimentary" and "amendable." In response to this criticism, premier Ciubuc urged the PDAM deputies to rally behind that program. The main bone of contention appeared to be the draft of a law on reforming the farming sector, mainly by allowing the purchase of land—a piece of legislation that was opposed by some radicals within the PDAM. That law was bitterly attacked by the communists as well. By early August, they had already collected 200,000 signatures in favor of staging a national referendum on the issue, but their initiative failed to materialize, and the law was finally approved by parliament on 25 July and promulgated by Lucinschi on 27 August. The communists, however, did not abandon the fight. Together with the Socialist Unity faction, they proposed a package of three referenda—against selling land, raising the retirement age from 60 to 65 years, and reforming the country's administrative division. The parliament turned down the proposal on 10 October, much to the dismay of Voronin, who accused it, in the purest Bolshevik style, of "betraying the interests of the people."

Such attacks, coming from the left end of the political spectrum, helped to consolidate the solidarity between the presidency and the executive, despite Lucinschi's initial doubts about the new team's professionalism. This, in turn, prompted Voronin to speak (as far back as April) of a "pocket cabinet," which was merely executing Lucinschi's orders.

At the same time, the conservative/leftist majority in parliament focused on putting their own house in order. Following a proposal by Motpan, Diacov was dismissed as deputy chairman on 17 July. The move came in retaliation to Diacov's repeated calls for early elections, meant to bring the parliament's structure in line with a changing political environment. However, the PDAM majority faction was not exempt from infighting and even splits. On 22 July, eleven deputies announced they were leaving the faction; and on 10 November, the PDAM Council expelled 15 dissident deputies from the party.

The opposition, on the other hand, made some attempts to overcome its own divisions, with an eye on the 1998 parliamentary elections. Snegur's Party of Revival and Accord (PRCM) and the pro-Romanian Christian Democratic Popular Front (FPCD) formally joined forces in the Democratic Convention of Moldova (CDM) on 19 June. Another important center-right organization, the Party of Democratic Forces, lead by Valeriu Matei, refused to join the alliance. The idea of a right-wing bloc had been launched by Snegur on 25 March and further developed in an "Appeal to the Nation," issued in early June.

The far-left forces were quick to react to this challenge by closing their own ranks. At a constituent congress held in the town of Balti on 21 June, the Unitate/Edinstvo Movement for Equal Rights, the Socialist Party, and the Union of Moldovan Communists (a group of hard-liners which had split from the PCRM in February) decided to set up a Bloc of Popular-Patriotic Forces. The new alliance harshly criticized the government, accusing it of keeping the population in "a labyrinth of destructive reforms."

Political confrontation intensified after the campaign for the next parliamentary election was officially launched. On 19 November, President Lucinschi set the date for the election on 22 March 1998; and on 24 November, the parliament passed the new electoral law, which was promulgated by the president on 6 December. On 16 December, the parliament approved the make-up of the Central Electoral Commission, whose task was to supervise both the campaign and the election itself. The first formation to register with the panel was the CDM on 23 December, followed by the PCRM on 26 December.

Lucinschi took advantage of the first anniversary of his own victory in the 1996 presidential race to state on 1 December that the pre-electoral struggle was "heating up the atmosphere" within society at large and even had a "negative impact" on economic life at local levels. He repeated his view that the current semi-presidential system hindered the promotion of reforms, urging Moldovans to opt for either a full presidential or a full parliamentary system.

ECONOMY AND SOCIETY

Despite his rather limited powers, Lucinschi tried to encourage reforms as much as he could. On 24 January, he signed a decree providing for urgent measures to be taken in order to improve the social and economic situation in Moldova; and on 5 March he urged the parliament and all political forces in the country to help create legal, economic, organizational, and political conditions for speeding up reforms. The appeal was repeated in a further address to parliament on 27 June. More specifically, he called upon the parliament (on 26 May) to pass the privatization program for 1997–1998 without delay. The bill, which was adopted in an amended form on 25 June after heated debates, envisaged the privatization of 580 state enterprises. But the privatization drive was overshadowed by suspicions of preferential treatment for well-connected bidders. On 10 June, Privatization Minister Ceslav Ciobanu was forced to resign over his role in the sale of a sanitarium to a private university in which his wife had a 16-percent share.

The state of Moldova's economy remained rather desolate throughout the year, with few signs of recovery in sight for the near future. In early November, the IMF and the World Bank warned they would withhold further loan installments, pointing at a budgetary deficit expected to reach 7 percent of GDP in 1997 (as against the 4.5 percent agreed on with the international financial organizations). But on 12 December, Moldova's main international creditors decided at a meeting in Paris to continue supporting the country's economic modernization, despite its rather poor performance.

The trade deficit continued to grow, reaching nearly $344 million in 1997 (or 17 percent of the total foreign-trade volume). Moldova's external debt mounted up by $60 million, reaching $709 million by the end of the year.

The government, however, claimed to have achieved a certain degree of macro-economic stabilization. Moldovan officials (including Lucinschi) maintained not only that the economic decline of the last six years was halted in 1997, but also that 1.3 percent growth was registered as against 1996. Yet they admitted that a true recovery could not be expected in the next several years. Among other positive aspects in 1997, the government cited the stability of the national currency, the Moldovan leu; a reduction of the annual inflation rate from 15.1 percent in 1996 to 11.2 percent in 1997; and a near doubling of foreign investments, which reached some $275 million. Economic experts, however, expressed doubts about the accuracy of the modest growth assumption, pointing at the huge (by Moldovan standards) losses in agriculture caused by bad weather in spring and summer (some $150 million).

Some analysts noticed that reforming the economy was apparently not the number-one priority for the new administration, which seemed more interested in ways to soothe the social grievances provoked by the transition from a state-controlled to a free market economy. As in the Russian Federation, one of the most serious issues was the accumulation of huge salary and pension arrears. Though Ciubuc's team was quite successful in paying back some 85 percent of the debts, some reports indicated that the arrears were again on the rise by December. At the same time, the average monthly salary remained low (some $50), less than half the minimum consumer budget ($103 in December), which places Moldova among Europe's poorest nations.

Lucinschi tried to take steps against another scourge affecting the society, namely rampant corruption at all levels. On 10 April, he approved the creation of a department specializing in the prevention of organized crime and corruption and designated its head. But his decrees were reversed on 21 July by the Constitutional Court, which ruled that the president had exceeded his prerogatives.

In view of continuing social hardship, the outcome of a poll conducted in late December came as no surprise for observers of the Moldovan scene. According to it, nearly half of the population (49 percent) considered 1997 a more difficult year than the previous one.

THE DNIESTER ISSUE

Lucinschi's initial optimism over the possibility of reaching a final settlement of the Dniester conflict in 1997 proved unrealistic. The year brought only modest progress in negotiations, despite the occasional feeling that a breakthrough was closer than any time since the region's separation from Moldova in 1990–1991. That feeling was particularly strong after the visit of Russian Foreign Minister Yevgenii Primakov to Chisinau on 10–11 April. Primakov succeeded in convincing the two sides to resume negotiations over the text of a "Memorandum on the Principles of Normalizing [Mutual] Relations." The document had been initialed in June 1996, but Moldova later refused to sign it, suggesting that the memorandum was encroaching on Moldova's sovereignty and territorial integrity. This view was shared in late February by the head of the mission of the Organization for Security and Cooperation in Europe (OSCE) in Moldova. This caused an angry reaction in Tiraspol, the capital of the Dniester region, which materialized in a ban on OSCE activities in the region in March and early April. At Primakov's insistence, an article was added to the original document, proclaiming the idea of a "common state" within the borders of the Moldovan Soviet Socialist Republic as of January 1990, i.e., before the separation took place.

Lucinschi and the Dniester leader Igor Smirnov signed the memorandum on 8 May in Moscow, in the presence of Russian President Boris Yeltsin and his Ukrainian counterpart, Leonid Kuchma. In a supplementary statement, Russia, Ukraine, and the OSCE committed themselves to act as guarantors in the peace process. But within days of the signing ceremony, the two signatories started offering conflicting interpretations of the document. Tiraspol repeatedly stressed its determination to retain all attributes of distinct statehood, including its presidency, parliament, army, constitution, and state symbols. Besides, the maverick Smirnov never retracted earlier statements, according to which his land was seeking to join the Russian-Belarus Union and to be accepted as a distinct member of the Commonwealth of Independent States (CIS). In the Moldovan capital of Chisinau, the opposition accused Lucinschi of giving in to the separatists' pressure and accepting the de facto confederalization of the republic.

Consequently, Chisinau and Tiraspol failed to sign a further agreement intended to regulate the division of powers between central and local authorities. The text had been agreed to by a meeting of experts in a Moscow suburb on 5–9 October. But Smirnov snubbed the 23 October CIS summit in Chisinau at which the document was supposed to be solemnly signed.

The only encouraging development appeared to be the signing in Chisinau on 10 November of an understanding aimed at exploring the ways to restore a minimum of economic and social cooperation between the two sides. Again, analysts warned against overwrought expectations.

In the meantime, the Russian military presence in the Transdniester region continued, though the contingent (formerly the 14th Army) was down-sized in the first months of 1997 from 5,000 to some 3,000 men. Tiraspol strongly opposed any withdrawal of Russian troops, military equipment, or ammunition from the region. The self-proclaimed "Dniester Moldovan Republic" received logistic support from leftist and conservative political circles in Moscow, and especially from the State Duma, the lower chamber of the Russian parliament. In February, the Duma set up a special panel to deal with the Dniester issue, a fact resented by Chisinau as interference in its domestic affairs. And in late October, Duma Chairman Gennadii Seleznev visited both Chisinau and Tiraspol in what was perceived as a show of support for the separatists.

FOREIGN RELATIONS

Russia's stance on the Dniester issue inevitably cast some shadow on Russo-Moldovan relations. In an address delivered to the UN General Assembly on 29 September, Moldovan Foreign Minister Nicolae Tabacaru charged Moscow with dragging its feet over the agreed withdrawal of its troops and weapons from the Dniester area. Lucinschi, in turn, said in an interview in October that bilateral ties, including mutual trade, were strongly affected by the fallout of the Dniester conflict. Despite this rhetoric, Lucinschi did not hesitate to repeatedly call Russia Moldova's "strategic partner." He also advocated on every possible occasion boosting relations with both the Russian Federation and the CIS. Lucinschi discussed bilateral relations with Yeltsin in Moscow on 25 February; spoke up in favor of closer integration at a CIS summit in Moscow on 28 March; and asked Yeltsin to intercede in the Dniester issue on 8 May and again on 8–9 September, when he attended the celebrations for Moscow's 850th anniversary.

This prompted the opposition to accuse Lucinschi of pro-Russian sentiments and to recall that he had been the ethnic Moldovan who had occupied the highest position in the hierarchy of the former Communist Party of the Soviet Union (that of Central Committee secretary). In response to such attacks, Lucinschi used to stress his country's economic dependence on the former Soviet space, and especially on Russian energy. Moldova's debts for natural gas deliveries from Russia rose, indeed, to some $500 million, of which the Dniester region had the lion's share (though not the slightest intention to assume responsibility for them). Threats by the almighty Russian Gazprom company to cut gas supplies to Moldova were denounced by the Moldovan opposition as an attempt to blackmail the country, both economically and politically. On 23 September, visiting Russian Deputy Prime Minister Valerii Serov signed an agreement providing for deliveries of Moldovan agricultural products in exchange for Russian gas supplies.

According to some commentators, the number of high-ranking Russian officials who visited Moldova in 1997 was higher than in all previous five years of independence combined. Apart from Primakov and Serov, the list included, among many others, Russian Defense Council Secretary Yurii Baturin (February) and the ministers for CIS affairs Aman Tuleev and Anatolii Adamishin (April and November, respectively). Yeltsin was also in Chisinau, to attend the 21st CIS heads of state summit, on 22–23 October. He was accompanied by Defense Minister Igor Sergeev, who seized the opportunity to visit Tiraspol on 23 October.

Russia jealously watched Ukraine's attempts to step up its mediation efforts in the Dniester conflict, as well as its relations with Moldova in general. In March, President Kuchma was in Chisinau to discuss, among other things, the possible participation of Ukrainian troops in the Dniester peacekeeping forces. On 22 July, the Russian representative on the Joint Control Commission stated that his country was opposed to the presence of a Ukrainian contingent in the security zone on the Dniester river. Earlier that month (July 3), Kuchma met Lucinschi and the Romanian President Emil Constantinescu in the Ukrainian port of Izmail on the Danube to boost cooperation among the three countries. The presidents agreed to set up two Euro-regions: the Lower Danube and the Upper Prut—a project which remained largely on paper. They also signed an agreement on combating organized crime, as well as weapons and drugs smuggling. The accord was followed by a joint declaration of the interior ministers of the three countries, issued in Chisinau on 14 November.

Relations with the CIS were another priority of the Lucinschi administration. Chisinau played the host to sessions of the CIS Councils of Interior Ministers and of Heads of Security and Secret Service Agencies, in March and October, respectively. As for the 22–23 October CIS summit in Chisinau, it was the first of the kind to take place in Moldova. FPCD leader Iurie Rosca denounced the meeting as a further step toward Moldova's "incorporation into a Russian-dominated economic, political, military, and informational space." The summit's outcome, however, was far from encouraging for the future of the organization.

For its part, Moldova had a strong interest in reviving trade ties with other CIS countries, which were declining following a decision by Ukraine to impose tax deposits for Moldovan exports transiting its territory. Economic reasons were also behind Moldova's decision to join a closer partnership with Georgia, Ukraine, and Azerbaijan, the "GUAM" group. The decision was taken following a series of meetings of the four countries' presidents on the sidelines of the Council of Europe summit in Strasbourg on 10–11 October. Moldova hoped to be chosen as a transit country for possible exports of Azeri oil via Georgia and Ukraine. Lucinschi stressed the importance of the Caspian oil issue while addressing in Chisinau on 10 October the 10th Parliamentary Assembly of the Black Sea Economic Cooperation, an organization set up in 1993 to which all four countries belong. And on 26–29 October, he paid a visit to Azerbaijan and Georgia.

Conservative forces, for their part, seemed more interested in other forms of closer cooperation: 57 out of parliament's 104 members on 21 April welcomed the Russian-Belarus Union Treaty as a positive example of "further integration within the CIS." This prompted an outcry from the opposition. Snegur's PRCM described the appeal as a "cynical betrayal" of Moldova's interests and an indication that those forces were striving to turn the country into a [Russian] "colony." Lucinschi tried to calm down the spirits by stating that his country had no intention of pursuing the Russian-Belarus model.

Moldova's relations with neighboring Romania were less dominated by big words and more by a policy of small steps. The two sides resumed talks on concluding a bilateral basic treaty that had ground to a halt in fall 1996. They were unable to complete the draft document, mainly because of Romania's insistence that the treaty include a clause denouncing the 1939 Molotov-Ribbentrop pact which forced Romania to cede the province of Bessarabia to the Soviet Union. (Parts of that province make up the core of today's Republic of Moldova.) In addition, Romania wanted the document to mention the "special relationship" of the two countries, based on their common culture, history, and language. Chisinau, on the other hand, was reluctant to sign a treaty of "fraternity" instead of one of "friendship and cooperation," for fear of letting the door open to future territorial claims on behalf of Romania.

Such apprehensions were visible in spiritual life as well. Throughout 1997, the Moldovan authorities stubbornly refused to officially recognize the Bucharest-subordinated Bessarabian Metropolitan Church (reestablished in 1993), and continued to support by all means the Moscow-subordinated Moldovan Metropolitan Church. The religious conflict led not only to a schism within the Orthodox community but also to a deep division in the society at large.

Other developments suggested that Chisinau was trying to balance every overture toward Romania by further strengthening its traditional ties to Moscow. On 24–25 July, Defense Minister Valeriu Pasat went to Bucharest, where he signed an agreement on cooperation in military transportation and agreed to set up a joint peacekeeping unit with Romania. On 28 July he was in Moscow, leaving the impression that he was reporting on his recent Romanian visit. There, he signed an agreement on military cooperation with Russian Defense Minister Sergeev. The document provided for the training of Moldovan officers in Russia and for conducting joint maneuvers of peacekeeping units.

Duplicity seemed to hang over Moldova's increased appetite for closer relations with the West as well. While visiting Chisinau on 10 February, NATO Secretary General Javier Solana was told that Moldova was sticking to its neutrality. The country was nevertheless eager to seek closer cooperation with NATO and to serve as a bridge between the alliance and Russia. Only two days later, Baturin arrived in Chisinau to criticize NATO and its expansion plans. This did not prevent Moldova from organizing in May the first Partnership for Peace exercise to take place in a former Soviet republic. Some 80 U.S. medical troops took part in the exercise, bearing the name Medceur '97. Together with about 250 Moldovan troops, they simulated an emergency rescue operation. Moreover, U.S. Deputy Defense Secretary John White signed an agreement in Chisinau on 23 June on preventing the proliferation of mass destruction weapons. And in November, Moldova was in the news when the United States announced that it had bought 21 Soviet-built MiG-29C jets from Moldova in order to prevent their sale to "rogue nations."

Lucinschi attended the NATO summit in Madrid on 9 July and addressed the next day the economic summit of Eastern and Central European States in Salzburg. In order to stress Moldova's interest in developing relations with the West, the president also paid official visits to France and Italy in September and received Council of Europe Secretary General Daniel Tarschys in early July, as well as the presidents of two countries with a good prospect to join both NATO and the European Union (EU) in a predictable future: Arpad Goncz of Hungary in October and Aleksander Kwasniewski of Poland in December. On 12 December, Lucinschi addressed an appeal to the heads of the EU member states to support his country in launching negotiations on associate membership. According to the letter, Moldova's strategic target was to become a full EU member, since, it argued, historically and culturally the country was an "integral part of European civilization." The appeal failed to convince Lucinschi's critics at home, who said it was designed to divert attention from the administration's pro-Russian policies.

GLOSSARY

CDM	Democratic Convention of Moldova
FPCD	Christian Democratic Popular Front
MPMDP	Movement for a Democratic and Prosperous Moldova
PCRM	Communist Party
PDAM	Agrarian Democratic Party
PRCM	Party of Revival and Accord

RUSSIA

VII

Domestic Affairs

Foreign and Military Policy

Economy and Society

Domestic Affairs

Population:	147,700,000
Capital:	Moscow (1994 pop. 8,793,000)
Major cities:	St. Petersburg (pop. 4,883,000), Nizhnii Novgorod (pop. 1,425,000), Novosibirsk (pop. 1,418,000)
Area:	17,075,400 sq. km.
Major ethnic groups:	Russian 81.5%, Tatar 3.8%, Ukrainian 3%, Chuvash 1.2%, Bashkir 0.9%, Belarusian 0.8%, other 8.8%
Economy:	GDP growth: 0.8%
....	Inflation rate: 11.0%
....	Average monthly wage: $205
....	Unemployment rate: 8.9%

A YEAR OF DISCORD

by LAURA BELIN

To no one's surprise, 1997 failed to live up to the title of the "year of accord and reconciliation," which President Boris Yeltsin had conferred on it by decree. But unexpectedly, the most acrimonious battles of the year were fought not between the "winners" and "losers" of the post-Soviet period, but among financial groups that had gained power and wealth during Yeltsin's tenure as president. Government ministers who were political allies of competing business groups were increasingly caught in the crossfire as the year wore on.

In contrast, relations between the executive branch and the legislature slowly improved over the course of 1997, at least on the surface. For much of the year, confrontation reigned between the executive and the State Duma, or lower house of parliament. The upper chamber, the Federation Council, also proved more willing to challenge the Kremlin. In the autumn, Yeltsin agreed to various concessions to the Communist opposition, which formed the largest group in the Duma, and to regional leaders, who make up the Federation Council. Although there were few discernible changes in policy, new arrangements promising greater consultation gave parliamentary leaders an incentive—or at least a fig leaf—for cooperating with Yeltsin and his government.

OUTBREAK OF CLAN WARFARE

The political and financial elite that helped re-elect Yeltsin in 1996 remained united at the beginning of 1997, not least because new presidential elections seemed a not-so-distant prospect due to Yeltsin's poor health. Yeltsin had been mostly out of public view during the second half of 1996, as he prepared for, and recovered from, open-heart surgery. During the first week of 1997, he fell ill again with what aides said was the flu. Once his health improved enough for regular work in the Kremlin, Yeltsin began preparing to reshuffle the government that he had appointed after his inauguration in August 1996.

Yeltsin's new cabinet appointments in March planted the seeds for the conflict that became increasingly bitter and public later in the year. Contrary to widespread speculation, Yeltsin left the veteran Viktor Chernomyrdin in place as prime minister. However, he dismissed several senior officials, including all three first deputy prime ministers: Aleksandr Bolshakov (who had been in charge of industrial policy), Viktor Ilyushin (social policy), and Vladimir Potanin (economic policy). After only seven months in government, Potanin returned to the private sector to head Oneksimbank, the commercial bank he founded in 1993. Finance Minister Aleksandr Livshits returned to the presidential administration as Yeltsin's chief economic advisor.

The new government's economic policy team was headed by Anatolii Chubais, who had arguably been the most powerful Russian politician during Yeltsin's protracted illness, when he was the president's chief of staff. Chubais joined the new government as finance minister and first deputy prime minister in charge of economic policy. Yeltsin charged him with solving the problem of wage and pension arrears—the same problem for which he had blamed Chubais when dismissing him from the government back in January 1996.

The big surprise in March was the appointment of Boris Nemtsov, the 37-year-old governor of Nizhnii Novgorod, as first deputy prime minister in charge of social issues. Nemtsov was the first governor to join the federal government, and his appointment was seen as a signal to other regional leaders that Moscow would take their needs into account. Nemtsov was also widely tipped as the man Yeltsin would like to succeed him as president.

The cabinet reshuffle had far-reaching consequences. When Chubais had been first deputy prime minister in 1994 and 1995, the conservative industrialist Oleg Soskovets had equal cabinet rank and sometimes diametrically opposed views. Chernomyrdin was consequently seen as the balancing force between their competing factions. In contrast, Chubais and Nemtsov found common cause in 1997 and seemed to gain ground at Chernomyrdin's expense. In a "spring offensive" from March through May, one senior official after another was forced out and replaced by allies of Chubais and Nemtsov, whom the media soon dubbed the "young reformers."

Aleksandr Pochinok, like Chubais a high-ranking member of the Russia's Democratic Choice party, was appointed to head the State Tax Service. The 44-year-old mayor of Samara, Oleg Sysuev, joined the government as a deputy prime minister and soon became labor minister as well. Nemtsov removed Chernomyrdin ally Petr Rodionov as fuel and energy minister and took over the post of minister himself, bringing a colleague from Nizhnii Novgorod, Sergei Kirienko, as his first deputy in that ministry. Boris Brevnov, a 29–year-old Nizhnii Novgorod banker, was appointed chief executive of the electricity monopoly, Unified Energy System.

Yeltsin made clear that the first deputy premiers had his blessing, and even advised Chernomyrdin in one radio address not to be afraid of letting younger politicians assume positions of power. Chubais and Nemtsov even threatened to force the sacred cow Gazprom, the gas monopoly that Chernomyrdin ran before he became prime minister in 1992, to settle its large tax debts, and pledged to strengthen the state's role in managing the company. By June, some Russian commentators were beginning to view Chernomyrdin as little more than a figurehead.

Out of public view, a conflict was brewing over privatization. As tax collection remained far too low to cover government expenditures, Chubais and Nemtsov promised to replenish state coffers through a new round of auctions of state-owned property. They pledged to do away with the rigged deals of previous years, in which well-connected banks—with Chubais's blessing—bought property for a fraction over the (undervalued) minimum price.

The strains began to show in late July, after a consortium led by Potanin's Oneksimbank won an auction for a stake in the telecommunications giant Svyazinvest. Market analysts said the auction was relatively fair, and most agreed that the state got a reasonable price for the shares. Those involved in the losing consortium did not agree. They included Vladimir Gusinskii, the founder of the Most Bank, and Boris Berezovskii, who had ostensibly delegated his business affairs when he became deputy secretary of the Security Council in late 1996.

Critics of the Svyazinvest sale charged that it had been rigged and that the Oneksimbank empire was becoming too powerful. Media financed by Berezovskii and Gusinskii led the chorus. Berezovskii had substantial leverage over the 51 percent state-owned Russian Public Television (ORT) network, the newspaper *Nezavisimaya gazeta,* and several other outlets. Gusinskii's Media-Most company owned a controlling stake in the leading private network NTV, the influential radio station Ekho Moskvy, and print media including the newspaper *Segodnya.*

Nemtsov slammed the media "hysteria" over Svyazinvest as the work of sore losers. He even accused unnamed businessmen of having tried to blackmail the government before the Svyazinvest sale. But Berezovskii and Gusinskii found more ammunition during the first week of August, when a small company linked to Oneksimbank won a controlling stake in the metals giant Norilsk Nickel. That auction was fraught with apparent conflicts of interest: Oneksimbank had acquired the right to manage the shares in Norilsk Nickel in late 1995 in exchange for a $170 million loan to the government. Analysts criticized both the terms of the auction and the relatively low price for which the shares were sold. To add to the stench, the sale was nearly halted at the eleventh hour but allowed to go ahead following secret meetings between Potanin and top officials including Chernomyrdin.

The media uproar did not lead to the reversal of either the Svyazinvest or the Norilsk sales, but it claimed one casualty. In mid-August, Yeltsin fired State Property Committee Chairman Alfred Kokh, a close Chubais ally. Oneksimbank returned fire through newspapers over which it had financial leverage. Potanin's bank had acquired major stakes in the dailies *Izvestiya* and *Komsomolskaya pravda* in spring 1997, and they portrayed Kokh as a "victim" of the government's drive to enforce fair rules in privatization. (That argument was quite a stretch considering Kokh's role in preparing earlier sweetheart privatization deals.) *Komsomolskaya pravda* accused Chernomyrdin of having "become a hostage of financial groups" and ran an interview with Nemtsov in which he accused Berezovskii of using his government post to further his private business interests.

The rhetoric escalated in September, with *Nezavisimaya gazeta* accusing Chubais of "striving for complete control over Russia" and strengthening "oligarchic" rather than "democratic" trends in society. Two days after that article appeared, Yeltsin summoned six top bankers to the Kremlin to urge them to stop "slinging mud" against each other and government ministers. (Berezovskii, who formally was not engaged in business, did not attend that meeting.) The president announced triumphantly after the conclave that the bankers had agreed "to end their battle against Chubais, Nemtsov, and the government."

But Yeltsin's peacemaking effort did not end the "information war." Within days, *Nezavisimaya gazeta* published another blistering attack on Oneksimbank. Soon thereafter, media financed by Berezovskii and Gusinskii pounced on allegations that Kokh had accepted $100,000 from a small Swiss publisher, Servina, that was linked to Oneksimbank, for an as yet unwritten book on privatization. In early October, *Nezavisimaya gazeta* accused Chubais of "fulfilling the instructions of the U.S. Finance Ministry [sic]" and argued that "the real threat of dictatorship in Russia comes not from the Communist revanchists . . . but from the Chubais team."

Newspapers financed by Oneksimbank—which by this time included the new daily *Russkii telegraf*—steadfastly defended Chubais and Nemtsov and aimed fire at their opponents. They also published occasional criticism of Chernomyrdin, who enjoyed favorable treatment in media financed by Berezovskii and Gusinskii.

For a brief time in November, Yeltsin appeared to settle the argument in favor of the "young reformers." He sacked Berezovskii, giving no official reason, shortly after returning from a trip to Krasnoyarsk Krai, on which Nemtsov had accompanied him. Berezovskii refrained from criticizing the president and blamed his ouster on Chubais. Nemtsov said firing Berezovskii was an important step toward leaving "oligarchy capitalism" behind.

Revenge came swiftly. In mid-November, it emerged that Chubais and several close associates, including Kokh, received honoraria of $90,000 each for an unpublished book on the history of Russian privatization. Even more suspicious, the book's publisher, Segodnya Press, was part-owned by Oneksimbank. (This was in addition to the earlier scandal surrounding the book of which Kokh was the sole author.) Journalist Aleksandr Minkin broke the story of the "book scandal" during an interview on Ekho Moskvy—which is itself part of rival Gusinskii's media empire.

Yeltsin fired the three book authors who were still in public service: Aleksandr Kazakov, the deputy head of the presidential administration, Petr Mostovoi, the head of the Federal Bankruptcy Service, and Maksim Boiko, who lasted just three months as head of the State Property Ministry. Yeltsin refused to accept Chubais's resignation but clipped his wings by replacing him as finance minister with Mikhail Zadornov, formerly the Duma Budget Committee chairman and a prominent member of Grigorii Yavlinskii's Yabloko movement. Nemtsov, who was not directly involved in the scandal but was tainted by his association with Chubais, was replaced as fuel and energy minister by Kirienko.

The mini-reshuffle in November damaged Chubais's reputation and strengthened Chernomyrdin's hand. In one telling detail, Zadornov was to report directly to the prime minister rather than to Chubais. Chernomyrdin downplayed the significance of the changes, saying they were designed to alleviate Chubais's heavy workload. However, Nemtsov argued that the shakeup reflected an "ideological" crisis, a choice between privatization "benefiting a narrow circle of people" or privatization with equal rules for all.

Chernomyrdin's star continued to rise in December, and media financed by Berezovskii and Gusinskii did their best to bolster his image as a "professional." They squandered few opportunities to take swipes at the "young reformers." Russian Public Television, NTV, and *Nezavisimaya gazeta* aired allegations that Chubais was leaking information to Western financial institutions. The "smoking gun" was letters Chernomyrdin received from World Bank President James Wolfensohn and IMF Managing Director Michel Camdessus, who were said to be giving "instructions" on economic policy.

The conflict showed no sign of blowing over at year-end. During the last week of December, Berezovskii continued to assail Chubais as a "Bolshevik," while Chubais charged in an interview with *Izvestiya* that Berezovskii viewed the government as a "housemaid" for big business.

EXECUTIVE AND LEGISLATIVE BRANCH REACH WARY COEXISTENCE

In contrast to the bank war, which shattered taboos on squabbling within the elite, legislative–executive relations became more civil over the course of 1997. Extra-constitutional arrangements gave the appearance of greater influence for the legislature, although in practice presidential power was not diminished. Yeltsin's concessions to parliament were superficial, but served to provide a fig leaf for the Communists and other deputies who did not want a showdown with the Kremlin.

The Duma began the year with an embarrassing climb-down on the 1997 budget. The document was adopted with the backing of many Communist deputies, even though the government and Yeltsin pointedly refused to meet 11 demands the Communists had put forward as conditions for their support. Only the Yabloko faction unanimously voted against the 1997 budget, and its leader, Yavlinskii, repeatedly accused the Communists of being a phony opposition.

Perhaps in order to counter such accusations, the Communists and their allies, who commanded a near majority in the Duma, passed several important laws during the first half of 1997 that displeased the Kremlin. For instance, the Duma approved a law prohibiting the transfer abroad of all cultural valuables seized during World War II. Yeltsin vetoed this so-called "trophy art law," but the Duma overrode his veto in April, embarrassing Yeltsin shortly before he was to visit Germany. The Duma also approved a federal constitutional law on the government, designed to increase parliamentary oversight over the cabinet. In June, the lower house passed a land code that prohibited the purchase and sale of farmland.

Meanwhile, deputies voted down various high-profile government proposals, including a package of laws on cutting social benefits and a bill to authorize cuts of some 20 percent of planned 1997 budget expenditures. (That bill would have slashed by 55 percent some programs dear to the hearts of opposition deputies, such as agriculture subsidies.)

During the first half of the year, the Duma was aided by the more assertive posture of the Federation Council. By the beginning of 1997, nearly all regional leaders had been elected and could no longer be removed by presidential decree. Consequently, the upper house proved willing to approve legislation it had blocked in 1996, such as the law on the government and the trophy art law. In July, the upper house also approved the land code, which, while somewhat different from the version it rejected in 1996, was still opposed by the Kremlin since it did not allow free sale of land.

The executive branch was not inclined to compromise. Disregarding the Duma's objections, the government imposed its planned budget cuts unilaterally in June. Faced with a less loyal Federation Council, Yeltsin used his veto even more often than he had in 1996. In apparent violation of the constitution, he returned the trophy art law to parliament twice, charging that both the Duma and the Council used unconstitutional voting procedures when they overrode his veto. On similar grounds he refused to sign the law on the government (although the constitution indicates that the president has to sign federal constitutional laws within 14 days of their approval by the upper house). In July, Yeltsin vetoed the land code and a religion law that had cleared both houses of parliament with huge majorities. The following month, Duma Speaker Gennadii Seleznev, a prominent Communist, accused the president of "abusing his constitutional right" to veto laws in order to block the legislature's work.

The Duma remained defiant after returning from its summer recess in September. Although the legislative and executive branches managed to agree on a revised version of the religion law, the Duma overrode Yeltsin's veto of the land code rather than forming a conciliatory commission to revise the document. Soon after, deputies again rejected government-backed laws to cut expenditures on social benefits.

At this point, Yeltsin sought to drive a wedge between the two houses of parliament, contrasting the "responsible" Federation Council with the "politicized" Duma. In an address to open the fall session of the Council, he praised the upper house as a "stabilizing force." He also promised concessions in tax policy to regional leaders. For instance, he endorsed legislation to force regional branches of corporations to pay taxes to the regions where they are located rather than to Moscow, where most company headquarters were located.

Meanwhile, confrontation between the executive branch and the Duma continued to grow. In early October, Yeltsin lambasted the Duma in a nationwide radio address. He warned deputies that his patience and the patience of the Russian people were not "limitless." Communist Party leader Gennadii Zyuganov decried Yeltsin's "confrontational ultimatum" and accused the president of "blackmail," while Seleznev reminded Yeltsin that the Duma "is not an appointed bureaucratic apparatus."

The following week, the Duma passed a resolution declaring the government's 1997 performance "unsatisfactory" and rejected the draft 1998 budget in the first reading. Deputies also put a confidence motion, proposed by the Communist faction, on the agenda for 15 October.

A showdown appeared to be looming. Chernomyrdin hinted that if the confidence motion passed, the government would immediately demand that the Duma hold a second confidence vote. (The constitution gives the president the right to dissolve the Duma and call new parliamentary elections if two no-confidence votes are passed within three months.) Chubais and Nemtsov warned the Duma that if it provoked a government crisis, share values for Russian companies would plummet.

In fact, neither Yeltsin nor the Duma stood to gain from forcing the issue. Opinion polls consistently showed that if new parliamentary elections were held, pro-government groups would do poorly, and the Communists—while still more popular than any other single party—would likely lose some Duma seats to other opposition groups.

On both sides the search began for a face-saving way out. The day before the scheduled no-confidence vote, Chernomyrdin promised that the parliament would get its own newspaper and more air time on state-owned television and radio. Yeltsin sealed the deal by making two last-minute phone calls to Seleznev on the day of the vote and agreeing to hold "roundtable talks" on various controversial issues (a longtime Communist demand). Yeltsin also agreed to revive meetings of the "big four": president, prime minister, and speakers of both houses of parliament. The Duma postponed the no-confidence vote, and the Communist faction eventually withdrew the motion altogether after Yeltsin convened a meeting of the "big four" and held consultations with the leaders of all seven Duma factions.

Within the opposition camp, some criticized the Communists for "appeasing" the government. Duma Deputy Speaker Sergei Baburin derided the deal as a "pseudo-compromise." The Kremlin's concessions were indeed flimsy. Although Yeltsin agreed to "big four" meetings, roundtable talks, and a few hours per week of media coverage for parliamentary activities, he did not meet any of the Communists' concrete policy demands, such as a freeze on rent and utility rates, or increased compensation for citizens who lost their life savings because of high inflation in the early 1990s. Yeltsin agreed to sign the law on the government (which he was constitutionally obliged to do) only if certain amendments were approved. He also promised that opposition figures would be represented on new supervisory boards for Russia's two main television networks, although there was no guarantee that such boards would in fact be appointed.

Yeltsin continued his persuasion offensive by paying a surprise visit to the Duma on 6 November to give Seleznev an award on his 50th birthday. On more substantive matters, the government made concessions to representatives of the Duma and Federation Council in talks over the 1998 budget. Planned spending was increased by a total of 2.8 trillion rubles ($4.6 billion), although there were doubts whether this spending would materialize. After Zyuganov announced that the Communist faction would again vote against the budget in the first reading, Yeltsin came to the Duma on 5 December, the day of the vote, to urge deputies to support the document. The budget passed by just five votes. Among the supporters were 29 Communist deputies and many members of the Communist-allied Agrarian and Popular Power factions.

Yeltsin signed the law on the government in mid-December, after receiving assurances from Seleznev and Federation Council Speaker Yegor Stroev at a "big four" meeting that parliament would approve the agreed amendments. A week later, the Duma approved the 1998 budget in the second reading. As in the first reading, the budget passed by only five votes, and would have been rejected without limited Communist support. The Yabloko faction remained unanimously opposed, and Yavlinskii insisted that compromises with the Communists had only made an already unrealistic budget worse. Roundtable talks on land reform were held in the Kremlin on 26 December, and all sides signed a protocol calling for a compromise on the land code within three months.

The left opposition in the Duma did not stop speaking out against what Zyuganov sometimes called the "criminal regime." Communist leaders continued to insist that Yeltsin appoint a "government of national trust," and through the end of the year, the lower house occasionally passed harsh resolutions against government ministers or specific polices. But such resolutions were non-binding and failed to conceal the fact that the Communist-led opposition—like Vladimir Zhirinovsky's Liberal Democratic Party of Russia—supported many of the government's key initiatives in exchange for superficial concessions. While "reconciliation and accord" were not achieved, the executive and legislature at least arrived at a dance of accommodation.

LOOKING TOWARD THE NEXT PRESIDENTIAL ELECTION

Although Yeltsin's term was not scheduled to end until the summer of 2000, speculation about the next presidential race frequently appeared in Russian media in 1997. Only a few Russian politicians, all of whom ran for president in 1996, openly acknowledged plans to run again in 2000. One of them, former Security Council Secretary Aleksandr Lebed, fought to stay in the limelight by founding a new political party, the National Republican Party of Russia, in March. During the remainder of the year, he traveled frequently within Russia and abroad, although the Russian media generally overlooked him. Zhirinovsky and Yavlinskii also vowed to repeat their presidential bids.

Most of the leading contenders downplayed or denied their aspirations to succeed Yeltsin. Chernomyrdin and Nemtsov, the two most promising candidates from the "party of power," repeatedly denied having plans to run for president. Zyuganov, who continued to lead other likely candidates in opinion polls, said only that the "popular-patriotic forces" would nominate a candidate.

Moscow Mayor Yurii Luzhkov denied having presidential ambitions but quietly laid the ground for a future candidacy. The Moscow city government founded a television network that began broadcasting in June (coverage of Luzhkov on other major Russian television networks ranged from neutral to hostile). To raise his profile outside the capital, Luzhkov organized lavish celebrations in September to mark the 850th anniversary of the first recorded mention of Moscow. He made frequent trips abroad and to the regions, where he invariably concluded economic cooperation agreements with political and business leaders. He sought to bolster his image as a patriot and a state-builder by calling for closer ties with Belarus and laying claim to Sevastopol, the Ukrainian port where the Black Sea Fleet is based. Luzhkov was also a vocal critic of Chubais, Nemtsov, and the federal government's economic policies as a whole. For instance, in December he termed Russia's dependence on foreign economic institutions such as the IMF a "national disgrace."

In autumn 1997, the Kremlin gave mixed signals about whether Yeltsin might run for president again in 2000. Yeltsin appeared to rule out such a prospect in October, saying he would not violate the constitution, which allows the president to serve only two consecutive terms. But several Kremlin officials suggested that since Yeltsin was first elected in 1991, when Russia was not yet independent and had a different constitution, his term that began in 1996 should be considered his first. The Duma asked the Constitutional Court to consider the matter, and it accepted the case for consideration sometime in 1998.

NEWLY ELECTED REGIONAL GOVERNORS GRAPPLE WITH MOSCOW

by ROBERT ORTTUNG

For the first time in Russian history, elected governors ruled every region of the country except for the republic of Karachaevo-Cherkessiya. The rise of a regional elite beholden to the electorate rather than to the will of the president set off a struggle for power between the presidential administration and the governors, with victories for both sides during the year. The regions also continued to develop at different paces, and the differences between them became more apparent as some pursued market reforms while others fought them.

CENTER REASSERTS LOST AUTHORITY

Russia finished 1996 with a marathon series of gubernatorial elections that brought elected officials to power in more than fifty regions, complementing the regional executives who had already been elected. The governors also demonstrated their importance in 1996 by helping President Boris Yeltsin win his presidential election against the competitive Communist challenger Gennadii Zyuganov.

With the election season over and the victors settling down to the task of dealing with local problems, Moscow sought to restore its traditional control over regional affairs while the newly elected regional elite sought to transform its popular mandate into greater leverage over the federal government. Although the Russian government clearly had lost much of the control over the regions that the Soviet Union exercised before 1991, in 1997 the federal government reasserted some of its lost authority. It would be an over-simplification to see this as a straightforward battle between the Kremlin and the governors. President Boris Yeltsin had a strong interest in using regional executive and legislative leaders, who collectively make up the Federation Council (the upper house of the national parliament), to oppose the Communist-dominated State Duma, the lower chamber.

The federal government had a powerful arsenal at its disposal in its battle to control the periphery. Since the vast majority of regions continued to receive subsidies from the federal budget, they had to maintain good relations with the Kremlin to ensure the continued flow of funds. The Federation Council thus voted to approve the 1997 federal budget on 12 February, since giving formal backing to the document improved the chances that the regions would receive transfers from the federal government. Passing the budget was a bitter pill to swallow because the governors objected to the way federal funds were to be distributed in the budget, and questioned the statistics being used and the criteria for determining allocations. The governors' objections were borne out a few months later when the administration had to admit that the budget had little relationship with reality.

Yeltsin's cabinet shakeup in March created a more consolidated executive under the leadership of two new first deputy prime ministers, Anatolii Chubais and Boris Nemtsov. The two reformers tightened the Kremlin's grip on the federal purse strings and sought to rein in the natural monopolies, boosting the Kremlin's power over the regions. Yeltsin's appointment of Nemtsov, the former governor of Nizhnii Novgorod, put him in a good position with the remaining governors, who generally supported Nemtsov's promotion. Chubais used his new power base to fill federal coffers and rescind the advantages previously given to the ethnic republics. He forced Sakha (Yakutiya) to contribute a significant share of its diamond sales to the federal budget and revoked Ingushetiya's status as a tax-free trade zone.

Additionally, the federal government worked to strengthen local governments as a counterweight to the governors' power. Governors and mayors often fought over the distribution of budgetary funds and property, giving the federal government an opportunity to keep regional leaders from becoming too powerful by siding with the mayors. On 25 September, Yeltsin signed a law on local government financing to make local governments more independent of the regional and federal governments above them. Earlier in the year, on 29 May, the president created a Council on Local Government that gave him direct access to the country's mayors. Additionally, the Kremlin took the side of Izhevsk Mayor Anatolii Saltykov, who was battling to protect his office in the Constitutional Court after Udmurtiya's parliament had sought to arrogate the power to appoint mayors in the republic. On 24 January, the court ruled in favor of the mayor, but Yeltsin had to issue a decree on 21 February to compel the Udmurt parliament to enforce the ruling. The court decision had broad implications for other regions because it defended local government as an independent third level in the overall hierarchy.

An abortive tax strike in the spring also demonstrated the limits of the governors' powers. Sakhalin and Irkutsk declared that they would withhold payments to the center until the Kremlin paid all the money they felt that they were owed. The center quickly squashed the uprising, however, and Irkutsk Governor Yurii Nozhikov resigned in frustration on 21 April. He was only the second regional leader to willingly leave office after Moscow Mayor Gavriil Popov resigned in June 1992 under a cloud of corruption allegations.

Despite these setbacks, the governors were able to assert themselves at key moments. In a Federation Council meeting on 2 July, the governors stood behind Primorskii Krai Governor Yevgenii Nazdratenko when Yeltsin tried to fire him. While objecting to Nazdratenko's inability to resolve the severe energy crisis facing his Far Eastern region, the governors made clear that they would not let Yeltsin remove a regional executive who had been popularly elected. The administration's withdrawal from the battle showed that there were now limits on the Kremlin's ability to punish governors it no longer liked. The administration fought back by issuing a decree on 9 July strengthening the powers of the presidential representatives, handing them the authority to monitor the implementation of federal programs, the use of federal property, and the way federal money is spent in the region. Additionally, Yeltsin transferred much of

Nazdratenko's power to his newly appointed representative in Vladivostok, Viktor Kondratov, who simultaneously served as head of the regional Federal Security Service, the successor to the KGB.

The rise of Nemtsov and former Samara Mayor Oleg Sysuev to Yeltsin's cabinet gave much greater prominence to the regional leadership and demonstrated that regional leaders could gain access to the highest levels of power. The regions also gained as the administration signed power-sharing agreements with an additional 14 regions, bringing the total number of regions that had signed such treaties to 40 (out of 89). In a 31 October radio address, Yeltsin praised the treaties as "strengthening the federal state," but with their secret protocols the treaties often create friction between regions when some leaders become convinced that their neighbors are getting better deals.

A war of words broke out in October with Tatarstan, North Ossetiya and other ethnic republics over the new Russian internal passport, which does not include information identifying the holder's republic or ethnicity. (The old Soviet passport required the holder to record his or her ethnicity: the infamous point number 5.) In 1996, President Yeltsin vetoed a parliamentary bill that stipulated listing ethnic identity in birth certificates. In October 1997 the Interior Ministry started issuing the new passports, which lack ethnic identification (and which have the Tsarist double-headed eagle on the cover). Tatarstan's President Mintimer Shaimiev objected, claiming that the new document "violates citizens' constitutional rights to both Tatarstan and Russian citizenship." Protests also came from the leaders of other ethnically non-Russian peoples, who make up 18 percent of the population of the Russian Federation. Some of them also wanted the new passports to be printed in the language of the titular nationality as well as Russian. Communist Duma deputies urged that citizens be given the option of recording their ethnicity. Tatarstan's parliament announced its intention to adopt its own law on citizenship and to issue its own passports, but in December decided to postpone the question until the next year. A compromise would be to allow the republics to print inserts for the passports, or to issue their own passports in parallel.

GROWING REGIONAL DIFFERENTIATION

Russia's regions became increasingly differentiated over the course of the year. Strong, reform-minded leaders seemed to be the key to success for the regions that were best able to adjust to the new economic conditions. Above all, conditions in the city of Moscow remained wildly different from the situation in the rest of the country. Despite concern over the fate of the losers, the federal government's limited resources prevented it from taking much direct action. By the end of the year it was discussing a policy of helping those regions that could pull up the overall economy and succoring the neediest victims of change, leaving little for the many regions somewhere in the middle.

The richer regions of Moscow, St. Petersburg, and Nizhnii Novgorod took advantage of their sounder finances as they followed the national government's lead by issuing their own Eurobonds to finance investment projects—at rates of interest far below those charged on the domestic Russian capital market. Yeltsin authorized several more regions to do so, but the economic crisis in Southeast Asia forced many of these regional leaders to put their plans on hold. Before the crisis, however, Moscow celebrated its 850th birthday in grand style, launching a potential presidential bid by Mayor Luzhkov. The capital's celebrations contrasted with the poverty of many other regions, where teachers and doctors went unpaid and the decaying defense industries left numerous environmental hazards.

Saratov took the lead in a crucial component of reform when Governor Dmitrii Ayatskov signed a law into force on 14 November that allowed the buying and selling of land. The State Duma had stymied Yeltsin's attempt to get such private property guarantees approved at the national level. The move dramatically increased the interest of Moscow banks and foreign investors in Saratov, but it will be some time before an active real estate market develops in the region, not least because legal provisions for mortgages are lacking.

Ayatskov was successful in obtaining legislative approval for the bill because the Communists did not win a single seat in the 31 August elections to the Saratov oblast legislature, while supporters of the governor took a majority. Many other regions were preparing to copy and expand on the Saratov example, while in places like Rostov land privatization is happening spontaneously, as residents simply divided the soil among themselves while ignoring the legal nuances. Luzhkov, however, bucked the national trend in Moscow by vetoing a municipal law to privatize the land under large enterprises.

A series of more than thirty elections to regional legislatures during the fall forced out many of the leftist incumbents and replaced them with more pragmatic entrepreneurs and factory managers. As a rule, the governors were able to win the election of supportive legislatures, pleasing the Yeltsin administration, but there were some exceptions such as Primorskii Krai, Samara, and Krasnoyarsk, where more opposition-minded local parliaments were elected. Although no Communist won in the so-called "red belt" province of Saratov, they were able to dominate in Stavropol, Chelyabinsk, Smolensk, and Penza. In general, all political parties did badly in the regional elections, particularly Vladimir Zhirinovsky's Liberal Democratic Party of Russia, which nominated numerous candidates and was shut out almost everywhere, even in Novosibirsk, where it had won 11 seats in the December 1996 city council elections.

Conditions seemed to worsen in many of the most troubled regions. Coal miners' strikes in Primorskii Krai deprived residents of electricity for as much as 18 hours a day during the spring and early summer. Numerous federal commissions that descended from Moscow were unable to resolve the underlying problems. The battle between reinstated Vladivostok Mayor Viktor Cherepkov and Governor Nazdratenko also continued unabated. On 26 September the Nazdratenko-dominated krai duma voted to remove Cherepkov from office again, but was overruled by the courts. In a surprise move, Cherepkov resigned on 12 November, setting mayoral elections for 1998, and began an abortive hunger strike. He rallied by the end of the year, however, and won a decisive victory in the 7 December elections to the krai duma, replacing his enemies with allies. Although Cherepkov took back his resignation just after the New Year, the struggle was set to continue, with further deterioration in the region's economy the only predictable result.

RISKY BUSINESS

The year proved mixed for many of Russia's major enterprises and foreign investors. In a move forward, the State Duma on 24 June approved a list of seven natural resource deposits for development on the basis of production-sharing agreements. The original list proposed by the government had contained 230 sites, but the parliamentarians were wary of selling off Russia's valuable resources to rapacious Western firms. The approval of lists did not immediately lead to any major new investments.

There were some bright spots on the economic front. Arkhangelsk authorities began publicizing the Lomonosov diamond deposit that could hold up to $12 billion worth of precious stones. Some major enterprises like St. Petersburg's Kirov Factory were able to score major turnarounds and the number of car assembly projects jumped dramatically, capped by a year-end deal between Fiat and Nizhnii Novgorod's Gorkii Automobile Plant. Foreign investors scored big successes in some areas: Cadbury and Stollwerck, for example, built chocolate factories in Novgorod and Vladimir oblasts respectively.

Many foreign investors faced difficulties, though. Sweden's AssiDoman pulled out of the Segezhabumprom Cellulose and Paper Plant at the end of the year after complaining that the Russian authorities made it impossible to work there. Britain's Trans World Group also lost control of its empire of steel and aluminum plants, including the one in Novolipetsk, where other shareholders were finally able to gain seats on the board of directors after a multi-year battle. In another well-publicized struggle, Exxon fought Nenets Autonomous Okrug authorities to retain control of rights it had won to pump oil from the Timano-Pechora basin.

Many of Russia's behemoth producers continued to sink. Tatarstan truck-maker KamAZ, for example, fell far short of producing enough trucks to be profitable and had to shut its production line for weeks at a stretch for lack of ready financing. This failure came despite an attempt by the Tatarstan government to pay off the plant's debt to the federal government.

In a troubling development, the number of small businesses in Russia dropped by nearly 50,000 between 1995 and 1997, from 877,300 to 829,400. Despite the national trend, however, the number of small businesses in Moscow grew by more than 7,000, to 183,000.

Communal services took up 30–50 percent of regional budgets while households paid only 30 percent of the cost of their housing and utilities. Following the cabinet shakeup in March, the government tried to reduce this burden by raising rents and utility prices, forcing residents to be more efficient by measuring their utility usage, and lowering prices by breaking up natural monopolies. (See also the accompanying article by Penny Morvant, "Tensions Ease in the Social Sphere.")

Luzhkov resisted the program in Moscow, saying that it underestimated the number of people that would need assistance and overestimated the savings likely to be generated. Nemtsov on 12 May conceded that the regions would be free to implement their own policies. However, when St. Petersburg Governor Vladimir Yakovlev doubled rents at the beginning of the year, he faced a Communist attempt to recall him. Only a 5 June court ruling prevented the issue from going to a popular vote. In Samara, where housing reform had begun in 1996, newly elected Mayor Grigorii Limanskii announced that he would lower rents, when it became apparent that increased charges did not greatly reduce state expenditures since many tenants were unwilling or unable to pay. By the end of the year, many regional leaders were increasingly opposed to the reform plans, and utilities refused to introduce meters.

REGIONAL FOREIGN POLICIES

Foreign policy became another area for dispute between the Kremlin and regional leaders as well as among regional leaders themselves. Luzhkov supported the Kremlin-initiated policy of unification with Belarus, but upset federal foreign policy makers by embracing the return of Crimea to Russia, thereby offending Ukraine. Tatarstan President Mintimer Shaimiev, in contrast, denounced the idea of including Belarus in the Russian Federation, warning that such a move would lead him to reexamine his republic's bilateral treaty with Moscow. Growing weary of Belarusian President Alyaksandr Lukashenka's authoritarian tactics in arresting Russian journalists reporting from Minsk, the Kremlin blocked his visit to Yaroslavl and Lipetsk just hours before the Belarusian leader was set to go, on 2 October. Lukashenka had planned the trip hoping that the "red belt" leaders might give him a more sympathetic hearing.

The Russian regions also became more vocal in pressing their interests, creating potential for international conflict. In the Northwest, Leningrad Oblast began construction of three ports that it hopes will be able to redirect the $1 billion in transit fees that now goes to the Baltic states. The struggle for this revenue could lead to greater friction between Russia and its Baltic neighbors. Kaliningrad Governor Leonid Gorbenko has already offended the Poles and Lithuanians by his protectionist measures to help local bankers. In the Far East, Nazdratenko continues to protest the signing of a Moscow-approved, Russian-Chinese border treaty that would cede some land to China.

Both Moscow and the regions have an interest in attracting greater foreign investment, however. A 1 November summit "without neckties" between Yeltsin and Japanese Prime Minister Ryutaro Hashimoto seemed to open up the possibility of greater Japanese activity in Russian regions, while sidestepping the return of the Kuril islands, a dispute that has prevented the two countries from signing a World War II peace treaty.

In general, the election of Russia's regional elite did not give the governors considerably greater power in the struggle with Moscow. The regions were pursuing too many different interests to present a united front against the Kremlin. The process of increasing differentiation, with some regions succeeding and some falling farther behind, is likely to make such unity even more difficult in the future.

Sidebar: CHANGES IN EDITORIAL POLICY AND OWNERSHIP AT *IZVESTIYA*

by LAURA BELIN

Izvestiya is one of the oldest Russian publications. It was a stalwart of the Soviet political system, and then emerged as a reliable and authoritative organ in the era of glasnost. In August 1997, it published its 25,000th edition. From 1991 to early 1996, the newspaper had a predictable and stable editorial line. It supported the economic reforms associated with Yegor Gaidar and Anatolii Chubais. It generally supported President Boris Yeltsin, although it criticized certain presidential associates, government ministers, and policies (especially the war in Chechnya). It strongly opposed the Communist Party and Vladimir Zhirinovsky's Liberal Democratic Party of Russia.

This article documents the shifts in ownership and editorial policy at *Izvestiya* over the period 1996–97. Its vicissitudes are a microcosm of the shifts in Russian politics and the growing encroachment of political and business interests over the independent media.

24 January 1996: In the aftermath of the hostage crisis in Pervomaiskoe, Dagestan, *Izvestiya* publishes open letter to Yeltsin from human rights defender Sergei Kovalev. In the letter, Kovalev explains why he is resigning from the presidential human rights commission and reproaches Yeltsin in extremely harsh terms. ("At times of crisis [. . .] you and the leaders of state departments appointed by you deign to offer us lies so obvious and hopeless that it is simply staggering. [. . .] You began your democratic career as a feisty and vigorous fighter against official lies and party despotism and are ending it as the docile performer of the will of cynical power-lovers from your entourage. [. . .] I am not going to vote for you. And I will not advise other decent people to do so." Soon after, *Izvestiya* commentator Otto Latsis follows Kovalev's lead and resigns from a presidential commission.

February–July 1996: *Izvestiya* supports Yeltsin re-election effort, publishes favorable coverage of the president and unrelenting negative coverage of Communist candidate Gennadii Zyuganov. Yeltsin's disappearance from public view a week before the second round of the election is not reported. Pro-Yeltsin television commercials feature the well-known *Izvestiya* logo above the mock headline, "Boris Nikolaevich Yeltsin: President of All Russians."

July 1996: Criticism of Yeltsin's policies gradually reappears in *Izvestiya*. However, Sergei Kovalev complains that the newspaper refused to publish his open letter to Yeltsin and then-Security Council Secretary Aleksandr Lebed, demanding that they keep their campaign promises to end the war in Chechnya.

August–September 1996: *Izvestiya* publishes criticism of Yeltsin more frequently, and eventually begins to cover the president's health problems.

November 1996: Oil company LUKoil, in which the state is the largest single shareholder, purchases a stake in *Izvestiya.* Editor in chief Igor Golembiovskii declares that the sale will bring capital investment to the newspaper but will not affect editorial policy.

1 April 1997: *Izvestiya* reprints, without comment, an article from the French newspaper *Le Monde* alleging that Prime Minister Viktor Chernomyrdin has amassed a $5 billion fortune. The article erroneously describes a question on Chernomyrdin's wealth asked by a representative in the U.S. Congress as a statement by a U.S. official.

2 April 1997: Government spokesman Igor Shabdurasulov denies the *Izvestiya* report on behalf of the prime minister.

7 April 1997: LUKoil President Vagit Alekperov complains about the *Izvestiya* publication concerning Chernomyrdin. He charges that the paper's sloppiness hurt LUKoil's business reputation, as readers might assume the article was an attempt by LUKoil to discredit the prime minister. Alekperov says the company may sell its stake in *Izvestiya.* He adds that LUKoil is not trying to influence the paper's editorial policy but is merely looking for a better investment.

15 April 1997: *Izvestiya* publishes an editorial charging that the government sought to impose "political censorship" after the newspaper reprinted the article from *Le Monde* on Chernomyrdin's alleged vast wealth. The paper says government officials pressured the 36 percent state-owned LUKoil to act as Chernomyrdin's "censor."

17 April 1997: *Izvestiya* claims LUKoil is seeking to replace the paper's top journalists, in violation of an earlier commitment not to interfere in the paper's editorial policy.

18 April 1997: *Izvestiya* journalist Stepan Kiselev writes that there is a trend toward diminishing press freedom in Russia. He claims that officials in the government and presidential administration have recently sought to punish newspapers for publishing criticism of leading politicians. The same day, *Izvestiya* publishes an appeal signed by several intellectuals and cultural figures denouncing attempts to turn the paper "into an obedient mouthpiece for its new masters."

22 April 1997: *Izvestiya* publishes a front-page appeal asking Yeltsin to help resolve the conflict between the paper's journalists and LUKoil. The chief editors of more than a dozen publications sign the appeal, which also asks Yeltsin to prevent shareholders from forcing *Izvestiya* and *Komsomolskaya*

pravda to change their political lines. The open letter notes that Yeltsin promised in a recent radio address not to allow censorship to return to Russia. (*Komsomolskaya pravda* had agreed to sell a 20 percent stake to Oneksimbank, Russia's third largest bank, in March 1997. In May, shareholders voted to replace that paper's top editor, who had lobbied for selling the shares to Gazprom instead.)

23 April 1997: At a shareholders' meeting, LUKoil appoints a new *Izvestiya* board of directors, composed of four representatives from the oil company and three from the newspaper. *Izvestiya* staff had sought unsuccessfully to delay the shareholders' meeting.

14 May 1997: *Izvestiya* announces that it has sold shares to Sidanko, an oil company in which Oneksimbank holds a controlling stake. The article denies LUKoil's claim to own a majority of *Izvestiya* shares. Journalists presumably hope that Oneksimbank, considered close to the paper's longtime ally Anatolii Chubais, will be a buffer against LUKoil.

15 May 1997: *Izvestiya* publishes an article alleging that some influential officials in LUKoil have criminal ties. The article, signed by the newspaper's "analytic center," claims that Prime Minister Chernomyrdin's personal patronage has allowed LUKoil and its subsidiaries to escape punishment for owing at least 1.2 trillion rubles ($208 million) to the federal budget.

4 June 1997: *Izvestiya* publishes a charter signed by the paper's journalists with major shareholders LUKoil and Oneksimbank. The charter calls for the creation of a seven-member board of directors, with three representatives from the newspaper's editorial collective and two each from LUKoil and Oneksimbank. The editorial collective retains the right to nominate candidates for editor in chief, who must be confirmed by the board. The journalists declare a victory for media freedom. The charter promises that the paper's editorial policy will be determined by its journalists "without any outside influence." It says the paper's objectivity is not tainted by any "conflict of interests" or "corporate goals."

23 June 1997: The seven-member board of directors is elected for *Izvestiya.*

1 July 1997: In an unsigned commentary, *Izvestiya* accuses LUKoil of failing to respect the charter it signed with the paper's journalists. *Izvestiya* says LUKoil is now insisting that it, Oneksimbank, and the journalists each propose a candidate to become editor in chief. The oil company wants the board to have the right to choose an editor from among the three nominees.

1 July 1997: *Izvestiya* publishes an article by Leonid Krutakov accusing First Deputy Prime Minister Anatolii Chubais of accepting an interest-free $3 million loan from Stolichnyi Bank in February 1996 (a time when he did not

hold a government post). The article alleges that the bank credits went to the Center for the Defense of Private Property, which Chubais had created shortly before. The center reportedly put up no collateral for the loan, the stated goal of which was the "development of civil society." The bank credits were allegedly used to speculate on the lucrative treasury bill market. Krutakov's article charges that as presidential chief of staff later that year, Chubais helped Stolichnyi acquire Agroprombank. Some analysts believe Oneksimbank is behind the article; others view the article as a "parting shot" from outgoing editor in chief Igor Golembiovskii.

4 July 1997: The *Izvestiya* board sacks Golembiovskii and approves a process for selecting Golembiovskii's successor that reduces the influence of the paper's journalists. Journalists will vote for the editor, and then the board will select their candidate from among the top three vote-getters in the balloting.

5 July 1997: *Izvestiya* publishes a letter from First Deputy Prime Minister Anatolii Chubais refuting the allegations published in the newspaper on 1 July. Chubais remarks that he would have expected to see such accusations published in the pro-communist newspaper *Sovetskaya Rossiya.* He also notes that he personally helped *Izvestiya* fend off attempts by the opposition-dominated Supreme Soviet to take over the paper in 1992.

10 July 1997: *Izvestiya* reports that its journalists are forming a trade union after not being unionized for the last five years.

18 July 1997: *Izvestiya* board of directors appoints Vasilii Zakharko as the paper's new editor in chief. Zakharko had served as deputy editor of *Izvestiya* since February 1996 and had been acting editor in chief since Igor Golembiovskii was forced out. Shortly before Zakharko's appointment is announced, Radio Free Europe/Radio Liberty correspondent Anna Kachkaeva reports that most *Izvestiya* journalists were discouraged by the selection process and have little hope that the new editor will be independent of LUKoil and Oneksimbank.

July–August 1997: *Izvestiya*'s coverage of conflicts over the privatization of the telecommunications giant Svyazinvest and Norilsk Nickel are noticeably biased in favor of Oneksimbank's point of view. However, two commentaries published on 7 August argue that the Norilsk sale took place under unfair conditions that contradicted Russia's national interests. (Those commentaries were a parting shot by journalists who soon quit *Izvestiya.*)

August 1997: Golembiovskii announces plans to create new newspaper, *Novye izvestiya.* He promises that the paper will be truly independent. Some 30 journalists from *Izvestiya,* including some of the paper's most prominent commentators, quit in order to join Golembiovskii's new project. Mikhail Berger, former chief economic correspondent for *Izvestiya,* takes a senior post at the newspaper *Segodnya.* That paper is owned by Vladimir Gusinskii's Media-Most company, a leading rival of Oneksimbank.

October 1997: *Novye izvestiya* publishes its pilot issue. The newspaper is reportedly financed in part by Boris Berezovskii's LogoVAZ group. Berezovskii attends a 26 October party to celebrate the appearance of the pilot issue.

29 October 1997: Journalist Leonid Krutakov claims he was fired from *Novye izvestiya* for publishing an article criticizing Berezovskii in *Moskovskii komsomolets.* Krutakov tells *Komsomolskaya pravda* (like *Izvestiya,* part-owned by Oneksimbank), that Golembiovskii refused to publish criticism of Berezovskii in *Novye izvestiya.*

6 November 1997: *Novye izvestiya* publishes an article on alleged bribery of State Duma deputies by financial and industrial groups. The article singles out LUKoil and Oneksimbank, accusing them of buying votes to get key legislation passed in the lower house of the parliament.

Sidebar: BANKERS AND OIL TYCOONS USE THE MEDIA AS A BUSINESS WEAPON

by ANDREI FADIN

A short but fierce tussle between Russian banks over privatization of a state enterprise in the summer of 1997 exposed the flagrancy with which financial groups are using their newspapers and television stations to wage war on one another.

The ostensible prize was an attractive piece of the state property pie—Svyazinvest, the largest Russian telecommunications holding—but what was ultimately at stake was the reallocation of property, financial might, and political influence. For the first time, a political offensive was waged by appeal to public opinion through the media rather than by the secret Kremlin intrigues of days gone by. But because the press has been almost entirely taken over by the banks, independence of media and ultimately freedom of speech—one of the few indisputable achievements of the post-Soviet regime—has been seriously deformed.

The blatant spread of propaganda through private newspapers and television was not entirely new in post-Soviet Russia. In the 1996 elections, the bankers who controlled the most media outlets were the main winners. Vladimir Gusinskii and Boris Berezovskii, businessmen who controlled the two main information empires in the country, were still reaping the benefits of the good press they gave Yeltsin and his crowd.

Gusinskii's media concern, owned by his Most-Bank group, consists of Independent Television (NTV), Ekho Moskvy radio, the daily newspaper *Segodnya,* and a weekly television guide called *7 Dnei (7 Days).* It also partly owns several publications, such as *Novaya gazeta* and *Obshchaya gazeta.* Boris Berezovskii, de facto head of the LogoVAZ concern and one of the richest people in Russia, managed to establish control over Russian Public Television (ORT), which reaches more than 100 million people, *Nezavisimaya gazeta,* and *Ogonek* magazine. Berezovskii and Gusinskii are consulted on practically every decision of national importance, and Berezovskii was appointed deputy secretary of the Security Council and became Moscow's main negotiator with Chechnya.

Other members of the so-called Davos alliance (the seven largest banks that in early 1996 joined efforts to prevent a communist return to power) later realized that having one's own press was an asset in the struggle for access to privatized state property. They wielded influence by contributing to Yeltsin's campaign. Vladimir Potanin, head of Oneksimbank, one of the most powerful Russian banks, became a deputy prime minister in Yeltsin's first postelection government. The appointment was widely considered a thank-you to the Davos alliance. When he left the government, Potanin was much stronger than before. But his main achievement was his friendship with the powerful First Deputy Prime Minister Anatolii Chubais. With Chubais on its side, the financially and politically strengthened Oneksimbank could enter the battlefield of the financial giants: the sphere of oil, gas, and information. Under the previous tacit arrangement, every privatization was agreed upon by the main players, but now Oneksimbank was strong enough to outbid its competitors without having to make a deal.

In preparation, Oneksimbank began creating its own information empire. It bought the best national daily newspaper, *Izvestiya,* established control over *Komsomolskaya pravda, Ekspert* magazine, and several other Moscow publications, and founded a new business daily, *Russkii telegraf,* to be launched as "the *Russian Wall Street Journal*" with enormous funding by Russian standards: $20 million over three years.

CLASH OF THE TITANS

The auction of the block of shares of the Svyazinvest state telecommunications holding was the battleground. The Davos alliance was an alliance no more. Potanin's main rivals, Gusinskii and Berezovskii, tried to pull all their political strings to reach a compromise at the Svyazinvest auction. But attempts to talk Chubais into making a secret deal failed. He was now in a position to insist: "Everything should be solved in an honest and open auction where the winner is the one who offers more. There will be no more covert deals. The budget needs money to pay debts to the army, teachers, and doctors." The bankers reportedly threatened to start a public campaign against Chubais on the television channels under their control, but he countered that in that case they would have to face the whole might of the state machine.

An even harder stand was taken by the new Kremlin favorite, the other first deputy prime minister, Boris Nemtsov, who espoused the principle of open competition as his personal creed. "There will be no bandit capitalism and unfair privatization anymore. Everything will be done honestly," Nemtsov said.

Under those circumstances, Oneksimbank's rivals had no choice but to move the struggle to the public sphere. Using their connections at the top as well as their mass media outlets, they tried a preemptive strike. The weapons were public accusations of corruption, financial abuse, and theft. The banks made public confidential information that was compromising to their rivals. With the help of their cronies in the Kremlin, they initiated legal actions and investigations.

The main battles took place in July and August. At first, the head of the Central Bank, Sergei Dubinin, accused two banking structures connected to Oneksimbank of gross mismanagement, causing a loss of millions of dollars to the budget. The head of one of the accused banks, influential ex–Deputy Finance Minister Andrei Vavilov, retaliated by giving the procurator's office materials compromising the head of the Central Bank. Still, the procurator's office and Prime Minister Viktor Chernomyrdin demanded a stop to the final sale to Oneksimbank of a controlling interest in a very lucrative company. Nevertheless, the deal went through, apparently with Chubais's support.

Having lost the battle in the corridors of power, Gusinskii and Berezovskii turned to the media to attack Potanin and Chubais. The weekly analytical television program *Vremya*—owned by Berezovskii—investigated Oneksimbank's machinations during the privatization of some state enterprises. Moderator Sergei Dorenko directly accused Potanin of swindling and stealing state money. The expose generated a stream of materials compromising Alfred Kokh, the chairman of the State Property Committee.

ORT, NTV, Ekho Moskvy radio, *Nezavisimaya gazeta, Novaya gazeta, Segodnya,* and *Obshchaya gazeta* concentrated on exposing corruption in the sphere of privatization—in most cases, through authentic and truly compromising materials. And they paid special attention to the roles of Chubais, Kokh, and Nemtsov.

The focus of the campaign was that Oneksimbank received unfair privileges due to its "special relations" with the Chubais team. The media suggested—and proved in the case of Kokh—that the "special relations" had a purely financial dimension. Kokh had to resign, and the Customs Committee account was taken from Oneksimbank. Nevertheless, Oneksimbank and its foreign partners won a 25 percent stake at the Svyazinvest auction.

THE OWNERSHIP DIVIDE

Alas, the media failed to demonstrate the minimum of independence of opinion necessary for preserving self-respect and enjoying the confidence of the public. Moscow's main press outlets were divided into camps—not according to ideological or political orientation, but according to ownership. Independence of commentary was evident only in those newspapers supported by banks that did not participate in the "clash of the titans": *Kommersant-Daily, Moskovskii komsomolets,* and a few others.

The papers that were critical of Chubais and Potanin harped on the danger of concentrating so much power and money in one organization. Instead of the old oligarchy of seven major banks, one super-monopoly had emerged. The opposite side interpreted the victory of Oneksimbank and the reformers' team as the victory of open market rules over secret political bargaining. *Izvestiya,* purged of "disloyal" journalists after it was bought by Oneksimbank, declared it a victory of national interests over private.

The criticisms on both sides were absolutely right. The irony is that the mutual accusations and exposures of the bank's presses somehow ensure a peculiar freedom of information. For ordinary Russians, though, that freedom is exhausting; in order to get the complete picture, you have to read at least half a dozen newspapers a day.

NOTE

Reprinted with kind permission from *Transitions* magazine, October 1997.

Foreign and Military Policy

HOLDING THE FORT

by SCOTT PARRISH

In a 23 December 1997 press conference, Russian Foreign Minister Yevgenii Primakov painted an upbeat picture of Russian foreign policy during the past year. Primakov said that Russia had managed several significant achievements, including defending national interests without provoking confrontation with other states, and diversifying contacts with a wide range of countries beyond the West. One critical Russian newspaper quipped afterwards that Primakov had sounded like a "pupil in the fifth grade who claims he could read at the age of three and learned to swim at five." Indeed, Russian diplomacy in 1997 managed only a few concrete accomplishments. As the national economy remained in crisis and the military continued to collapse, Primakov and his boss, Russian President Boris Yeltsin, found themselves with few diplomatic cards to play. In general, it took their best efforts to stave off a continued erosion of Moscow's international position.

During the year Yeltsin and Primakov swallowed NATO expansion, and found their ties with the former Soviet republics in the Commonwealth of Independent States (CIS) crumbling around them. Links with the Baltic States and Eastern Europe also stagnated. The critics of Primakov had some points, since a more astute Russian policy in Eastern Europe and the CIS could probably have ameliorated the current problems there. Ties with the United States also continued to falter. Primakov tried vainly to bolster Russian standing in the Middle East, but the settlement he mediated between Iraq and the West collapsed within weeks, unintentionally underlining Russian weakness. On the other hand, Primakov and Yeltsin did manage to shore up Russia's position in some areas. In Asia, ties with Japan, China, and South Korea were improved. And in the West, while the NATO-Russia charter Primakov and Yeltsin signed in May did not halt NATO expansion, it did at least defuse a potential confrontation over the issue for the time being.

For the Russian military, 1997 was another dismal year. The collapse that had begun before the break-up of the Soviet Union continued unabated. As in 1996, the year was full of financial shortfalls, suicides by unpaid officers, and shooting sprees by crazed soldiers. The only bright spot was the prospect that Igor Sergeev, the new Defense Minister appointed in May, would begin serious military reform that would create a smaller, but more effective military force. Sergeev faced a monumental task, as downsizing the demoralized and decrepit Russian military would clearly be a long, painful, and expensive process. Nevertheless, a blueprint was laid down in the fall of 1997, and organizational reform was begun, which is more than had been accomplished in previous years.

NATO EXPANSION: SWALLOWING A BITTER PILL

NATO enlargement remained the dominant issue in Russian foreign policy during the first half of 1997. The first few months of 1997 saw frenzied negotiations between Russian diplomats and their counterparts in the major capitals of the Western alliance, as both sides strove to defuse a potential confrontation over NATO plans to invite several former members of the now-defunct Warsaw Pact to join the alliance. Russian politicians of all ideological stripes continued to vehemently oppose NATO expansion, viewing it as directed at the long-term "containment" of Russia. Russian Foreign Minister Yevgenii Primakov, while publicly maintaining that Russia would not accept NATO enlargement, continued his 1996 policy of bargaining with NATO over the terms of that enlargement.

The ensuing diplomatic haggling focused on negotiating a NATO-Russia charter. In these talks, Primakov demanded that NATO promise not to deploy nuclear weapons or additional conventional forces on the territory of new members, a demand that NATO leaders rejected. Moscow also wanted the agreement to place geographical limits on NATO enlargement, a demand NATO also rebuffed. Subsequently, at his March 1997 summit meeting in Helsinki with his U.S. counterpart, Bill Clinton, Russian President Yeltsin settled for pledges by NATO that it had "no intention, no plan, and no reason" to deploy nuclear weapons or additional conventional forces on the territory of new members, rather than insisting on binding promises. Yeltsin also "agreed to disagree" with Clinton about the geographical scope of NATO enlargement. About six weeks later, on 14 May 1997, Primakov and NATO Secretary-General Javier Solana announced the conclusion of the "Founding Act on Mutual Relations, Cooperation and Security Between NATO and the Russian Federation." Yeltsin, Clinton, and other Western leaders formally signed the Founding Act at a ceremony outside Paris on 27 May.

In the face of domestic criticism that he had capitulated to NATO, Yeltsin contended that the Founding Act represented the best way to "minimize" the negative consequences for Russia of NATO enlargement. Russian supporters of the agreement especially pointed to its provisions establishing a Russia-NATO Permanent Joint Council, which would give Moscow an institutional forum for discussing security issues with the alliance. Critics, however, countered that Russia had accepted the "illusion" of non-binding pledges from NATO, which would not sufficiently restrain the alliance. These critics said that the new joint council would become a mere "talking shop."

Indeed, the Founding Act, while defusing the immediate danger of a confrontation, did not address the underlying issues that make the addition of new members to the alliance potentially destabilizing in the future. NATO leaders formally agreed at their Madrid summit on 8–9 July that the first "wave" of enlargement would be limited to Poland, Hungary, and the Czech Republic. But they also left the door "open" to other European democracies in the future, including former republics of the Soviet Union such as the Baltic states, Moldova, and Ukraine. Primakov and Yeltsin, however, made it clear that Moscow will "reconsider" its relationship with the alliance if any of the former Soviet republics are asked to join. Meanwhile, Romania, Bulgaria, Slovenia, and the Baltic states, denied invitations to join in the current round, continued to lobby hard for future admission. In January 1998, Clinton and his three Baltic counterparts signed a U.S.-Baltic charter in which Washington pledged to push for Baltic membership in NATO, setting the stage for future difficulties that may be difficult to finesse. Meanwhile, media reports suggest that at its initial meetings during 1997, the NATO-Russia council did not made much progress toward resolving these problems, but instead was becoming a battleground for continued disputes. Following a pattern set since 1991, Russian diplomacy in Eastern Europe during 1997 remained moribund, and failed to offer any real alternatives to NATO enlargement.

U.S.-RUSSIAN RELATIONS: THE CHILL DEEPENS

Like the 1993 START II treaty, which has languished unratified in the Russian legislature for five years, a wide range of issues in U.S.-Russian relations remained unresolved during 1997. The overall tenor of the relationship became chillier, despite attempts by Presidents Clinton and Yeltsin to improve ties. NATO expansion, which fueled distrust in both Washington and Moscow, a stalled arms control process, and nagging disputes over regional issues like Iran and Iraq combined to sour the bilateral climate. The domestic political situation of the two presidents, who faced legislatures dominated by their political opponents, further complicated matters. While bilateral ties were still nowhere near the deep-freeze of the Cold War, emergent trends suggested that the relationship would remain rocky in the near future.

In an attempt to break the ongoing arms control logjam at their Helsinki summit in March, Yeltsin and Clinton announced that they had agreed on the outline of a START III treaty, which would reduce the strategic forces of each country to 2,000–2,500 warheads. They also declared that they had resolved their long-standing differences over theater missile defense (TMD) systems. Coming at the same summit where Clinton and Yeltsin outlined the terms of a NATO-Russia charter, these agreements appeared to clear the way for further progress in the long-stalled U.S.-Russian arms control process. This impression was reinforced on 26 September 1997, when Russia and the United States signed a package of agreements implementing the political understanding reached by

Clinton and Yeltsin at Helsinki. The package included a protocol extending the destruction deadlines in START II, and two agreements on theater missile defense (TMD) systems which outlined what systems are considered prohibited under the 1972 ABM Treaty. The agreements, together with the START III framework outlined at Helsinki, were designed to mollify Russian parliamentary critics of START II.

The impact of this package on the communist-dominated Duma was negligible, however, and lobbying efforts in October by Defense Minister Igor Sergeev and Foreign Minister Primakov also had no visible effect. As a result, the deadlock persisted, since the political climate in the United States would not allow further arms control measures to move forward until START II is ratified. Yeltsin pledged to press hard for START II ratification in the spring of 1998, but his repeated promises to do so in the past had not produced results.

The 1997 work of the U.S.-Russian Joint Commission on Economic and Technical Cooperation, led by Vice President Al Gore and Prime Minister Viktor Chernomyrdin, produced some promising economic agreements and a few small achievements in the security field, including an agreement by Russia to convert its last three military plutonium production reactors to purely civilian uses. Despite this progress, Russian officials complained that Washington was hampering the development of bilateral trade by failing to repeal the Jackson-Vanik Amendment, refusing to recognize Russia as a country with a market economy under U.S. law, and failing to support Russia's bid for entry into the World Trade Organization.

Regional issues also continued to divide Moscow and Washington during 1997. Primakov's attempts to rebuild Russian influence in the Middle East often catalyzed these tensions. In Iran, for example, Russia continued working on the Bushehr nuclear power plant, despite charges from the United States that the reactor could aid Iran in building nuclear weapons. Russian and American officials also sparred for much of 1997 over allegations that Russian firms were assisting Iran's ballistic missile program. Russian officials angrily denied that any militarily significant missile technology had been sent to Iran, but did acknowledge that Iranian agents had sought such technology. Beginning in October 1997, Republican legislators repeatedly urged the Clinton administration to sanction the Russian firms suspected of involvement in missile deals with Iran.

Disagreement over how to handle Iraq also strained ties. Russia, together with France and China, continued to advocate lifting the UN embargo against Iraq as soon as possible, and opposed using force to compel Baghdad to comply with the terms of UN Security Council resolutions passed after its 1991 invasion of Kuwait. Russian diplomacy during the November 1997 crisis over Iraq's refusal to allow UN disarmament inspectors to continue their work was regarded as "appeasement" by many in Washington, who would prefer that the UN sanctions remain in place until Iraqi dictator Saddam Hussein is removed from power. Since Russia was owed some $8 billion by Iraq, and Russian oil companies have concluded several lucrative deals to explore Iraqi fields which are contingent on the sanctions being lifted, this divergence of approach seemed well-entrenched.

Some Western analysts argue that Russian ties with the West will remain relatively cordial, because the powerful financial-industrial groupings which now dominate the new Russian economy need access to Western markets and Western capital. This theory has some surface plausibility, but these interests do not seem to have exerted themselves to solve the many outstanding issues in U.S.-Russian relations. Some of their actions, such as the November 1997 gas pipeline deal between Iran and Gazprom (which could trigger U.S. economic sanctions), complicated relations with the United States even more.

TROUBLE IN THE CIS

In terms of rhetoric, the territory of the former Soviet Union has been a "priority area" in Russian foreign policy for the past several years. In reality, however, progress toward cementing Russian influence in the region was mixed, at best. There was still no consensus within the Russian elite over how to best construct links with the other former Soviet republics. Some wanted Russia to actively promote and finance political and economic re-integration of the region, while others believed that market-based economic links, not government-financed political and economic integration programs, are the only glue that can hold together a new type of regional cooperation over the long run. For the most part, the latter group—often led by First Deputy Prime Minister Anatolii Chubais—has held the upper hand, and Russia has taken few concrete actions to promote integration. 1997 saw this pattern continue, as organizations ostensibly created to promote regional integration—like the Commonwealth of Independent States (CIS), the Russo-Belarusian Community, and the Customs Union of Russia, Belarus, Kazakhstan, and Kyrgyzstan—remained largely moribund. In fact, by the end of the year, many Russian commentators believed that the CIS itself was on the verge of disintegration, after an acrimonious summit meeting in Chisinau in October 1997.

Russia did score some successes on the bilateral level with its former Soviet neighbors. Links with Ukraine, for example, improved significantly during 1997. In May, Yeltsin and his Ukrainian counterpart Leonid Kuchma signed two long-anticipated agreements: an accord on the division of the Black Sea Fleet, and a bilateral friendship treaty. The dispute over the fleet had been one of the prime irritants in Russo-Ukrainian relations since 1991, while the friendship treaty addressed one of Kyiv's biggest concerns by including a clause in which Russia pledged to respect Ukrainian territorial integrity, in effect ending any possible dispute over the Crimea. The treaty did not fully resolve many thorny economic disputes between the two countries, however. And while the Ukrainian legislature moved fairly quickly to ratify the agreements, the Russian Federal Assembly, which includes many deputies who still view the Crimea as Russian territory, has not done so. (And the Ukrainian parliamentary ratification specifically excluded some of the clauses pertaining to Crimea.)

Russian relations with the Baltics remained difficult during 1997. Russia and Lithuania did sign a border treaty in October 1997, making Lithuania the first former Soviet republic to formalize its border with Russia. Similar agreements with Latvia and Estonia remained stalled, however, largely because Moscow continued to link their signature with what it views as continued discrimination against the Russian minority in those two states. Relations with all three Baltic states remained strained over the issue of NATO enlargement, as Tallinn, Riga, and Vilnius rejected offers of Russian security guarantees made by Yeltsin during a December 1997 visit to Sweden as an alternative to NATO enlargement.

Russian ties with the Caucasian republics of Georgia, Azerbaijan, and Armenia remained mixed, at best. Relations with Georgia were strained by the failure of efforts to mediate a solution to the Abkhaz conflict and a trade dispute over vodka imports. Ties with Azerbaijan were dominated by the conflict over how to manage the resources of the Caspian Sea basin, while efforts to compel Armenia and Azerbaijan to settle the Nagorno-Karabakh dispute remained stalemated. Russia scored a small victory in the struggle for control over Caspian oil in November 1997, when "early oil" from the first offshore field in Azerbaijan began to flow through an export pipeline leading to the Russian port of Novorossiisk. However, the "major" route for exports from the region remains undetermined and is unlikely to run through Russia.

MORE PROGRESS IN THE FAR EAST

As in 1996, the bright spot in Russian diplomacy was in the Far East. Efforts to bolster ties with China, Japan, and South Korea all bore fruit, and ties with India—a major partner of the Soviet Union—also continued to advance. Yeltsin met twice during 1997 with Chinese leader Jiang Zemin. At their Moscow meeting in April, the two, joined by the leaders of Kazakhstan, Kyrgyzstan, and Tajikistan, signed an agreement on the mutual reduction of military forces along the CIS-China border, which set limits on deployments within 100 km of the frontier. In their November meeting in Beijing, the two leaders settled a nagging dispute over islands along their border, further cementing their declared "strategic partnership." Moscow also continued sales of sophisticated military hardware to China in 1997, including two advanced type-636 Kilo class diesel submarines and a licensing agreement for the manufacture of 200 SU-27 fighters. Reports also surfaced that Russia was aiding China in its naval nuclear propulsion program.

Nevertheless, Russo-Chinese cooperation had its limits. Bilateral trade during 1997 actually decreased by 10 percent, dropping to $6.1 billion, which accounts for less than 2 percent of China's $325 billion in foreign trade last year. Despite plans to boost bilateral trade to $20 billion by 2000, major Chinese civilian development projects are often completed with Western, rather than Russian assistance. While the Russian Ministry of Atomic Energy won a contract in December to build a nuclear power station in China, Russian contractors lost out on their bid to participate in the huge Three Gorges hydroelectric project. For both countries, ties with the other cannot replace ties with the West, and so their partnership, while mutually beneficial, does not signal the foundation of a new anti-Western alliance.

As if to demonstrate this point, Moscow redoubled its efforts during 1997 to improve relations with Japan, which have long been hindered by the dispute over the southern Kuril islands and the consequent failure to conclude a peace treaty between the two countries formally ending World War II. A visit to Japan by Defense Minister Igor Rodionov in May was followed in June by the first visit of a Russian warship to a Japanese port in 103 years, and a pledge by Moscow to de-target all strategic nuclear weapons which were previously aimed at Japan. Meeting on the sidelines of the G-8 summit in Denver, at which Japanese support helped Russia become a full member of the group, Yeltsin and Japanese Prime Minister Hashimoto agreed to hold a summit meeting in the fall. The "no neckties" summit between the two leaders held in November in Krasnoyarsk had the best atmospherics of any Russian-Japanese meeting since the collapse of the Soviet Union, and produced an agreement by the two leaders to press for the conclusion of a peace treaty by 2000.

Moscow also moved to bolster its links with South Korea, agreeing to increase military shipments as part of a barter agreement aimed at repaying Russia's substantial debt to Seoul within 10 years. Reversing previous objections and moving to put Russian policy more in harmony with Seoul's, Primakov expressed support in July for the four-power talks (involving South Korea, North Korea, the United States, and China) which were discussing a framework for a peace treaty formally ending the Korean War. Relations with North Korea, by contrast, remained relatively cool, and talks on a new bilateral friendship treaty to replace the 1961 pact that expired in 1996 did not make any visible progress. To the south, Russia also continued building ties with India, coming close to concluding a $2 billion deal for the construction of a nuclear power plant there, despite objections from Washington. While these links with Asia cannot fully compensate for the shortcomings in ties with the West, they did demonstrate that Primakov's rhetoric about a "multipolar" world was having a concrete impact on Russian foreign policy.

MILITARY POLICY: REFORM BEGINS, BUT THE CRISIS CONTINUES

1997 was another year of turmoil in the Russian military. Financing shortfalls remained severe, despite repeated government promises of repayment. Media reports indicated that the government still owed the defense ministry some 25 trillion old rubles ($417 million) at the end of 1997. This debt represented about one-third of the 81 billion new rubles (equivalent to 81 trillion old rubles) allocated to defense in the 1998 draft budget. This in itself was a significant reduction over the 104 trillion rubles allocated to the defense budget in 1997, and is even lower than the 83 trillion rubles allotted to defense in the austerity budget issued by the government in May 1997.

In this climate, where military salaries often went unpaid for months, personnel problems also remained dire. Suicide was the leading cause of death in the armed forces, with 487 cases reported in 1997. Shooting incidents in which servicemen broke under the pressure of their extreme conditions and killed their comrades also proliferated. Draft evasion remained a serious problem.

The picture was not entirely bleak, however, as the appointment of Igor

Sergeev as defense minister in May 1997 and the approval of a military reform plan in the fall revived hopes that the military could be downsized and rebuilt into a smaller, cheaper, but more effective force. Yeltsin fired the previous defense minister, Igor Rodionov, in May, blaming him for failing to develop an effective military reform program. Rodionov's approach had been rather unproductive. During his short tenure in office (he was only appointed defense minister in July 1996) he had spent most of his time complaining publicly about military budget problems, and insisting that reform could not begin unless financing was increased. But Yeltsin must also shoulder the blame for the military's plight, having largely neglected the military reform issue since 1991.

In July 1997, based on recommendations by Sergeev and Defense Council Secretary Yurii Baturin, Yeltsin issued a decree on "Principal Measures for the Reform of the Armed Forces of the Russian Federation and the Improvement of Their Structure." Under the terms of this decree, the military was to be reduced from its current strength of about 1.4 million to 1.2 million by January 1999. Most of the service branches will be restructured. The Strategic Rocket Forces have already absorbed the Military Space Forces and the Space-Missile Defense Troops of the Air Defense Forces. The Air Defense Forces are to merge in 1998 with the Air Force, and the Ground Forces command will be significantly reduced and most of its functions transferred to the commands of Russia's eight military districts. The Navy and the Airborne Forces will also suffer significant cutbacks. The reform also called for the Russian General Staff to assume greater responsibilities over all the armed forces, including the uniformed servicemen of paramilitary forces like the Internal Troops and the Federal Border Service. One of the principal objectives of the reform was to create a smaller number of fully staffed and combat-ready units, rather than the larger, understaffed ones that currently predominate.

In terms of doctrine, the Russian military, given the lamentable condition of its conventional forces, chose to increase its emphasis on the importance of nuclear deterrence. The appointment of Sergeev, who previously commanded the Strategic Rocket Forces, reflected this change, as did the initial test deployment of the new SS-X-27 Topol M intercontinental ballistic missile in December 1997. The official Russian national security concept issued in December 1997 made it clear that "Russia reserves the right to use all the forces and systems at its disposal, including nuclear weapons, if the unleashing of armed aggression results in a threat to the actual existence of the Russian Federation as an independent sovereign state." Articles in Russian military publications began discussing the renewed importance of tactical nuclear weapons to Russian defense. These developments effectively reversed the former Soviet declaratory policy of "no first use" of nuclear weapons, formalizing a change that Russian officials have hinted at for several years. This doctrinal change may affect the Russian stance in future arms control talks.

Despite having laid out the basis for a reformed military, Sergeev faced seemingly insurmountable obstacles to rebuilding an effective force. The financial costs of downsizing are likely to swamp efforts to create, man, and train an effective military. Downsized officers and soldiers must be offered social benefits and re-training, while the costs of dismantling the legacy of the Soviet military, such as the 156 decommissioned nuclear submarines that will be awaiting dismantling by 2000, are severe, even considering the possibility of foreign financial assistance. Procurement of new hardware has almost ceased, and training levels are abysmally low. Western experts believe that even under the best circumstances it will take at least a decade before Russia can reconstitute a combat-ready military.

As in 1996, some commentators suggested that these conditions might spark a military revolt. Such predictions appear unfounded. Duma Defense Committee Chairman Lev Rokhlin and former Defense Minister Igor Rodionov did form a "Movement to Support the Armed Forces, Defense Industry, and Military Research," which held its founding congress in September 1997. Rokhlin denounced Yeltsin's and Sergeev's reform plans and called for Yeltsin's ouster. However, it was unlikely that his movement would be any more effective than the plethora of other such movements formed since 1991 to defend the interests of the military. The military seemed fated to remain one of the big "losers" of the ongoing political, social, and economic changes in Russia.

NEITHER WAR NOR PEACE IN CHECHNYA

by PETER RUTLAND

The year 1997 saw Chechnya make the transition from a state of war to an uneasy peace. Moscow honored the peace accords signed at Khasavyurt in August 1996, to the extent that the last Russian soldier was withdrawn from Chechnya on 4 January 1997. However, Moscow obstinately refused to recognize the independence of Chechnya, and continued to adhere to the legal fiction that it was an integral part of the Russian Federation.

FIRST STEPS TOWARD DEMOCRACY

There was a semblance of consolidation in the political leadership of Chechnya. Presidential elections were held on 12 February, with 16 candidates in the running. The main contenders were former chief of staff and architect of the Khasavyurt peace Aslan Maskhadov; the charismatic field commander Shamil Basaev, who had led the June 1995 raid on the Russian town of Budennovsk; and Zelimkhan Yandarbiev, who had taken over as Chechen president following the death of Djohar Dudaev in April 1996. Maskhadov was an acceptable interlocutor for Moscow—unlike Yandarbiev, an Islamic intellectual who had plans for a broader Confederation of the Caucasus Peoples, or Basaev, still a wanted man in Russia for his role in the June 1995 terrorist raid on Budennovsk in southern Russia, which left 100 dead.

The elections took place under difficult circumstances. In the run-up to the election two Russian ORT journalists were kidnapped, and 26 Cossack inhabitants of a village in Naurskii district in northern Chechnya were slain. That the elections took place at all was only thanks to a $350,000 grant from the Organization for Security and Cooperation in Europe (OSCE), whose mission leader, Tim Guldimann, had been instrumental in bringing about the Khasavyurt accords. The OSCE also provided 70 international observers, which gave a sort of legitimacy to the proceedings. Chechen authorities refused to allow polling stations to be set up in Russia to enable the 140,000 refugees to vote (out of a total electorate of 640,000), although some of these refugees were brought by bus to polling stations at the borders of Chechnya.

Much to Moscow's relief, Maskhadov emerged the victor, with 59 percent of the vote, trailed by Basaev with 24 percent and Yandarbiev with 10 percent. Voting seems to have been largely along regional/clan lines, with Maskhadov polling heavily in the northern districts. There were fears that the defeated candidates would refuse to accept the results of the election, as was the case with Salman Raduev, son-in-law of the slain president Dudaev. However, Maskhadov's inauguration on 12 February passed without incident.

Maskhadov took on the post of prime minister as well as president. He brought several of the defeated candidates into his government, most notably Movladi Udugov, the 34-year-old former information minister and leader of the Islamic Path party, who had thrown his support behind Maskhadov in the week before the election. Udugov was appointed foreign minister, and later first deputy prime minister. Basaev initially announced his withdrawal from politics. In a surprising turnaround he joined the government as first deputy prime minister on 1 April, but resigned on 9 July, complaining about Russia's failure to pay compensation to Chechnya for the damage and loss of life inflicted by the war.

Parliamentary elections were also held on 17 January, but with 830 candidates from 40 parties competing for 63 seats, only 5 of the candidates won the required 50 percent of votes in the first round, and only 30 more in the second round a month later. The last round of elections for the 20 remaining seats took place on 31 May. The powers of the parliament seemed even vaguer than those of the president. Three times in the course of the year Maskhadov asked the parliament to grant him extraordinary powers, but was rebuffed each time. On 1 January 1998 Maskhadov asked Basaev to take over as prime minister and form a new government, with Maskhadov declaring his intention to concentrate on foreign policy.

STAND-OFF WITH MOSCOW

Under the Khasavyurt accords of August 1996 Russia promised to withdraw its forces, while the vexed question of Chechnya's legal status was left undecided, to be resolved sometime before December 2001. In November 1996 Maskhadov signed the Moscow accords with Russian Prime Minister Viktor Chernomyrdin, under which Russia pledged to restore communications, restart the oil pipeline across Chechnya, and provide aid for the reconstruction of its shattered economy.

The Chechens regarded the Khasavyurt agreement as de facto recognition of their independence, but Moscow insisted that Chechnya was still one of the 89 subjects of the Russian Federation. The last Russian troops withdrew on 4 January, and most communication links were re-established, but reconstruction aid never arrived and even Russian payment of pensions only began late in the year.

In the wake of the 21 months of fighting some 1,200 Russian troops were still missing. Most were presumed dead, but at least 200 were thought to be held as hostages by independent Chechen bands. 1,340 Chechens were still held in Russian prisons for war-related activity, and the Russian State Duma was eventually persuaded to approve (on 11 March) a partial amnesty in the hope that some of these prisoners could be exchanged for Russian detainees. Only a handful of such exchanges took place during the year: Russians travelling to Chechnya to make such arrangements were themselves liable to be kidnapped.

On 12 May Maskhadov met Russian President Boris Yeltsin and signed a treaty "On Peace and Relations between the Russian Federation and the Chechen Republic of Ichkeria" which formally affirmed the results of the Khasavyurt accords. Maskhadov interpreted the May treaty as Russian recognition of Chechnya's independence, on the grounds that the treaty was signed between two equal subjects. Hence for example Chechnya did not send any representatives to the Russian parliament. However, Russian Security Council Secretary Ivan Rybkin scotched such assertions, insisting that the Khasavyurt accords had frozen the status of Chechnya till December 2001. Moscow was playing something of a balancing act. They wanted to support Maskhadov in his struggle to control more radical elements inside Chechnya, but they did not want to give too much away in the process.

There was no further progress toward resolving Chechnya's constitutional status over the course of the year. Yeltsin and Maskhadov met on 17 August and agreed to set up a task force to discuss the issue. Yeltsin urged Chechnya to accept a deal along the lines of the 1994 treaty with Tatarstan, under which Moscow would pay lip-service to Chechen sovereignty while Grozny agreed to preserve a "common economic, defense, and air space" with Russia. One of the few dissenting voices in the Russian government was Deputy Prime Minister Ramazan Abdulatipov, who publicly questioned whether Chechnya would settle for Tatarstan-type status.

The signing of the May peace agreement cleared the way for negotiations over the economic revival of Chechnya. The carrot which dangled before Moscow and Grozny was the prospect of "early oil" from Azerbaijan flowing north through the 150-kilometer-stretch of pipeline across Chechnya, which would carry the oil from Baku to the Russian Black Sea port of Novorossiisk.

The Russians insisted on Chechnya accepting their terms for banking and customs relations as a precondition for the pipeline deal. It looked as if Grozny (and Baku) needed the oil revenue more than Moscow. Chechnya reluctantly agreed that all banking transactions with Russia would go through a special account at the Central Bank of Russia. (Chechnya continued to use the Russian ruble as its currency.) Maskhadov also accepted Russian customs controls on external trade, including jointly operated customs at Grozny's Sheik Mansur (formerly Severnyi) airport, and Russian policing of Chechnya's only external border, with Georgia. After these points were accepted, a tripartite deal was signed in Baku on 12 July under which Russia, Chechnya, and Azerbaijan agreed to start the export of early oil across Chechnya.

Haggling continued over the terms of the deal. Moscow offered to pay Chechnya their standard internal transit fee of 43 cents a ton: Chechnya asked for $4. The negotiations continued in fits and starts throughout the year, with Moscow threatening to build a new 280-kilometer pipeline bypassing Chechnya if agreement was not reached.

Finally on 8 September the two sides compromised on a transit fee of $2.20 a ton, with Moscow also providing $10 million to help pay for the rehabilitation of the pipeline. The Chechen government promised to provide security for Russian oil workers and to crack down on the hundreds of backyard refineries which had run on pilfered oil from the pipeline when it was operating. On 9 November the first oil arrived from Azerbaijan at the Chechen border, although volumes were expected to be quite modest—200,000 tons in the first year. First Deputy Prime Minister Boris Nemtsov continued to advocate the new pipeline option, showing the persistence of serious rifts within the Russian leadership on this issue.

LAW AND DISORDER

The Maskhadov government struggled to establish law and order in the devastated country, which was effectively a conglomerate of a hundred autonomous villages, each with its own leaders who paid scant regard to the orders of the government in Grozny. Despite repeated efforts to disband all armed groups and subsume them into the Chechen national army, several large independent bands continued to move at will through the republic and wage terroristic acts on neighboring territories. Repeated orders from Maskhadov seeking to disband these groups went unheeded.

The two most prominent groups were Salman Raduev's "Army of General Dudaev" and the "Islamic Battalion" formed by Jordanian-born fighter Emir Khattab, an adherent of the Wahhabi sect. Raduev refused to accept that the war with Russia was over and pledged to continue a terrorist campaign until the whole Caucasus was free. Raduev claimed responsibility for two blasts in the Russian cities of Armavir and Pyatigorsk on 23 and 28 April, each of which claimed two lives. Neither Moscow nor Grozny was able to shut down Raduev's operations: Raduev himself survived his fourth assassination attempt in October. Otherwise, the Chechen warlords generally avoided attacking each other. An exception was the assassination of a leading candidate for the post of mayor of Grozny, Yakub Usmanov, on 23 May.

The most terrible act of terrorism, the killing of six Red Cross workers in Novye Atagi in December 1996, remained unsolved, although Chechen authorities laid the blame on Adam Deniev, a pro-Russian Chechen then living in Moscow.

The main indicator of lawlessness was the endemic practice of kidnapping, either for ransom or for political reasons. During the course of the year about 50 foreigners were kidnapped. The most publicized case was the seizure of NTV journalist Yelena Masyuk and her two assistants on 10 May—just days before the signing of the peace treaty with Moscow. Masyuk was a popular figure whose objective reporting of the war had greatly helped the Chechen cause. Four other Russian journalists had been seized on 4 March, and were released on 6 June. Four days later two journalists from the ORT TV show *Vzglyad* were captured: one of their last assignments had been interviewing the four kidnapped journalists. July saw the killing of nine Russian policemen in Khasavyurt, just over the Dagestan border, and further kidnappings, including the seizure of aid workers from Medecins Sans Frontieres. (Nearly all other international aid organizations had pulled out of Chechnya after the Red Cross killings in December 1996.)

Masyuk and her TV crew were freed on 18 August. Her boss, NTV chief Igor Malashenko, went public with claims that he had paid a ransom of $1 million for her release, and accused Chechen Vice President Vakha Arsanov of being behind the kidnapping. He was supported in these accusations by former Security Council Deputy Secretary Boris Berezovskii, who had himself negotiated the release of the two ORT journalists earlier in the year. Cynics suggested that Malashenko and Berezovskii were merely trying to discredit the Russian government. Their corporations had lost out in the bidding for the privatization of Svyazinvest and had launched a media war against First Deputy Prime Ministers Anatolii Chubais and Boris Nemtsov.

Many violent clashes occurred across the border in Dagestan. At a forum in July First Deputy Prime Minister Udugov called for the "restoration of Dagestan to its historic borders," by which he meant the return to Chechnya of the Aukhovskii district, populated by Akin Chechens, which was ceded to Dagestan when the Chechen Autonomous Republic was dissolved in 1944 and its inhabitants deported.

In early November eight policemen were abducted in Akrai, just across the border with Dagestan, in response to which Russian interior ministry forces tried to seal off the border. On 21 December a group of up to 100 men attacked a Russian military base at Buinaksk in Dagestan, after which Interior Minister Anatolii Kulikov threatened "preemptive strikes" against Chechen guerrilla bases. The Buinaksk raid was attributed to Khattab's "Islamic Battalion."

First Deputy Prime Minister Udugov used the prevailing lawlessness as a reason to push for the introduction of an Islamic state, arguing that the Shariat or Islamic code would eliminate crime. On 23 April Chechen TV screened the first public execution under Shariat law: the condemned man had his throat cut. Another public execution by shooting on 3 September drew further international protests. The Russian Federation (of which Chechnya was still technically a part) had suspended the death penalty as a condition of its entry to the Council of Europe.

Maskhadov himself, although of secular bent, went along with the Islamicization, announcing a new set of measures on 8 June that included a plan to switch from Latin to Arabic script. In July as a further step toward eliminating Russian influences Udugov cut all Russian TV broadcasts in the republic. While

Maskhadov was travelling to Washington in November his erstwhile vice president Arsanov went a step further, advising women to cover themselves in public.

INTERNATIONAL ISOLATION

Perhaps the greatest disappointment of the year was Chechnya's failure to win international recognition. Russian Foreign Minister Yevgenii Primakov made it clear that Moscow would cut all ties with any country which gave diplomatic recognition to Chechnya. This served to deter all countries from acknowledging Chechen independence, except Tatarstan, which signed a Treaty of Friendship with Chechnya on 21 May. Tatarstan's own status as a "subject of international law" was only ambiguously acknowledged in the treaty it signed with the Russian Federation in 1994.

Chechnya still relied on Russia for communication with the outside world. Chechens had to travel abroad on Russian passports and pass through Russian customs. The Russians used their control of the airspace around Chechnya to enforce compliance. In early April Moscow allowed seven planes of pilgrims, including President Maskhadov, to fly to Mecca, and provided 3,000 new Russian passports for them. On 20 May a plane carrying Vice President Arsanov to a conference in the Hague was turned back by Russian fighters, an action which Security Council Secretary Ivan Rybkin later attributed to "overzealous officials" in the border guards service. The delegation got as far as Odessa, but then refused to travel on to the Hague using the new Russian passports they had been issued, with the imperial eagle on the cover. On 1 October Russia refused to let a plane with Vice President Arsanov fly to Baku, on the grounds that it was not licensed with the Russian authorities. In response Arsanov expelled all 80 Russian officials (including the mission representing President Yeltsin) from Grozny.

Despite these tensions, Russian and Chechen negotiating teams continued to hold meetings in the town of Dagomys in a bid to come up with a formula to resolve Chechnya's ambiguous legal status. Chechnya experienced a most unsettled year of peace, but this was still better than the alternative.

Economy and Society

WAITING TO GROW

by PETER RUTLAND

1997 was supposed to be the year that the Russian economy took off into sustained growth. Alas, it was not to be. GDP growth was registered at an anemic 0.8 percent for the year.[1] Although monetary stability was achieved, the government's capacity to raise taxes remained disturbingly low. There was also a deterioration in Russia's foreign trade performance, as the output of key commodities was static while the world prices for energy and metals fell. The main story of the year was the abortive attempt to launch a second "liberal revolution" by a team of reformers appointed to top government posts in March. Their aim was to break the privileges of the financial and industrial oligarchs who dominate the Russian economy and complete the structural market reforms that had not been carried out in 1992–94. One positive development was the conclusion of a favorable agreement with the Paris Club on the restructuring of Russia's debts to commercial creditors. More ominous was the economic turbulence that hit Asia in the fall, which was sure, sooner or later, to send waves crashing against the flimsy financial structures on Russia's shores.

Experience in East-Central Europe suggests that economic growth resumes two years after financial stabilization has been achieved. Russia managed to rein in the money supply and bring inflation under control in 1995–96: hence, it was expected that 1997 would be a year of strong recovery. However, this did not occur. There are at least three possible explanations for this failure. First, some argue that the government's monetary stabilization was illusory, that it had been achieved by allowing the spread of money substitutes, from physical barter to bills of exchange (*vekselya*). Second, the blame could lie with the poor management of the newly privatized enterprises which now accounted for 70 percent of the economy. The new owners had ill-defined property rights and chose to loot their enterprises for short-run gains rather than plow surplus revenues back into investment. Third, Russia's ongoing economic stagnation could be due to yet deeper structural problems, the legacy of an economy that had been developed over 75 years with the primary purpose of sustaining the world's second largest military machine.

THE ECONOMY STABILIZES

1997 saw the most encouraging macroeconomic results since 1990. Annual inflation was 11 percent, its lowest level since 1990. GDP grew by about 0.8 percent and stood at 2,675 trillion rubles ($450 billion): a welcome contrast to the 5 percent fall recorded in 1996. Industrial output grew by 1.9 percent, leading most commentators to suggest that Russia's seven-year slump had finally ended. Industrial growth was led by the metals and forestry sectors, but there was also growth in some manufacturing industries, such as automobiles. Real incomes rose by 2.5 percent and real wages 4.2 percent, while real personal consumption crept up 1.2 percent and retail trade 2.4 percent. Natural gas output fell 5 percent but crude oil output rose 1.4 percent. All these growth trends strengthened in the second half of the year, but there was a strong chance that the financial crisis that hit in October would derail these fragile gains.

The unofficial economy may have been growing faster than the official economy, but in the absence of reliable data no one can say for sure. In 1997 Goskomstat (the State Statistics Committee) raised its official estimate for the black economy's share of GDP from 23 percent to 28 percent, although most observers put it higher still, at around 40 percent. Agriculture continued to be a drag on economic recovery. Good weather led to a bumper grain harvest of 89 million metric tons—28 percent higher than 1996—but meat and dairy production fell by 10 percent and 5 percent respectively, so overall output showed little change. The financial situation in the sector was dire: farms may have run up 25 trillion rubles ($4 billion) in losses. The private plots of urban and rural residents continued to be an important source of food for most families.

Capital investment showed no sign of recovery, dropping another 5 percent in 1997. There was a boom in investment in communications, rising 28 percent, but even in this sector the absolute level of investment was still only half the 1990 level. Between 1991 and 1997 investment as a share of GDP fell from 36 percent to 23 percent, and in real terms it fell by three quarters. The average age of Russian factory equipment was 15 years. Commercial banks did very little lending to the private sector; capital investment was squeezed out of the state budget; and there was no substantial influx of foreign investment beyond short-term and speculative portfolio lending.

Unemployment declined from a high of 9.6 percent in April to 8.9 percent at year's end, representing 6.5 million out of a workforce of 72 million. This is using the broad International Labor Organization definition based on survey data: only 2 million workers were actually registered as unemployed. At least another 4 million workers were temporarily laid off and did not show up in these figures.

SPRING OFFENSIVE BOGS DOWN

Having apparently recovered from his winter bouts of illness, President Boris Yeltsin launched an extensive government reshuffle in March. Yeltsin appointed two new first deputy prime ministers: long-time reformer and since July 1996 presidential chief of staff Anatolii Chubais (age 41) and Nizhnii Novgorod governor Boris Nemtsov (age 37). Chubais also took over the finance ministry. Oleg Sysuev, the 44-year-old mayor of Samara, became deputy prime minister with responsibility for labor and social questions. It was thought that the infusion of new blood from the provinces would give the technocrat Chubais the political support he needed to complete the economic liberalization of Russia. Viktor Chernomyrdin stayed on as a figurehead prime minister: Yeltsin had stripped him of virtually all his power.

Former Oneksimbank chief Vladimir Potanin left the post of deputy prime minister which he had held for seven months. The ministries of industry and defense industry were abolished and merged into Yakov Urinson's economics ministry. April saw the departure of more ministers—those for energy, railways, and the State Tax Service. Nemtsov took over the energy ministry, and the 39-year-old Aleksandr Pochinok took over the tax agency. The 36-year-old Alfred Kokh, head of the State Property Committee, was promoted to deputy prime minister. Irina Khakamada, 42, was named Russia's first minister for small business. Other cadres were drafted in to be deputy ministers in the finance and energy ministries. The agenda of the new reform team was summarized in a seven-point action program launched by Yeltsin on 19 May. The program promised to improve tax collection; to battle corruption; to reform pensions and social welfare; and to cut tariffs in the "natural monopolies" of gas, electricity, and railways.

The reformers wanted to dismantle the privileges which were enjoyed by the leading bankers and industrialists, and which had enabled them to consolidate their political and economic power in the course of Russia's market transition. This was politically dangerous, since it was the "seven bankers" who had pooled their resources to secure President Yeltsin's re-election in 1996; while the energy lobby was represented in government by none other than Viktor Chernomyrdin, prime minister since 1992.

Boris Nemtsov described his approach as that of "popular capitalism," to be distinguished from the oligarchic capitalism of the bankers and the corporatist capitalism of Moscow Mayor Yurii Luzhkov (built around cronyism and state patronage). One of his first acts was to order all government officials to sell off their foreign-made limousines and instead ride in Russian Volgas. A few symbolic car auctions were held, but within weeks the idea was dropped. May saw another populist gesture: a new law and a presidential decree requiring ministers to submit income declarations. Most of the published declarations were suspiciously modest.

Chubais vowed to crack down on the hitherto cozy relations between banks and the state budget. In March the finance ministry announced it would stop providing guarantees for commercial bank credits to organizations funded from the state budget. Chubais also strove to create a network of state treasury branches so that budget funds would not have to be spent through "authorized" commercial banks—a source of rich commissions and more nefarious diversions of funds. But this process dragged on, and was not completed by year's end.

Nemtsov's first target was the natural gas monopoly Gazprom. In April he declared his intention to reaffirm state control of the company, which was behind with its tax payments. Nemtsov suspected that Gazprom and the other utilities were using non-payments by their customers as an excuse to hide income, siphon off profits, and evade taxes. Only about 10 percent of Gazprom's domestic customers paid for their deliveries in cash. Under a 1994 agreement with the privatized company, management of the state's 35 percent shareholding was delegated "in trust" to the Gazprom board. Gazprom chief Rem Vyakhirev mobilized support in the Russian parliament. Gazprom claimed to be owed 83 trillion rubles ($14 billion) by Russian customers: this gave it considerable leverage over leading companies and regional politicians. Gazprom also made some effort to pay off its tax arrears, transferring 14.5 trillion rubles ($2.5 billion) to the budget in May and June. Nemtsov backed off: Gazprom was providing 25 percent of federal budget revenue, and he did not want a knockdown struggle with Vyakhirev. On 22 December the trust agreement with Gazprom was renewed, symbolizing the failure of Nemtsov's "spring offensive" against the giant energy corporation.

Nemtsov also targeted the electricity monopoly, Unified Energy System (EES). In May an ally of Nemtsov from Nizhnii Novgorod, the 29-year-old banker Boris Brevnov, was appointed to head EES. Nemtsov wanted to introduce more competitive pricing by allowing power plants to sell directly to large customers without going through EES. It was hard to implement these ideas since the regional electricity utilities were uncooperative. Nemtsov also put pressure on the railways to cut rates while insisting that customers pay in cash. From 1 July freight rates for timber and coal were cut by 50 percent and for food and oil cargoes by 40 percent and 25 percent.

The IMF and World Bank urged the reformers to tackle social welfare spending, which was still structured along Soviet-era lines and was not targeted on those in real need. (See the accompanying article by Penny Morvant.) Nemtsov and Sysuev tried to design a program to ease the burden of subsidizing housing and public utilities which had fallen on municipal budgets as state-owned firms were privatized. Yeltsin signed a decree in April outlining a plan for tenant contributions to rise from the current level of 27 percent of the cost of services to 50 percent in 1998 and 100 percent in 2003. The government would grant subsidies to low-income families. Many regional leaders protested: Moscow mayor Yurii Luzhkov refused to implement the scheme, and in May he was granted an exemption. Other regions tried to follow suit.

The reformers also hoped to tackle the problem of pension reform. They introduced plans to cut the special privileges (such as free transport and housing) for various categories of officials; but these were rejected by the State Duma. A draft program for shifting from the existing system of pensions based on labor records to one based on individual pension accounts did not even get as far as the Duma. It was rejected when Sysuev presented it to a cabinet meeting in October.

The reform team was tarnished by accusations of corruption in summer. The discontented bankers launched a media blitz against their political opponents, which led to the resignation of Kokh from the State Property Committee in August. (See the accompanying articles by Andrei Fadin and Laura Belin.) November saw the dismissal of industrialist Boris Berezovskii from his post as deputy secretary of the Security Council, and the book advance scandal which led to the resignation of Kokh's replacement, State Property Minister Maksim Boiko, and Federal Bankruptcy Service Chairman Petr Mostovoi. (Boiko was replaced by Farit Gazizullin, and Mostovoi by Georgii Tal.) As a result of the scandal Chubais had to give up his post as finance minister, although he stayed on as first deputy prime minister. The new finance minister was the 34-year-old Mikhail Zadornov, the Yabloko party economist and former head of the Duma budget committee. At the same time Nemtsov gave up his post as energy minister, which was taken by his ally from Nizhnii Novgorod, the banker Sergei Kirienko. The net result of these demotions appeared to be a strengthening of the authority of Chernomyrdin.

It was clear that the spring action program was over-ambitious and failed to produce the intended structural reforms. Despite the firm backing of President Yeltsin and an infusion of cash from the IMF, the young reformers lacked the political and/or administrative capacity to push through their agenda. Many of the ideas were derived from contemporary Western practice, and were fine in principle but did not, as the saying goes, suit the "Russian climate." The opposition came from all sides—from the State Duma; from regional leaders; from leading bankers and industrialists; and from much of the media, most of which was controlled by the oligarchs. Already by the summer most of the reformers' policy initiatives were in abeyance, and even Nemtsov himself was disavowing the concept of popular capitalism as an oversimplification of what he was trying to accomplish.

MONETARY AND FISCAL POLICY

Following the pattern of previous years, monetary policy continued to be one of the few positive features of the Russian economy. While inflation was held to 11 percent over the year, the Central Bank of Russia (CBR) ran a more relaxed monetary policy, allowing money supply (M2) to rise by 30 percent, which helped bring down interest rates. However, this softening of monetary policy (mainly in the first half of the year) was not sufficient to end the investment slump nor to re-monetize Russian industry. In the final months of the year the CBR had to hike interest rates once again to protect Russia from the effects of "Asian flu."

Monetary policy was only relaxed in comparison with previous years. The Russian economy still faced an acute shortage of liquidity. M2 made up only about 14 percent of GDP (compared to 50 percent plus in other economies), and non-cash transactions accounted for about half of industrial sales. Reliance on barter had increased since 1992, as the tighter monetary policy took hold. Despite the apparent stability in monetary policy, arrears remained a chronic problem throughout the economy. At year's end debts to suppliers amounted to 12.5 percent of GDP, to tax authorities 6.6 percent, to off-budget funds 4.9 percent, and to workers in the form of unpaid wages 1.8 percent. This came to a grand total of 700 trillion rubles ($120 billion), or 26 percent of GDP (up from 22 percent at the start of the year).

Fiscal policy was a source of growing concern. The federal budget deficit declined slightly to 6.8 percent of GDP, down from 7.7 percent of GDP in 1996. (This figure includes interest payments on the government debt.) Actual spending ran at 17.8 percent of GDP and revenues at 11 percent: these were 2 percent and 4 percent below the levels planned in the 1997 budget law. In May government submitted a 108 trillion ruble ($19 billion) sequestration plan to close the gap: federal spending arrears mounted. One quarter of federal spending was on debt service. The flow of federal revenue was highly uneven, with twice as much collected in taxes in the final quarter as in the first quarter. In June George Soros extended a two-week $700 million loan to the Russian government to tide it over until the end of the month.

In addition to the federal budget, regional and municipal authorities raised (and spent) about 15 percent of GDP, running a small deficit (1.2 percent of GDP). Regional governments started to enter the international capital market. In May Moscow issued a $500 million bond, followed by St. Petersburg ($300 million) and Nizhnii Novgorod ($100 million). "Off-budget funds" for pensions, social security and unemployment) raised and spent another 7 percent.

The deficit was financed through the sale of about $50 billion worth of treasury bills (GKOs), about $16 billion of which were held by foreigners. The government also sold $4 billion of Eurobonds. As a proportion of GDP, GKOs rose from 2.4 percent in 1995 to 15 percent of GDP at the end of 1997. Yields, which had peaked at 180 percent during the June 1996 presidential election, fell to 39 percent by December 1996 and 18.4 percent in July 1997, before nudging back up to 19.1 percent in October. The CBR reduced its re-financing rate from 48 percent at the beginning of the year to 21 percent in October, raised to 28 percent in early November. The Asian crisis caused steadily increasing pressure on the ruble, as funds were pulled out of the stock and GKO markets. On 27 October trading was halted for several hours on the Russian trading system (RTS) after prices dropped 8 percent.

Despite the drop in stock values after the October crisis, the Russian stock market was still the best performer worldwide in 1997, having risen 180 percent in the first ten months of the year, then falling 30 percent. Market capitalization rose from $36 billion in January to $86 billion as of October 20 before falling to $60 billion at year's end. In comparison with Western markets this is extremely low given the potential value of the assets of some of the companies (in oil and gas for example). Trading was concentrated in a narrow range of stocks, however: 40 percent of turnover was in LUKoil and the electricity utility EES. The situation in the banking system was fairly static: no major crises, but lingering doubts about the stability of the banking system given the banks' lack of usual banking operations (like lending to private businesses) and their dependence on the GKO market. The CBR withdrew banking licenses from 282 credit institutions in 1996 and 290 in 1997, reducing the number of banks to 1,675.

The IMF was pressing the government to introduce a new tax code in order to decrease the opportunity and incentive for tax evasion and thus increase federal revenues. A new draft code was prepared which aimed to reduce the number of taxes from more than 100 to around 30, and to shift the burden from the producer toward consumers. The Duma initially accepted the new draft tax code on first reading in June, but became more combative as the summer wore on. In August the government issued its draft budget for 1998. Revenues were to be 11.8 percent of GDP and expenditures 16.9 percent, leaving a deficit of 5.1 percent. The Duma rejected the draft 1998 budget in October and threatened the government with a vote of no confidence. Chernomyrdin persuaded the Duma to accept the 1998 budget, but only by agreeing to postpone the much-needed introduction of a new tax code, and by accepting the Duma's overly optimistic GDP projections when calculating the 1998 budget. The revised draft had revenue at 12.5 percent of GDP, spending at 17.4 percent, and a deficit of 4.7 percent. By year's end the Duma had only adopted the 1998 budget on second reading, and the haggling continued into the New Year. Both sides knew the budget assumptions were unrealistic. As the saying goes, "We pretend to approve the budget and the government pretends to implement it."

Anatolii Chubais spent much of the year trying to "beat out" taxes from delinquent companies in order to raise the funds to pay the pensions and wages owed to state employees. (On wage arrears, see the article by Penny Morvant.) In late 1996 President Yeltsin had formed the Temporary Extraordinary Commission for Tax Collection (whose initials mimicked those of Lenin's Cheka secret police) with Chubais at its head. The new Cheka was less effective than its Leninist counterpart: most of the firms on its hit list continued to accumulate tax arrears in 1997. Tax receipts amounted to about 75 percent of the planned level. In March a presidential decree called upon firms to hand over to the government shares equal to their tax debts. A new scheme to restructure old tax debts was slowly implemented: in October the auto giant AvtoVAZ signed a deal to pay back 8 trillion rubles in tax arrears over 10 years. One hundred major enterprises owed around 40 percent of all tax arrears, and two thirds of these arrears were generated by the energy sector. Part of the problem was that penalties for tax arrears accumulated at the rate of 3 percent per day, and often the penalties exceeded the initial debt.

In early December the Cheka announced that it had decided to declare two tax laggards bankrupt—the Omsk and Angarsk oil refineries, which owed federal taxes of 766 billion rubles ($128 million) and 526 billion, respectively. The move had clear political implications. The Angarsk refinery belonged to Sidanko, part of Vladimir Potanin's Oneksimbank empire, while Omsk belonged to Sibneft, owned by Boris Berezovskii's group. However, the seizure of the firms's assets was blocked by Chernomyrdin. Chubais scored a victory on 23 December, when the Constitutional Court struck down the clause in the Civil Code which required firms to pay wages before paying taxes.

Chubais also tried to put the squeeze on regions that were withholding taxes, especially the republics of Tatarstan, Bashkortostan, and Sakha (Yakutiya). An attempted tax revolt by Irkutsk Oblast in March was easily squashed. To clear the 1997 budget Chubais, gritting his teeth, agreed to what he described as "disgusting" tax offsets (where firms' tax arrears are set against debts to them from state organizations) worth 60 trillion rubles. The government warned—as it had in 1996—that in the next year, no tax offsets would be allowed.

RUBLE HOLDS STEADY

Maintaining the stability of the ruble was one of the central planks of the government's economic policy. The ruble lost 7 percent of its nominal value against the dollar over the year, falling from 5,482 at the end of 1996 to 5,908 at the end of 1997. This meant a slight appreciation in real terms (given 11 percent inflation). The ruble corridor was set at 5,500—6,100 at the beginning of the year, shifting to 5,750—6,350 by the end. One sign of confidence was the December announcement that from 1 January 1998 the ruble would be redenominated, with one new ruble worth 1,000 old rubles. (Previous monetary reforms had caused public panic.) The CBR announced that for 1998 it would scrap its sliding band in favor of a more flexible regime, allowing 15 percent fluctuation around a target rate of 6.2 (redenominated) rubles/dollar for 1998–2000. The CBR had to step in to defend the ruble in December, hiking its interest rate to 45 percent and spending $3 billion from its reserves. The bank rejected suggestions (from Berezovskii among others) that it was time to devalue the ruble. Gross foreign reserves, which had peaked at $24.5 billion in July, fell to $17.8 billion at the end of 1997. A new 0.5 percent tax on hard currency purchases was introduced in July 1997, sending much of the ruble/dollar trading underground. People turned an estimated 22 percent of their earnings into dollars, most of it for purchases or foreign trips rather than savings.

The IMF welcomed the appointment of the reform team but was worried by the state of the federal budget. The November and December tranches of the three-year Extended Fund Facility (each about $670 million) were paid out in February. It showed its displeasure at the slow pace of tax collection by delaying payment of the January tranche, which was released in May, and the September installment, released in December. Similarly, the World Bank declined to extend a $1.1 billion loan in the fourth quarter.

PRIVATIZATION: FAIR OR FOUL?

Privatization continued to be a source of controversy in 1997. Postponement of adoption of the new tax code and the lack of effective bankruptcy procedures meant that even though 70 percent of Russian industry was privately owned few firms faced incentives to behave like their profit-maximizing equivalents in other capitalist economies. Only a minority of the privatized firms had tried to restructure their operations: shedding excess labor and seeking new products and new markets. Most firms used arrears as their survival strategy—reneging on payments to suppliers, workers, and tax authorities. This reflected the fact that most firms had been bought by their managers and workers: only one in ten was controlled by an outside owner.

The government turned to privatization in the second half of the year as a way of plugging the federal budget deficit. By year's end privatization revenues had reached 23 trillion rubles ($3.8 billion)—well above the target level. In January 8 percent of the electricity monopoly EES was sold for $335 million. The sale of shares in the oil company Surgutneftegaz raised $73 million cash and $211 million investment in February, and the Sibneft auction raised $110 million cash and $50 million investment in May.

Pride of place went to the sale in July of 25 percent of shares in Svyazinvest, a telecom company which had been created to hold a controlling interest in 85 of Russia's 87 regional telecom companies as well as the long-distance and international telephone lines. Oneksimbank, in alliance with George Soros's Quantum fund, won the auction with a bid of $1.875 billion, well above the starting price of $1.18 billion. The reformers hailed the sale as a breakthrough: competitive bidding finding new owners for state companies while filling federal coffers. Others were more skeptical. Some suspected that information about the rival bids had been leaked in advance to Oneksimbank, and even that the bank was lent state money in order to make the purchase. Many countries had sold their state-owned telecoms in the 1990s: in nearly all cases they were bought by foreign telecom operators, and not by banks. It was suspected that Oneksimbank was just speculating, hoping to sell off the shares at a later date. The price was relatively modest: in 1996, the sale of 100 percent of Mexico's state telecom raised $23 billion.

There were a series of high-profile auctions following the Svyazinvest sale. In July, 40 percent of the Tyumen oil company was sold to Alfa bank in return for a pledge to invest $810 million, much to the chagrin of the local oil managers who tried to block the sale. In August, 38 percent of the metals giant Norilsk Nickel was sold to Oneksimbank for $256 million cash and a $310 million investment pledge. The October crisis put a financial squeeze on the banks, and sales of three further tranches of oil company shares in November–December had to be postponed due to lack of bids. In December the Rosprom-Yukos concern, controlled by the bank Menatep, bought a 42 percent stake in the Eastern oil company, but paid only $800 million—half of what had been expected.

The bankers started to quarrel among themselves—angry that Oneksimbank had done so well in these sales. The feuding grew more intense after the sacking of the business tycoon turned politician Boris Berezovskii from his post as deputy secretary of the Security Council in early November (to which he had been appointed in October 1996). Opposition figures criticized the wave of auctions as crony capitalism in action, seeing them as payoffs for the oligarchs who had bankrolled Yeltsin's election campaign. In July Yeltsin bowed to Duma demands and signed a new law on privatization that required the government to submit its annual privatization program for Duma approval and tightened up the enforcement of investment pledges made by the winners in privatization auctions. In December, the Duma's Audit Chamber recommended that the auctions earlier in the year of shares in Svyazinvest, Norilsk Nickel, and Sibneft be canceled due to cronyism in the bidding process.

Yeltsin failed in his repeated efforts to persuade the Duma to adopt a land code that would legalize the private ownership of land. As a result the restructuring of Russia's farms involved only a paper shift in the status of the old collective and state farms. A few regions, such as Nizhnii Novgorod, pressed ahead with experimental privatization of farms on their own. The number of private farmers stayed at around 280,000, the same level reached in 1993. These farmers were able to hold land based on a 1993 Yeltsin decree that allowed any collective farm employee to remove a small allotment of land for private use, and to rent plots from other collective farm employees. These farmers faced problems obtaining bank loans to buy equipment, and in gaining access to the wholesale network to sell their produce. On 27 November Yeltsin signed a decree allowing the sale of land in cities.

FOREIGN TRADE

Russia's export earnings fell 2 percent in 1997 to $87 billion, while imports rose 8.5 percent to $67 billion. This left a trade surplus of $20 billion—a robust figure, but down from $27 billion in 1997. The fall in export revenue was due to a slump in world oil prices: crude oil export volume was static but revenue fell 8 percent. Energy accounted for 45 percent of exports and metals another 16 percent. CIS countries accounted for 23 percent of the trade turnover. Goskomstat includes an estimate of individual "shuttle trade" in its figure for imports, which amounts to 22 percent of the $67 billion cited above. The share of imports in retail sales eased slightly, falling from 54 percent in 1995 to 49 percent in 1997, but still a sign of a very open economy.

Foreign direct investment shot up in 1997, mainly because of the privatization auctions. FDI totaled $5 billion in the first nine months, an amount equal to the entire sum of FDI over the preceding three years. The parliament continued to drag its feet over implementing the 1995 law on production sharing agreements. In July the parliament approved seven sites under the law, but only two were open to foreigners. One positive step for foreign investors was the lifting of VAT from foreign capital equipment imports in March. In November President Yeltsin signed a decree allowing foreigners to take full ownership of domestiç oil companies—previously, foreign ownership had been limited to 15 percent. The same month British Petroleum announced it was buying 10 percent of Sidanko from Oneksimbank for $570 million.

Some earlier investors continued to have problems enforcing their ownership rights. In August the government unexpectedly canceled Exxon's tender for developing an oil field in the Nenets district. Despite three rulings in its favor from the Stockholm International Arbitration Tribunal, the Canadian IMP group was not able to get control of the Aerostar Hotel from its former Russian partners, nor collect the $6 million in damages awarded by the court. In December the Moscow banks Renaissance Capital and MFK and their international partner Cambridge Capital Management finally won a court case giving them five seats on the board of Russia's largest steel mill in Novolipetsk, in which they had a minority stock holding. In October unions at the Novomoskovsk detergent plant (near Tula) forced Procter and Gamble to abandon a plan to fire half the workforce, and promise to raise the minimum wage to 850,000 rubles.

Foreigners were far more active in lending money than investing it in Russia. Foreigners advanced $15 billion in short-term loans to the government in the first nine months of the year (up from $6.5 billion in 1996). Despite this influx of lending, repayment of loans, purchases of foreign currency, and the shrinking trade surplus meant that in the third quarter of the year Russia's current account ran a $1 billion deficit—for the first time ever. This was a worrying sign of potential financial squeeze, caused mainly by the explosion in short-term government borrowing.

In June 1996, Russia had concluded a deal rescheduling its $39 billion debt to members of the Paris Club of official creditors. Separate deals were signed over the course of 1997 dealing with supplementary official loans from Germany and Japan. An agreement with the London Club of commercial creditors was signed in December 1997, under which Russia's $32.5 billion debts to the club will be repaid over 25 years, with a seven-year grace period. In September 1997, Russia joined the Paris Club as a creditor, although realistically its chances of getting back some of the $140 billion the Soviet Union claimed to have lent to third world states appears slim. On 1 December 1997 the Partnership and Cooperation Agreement signed by the European Union and Russia at the June 1994 Corfu Summit went into force. An interim agreement covering trade had been in force since February 1996.

Russia's foreign obligations totaled $127 billion, of which $102 billion were pre-1991 Soviet debts and $25 billion new post-1991 borrowing. Russia repaid about $7 billion in interest and capital in 1997: thanks to the reschedulings, the heavy repayments will not begin until 2003. The ratio of Russia's total foreign debt to GDP was about 30 percent, while debt service payments ran at 3 percent of GDP and the ratio of debt payments to exports was only 6 percent. These figures are modest by international standards, but the rapid increase in borrowing at high interest rates to fund the federal budget deficit could change the picture very quickly.

NOTES

[1]The macroeconomic data cited in this article come from the monthly and quarterly reports of *Russian Economic Trends*, produced by the Center for Economic Reform, supplemented by data from the State Statistics Committee.

TENSIONS EASE IN THE SOCIAL SPHERE

by PENNY MORVANT

Judging by opinion polls, most Russians found life easier in 1997 than they had in 1996. Official statistics showed an overall improvement in living standards, although many people continued to experience great poverty. The government launched a high-profile campaign against delays in the payment of wages and pensions, which scored some successes in the short term, but arrears continued to build up in the non-state sector. Looking to the longer term, cabinet reformers sought to restructure welfare provision to target benefits on the poorest strata, but progress was limited. As in previous years, social policy tended to take a back seat to immediate political and economic considerations or to fall victim to tussles between the executive and the legislature.

The government proclaimed several anti-corruption campaigns during 1997, but it was largely a phony war. While overall crime figures declined for the second year running, reports of high-level abuse of office multiplied—surely a reflection of deep-seated corruption as well as of public feuding between rival business and political elites. It was a mixed year for human rights. There were some positive developments in the reform of the criminal justice system, but a highly controversial law was approved in September that could restricted the work of many religious groups in Russia.

LIVING STANDARDS IMPROVED. . .

In a poll conducted by the All-Russian Center for the Study of Public Opinion (VCIOM) in late December, 63 percent of respondents said 1997 had been easier or no more difficult than 1996. Similar surveys by VCIOM in previous years had always found a majority classing the current year as harder than the last. In another end-of-year survey, 56 percent of respondents described their material situation in 1997 as good or satisfactory, up from 49 percent in 1996. Nevertheless, three-quarters of those polled still regarded 1997 as a bad year for themselves and their families.

The perceived improvement in 1997 was reflected in official statistics on living standards. According to the State Statistical Committee (Goskomstat), average per capita real income increased by 2.5 percent, after remaining stable in 1996 and falling sharply in 1995. The share of the population living in households where average per capita income was below the minimum subsistence level (the Labor Ministry's estimate of the level of income needed to get by for a month) fell slightly, from 21.4 percent in 1996 to 20.9 percent in 1997. Families with several children, non-working single pensioners, and the unemployed were among the poorest.

Income differentials increased. According to the All-Russian Center for

Table 1. Positive Events of the Year
(percent of respondents mentioning as a positive achievement)

Elimination of wage and pension arrears	82%
Signing of treaty of union with Belarus	57%
Celebration of 850th anniverary of Moscow	41%
Compromise between president and parliament	41%
State Duma approval of 1998 budget	37%

Source: Nationwide poll conducted by Russian Independent Institute of Social and National Problems, reported in *Nezavisimaya gazeta*, 16 January 1998.

Living Standards, the income of the richest 10 percent of the population was 12.3 times that of the poorest decile, up from 11.8 times in 1996. As in previous years, there were also considerable regional differences in living standards. The populations of the North Caucasus republics were the worst off, while living standards were highest in Moscow and the natural resource–rich Tyumen Oblast.

Unemployment (measured according to the International Labor Organization methodology) declined slightly, from 9.3 percent of the labor force at the end of 1996 to 9.0 percent a year later. The number of unemployed officially registered with the Federal Employment Service also fell, from 3.4 percent to 2.8 percent. Long delays in the payment of benefits were one disincentive to register. But the downward trend in unemployment was not expected to last, and VCIOM polls showed that the prospect of being out of work overtook delayed wages and pensions as the nation's no. 1 worry.

It is important to remember that all figures relating to living standards in Russia are extremely unreliable. On the one hand, official data tend to understate poverty, because the official subsistence minimum is artificially low, and because delays in the actual payment of wages and social benefits are not taken into account. On the other hand, under-reporting of income by companies and individuals to avoid taxes is rife. In December 1997, a study commissioned by the U.S. Treasury Department contended that Goskomstat badly underestimated the size of the shadow economy, by putting it at 25 percent of GDP when the correct figure would be closer to 50 percent. The report's authors argued that as a result real personal income levels were about 50 percent higher than the official statistics suggested. Whatever the exact size of the shadow economy, there can be no doubt that many Russians relied on strategies such as moonlighting, growing their own food, and engaging in unregistered trading to improve their living standards and those of their families.

. . . BUT WAGE ARREARS CONTINUED TO MOUNT

President Boris Yeltsin began 1997 vowing to wipe out delays in the payment of state-sector wages and pensions, which were caused by poor tax collection, inter-enterprise debt, and the misappropriation of funds. A similar campaign had been proclaimed ahead of the 1996 presidential election, but that year ended with a 9.3 trillion ruble ($1.7 billion) debt to public-sector employees and a debt of

$6.2 billion in the non-state sector. The 1997 drive to eliminate the pension backlog was more successful than that of the preceding year. Most pension arrears were paid off by the 1 July deadline, thanks to large transfers to the Pension Fund from the federal budget and, following government pressure, from large companies behind on their taxes.

Soviet-style storming to meet the end-of-year deadline for paying off wage arrears proved inadequate. Despite massive transfers to the regions in December, public-sector workers were still owed some $820 million at year's end. Back pay owed in the non-state sector was estimated at a record $6.9 billion on 30 November. Moreover, while the year-on-year rate of growth in private-sector arrears gradually declined throughout 1997, there were fears that a December Constitutional Court ruling stipulating that companies should give tax liabilities priority over wage payments would reverse that trend.

As in previous years, persistent wage delays were the main trigger for labor strikes and more desperate forms of protest, such as hunger strikes and railroad blockades. The number of working days lost increased from about 4 billion in 1996 to 6 billion in 1997, with education the worst affected sector in both years. But most strikes continued to be short-lived and often confined to a single region, posing no real threat to social stability. A national day of action organized by the umbrella Federation of Independent Trade Unions of Russia (FNPR) in March attracted a lower turnout than expected, and the federation's traditional November day of protest was not held. The FNPR's inability to organize effective national action was typical of the experience of public associations in general. While the number of organized groups in civil society has mushroomed since 1991, they tend to be fragmented and weak. Narrowly focused initiatives, such as environmental groups dedicated to a single issue, have had more success in influencing policy than broader-based national movements.

WELFARE REFORMS GET UNDER WAY

One of the priorities of the new ministers appointed during the government reshuffle in mid-March was to reform Russia's social welfare system. Their aim was to eliminate costly universal subsidies and to target benefits to support the most vulnerable groups. This was not a new policy, but reforms received a higher profile and priority, even if actual achievements turned out to be limited.

One of the most expensive legacies of the Soviet welfare system was subsidized housing services, such as heating, water, and building maintenance. In 1993 the government issued a resolution gradually phasing out subsidies by 1998, but that target fell by the wayside as it became clear that the vast majority of the population could not afford to absorb the costs. By 1997, utilities and maintenance subsidies were still costing the state about $18 billion a year. Households paid on average only about 27 percent of costs, a situation that benefited well-off families disproportionately and encouraged wasteful consumption. The picture varied considerably from region to region, however. In St. Petersburg and Samara, for example, charges to domestic consumers had already been raised sharply, while in Moscow households were still picking up only a fraction of the bill. On 28 April Yeltsin issued a decree establishing the general principles for further reform of the sector. According to First Deputy Prime Minister Boris Nemtsov, the aim was to eliminate state subsidies and to introduce competition into the provision of services in the hopes of reducing charges and improving standards. He said the share of costs borne by tenants should increase to 35 percent by the end of the year and then rise in steps to 100 percent by 2003. No family, however, would be expected to spend more than 16 percent of its income on housing in 1997, with the share rising to 25 percent by 2003. Special centers would be created in the regions to pay allowances to low-income households. To work, the reforms require the backing of regional and local authorities, which are responsible for running the services. All are supposed to ensure the 2003 target is met, but Moscow Mayor Yurii Luzhkov wasted no time in expressing his opposition and setting out his own, more gradual program. Other regional bosses were just as recalcitrant, not least because popular opposition to the withdrawal of subsidies was fierce. At year's end, reforms appeared likely to continue at a slow and uneven pace.

The government also sought to abolish a string of special benefits, such as free travel and supplemental allowances, enjoyed by certain categories of the population by dint of where they lived or the type of work they performed, irrespective of their financial status. By 1997, almost two-thirds of the population were entitled to some sort of special benefit, although payments often failed to materialize. In mid-May the government submitted eighteen bills eliminating many of these privileges, arguing that this would free up funds to pay off the wage and pension backlog, help prevent new arrears from accruing, and allow benefits to be targeted more effectively. But the Duma, locked in a struggle with the executive, rejected all but one of the spring drafts as well as an amended package of bills submitted in the summer.

An important step toward means-tested benefits was taken in the autumn, with the passage of a law on the minimum subsistence level. Since 1992, the Labor Ministry had calculated a subsistence level for pensioners, children and people of working age on the basis of a basket of basic necessities (foodstuffs, goods, and services), but the measure was not linked to the payment of benefits. Moreover, the basket was widely criticized as inadequate, because it provided for little more than physical survival; and other organizations, such as the trade unions, came up with their own figures. In April 1994 the Duma began drafting legislation aimed at forcing the authorities to pay benefits to households falling below the poverty line, but successive drafts were quashed either by the president or by the Federation Council on the grounds that they would be too expensive to implement. In October 1997, however, a compromise was reached. The new law called for national and regional subsistence levels to be issued quarterly and a gradual increase in the minimum pension, minimum wage, and other social benefits to bring them into line with the subsistence level. The minimum wage is currently no more than an accounting unit. In May 1997, it was set at a mere 83,490 rubles a month, while the national minimum subsistence level for a person of working age was calculated to be 469,000 rubles. Although the law established an important principle, further legislation was required to determine the composition of the consumer basket and how quickly benefits are to be indexed to it. It also ignored the tricky question of how to assess a household's income accurately. Given the size of the shadow economy, ensuring means-tested benefits are not abused is likely to prove a serious problem.

Turning to pensions, reformists argued that Russia's aging population made the existing system unsustainable even if mandatory employer and employee contributions to the state Pension Fund were paid on time. They also viewed the system as unfair in that a person's own work history played very little role in determining the size of his or her pension. The issues most hotly debated were: the weight to be given to personal, cumulative pension accounts based on an individual's own contributions; the role and regulation of private pension funds; the retirement age, currently a low 55 for women and 60 for men; and policies toward Russia's 7 million working pensioners. All these issues were politically sensitive, and there was considerable dissent within the government. On 18 December the cabinet approved a reform concept that, if endorsed by the president, would go into effect in 2000. By no means as radical as the Labor Ministry's first draft, it envisaged the gradual transition to a three-tiered system consisting of earnings-related state pensions, financed by the Pension Fund from current contributions; state pensions funded by the federal budget for individuals who had made insufficient contributions and for certain special categories of state-sector employees; and supplementary personal pensions funded by voluntary contributions to state or non-state pension schemes. The plan also called for an increase in employees' contributions to the Pension Fund (from 1 percent to 7 percent of salary by 2009) and a parallel reduction in employers' obligations (currently 28 percent) as well as providing for the creation of a personalized register of contributions. A preliminary step toward making pensions reflect an individual's years of service and salary level was scheduled to take effect in February 1998 under separate legislation.

CORRUPTION FLOURISHES

Cracking down on corruption was a constant refrain in 1997, but the measures enacted had no teeth. A May presidential decree forced senior officials to make declarations of their income and assets, but the accuracy of their statements could not be checked and they were widely regarded as a joke. Allegations of corruption, or *kompromat*, featured prominently in the battles between rival elite groups, but only a few cases went to trial. The president and the parliament again failed to agree on anti-corruption legislation. Meanwhile, the media were filled with reports detailing the sort of bribes routinely accepted by officials at every level, from Duma deputies and ministry mandarins to local police, and exposing the links between business, organized crime, and politicians.

According to the MVD, the crime rate fell by more than 8 percent in 1997, to

2.4 million recorded crimes. But the statistics are unreliable. Under pressure to demonstrate a high rate of solving crimes, police fail to register many complaints. Drug-related crimes increased, and there was considerable concern over the link between intravenous drug use and rapidly increasing rates of HIV infection.

CHANGES IN THE CRIMINAL JUSTICE SYSTEM

On 9 October, on the eve of a trip to Strasbourg, Yeltsin issued a decree transferring jurisdiction over Russia's prison service from the Ministry of Internal Affairs (MVD) to a beefed-up Justice Ministry under a former head of the Federal Security Service (FSB), Sergei Stepashin. The transfer, based on the principle that the same department should not be in charge of both the investigation and internment of criminals, had been under discussion since 1991 and was in line with obligations Russia assumed when it joined the Council of Europe in February 1996. The decree, however, did not set out a timetable for implementing the changeover, which mandated amendments to more than forty laws. Nor did it make any mention of the pre-trial detention centers under the jurisdiction of the FSB. Russia's million or so prisoners, particularly the 300,000 remanded in severely overcrowded FSB or MVD prisons, continued to endure appalling conditions and to suffer high rates of disease, including tuberculosis.

Another positive step was the repeal of an unconstitutional 1994 presidential decree allowing suspects to be remanded in custody for up to 30 days without being charged. But activists said torture was still routinely used to extract confessions. Progress on the abolition of capital punishment was slow. Although Russia signed Protocol 6 of the European Convention on Human Rights banning executions in peacetime, the new Criminal Code, which went into force on 1 January 1997, retained the death penalty, albeit for a reduced number of crimes, and the Duma blocked legislation imposing an official moratorium. No executions were carried out, however, in line with the unofficial moratorium Yeltsin instituted the previous summer. The only exception was Chechnya, where the implementation of Shariat law led to public executions.

RESTRICTIVE RELIGIOUS LAW APPROVED

It was a mixed year for human rights in general. In February the executive and the legislature finally reached agreement on a law governing the post of Russian Federation human rights commissioner (responsible for overseeing state protection of individuals' rights and freedoms), but the position was still vacant at year's end. Conditions in the armed forces continued to deteriorate, and there were reports of increasingly authoritarian policies by legal organs in certain regions, such as Krasnodar Krai.

The most controversial development of the year was the passage of new legislation on religion making it more difficult for foreign missionaries to operate in Russia. On 23 June the Duma approved a bill granting unregistered "religious groups" that had been operating in Russia for less than fifteen years fewer rights than accredited "all-Russian religious organizations," which were identified as Orthodoxy, Islam, Judaism, and Buddhism. The legislation, strongly supported by the Orthodox Church, was ostensibly aimed at controlling the activities of so-called totalitarian sects, whose teachings found fertile ground in Russia after the collapse of communism. The bill's opponents warned, however, that it would re-institutionalize Soviet-era discrimination against all but the small number of officially sanctioned religions. Yeltsin vetoed the draft in July under heavy pressure from foreign governments, but following intense lobbying by the Orthodox Church the new version, drawn up by a conciliation commission and signed by the president on 26 September, was little different. It expanded the list of "traditional" Russian faiths to include other Christian denominations but retained the fifteen-year requirement for religions to receive full rights. Groups that failed the test would not be allowed to run businesses, schools, or media and were required to re-register every year until they qualified. It was too early to assess the impact of the law at year's end. Mechanisms to implement it were not scheduled to take effect until 1998, ironically decreed by Yeltsin to be "the year of human rights."

TRANSCAUCASUS & CENTRAL ASIA

VIII

Georgia

Azerbaijan

Armenia

Kazakhstan

Uzbekistan

Tajikistan

Kyrgyzstan

Turkmenistan

Georgia

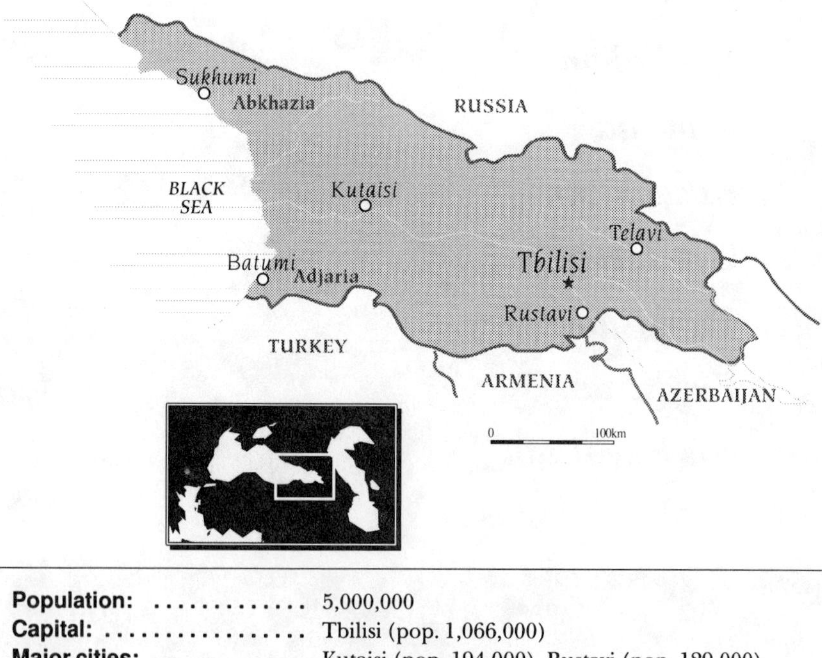

Population:	5,000,000
Capital:	Tbilisi (pop. 1,066,000)
Major cities:	Kutaisi (pop. 194,000), Rustavi (pop. 129,000), Batumi (pop. 123,000)
Area:	70,000 sq. km.
Major ethnic groups:	Georgian, Armenian, Russian, Azerbaijani, Ossetian, Greek, Abkhaz (percentage breakdown unavailable)
Economy:	GDP growth: 11.3%
....	Inflation rate: 7.9%
....	Average monthly wage: $50
....	Unemployment rate: 2.6%

PROGRESS AMID PRIVATION

by STEPHEN F. JONES

Since Georgia declared its independence in 1991, every year has been filled with tragedy, scandal, and public misery. At the same time, particularly since the elections and the new constitution of 1995, Georgia has begun to reassemble the state, reform government, and establish the legislative basis for democracy. In 1997, the local press, with its ear to the ground and its nose for scandal, continued to represent the first view, a picture of mass poverty, struggle, and government corruption. In the Western press there was more of the second tendency—Georgia on the road to economic recovery and democratic progress. Both are right. Georgian citizens who live the grind of everyday life might justifiably challenge the views of optimistic Western observers, but Georgia's continuing steps toward stability and democracy, despite the accompanying corruption, party intrigue, and lagging civic consciousness, are undeniable. Of all the Caucasian republics, Georgia has been most successful in overcoming the post-Soviet crisis of authority.

In 1997, these two tendencies—continuing misery and continuing progress—took various forms. Economic polarization, oligarchic monopolies, and a devastated health and welfare system came alongside better laws (with improved implementation), popular organization from below (reflected by extraordinary growth in the local NGO community), and greater economic opportunities. Foreign affairs saw increasing independence from Russia and rapidly multiplying economic and political links with the West, but no progress in separatist Abkhazia or South Ossetia. The plight of the 250,000 refugees from these regions was acute, and Russian obstruction of a solution to the Abkhaz problem led to tense relations with Moscow.

At the same time, the country's political system became better regulated and the rules of behavior better understood. President Eduard Shevardnadze continued to set the standard in political life as well as control the country's legislative direction. In his May 1997 state-of-the union address Shevardnadze described his vision for Georgia. His "national philosophy" has not always corresponded to Georgian reality, but his language—pluralism, constitutionalism, citizenship, tolerance, and human rights—has profoundly shaped the country's political behavior and expectations. In his speech, he emphasized a number of themes for 1997. The first goal was national reconciliation and consensus, to be achieved through further democratization. This included strict protection of legal rights for individuals and groups, adherence to the constitution, judicial reform, and a deepening of civil society. Second, more economic reform with particular emphasis on the fulfillment of a realistic budget, macroeconomic restructuring as part of a continuing three-year plan, and a move to a "civilized market economy" with greater emphasis on social welfare and employment. Third, a continuing campaign against corruption, especially in the executive branches (the Ministries of the Interior and of Security were singled out). The fourth goal was territorial unity and the regulation of center-regional relations; and the fifth, a European foreign policy orientation, regional cooperation (a "Caucasian home"), and strategic partnership with Russia.

NATIONAL RECONCILIATION AND DEMOCRACY BUILDING

The day before Shevardnadze's address to parliament and his call for national conciliation, there was a demonstration of approximately 300 supporters of former President Zviad Gamsakhurdia. The demonstration was crudely dispersed by the Tbilisi police, and a number of journalists were beaten. The demonstration showed legislative progress on human and civil rights still relied on ex-Soviet personnel to implement the new measures. Laws passed in 1997 designed to defend citizens' rights included a law on peaceful assembly, new Civil and Criminal Codes, a law "On the State Security Service," a bill on the press (controversial and not passed until March 1998), and finally, after much delay, a law on local self-government. In June Shevardnadze issued a decree that emphasized the need to rectify human rights violations in preliminary detention and penitentiary systems.

The new legislation, while welcome, was often flawed. The original bill on peaceful assembly severely restricted where demonstrations could take place and allowed the authorities to ban them if they were considered a potential threat to public order. Many of the restrictions were removed in the final version. The law on the state security service restricted the much-abused right of telephone surveillance (it removed it from the jurisdiction of the Ministry of the Interior). The new Criminal Code abolished capital punishment (finally legislating Shevardnadze's moratorium introduced in December 1996), introduced a criminal penalty for those impeding the professional work of journalists, and transferred many of the Ministry of the Interior's investigation responsibilities to the Procuracy. Earlier in the year, in an act seen as a victory for press freedom, Rustavi 2, an independent TV station critical of the government and closed down by order of the Ministry of Communications on a technicality, was permitted by order of the Supreme Court to resume broadcasts.

On 29 October after vetoes of two previous candidates by parliament, a national ombudsman was appointed to supervise human and minority rights. The appointment of David Salaridze to the position of national ombudsman was poorly received by many in the human rights community. Salaridze, head of the government's tax department and a former police official, had few obvious qualifications. His appointment reflected political deals in parliament and a persistent lack of judgment in Shevardnadze's personnel policies.

The new law on "General Courts" enhanced the independence of the judiciary by transferring the supervision of judges from the Ministry of Justice to an independent twelve-man consultative council attached to the President's office and consisting of judges appointed by the president, justice ministry, and parliament. A new three-tier judicial system was designed not to coincide with administrative divisions, to prevent pressure from local politicians. These steps came in the wake of the setting up in 1996 of a Constitutional Court to arbitrate constitutional disputes between different branches of government and to hear claims for protection of civil rights (something it has in reality tried to avoid). At least in principle the legislation for protecting citizens' rights was up to European standards.

The law on local self-government met stiff opposition in parliament. The Majoritarian, Labor, All-Union Revival, and both National Democratic factions opposed the clause permitting the president to appoint all the district governors (*gamgebeli*) and the mayors of six major cities. The extra-parliamentary opposition led by the Traditionalists and Charter '91 called for a referendum on the issue. The required 200,000 signatures were collected, but the request was denied by the Central Electoral Commission (CEC) on the grounds that a national referendum could only take place in a territorially united Georgia. The Supreme Court rejected the opposition's appeal against the CEC decision. The law's supporters argued that at a time of strong centrifugal forces in the country, it was a necessary precaution. They were afraid that in regions like the Armenian-dominated Akhalkalaki, or in Samegrelo, a region hostile to Shevardnadze, anti-government candidates would be elected. The opposition called the law undemocratic and insisted all posts should be elective, but failed to extract any concessions despite popular support.

Despite such controversy, Georgian parliamentary life was broadly democratic. Even the manipulation of parliamentary procedure by the majority Citizens Union of Georgia, a pro-Shevardnadze party formerly chaired by the president himself, was in keeping with Western parliamentary systems. Yet reconciliation has been hard to attain in parliament or among the extra-parliamentary opposition. In 1997, the arrival in Tbilisi of Zviad Gamsakhurdia's widow, Manana Archvadze-Gamsakhurdia, temporarily galvanized the extra-parliamentary opposition, but despite an increase in demonstrations and clashes with the police, her former husband's supporters, known as the "Zviadists," have had little impact. In October, their party, Round Table–Free Georgia, split. They still had some support in Samegrelo (Western Georgia) however, which Shevardnadze acknowledged as a problem in his May parliamentary address.

The legislative achievements in 1997 are impressive and the legislative process, though dominated by Shevardnadze and the CUG, was relatively open. Members of the non-governmental community were involved, particularly in the committees on economic policy and judicial issues, led by two well-known reformers. The meeting of the chairman of parliament, Zurab Zhvania (himself a former leader of the Greens), with over 500 representatives of non-governmental organizations (NGOs) was an indication of a growing government acceptance of civil society institutions. NGOs such as Horizonti, the Business Law Center and the Young Lawyers Association were particularly influential in legislative writing and revision in 1997.

The greatest weakness of Shevardnadze's legislative program was implementation. The economic misery of the majority of the population inspired little confidence and support for the government. In 1997, police abuses, including illegal extension of pre-trial detention, beatings of prisoners, torture, and a high incidence of deaths in custody from disease (mostly TB) and "accidents," continue to occur. Most judges, despite the new law, were either incompetent or corrupt and the increased rights of defense attorneys as defined by the law on the procuracy were rarely exercised. Many of these weaknesses were evident in the trials of former members of opposition groups (Mkhedrioni and Zviadists) in 1997. These flaws are serious and cannot be cured by legislation alone.

PARTIES AND POLITICS

Parliament served as an important check on the executive, despite its control by the CUG, a heavy workload, an often-superficial discussion of important bills, and violations of quora. The opposition continued to fragment (the third largest party, the All-Union Revival, split in August), although speaker Zurab Zhvania exercised masterful control over the legislative agenda. Legislation introduced by the president's office or the CUG was often challenged, amended, or delayed on the floor and in the powerful parliamentary committees. In 1997, Shevardnadze's choices for national ombudsman and chairman of the National Bank were overturned. Laws such as those on executive power, the media, public demonstrations, and the Criminal Code were successfully amended by the opposition. Parliament was an important forum for investigations into government corruption, human rights violations, and continuing policy failure in Abkhazia.

Despite the government's hope that its own anti-corruption campaign might increase its popularity, scandals continued to undermine its reputation. In January there were accusations against corrupt and incompetent ambassadorial appointees, then in March, Fuel and Energy Minister Davit Zubatishvili came under scrutiny for mishandled credits from Russia. In June, a parliamentary commission found evidence showing the security minister, Shota Kviraia, was tapping newspaper phones. Djemal Gakhokidze took over the revamped ministry in July after Kviraia's resignation, although Gakhokidze was himself accused of past involvement with the Soviet KGB. Rocked only two years earlier by Minister Igor Georgadze's participation in an assassination plot against Shevardnadze, the new minister promised fundamental changes, including a reduction in staff, the transfer of its special forces to the defense ministry, and an emphasis on information and analysis. His new deputy, Avtandil Ioseliani, was put in charge of a new intelligence division, which along with the National Security Council was designed to counter the concentration of power in the security minister's hands. In the summer, Kakha Targamadze, the interior minister, was accused of involvement in cigarette smuggling and alleged links with the "gasoline Mafia," but evidence was insufficient. Corruption was not new to Georgia, but was one of the most pervasive threats to effective democracy at all levels of government and business. It remained a way of life for inadequately paid officials, underpaid professors, opportunistic customs staff, and ex-Soviet judges.

The CUG, despite prominent defections and poor discipline, maintained its dominance over parliament and emerged as the establishment party. The new finance minister, Mikhail Chkuaseli, was a former head of the party's youth branch. The party gained additional parliamentary support after the All-Union Revival party split over the "separatist" policies of its leader, Aslan Abashidze. Seven All-Union Revival dissenters formed Mamuli (Homeland), and declared allegiance to the CUG. (The rump changed its name to the All-Union Democratic Revival in December). The parliamentary opposition remains disunited on most issues, and their national party organizations, with the exception of the National Democratic Party faction led by Irina Sarishvili-Chanturia and the Socialist Party led by Vakhtang Rcheulashvili, were ineffective. Vakhtang Rcheulashvili, former deputy speaker of parliament and leader of the Socialist Party and the Majoritarian faction, became one of the most vociferous critics of the government in 1997. Comparing himself to Moscow Mayor Yurii Luzhkov, he was an effective populist and orator who claimed to represent the interests of ordinary people against the IMF and the government's monetarist policies. The Stalin Society joined his left-socialist bloc in April, and his humanitarian gestures, such as the provision of a free ambulance service, gained him popular recognition.

Parliamentary machinations and mutual accusations of corruption are not unique by Western standards, but the repeated whiff of conspiracy and murder in Georgia reminds one of Papal politics under the Borgias. Igor Georgadze, safely protected in Moscow, continued to accuse Shevardnadze in Georgian newspaper interviews of stage-managing his own assassination attempt and murdering his opponents. In April, two parliamentary deputies accused Shota Kviraia of attempting to poison them, and Aslan Abashidze regularly blamed Tbilisi for plotting his death. In October, the former mayor of Batumi, Tamaz Kharazi, accused Zurab Zhvania of conspiring to oust Aslan Abashidze. That same month, Temur Maskhulia told journalists he had been pressured by senior Georgian security officials, including the new Deputy Security Minister Avtandil Ioseliani, to frame the Georgian Ambassador to Russia, Vazha Lortkipanidze, and parliamentary deputy Vakhtang Goguadze, for the assassination plot against Shevardnadze in August 1995. The plots thickened in 1997, but there was rarely any resolution.

ETHNIC DIVISIONS

In 1997, internal ethnic divisions remained Georgia's most serious national security issue. Abkhazia and South Ossetia still dominated domestic politics, though an Armenian autonomist movement in Samtskhe-Javakheti and a Meskhetian campaign to return to Georgia also attracted government attention. Russia was involved in all four issues and had no wish to see them resolved. Russian-led negotiations to determine the status of Abkhazia and return the quarter of a million Georgian internally displaced persons and refugees who fled the 1993 conflict made no progress in 1997. Russian peace-keeping troops in South Ossetia continue to profit from a corrupt trade in drugs and alcohol. Stability in Armenian-dominated Samtskhe-Javakheti was undermined by Russian troops stationed there, tacitly supporting local Armenian claims for autonomy.

Abkhazia, as in previous years, brought parliament to the verge of hysteria, undermined Shevardnazde's popularity, and gave the opposition an opportunity to exploit discontent among refugees. It also antagonized Georgian-Russian relations and remained a considerable burden on the economy (the loss of agriculturally productive Abkhazia, budgetary increases for the military, and welfare support for refugees). The year began well with a 28 March summit of the Commonwealth of Independent States (CIS) agreeing to extend the security zone in Abkhazia and add policing powers to the duties of the Russian CIS Peace Keeping Force (PKF), something Georgia had been urging for some time. A few days earlier, the Abkhazeti faction in parliament (mostly Georgian deputies from Abkhazia) ended a hunger strike protesting the delay in returning Georgian refugees to Abkhazia. However, at the Abkhazeti faction's urging and under pressure from street rallies of refugees, parliamentary resolutions followed in April and May declaring that the Russian peace-keeping mandate would end on 31 July unless Russia implemented the CIS resolution. In April, the Georgian government raised the economic pressures on Abkhazia by routing telephone connections through Tbilisi rather than Moscow. The Abkhazians retaliated by cutting off electricity supplies to Georgia from the Ingur Hess power station and by a military build-up. As 31 July approached and there was no progress in Georgian-Abkhazian talks in Moscow, partisan activity by the Georgian White Legion in Abkhazia increased. There was fighting in the Kodori valley, a region in Abkhazia still occupied by Georgians.

Shevardnadze called for an international conference on Abkhazia and urged the Organization for Security and Cooperation in Europe (OSCE) and the Friends of Georgia (an informal group of countries consisting of the United States, Russia, Germany, UK, and France) to help break the deadlock. He encouraged international involvement in the peace-keeping force, including Ukraine and Turkey. At the end of July, Georgia did not officially renew the Russian peace keeping mandate, but agreed to an extension of the Russian PKF mandate at the CIS summit in October. A war would have been disastrous for the Georgian economy and would have reopened the divisive passions that had threatened Georgian statehood in 1993–95.

Hopes rose in the second half of the year as bilateral contacts between Abkhazia and Georgia multiplied, culminating in the dramatic visit of separatist leader Vladislav Ardzinba to Tbilisi in August. Despite return visits by the chairman of the Georgian parliament and Georgia's foreign minister; an agreement by both sides to renounce force; a visit by the Abkhazian "prime minister" Sergei Bagapsh to Tbilisi in September; and renewed talks in Sukhumi, Moscow, and Geneva, there was no progress beyond limited cooperation on economic issues. Hostage-taking and bombings by both sides continued in Abkhazia and Samegrelo. In October there were large-scale Georgian maneuvers in Khulevi, bordering Abkhazia, involving 10,000 soldiers and 21 warships.

In South Ossetia (which Georgians call Tskhinvali), despite the bombing of a Georgian national monument in the summer, tensions on the South Ossetian border with Russia, a serious drug transit problem, "Mafia" killings, and an absence of progress on the status of the region, the situation improved. Georgia had no authority in most of South Ossetia, and refugees on both sides had not returned in significant numbers, but in contrast to Abkhazia, security was better and travel to the capital of Tskhinvali by Georgians was possible. In September, the Joint Control Commission responsible for security in the region decided, despite Russian protests, to halve the number of Russian army peace-keeping posts.

Earlier, in May, after a visit to the region by Zurab Zhvania, inter-parliamentary links were set up between the Georgian and South Ossetian legislatures. In talks between the two sides, which culminated in a meeting between the "President" of South Ossetia Ludvig Chibirov and Shevardnadze in the South Ossetian village of Java on 14 November, both agreed to start the repatriation of refugees to the region in 1998. But without economic improvements in South Ossetia, the 20,000 South Ossetians in the North Ossetian capital of Vladikavkaz—who were not welcome there and had their refugee allowances revoked by the North Ossetian authorities in June—will not return. Chibirov, despite his wish to unite South and North Ossetia, and his links with Russian nationalist politicians, recognizes the need to compromise on the political status of the region, although talks between both sides were postponed in December precisely due to continuing disagreements on this issue.

Decisions in South Ossetia will have a direct bearing on Samtskhe-Javakheti. This region, one of the poorest in Georgia and whose inhabitants are 55 percent Armenian, is a potential route for the Baku-Ceyhan pipeline and a proposed Georgian-Turkish railway link. Led by Javakh, the most influential Armenian organization in the area, local Armenians are demanding a division of the region. They want Akhalkalaki, the overwhelmingly Armenian part, to have distinct status within a Georgian federation. A presidential decree in January calling for social and economic aid to Samtskhe-Javakheti, and regular ministerial visits did not stem Armenian demands for a referendum on the issue. Should the Meskhetians, a largely Muslim population expelled from the region in 1944, succeed in returning to Samtskhe-Javakheti, the situation could become explosive. Cossack groups in Krasnodar, where many Meskhetians located after their expulsion from Uzbekistan in 1989, were pressuring the Meskhetians to leave for Georgia. Meskhetians continued to protest in Georgia at the slowness of promised repatriation in Georgia following a presidential decree in 1996. The Georgian government fears that a Meskhetian return to Samtskhe-Javakheti could generate an Armenian-Muslim clash which would sabotage the Baku-Ceyhan pipeline and end Georgia's image as a beacon of stability and democracy in the Caucasus.

FOREIGN POLICY

Under the shrewd direction of Shevardnadze, Georgia has continued to diversify its international alliances and promote itself to both Europe and Central Asia as a vital transit link. In 1997, Georgia deepened its regional economic interests in the Black Sea Economic Cooperation organization (BSEC); explored with the Chechens and Azeris plans to establish a Caucasian framework for security and economic cooperation; and strengthened regional cooperation with both Armenia and Azerbaijan. Further afield it developed its partnership with Ukraine; pursued its common economic interests with Turkey and Central Asia; encouraged greater U.S. commitment to the region; and pushed for integration with European institutions. These policies were marred by a continuing cold war with Russia, which used its influence in Achara, Abkhazia, and South Ossetia to restrict Georgia's increasing foreign policy boldness.

In April parliament passed a resolution blaming Russia for the lack of progress in Abkhazia and declaring integration with Europe to be Georgia's highest foreign policy priority. The same month Shevardnadze attended two major international conferences, one in Tbilisi of the BSEC and EU transport ministers devoted to the Euro-Asia Corridor (known officially as TRACECA—Transport Corridor, Caucasus, Central Asia). The second was a BSEC gathering of seven presidents in Istanbul. In 1997 Turkey was Georgia's third-largest trading partner, after the United States and Azerbaijan. The CIS accounted for only 38 percent of the country's foreign trade in 1997—of that, Russia was 17 percent. A decision at the BSEC meeting to build a Georgian-Turkish, Kars–Akhalkalaki railway, a visit by a Turkish parliamentary delegation in February, a military delegation in May, and finally the visit of President Suleiman Demirel in the summer, all reaffirmed the close strategic and economic interests of both countries. Turkey promised Georgia military aid, signed an extensive military agreement, promised a peace-keeping contingent in Abkhazia if asked for, and fully supported Georgian territorial integrity. Both Georgia and Turkey support the main oil pipeline route of Baku–Georgia–Ceyhan.

Relations with the United States and Europe were a priority in 1997. Shevardnadze visited France in February and Italy in May. In July he attended the NATO Madrid conference and visited the United States. In September, he was in Greece, and he addressed the Council of Europe in Strasbourg in October. Extensive bilateral economic and, in some cases, military agreements of cooperation and assistance were signed during these trips. Greece, like Turkey, signed a series of military agreements and the United States promised military training, joint exercises, arms supplies and help in frontier defense. But neither the United States, nor any other country, would commit itself to provide troops for peacekeeping in Abkhazia without UN sanction. Georgia remained a "special guest" at the European Union and Leni Fisher, president of the parliamentary assembly of the Council of Europe, warned during a visit to Georgia in May that until the Abkhazian issue was solved, Georgian admission to the Council would be delayed. However, Georgia was granted most-favored-nation status for trade purposes and received praise for its economic and political reforms.

Georgia continued to participate in NATO's Partnership for Peace (PfP) and was a member of the Council of Euro-Atlantic Partnership Council. In May parliament ratified agreements with NATO and the PfP which, among other things, permitted joint U.S.-Georgian exercises. John Shalikashvili, the Chairman of the U.S. Joint Chiefs of Staff, and himself of Georgian origin, visited Georgia in August to promote U.S.-Georgian strategic relations, followed by the U.S. ambassador to

NATO Robert Hunter, in October. Georgia took the lead in furthering Caucasian partnership in 1997 and Shevardnadze offered his services as mediator between Azerbaijan and Armenia, and between Armenia and Turkey. Following the June 1996 summit meeting of Russia and the three Caucasian republics in Kislovodsk, Georgian parliamentarians (notably the Georgian Abkhazeti faction and the Chairman Zurab Zhvania) pursued separate talks with Azerbaijan, Chechnya, and other North Caucasian nations. In 1997, the Abkhazeti faction signed an agreement with fellow parliamentarians from Azerbaijan, Ingushetia, and Dagestan on a Caucasian parliament, although Zhvania, with Shevardnadze's backing, was proposing a looser Caucasian Inter-Parliamentary Assembly. In March Georgian Defense Minister Vardiko Nadabaidze held talks with the presidents of Ingushetia and Chechnya, securing their neutrality in any future conflict with Abkhazia. In May, again in Kislovodsk, there was a meeting of Caucasian governmental leaders where a permanent Coordinating Council was established, although the Chechen proposal for a Caucasian security organization was not taken up.

Chechnya, dependent on Georgia for transit to Turkey and access to the Black Sea, wanted to strengthen its bilateral relations with Georgia. Publicly recognizing Georgia's territorial integrity and denouncing former Chechen support for Abkhazia, the Chechen government sent its first official delegation to Tbilisi in May. This led to further parliamentary visits on both sides, including a visit by the Chechen president in the summer and the vice president in November. Georgia promised not to permit Russian troops on the Georgian-Chechen border and both sides agreed to build a new highway link between the two states.

Armenia, although it refused to participate in the dialogue with North Caucasians, followed Georgia's lead for greater regional cooperation. Relations with Georgia improved, despite a Georgian-Azerbaijani strategic partnership signed in February, a secret shipment of Russian arms across Georgian territory to Armenia revealed in April, and Armenian concern with the socio-economic situation in Samtskhe-Javakheti. A visit to Armenia by Shevardnadze in May led to agreements on energy and customs cooperation, discussions on border demarcation, and cooperation in Samtskhe-Javakheti, and promised Armenian participation in the Euro-Asia corridor through a special transport link to Batumi across Georgia's southern regions. Although Georgia tried to take a neutral position on the Armenian-Azerbaijani conflicts, Georgia had closer economic and strategic interests with Azerbaijan. In February, Georgia and Azerbaijan signed a strategic partnership agreement and in December a visit by the Azerbaijani prime minister led to agreements in the fields of power supplies, currency, export control, and taxation. In October in Strasbourg, both Georgia and Azerbaijan, along with Moldova and Ukraine, established a new consultative body known as GUAM (Georgia-Ukraine-Azerbaijan-Moldova), an organization which reflected the common economic and geopolitical interests of those countries and was seen as a counterbalance to the CIS.

Of all its neighbors, Georgia had the most trouble with Russia. The sources of distrust were numerous: Russian passivity in the Abkhazian dispute; poorly behaved Russian troops in Akhalkalaki and South Ossetia; Russian control of Georgian borders; the illegal transit of arms to Armenia; support of the anti-Shevardnadze leader Aslan Abashidze in Achara; and protection of former Security Minister Igor Georgadze in Moscow. Russia was alarmed at the growing Western and U.S. presence in the region. Economic recovery in Georgia and Azerbaijan, accompanied by increasingly assertive foreign policies, was slowly removing them from CIS influence. In 1997, Georgia continued to resist economic integration into the CIS. In January at a meeting of CIS heads of government, Georgian State Minister Niko Lekishvili rejected proposals for CIS supra-national organizations, and refused to sign over half of the fifteen economic proposals at the meeting designed to foster closer integration. In May, after the failure of Russian forces to implement the March CIS agreement on Abkhazia, Shevardnadze condemned the CIS's "helplessness" and "indifference" to Georgian problems.

Shevardnadze's condemnation of Russia was persistent in 1997. Georgia was alarmed by a series of incidents. In February and March shots were fired at Turkish fishing boats by Russian coast guards, who still patrolled Georgia's marine borders. In August Russia imposed a blockade on alcohol exports from Georgia on the Georgian–North Ossetian border (in response, Shevardnadze canceled a trip to celebrate Moscow's 850th anniversary). Other bones of contention included Russia's unilateral move of its border 1.5 kilometers into the neutral zone at Larsi on the Georgian-Russian border; the alleged nuclear contamination of Georgian training camps by departing Russian troops; and the Russian refusal to give Georgia a portion of the Black Sea Fleet. In 1997, Georgia was increasingly exasperated with Russian policies and in March, Zurab Zhvania warned a visiting Russian Duma delegation that Russia was in danger of losing Georgia as a friendly neighbor. Until progress is made in Abkhazia, it is unlikely that Russian-Georgian relations will improve. Georgia will continue to pursue its interests with more reliable partners.

A MIXED PICTURE IN THE ECONOMY

In a January 1997 radio address, President Shevardnadze declared 1997 would be a turning point for the Georgian economy. Social welfare, manufacturing industry and the energy sector, all of which affect citizens directly through pensions, health care, employment, and domestic heating in the winter, would be the foci of the second stage of economic reform. However, reforms, along with institutional and personnel changes, brought no significant economic improvement to the population in 1997.

There were two pictures to draw from: that of the IMF and World Bank lauding Georgian economic growth and macroeconomic stability, and that of the ordinary Georgian receiving an average monthly salary of 44 lari ($35), significantly below the official subsistence level of 112 lari ($87). Official Georgian figures suggested that 65 percent of the population lived in poverty, but the IMF, taking the black market economy into account, put the figure at 25–30 percent.

Shevardnadze's government could certainly boast impressive macroeconomic gains in 1997. With a GDP growth rate of over 10 percent, Georgia was the fastest-growing economy in the CIS even without taking into account the estimated 60 percent of the economy operating illegally. The tight monetary policy insisted on by the IMF and World Bank brought inflation down from 14.5 percent in 1996 to 7.9 percent in 1997. State enterprise credits and bread, utility, and transportation subsidies were cut, as was state employment (by 10 percent). Zero cash auctions were held to dispose of over 250 unsold state enterprises (with no minimum price) and 51 of the largest companies from the government's list of "strategic" firms which were not to be privatized. The final phase of privatization of small enterprises took place in 1997. 330 were sold between July and September bringing the total number of privately owned to 10,423. By the end of the third quarter of 1997, 54 percent of all arable land had been privatized, and the U.S. Department of Agriculture described Georgia and Armenia as the two most agriculturally reformed states of the former USSR. There were also institutional and personnel changes. November saw a massive purge of the corrupt energy ministry (four top officials were removed, including the deputy minister). The industry ministry was reestablished and the 26-year-old banker Mikhail Chkuaseli was appointed finance minister.

The 1997 budget, rejected in September 1996 by parliament, was finally approved in February 1997. It anticipated a deficit of 2.8 percent of GDP (down from 4.4 percent in 1996) and an increase in revenue to 8 percent of GDP—up from 5.4 percent in 1996, but still very low. The new version did not include measures to boost tax revenues, mostly because of corruption, but partly because the new tax code, while tightening loopholes, reduced penalties for evasion. It has been estimated that of 37,000 economic entities in Georgia, only one third are registered and thus pay taxes. Lags in tax collection led to arrears in the payment of state wages and pensions. In August, there was a strike in the manganese-producing town of Chiatura over non-payment of wages, which led to the mayor's flight from the city. In line with Shevardnadze's stated priorities, the 1997 budget increased social spending by 10 percent over 1996, to 45 percent of the total.

But the impressive macroeconomic picture hid serious weaknesses. The IMF's figures were challenged by Georgian economist Vazha Marulava, who suggested that the government manipulated data to stress growth in trade and services (45 percent in the first six months of 1997) rather than industrial production. At the end of April 1997, 990 industrial enterprises, or one third of the total, were idle. At year's end despite a small increase in production, most enterprises were working at 8–10 percent of their capacity. In agriculture, despite a record grain harvest in 1997, there was a disastrous decline in the traditionally strong grape harvest. Farmers were plagued by a lack of credit sources, utility breakdowns, and a poor transport and trade infrastructure.

The high GDP growth rate was relative to the economic downturn of the first half of the decade: in 1997 GDP was still only 40 percent of its 1989 level. Apart from severe structural problems associated with tax collection and energy production, Georgia was unable to meet its external debt repayments. Its foreign debt in 1997 was over $1.5 billion, and although trade figures are unreliable due to massive underreporting, the trade deficit in 1997 also increased. Between January and August 1997, of a total $702 million trade turnover, only $141 million was exports. The balance-of-payments deficit in August ($419 million) was almost double the 1996 figure. Foreign direct investment, despite some prominent new investors such as McDonald's and Chevron, fell off dramatically in 1997. Shevardnadze established a Foreign Investment Advisory Council to promote a more hospitable climate for foreign investors.

Economic growth, despite low inflation and a steady exchange rate, did not have much impact on living standards, though it helped to prevent them from falling. The government tried to make up the shortfall in its revenues through reductions in the social security payments. At the beginning of the year, child allowances were replaced by a family allowance of 9 lari per person for a much smaller eligible group. Utility charges increased dramatically, with a 50 percent increase in water rates, 66 percent in trash collection and 80 percent in electricity charges. Pensions, though they increased twice in 1997, remained at a pitiful 11.8 lari, and benefits for the 139,600 officially unemployed—the real figure, though hard to define, is probably around 20 percent—are one tenth of the minimum subsistence level. Health care for most Georgians was prohibitively expensive and few subscribed to the state medical insurance company, which could not provide decent health care. Poorly paid health-care workers, including doctors, depend on informal payments to survive.

The serious difficulties faced by ordinary Georgians were reflected in an April poll (although polls in Georgia must always be treated skeptically). Eighty-six percent of a sample of 500 felt the most acute social problem was the low level of pensions and salaries, 67 percent pointed to the absence of a guaranteed subsistence minimum, 36 percent saw unemployment as most threatening, and 25 percent, the absence of good medical care. Georgia's residents voted with their feet: some 1,384,000 persons emigrated between 1991 and 1996 (550,000 of them ethnic Georgians). Yet at the same time another April poll suggested 4.4 percent of Georgians had significantly improved their economic situation, 31 percent slightly improved it and 30 percent had remained the same. Forty-three percent also believed the situation would get better (27 percent thought it would remain the same and 13 percent thought it would get worse). Such polls do not reflect an economic turnaround, but perhaps its fragile beginnings.

Azerbaijan

Population:	7,529,000
Capital:	Baku (pop. 1,550,000)
Major cities:	Genje (pop. 232,000), Sumgait (pop. 190,000)
Area:	86,600 sq. km.
Major ethnic groups:	Azeri 90%, Russian 5%
Economy:	GDP growth: 5.3%
....	Inflation rate: 4%
....	Average monthly wage: $31
....	Unemployment rate: 13%

AZERBAIJAN IN 1997

by ELIN SULEYMANOV

The figure of President Heydar Aliev continued to be the dominant feature of Azerbaijan's political landscape in 1997, Aliev's fourth year in office. While Aliev strengthened his position, the year saw further confusion among the opposition parties. Meanwhile, an active, Western-oriented and oil-driven foreign policy activity was aimed at building alliances both in the region and outside.

Despite the positive developments and public optimism of the second half of the year, no breakthrough was achieved in the resolution of the Nagorno-Karabakh conflict, which remained the main, immediate challenge facing the leadership of Azerbaijan. Armenia continued to occupy some 20 percent of Azerbaijani territory, and the government in Baku faced the political and economic challenge of dealing with the presence of an estimated 900,000 refugees and internally displaced persons from those regions and from Armenia itself.

According to the State Committee for Statistics, Azerbaijan's GDP rose 5.3 percent in 1997 while the inflation rate of 4 percent was the lowest among the members of the Commonwealth of Independent States (CIS). A program of voucher privatization was launched in the second half of 1997. Foreign investment, mostly in oil-producing infrastructure, doubled to around $1.2 billion, making Azerbaijan one of the top ten recipients in Eastern Europe and the CIS. Average monthly pay was a mere $31 in August—44 percent up on the August 1996 figure, but still only one quarter of the 1991 level. The officially reported unemployment rate was 13 percent, but the real rate was considerably higher. And these figures did not allow for the minimal living standards of the country's numerous and destitute refugee population.

DEADLOCK OVER NAGORNO-KARABAKH

Peace negotiations over the disputed region of Nagorno-Karabakh were on hold in the first half of 1997 after Armenia withdrew from direct talks with Azerbaijan following the endorsement of Azerbaijan's territorial integrity by the Lisbon Summit of the Organization for Security and Cooperation in Europe (OSCE) in late 1996. Moreover, Azerbaijan objected to the nomination of France as second co-chair of the OSCE Minsk Group because of its perceived pro-Armenian position. The co-chairmanship dispute was resolved by the U.S. becoming the third co-chair of the Minsk group in addition to France and Russia, as suggested by the Danish president of the OSCE.

In April there were shooting incidents around the borders of Nagorno-Karabakh, the worst since signing the cease-fire agreement in 1994. These came against the background of the scandal over illegal Russian shipments of $1 billion worth of arms to Armenia, and the appointment of Robert Kocharian, former president of the self-proclaimed Nagorno-Karabakh Republic, as prime minister of Armenia. In one of these incidents the car of the OSCE special representative was fired at from the Armenian side. Later the same month, the presidents of Armenia and Azerbaijan issued reconciliatory statements and met in Istanbul.

In the second half of 1997, the peace negotiations intensified when the OSCE submitted a new proposal based on the "phased" approach. This would involve the withdrawal of Armenian forces from currently occupied areas around Nagorno-Karabakh; the return of the displaced population; and re-establishing communications and links between Armenia and Azerbaijan as well as between Nagorno-Karabakh and the rest of Azerbaijan. All this was to take place in the first phase of the settlement. The second phase of the settlement would then include determination of Nagorno-Karabakh's status and a decision on Shusha, the former center of Nagorno-Karabakh's Azeri community, and Lachin, a region of Azerbaijan between Armenia and Nagorno-Karabakh that was seized by Armenian troops in 1992.

The "phased" proposal was accepted in principle by Baku and Yerevan but rejected by the Karabakh Armenian leadership under Arkady Gukasyan, who was elected in September to replace Kocharyan. Gukasyan continued insisting on the "package," i.e. one-phase, solution. Aliev and Ter-Petrossian met briefly at the October summit of the Council of Europe in Strasbourg. In early December the Tehran summit of the Organization of Islamic States called for the withdrawal of Armenian troops from the occupied regions. However, despite the OSCE's mediating efforts and the United Nations adopting a resolution in support of the "phased" solution, no progress was made at the Copenhagen meeting of OSCE foreign ministers in December. Not surprisingly, in sharp contrast with the euphoria around the OSCE Lisbon summit the previous year, the Azeri media virtually ignored the results of Copenhagen.

DIVIDED OPPOSITION POSES NO THREAT TO ALIEV

The presidency of Heydar Aliev concentrated power in the hands of the national leader, with the other branches of government merely serving to implement his decisions. The Cabinet of Ministers was not an independent decision-making body, and while the parliament, or Milli Meclis, was active, it was largely irrelevant. Aliev relied on a solid core of loyalists, many of whom came from his home Nahchivan region and from the currently displaced Azeri population of Armenia. However, his base of support was significantly wider than any specific regional group. In fact, the notion of clan politics also seems somewhat superficial because many opposition leaders represented the same would-be regional clans.

Opinion polls conducted by the independent Turan news agency showed the 74-year-old Aliev with a strong lead in public support, far ahead of any other politician in the country. The Milli Meclis voted to institute 15 June, the day when Aliev came to power in 1993, as the Day of Salvation. In October, the president's office felt obliged to call upon the media to cut down on their excessive eulogies for Aliev. The strong figure of Aliev underscores the fact that

Azerbaijan's politics was that of personalities, and not parties. There seemed to be no credible alternative to the current leader in the public's perception. A poll conducted by ANS-TV, an independent TV channel in Baku, at the end of 1997 showed that the majority of respondents named foreign minister Hasan Hasanov, a long-time Aliev ally and not an independent political actor, as the second-most influential politician in Azerbaijan.

Most of Azerbaijan's political parties, both pro-government and opposition, were undergoing a certain identity crisis. The nominally ruling Yeni Azerbaycan (New Azerbaijan) Party had initially been created to bring Aliev to power. The party, which celebrated its fifth anniversary in November, failed to produce a new program. Tension between various groups within the party grew into open confrontation, and Aliev was its only obvious consolidating factor.

In October after long preparations Abulfaz Elchibey, ex-president and currently chairman of the opposition Popular Front Party of Azerbaijan (AXCP), returned to Baku from his native village of Keleki in Azerbaijan's exclave of Nahchivan. (He had fled there in 1993 after being deposed from the presidency in the wake of military defeat at the hands of the Armenians in Nagorno-Karabakh.) His return apparently followed behind-the-scenes negotiations with the authorities, and coincided with expiration of the term he was elected for in June of 1992. In this way opposition was finally able to recognize Aliev's legitimacy, which it had been refusing to do earlier. Elchibey was democratically elected to the presidency in 1992, and had a certain following in the West, so his participation in the 1998 presidential elections would make them much more legitimate, without seriously undermining Aliev's chances of victory judging by the opinion polls.

Elchibey said that he returned from his internal exile in order to consolidate the opposition forces and to promote democracy. However, his return seemed to have divided the opposition more than uniting it. At times he embarrassed the Popular Front Party, run by Deputy Chairman Ali Kerimov in his absence, with his radical remarks. Elchibey's return emphasized the disagreements between the faction led by the younger Kerimov and AXCP's old guard within the ranks of the party, once the core of Azerbaijan's national movement. A split was avoided in 1997, but the AXCP had yet to complete its transformation from the broad, nation-wide movement which emerged from the democratic transition of the early 1990s into a party with a clear vision and specific program.

Drift continued between the AXCP and its closest ally, the Musavat party, led by Isa Gambar, the former parliamentary speaker during Elchibey's presidency. Musavat's October congress was riven by disagreement between its nationalist and liberal wings and failed to produce a unified program. With Elchibey and Gambar competing to be the opposition's single candidate in the 1998 presidential elections, the rivalry between AXCP and Musavat, two of the strongest democratic opposition forces, was likely to deepen. Confrontation within the nominally opposition Party of National Independence under Etibar Mamedov once again underlined the crisis of Azerbaijan's political parties. Some of the smaller parties, including those united in the Democratic Congress, merged together and were mostly ignored by both the authorities and the larger opposition groups.

Rasul Guliev, ex–parliamentary speaker and once Aliev's close associate, returned to politics in late 1997. Guliev had resigned from his position in October 1996, officially for health reasons, and had been residing abroad. He harshly criticized the current leadership of the country in his second book *The Path to Democracy* (the first one was *Oil and Politics*). The former director of Baku's main oil refinery, he was rumored to be one of the richest people in the CIS, and was considered to be a free market supporter. Guliev's re-emergence, even if from abroad, in Azerbaijan's politics and his stated intention to run in the upcoming elections added a new figure to the opposition's camp, although it was not really clear where he fitted into the ranks of his former political opponents. However, it did serve to energize his supporters in the not-so-numerous Democratic Party of Azerbaijan and in the Committee for Rasul Guliev's Rights. The latter organization had been set up after Guliev was stripped of his parliamentary seat, technically for failing to attend sessions of the parliament for more than a year. Guliev's supporters came under pressure from the authorities and, while Aliev himself did not comment on his former ally, the Ministries of Security and of the Interior in a joint statement with the prosecutor general's Office accused the ex-speaker of plotting a coup.

On the subject of coups, Aliev continued his efforts to track down opponents who had taken refuge abroad. After repeated demands from Baku, Russia extradited former Prime Minister Suret Huseinov, who had ousted Elchibey in the 1993 rebellion and who had been hiding in Russia since the failed coup attempt against Aliev in 1994. Russia, however, refused to extradite Ayaz Mutalibov, the former president living in Moscow since 1992, on the grounds that he had acquired Russian citizenship.

High-profile political trials continued throughout the year. Several OPON (Special Police Force) members and associates of former Prime Minister Huseinov, implicated in coup attempts in 1994 and 1995, were sentenced to various terms. Supporters of Mutalibov, including his former press secretary Rasim Agaev, went on trial as well. Azerbaijan's supreme court also convicted the terrorists (supporters of secession for the Lezgin ethnic minority) allegedly responsible for the 1995 bomb attack in Baku's subway in which more than 200 people died.

In a move clearly aimed at curbing Iranian influence, the Supreme Court sentenced the leader of the Tehran-financed Islamic Party, Aliakram Aliev, to 11 years for high treason and spying for Iran. At the same time, the former prime minister in Elchibey's government, Panah Guseinov, who had been arrested earlier, was released early in the year. The investigation into the murder of the academician and vice-chairman of President Aliev's New Azerbaijan Party, Ziya Buniadov, made no progress in 1997.

Various international human rights groups criticized Azerbaijan's government for violating the rights of its citizens, and Human Rights Watch called upon Azerbaijan to fulfill its obligations under the Universal Declaration of Human

Rights. Media censorship, although officially abolished except for military secrets, persisted in Azerbaijan. While the third independent TV channel, SPACE-TV, was allowed to begin broadcasting in the Baku area, the existence of smaller independent TV stations in the regions was repeatedly threatened by local authorities.

Azerbaijan failed to make substantial progress in reforming its political institutions. Steps in the right direction included suspending the death sentence, adopting a law introducing the jury system for courts, a new law on municipal elections, and a law on the constitutional court, as well as continuous high-level consultations with the Council of Europe. Given Azerbaijan's aspiration to join the latter body, 1998 is likely to be a year of more active institutional reforms.

PIPELINE POLITICS

President Aliev's visit to the United States in August, the first official visit by an Azerbaijani leader, was, perhaps, the most significant foreign policy event of 1997 and a clear indication of the strong Western orientation of Azerbaijan. Aliev received a red-carpet reception in Washington, and three major oil contracts between the State Oil Company of Azerbaijan (SOCAR) and leading U.S. companies were signed in the White House. Aliev apparently succeeded in his goal of achieving U.S. recognition of Azerbaijan's strategic importance in the Caucasus, and secured the Clinton administration's support for lifting Amendment 907 to the 1992 Freedom Support Act which prohibited U.S. aid to Azerbaijan's government. However, to Baku's displeasure, the U.S. Congress not only refused to rescind clause 907, but also introduced direct aid to Nagorno-Karabakh for the first time. This led even the usually pro-Western ex-president Elchibey to call for suspending the oil contracts with the United States.

Aliev's visit to the United States was preceded by a visit to Moscow in July in an apparent attempt to improve the deteriorating relationship with Russia following the scandal over Russian arms shipments to Armenia. At the meeting, Yeltsin asked Foreign Minister Yevgenii Primakov to make solving the Nagorno-Karabakh issue a matter of daily concern "as he did with the issue of NATO expansion." No dramatic improvement in Azeri-Russian relations was immediately visible, and the unexpected visit to Baku by Chechen President Aslan Maskhadov just before Aliev's departure for Moscow did not make relations any easier. During Aliev's Moscow visit the Caspian Sea Kyapaz oil field contract was signed in Moscow between the State Oil Company of Azerbaijan (SOCAR) and Russia's LUKoil and Rosneft. The contract was suspended later in the year due to Turkmenistan's territorial claims on the field. Furthermore, Aliev canceled a planned visit to mark Moscow's 850th anniversary celebrations, apparently in reaction to the August signing of the Russo-Armenian Strategic Cooperation Treaty, which included a clause pledging military assistance. Aliev also paid a visit to France in the beginning of the year, where SOCAR signed contracts worth $2 billion with Elf and TOTAL on developing the Lenkoran-Deniz and Shah-Deniz oil fields in the southern part of Azerbaijan's sector of the Caspian.

Azerbaijan's foreign policy was not limited to the capitals of the Minsk group co-chairs, but was increasingly diverse. Aliev's itinerary included Turkey, Italy and the Vatican, and Poland, in an apparent move to restore relations with the Central European states, which had faded after the collapse of the USSR. Later in the year, high-ranking delegations from Romania and Bulgaria visited Baku. Following Israeli Prime Minister Benjamin Netanyahu's swift but cordial meeting with Aliev during his stopover in Baku, Foreign Minister Hasanov toured Syria and Lebanon to promote bilateral ties.

1997 brought no improvement of relations with Iran, angered by Azerbaijan's growing U.S. and Israeli ties, and by Baku's active development of Caspian Sea resources. Iran repeatedly warned Azerbaijan not to act unilaterally in the Caspian and even sent a letter to the UN secretary general to that effect. During the year Baku suspended re-broadcast of Iranian TV programs.

Relations also soured with another Caspian littoral state, Turkmenistan, over the division of the Caspian. Russia seemed to be abandoning its earlier insistence on common development of the Caspian Sea's resources. It appeared to be more open toward the position of Azerbaijan and Kazakhstan, which favored a sectoral division between the littoral states—not least because Russian oil companies were offered a share in some of the Azerbaijani projects. This development would appear to leave Iran as the only state holding out for a sectoral division (despite its State Oil Company participating in two of the offshore oil deals).

The summit of leaders of members of the Commonwealth of Independent States in Chisinau, Moldova in October 1997 seemed to be a turning point in that organization's development. Sharp charges were leveled at Russia, and a new informal group consisting of Georgia, Ukraine, Azerbaijan, and Moldova, known as GUAM, was created, and was reinforced further by the Ukrainian and Moldovan presidents' visits to Tbilisi and Baku respectively. The four countries were the ones most concerned by amendments to the 1990 Conventional Forces in Europe (CFE) flanks agreement that allowed Russia to increase its military presence along its southern frontiers. Azerbaijan was the last country to ratify the change in the CFE, just hours before the deadline of 15 May 1997, after the personal intervention of U.S. Vice President Al Gore.

Developing a common understanding with the other post-Soviet republics opposed to Russian domination was an important element of Aliev's regional policy and included visiting Kazakhstan and Uzbekistan to secure support of the two major Central Asian states for Azerbaijan's initiatives in the Caspian and within the CIS. In the Caucasus, Azerbaijan enjoyed increasingly cordial relations with Georgia and an understanding with the Chechen leadership. Not surprisingly, Aliev called for NATO's greater involvement in the Karabakh peace process and possibly even in guarding the oil pipeline.

Surveys conducted by Turan throughout the year showed that while the majority of respondents supported the foreign policy of the current authorities, its domestic policy accomplishments enjoyed much less support. Azerbaijan's current foreign policy was a more balanced version of the one advocated by the national movement, and in fact incorporated many of the Popular Front's foreign policy priorities such as strengthening independence, a pro-Western and specifically pro-U.S. orientation, and the steadfast rejection of a Russian military presence in Azerbaijan. On the other hand Aliev, formerly one of the top members of the Soviet leadership, is himself a somewhat grander politician and seemingly prefers geopolitics over domestic issues.

This was especially evident during the "First Oil Day" celebrations, one of the most significant events of the year and, according to some (such as American journalist Thomas Goltz), the "finest hour" of Heydar Aliev. Azerbaijan's Constitution Day, 12 November, marked the official opening of the "Northern pipeline," the one passing through Russian territory, including Chechnya. The pipeline was to carry the so-called "early oil" produced by the Azerbaijan International Operating Company (AIOC), the first international oil consortium to start operations in the Caspian, to the Russian Black Sea port of Novorossiisk. This meant Azerbaijan for the first time since 1920 was returning to the ranks of the world's oil exporters. Various foreign dignitaries including Georgian President Edvard Shevardnadze, Turkish Prime Minister Mesut Yilmaz, Russian First Deputy Prime Minister Boris Nemtsov, U.S. Energy Secretary Federico Pena, and others attended the celebration ceremony.

In speeches reminiscent of the nineteenth-century "Great Game" between Britain and Russia for control over Central Asia, foreign guests praised Aliev and advocated the pipeline option they prefer for the main export route. (A decision on the main route was expected by October 1998.) The U.S. energy secretary explicitly backed the Turkish Prime Minister's insistence on building a Baku-Ceyhan pipeline (the "Western" route, through Georgia and Turkey). Russian First Deputy Prime Minister Nemtsov, the author of the long-negotiated agreement among Baku, Grozny, and Moscow allowing the early oil to pass through Chechnya, urged the "northern" pipeline as the most economical export route. Perhaps the most revealing were Shevardnadze's words: "Let the oil flow through Russia, for now." As expected, Kazakhstan and Uzbekistan endorsed Azerbaijan's position on dividing the Caspian, while Iranian and Turkmen representatives declined the invitation to attend the ceremony.

Interview: **"OIL IS OUR DESTINY"**

by ANNE NIVAT

The oil under the Caspian Sea was a political resource as well as a natural one, Azerbaijani Foreign Minister Hasan Hasanov told Transitions' *Anne Nivat in an interview in Baku.*

Nivat: How do you judge Azerbaijan's place on the international political scene today?

Hasan Hasanov: Azerbaijan's role is defined by its geostrategic situation and its domestic politics. Due to its geostrategic position, Azerbaijan is a target of interest for several countries in the world, because we are at the crossroads between Europe and Asia, on the Caspian Sea. We now also appear to be a real bridge between Central Asia and Europe. The fact that we can transport Kazakh and Turkmen oil and gas to world markets makes us even more important on the world scene. Moreover, we have borders with very serious and powerful states like Russia, Turkey, and Iran, which means that the border between the CIS [Commonwealth of Independent States] system of security and NATO is our border with Turkey. That very simple fact defines our relationship with most of our neighbors.

After we gained independence, our relationship with Russia grew dynamically from a pretty bad level to a normal one. With Georgia we never had a single problem, and Georgia is now our strategic partner in the region. Our other strategic partners in the region are Ukraine, Turkey, Kazakhstan, and Uzbekistan. Of course, there is not a single definition of "strategic." With Kazakhstan, the most important question is that of the status of the Caspian Sea and our right to exploit our oil; the question of the rights of minority populations of Kazakhs here and Azeris there is also of concern. We don't have a direct border with Uzbekistan, but we appear to be their unique bridge to gain access to Europe. We also agree that neither Azerbaijan nor Uzbekistan will enter any kind of new union that could cancel either's independence.

With Georgia, we belong to the same geographical space, the Caucasus, which is formed from three countries. We share the same view about how East and West can live together. We both want to integrate into European structures, yet without giving up our Eastern values. And together we form this geographical corridor that leads from Central Asia to Europe. The third of the Caucasian countries, Armenia, is our enemy and still occupies 20 percent of our territory [captured in the Nagorno-Karabakh war].

With Turkey, we share ancient history, a lot of traditions, a common language, and also a common point of view on foreign affairs. Through Ukraine, we have access to the Central European region, which is also possible through Turkey. Up to now, we have had a very good relationship with all the countries along the Black Sea.

What about Iran?

Our relationship is absolutely normal. Disapprobation is the same on both sides. Iran judges our European orientation as a mistake; it also dislikes our relations with the United States and Israel. And we judge as a mistake their relations with Armenia. Therefore it is quite difficult to maintain a good relationship with Iran. A certain euphoria appeared in the Western press after the election of the new Iranian president. That [euphoria] is now over, and we are all waiting to see how he will behave in practice. But despite the fact that between 20 [million] and 30 million ethnic Azeris live in Iran, we don't have a single direct problem with Iran.

The war between Azerbaijan and Armenia seems to be over, but relations remain very cold. On which level do you think they could be improved?

I would not say the war is over. It is not. There is only a cease-fire. We are ready to give Nagorno-Karabakh autonomy within Azerbaijan, but, unfortunately, the Armenian state thinks that such autonomy is not enough and insists upon the total independence of this part of our country. But we cannot give Nagorno-Karabakh its independence because, as our president [Heidar Aliev], says, there cannot be two Armenian states in the Caucasus.

The geopolitical situation of Azerbaijan and its oil reserves more or less define its external politics.

They don't only define our foreign affairs policies but also the attitudes of other countries toward us. This is what I want to stress.

But don't you think that oil is playing too big a role in your politics?

Every country has, more or less, one particularly strong feature [that it uses in] its politics. For some, it is nuclear weapons, for others it is a strong army, a vast territory, or a huge population. We did not choose oil to be one of our main factors in external politics. Oil plays the role it must play. That doesn't please Armenia, but it is a simple fact. What do we do here in Azerbaijan against the fact that Armenia is using its strong and very powerful diaspora all around the world against us? They use their diaspora, we use our oil. It could also have happened that they would have oil and we would have a diaspora. The oil is not something we created; we only received it by chance. It is our destiny.

What will oil revenues and control of a pipeline give your country?

As you have been traveling all around the former Soviet republic capitals, you can judge for yourself Azerbaijan's position regarding openness to the world. [You can see] how many more foreign companies are present here, how many foreign shops, foreign people, and the volume of foreign investment here. Of course, this cannot be felt by every single inhabitant of this country, just as not every American can understand and feel the importance of the $10 billion U.S. investment in Azerbaijan. We don't count on any miracle happening because of oil or because of the pipeline. There will be no miracle. There will only be a normal, slow movement forward.

How do you judge domestic politics? People seem to be happy with the recent stability, but at what price has it been launched?

These people grew up with and are still used to socialism. They think the government has to guarantee each of them a decent salary. In fact, under a market economy, the state can guarantee ideal conditions to earn money, but it can in no case simply give money to people as a gift. There is a specific group of people who like to live in this new world under capitalism but still demand the state guarantee them a salary [as it did] under socialism.

Do you think there is an alternative to Aliev? What is Azerbaijan's future after him?

I see the future of our country after Aliev like the future of the United States after Clinton or the future of France after Chirac. Aliev managed to create a stable state mechanism; he is very energetic, and, according to our constitution, he is allowed to be president for the next ten years. So it is too early to make any prognosis.

How do you explain the fact that state television constantly broadcasts pro-Aliev propaganda?

What you saw on television is not a permanent propaganda but only a commemoration of what happened in our country in 1993. At that time, our country was in a deep crisis and needed help. That's when people appealed to Aliev. It has nothing to do with propaganda. Around 600 newspapers are registered in Azerbaijan, among them 30 or 40 serious opposition newspapers. I don't think such a high level of criticism of the government is allowed in any other country in the world. One of those newspapers is *Mukhalifat,* which means opposition. Isn't that enough? All the parties publish their own newspapers, including opposition parties. So why shouldn't the government reserve the right to defend itself against these critics? That's why censorship exists. But in any case, our censors don't change the lies published in the opposition press. They can really write what they want."

NOTE

Reprinted with kind permission from *Transitions* magazine, September 1997.

NAGORNO-KARABAKH CONFLICT STILL IN IMPASSE

by EMIL DANIELYAN

1997 saw significant events in relation to the Nagorno-Karabakh conflict, which, nevertheless, did not result in any tangible progress in the talks. Growing discord between Armenia and the unrecognized Republic of Nagorno-Karabakh that came to light in September had repercussions on the mediation process sponsored by the Organization for Security and Cooperation in Europe's (OSCE) Minsk Group.

The year started out in an acrimonious atmosphere following the OSCE's December 1996 summit in Lisbon. Armenia found itself alone in vetoing a provision in the summit's final document that upheld Azerbaijan's sovereignty over the disputed enclave. The controversial wording was included in a separate statement by the OSCE acting chairman. Later, the Armenian side claimed that the statement predetermined the outcome of the peace process, and thus encouraged Azerbaijan to toughen its position.

The first and sole face-to-face talks between the warring sides in 1997 took place in April but were again fruitless. Apparently due to their failure, the Russian, U.S., and French co-chairs of the Minsk Group began relying more on shuttle diplomacy. Their first coordinated effort came in early June when a high ranking delegation including U.S. Deputy Secretary of State Strobe Talbott and Russian Deputy Foreign Minister Boris Pastukhov visited the region to seek approval for their "package" plan. The plan proposed settling all contentious issues by a single framework accord, as opposed to trying to resolve issues one at a time. Even though it was kept secret, some of its details emerged in the Armenian and Azerbaijani media. Nagorno-Karabakh would be granted broad autonomy within Azerbaijan, having its own government, parliament and armed forces. According to Azerbaijani officials, the latter's role would be confined to policing. The Lachin corridor, the region's main and shortest connection with Armenia, would reportedly be placed under international control.

Despite further behind-the-scenes diplomatic efforts, it became evident by the end of August that the Group's initiative had failed. Nagorno-Karabakh rejected the plan in line with its policy of no "vertical subordination" to Baku and no concessions on Lachin, currently controlled by Karabakh's army. The enclave's leadership also rebuffed the plan for what it saw as insufficient security guarantees. Armenia and Azerbaijan, in turn, had unspecified reservations.

Those developments coincided with the 1 September presidential election in Nagorno-Karabakh. With over 90 percent of the vote, Nagorno-Karabakh Foreign Minister Arkadii Ghukasian won the election. The previous president, Robert Kocharian, had been appointed Armenian prime minister in March 1997. During his election campaign, Ghukasian denounced the peace plan because it allegedly involved "unilateral concessions" to Azerbaijan. Baku and the international community for their part refused to recognize the legitimacy of the election on the grounds that the region's status is not determined and its Azerbaijani minority, which fled from the region during the war, was unable to participate in the vote.

The failure of the "package" plan forced the Minsk Group to change its strategy and come up with the so-called "phased" approach. New peace proposals unveiled in September would delay resolution of Karabakh's status until the last phase of the peace process. And this would be preceded by the release of the occupied Azerbaijani territories, the lifting of Azerbaijan's blockade of Armenia, the repatriation of displaced persons, and other confidence-building measures. Armenian President Levon Ter-Petrossian's 26 September news conference brought a new turn of events. As well as supporting the plan as a basis for further negotiations, Ter-Petrossian said "unilateral demands" for Nagorno-Karabakh's secession from Azerbaijan were unrealistic and would not be tolerated by the international community. He said the Armenian side must be ready for serious concessions if it is to live in a "normal country" and if it is not to lose more in the long run, drawing parallels with the intransigent Croatian Serbs who lost their self-proclaimed republic in 1995. Ter-Petrossian's remarks were welcomed in Baku but strongly condemned by the Armenian opposition, and caused covert discontent in Karabakh.

Developments in the following months showed that Armenia and Nagorno-Karabakh were drifting apart in their positions on the conflict. The "phased" plan was approved by Azerbaijan and Armenia, but was rejected by the Karabakh Armenians. They said the phased solution was dangerous because it would oblige them to withdraw from the occupied six districts of Azerbaijan adjacent to Karabakh (their main bargaining chip) but did not guarantee that Baku would not attack Karabakh after the first stage of the peace process. Having regained their territories, they argued, the oil-rich Azerbaijan would be tempted to try to solve the dispute by force. In September, the commander of the powerful Karabakh armed forces, Lt.-Gen. Samvel Babayan, predicted that if the deadlock drags on for a year or two, another war with Azerbaijan will be inevitable, in which case he threatened Baku with complete military defeat.

But even securing his own government's support was not an easy task for the Armenian president. Prime Minister Kocharian repeatedly said he preferred the package solution to the phased one. Two other key officials, Interior and National Security Minister Serzh Sarkisian and hard-line Defense Minister Vazgen Sarkisian (not related to Serzh), also opposed concessions. The defense minister, in particular, said Azerbaijan should forget about getting back not only the Lachin but also Kelbajar districts. The two districts lie between Armenia and Karabakh and equal the latter in their size. During their further visits to the region in November and December, the Minsk Group co-chairs were again unable to get Stepanakert (the Karabakh capital) to accept the plan. Karabakh was still insisting on direct talks with Baku as the shortest way to peace. Hence, there was growing speculation that the Armenian side may face increased international pressure to change their position. International mediators tried to assure the Armenians that they did not intend to impose a solution on any of the sides and would try to reach a consensus.

Indeed, nothing alarming was going on in the international arena for the Armenians. For instance, the pro-Azerbaijani oil lobby in the United States failed to reverse Armenian gains in the U.S. Congress. Not only did Congress keep the sanctions against Azerbaijan in place, but also earmarked $12.5 million in direct assistance to the Nagorno-Karabakh government. That unprecedented decision was passed over objections from the Clinton administration. Troubles were expected from the 17–19 December OSCE Council of Ministers meeting in Copenhagen. In the run-up to the meeting, Armenian diplomats were lobbying for the OSCE countries to "eradicate the consequences of Lisbon" amid a domestic outcry against the threat of "another Lisbon." But the meeting did not mention Karabakh in its final document. For the Armenian diplomats this very fact was a success. The government claimed credit for it in a bid to counter-attack the opposition, which speculated the international community simply gave the Armenian side a time-out to make a final decision.

In Azerbaijan the reaction to and discussions preceding the statement were much calmer. It appears that the Azerbaijani leadership more and more banked on Ter-Petrossian, who it was hoped would rein in the hard-liners. This was quite natural given that both Baku and Ter-Petrossian accepted the Minsk Group's peace plan. The most vocal Azerbaijani critic of the Karabakh policy of President Heydar Aliev was the country's former President Abulfaz Elchibey. He was ousted as president in 1993 as a result of a military coup and returned to Baku in the fall of 1997. He spoke out against the idea of granting the Karabakh Armenians the "broadest possible" autonomy in Azerbaijan, a policy favored by Aliev. Elchibey's party, the Popular Front of Azerbaijan, was a leading opposition force. Its chances of success were not very high, given Aliev's autocratic rule and unlimited power. Despite his advanced age (he is 74), the powerful Azerbaijani president was full of energy and likely to rule the country for another five-year term after elections in October 1998. That is why Ter-Petrossian played such a pivotal role in the Nagorno-Karabakh peace process. For Azerbaijan and the international community his success was the key to peace. But if the Armenian president was really keen to press on with his ideas on Karabakh in 1998 he would face the strongest challenge yet from the Nagorno-Karabakh authorities, the Armenian opposition, and most importantly his own key ministers. The very army and police that helped secure his dubious reelection in September 1996, may not stand behind him. The only force likely to support his Karabakh policy would be the unpopular Armenian Pan-National Movement (HHSh).

Armenia

Population:	3,754,300
Capital:	Yerevan (pop. 1,200,200)
Major cities:	Gyumri (pop. 207,000), Vanadzor (pop.146,000)
Area:	29,800 sq. km.
Major ethnic groups:	Armenian 93.3%, Kurdish 1.7%, Russian 1.5% (est.), other 3.5%
Economy:	GDP growth: 2.7%
....	Inflation rate: 22.0%
....	Average monthly wage: $22
....	Unemployment rate: 11.0%

BACK TO POLITICAL STANDSTILL

by EMIL DANIELYAN

Those who expected to see radical political change in Armenia in 1997 were disappointed. A major split in the opposition and re-consolidation of the ruling circles pushed back the country to the status quo that had existed before the troubled September 1996 presidential elections. The elections, despite their dubious results and violent aftermath, raised hopes of a democratization of Armenia's political system.

The year began with the anticipation of imminent opposition mass protests scheduled for the spring. An alliance of the leading Armenian opposition forces, the National Accord Bloc (AHD), was recovering from the government's post-election crackdown, and was preparing to campaign for fresh elections at all levels. The parties making up the AHD still believed that their candidate, former Prime Minister Vazgen Manukian, was the rightful winner of the 1996 ballot as opposed to the official results that had given victory to the incumbent President Levon Ter-Petrossian. The opposition hoped that through staging repeated mass demonstrations throughout the country (as had occurred in Serbia in 1996–97) it would force the authorities to hold free and fair elections.

Plans for the spring campaign failed to materialize, however, due to the emergence of serious differences among the main AHD parties. With Manukian's National Democratic Union (AZhM) calling for radical actions but the Self-Determination Union (IM) and the banned Dashnak party (HHD) taking a softer line on the regime, it was obvious that no concerted opposition effort would be possible. The IM and the HHD were strongly criticized by the AZhM and its allies for their closed-door meetings with the authorities. The leader of the IM, prominent Soviet-era dissident Paruyr Hayrikian, defended such meetings, arguing that a dialogue with the Ter-Petrossian regime could result in reforms in election law that would improve the opposition's electoral prospects. As regards the Dashnaks, they appear to have been mainly concerned with trying to lift the 1995 ban that forbade them from operating inside Armenia. As a result of these tactical differences, the AHD ceased to be the formidable force that had caused so many problems for Ter-Petrossian in September 1996. The more radical opposition parties apparently realized that without having the influential Dashnaks and Hayrikian on board they would be unable to mobilize the public.

Equally dramatic developments followed in the camp of the authorities, who were regaining their pre-election self-confidence. By mid-July a struggle between the hard-line and reform-minded wings of the ruling Armenian Pan-National Movement (HHSh) ended with the complete victory of the former. At a party congress held on 11–13 July the leader of the hard-liners, controversial former Interior and National Security Minister Vano Siradeghian, was elected the chairman of the HHSh. Siradeghian played a key role in the 1996 crackdown on the opposition. He was subsequently sacked as the minister, but then made a quick political comeback, being appointed Yerevan mayor. His takeover of the HHSh was seen as the logical outcome of the regime's re-consolidation.

Siradeghian's main rival was the reformist leader Eduard Yegorian, the chairman of a key parliamentary committee. A former anti-opposition "hawk," Yegorian drastically changed his political views after the presidential elections. He now admitted that Armenia is far from democracy, calling it a "nomenklatura capitalism." He called for a sweeping political reform, arguing that early, free, and fair parliamentary elections would be a face-saving solution to the bitter standoff between the authorities and the opposition. Speculation that Ter-Petrossian would announce early elections as a gesture of reconciliation was dashed by the election of Siradeghian. It was assumed that Siradeghian would use the governmental apparatus to try to set up a strong party machine capable of winning the next parliamentary elections, scheduled for July. He unveiled plans to found a new powerful center-right force on the basis of the pro-government Hanrapetutyun (Republic) bloc, dominated by the HHSh.

Meanwhile, inside the HHSh, purges of Yegorian supporters began with the dissolution of a number of local party branches. Yegorian subsequently left the HHSh and set up his own 12–member parliamentary group named Hayrenik (Fatherland). Another major setback for the renegade HHSh leader was his dismissal as the chairman of the parliament committee on state and legal affairs in September after the Hanrapetutyun-led parliament majority scrapped Yegorian's draft electoral code.

By the fall of 1997 it became clear that the expectations of political liberalization were premature. Ter-Petrossian confidently assured the HHSh congress that "the internal political crisis in Armenia has been fully overcome." Growing squabbles within the opposition only reinforced the regime's grip on power. They culminated on 24 September in the formal dissolution of the AHD. Manukian's AZhM, Hayrikian's IM, and the Dashnaks openly admitted having differing agendas. The more radical AZhM could no longer get along with the more conciliatory IM and HHD. The Dashnaks' first confidential meeting with Ter-Petrossian's representatives in April was the beginning of the AHD's break-up. Another similar meeting took place in September. Prior to that, in an unprecedented move Prime Minister Robert Kocharian visited the HHD's ruling bureau in Athens. Furthermore, Foreign Minister Aleksandr Arzumanian and other diplomats publicly praised and thanked the Dashnaks for their pro-Armenian lobbying efforts in the U.S. Congress. The party got back most of its confiscated assets by the end of October, and commentators suggested that its reinstatement was just a matter of time. But the conclusion of the trial of 31 members and supporters of the HHD led to further uncertainty about prospects for the reinstatement of the Dashnak party. On December 12 the popular and prominent Dashnak leader Vahan Hovannisian was sentenced to four years in prison, having been found guilty of calling for the "violent overthrow of the government." Four other defendants were sentenced to death for murdering two policemen during their arrest in 1995, and 18 others received prison terms of two to seven years. With Hovannisian in prison it is hard to think of a full reconciliation between the authorities and the Dashnaks. Nevertheless, the Dashnaks were accused by the AZhM and its allies of making a secret deal with Ter-Petrossian, involving a pull-out from the opposition alliance in exchange for a re-legalization. What is certain is that the Armenian president did benefit from the collapse of the alliance regardless of whether he and the Dashnaks actually caused it.

DISSENT IN RULING CIRCLES OVER THE KARABAKH PEACE PROCESS

In 1997 all the signs were that political changes were more likely to come not from opposition mobilization, but as a result of discord within ruling circles over developments in the Nagorno-Karabakh peace process. On 26 September, in a departure from previous policy Ter-Petrossian stated that "unilateral demands" for Karabakh's secession from Azerbaijan were unrealistic and would not be tolerated by the international community. He said that Armenia's economic recovery would not take place until the decade-old conflict was settled in agreement with the international community.

Ter-Petrossian's remarks caused an explosive public debate, which redrew the political battle-lines and gave the divided opposition a cause around which they could unify. Opposition leaders promptly condemned his comments as a "defeatist" posture, and a series of opposition rallies against any "sell-out of Karabakh" ensued. Within the government itself, the president's ideas were challenged by three key politicians: Prime Minister Kocharian, Defense Minister Vazgen Sarkisian, and Interior and National Security Minister Serzh Sarkisian. Consequently, speculations grew about a possible alliance between Prime Minister Kocharian, the wartime leader of Nagorno-Karabakh, and the two "power" ministers. The opposition said that it would not be averse to cooperating with the three men on Nagorno-Karabakh—an unprecedented act, given that Defense Minister Sarkisian was a leading opposition foe. Meanwhile, the Siradeghian-led HHSh lent its support to Ter-Petrossian's Karabakh policy. The move underscored existing differences between the HHSh-controlled parliament and Kocharian's cabinet. The ruling party was unhappy with its perceived lack of influence with the government. Kocharian and Siradeghian were rumored to be at odds with each other. The estrangement reached its climax in December during parliamentary debates on the government's draft budget for 1998. The majority Hanrapetutyun bloc openly criticized the draft for its alleged failure to attain the bloc's 1995 election promises. A last-minute compromise pushed the budget through, but the clash illustrated that the government was finding it increasingly difficult to get its legislative initiatives passed by the National Assembly.

FOREIGN AFFAIRS

The year began with an embarrassment for Armenia's foreign policy, related to a scandal with alleged clandestine Russian arms supplies to Armenia. Two well-known Russian politicians, Minister for Commonwealth of Independent States

(CIS) Affairs Aman Tuleev and the chairman of the State Duma's defense committee, Lev Rokhlin, alleged that over the previous three years the Kremlin secretly delivered weapons worth $1 billion to Armenia. Official Yerevan and the Russian military denied the charges, but this did not prevent Russian President Boris Yeltsin from ordering an official inquiry, following strong protests from Azerbaijan. In the following months, the scandal finally bogged down, and as both Tuleev and Rokhlin left office, it seemed finally forgotten.

On 29 August Ter-Petrossian and Yeltsin signed a landmark treaty in Moscow on "friendship, cooperation and mutual defense," widely interpreted as a sign that Yerevan was abandoning its policy of "balance" between the West and Russia. Some analysts argued that Armenia hoped to check any future international pressure to recognize Azerbaijan's territorial integrity by strengthening its bonds with Russia. Apart from military matters the treaty did not envisage any other mutually binding obligations, and a campaign to collect signatures calling for Armenia to join the Russia-Belarus union did not receive support from either the authorities or the main opposition parties. Two rival groups, the Armenian Communists and a union of small leftist forces, were claiming by September to have each collected around one million signatures in support of joining the union, but for unknown reasons the Communists did not raise the issue in parliament.

As for Armenia's relationship with the West, the crisis caused by Ter-Petrossian's dubious reelection seemed to be over. He was still regarded as an acceptable figure to the international community and especially the United States, perceived to be both predictable and to a degree flexible in the Nagorno-Karabakh conflict—especially in comparison with other potential Armenian leaders. The Dashnaks, who control one of the two main Armenian-American lobbying groups in Washington, did not try to lobby against Ter-Petrossian. As a result, the U.S. Congress kept the ban on direct American aid to Azerbaijan, despite mounting opposition to the ban from U.S. oil interests.

In the fall, Armenian soldiers took part for the first time in military exercises held in Greece under NATO Partnership for Peace auspices. The year generally saw a greater emphasis on the European direction of Armenian foreign policy. Several visits by Council of Europe delegations boosted hopes that Armenia would finally become a full member of the organization in 1998. In November Armenia proposed to the European Union that it begin a "political dialogue" aimed at further integration. According to First Deputy Foreign Minister Vartan Oskanian, Armenia's ultimate aim is to become a full member of the EU, but the more immediate task is to secure an associate membership.

ECONOMIC SLOWDOWN

In 1997 the Armenian government fell short of its macroeconomic targets as the economy grew by only 2.7 percent and inflation totaled 21 percent, against the forecast 6 and 10 percent, respectively. Particularly noteworthy was the rise in the inflation rate, considering that it had been just 5.8 percent in 1996. The rise in inflation was partly due to price hikes in housing utilities but also to the deplorable state of local industry, which remained stagnant throughout the year.

The Armenian Bank Association estimated that the 20 largest Armenian enterprises need some $2 billion in long-term loans and investment in order to become viable. Armenian banks had generated just $80 million in industrial investment by year's end.

The trade deficit widened in 1997: exports fell 25 percent while imports went up by 4 percent. In the first nine months of the year imports ran at $627 million and exports $155 million. The fact that the country got by with such a huge trade deficit for six consecutive years was due to substantial money transfers from the diaspora and from the hundreds of thousands of Armenians who are working abroad to support their families. The CIS countries accounted for only a third of Armenia's foreign trade turnover. Incidentally, Belgium remained Armenia's number one Western partner, with the Armenian diamond polishing industry the key reason. Diamonds were the country's major export.

The large-scale privatization was cited as another reason for the industrial stagnation. Privatization got underway back in 1991 and gained momentum in 1995. It was carried out mainly through vouchers, distributed to citizens. Sixty-five percent of medium and large state enterprises (1,200 in absolute terms) and 90 percent of small (about 6,000) state enterprises were privatized as of late 1997. It appeared that the new owners made little effort at a serious restructuring of their enterprises, which needed to find new markets. The new government of Prime Minister Robert Kocharian thus decided to change tack and auction off the remaining industrial giants in return for investment tenders. In December the Greek telecom company OTE won a tender for 90 percent of the ArmenTel company which ran the country's entire telephone network. As well as paying $80 million to the national budget, OTE promised to invest $300 million in local telecoms. Encouraging developments occurred in the mining sector too. A U.S. and a Canadian firm planned to invest $200 million in the local gold industry over 10 years. Also, the Yerevan Cognac Factory, whose famous product is considered the most competitive Armenian commodity, was put up for international tender. The Russians were particularly active in the Armenian energy sector. A major Russian stake in the Medzamor atomic plant was complemented by a $270 million deal between Russia's Gazprom and the government. The new joint venture will handle Russian natural gas deliveries to Armenia.

An investment fund set up by an Armenian-American billionaire was another source of much-needed oxygen for the Armenian economy. The businessman, Kirk Kirkorian, in September earmarked $100 million for a special fund, designed to provide Armenian enterprises with low-interest loans. The fund was managed by retired U.S. pro-Armenian Senator Bob Dole. A similar scheme worth $17 million was launched by the World Bank. Despite the worse-than-expected economic performance, the World Bank and IMF continued to praise and support the government. By the end of 1997 Armenia had received a total of $360 million in interest-free loans from the World Bank for financing its budget deficit and rebuilding its battered infrastructure.

The year also saw a further liberalization of the country's banking sector. In November the parliament reinforced the confidentiality of bank deposits of physical persons. This meant that only courts could order banks to disclose information about their accounts. Armenia was the first CIS country to introduce virtually absolute bank confidentiality. The move was part of the government's wider effort to turn the country into a sort of safe haven for international banking capital. Perhaps the main achievement of the Kocharian government was much-improved tax collection. By September tax revenues were twice as much as in September 1996. This was the result of a government crackdown on the shadow businesses close to the ruling circles that had previously managed to evade taxes. Officials said the shadow economy, which is estimated to comprise 50 to 70 percent of all economic activity in Armenia, was hit badly by these measures. Accordingly the authorities expected the officially reported economy to show steady growth of around 5 percent in 1998.

GLOSSARY

AHD National Accord Bloc
AZhM National Democratic Union
HHD Dashnak Party
HHSh Armenian Pan-National Movement
IM Self-Determination Union

Kazakhstan

Population:	17,300,000
Capital:	Almaty (pop. 1,200,000). The capital moved to Akmola in December 1997.
Major cities:	Karaganda (pop. 613,000), Shymkent (401,000), Akmola (pop. 280,000)
Area:	2,717,300 sq. km.
Major ethnic groups:	Kazakh 43%, Russian 36%, Ukrainian 5.2%, German 3%, Uzbek 2%, Tatar 2%
Economy:	GDP growth: 2.3%
....	Inflation rate: 15.0%
....	Average monthly wage: $110
....	Unemployment rate: 5.6%

A YEAR OF GROWING UNREST AND OPPOSITION

by BHAVNA DAVE

Appearing stable and fully in control, and resolutely gaining new international partners and integration with the global economy all through 1997, President Nursultan Nazarbaev grew increasingly authoritarian, scornful of public debate, suspicious of free flow of information, and profoundly insecure about any level of opposition.

After installing a new government headed by Nurlan Balgimbaev following the resignation of Prime Minister Akezhan Kazhegeldin on "health grounds" in October, Nazarbaev confidently launched his Strategy for Economic Development up to the year 2030. He reiterated his appreciation for the economic liberalization model of the South East Asian "tigers," and envisions his own brand of Eurasianism and state-regulated privatization progressing along a similar path such that Kazakhstan will emerge as the "Central Asian snow panther."

Behind the confident facade of "social stability and concord" and grandiose vision there lurked the insecurity of an authoritarian presidency, undertaking a continuing reshuffling of ministers, oblast heads (*akims*), and personnel at all levels, all of whom were held strictly accountable to the president. The presidency was challenged by the emergence of an opposition coalition National Front, led by the Azamat movement, and countrywide protests over unpaid wages and pensions, supported by the 500,000-member Association of Independent Trade Unions.

The most dramatic event of the year was the rapidity of the transfer of parliament, ministries, and state symbols in severe, sub-zero temperatures to the new capital Akmola (formerly named Tselinograd), which as yet lacks an infrastructure or the necessary accouterments to fulfill its role.

A NEW CAPITAL

Just over 40 years ago, Nikita Khrushchev's proposal to move Kazakhstan's capital to what he fondly named Tselinograd (Virgin Land City) was dismissed as one of his numerous hare-brained schemes, which subordinated the republic's interests to the vagaries of Moscow's central plan. However, Nazarbaev found a set of new justifications to this idea in the profoundly altered political and ethnic climate of the 1990s, linking it with his conception of Kazakhstan as a mighty Eurasian state, with its new capital located in greater proximity to "Europe."

Akmola is the fourth capital that Kazakhstan has had since its administrative boundaries were created in 1920. Few were convinced by the official rationale for the latest transfer—that the capital should be located in a "central" as well as a seismic-free zone (all other Central Asian capitals are on shaky grounds, for that matter), or in less polluted and less crowded environs. Still fewer believed in the vision of a harmonious relationship between the two cities, with Akmola emerging as the political and administrative center and Almaty remaining the cultural and business center and the "southern capital." What lay behind the transfer were the geopolitical concerns of a vast, virtually landlocked state buffered between the mighty China and Russia, anxious to deter any potential irredentist demands on the part of the Russians, who dominate the northeastern regions, and struggling to rectify the imbalance between the various regional and clan interests. The absence of a natural, indigenous urban center in Akmola, the sparse population, and isolated location are obstacles to Nazarbaev's efforts to consolidate its fragile statehood around the newly invented Eurasian core.

Determined against all odds to greet the New Year in the new capital, Nazarbaev inaugurated Akmola as the capital on 10 December 1997 at a joint session of the government and the parliament, with most ministries yet lacking buildings and deputies living in dormitories. Speculation had been rife whether the move was attainable before 2000, or feasible at all, due to the lack of funds, poor infrastructure, and inhospitable climate of Akmola. There was no serious debate on the implications of the transfer, nor reliable information on the expenditure and its source. Nazarbaev insisted that not a *tiyin* (cent) would be spent out of the public budget, arguing that the construction is to be funded entirely from extrabudgetary funds, with significant contributions from domestic, CIS, and international investors. It is hard to imagine enthusiastic international interest in developing a city with Siberian winters, gusty winds, and mosquito-infested summers.

In the absence of public accountability, it was widely speculated that the lion's share of the state budget, foreign investments, and contributions for other socio-economic projects (such as the pension fund), were siphoned off to develop Akmola. The State Investment Committee (Goskominvest), headed by Nazarbaev's relative and confidant Akhmetzhan Yesimov, and one of the numerous committees accountable to the president alone, oversees the task of attracting investment to Akmola.

Could there be yet another change, a reversal of the decision in the next millennium if a new leadership comes to power? Nazarbaev remained unfazed by such concerns, asserting with great optimism that Akmola "will become one of the most powerful communicative centers of the Eurasian super-mainland" in the twenty-first century.

COMPROMISE OVER LANGUAGE?

A major breakthrough in parliamentary affairs was the passage of the language bill that had led to a near-deadlock between both houses of parliament. The parliament finally endorsed the language bill in July, recognizing Kazakh as the sole state language, and Russian as an official language on par with Kazakh, dropping the additional clause "only when absolutely necessary" (*pri neobkhodimosti*). The final version of the law scrapped the initial time scale requiring Kazakhs to master their language by the year 2003 and all others to gain a proficiency in the state language by 2006, as well as the proposal to create a list of positions in the government where Kazakh would be mandatory. The new law mandated that at least 50 percent of broadcasts in both state and independent media be in Kazakh. The law also deemed that learning Kazakh is "the duty of each Kazakhstani" but there was no clear statement of what resources the state proposed to invest in order to facilitate the learning of Kazakh. Still, Kazakh language made further inroads at all levels of administration and society, thanks to the ongoing indigenization and state patronage. While state protection will continue to enhance its symbolic appeal and status, Kazakh is unlikely to become the natural lingua franca or the de facto state language in the foreseeable future. The declining hegemony of Russian is offset by globalization, with English spreading as the most neutral option and the undisputed marker of prestige. Indeed, in his *Strategy—2030* Nazarbaev envisioned Kazakhstanis as having an equally good command of all three languages.

The language issue was inextricably linked with the status as well as the demographic share of Kazakhs in the country's population. Though Kazakhs were estimated to constitute a clear majority, the country's total population dropped from 16.9 million in 1994 to 15.8 million at the end of 1997. The continuing emigration of Russian-speakers and Germans was not offset by the return of the Kazakh diaspora from Mongolia, Turkey, and other neighboring countries. These returning Kazakhs, fluent Kazakh speakers who do not know the Cyrillic script, are symbolic and demographic assets but an economic liability to the state.

MORE CENTRALIZATION AND SHUFFLING OF PERSONNEL

The year saw numerous administrative changes and personnel reshuffles, motivated by the dual objective of replacing the notorious internationalism cultivated under the Soviet era with a distinctively national profile and deterring regional leaders from building an independent power base.

Five oblasts were merged with the neighboring larger entity on grounds of economy and efficient governance. Taldy-korgan, Turgai, Zhezkazgan, Semipalatinsk, and Kokshetau were merged with Almaty, Kustanai, Karaganda, East Kazakhstan, and North Kazakhstan oblasts respectively. As a result of this gerrymandering, which was expected to continue, Kazakhs formed a majority in each of the newly constituted oblasts except North Kazakhstan.

Unlike Russia, the trend has been toward a greater centralization rather than any devolution. The center's mandate that revenues from more prosperous oblasts be transferred to the less developed ones deprived the oblast akims of an incentive to work for their oblasts. Their frequent transfers and short tenures—the average tenure of an akim was about a year—deterred them from building any base in the region and thus challenging the authority of the center, vested and personified in the institution of the president.

The dismissal of Akezhan Kazhegeldin as prime minister in October was an important example of this reshuffling. There were growing rumors of a latent power struggle between the prime minister and the president, coinciding along regional and *zhuz* (horde) divisions—with Nazarbaev representing the more assertive elder horde from the south and Kazhegeldin the more numerous middle horde in the central and northeastern part of the country. International observers noted a struggle between supporters of liberalization, headed by Kazhegeldin, and its more numerous and powerful opponents, who sought to maintain a state monopoly, especially over the strategic oil and gas sectors. Neither differences over economic policy nor the "zhuz factor" alone account for Kazhegeldin's exit. It was a combined outcome of the steady measures taken by the presidential apparatus to circumscribe the prime minister's authority and the growing criticism of his economic policies by forces within as well as outside the government.

In a further bid to consolidate his virtually unlimited constitutional mandate, Nazarbaev continued to create extra-constitutional bodies, appointing his close emissaries, kith, or "clients," as well as nominating his own people to the prime ministerial team. In 1996 Nazarbaev created the extra-constitutional post of secretary of state, appointing his closest ally Yesimov to a position that effectively superseded that of the prime minister. A subsequent presidential decree reduced the power of the state secretary, and Yesimov was appointed deputy prime minister, a position accountable to neither the prime minister nor the cabinet but to the president, and thus de facto more influential. Continuing to serve as the head of Goskominvest, Yesimov served as a trusted figure, occupying numerous strategic posts during the transitional phase.

Nazarbaev sacked a third of the ministers in Kazhegeldin's team in March to "streamline the unwieldy administration" in face of the economic crisis. At the same time he created yet another extra-constitutional body called the Agency for Control of Strategic Resources, headed by his protégé and a critic of Kazhegeldin, the young akim of Semipalatinsk Galymzhan Zhakianov. The key task of this agency was to exercise supervision over contracts with foreign firms and over the allocation of resources—the domain controlled by the prime minister and his staff. The net effect was a further strengthening of the authority of the presidential apparatus at the expense of the prime minister and the cabinet.

Kazhegeldin's relative popularity with foreign business and investors, and his image as an opponent of state monopoly, brought him few kudos within the government or in parliament. Among his strongest opponents outside the government was the self-standing powerful figure Zamanbek Nurkadilov (a deputy of the parliament), who accused him of selling off the country's wealth to foreign firms, often of dubious origins, and promoting a hasty and indiscriminate privatization, especially of strategic sectors such as oil, mining, and metallurgy. As the influential mayor of Almaty in 1993, Nurkadilov had successfully engineered the ouster of the then premier Sergei Tereshchenko. He published information on the allegedly illegally acquired financial assets of Kazhegeldin, held in various foreign banks, and claimed that the so-called foreign investments procured by Kazhegeldin (deals such as Ispat-Karmet) and investment by Samsung were "dummy" deals, in reality financed by the government with the premier's complicity.

In September, just weeks before his dismissal, Kazhegeldin gave an interview to *Karavan* in which he confessed to working for the KGB in the 1980s as a secret envoy involved with arms sales to the Balkans and the Middle East. He further substantiated this claim in an interview to *Komsomolskaya pravda* a couple of weeks later. Why he chose to reveal these activities is unclear; very likely it was a preemptive move directed at his opponents and possibly intended to shift the attention away from his recent role. Kazhegeldin disappeared from public view for a few weeks to undergo a surgery in Switzerland and resigned on "health grounds."

Deputy Prime Minister Yesimov once again played his role as a stock figure until Nurlan Balgimbaev, an oil engineer and former oil and gas minister who was head of the newly formed state agency Kazakhoil, was appointed prime minister. Proficient in English, trained at MIT and boasting significant experience with Chevron, Balgimbaev promised a continuation of economic reforms and privatization begun under Kazhegeldin. His association with Kazakhoil, whose deputy president was Nazarbaev's son-in-law Timur Kuligov, and his image as a hand-picked client of the president, occupying a highly circumscribed position, cast doubt on the extent to which the strategic oil, gas, and mining sectors will be privatized.

THE RETURN OF NURKADILOV: SHADOW ZONE BETWEEN GOVERNMENT AND OPPOSITION

Nurkadilov returned to the political center-stage in December as akim of Almaty oblast. He is a political maverick with an independent economic base and regional clientele, possessing traits of outspokenness and political ambition uncharacteristic for a parliamentary deputy. Over the preceding year and a half Nurkadilov had closely allied with Azamat, endorsing its demands for regional autonomy and direct elections of akims and the oblast assembly, and praising its leaders and other critics of Nazarbaev in public and in print. Rather than a reward for compliance, Nurkadilov's appointment was an acknowledgment of his stature as the most influential of Nazarbaev's rivals, operating in a shadow-zone between the government and the opposition.

As Almaty's mayor, Nurkadilov had opposed the transfer of capital to Akmola, and was dismissed weeks before this decision was made public in 1994. Notorious for his alleged close links with the Mafia, ownership of a vast economic empire, and clientele in the south, Nurkadilov had retained a high visibility and clout in national politics in his ordinary capacity as a deputy of the lower house of the Majilis.

Within weeks of his becoming the oblast akim, Nurkadilov appointed the Azamat leader Murat Auezov as chief of the Information and Social Concord Department in the Almaty oblast administration. This may well herald the consolidation of a new tactical alliance of Nazarbaev's rivals within the state organs and the opposition forces outside. There is a distinct likelihood that Nurkadilov will run as a presidential candidate against Nazarbaev in the elections scheduled for the year 2000.

COALESCENCE OF OPPOSITION GROUPS

The opposition groups, headed by Azamat, organized numerous demonstrations and rallies in the latter half of the year, often defying the restrictions on public gatherings, and protesting against the worsening socio-economic situation and the lack of civil rights. Azamat continued to present a coherent and unified opposition platform under the leadership of its triumvirate Murat Auezov, a sinologist and former Kazakhstani ambassador to China; Petr Svoik, head of the socialist party and former head of the State Anti-Monopoly Committee (dismissed in 1995); and Galym Abilseitov, a scientist who worked in Moscow for 18 years before being invited by Nazarbaev to head the Ministry of Science and Technology (dismissed in 1996).

Azamat appealed for a devolution of power, regular local elections (which had not been held in numerous councils since 1991), accountability of akims to the electorate rather than to the president, repeal of regulations on public organizations, and amendments to the near absolute powers vested in the presidency by the constitution. It has also attacked the economic policies of the government, especially the "nomenklatura privatization" of the oil and mining sectors, and what it regarded as sell-out deals (such as the pipeline deal with China signed in September).

To counter the flurry of opposition activities, Nazarbaev again resorted to his strategy of generating pluralism and multiple party structure from above by sponsoring yet another group called the Liberal Movement of Kazakhstan, headed by Asylbek Bisenbaev, an ex–staff member of the presidential administration. Declaring its intent to cooperate with all who "respect the constitution" and offer "constructive" support for the government, the Liberal Movement has published lengthy anti-Azamat treatises in the pro-government newspapers *Kazakhstanskaya pravda* and *Panorama.*

The public rally by Azamat in November, held despite the denial of permission by the procurator, led to the arrest of Auezov and Abilseitov and an attack on Svoik. Auezov was fined some 3,000 tenge ($35) and released a week later whereas Abilseitov spent two weeks without any hearing in prison, where he went on a hunger strike. A couple of days later, Svoik and his wife were beaten up, allegedly by Kazakhstani state militia, in their hotel room in Bishkek, where he was attending a conference on human rights.

In late November Nazarbaev warned the opposition that criminal charges might be brought if it continued to hold unsanctioned rallies. He dismissed demands for amendments to the constitution, urging the opposition to "let people live peacefully," as the parliament already had its hands full with the spate of pending legislation. As for the question of the legality of the law on public meetings and rallies, he contended that this matter was to be decided by the Constitutional Court and not the president. However, the Constitutional Court is not an independent body: its chairman and members are appointed by the president.

The growing stature of Azamat and the clean public image of its leaders brought together disparate oppositions groupings such as the right-wing Azat; the Republican Party; the Association of Independent Trade Unions (with some

500,000 members); Pokolenie, the pensioners' organization; and the Communist Party, headed by former speaker Serikbolsyn Abdildin. These groups had a common interest in opposing the growing authoritarianism of the presidency. The new Azamat-led coalition National Front, formed in December, was bolstered by Nurkadilov's appointment as the head of Almaty oblast.

ECONOMY CONTINUES TO DISAPPOINT

President Nazarbaev repeatedly stated that Kazakhstan must aim for intensive rather than extensive economic development and should emulate the example of the Southeast Asian economies and develop its own distinct path. In his Strategy for Economic Development up to the year 2030, he envisioned Kazakhstan as "a Central Asian snow panther [in contrast to the Asian "tigers"], which would serve as a fine example to other developing countries."

Kazakhstan's GDP grew 2.3 percent in 1997 compared to 1996; it claimed the highest per capita GDP rating ($1,500) of any country in the CIS beyond Russia. Inflation ranged between 12 and 15 percent during the year. Direct foreign investment totaled $1.7 billion, with the two biggest investors being the South Korean companies Daewoo and Samsung. The metallurgical sector continued to outrank the oil and gas sector as a recipient of foreign investment.

Unemployment was officially at 5.6 percent, though the real rate may have been over 20 percent, and was especially high among rural youth in the southern oblasts. Unrest over unpaid wages and pensions—the total amount owed by the state was estimated to have reached almost a billion dollars—broke out in several parts of the country, with strikes continuing for several months in Zhanatas phosphorus plant, Achisay polymetal plant, and Kentau in the south. Inhabitants of the three southern oblasts of Shymkent, Almaty, and South Kazakhstan demonstrated against the lack of gas and electricity due to the wrangle over non-payment to Uzbekistan and Turkmenistan.

INTERNATIONAL PARTNERS AND PIPELINES

Nazarbaev continued to seek closer ties with the West while developing cooperation with the Asian tigers, as well as China and Iran. He also became more critical of Russia and the CIS. He blamed Russia's "imperial ambitions" and heavy military involvement in Tajikistan, Georgia, and Trans-Dniester for the "lack of trust" between the CIS members.

In September, with negotiations with the Caspian Pipeline Consortium getting periodically stalled, Kazakhstan quickly moved on to sign a $9.5 billion deal with China on oil shipment and the construction of two pipelines. China's National Oil Corporation will develop the Uzensk and Aktyubinsk oil fields in western Kazakhstan, and build one 3,000-km pipeline from there to Xinjiang and another 250-km pipeline south to the Turkmen border. Both pipelines will begin operating within five years. Chinese premier Li Peng called it a "new page" in Sino-Kazakhstani relations, while Nazarbaev said it was "the contract of the century"—a phrase that had previously been used to characterize the Chevron deal for the Tengiz field. Bilateral governmental relations continued to improve, as attested by agreements on military cooperation and border demarcation and Kazakhstan's support for China in its clampdown on the Uighur separatists in Xinjiang. Behind this rhetoric of friendship, however, there were some apprehensions on the Kazakhstani side about inferior Chinese goods glutting the markets and Chinese migrant workers flocking into their depopulating and potentially labor-scarce cities.

Kazakhstan signed a $750 million contract with Turkey to develop oil fields in Kazakhstan's Aktyubinsk province. During Nazarbaev's visit to the United States in November, a major agreement on production sharing for the vast Karachaganak oil and gas field in western Kazakhstan was signed by representatives of Texaco, Italy's Agip, British Gas, and the Russian LUKoil. If oil exploration and pipeline construction continue as planned, this deal is expected to bring Kazakhstan a total of $500 billion over the next 40 years and help it realize its dream of becoming the sixth largest oil exporter in the next decade. So far, Kazakhstan has the capacity to export only about 40 percent of the oil from the Tengiz fields via existing pipelines. The dispute over legal ownership of Caspian resources between the littoral states continued, limiting Kazakhstan's ability to attract more foreign investment. Meanwhile, Kazakhstan kept its option open on another major pipeline through Turkmenistan and Iran. "Iranians are asking me constantly about it," Nazarbaev announced two days after concluding the major deals with the United States.

Kazakhstan's economic liberalization and handling of foreign investment in oil, gas, and mining sectors came under increasing questioning by forces within the government and the opposition. In order to become a vibrant economic "panther" and maintain its image as a society based on interethnic peace and concord, the Nazarbaev leadership needs to pursue more coherent economic liberalization and devolution of authority at the same time. 1997 showed dubious progress on the liberalization front and a total clampdown on devolution.

Sidebar: THE CLAN FACTOR

by NURBULAT E. MASANOV

Traditional Kazakh society was divided into three *zhuz* or "hordes"—the Greater, Middle, and Small. Underlying this division is the principle of genealogical seniority—elder, middle, and younger brothers. According to this complex and widely branched system, each zhuz is divided into tribal groups which are, in turn, divided into smaller clans, and so on, all the way down to the concrete individual. According to the norms of customary law, every Kazakh should know his ancestors for forty generations back. The norms of exogamy, claims to property, leviratic norms (according to which a widow must sometimes be married by a brother of her deceased husband) and many other things are based on the degree of genealogical kinship.

This is a product of the traditional Kazakh mentality which, by virtue of the specific character of the transmission of information (as something secret, only for "one's own") and property (from father to son, from son to grandson, and so on), fosters a clan-based identification of the individual's social space.

The zhuz-clans in Kazakhstan were never, however, functional organizational structures, such as existed in medieval Scotland and still exist in some African and Asian countries. Kazakhstan's zhuz-clans are more a way of thinking, a way of interpreting ongoing processes through the prism of the genealogy of the individual or group.

In Soviet times, this traditional principle of interpreting social phenomena was transformed into a universal way of identifying and interpreting political processes and personnel reshuffles. Kazakhs of the Greater zhuz, for example, mythologized the figure of Kazakhstan's Communist Party First Secretary Dinmukhamed Kunaev. Since he was a member of the Sty tribe of the Greater zhuz, they saw him as one of their own. The Kazakhs of the Middle zhuz, by contrast, did not see him as one of their own.

To this day, clan is an important (though not the only) prism for interpreting and classifying the social and political processes taking place in Kazakhstan. It is an important psychological factor that finds its greatest application in the selection and career paths of public officials. The clan factor underlies the legitimacy of an individual's claim to this or that public post, feeds his hopes, and determines his ability to play an independent role in political life. It is the clan factor that largely defines the extent of an official's authority, his power, how high he is likely to move in government service, the bounds of his social space, and the length of time he stays in power.

In Kazakhstan, where President Nursultan Nazarbaev has established a regime of personal power, clan considerations enable the president to manipulate personnel policy in his personal interest and to exclude competition, corporate consolidation, or the appearance of political opponents within the government.

Back when Kunaev was Communist Party leader in Kazakhstan, he could afford to appoint members of the Small zhuz to the ruling Bureau of the republic Communist Party. He knew that they were so few in number, so rooted in the countryside, and so lacking in influence in the capital, that they would never be able either to challenge him for power or to become his successors.

Kunaev's main rivals came from the Middle zhuz. He was careful to keep them in positions that looked important but were in reality second-tier, such as Chairman of the Council of Ministers, Party boss of a region. He never allowed them access to the serious jobs, that is, to posts in the Bureau of the Central Committee of Kazakhstan's Communist Party.

President Nazarbaev has taken a leaf out of Kunaev's book and runs his personnel policy along similar lines. Nazarbaev fully understood the dissatisfactions and frustrated ambitions of the political elite and intelligentsia of the Middle zhuz—the most populous and most urbanized zhuz—when the country gained its independence. He kept representatives of the Middle zhuz close to him in order to prove how balanced his personnel policy was. This was the role played by Vice President Erik Asanbaev, who has since been "demoted" to Kazakhstan's ambassador to Germany. Later, the appointment of Prime Minister Akezhan Kazhegeldin was also supposed to prove that all the zhuz-clans were equal in the president's eyes. In the eyes of the Middle zhuz intelligentsia and political elite, however, it proved nothing, since Kazhegeldin was from one of the least influential tribes of the Middle zhuz—the Uak tribe.

The Middle zhuz bureaucracy, both during Kunaev's time and now under Nazarbaev, was supposed to play the role of an obedient creature, a symbol of the purportedly equal representation of all zhuz-clans in the upper reaches of the government. Reality was and remains different. Those holding key positions today are either representatives of the Greater zhuz (for the most part, Nazarbaev's close relatives) or people from the Small zhuz. The latter are not, in the eyes of public opinion, legitimate contenders for power and cannot, therefore, play an independent role in political life. This phenomenon, which was less noticeable in Kazakhstan's first years as a sovereign state, has grown more visible over time, as power has been increasingly concentrated in the hands of President Nazarbaev.

The following members of the Greater zhuz are currently to be found in the ranks of those with real decision-making power in Kazakhstan: the president himself and his closest relatives or members of the same clan, including Deputy Premier Akhmetzhan Yesimov, who has control over the receipt of foreign investment, presidential advisor Nurtay Abykaev, Defense Minister Mukhtar Altynbaev, Senate Speaker Umirbek Baigeldi, and Director of the Press and Information Agency Altynbek Sarsembaev.

Representatives of the Small zhuz in the top levels of government include: Prime Minister Nurlan Balgimbaev, State Secretary Abish Kekilbaev, Majilis [lower house of parliament] Speaker Marat Ospanov, and Director of the president's Scientific-Analytical Center Marat Tazhin.

The Middle zhuz is not seriously represented in the top level of government at present. It did, however, receive peculiar and, as always, purely formal compensation in the movement of the capital from Almaty, which is located on territory traditionally settled by Kazakhs of the Greater zhuz, to Akmola, on territory traditionally settled by Kazakhs of the Middle zhuz. Meanwhile, all the best-known political leaders from the Middle zhuz are either in respectable "exile" as ambassadors (Nazarbaev's former rival, Olzhas Suleimenov, in Italy; former vice president Erik Asanbaev in Germany; and former deputy premier Baltash Tursunbaev in Turkey), or out of a job (former prime minister Akezhan Kazhegeldin).

As political power is increasingly concentrated in the hands of Nursultan Nazarbaev, less effort is being made to ensure that all the zhuz-clans receive equal representation in the top levels of government (as was the practice during Soviet times and in Kazakhstan's first three or four years as a sovereign state). More use is being made of the clan factor to eliminate political opponents and to create a neutral "vacuum" around the figure of the president. The president dominates this vacant space to such an extent that no room is left for possible opponents and competitors. The fact that the president prefers officials from the Small zhuz, who are illegitimate in the eyes of society, for appointment to key government posts enables him both to strengthen his own influence and to exclude possible opponents from political life.

Translated by Mark Eckert

NOTE

Reprinted with kind permission from Jamestown Foundation's *Prism,* vol. IV, no. 3 (February 6, 1998). Jamestown publications can be found on the web at www.jamestown.org.

Document: KAZAKHSTAN—2030

Excerpts from "Kazakhstan—2030," Nursultan Nazarbaev's strategy for economic development of Kazakhstan up to the year 2030.

I have no doubt that by the year 2030 Kazakhstan will have become a Central Asian snow panther and will serve as a fine example to other developing countries. True, tigers are not found in Kazakhstan, while the snow panther inhabiting our mountains is a stranger to the world community. Though a relation to the tiger in the animal kingdom, the panther bears some substantial distinctions. It will be a distinctly Kazakhstani panther with inherent egalitarianism, sense of independence, intelligence, courage and noblesse, bravery and shrewdness. [. . .] The Kazakhstani panther will possess Western elegance reinforced by an advanced level of development, oriental wisdom and endurance. [. . .] He will be united in his strivings, victories and failures with his brother Uzbek, Kyrgyz, and other Central Asian panthers, nursed by a single mother.

[. . .] In previous years we actively followed the Anglo-Saxon variant and strove to attain rapid changes. Today we face a range of strategic alternatives—there is no consensus as yet on which one to choose. In a small way but nonetheless we are part of Europe and have historically gravitated toward the Western civilization—that's what some will say. Others argue that we are predominantly an Asian country and should thus emulate the experience of the "tigers" such as Japan and Korea. The third view claims that given the strong legacy of Russian culture and its principles of collectivism our model must coincide with that chosen by Russia. The fourth view would propose that we lean toward a neo-Turkic variant, having a predominantly Muslim population.

Paradoxically, all these views are right and wrong at the same time. We are a Eurasian country with its own specific history and specific future. That's why our model would bear affinity to none of these models; instead it would assimilate the achievements of various civilizations.

Uzbekistan

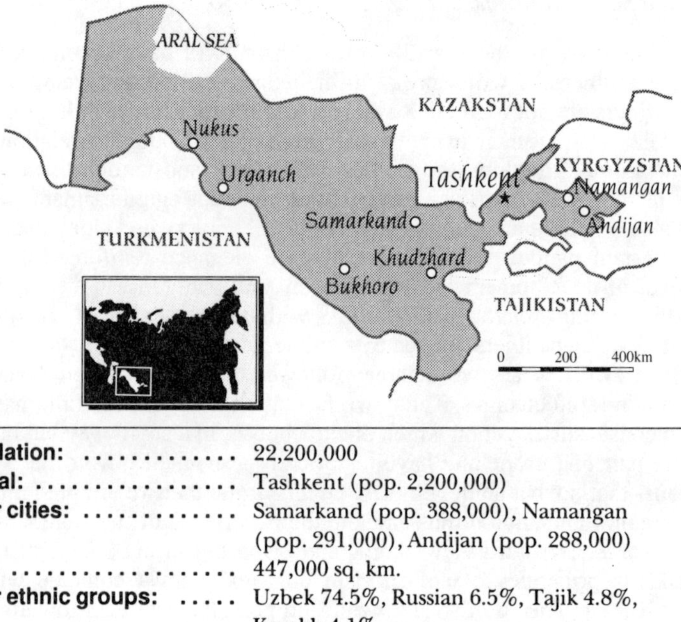

Population:	22,200,000
Capital:	Tashkent (pop. 2,200,000)
Major cities:	Samarkand (pop. 388,000), Namangan (pop. 291,000), Andijan (pop. 288,000)
Area:	447,000 sq. km.
Major ethnic groups:	Uzbek 74.5%, Russian 6.5%, Tajik 4.8%, Kazakh 4.1%
Economy:	GDP growth: 5.2%
	Inflation rate: not available
	Average monthly wage: $50
	Unemployment rate: 0.3%

THE SEARCH FOR STABILITY

by BRUCE PANNIER

For Uzbekistan 1997 was the year the country began to emerge as the regional power many expected it to become. Despite some setbacks in agriculture, troubles on its eastern and southern borders, and lingering doubts about the commitment of President Islam Karimov to democracy, Uzbekistan by year's end was clearly the most securely independent of the Central Asian states.

FOREIGN POLICY

There were some notable successes in foreign policy for Uzbekistan in 1997, following up the recognition symbolized by President Islam Karimov's 1996 visit to Washington. Part of a military exercise, Centrazbat, was held under NATO's Partnership for Peace Program on Uzbek soil in September. This not only helped Uzbekistan's relations with the NATO countries participating in the exercise (Turkey and the United States) but also with the Commonwealth of Independent States (CIS) members that took part (Kazakhstan and Kyrgyzstan). In November American First Lady Hillary Clinton stopped in Tashkent as part of her Central Asian tour. President Karimov extended an invitation through Mrs. Clinton to the American President to visit Uzbekistan. But matters much closer to home dominated the attention of officials in Tashkent.

A good deal of Uzbekistan's foreign policy in 1997 had to do with its southern neighbor Afghanistan.[1] Uzbekistan was seen as a supporter of the strongman of the northern Afghan city of Mazar-i-Sharif, General Abdul Rashid Dostum. The Uzbek government looked on Dostum as a buffer against the religious army of the Taliban movement and supplied the area under Dostum's control with electricity for several years past. Rumors suggested that more than just electric power was crossing the border. The general and his supporters were well-armed and often were on the offensive against Taliban forces. However, a betrayal within the ranks sent Dostum fleeing to the Uzbek border in late May, and from there he quickly flew to Turkey. When the man responsible for ousting Dostum, Abdul Malik, invited the Taliban to come help govern Mazar-i-Sharif, it appeared only a matter of days if not hours before the Taliban forces made their way to the Uzbek border. Fortunately for the Uzbek government, the man who betrayed Dostum proved equally untrustworthy to the Taliban, luring them into a trap where thousands were slaughtered. But the Uzbek government, as it had done in September 1996 when the Taliban captured the Afghan capital Kabul, sounded the alarm and looked to Russia for reassurances. The border was closed, including the "friendship" bridge over the Amu-Darya, the river which divides Uzbekistan and Afghanistan.

Malik's double treachery soon calmed fears in Uzbekistan, but the respite was only temporary. In early September fighting once again crept toward the Uzbek border. This time the Taliban were attempting to cut off the reopened supply line from Uzbekistan to Mazar-i-Sharif by capturing the town of Khairaton lying on the Afghan side of the Amu-Darya. Taliban forces succeeded in occupying some areas of the city and in the fighting stray shells landed on the other side of the Amu-Darya in the Uzbek town of Termez. For the second time in less than four months the "friendship" bridge over the river was closed and Uzbekistan increased its military presence along the border. Dostum returned from Turkey shortly thereafter, presumably via Uzbekistan, and restored the buffer zone in northern Tajikistan. Along the Afghan-Uzbek border the year ended much as it began.

There were also alarming events on the eastern border with Tajikistan. In Tajikistan the five-year civil war finally ended when the two principal antagonists, the Tajik government and United Tajik Opposition (UTO), negotiated a peace treaty, which was formally signed in June. The Uzbek government helped the Tajik government fight the war against the UTO in a bid to prevent the Islamic parties, which form a majority of the UTO, from coming to power. There was little surprise therefore when the Uzbek government unenthusiastically greeted the peace deal which provided for these very people to share power in a reformed Tajik government. At first Uzbekistan even refused to sign on as a guarantor nation of the peace. Later Uzbekistan joined other countries in the Central Asian region as a guarantor nation, justifying its earlier reluctance by explaining it was inappropriate for Afghanistan to be a signatory as that country was in no condition to guarantee anyone else's peace.

However, Uzbekistan's earlier stubborn refusal to give a blessing to the peace deal resulted in unpleasant rumors being circulated. When an assassin tried to kill Tajik President Imomali Rakhmonov on the last day of April in the northern Tajik city of Khujand there was talk the Uzbek government had sponsored the assassin. Later toward summer's end fighting broke out in Tajikistan between the government and one of its former allies, Colonel Mahmud Khudaberdiyev, near the Uzbek border. Khudaberdiyev very much opposed any power-sharing deal with the UTO and refused to allow any members of the UTO into the area where his army unit was quartered. Tajik government forces chased Khudaberdiyev toward the border, and during the running gun battle, stray shells landed on Uzbek soil, prompting protests from Tashkent. Dushanbe countered that Uzbekistan might be helping Khudaberdiyev, who is half Uzbek, and suggesting that Khudaberdiyev may have escaped to Uzbekistan. Some of that damage may have been repaired when Karimov and Rakhmonov met in Tashkent just after New Year's Day in 1998. However, the Uzbek government was still suspicious of UTO motives and barely concealed its discontent with the fact that UTO representatives were allowed into the Tajik government.

TIGHTENED GRIP ON RELIGIOUS MOVEMENTS

The events in eastern Uzbekistan around the city of Namangan in late November and early December demonstrated just how sensitive the Uzbek government was to Muslim groups, which it termed "fundamentalists" or "extremists." A high-ranking officer in Uzbekistan's Government Auto Inspection force was decapitated and his head left on a fence. In the following days three more auto inspection officers were killed. The crime had all the markings of a Mafia assassination: the Namangan region is known as one of the main drug smuggling routes of Central Asia. But the Uzbek government blamed members of an Islamic religious group, the Wahhabis, for the crime. The Wahhabis have come to be seen as the leading fundamentalist movement of the CIS since violence in the Caucasus involving this group in the spring of 1997.

The Uzbek government's response was swift and strong. Uzbek elite militia troops poured into the Namangan area, and by some accounts arrests were in the thousands. No media were allowed into the area, so full details of what happened are sketchy. It is probably more than a coincidence that Namangan is in the Uzbek section of the Fergana Valley. Kyrgyzstan and Tajikistan also have territory in the valley, and it may be that the Uzbek government's heavy hand was directed more toward the Tajik government's new peace arrangement with the UTO than toward a perceived threat from the Wahhabis. A reminder that some religious groups have no place in Uzbekistan came with the events surrounding a Tashkent Imam in late April. Obid Khan Nazarov was the Imam of Tashkent's Tokhtoboy mosque until his dismissal in 1995. Nazarov was then evicted from his apartment, but promised a new one. By 1997, when he had not received a new apartment, he took the government to court. In early April when the court was hearing Nazarov's case against the government some 300 people gathered outside the court building as a sign of solidarity with Nazarov. At the end of April, the state brought charges against Nazarov, saying he had violated the criminal codes on slander and on inciting ethnic, racial, or religious hatred. The U.S.-based Human Rights Watch criticized the charges as a throw-back to the country's Soviet past, but probably more alarming for the Uzbek government was the small group of clerics (about 15) who were bold enough to gather outside the courthouse where Nazarov was appearing.

Interestingly, while showing intolerance for potential religious (Islamic) opposition, the government made gestures indicating that limited political opposition would be allowed. At the opening of the eighth session of the Uzbek parliament in late April, Karimov told government officials to "speak more freely about what is happening in the provinces, where, when, and how human rights are violated." There was not a visible surge of "whistle blowers" following this statement, although some opposition groups did take small advantage of the opportunity presented.

In early September, the Independent Human Rights Society, led by Mikhail Azdzinov, met in Tashkent. The next month, about 30 members of the banned opposition movement Erk (Freedom) were allowed to meet in Tashkent to elect their secretary and were apparently undisturbed by the authorities. The Coordinating Council of the Democratic Opposition of Uzbekistan also met that month. Dissident figure Shukrullah Mirsaidov, a former vice president of Uzbekistan who had spent several months under house arrest, was again allowed to receive visitors at his home outside Tashkent. None of these developments received any republican press coverage on television or in print, but that they happened at all represented, on the surface at least, a marked improvement in a generally intolerant attitude by the Uzbek government toward any manifestation of opposition. However, it was probably not coincidental that these gestures came in the run-up to the November visit by Hillary Clinton.

ECONOMY MARKING TIME

Disastrous storms ruined a good portion of Uzbekistan's cotton crop in May, ensuring another bad harvest. This in part accounts for the poor year that the Uzbek economy experienced. How much damage the cotton crop suffered is difficult to tell, but in some areas the claim was about one-third ruined and another third possibly salvageable. In August the government reported that for the third year in a row the country failed to meet the target figure for grain. Of the 4.5 million tons planned, only 2.86 tons were harvested. Since 1991 Uzbekistan has relied on cotton sales to keep the country from falling into debt. Cotton sales may account for as much as 60 percent of Uzbekistan's hard currency earnings. But cotton prices fell in 1996, while the price of grain, which Uzbekistan imports, rose.

Following the storms in May the decision by the Kyrgyz government to begin charging for the water from its reservoirs which feed northern Uzbekistan's main river, the Syr Darya, added insult to injury in Tashkent. The deterioration in the agricultural situation helped to send the national currency, the som, plummeting. On the official market the som fell significantly against the dollar and other hard currencies (from $1 buying 56 som in January, to 100 som in December). The black market rate for dollars nearly doubled (from $1 for 118 som in January to 180 som in December) and the government was unable to stem illegal currency trading at bazaars. Compounding the problem was the Uzbek government's refusal to back down and fully implement the recommendations of international financial organizations, especially with regard to making the national currency convertible. That left Uzbekistan no closer to receiving the last half of a $185 million loan that was suspended by the International Monetary Fund (IMF) in December 1996 after Uzbekistan had reintroduced currency controls. President Karimov's comments early in 1997 that IMF loans were "slavery" suggested that no resolution of the impasse was likely in the immediate future, although IMF Vice President Stanley Fisher did visit in May and noted some encouraging signs. The failure to release full and accurate data on the economy to international financial organizations and obvious doctoring of what data the Uzbek government did make available was a further disincentive to international lenders.

In late July Karimov stated that 1997 would be a year of growth in practically all sectors of the Uzbek economy. According to Karimov, industrial output had risen in the first half of the year by 5.4 percent compared to the period in 1996, and agricultural output (two months after the storms hit) was up by 23 percent. He also said that "macroeconomic stabilization measures" had brought inflation down from 13 percent in December 1996 to 2.9 percent in May 1997. But reports indicated there were controls on the sale of sugar, flour, and basic foodstuffs, which led to food shortages and the accompanying queues at stores.

The Uzbek som, as mentioned, remained inconvertible, which also had a detrimental effect on the Central Asian Union (Uzbekistan, Kyrgyzstan, and Kazakhstan) in formulating tariffs or payment plans among these three governments. Still, the three countries' combined efforts in guarding the Tajik-Afghan border and participation in the peacekeeping exercises in September suggested that defense was one area where Uzbekistan did cooperate with its neighbors.

This picture contrasts with Uzbekistan's relations with its western neighbor, Turkmenistan, during 1997. President Karimov and Turkmen President Saparmurad Niyazov were never close friends. Among other things, the Uzbek government was concerned that Afghanistan's Taliban movement may have been acquiring weapons via Turkmenistan. Uzbekistan's quick move to supply Ukraine with natural gas after Turkmenistan cut off Ukraine for non-payment certainly did not improve the situation.

Karimov has never been able to resist taking shots at Niyazov in front of the press. Though Karimov criticized parliament for passing unimportant laws, there is a law in Uzbekistan, passed with Karimov's full blessing, prohibiting erecting a statue to any living person. Only one living person in the region has monuments to himself, Turkmenistan's president. For this and other such irritations, Karimov's plane was diverted en route from Tashkent to a conference in Ashgabat in May. The Uzbek president's new Boeing had to wait at an airport in eastern Turkmenistan before continuing to its destination, though flight time between the two capitals is one hour.

DISTANT FRIENDS

Despite the problems Uzbekistan suffered in 1997, toward year's end its neighbors appeared to be somewhat envious. Though there is likely more than meets the eye in Russian-Uzbek relations, at home President Karimov seems to have no problem criticizing Russia's policies. At the April session of parliament, when Karimov was calling on the Uzbek parliament to report human rights violations, he also criticized legislative practices. Stressing that the quality of legislation is more important than the quantity, he said Russian "legislators are fond of boasting that they have passed, say, 500 laws in a year," but "such mass scale" creation of laws "hardly makes sense." In previous years Karimov said Russia's greater democracy had produced virtual lawlessness and also that the presence of Russian troops on one's soil was tantamount to slavery. All the other CIS Central Asian states save Uzbekistan have Russian guards on their "external" borders.

While there were hasty discussions between Moscow and Tashkent during both the Afghan episodes, the Uzbek government did not request Russian troops to bolster its own. Nor did Uzbekistan look to Russia after the cotton crop failure. Uzbekistan is not part of the power grid that knots its way through Kazakhstan and even into Kyrgyzstan, and has minimal Russian investment.

Thus Uzbekistan has been far and away the least encumbered by Russian politics of all the Central Asian states. That has not escaped the notice of the neighboring countries. In the midst of difficult negotiations with Russia, officials of Kazakhstan and Kyrgyzstan more than once alluded to Uzbekistan's policies as an option.

Another reason Uzbekistan was able to so distance itself from Moscow was the friendship Tashkent was developing with Washington. Tashkent went to strange lengths to prove its loyalty, such as voting in favor of the U.S. position on embargoes against Cuba (the only other country to back the United States on that vote was Israel).[2] The visit of Mrs. Clinton to Uzbekistan in November was symbolic of that friendship, though she was also in Kazakhstan and Kyrgyzstan. The more relevant event was the agreement to form the joint U.S.-Uzbek commission in June, chaired by Deputy Secretary of State Strobe Talbott. A U.S. State Department spokesman (Nicholas Burns) said during the meetings leading up to the agreement, "The United States expressed very clearly our support for the independence and sovereignty and integrity of Uzbekistan."

But the closer Uzbekistan gets to the United States, the heavier will be the demand for Tashkent to clean up its human rights record, to meet the demands of international financial organizations, and to show clearer signs of moving toward democracy.

One last reason for Uzbekistan's rise to a dominant position in the region was the country's positive relations with Turkey. Turkey has given more aid to Uzbekistan than to any other Central Asian country since 1991. Turkey is one of Uzbekistan's leading trading partners. Bilateral trade was over $400 million in 1996, though it dropped in the first nine months of 1997 to about $200 million. President Karimov paid a visit to Turkey in November and, with Turkish President Suleiman Demirel, signed a Treaty of Eternal Friendship. Though that has been the vogue for treaties in Central Asia recently, the Turkish-Uzbek treaty of friendship was apparently among the most sincere.

President Karimov is arguably the most resolute, perhaps intractable, leader in Central Asia. Having charted his political course, he has held fast despite numerous objections from many who would like to help Uzbekistan if only there were some marked signs of true change. Unfortunately, Karimov is more likely to see such advice as meddling or possibly good for one country but not suitable for his own. Uzbekistan faces unique geopolitical challenges due to its extreme geographical isolationism. Along with Liechtenstein, it shares the dubious honor of being one of the world's few double land-locked countries (that is, a country surrounded by countries that are themselves landlocked). That Karimov rules supreme is beyond doubt. But given the economic and security challenges that Uzbekistan faces, even a strongman ruler will need friends. The country would seem destined to play a leading role in Central Asia, given that it has the largest population of the region (22 million), and a wealth of natural resources. If the coming years bring the same policies as 1997, however, Uzbekistan may not reach its full potential. Cautious cooperation, on the other hand, could propel Uzbekistan into being the most influential state between Iran and China.

NOTES

[1]Of course one could easily point out that except for a relatively small section of the Uzbek border which adjoins Afghanistan the entire length is contiguous with other CIS states. The others all have much longer stretches with non-CIS countries—witness Tajikistan's and Turkmenistan's border with Afghanistan, and Tajikistan's, Kyrgyzstan's and Kazakhstan's border with China.

[2]After the resolution of the "Persian Gulf crisis" of February 1998, Uzbekistan came out publicly as giving the United States credit for its "strong stand" in the Gulf which made Iraq give in to further UN inspections. Most everybody else gave the credit to UN Secretary General Kofi Annan (and Russia).

Tajikistan

Population:	6,000,000
Capital:	Dushanbe (pop. 600,000)
Major cities:	Khojent (Leninabad) (pop. 180,000), Kulyab (pop. 70,000), Kurgan-Tyube (pop. 45,000)
Area:	143,100 sq. km.
Major ethnic groups:	Tajik 64.9%, Uzbek 25%, Russian 3%, other 7.1%
Economy:	GDP growth: –8.9%
	Inflation rate: 280%
	Average monthly wage: $50
	Unemployment rate: not available

EXERCISING PEACE

by BRUCE PANNIER

For the Central Asian nation of Tajikistan, 1997 was the best year in its short history as an independent country. Barely six months after Tajikistan obtained independence in 1991 the country crept and then plunged into civil war. Though the first year was the worst, the continued guerrilla campaign waged by the supporters of ousted political groups kept Tajikistan from achieving any form of stability. Peace between the principal antagonists finally came in 1997, and the foundations for a unique experiment in coexistence between government and opposition were laid. But as the two sides found out, before any semblance of order could be restored some housecleaning was needed.

The coalition organization known as the United Tajik Opposition was made up of several parties: the Democratic Party, the Rastokhiz People's Movement, and the Laali Badakhshan, but the bulk of this opposition group was from the Islamic Renaissance Party. The UTO was driven out of Tajikistan in the winter of 1992–93 by government forces supporting the former speaker of the Tajik Soviet Republic's parliament, Imomali Rakhmonov. Temporarily chased from the country, the guerrilla campaign began with the UTO using areas in Afghanistan as bases for forays into Tajikistan. The UTO forces gained footholds which gradually expanded inside Tajikistan. The UTO and the Tajik government ground each other down in costly battles, which broke out in one section and died down only to reappear in a different part of the country.

The fighting in central Tajikistan in 1996 was the worst anywhere since 1992. A cease-fire agreement signed between the two warring factions in September 1994 in Tehran had never really had any effect. However, the advances of the Taliban in Afghanistan spurred the two sides to seek agreement. (See the accompanying article, "Thank the Taliban for the Tajik Peace Agreement," by Rasheed Abdullaev and Umed Babakhanov.) In mid-December 1996 the leader of the UTO, Said Abdullo Nuri, met Rakhmonov in the northern Afghan village of Khostdeh. They followed that meeting up two weeks later in Moscow and a genuine cease-fire went into effect in time for the New Year.

With the shooting stopped, the process of negotiating an acceptable treaty began. Two issues invariably complicated every round of talks, the remake of the government and the conditions for UTO fighters to return to their homeland. That the division of the government would be a problem was obvious. There was little trust between the two sides, so the UTO insisted its fighters be allowed to return to Tajik soil armed. Naturally the government, which had been trying to keep these fighters out of the country for several years, was reluctant to suddenly open the door to the same armed men.

As this dragged on, an unexpected event occurred. On the last day of April,

President Rakhmonov traveled to the northern Tajik city of Khujand to celebrate the anniversary of the university there. A young man in the crowd of people threw a hand grenade at Rakhmonov. Rakhmonov escaped with a leg injury but two people were killed and dozens injured.

Khujand had never been viewed as supporting the Tajik president. Rakhmonov's rival in the 1994 presidential elections was Abdumalik Abdullajonov from the Khujand area. In the days that followed the assassination attempt a large number of government security forces were sent to the north, where they rounded up hundreds of people. Some were sent to Dushanbe for questioning, Abdullajonov's brother among them.

Far from complicating talks between the government and the UTO, after these events negotiations picked up speed. Khujand did not support Rakhmonov, but neither did it support the UTO, so the wave of arrests there received little attention from the UTO. However, had Rakhmonov died the situation would likely have grown worse throughout the country very quickly. So both sides accepted an invitation from neighboring Kyrgyz President Askar Akayev to meet in Bishkek. That meeting took place in the second half of May and was hailed as a major breakthrough. It was announced that a peace accord would be signed in June. As efficacious as the countryside outside Bishkek may be, events unfolding in Afghanistan were probably at least as influential in the Tajiks, finally resolving their differences.

In the latter half of May, Afghanistan's Taliban religious army were well into their spring offensive to capture the remaining 15–20 percent of the country not already under their control. Part of that unoccupied territory was the province of Mazar-i-Sharif. The warlord of Mazar-i-Sharif, General Abdul Rashid Dostum, fled in late May after some treachery by one of his trusted commanders. The same commander, Abdul Malik, invited the Taliban to come to Mazar-i-Sharif and help occupy the city, the last big city not under the Taliban's control. The only thing which prevented Uzbekistan and Tajikistan from having Taliban neighbors was that Malik couldn't be trusted by anyone. He turned on his former Taliban allies and, as investigations months later would prove, put to death some of the Taliban fighters in horrible fashion.

The message surely was received by the Tajiks. Some problems might not wait for them to patch up their differences.

Despite some "technical delays" the Tajik National Peace Accord was signed in Moscow on 27 June. The agreement called for the government to give 30 percent of the government positions to UTO representatives. A 26-member National Reconciliation Commission was established with equal representation from both sides. Said Abdullo Nuri was the chairman. The armed forces were to be integrated, banned parties could re-register, a review of prisoners would take place, amnesty would be given to those in jail for political reasons, and prisoners of war would be exchanged. Later it was agreed that when the commission began work in Dushanbe its UTO representatives would be allowed to bring with them a "body guard" of 460 armed men chosen from their own ranks.

It was planned that elections to parliament would take place 18 months after the work of the Reconciliation Commission began. The commission in the meantime would be recommending amendments to the constitution that would guide the country through the transition stages.

But everything was delayed from the start. The commission could not begin work until its chairman, Nuri, arrived in the Tajik capital. Nuri did not want to return until he had been cleared of charges made against him after he left Tajikistan during the war and went to Tehran. An official pardon took longer than expected, coming only in early August. Nuri eventually arrived in Dushanbe on 10 September. Then started the long debate over which positions in the government the UTO would get. The debate was still going at year's end, while the deputy leader of the UTO, Khoja Akbar Turajonzoda, waited in Tehran for an official announcement of his expected government post. There would be no elections to parliament in 1998.

Amazingly, the longest period of peace in Tajikistan's short history as an independent country was not the biggest story of the year, at least not for the international media. Peace was still a relative term in Tajikistan. Now that enemies were trying friendship, both sides had to deal with allies from the war who were no longer desirable.

MAVERICKS ON THE LOOSE

At the beginning of 1997, Colonel Mahmud Khudaberdiyev was the commander of the Tajik Army's First Brigade. The brigade was by all accounts the best trained and equipped in the Tajik army. The unit was based in the southwestern town of Kurgan-Tyube. In return for his loyalty to the government, Khudaberdiyev was allowed to run things in the Kurgan-Tyube area. His exaction from the civilian population appears to have been light, but few resources from the area made their way to Dushanbe.

Khudaberdiyev had forced changes in the government in January 1996 when he mobilized his unit and marched on the capital. One month later, good soldier that he was, he sent his unit to fight alongside government troops in central Tajikistan against UTO forces. By the end of 1996 the unit was back in Kurgan-Tyube. Just prior to the New Year the leader of an outlaw group controlling the town of Tursun Zade, about 120 kilometers north of Kurgan-Tyube, ordered some of his group to obtain some more weapons. They chose to raid the First Brigade, and in the process of stealing weapons, killed one of the officers there.

Khudaberdiyev ordered his unit to Tursun Zade to take back what was theirs and obtain justice. It is unclear whether this was out of a sense of honor or opportunity: Tursun Zade is home to the biggest aluminum plant in Central Asia, which—amazingly—carried on production throughout the war. It was almost one year exactly since Khudaberdiyev had marched on Dushanbe. Once President Rakhmonov heard of the unit's movement he ordered them back to barracks, just as they were approaching the outskirts of Tursun Zade. Khudaberdiyev ignored the deadline from the president and instead advanced into the town. Rakhmonov ordered the presidential guard to force Khudaberdiyev out of the town. As the guard approached Tursun Zade the residents of the area, long tired of changing warlords and outlaws, sat in the road and blocked the guard's passage. While they were stopped outside of town, Khudaberdiyev chose to comply with the president's orders. As a result of defying presidential commands and restoring order in Tursun Zade, the First Brigade was made the rapid reaction force of the presidential guard, with Khudaberdiyev remaining its commander.

The only bright side was that the UTO did not take advantage of the situation, and stayed committed to the cease-fire throughout the trouble.

Khudaberdiyev grew bolder as the year went on. In June, less than two weeks before the signing of the Peace Accord, he disarmed the soldiers at a government checkpoint in the Fakhrabad mountain pass, 30 kilometers south of Dushanbe. He demanded the governor of Khatlon Oblast be replaced with one of his men. He also said that not a single armed fighter from the UTO would be allowed to enter the country.

Khudaberdiyev maintained his position, as the government and UTO slowly put into practice the first steps of their peace agreement. In July he declared the governor of Khatlon dismissed and convened a council of local field commanders to announce the separation of Kurgan-Tyube and Khatlon. Still part of Tajikistan, the areas under Khudaberdiyev's control were no longer responsible to Dushanbe.

In early August, fighting erupted in northern Dushanbe. The chairman of Tajikistan's Customs Committee, Yakub Salimov, and forces loyal to him were battling elements of the presidential guard. Salimov had been head of the Interior Ministry but became so powerful he was dismissed in August 1995 and sent off to Turkey as ambassador. He was chased from Dushanbe westward toward Tursun Zade. Mahmud Khudaberdiyev decided to come to Salimov's aid.

This time Khudaberdiyev had overplayed his hand. While the capability of other units in the Tajik army had not improved, the situation with political support for the government in Dushanbe had substantially changed. Previous actions by Khudaberdiyev had been viewed as internal affairs of the Tajik government. The unit was after all a part of the Tajik army. Now the war was officially over and Khudaberdiyev was threatening a peace that nearly all the countries in the region had an interest in preserving. This time government forces, led by the presidential guard, came out to fight. The First Brigade was defeated in surprisingly short time, but there are reports (from Khudaberdiyev) of air support being used, although the Tajik armed forces themselves do not have much in the way of an air force. Salimov's force, too, was shattered and fled to the hills north of Tursun Zade.

In battles with the retreating Khudaberdiyev two months later near the Uzbek border government forces suddenly lost the Colonel. The Uzbek government was worried about the fighting so close to its border, and complained loudly. The Tajik government's reaction was as amazing as the advance of the government forces against Khudaberdiyev. Usually very careful, at times almost obsequious in relations with Uzbekistan, the Tajik government made thinly veiled references to Khudaberdiyev's "foreign" supporter and it was said Khudaberdiyev had fled to the "safety" of Uzbekistan. There were even rumors that the "foreign" supporter, not satisfied with the coming peace arrangement in Tajikistan, may have sponsored the assassination attempt on Rakhmonov in April.

FAMILY VALUES

The UTO had a similar experience with renegade forces. In December 1996 an "outlaw" named Bahrom Sadirov took seven members of the United Nations Observer Mission on Tajikistan (UNMOT) hostage. He demanded that his brother, Rezvon, be transported back to Tajikistan from Afghanistan. Rezvon Sadirov was the Defense Coordinator for the UTO until 1994. His methods, especially executions, were deemed criminal by the UTO leadership. They intended to punish him but he escaped to Afghanistan. He wound up in a Kabul jail for the murder of several UTO members and was found by the long-time veteran of Afghan wars Ahmed Shah Masoud. Masoud knew of Rezvon's reputation as a field commander and had him released to join in Masoud's forces. That was before the Taliban captured Kabul in September 1996. Now Masoud was on the run and Bahrom felt his brother in Tajikistan would want to come home.

The December incident passed without tragedy though none of Bahrom's conditions were met. But a series of foreign workers went missing from the streets of Dushanbe in February. It became clear Bahrom, probably encouraged by the events with Khudaberdiyev in January, had kidnapped them. The demand again was passage for his brother and an armed party. After a crew of Russian journalists traveled to cover the story and also fell into Bahrom's hands, the government agreed to fly Rezvon and his party from Afghanistan to Tajikistan. Once the trade was completed the hunt was on for the Sadirovs. Bahrom was wounded and forced to give up in order to get medical aid. Rezvon fled into the mountains.

Rumors of Rezvon and his supporters ran through spring and summer. Anyone who disappeared was feared to have been taken by Rezvon. They did actually kidnap sons of the chief Mufti of Tajikistan Amonullo Negmatzoda. The demand was the release of Bahrom and other jailed supporters of the Sadirovs. One month later, in late August, they seized the Mufti himself when he came to negotiate with the kidnappers. They eventually freed the Mufti and his brother, but kept 18 others and disappeared again. Rezvon Sadirov came to epitomize the oft-mentioned "third force" in Tajikistan who were "not satisfied with the peace agreement."

He reappeared in November. A French couple, one of whom was working for the EU's aid program, were kidnapped from their apartment in Dushanbe. Rezvon was again asking for his brother's freedom. Frank Janier-Dubry was released but something went wrong and Karine Maine was killed along with several of Rezvon's group when firing started. Rezvon himself was killed by government forces that same day.

As the year ended Bahrom was still in jail. Relatives of Rezvon Sadirov came to the morgue to identify Rezvon's badly disfigured body and said it was him. However, prior to the New Year there were already rumors the body in the morgue was not Rezvon. He may yet "rise from the dead." The whereabouts of Colonel Mahmud Khudaberdiyev and Yakub Salimov are unknown, but they are presumed to be hiding in some rugged mountainous area of Tajikistan, probably in the west not far from the Uzbek border. It's almost impossible to believe 1997 was the last time these two will make news.

THE ECONOMY, WHERE TO START?

Sadly the best thing that can be said about Tajikistan's economic situation is "the war is over." At a conference of donor nations (specifically for Tajikistan) in Vienna on 24–25 November President Rakhmonov estimated war damage to Tajikistan at $7 billion. As examples of the problems, Rakhmonov noted the "industrial output has plummeted and living standards have fallen." Rakhmonov said there were more than 10,000 buildings, power lines, roads, bridges, and other facilities which needed to be rebuilt. Additionally, more than 10,000 Tajik refugees returned home in 1997 and a number of them no longer had a home in which to live or a herd or a farm to work.

Inflation was running the highest in the CIS, at a 280 percent annual rate. The cost of the "food basket" for one person per month was put at 14,230 Tajik rubles. The average wage was about 2,000–3,000 per month. The country's officially recorded GDP had declined by 8.9 percent compared to the previous year. Real income dropped by 38 percent between December 1996 and August 1997.

The donor conference in Vienna raised $57 million in pledges, and Switzerland promised to pay Tajikistan's admission fee to the Asian Development Bank. Aid from international organizations such as the European Union has been pledged as well. Perhaps more importantly, Tajikistan's CIS Central Asian neighbors are offering help or participation in regional projects.

It was a rocky start, but difficult first steps were taken in 1997. Though there were still outbreaks of violence, even between government soldiers and those of the UTO, they were quelled quickly by united efforts of the leadership on both sides. If the leaders can stop the violence, it should restore the confidence of potential foreign investors.

Russian troops were still needed to guard the border with Afghanistan, more against drug traffickers than any threat from the Taliban, but their presence freed up money and effort badly needed inside Tajikistan. The United Nations will increase its presence in Tajikistan during 1998 and that should help in keeping the peace throughout the country.

Tajikistan's leading warlords have been beaten, and while there are groups of outlaws still loose they do not represent the threat of a Mahmud Khudaberdiyev or a Rezvon Sadirov. If industry can begin in earnest Tajikistan's prospects are good, since the country has great wealth in rare and precious metals. So if the peace holds, 1998 should be an even better than 1997, which was in itself the best year of independent Tajikistan.

THANK THE TALIBAN FOR THE TAJIK PEACE AGREEMENT

by RASHEED ABDULLAEV *and* UMED BABAKHANOV

It's lunchtime in the filtration camp for repatriates on the Tajik bank of the river Panj on the border. Little Gulnoz is eating the traditional Tajik soup shurpo from an aluminum dish. One hour ago, a rusty old barge brought the Tajik refugees across the river from Afghanistan to Tajikistan, and the girl seems to be enjoying her first encounter with her motherland. This repatriation of Tajik refugees, on 17 July, was the first since the signing of the 27 June peace agreement.

Gulnoz was born four years ago in the Kampi Sahi camp for Tajik refugees, not far from Mazar-i-Sharif, the capital of northern Afghanistan. Every night as she settled down for sleep in her family's blue canvas tent—a gift of the United Nations—she would listen to her grandfather's stories about the motherland. For him, Tajikistan is the best place in the world: it has electricity, asphalt roads, and nice, large schools. And most important, there is the family's house with its television. It was always hard for Gulnoz to understand why, if Tajikistan were so wonderful, the family could not live there. It would be even harder for her to understand the paradox that brought her to her motherland: the peace agreement in Tajikistan was a result of the military offensive by the Taliban in Afghanistan.

YEARS OF WAR

Tajikistan had become unstable immediately after declaring independence on 9 September 1991. The collapse of the once-strong Soviet communist system revealed and aggravated the internal contradictions in the only Farsi-speaking republic of Central Asia. After a few months, a civil war was burning. For most people in this poor country, the Tajik word *ozodi* (freedom) had the salty taste of blood and tears.

From the very beginning, the media in Russia and the West defined the war simplistically as a struggle of "good democrats" against "bad communists." Yet the real conflict was far more complicated. Ideological struggle on the global and regional levels as well as the geopolitical confrontation of the regional powers and the superpowers accompanied Tajikistan's plunge into fratricide. Ultimately, it was Tajik regionalism in all its forms that caused the war. The huge disparity in the economic development of Tajikistan's regions exacerbates the acute differences in the mentalities of its people. Representation in power structures and decision making is unfairly distributed among the regions.

For many decades, the regions of the north dominated in the economic and the political life of the country. But that situation changed by the end of the 1980s, when the once-backward south gained strength. The south turned into the main base for production of cotton and electricity, and the center of machinery construction and the electrochemical industry. Gradually, the southerners came to outnumber northerners, especially in the capital city of Dushanbe.

Naturally, with the growing role of the south in the life of the country, the new elite demanded greater access to power. Also naturally, the entrenched north did not want to give anything up. Open confrontation between the two regions began in the autumn of 1991. The "communist north" had, by that time, lost the support of Moscow due to the disintegration of the USSR. The new Russia supported the south, which had reoriented quickly and adopted democratic slogans along with Islamic ones.

The situation changed by March of 1992. Representatives of the northern Leninabad region found supporters among the southerners in the poorest Kulyab region. Thus the north-south conflict transformed into a conflict between the southerners of Kulyab and their allies and the eastern region of Karategin-Badakhshan. The organizational structure of the former became the Popular Front. The political leader of the latter became the Islamic Renaissance Party.

Neighboring countries exploited the war in Tajikistan for political ends. For Russia, the war provided an excuse for preserving its military and political presence in the region. Some of the post-Soviet Central Asian states used the pretext of maintaining stability on their borders to toughen their regimes. Only Allah knows how long the outside forces would have fed the bonfire in Tajikistan had the situation remained unchanged.

UNLIKELY PEACEMAKER

The blitzkrieg of the armed Talibs through the Afghan provinces and the seizure of the Afghan capital, Kabul, drastically changed the military and political situation in the country. The advance of Taliban troops toward Hindukush and to the Salang Pass in September 1996 made the leaders of neighboring countries shudder. An urgent summit of the Central Asian leaders in Almaty, attended by Russian Prime Minister Viktor Chernomyrdin, signaled serious concern.

Why would Russia and its partners in the Commonwealth of Independent States (CIS) react with such alarm? The answer is quite simple. In recent years, many countries had been trying to influence the situation in Afghanistan. Russia and Tajikistan made their stake for a moderate Islamic society in Afghanistan headed by President Burhanuddin Rabbani and Ahmad Shah Masoud (both ethnic Tajiks); Pakistan and its overseas patron, the United States, hoped for the Pushtuni movement of Taliban; Uzbekistan supported the ethnic Uzbek leader General Abdul Rashid Dostum. Iran chose to work through the formations of the Shii Hazari movement Vahdat.

The Taliban caused a commotion within CIS corridors of power not merely because it was a radical Islamic group, but, more important, because it was supported by non-CIS countries: Pakistan, Saudi Arabia, and at one time even the United States. The reaction to the military and political advance of the Taliban revealed the old struggle for influence between the notably weakening Moscow and the energetic-as-ever Washington. The threat of the Taliban coming to power forced the countries of the region, including Russia and Iran, to unite their efforts, which was impossible with a war going on in Tajikistan. It was obvious that if Russia were to lose position and influence in Afghanistan, it would not be able to maintain them in Central Asia.

So the war in Tajikistan had to be quickly resolved. With energetic diplomatic effort, the Kremlin persuaded official Dushanbe to compromise with the United Tajik Opposition. Similar work was done on the other side by Tehran, which has considerable influence with the leaders of the opposition and forced them to make certain concessions. Thus, one could say that the Tajiks were reconciled by the Talibs.

ENEMY OR PARTNER?

The Taliban offensive changed attitudes toward the Tajik civil war not only in neighboring countries, but also within Tajikistan. Tajikistan is separated from the Afghan turmoil only by a narrow strip of river, and all the forces involved in the five-year confrontation in Tajikistan saw that the Afghan conflict could threaten the existence of Tajikistan as a state and the Tajiks as a nation.

Outwardly, official Dushanbe was restrained; it professed a refusal to interfere in the internal affairs of a neighboring country. At the same time, the leadership of the country developed a three-pronged strategy. First, it introduced peaceful initiatives for resolving the conflict through resuming the inter-Afghan negotiations. Dushanbe asked the UN and other organizations to call an international conference on Afghanistan. Second, it worked to build consensus among the states of Central Asia and Russia. Third, in negotiations with the opposition, the Tajik government began emphasizing the need to unite Tajiks to face the hostile forces.

The ordinary people of Tajikistan had a more emotional reaction. Most were frightened at the prospect of a Taliban approach toward their borders. Many saw in the Taliban movement a direct threat to the secular character of their state, because a Taliban victory would seriously strengthen the position of the Islamic radicals of Tajikistan. And most important, they viewed the Talibs as a Pushtu threat to the Tajiks of Afghanistan.

The Tajik opposition had a different view of the Talibs. As far as religion and ideology went, the leading Islamic part of the Tajik opposition had few problems with the Taliban. But the political side was ambiguous. Most of the Tajik refugees in Afghanistan, de facto opposition supporters, were in territories controlled by anti-Taliban forces. And because of the Taliban offensive, the Tajik opposition's training centers, military bases, and infrastructure were thrown into disarray. At the end of May, when the Taliban was already in Mazar-i-Sharif and Kunduz, the leaders of the Tajik opposition were between the hammer of the Taliban and the anvil of the anti-Taliban coalition. A single careless word could threaten all Tajik citizens in Afghanistan. The delicacy of the situation and the pressure of the nationalist-minded elements in the United Tajik Opposition, multiplied by outside pressure, prompted the opposition leaders to take steps toward peace with Dushanbe.

All countries of the region want Afghanistan to be a stable country. The question is how to achieve that. Some local political commentators believe the answer lies in Afghanistan's history. In the late 1920s, Emir Habibulla came to power in Afghanistan as the result of a coup. The brief (less than a year) rule of the emir, an ethnic Tajik, led to chaos in thc country. Like today, the process of overcoming that anarchy began in the Pushtu south of Afghanistan. Local tribal formations led by Nadir Shah ousted Habibulla and restored the monopolistic rule of the Pushtu tribe Durrani. The new king of Afghanistan cruelly suppressed all centers of national separatism that opposed the Pushtu, providing unity and political stability for almost half a century. Drawing a historic parallel, some experts assert that only the Pushtu, the main ethnic group in the country, can restore order in Afghanistan. By that logic, the problem can be solved only if the foreign partners of the anti-Taliban coalition cease their assistance.

Opponents to such an approach say that, first of all, no census has been carried out in Afghanistan for many decades and it is unclear what group makes up the ethnic majority. Second, to provide equal terms for the warring sides, interference in the Afghan conflict should end on both sides: by the states that support the Taliban movement and by those that help the anti-Taliban coalition. The question is, How realistic are such terms in the dirty business called politics?

The fighting that broke out in August was not between the government and the United Tajik Opposition but among forces that had been, albeit shakily, loyal to the government. Having learned from the past few years, this time the government and the opposition's leadership were politically and morally united because the mutiny was a threat not only to the government but to the whole course of national reconciliation. Both sides have come now to the common understanding that technical obstacles must be overcome before they turn into a deeper challenge for the Commission for National Reconciliation.

More Tajik refugees have joined Gulnoz at home now. Some died waiting and are buried in Afghanistan. Some still await repatriation. Meanwhile, neither Tajikistan nor Afghanistan is stable. If the tenuous peace inspired by the fear of the Taliban doesn't hold, where will the next initiative come from?

NOTE

Reprinted with kind permission from *Transitions* magazine, October 1997.

Kyrgyzstan

Population:	4,698,108
Capital:	Bishkek (pop. 650,000)
Major cities:	Osh (pop. 220,000), Jalalabad (pop. 75,000)
Area:	198,000 sq. km.
Major ethnic groups:	Kyrgyz 52.4%, Russian 21.5%, Uzbek 12.9%, German 2.4%, other 8.3%
Economy:	GDP growth: 10.4%
....	Inflation rate: 25.0%
....	Average monthly wage: $30
....	Unemployment rate: 3.1%

THE EARLY DAWN OF A BRIGHT DAY?

by BRUCE PANNIER

For the mountainous Central Asian state of Kyrgyzstan, 1997 seems to be the year when it started to turn the corner. When compared to its Central Asian neighbors which were also once republics of the Soviet Union (Kazakhstan, Tajikistan, Uzbekistan, and further west, Turkmenistan), Kyrgyzstan maintained its image as the most democratic state in the region. A relative statement, true, but peaceful public demonstrations were held and some criticism of the government found its way into print. However, the government again demonstrated its sensitivity to republican media in several cases against journalists. Opposition political parties continued their work, but continued lack of unity or common purpose left them, once again, easily ignored. "Extremist" religious groups also made news prior to the year's end. But Kyrgyzstan's big stories in 1997 concern the economy, though here too, events did not progress without controversy.

On the domestic political front, Kyrgyzstan's policies followed the pattern that had developed following independence. There were a number of political parties and movements, but none had emerged as a clear popular favorite. Some groups, such as Kyrgyzstan's Assembly of Peoples, which had representatives from 24 of the country's ethnic minority groups, were clearly supporters of President Askar Akayev. Other nationalist groups, such as the Ata-Meken (Fatherland) Party, were neutralized by representing the interests of a specific ethnic group and so were unable to rely on a majority of the population of Kyrgyzstan. So while parties and movements may have had members in parliament, the divisions between them mitigated most efforts at reforming the government from within the legislature. In such an atmosphere President Akayev, who already had expanded presidential powers following the constitutional amendments of early 1996, remained the unfettered navigator of Kyrgyz politics. Though Akayev was limited by the constitution to two terms in office, there was no real alternative candidate on the horizon to replace Akayev when presidential elections are held in the year 2000. That being the case, the first murmurs of amending the constitution to enable him to run for a third term were heard toward year's end.

PESKY JOURNALISTS

The only real problem that the government faced was the press. While allowing a relatively free press, mainly in the form of the lone opposition newspaper *Res Publica,* government officials resorted to the country's court system to discipline "rogue" reporting. The country's president, Askar Akayev, was the first to do so in 1995, and ever since journalists often found themselves defendants in libel or slander trials. The disturbing new aspect of this process was the enforcement of jail sentences in what should have been civil, and not criminal, cases. Zamira

Sydykova, the editor of *Res Publica,* was found guilty of libel in a case filed by the head of Kyrgyzstan's gold industry (Kyrgyzaltyn), Dastan Sarygulov. On May 23, Sydykova and another journalist from the same paper, Aleksandr Alyanchikov, were sentenced by the Pervomayskii district court to eighteen months in penal colonies for articles they had written alleging corruption in the gold mining industry. Two other journalists who played a part in the publication of the article, Marina Sivasheva and Bektash Shamshiev, were barred from practicing journalism for eighteen months and given 2,000 som ($115) fines. Despite pressure from human rights organizations that pointed out that no other democratic country put someone in prison for their words, Sydykova and Alyanchikov were jailed.

Other journalists fared no better. Yrysbek Omurzakov also found himself in the custody of the authorities. Omurzakov, also from *Res Publica,* reported on conditions at a Bishkek factory hostel. Based on the accounts of 108 workers from the factory Yrysbek wrote about "shortcomings in the privatization process and corruption in the factory." The factory director took Omurzakov to court. Omurzakov had already received a two-year suspended sentence in 1996, when he was found guilty of insulting president Akayev. In 1997 Omurzakov was found not guilty at his first trial in May, but was held while his case went for re-investigation. In late September Omurzakov was again in court but this time was found guilty. Strangely, Omurzakov was detained while awaiting the trials, but later when found guilty he was freed immediately under an amnesty law.

In an arguably less dramatic case the opposition newspaper *Kriminal* was ordered pulled from the stand in February, after two issues, by decision of a district court. The paper had printed articles criticizing the government and referring to well-known politicians by the unflattering nicknames used for them among the population. The justice ministry was responsible for the paper's being banned. Initially, the ministry ordered the publishing house printing the paper to stop. Later the Kyrgyz parliament's commission on media and information denounced that action as illegal. So, Kyrgyzstan's justice ministry sued *Kriminal.* To no one's surprise, the district court that heard the case in early May approved the earlier decision to ban the newspaper from publication. The paper's chief editor, Beken Nazarliyev, filed an appeal.

There were several demonstrations in front of the government building in Bishkek. On June 3, about one week after the trial of the four journalists from *Res Publica,* a group of 250–300 people gathered outside the government building. Four of them decided to start a hunger strike and remained on the square in front of the government building, but during the night of 4 June police tore down their tents and beat them. One of them, Kokon Rysaliyeva, was hospitalized.

But this was an exception. Pensioners assembled and so did the homeless. The demonstrations were mostly peaceful, and on occasion government officials went out to speak with demonstrators. But the reaction of Kyrgyz authorities, excepting the early June incident, to such demonstrations sets them apart from the other Central Asian states. Such events were unthinkable in Turkmenistan and Uzbekistan, where the law enforcement authorities were sure to step in immediately. In Kazakhstan, while protests and demonstrations did take place, they were always without official sanction and so participants and organizers were constantly at risk of imprisonment.

The one group the government was not so tolerant toward was the Wahhabis in southern Kyrgyzstan. Though they had been active in Central Asia since the former Soviet republics became independent in 1991, the Wahhabis aroused only occasional interest until 1997. Conflicts in the north Caucasus in May 1997 brought new attention to the Wahhabis, a purist sect of Islam. The Islamic spiritual board of Kyrgyzstan, the Muftiat, met to officially denounce them in late autumn, then Kyrgyz Security Minister Feliks Kulov announced the government was establishing a special committee to deal with "extremist" religious groups, mainly located in the Fergana Valley around the city of Osh. About the time Kulov was announcing the committee, there was unrest, allegedly caused by Wahhabis in Namangan, Uzbekistan, also in the Fergana Valley. The Kyrgyz government may have reacted more to this than any "extremist" problems at home.

FOREIGN AFFAIRS

Kyrgyzstan's foreign policy noted some successes. Akayev was in Moscow in April, along with the presidents of Kazakhstan and Tajikistan, to sign the border treaty with China. Though Akayev was not party to the joint statements made by Russian President Boris Yeltsin and Chinese leader Jiang Zemin, his presence as a leader of state was symbolic.

Akayev also visited Washington. Though U.S. President Bill Clinton was in Europe at the time, Akayev watched while the chairman of the Kyrgyz National Bank (Taaliaibek Koichumanov) signed an agreement with the president of Eximbank (James Harmon). A deal was signed with Case Corporation for delivery of tractors and "important" talks were held with Newmont Mining and Phelps Dodge on future gold mining projects. Akayev met with the president of the World Bank, James Wolfensohn, to talk about further cooperation (the World Bank was already helping in 13 projects in Kyrgyzstan worth $264 million). The country also received additional loans from the International Monetary Fund to the tune of $44 million in 1997.

At the same time Kyrgyzstan promoted relations with the Islamic states. Prime Minister Apas Jumagulov attended the May meeting of the Economic Cooperation Organization (grouping Turkey, Iran, Pakistan, Azerbaijan, Kazakhstan, Tajikistan, Turkmenistan, Uzbekistan, and Afghanistan) in Ashgabat. The declaration at the end of the conference included four transport projects (two rail lines, two highways) which affect Kyrgyzstan and should improve trade with neighboring countries. Later, Kyrgyzstan's secretary of state and foreign minister attended the meeting of the Organization of the Islamic Conference in Tehran.

Kyrgyzstan's parliament debated and then approved the "sale" of water from Kyrgyz reservoirs to the neighboring states of Uzbekistan and Kazakhstan. Neither country had ever paid for water before, but Kyrgyzstan claimed that maintenance of the reservoir system through the severe mountain chains was beyond the country's financial ability. Naturally, Uzbekistan and Kazakhstan were very much against paying for something they have been receiving on their lands for free throughout history. For Kyrgyzstan this may have been a shrewd move. Beyond the question of sharing maintenance costs, selling water may give Kyrgyzstan some leverage in negotiations for energy supplies for the winter months from Uzbekistan and Kazakhstan. However, playing with water in this region has historically proven a dangerous game.

Kyrgyzstan also played host in mid-May to a face-to-face meeting between Tajikistan's President Imomali Rakhmonov and the leader of the United Tajik Opposition Said Abdullo Nuri. Though peace between the rival groups had seemed close at hand for several months the meeting outside Bishkek was hailed as a breakthrough and indeed the final peace was signed just over one month later in Moscow.

Besides receiving praise for being a "peacemaker" Kyrgyzstan also had a chance to solve one of its internal problems connected with the five-year civil war in Tajikistan, that of refugees. The number of refugees living in Kyrgyzstan as a result of the wars in Tajikistan and Afghanistan was variously cited by officials as 20,000–30,000. Some, including President Akayev, say the real figure was over 50,000. Only 6–7 percent of Kyrgyzstan's land is arable, mostly in the south, and that is where most of the refugees are located. Finding plots of land for these people represented a real problem for the Kyrgyz government. A dispute over land was responsible for starting the ethnically charged riots outside Osh in 1990 and hundreds, certainly, died in the rampage there before Soviet troops poured in to restore order.

THE ECONOMY REBOUNDS

1997 was the year the Kyrgyz economy finally made a substantial leap forward. The upturn began in 1996. In a report released in April 1997, the European Bank for Reconstruction and Development noted, "After negative growth in the four years following independence, there are now unambiguous signs that output growth has resumed in 1996." 1997 was even better.

The national currency, the som, held its value: it began the year at a little over 17 to $1 and ended the year at the about same rate. Every economic factor indicates growth. Industry figures were up, agriculture was up, and the country's highly publicized joint venture gold mining operation Kumtor began operations and exceeded projections for its first year. More mines are scheduled to open in the next few years.

Statistics from the Commonwealth of Independent States (CIS) toward the end of 1997 showed Kyrgyzstan way ahead of the other CIS states in economic growth. According to Interfax, industrial output in Kyrgyzstan between January and November rose 49 percent compared to the previous year. Compared to the first eleven months of 1996 the gross domestic product in Kyrgyzstan in 1997 went up 11 percent, again the biggest increase in the CIS. Consumer price inflation decreased from 31 percent in 1996 to 25 percent in 1997. Also, Kyrgyzstan's trade deficit fell from $305 million in 1996 to $92 million in 1997 (also the January-to-November figure).

However, several experts on Kyrgyzstan noted that the country had a rather small industrial base when it became independent. Native industries which support construction and basic communications networks necessarily grew to meet the demands of gold-mining operations or new factories such as the monster silicon factory still being completed outside Tash Kumir. Reuters reported that the average nominal salary in 1997 actually fell by 1.7 percent, and in January 1998 the IMF's resident representative in Bishkek, Insu Kim, acknowledged that "average income (in Kyrgyzstan) is still lower than when the Soviet Union fell apart."

The privatization process was halted in May by President Akayev, after heavy criticism. Akayev said some enterprises had been sold for next to nothing. The head of Akayev's economic policy department, Batyrbek Davletov, said later the process had not been halted entirely but commented that something had to be done to stop the "offenses and outrages.

Successes in agriculture were similarly flawed. Though the country produced more barley and wheat, this was at the expense of land once used for cotton and tobacco that would have fetched more money when exported. More ominous was the sharp decrease in the sheep population, from 10 million to between 2–3 million, as mutton is the staple of the Central Asian diet. Kyrgyz reservoirs were reporting low levels toward year's end, which is bound to affect agriculture in 1998.

But gold was the big story in 1997. The Kumtor gold-mining operation, a joint venture between Kyrgyzstan's state gold company Kyrgyzaltyn and Canada's Cameco Corporation, began operation in 1997, and long-held expectations were finally realized. Gold production for the year was 17 tons, worth $176 million, of which more than 14 tons was produced by Kumtor. In 1996 gold production had been a mere 1.5 tons. The surge in gold output was responsible for the fall in the trade deficit and the increases in GDP and industrial output. Kyrgyzaltyn predicts that by 1999 production should reach 20 tons annually. The Kumtor site alone is estimated to hold 514 metric tons of gold. With other mining sites around the country scheduled to open in the next few years, 20 tons may prove a low estimate.

Turkmenistan

Population:	4,460,000
Capital:	Ashgabat (pop. 400,000)
Major cities:	Chardzhou (pop. 164,000), Tashauz (pop. 114,000)
Area:	490,100 sq. km.
Major ethnic groups:	Turkmen 77%, Uzbek 9.2%, Russian 6.7%, Kazak 2%, other 6.1%
Economy:	GDP growth: -35.0%
	Inflation rate: not available
	Average monthly wage: not available
	Unemployment rate: not available

ENERGY RICHES STILL LOCKED OUT OF WORLD MARKETS

by BRUCE PANNIER

The year 1997 was not kind to Turkmenistan. The country's leader, President Saparmurad Niyazov, continued his typical form of leadership. The lives of the Turkmen people did not improve, despite Niyazov's repeated promises that his country would become a second Kuwait thanks to its vast natural gas reserves. Human rights organizations also kept up their criticism of the Turkmen government for its tight control over society and recourse to prisons and psychiatric hospitals to quiet opposition.

Overall, the situation in the country as far as democracy and human rights were concerned was much the same as it had been since independence was gained in 1991. What really made a difference in 1997 was the deteriorating economic situation. Turkmenistan was in the unenviable position of having to export its biggest money-making resource, natural gas to customers via pipelines which run through Russia. Russia has been blocking Turkmenistan's access to solvent customers, as a result of which there was a catastrophic fall in natural gas exports: from 26 billion cubic meters in 1996 to 6.5 billion cubic meters in 1997. Correspondingly, output also fell, from 35 to 20 billion cubic meters, as it is difficult to store the gas. As natural gas is virtually the sole industry in Turkmenistan, this slump had a devastating effect on the overall economy.

Turkmenistan was selling its gas through an American corporation named ITERA. ITERA bought gas from Turkmenrosgaz, a joint venture between the Turkmen government and Russia's Gazprom, and sold it to Ukraine. Russia would not allow Turkmenistan to sell its gas to countries beyond Ukraine, such as Poland or Germany, who are more reliable customers when it comes to paying the bills. Ukraine was Turkmenistan's leading customer, but payments ran far behind deliveries until Ukraine's debt was in the hundreds of millions of dollars.

Ukrainian State Minister Anatoly Minchenko visited Turkmenistan in April and both sides laid the blame on the middleman, ITERA. They agreed to dispense with ITERA's services and start "direct gas supplies." However, the early May planned visit of Ukrainian President Leonid Kuchma to Ashgabat, the Turkmen capital, was postponed when Turkmenistan raised the issue of Ukraine's debt, which had reached $1 billion, and suggested that it be resolved before an official visit. Ukrainian Prime Minister Pavel Lazarenko responded by claiming that the debt belonged to private companies which supplied gas to Ukraine and had nothing to do with the Ukrainian government.

In late June Turkmenistan suspended supplies of gas to Ukraine, in view of a restructured debt from 1993–95 for $781 million, and a further $321 million for supplies from 1996 and the first quarter of 1997. (At the same time

Turkmenistan was asking Russia for the $71 million it owed.) Supplies would begin again when Turkmenistan received "full repayment of the entire amount of debt by Ukraine." Thus Turkmenistan cut off its biggest customer. One week earlier, by presidential order, it also had suspended the activities of Turkmenrosgaz.

Niyazov paid a visit to Moscow to meet with Russian President Boris Yeltsin in early August in an effort to get him to persuade Gazprom, Russia's monopoly producer and the company controlling the pipelines, to give Turkmenistan access to Western customers. Despite assurances of support from Yeltsin, nothing concrete came from the meeting. Observers speculated that Niyazov overestimated the value of Yeltsin's promises as, unlike Turkmenistan, in Russia the president does not have a decisive influence in the affairs of business corporations. Gazprom claimed that long-term contractual obligations require it to supply its own gas to customers in West Europe, and that there was no surplus pipeline capacity for additional deliveries of Turkmen gas. The simple fact is that the Russian government was unwilling to give up any export revenue in order to placate Ashgabat.

Turkmenistan's defiant stand left it with Georgia and Armenia as customers, both of whom were also in debt for previous supplies. Armenian President Levon Ter-Petrossian made a visit to Ashgabat in early June and managed to restructure his country's $40 million debt and keep the gas coming.

NEW OPPORTUNITIES

Part of the reason for Turkmenistan's tough line with Russia and Ukraine was the reassurances the country had been receiving from foreign governments and companies. The Economic Cooperation Organization (ECO), comprising Iran, Turkey, Pakistan, Azerbaijan, Kazakhstan, Kyrgyzstan, Tajikistan, Turkmenistan, Uzbekistan, and Afghanistan, held its annual meeting in Ashgabat in mid-May. The group called for quicker action in the construction of several pipelines at the hub of which lies Turkmenistan. Proposed routes were Turkmenistan–China–Japan (8,000 kilometers), Turkmenistan–Iran–Turkey–Europe (2,200 kilometers), Turkmenistan–Afghanistan–Pakistan (1,500 kilometers), and Turkmenistan–Iran–Persian Gulf (700 kilometers). In 1996 the U.S. Congress passed the Iran-Libya Sanctions Act (ILSA) mandating sanctions on companies, U.S. or foreign, doing business with Iran, which raises doubts over the feasibility of the Iranian routes. The Taliban government only controls about two-thirds of Afghanistan, and one would imagine that ongoing fighting would deter most companies from trying to build a pipeline through that country. That did not stop America's Unocal and Saudi Arabia's Delta Oil from signing a protocol on 14 May to move ahead with a feasibility study to build that pipeline. Accenting this problem was the appearance of 7,000 refugees from Afghanistan who crossed over into Turkmenistan at the end of May to escape fighting which had moved close to the northern borders of CIS.

Despite the threat of U.S. sanctions, visits by Turkish Prime Minister Mesut Yilmaz, and then Iranian President Mohammad Khatami just prior to the year's end emphasized the three countries's commitment to the Turkmenistan–Iran–Turkey route. The Anglo-Dutch company Shell was named to head an international project to build an oil pipeline, and it is possible that European and Russian companies may press ahead with the project despite the U.S. sanctions threat.

President Khatami's visit saw the most positive moment for Turkmenistan of 1997, when along with President Niyazov he oversaw the opening of the Korpedzhe–Kord Kuy pipeline connecting Turkmenistan to Iran's natural gas grid and providing Turkmenistan with its first opportunity to export natural gas through a country other than Russia. Under the U.S. presidential decree implementing the ILSA sanctions, trans-shipment of a third country's resources across Iran is not subject to sanctions.

Besides problems with Russia over gas shipments Turkmenistan had a continuing dispute with another CIS country, Azerbaijan. Back in November 1996 Turkmenistan had signed an agreement with Iran and Russia to develop the Caspian Sea jointly. In February 1997 Turkmenistan changed its position and started moving toward the Azerbaijani approach, which is that the Caspian Sea should be divided up into national sectors. The Russians continued to hold that the Caspian should be treated as a joint resource to be collectively developed by all the littoral states. However, while Turkmenistan wants the sea to be divided horizontally, based on equidistant points as measured by latitude, Azerbaijan wants to divide the sea on the basis of the physically nearest territory. This interpretation favors Azerbaijan since it has a peninsula that juts out into one of the most oil-rich parts of the sea.

However, the Turkmen position started shifting again later in the year. Ashgabat expressed outrage when Azerbaijan announced in July that a tender would be held for an offshore oil field which Azerbaijan calls Kyapaz, which lies in the disputed part of the sea. Turkmenistan calls the field Serdar and claimed it lies under Turkmen waters. A Russian firm that had been interested in the deal backed out quickly. The field, along with two other deposits, Chirag and Azeri, became a point of contention between the two from early summer to year's end. When Turkmenistan held its own tender in September there was little interest in the Serdar field. Despite this disagreement, on 6 November Azerbaijan's Transchart Co. brought in the first shipment of Turkmen oil by barge to a port at Baku, the first part of the oil's journey west to a Swiss buyer. Transchart's president said though the shipment was only 3,500 tons, he hoped to eventually ship 600,000–700,000 tons of Turkmen oil yearly.

TURKMENBASHI WINS U.S. APPROVAL

That some of these problems were not resolved is probably due to President Niyazov's disappearance from political life following his heart surgery in late August. Strangely, Niyazov made a scheduled, official visit to Germany in the last week of August, but only when the meetings with government and business representatives were over was it announced in the press that he was checking into a German hospital for open-heart surgery. The full medical details were never made public, though it appears he underwent multiple by-pass heart surgery. In any event, during his recovery he was not seen and it was unclear who was in charge in Turkmenistan for some time.

Niyazov did meet with the U.S. Secretary of Energy, Federico Pena, in November when the secretary paid a visit to Ashgabat. Again, the U.S. desire for multiple pipelines was the main topic of conversation. However, at the end of Pena's visit Niyazov was invited to make an official visit to the United States in 1998 and meet with American President Bill Clinton. While the U.S. government may have oil and gas in mind, the Turkmen press used the invitation as a symbol of success for Niyazov's policies.

There was bad news in agriculture, as cotton and grain harvests were far below target figures. The target for cotton was 1.5 million tons but only 620,000 tons were gathered. The grain target figure was 1.2 million tons but the harvest was 600,000 tons (up from a dismal 480,000 in 1996). This led to what is becoming the annual round of dismissals. Again, incompetence or poor management was the stated reason for sacking local officials, though it must be said that as a desert state there is little potential for agriculture in Turkmenistan.

Human rights organizations found more reasons to level criticism at the Turkmen government. A new civil code was passed in June, but it retained the death penalty. (Niyazov did, however, pardon 2,065 prisoners the same month, to mark his fifth anniversary in office.) At the end of October a journalist named Yovshan Annakurbanov was preparing to board a plane in Ashgabat and travel to Europe for a journalism seminar when Turkmen police stopped him. Though they reportedly found nothing suspicious on Annakurbanov when he was searched at the airport, police still took him into custody and later at the police station claimed to have found a computer disk with material from Turkmen opposition groups on it.

There was no shortage of examples of the glorification of President Niyazov, the *Turkmenbashi* (leader of the Turkmens), in 1997. (See accompanying profile, "The Dictator with the Personal Touch," by Avdy Kuliev.) There was an announcement of plans to build a 70-meter-high tower with a 12 meter revolving statue of Niyazov on top in downtown Ashgabat. Niyazov's new presidential palace was finally finished at an estimated cost of $80 million. And the Turkmen daily newspaper *Watan* reported in June that Turkmenistan's parliament, "taking into account numerous appeals" from workers and local officials, decided to officially change the name of Krasnovodskii Gulf to "Turkmenbashi Gulf."

Not all the economic news was bad. Turkmenistan and the European Union initialed an agreement on partnership and cooperation in late May. A few days later the country became the 172nd member of the World Bank's International Finance Corporation, which opened the way for further private sector investment. Still, the "Thousand-Day" economic program announced in April, corresponding roughly to the number of days remaining until the turn of the century, was troubled from its inception and disappeared from public view barely a month after it was launched.

As the year closed, the opening of the pipeline with Iran did bring hope that 1998 would be a better year for Turkmenistan. In any case some major changes are in order for the country in the near future if the vague dream of becoming a second Kuwait is not to be forgotten altogether. Much could be endured as long as it appeared that the country's oil and gas could keep it afloat in the face of international protests over poor human rights, the aversion of the government to cooperation with neighboring countries, and a low but stable and inexpensive standard of living for the Turkmen people. As 1997 ended, only a trickle of gas and oil was making its way out of Turkmenistan. Georgia was the only country even running up a debt for supplies. The dispute over ownership of sections of the Caspian Sea left small hope that any serious work would begin there until the littoral states come to an agreement over the sea's status. Failure to cooperate with the other CIS Central Asian states has left the latter with little if any reason to care about the situation in Turkmenistan. The tight grip Niyazov kept on domestic politics and his personality cult prevented most countries from even wanting to call Turkmenistan a friend.

If 1997 taught Saparmurad Niyazov anything, it is probably that being a neutral and autonomous country and wanting to compete on international gas and oil markets are not always compatible goals. The announcement at year's end that a meeting of the presidents of the five Central Asian states would be held in Ashgabat in the first week of the New Year is encouraging. Tajikistan is slated to join Kazakhstan, Kyrgyzstan, and Uzbekistan in the Central Asian Union sometime in 1998, which would leave Turkmenistan, the only country of the five not participating. It seems, then, Ashgabat will be forced to court better ties with its neighbors. If not, then Turkmenistan is destined to spend several more years like 1997, waiting for the potential salvation of pipelines.

Profile: THE DICTATOR WITH THE PERSONAL TOUCH

by AVDY KULIEV

He is president, prime minister, chairman of the upper house, chairman of the Council of Elders, president of the humanitarian association, chairman of the only political party, commander in chief of the armed forces, chairman of the Defense Council and the National Security Council, and head of civil defense. His parliament named him Turkmenbashi, the leader of all Turkmen in the world. His image is ubiquitous, adorning all banknotes and many town squares; he controls all newspapers and broadcast media; and his patronage is required for any government post. Saparmurat Niyazov has been supreme leader of Turkmenistan since the country's independence in 1991, and he is slated to remain supreme leader until at least 2002. He reigns over a personality cult in a manner evocative of Stalin in the 1940s. It is a world where personal devotion to the president is valued above all else.

Niyazov ensconced himself as father of his country with the semi-divinity of a Roman emperor by cannily manipulating Soviet-era institutions. Born in 1939 in the village of Gypjak in Turkmeniya, then part of the Soviet Union, he had a thoroughly Soviet childhood. He was brought up in a Soviet children's home because he was orphaned at an early age, his father a casualty of World War II and his mother and brothers killed in the Ashgabat earthquake of 1948. After studying in Leningrad, he worked as an instructor in the Central Committee of the Communist Party of Turkmeniya and was named first secretary of the city council in Ashgabat, the capital. Later, in Moscow, he was again an instructor in a party organization, working for the Central Committee of the Communist Party of the Soviet Union. In December 1985, at age 46, Niyazov became first secretary of the Communist Party of Turkmeniya.

Once at the top, he demonstrated a savvy understanding of the changing times and a talent for cultivating personal popularity. He often wandered through the markets, chatting about prices, how to supply kolkhozes with products, and other topics dear to the hearts of average people. Niyazov embraced the new era of perestroika, rehabilitating persecuted writers, scientists, teachers, artists, and doctors.

Shortly before the fall of the Soviet Union, in October 1990, Niyazov conducted the first presidential election in Turkmeniya—albeit in the Soviet style, with no candidates opposing him—and was elected with 97 percent of the vote. Dissent was not entirely absent while Niyazov was consolidating his rule. At a 1991 conference, many well-known Turkmen writers criticized Niyazov's policies, saying they were reducing the Turkmen people to material and spiritual bankruptcy. That December, the Communist Party of Turkmeniya was transformed into the Democratic Party of Turkmenistan and Niyazov was elected chairman. Niyazov ran unopposed in independent Turkmenistan's first presidential election, receiving 99.99 percent of the vote. By the second half of the 1980s and the early 1990s, an active movement for democracy and economic reform had taken root. Alternative political parties were formed, such as the Unity Party, the Party of Democratic Development, the Peasants Party of Justice, and others. But once Niyazov became president, those parties were quickly banned. Many democratic activists were forced into exile.

CLOSING THE FIST

During his five years of virtual dictatorship, the Turkmenbashi who had once rehabilitated dissidents has managed to create a tightly closed society. Censorship is more stringent than ever, and critical commentary has vanished from newspapers, magazines, radio, and television. The media are occupied exclusively with praising the president and the benefits of strong presidential power; the papers are full of accounts of government receptions and cabinet sessions, texts of presidential addresses, and official economic news. The covers of all newspapers and magazines are emblazoned with an oath of loyalty to the country that includes the words: "If I criticize you, may my tongue fall out!"

Propaganda supporting the cult of Niyazov has flourished ever since 1992, when a member of the president's council hung a portrait of Niyazov in his office. The governor of Mariiskii oblast (province) followed suit, naming a peasants' union after Niyazov. Niyazov was quite pleased with the initiative of the two men and gave them prominent positions in his inner circle.

Soon, government functionaries throughout the country were jumping on the bandwagon. The race to plaster the president's image everywhere was popular, not legislated. Portraits of Niyazov first appeared in offices and then sprang up everywhere, even in grocery stores. Regional governors begged Niyazov for permission to rename farms and factories after him (usually such institutions were named after Soviet heroes). Sculptures of Niyazov began appearing in oblast centers, on farms, and in cities. In the most picturesque areas, local councils began building palaces for him. A city; two agricultural areas; one of the districts in the capital; a ship; many hospitals and clinics; the Academy of Agricultural Sciences; the agricultural institute; a number of schools, streets, and squares; and many other things bear his name. In May 1993, the Council of Elders passed a motion to erect monuments to the president in every city and village in the country.

A few months later, parliament gave Niyazov the title of Turkmenbashi, and his birthday, 19 February, became a national holiday. The city of Krasnovodsk was renamed Turkmenbashi City. Twice Niyazov was awarded the government-sponsored Hero of Turkmenistan Award, which carries with it a gift of $100,000. Only he has ever received it. A special state award, the President's Star, has reportedly been given to heads of foreign oil companies doing business in Turkmenistan.

Like the Holy Family, the president's parents have been honored in the popular rush to exalt him: two streets in Ashgabat are named after them, a movie theater and a textile factory bear his mother's name, and a hospital is named after his father. Statues of both parents grace squares in several cities.

In 1994, the people voted overwhelmingly to extend Niyazov's term of office until 2002. At that point, orders from local governments, businesses, and other organizations began to pour in for songs, poems, and films about the Turkmenbashi as well as for sculptures, photographs, and portraits of him. Artists, composers, poets, and cinematographers are required to churn out such propaganda.

CHINKS IN THE CULT

But while Niyazov was genuinely popular, he was not immune to criticism. Most of it, however, must come from Turkmen exiles or foreigners. Throughout 1994, the Turkmen media continually reported that Niyazov had been nominated by the Russian Writers' Organization for a Nobel Prize and that a number of well-known poets, artists, and politicians, including Mikhail Gorbachev, supported his nomination. After the exiled Turkmen writer Akmukhamed Velsapar published several articles in Russian newspapers citing evidence that Niyazov had never even been considered for the prize (and that Gorbachev knew nothing of the matter), the media campaign ceased.

Knowing Niyazov's weakness for flattery, foreign businesspeople have appealed to his ego. Turkish publishers produced a multi-volume anthology of his speeches for distribution in the West, as several publishers had done with Leonid Brezhnev's speeches in Soviet times. Dutch horticulturists developed a special dahlia and called it the Turkmenbashi; a French perfumery created a scent of the same name. Such initiatives have brought enterprising businesspeople large profits and Niyazov false fame.

In 1993, Niyazov appeared frequently on television telling citizens not to worry about the future because he had $3 billion in foreign bank accounts. In December of the following year, *Turkmenskaya Iskra* published an incomprehensible article about the hard-currency reserves of the country: "With the goal of preserving the economic stability of the government, the president of Turkmenistan has decided that the hard-currency funds in the accounts of the Central Bank of the country are considered to be the hard-currency reserves of Turkmenistan." As money from the hard-currency reserves can be spent only on order from the president, the announcement bewildered most of the population. Had Niyazov transferred the hard currency the government held in foreign banks to Turkmenistan in order to finally carry out economic and political reforms, or did he mean that the Turkmen government's money in foreign banks did not belong to the Turkmen people?

With such immense wealth at his personal disposal, Niyazov lives like a king—and his family like a royal family. The London *Sunday Times* reported in October 1996 that Niyazov's son had lost 8 million British pounds at a Spanish casino in one night. Meanwhile, the average wage for a Turkmen worker is a dismal $10–$15 per month. Water, even in the capital, is often cut off during most of the day—although Turkmenbashi's palace boasts bubbling fountains surrounded by imported trees.

People devoted to the president are named to posts for which they have no training and are then left to manage as best they can. For lack of money, night schools and technical colleges have closed, and the Academy of Sciences has been practically dissolved; it is difficult for young people to find work. So far, the cult of personality has benefited few people other than the Turkmenbashi.

NOTE

Reprinted with kind permission from *Transitions* magazine, November 1997.

Contributors

Rasheed Abdullaev is a political analyst specializing in Central Asia and the Middle East. He studied at the Institute of Oriental Studies of the Russian Academy of Sciences in Moscow and had a Fulbright Fellowship to Georgetown University, Washington, D.C., in 1995.

Umed Babakhanov is a journalist and director of the Asia-Plus think tank in Tajikistan.

Laura Belin is studying for a Ph.D. at Oxford University. From 1995 to 1997 she worked as a research analyst on Russian domestic politics at the Open Media Research Institute in Prague. From 1997 to 1998 she covered Russian affairs for Radio Free Europe/Radio Liberty's Newsline.

Christopher Bennett is a political analyst with the International Crisis Group in Sarajevo and the author of *Yugoslavia's Bloody Collapse* (Hurst & Company, 1995).

Nebojsa Bjelakovic is a doctoral candidate at the political science department of Carleton University, Ottawa, Canada. He received a B.A. from Belgrade University, and an M.A. from the Institute of Central/East European and Russian-Area Studies at Carleton. He specializes in Russian foreign policy and Balkan issues.

Gerard F. Brillantes is a program specialist with the International Soros Science Education Program in Fairfax, Virginia. He has traveled extensively throughout Europe and Russia and writes frequently on European security issues.

Janusz Bugajski is director of East European studies at the Center for Strategic and International Studies in Washington, D.C. His books include *Ethnic Politics in Eastern Europe: A Guide to Nationality Policies, Organizations, and Parties* (M.E. Sharpe, 1994; 1995) and *Nations in Turmoil: Conflict and Cooperation in Eastern Europe* (Westview Press, 1995)

Jan Culik teaches Czech studies at Glasgow University and is a director of Inner Workings, a British multimedia company.

Emil Danielyan works for Radio Free Europe/Radio Liberty's Armenian service in Yerevan. From 1996 to 1997 he was an analyst intern at OMRI.

Bhavna Dave is a lecturer in Central Asian politics in the Political Studies department of the School of Oriental and African Studies, University of London. She previously worked as a research analyst at the Open Media Research Institute in Prague. Her major areas of research are ethnic relations, politics of language, religion, and clan networks in Central Asia.

Jeremy Druker is staff writer for *Transitions* magazine at the Institute for Journalism in Transition in Prague.

Andrei Fadin was a Moscow-based political analyst who was a staff writer for Moscow's *Obshchaya gazeta.* He died tragically in an auto accident on 19 November 1997.

Sharon Fisher is a Ph.D. candidate at the School of Slavonic and East European Studies (SSEES) at the University of London, writing on national identity and state-building in Slovakia and Croatia. She previously worked as the Slovak analyst at OMRI and the Radio Free Europe/Radio Liberty Research Institute.

Dan Ionescu is a broadcaster with Radio Free Europe/Radio Liberty, Prague, where he edits a daily program for the Republic of Moldova. He was formerly a research analyst with the RFE/RL Research Institute (1984–94), Munich, and a senior research analyst at OMRI, Prague (1995–97).

Stephen Jones is an associate professor of Russian and Eurasian Studies at Mount Holyoke College in Massachusetts, and is the author of over 50 articles and chapters in academic journals and books. He is currently completing a book entitled *Georgian Social Democracy: In Opposition and Power*.

Jakub Karpinski is an adjunct professor of sociology at Warsaw University. He was an OMRI senior research analyst specializing in Poland from 1995 to 1997. He has published a number of books on the postwar history and political system of Poland and has been a frequent contributor to *Uncaptive Minds* and *Transitions.*

Stefan Krause is a London-based expert on Balkan and East European history and current affairs. He is currently working toward a Ph.D. at the Free University of Berlin on the development of political symbols in independent Bulgaria. He is also working as a freelance elections analyst for the Office for Democratic Institutions and Human Rights at the Organization for Security and Cooperation in Europe.

Avdy Kuliev was minister of foreign affairs in Turkmenistan from 1990 to 1992 and then left the government to work with the Turkmen opposition in Moscow.

Until 1997 he worked for the Turkmen service of Radio Free Europe/Radio Liberty in Prague.

Joan Lofgren is a Ph.D. candidate at Columbia University in political science, writing a dissertation on nationalism and privatization in Estonia. She is currently a researcher at the University of Tampere, Finland, in a project on research and innovation in Russia.

Stan Markotich is a political analyst based in Vancouver, British Columbia. He previously worked at the RFE/RL Research Institute and OMRI as a research analyst specializing in Yugoslavia and Slovenia. He has a Ph.D. in history from Indiana University.

Ustina Markus is a specialist on the former Soviet Union with the Department of Defense. Before joining the DoD she worked for OMRI and its predecessor, the RFE/RL Research Institute, as a specialist on Ukraine and Belarus. She has a Ph.D. from the London School of Economics.

Nurbulat E. Masanov is a specialist on Kazakh nomadism and has been a professor of history at Kazakhstan State University since 1992. Banned from teaching for a while because of his critical stance toward government policy, he is now teaching again. He has received several international grants for the study of national minorities in Kazakhstan.

Michael Mihalka is currently teaching at the George C. Marshall European Center for Strategic Studies in Garmisch-Partenkirchen, Germany. He received a Ph.D. from the University of Michigan, and previously worked at the Open Media Research Institute in Prague, the Stiftung Wissenschaft und Politik in Ebenhausen, Germany, and the RAND Corporation in Santa Monica, California.

Penny Morvant is currently a research associate attached to the Post-Soviet States in Transition Research Program at Sidney Sussex College, University of Cambridge, England. From 1995 to 1997 she worked as a research analyst specializing in social issues in Russia at OMRI in Prague.

Anne Nivat was a staff writer at OMRI and *Transitions* magazine from 1995 to 1997. In 1997–98 she was a fellow at the Davis Center for Russian Studies at Harvard University.

Robert W. Orttung is a senior research analyst at the EastWest Institute in New York, where he is also senior editor of the EWI Russian Regional Report. He is the author of *From Leningrad to St. Petersburg: Democratization in a Russian City* (St. Martin's Press, 1995) and, with Laura Belin, *Russia's 1995 Parliamentary Elections: The Battle for the Duma* (M.E. Sharpe, 1997).

Artis Pabriks is an associate professor of political science in the Vidzeme University College, Latvia. He received his Ph.D. at Aarhus University, Denmark, with the dissertation, *From Nationalism to Ethnic Policy: the Latvian Nation in the Present and the Past.* In 1997–98 he was a Fulbright scholar at the New School for Social Research, New York.

Bruce Pannier covers Central Asia for Radio Free Europe/Radio Liberty's Newsline. From 1995 to 1997 he was an analyst at OMRI.

Scott Parrish currently works as a senior research associate at the Center for Nonproliferation Studies (CNS) of the Monterey Institute of International Studies, in Monterey, California. Formerly he covered Russian security and foreign policy at OMRI in Prague. He has a Ph.D. in political science from Columbia University and has taught at the University of Texas at Austin.

Slobodan Reljic is a writer with the Belgrade news magazine *NIN.*

David Rocks covers Central Europe for the *San Francisco Chronicle* and other newspapers.

Peter Rutland is a professor of government at Wesleyan University and an associate of the Davis Center for Russian Studies at Harvard. From 1995 to 1997 he was assistant director for research at OMRI in Prague. He has written *The Myth of the Plan* (Hutchinson, 1985) and *The Politics of Economic Stagnation in the Soviet Union* (Cambridge University Press, 1993).

Fabian Schmidt is working as the Tirana Project Director of the Institute for Journalism in Transition and was a media regulation advisor with the OSCE during the 1997 elections. He worked as a research analyst focusing on the southwestern Balkans at OMRI from 1995 to 1997. Schmidt is currently working on a Ph.D. thesis on democratic institution building in Albania.

Daria Sito-Sucic is a freelance journalist in Sarajevo. In 1995–97 she was an analyst at OMRI in Prague.

Ben Slay is a senior economist at PlanEcon, Inc., in Washington, D.C., a position he formerly held at OMRI in Prague. He is the author of *The Polish Economy: Crisis, Reform, and Transformation* (Princeton University Press, 1994) and the editor of *De-Monopolization and Competition Policy in Post-Communist Economies* (Westview Press, 1996).

Gale Stokes is Mary Gibbs Jones Professor of History at Rice University. He is a specialist in East European history, especially of the former Yugoslavia. His most recent book is *Three Eras of Political Change in Eastern Europe* (Oxford University Press, 1996).

Elin Suleymanov graduated from Moscow State University and has a Master's in Public Administration from the University of Toledo. He worked at OMRI from 1995 to 1997 and currently lives in Baku.

Matyas Szabo is academic coordinator of the Southeast European Studies program at the Central European University in Budapest. He has an M.A. in sociology, and worked as research fellow at the Center for Study of Nationalism in Prague. In 1995–96 he was an analyst intern at OMRI.

Zsofia Szilagyi is a freelance journalist based in Budapest, Hungary. She was formerly a Hungary analyst at OMRI in Prague.

Sava Tatic is the electronic publications editor at the Institute for Journalism in Transition in Prague. He holds a graduate degree in European studies from the Central European University (CEU) and a graduate diploma in international relations from the School of Advanced International Studies (SAIS) at Johns Hopkins University.

Milada Vachudova, a political scientist with a B.A. from Stanford University and a Ph.D. from the University of Oxford, is a fellow at the Center of International Studies at Princeton University. She wrote this chapter while a research associate at the EastWest Institute and a National Science Foundation–NATO postdoctoral fellow at Charles University in Prague, Czech Republic.

Oleg Varfolomeyev works for the BBC in Kyiv. In 1996–97 he was an analyst intern at OMRI.

Michael L. Wyzan is a research scholar in the Economic Transition and Integration project at the International Institute for Applied Systems Analysis in Laxenburg, Austria. Previously, he has been an associate professor at the Stockholm School of Economics and Illinois State University, and a senior economist at OMRI in Prague. He received his Ph.D. in economics from the University of North Carolina in 1979.

Index

D

F

G

J

K

Q

R

EastWest Institute

EWI New York Center
700 Broadway, Second Floor
New York, NY 10003
Tel: 212/824-4100
Fax: 212/824-4149
E-mail: iews@iews.org

EWI Prague Center
Rasinova nab. 78/2000
120 00 Prague 2
Czech Republic
Tel: 420-2/2198-4222
Fax: 420-2/294-380
E-mail: prague@iews.cz

EWI Moscow Center
Georgievsky pereulok, d. 1
kom. 320
Moscow 103009
Russia
Tel: 095/292-7258
Fax: 095/292-1869
E-mail: moscow@iews.org

EWI Kyiv Center
Hrushevsky st. 34a
Kyiv 252021
Ukraine
Tel/Fax: 38044/253-4489
38044/253-3176

EWI Budapest Center
Kalvaria ter 7
Budapest 1089
Hungary
Tel: 361/269-9300
Fax: 361/333-0315
E-mail: budapest@iews.org

EWI Brussels Center
53, rue de la Concorde
B-1050 Brussels
Belgium
Tel: 32-3/512-5902
E-mail: brussels@iews.org

EWI Košice Center
Hlavna 70
Košice 04001
Slovak Republic
Tel: 421-95/622-1160
Fax: 421-95/622-1150
E-mail: fdce@changenet.sk